JUDGMENTS

Queer Judgments

Editors

Nuno Ferreira
Maria Federica Moscati
Senthorun Raj

COUNTERPRESS
COVENTRY

First published 2025
Counterpress, Coventry
http://counterpress.org.uk

ISBN: 978-1-910761-21-2 (Paperback)
ISBN: 978-1-910761-22-9 (Ebook)

Typeset in 10.5 on 10pt Sabon

The cover art is the Queer Judgments Project's Flower logo, developed by Rose Gordon-Orr and Gabriel Purvis.

Global print and distribution by Ingram.

To queer people around the globe who deserve better justice.

Acknowledgements

This project has been possible because of the intellectual and emotional labour of many people. We thank Isabel Soloaga for curating videos and designing a website that show cases our work (https://www.queerjudgments.org/). We thank Rose Gordon-Orr for her research assistance in the initial development of the project, and Rose Gordon-Orr and Gabriel Purvis for the development of the project's logo. We thank Timothy Berard for his excellent editorial assistance when we were copyediting the collection.

We are grateful to Counterpress for their enthusiastic support for our project and giving us space to publish a collection that is accessible to those beyond academia.

We end with expressing our ongoing gratitude to our families, friends, lovers, communities, and contributors in this collection for sustaining us and reminding us why we keep fighting for justice with the tools available to us.

Contents

PART 2: PRIVACY AND DISCRIMINATION

PART 3: FAMILY AND PARENTHOOD

PART 4: HEALTH AND REPRODUCTION

PART 5: ASYLUM AND MIGRATION

List of contributors

Alex Powell is a Principal Lecturer in Law at Oxford Brookes University. He is also Co-Convenor of the Migration and Asylum section of the Society of Legal Scholars. Alex's research focuses on the intersections of gender, sexuality and the UK asylum system. His work to date has looked at how the UK Home Office addresses asylum claims made on the basis of the claimant's sexual or gender diversity, with particular attention being paid to how credibility is constructed. More information on Alex's work is available: https://www.brookes.ac.uk/profiles/staff/alex-powell

Alexander Maine is a Senior Lecturer, The City Law School, and specialist in family law. Alexander's research focuses on Family Law and Gender, Sexuality and Law, in particular relationship recognition, and the effect of law on the family life of LGBTQ people. His research has been published in leading journals including the Child and Family Law Quarterly, Sexualities, the Journal of Criminal Law, and he is Reviews Editor of the International Journal of Gender, Sexuality and Law. In 2022, Alexander and Professor Robin West (Georgetown University) were appointed co-editors of the Gender and the Law research handbook series (Edward Elgar).

Alexandra Grolimund is a doctoral candidate in Human Rights (Law) at the University of Essex. She is an Assistant Lecturer specialising in criminal law and criminology. She is also a research assistant in the Department of Sociology and Criminology. Her research concerns sexual consent in criminal law, LGBTQ+ rights and sadomasochism.

Alina Tryfonidou is Assistant Professor in Law at the University of Cyprus. Previously, she worked at the Universities of Leicester (Lecturer (2007-2011)) and Reading (Lecturer (2011-2013), Associate Professor (2013-2018), Full Professor (2018-2021)) in the UK, and Neapolis University Pafos (Full Professor (2021-2023)) in Cyprus. Alina's research focuses on EU law and the legal protection of LGBTIQ+ rights. She has authored (2023) and co-authored (2021) studies commissioned by the PETI Committee of the European Parliament and her work has been cited by several Advocates General of the Court of Justice of the EU. More information available on https://www.ucy.ac.cy/directory/en/profile/atryfo03.

Andrew Gilden is an Associate Professor of Law at Willamette University College of Law, where he teaches property, internet law, intellectual property law, and trusts & estates. His research focuses on the intersections of law, technology, and sexuality, as well as legal issues concerning free speech, equality, and creative expression. His scholarship has appeared in leading journals such as The Georgetown Law Journal, Washington University Law Review, Harvard Journal of Law & Technology, William & Mary Law Review, and Boston College Law Review.

Carmelo Danisi is Senior Researcher and Assistant Professor of Public International Law at Alma Mater Studiorum – University of Bologna (Italy) and Visiting Research Fellow at University of Sussex (UK). He was Research Fellow at the University of Sussex (2016-2020) working on the ERC Starting Grant Project 'SOGICA – Sexual Orientation and Gender Identity Claims of Asylum: A European Human Rights Challenge,' which ended with the co-authored monograph Queering Asylum in Europe (Springer, 2021). He has been involved in several research projects concerning international and EU law and has published widely on the protection of LGBTIQ+ people's human rights. More on www.unibo.it/sitoweb/carmelo.danisi2/en.

Carolynn Gray is Head of Accounting, Finance and Law at the University of the West of Scotland. Carolynn's background is as a legal academic specialising in legal gender recognition. Carolynn, influenced by Michel Foucault and Judith Butler, writes and presents on how the law can be used as a means of defining and creating legal identities and how the law can be used as a means of challenging these legal identities. Carolynn was a member of the Scottish Government's Non-Binary Equality Working Group providing recommendations to Scottish Ministers which were used to create an Action Plan for the Scottish Government.

Claerwen O'Hara is a Lecturer at La Trobe Law School, Co-Chair of the Australian and New Zealand Society of International Law (ANZSIL) Gender, Sexuality and International Law Interest Group, and a Managing Editor of the Australian Feminist Law Journal. Their research spans the fields of international human rights law and international economic law, with a focus on queer and feminist approaches to international law, alternative internationalisms, and law and political economy. They are currently editing two books on queer approaches to international law with Dr Tamsin Phillipa Paige to be published in the Routledge Feminist and Queer International Law series.

Claire O'Connell has recently been awarded her doctorate from University College Cork which examined how Irish law can recognise intending parentage while vindicating the child's right to identity in assisted human reproduction. Claire is also a board member of LGBT Ireland and is a member of the LGBT+ Parenting Alliance which is a group made up of LGBT Ireland, Equality for Children and Irish Gay Dads. The mission of the Alliance is to advocate for inclusive legislation on surrogacy and donor conception in Ireland.

Daryl WJ Yang is a Singapore-qualified lawyer, activist and independent researcher. He presently serves as the Honorary Secretary of the Disabled People's Association Singapore and has consulted for ILGA World, ILGA Asia and AWARE Singapore. His research interests span queer, feminist and disability legal studies as well as comparative constitutional and equality law. As a Fulbright scholar, Daryl pursued an LLM from the University of California, Berkeley's School of Law. He is also a proud graduate of the Double Degree Programme in Law and Liberal Arts jointly offered by Yale-NUS College and the National University of Singapore Faculty of Law.

Dianne Otto is Professorial Fellow at Melbourne Law School. She held the Francine v McNiff Chair in Human Rights Law 2013-2016 and was Director of the Institute for International Law and the Humanities (IILAH) 2011-2015. Dianne's scholarship explores how international legal discourse reinforces hierarchies of nation, race, gender and sexuality, and aims to understand how the reproduction of such legal knowledge can be resisted. Key publications include the edited collection Queering International Law: Possibilities, Alliances, Complicities, Risks (Routledge 2018) and, with Emily Jones, a bibliographic chapter 'Queering International Law' in Tony Carty (ed), Oxford Bibliographies Online: International Law (2023).

Fabienne Emmerich is Senior Lecturer at Keele University School of Law in the UK. Fabienne is Institutional Lead for the North West Social Sciences Doctoral Training Partnership and Lead for the Gender, Sexuality, and Law Research Cluster at Keele. Fabienne held a Leverhulme Fellowship for her project 'Swimming against the current: women, prison reform and resistance' (2019-2021). Fabienne's research interests include Punishment, Resistance and Gender; Transformative Justice and Abolition Feminism; and Queering legal studies.

Flick Adams (they/them) is an Associate Lecturer at The Open University, Fellow of the Higher Education Academy, Facilitator, and Doctoral Researcher at Keele University. Flick's research interests include queer and feminist theories, disability justice, gender, sexuality and the criminal legal system, and alternative, community, and transformative justice approaches. Flick's doctoral project examines how the prison system in England and Wales constructs and recognises identities, redistributes resources, and locates trans women within the prison – in cultural, spatial, and material terms. Flick's project sits at the intersection of Gender, Sexuality and Law, Carceral Geography, and Critical Prison Studies.

Frank Nasca (they/them) graduated from Osgoode Hall Law School in Toronto, Ontario, Canada as the gold medalist for the class of 2023. Frank has published award-winning research about Ontario's human rights system, which critically examines concerning practices regarding the premature dismissal of cases. As a transgender person, Frank has dedicated significant time and knowledge to pro-bono work that advances the legal rights of trans communities. Frank also holds a Master of Arts in Sustainability Studies (Trent University, 2016), and enjoyed a career in the not-for-profit sector before law school.

James Rooney is Teaching Fellow at the School of Law, Trinity College Dublin, and a practising Barrister, specialising in childcare, immigration, and equality law. Since 2022, James, along with Cillian Bracken BL, has run a weekly legal advice clinic for members of the LGBTQ+ community at the Free Legal Advice Centre in Dublin. https://www.flac.ie/news/flac-lgbtqi-legal-clinic/

Joanne Stagg (she/her) is a Lecturer at Griffith Law School, Gold Coast, Australia and a PhD Candidate at Deakin University, Melbourne, Australia. Her research interests have included gender, medicine and law, and more recently the application of queer theory to both domestic and international law, including theorising the application of queer theory to judging. She also developed an elective in Gender and the Law for the Griffith Law School. She is a member of the Editorial Board of the Australian Feminist Law Journal. You can find out more about Joanne's research at: https://experts.griffith.edu.au/16979-joanne-stagg/publications

Katie Jukes is a Senior Lecturer in Law at Manchester Metropolitan University and a poet. Her research interests are legal ethics, LGBTQI+ families and the law, and the use of creative methods in both research and teaching. She is a Fellow of the Higher Education Institute and was previously a contributing editor at EachOther, a UK focused charity that uses independent journalism, storytelling and film making to put the human into human rights. You can read Katie's poetry here: https://brokensleepbooks.com/product-page/ed-day-mattar-brendan-curtis-queer-bodies-queer-icons-anthology

Kay Lalor (she/her) is a Reader in Human Rights Law at Manchester Metropolitan University. Her work explores the growth of LGBTQI+ rights activism in international legal arenas, with a focus on how legally informed activism is translated into non- and quasi-legal projects and what this means for the development of human rights theory, law, and practice. More information can be found at https://www.mmu.ac.uk/staff/profile/dr-kay-lalor

Kseniya A. Kirichenko is an intersectional feminist activist, lawyer and researcher with two-decade experience in local, national, regional and international human rights movements and academia. Having a law degree from Novosibirsk State University, she completed her first PhD studies on comparative legal analysis of assisted reproduction, and was a Visiting Scholar at Columbia University. She has been leading various efforts around law, gender and sexuality, including strategic litigation, policy research, monitoring and documentation, education and coalition building. She is currently based in Geneva managing ILGA World's engagements with the United Nations, and pursuing her PhD at the University of Leicester.

Liam Davis (he/him) is a Teaching Associate and PhD Candidate at the University of Bristol Law School, UK. His PhD concerns reform of birth registration law, taking special account of non-traditional family structures (specifically trans/non-binary parents, LGBTQ+ polyamorous parents and gay fathers through surrogacy). His research interests span family and medical law, particularly the intersections between the two concerning parenthood and alternative family models. He has a growing interest in queer and abolitionist theory.

Lucas Lixinski is a Professor at the Faculty of Law & Justice, UNSW Sydney (Australia), and an Associate at the Australian Human Rights Institute. His work spans a number of fields, particularly international human rights law and international cultural heritage law. He is a co-founder and editor of International Law Agendas, a blog of the Brazilian Branch of the International Law Association devoted to Global South engagements with international law. You can find pre-prints of all his publications on his SSRN page: https://ssrn.com/author=2548995.

Lynsey Mitchell is a lecturer at the University of Strathclyde. Her research straddles international human rights law, women's rights, reproductive rights, feminist legal theory, and law and literature. She has published on the narrativisation of women's rights in law. She is currently working on a funded project entitled Scotland's Abortion Law: Understanding the Past to Inform Future Reform. She sits on the editorial board of Feminist Legal Studies and is a member of the European Commission on Sexual Orientation and the Law. She is also an Executive Committee member of Abortion Rights and Abortion Rights Scotland.

Malhar Satav (he/him) is currently a Third-Year Undergraduate student at the National Law School, Bangalore. He is a Constitutional Law and Commercial laws enthusiast with special interest in Intellectual Property Rights and Arbitration Law and, naturally, Queer Rights. Among other things, he has worked on landmark cases like *Supriyo v Union of India* (Plea in the Indian Supreme Court to legalise the right to marry for Queer individuals). He believes that Exclusive Legal Positivism must not be dispositive of disputes, but a normative critique anchored in Structural Intersectionality. More on Malhar can be found at https://www.linkedin.com/in/malhar-satav-a5ab76175/.

Maria Federica Moscati (Marica) is Reader in Law and Society at the University of Sussex. She is a qualified lawyer, trained mediator, and dancer. Her research explores issues concerning Dispute Resolution, Human Rights – especially LGBTIQ+ and Children's Rights, Reproductive Health, Dance/Law and their intersection in comparative perspective. She is co-director of the Centre for Cultures of Reproduction, Technologies and Health at University of Sussex. More can be found at: https://profiles.sussex.ac.uk/p355203-maria-moscati

Mariza Avgeri is a qualified lawyer in Greece and an Associate lecturer in Law, Culture and Society, International Law and Public Law at the Open University, UK. She has graduated with a Bachelor of Laws and a Master of Political Science from VU Amsterdam. She has completed her PhD in Maynooth University at the Law Department working on transgender asylum claims and jurisprudence in the context of the Council of Europe and the European Union. In the past, she has worked as a legal researcher, a case worker at the Greek Asylum Service and a member of the Appeals' Committees.

Miriam Schwarz started her PhD at the University of Cambridge in 2020. Before that, she taught as DAAD–Lektorin at the University of Oxford. She received a Master's Degree in Modern German Literature as well as a Bachelor's degree in German Philology and Social Anthropology at the Freie Universität Berlin. In between these degrees, she spent a year as a teaching assistant at the German Department of Shahid Beheshti University, Tehran. Miriam's PhD research is focused on the narratives of women's friendships in contemporary German and Anglophone literature.

Nuno Ferreira is a Professor of Law at the University of Sussex, UK. Previously, he was a Senior Lecturer at the University of Liverpool and Lecturer at the University of Manchester. Nuno's teaching and research focuses on refugee law, European law, and human rights – especially LGBTIQ+ and children's rights. Nuno has been a Horizon 2020 ERC Starting Grant recipient, leading the SOGICA project (2016-2020, www.sogica.org), as well as a co-investigator in the Horizon 2020-funded TRAFIG project (2019-2022, www.trafig.org) and Principal Investigator in the ESRC-funded project 'Negotiating Queer Identities Following Forced Migration' (2022-2024, https://iranqueerefugee.net/). More information available on https://profiles.sussex.ac.uk/p396218-nuno-ferreira.

Odette Mazel (she/her) is a Senior Research Fellow at the Poche Centre for Indigenous Health in the Faculty of Medicine, Dentistry and Health Sciences, and a PhD candidate at the Melbourne Law School. Drawing on feminist, decolonial and queer theories, her research focuses on the rights and experiences of minority populations including LGBTQIA+ people and Indigenous peoples and the cultural, social, political and legal avenues through which they pursue those rights. Odette is a Board Member of the Australian Feminist Law Journal. Further information on her work and publications can be found at: https://findanexpert.unimelb.edu.au/profile/12289-odette-mazel.

Paula Gerber is a Professor of Law at Monash University in Melbourne, Australia. She is an expert in international human rights law, with a particular focus on the rights of LGBTIQ+ people and children's rights. Paula is the editor of the 3-volume collection Worldwide Perspectives on Lesbians, Gays and Bisexuals (2021) Bloomsbury as well as numerous peer reviewed journal articles, book chapters and opinion pieces. More informations about Paula's scholarship can be found at www.paulagerber.com.

Po-Han Lee teaches at the Global Health Program and Institute of Health Policy and Management, National Taiwan University. He was trained in International Law and Sociology. He is a member of Feminist Review Collective and senior editor for Plain Law Movement, the first multimedia platform for human rights education in Taiwan. He co-edited Plural Feminisms: Navigating Resistance as Everyday Praxis (Bloomsbury, 2023) with Sohini Chatterjee, and Towards Gender Equality in Law: An Analysis of State Failures from a Global Perspective with Gizem Guney and David Davies (Palgrave, 2022). More information about him can be found here: https://scholars.lib.ntu.edu.tw/cris/rp/rp199740/information.html?locale=en.

Rafael Carrano Lelis is a Brazilian human rights lawyer and LGBTI+ activist. He is a Teaching Assistant and Ph.D. Researcher at the Geneva Graduate Institute, and a member of the Editorial Board of the Australian Feminist Law Journal. His current research focuses on the mobilization of human rights by transnational LGBTI+ activists, combining legal and anthropological approaches. Rafael worked as a research consultant for ILGA World between 2020-2021, during which time he co-authored the 2020 edition of the State-Sponsored Homophobia report. His latest book analyzes advocacy efforts by the Brazilian LGBTI+ movement in the 1980s. More information at: https://www.graduateinstitute.ch/discover-institute/rafael-carrano-lelis.

Raju Behara, a trans disabled Peer Support Provider with a decade of healthcare experience, holds a Masters in Pharmacology and a PG Diploma in Health Economics, Health Policy at the Indian Institute of Public Health. Aligned with the Safe Access Community Well-being project, Raju has contributed to LGBTQIA+ safety in Indian workplaces, drafting gender-neutral dress codes and working on sensitization. A published author and poet in various anthologies, Raju, through EQUAL fellowship, chronicled social histories of housing, healthcare and workplace discrimination for queer-trans individuals in India. They initiated 'Queer & Quarantine,' a crisis intervention program for trans folks facing housing challenges.

Sal is a lawyer graduated from NLS, Bangalore in 2021, Ex-Convenor, National Law School Queer Alliance, Founder Ace/Aro support group, and Law Schools' Queer Alliance. They have recently cleared the UGC-NET exam with flying colours.

Sanna Elfving is a Senior Lecturer in Lincoln Law School, UK. Her research focuses on EU law. She has published a co-authored research monograph Gender and the Court of Justice of the European Union (Routledge 2018). Sanna is currently working on a monograph that applies perspectives of queer and feminist studies to the case law of the European Court of Human Rights in areas such as family life, family reunification, and asylum. She is also a member of COST Action 'Transnational Family Dynamics in Europe' (2022-2026).

Senthorun Raj is a Reader in Human Rights Law at Manchester Law School, UK. He is passionate about glitter, pop culture, and social justice. His research explores the relationship between emotion, law, and LGBTIQ+ rights. His first book, Feeling Queer Jurisprudence: Injury, Intimacy, Identity (Routledge 2020), explored how law crystallises emotions through progressive judgments relating to LGBT people. He is currently working on his next monograph, The Emotions of LGBT Rights and Reforms: Repairing Law (forthcoming with Edinburgh University Press), which explores socio-legal conflicts over religious exemptions to anti-discrimination law, legal gender recognition, conversion practices, and sex education in schools.

Surabhi Shukla is a lecturer in law at the University of Sheffield where she runs the Lectures on Gender and Sexuality along with her team. She works on law and sexuality with a focus on India and is interested in exploring the social afterlife of legal judgments and the lived experiences of queer people with legal institutions. More here: https://www.sheffield.ac.uk/law/people/law-academic-staff/surabhi-shukla.

Thomas Crofts is a Professor in the School of Law and in the Department of Social and Behavioural Sciences at City University Hong Kong, and an Adjunct Professor at Northumbria University, Queensland University of Technology and the University of Sydney. His research in comparative criminal law and criminal justice focuses on criminalisation and criminal responsibility, particularly in relation to young people, gender and sexuality.

Titan Deng is an Attorney-in-Law and founded the law firm, Prisma Attorneys-at-Law, in 2016. The firm mainly provides legal services for LGBT+, sexual minority, HIV-positive, and substance-user clients. The areas of Deng's practice include gender equality, same-sex marriage and family, equality claims and criminal defenses for persons living with HIV/AIDS, and substance addiction cases; he has also been the executive director and legal counsel for various organisations such as the Taiwan Tongzhi Hotline Association, Taiwan Equality Campaign, Taiwan Rainbow Civil Action Association (Taiwan Pride), and Persons with HIV/AIDS Rights Advocacy Association of Taiwan. More information about him: https://www.prismalaw.com.tw/td (in Chinese).

Tsung-Han Yu obtained his LLB from the National Taipei University and LLM from the Graduate Institute of Health and Biotechnology Law of Taipei Medical University, and recently he just passed the bar exam in Taiwan. His master's research studies the socio-legal underpinnings of the sexual rights and joint responsibility of persons living with HIV/AIDS in Taiwan. He has been interested in public laws, the sociology of law, public health and medical laws, and queer and feminist legal theories.

Tzu-Wei Lin obtained his PhD in Law from National Chengchi University, Taiwan; his doctoral study looks at the impact of sentencing on the children of criminal defendants. He has been interested in the intersection of criminal law, the family, and gender and sexuality – particularly concerning the necessity and extent of state interventions using criminal punishment – through the critical lenses of human rights treaties and sociology. Lin is also the Director of Legal Affairs of the Taiwan Alliance to End the Death Penalty, having worked on many cases involving the death penalty and with convicts and their families. More information about him: https://lintwlaw.com/about/ (in Chinese).

Victoria McCloud, Judge (Dr), was a judge in the High Court, London until 2024 when she retired after threats, and abuse from 'gender critics.' She was the first judge appointed from the 'transgender' community, in 2006, and probably the first such practising barrister, from the late 1990s. She was one of the editors of the Equal Treatment Bench Book, is a Chartered Psychologist, Advisory Head of Interdisciplinary Collaborations at the EU Euro-Expert project (Sorbonne), and part of the RCPsych. Working Group on non-recent child abuse. She is an international speaker and commentator on legal tech and diversity, war crimes and extremism.

Waruguru Gaitho (she/they) is a human rights lawyer, Advocate of the High Court of Kenya, and PhD candidate at the University of Cambridge. Her socio-legal research project focuses on legal mobilization by Black LBQ+ (lesbian, bisexual and queer) activists in Kenya and South Africa. Previously, they were a lecturer of law at the University of Leiden, and hold a Masters in International Human Rights Law. Additionally, she engaged in and continues to be invested in LGBTIQ+ activism, in particular the struggle for the decriminalization of same-sex relations and the fight for non-discrimination, equality, freedom and joy for queer Africans generally.

Yàdad De Guerre is an expert of Media and Film, and an anti-fascist activist supporting the rights of LGBTQI+ people in Italy. He edited the Playing The Gender Card blog in which he analyses the results of a research on the anti-gender movement and its links with the extreme right in Italy. He has published on LGBTIQ+ issues in Italy for Il Post, Valigia Blu and Jacobin Italia. Together with Francesco Bilotta, he co-authored Favolosa - 2019 LGBTQI+ diary. His current research concerns Aldo Braibanti and the trial that saw him convicted of plagiarism of the mind in the 1960s.

Queerword to the first edition

As a young kid in suburban England in the early 1970s, I remember my dolls' house. It was a hand-me-down from much older cousins and was very much a thing of the 1960s. For a start it was a single floor construction, somewhat sprawling and with no roof. I could look down on its rooms, its tiny 1960s chairs and Formica worksurfaces. Its strange mix of slightly post-war taste in wall pictures and paper, combined with the Austin Powers-esque modernism of its day. It was a little run-down, to be sure. Here and there the wallpaper was torn: perhaps a sign of the 1970s recession on its way for my poor 1960s little dolls, stranded innocently in their own groovy era.

I also remember the visit paid to them by 'Action Man,' who I introduced to this scene of domesticity, even though he towered over the other dolls. People often criticise, say, Barbie for her range of career options, but poor Action Man—we must recall—never got anything other than a uniform. Maybe a diver's wetsuit. Not for him the role of mermaid. Nonetheless, I like to think that I had made some sort of childhood inroad into queering that mini-household space and expanding the social horizons of my plastic playmates by bringing them together, at least until in the end I dismembered the lot of them, a fate not unusual for even the best behaved of doll figures.

About 25 years later, and with no limb-ripping involved, I found myself standing up in court for the first time having come out as what we then called 'transsexual' (a strangely terrifying, stigmatizing yet powerful word perhaps ripe for reclaiming). I was now an advocate arguing my client's case in public and in a peculiar way feeling either like Action Man in my dolls' house, or alternatively like my dolls if they had been dropped behind enemy lines into bloody combat. Whilst I had always been clear from my earliest days as to my gender as female, flying in the face of the evidence of my body and the beliefs and behaviour of adults, this new transition to the distinctly non-queer zone of the court and the judge, the wig and the robes, left me feeling 'liminal,' in-between, *transforming* but not *transformed*. I was between worlds rather than firmly in one or the other. That changed only slowly, and traces of my memory of that organic journey are artefacts of my own personal history which I will cherish forever and which I hope have informed my outlook in my more recent years, as a judge.

What this book—this wonderful collection of highly diverse work—does is to embark on an important journey in which we re-examine mental spaces, the literal or metaphorical dolls' house of orthodoxy, and introduce into it a new eye, a new mode of expression, a re-interpretation which challenges us to consider the queered perspective, which may be one which challenges and reverses assumptions, or which moves our thinking into the sort of liminal space in which I found myself when starting out as (what is now called) trans openly in the world.

This book—which I hope is only the beginning of more work to come—could not emerge at a more significant time. Both in the UK and elsewhere, notably in the USA, the apparently accepting society which some had thought was built between the late 1990s and the early 2000s, is challenged in 2024 by the rise of more absolutist, distinctly de-queering ideologies sometimes rooted in religion, sometimes rooted in aspects of fascistic thinking, sometimes simply born of fear fuelled by falsehood and a distaste for all things not-understood.

The narrative of the 'queer' as abusive, as dangerous, as 'foreign' and as sick, is simple and easily swallowed by some, and feeds proposals to row back basic civil liberties. To the trans community, for example, proposals to restrict access to medical wards or to alter the legal sex of some against their will by statutory change are threats of immense structural violence and brings back memories—for those old enough to recall being trans in the 1990s—of proposals such as requirements for reproductive sterility of trans people in exchange for civil rights. Moves today to restrict diversity networks in some workplaces likewise feel like pending erasure and silencing of the voices of many. Little wonder then that human rights lawyer Victor Madrigal-Borloz said this after a visit to the UK in 2023 to examine the rights situation there in relation to LGBT+ people:

> I am deeply concerned about increased bias-motivated incidents of harassment, threats, and violence against LGBT people, including a rampant surge in hate crimes in the UK ... All of this is attributed—by a wide range of stakeholders—to the toxic nature of the public debate surrounding sexual orientation and gender identity.[1]

Leaving aside being an antidote to the 'anti-queer' or 'de-queering' movements in the public marketplace of ideas, this book also achieves a more subtle outcome. It advances our discussion of the changing notion of norms and of the antinormative simply by its approach of re-writing or re-telling existing narratives through the compound lenses of queerness. It marks one point in time in this field of thought, within an inevitable evolution of ideas. It is the kind of evolution one can see if I quote my trans-sister Christine Jorgensen in 1952:

> Nature made a mistake, which I have corrected,[2]

to which now I would say in 2024 instead:

> Nature made no mistake, but gave me a path to grow.

It is in works of pioneering critical scholarship such as this collection that 'queerness' can find its ongoing survival and expression, because it invites us to revisit examples of public discourse and thought and to see how 'the queer' can still find its place 'in court ,' whether literally or in the court of public opinion. The publishers and editors of this collection should feel immensely proud—as should all the chapter authors—of the academic contribution which they have made here.

Victoria McCloud, January 2024

1. UN Human Rights Office of the High Commissioner, 'UK: Keep calm and respect diversity, says UN expert,' 11 May 2023, accessed 22 January 2024, https://www.ohchr.org/en/press-releases/2023/05/uk-keep-calm-and-respect-diversity-says-un-expert.
2. Jorgensen, Christine (1952) reported in the Daily News, apparently in a leaked letter: Francine Uenuma, 'A gender-affirming surgery gripped America in 1952: "I am your daughter",' 12 June 2023, accessed 22 January 2024, https://www.washingtonpost.com/history/2023/06/12/first-transgender-surgery-christine-jorgensen/.

1

Queer(ing) Judgments

Nuno Ferreira, Maria Federica Moscati and Senthorun Raj

Introduction

Dear reader...
We are dancers. We are teachers. We are students. We are lovers. We are jokers. We are fighters. We are friends. We are...

We open *Queer Judgments* by opening our queer selves to you. As editors/contributors, we are embodied across the pages of this edited collection that give words to our queer emotions, identities, activisms, theories and doctrines. *Queer Judgments* is an opening. It is an invitation to collaborate, converse, critique, imagine, and create the possibilities of working queerly within and against law by becoming queer judges. We do this work because we seek to build a world where everyone can flourish without violence, exclusion, discrimination, and inequality.

The Global Scene

As we write the introduction to our edited collection, there are momentous changes across legal systems that seek to improve the lives of lesbian, gay, bisexual, transgender, queer, intersex, asexual, and other (LGBTIQA+) people. In the last decade, courts in countries like India, Mauritius, and Botswana have decriminalized homosexuality while parliaments in places like Singapore and Angola have done the same.[1] Jurisdictions like Australia, Taiwan, Chile, and United Kingdom (UK) have passed legislation to recognize same-sex marriages, with others providing civil unions.[2] Portugal, Pakistan, and Aotearoa New Zealand have made it possible for people to self-declare their gender without unnecessary medical, surgical, or bureaucratic procedures.[3] Malta was

---

1. Human Dignity Trust, 'A History of LGBT Criminalisation,' accessed 26 January 2024, https://www.humandignitytrust.org/lgbt-the-law/a-history-of-criminalisation/.
2. ILGA, 'Legal Frameworks: Same-Sex Marriage and Civil Unions,' accessed 26 January 2024, https://database.ilga.org/same-sex-marriage-civil-unions.
3. ILGA, 'Legal Frameworks: Gender Recognition,' accessed 26 January 2024, https://database.ilga.org/legal-gender-recognition.

one of the first nations in the world to explicitly prohibit surgical interventions that aim to 'correct' the bodies of intersex infants.[4] In 2017, the Yogyakarta Principles (an international document setting out how international human rights laws apply to issues of sexual orientation and gender identity) were revised and improved to recognize changing international norms, and explicitly recognized issues affecting intersex people.[5] This non-exhaustive list captures the scale and intensity of *progressive* reforms over the past decade for LGBTIQA+ people, which have been made possible by legal and social activisms in local courts, national parliamentary forums, and international committees.

Yet, law reforms have not been universally progressive when it comes to protecting LGBTIQA+ people from stigma, inequality, and discrimination. Under the guise of combatting 'gender ideology,' some states in the United States of America (USA), Russia, Hungary, and Poland have sought to further restrict the public visibility of queer and trans people.[6] Typically referred to as 'gay propaganda,' these jurisdictions seek to curtail freedom of speech and association by proscribing Pride marches, LGBTIQA+ organizations, and educational materials designed to facilitate acceptance of sexual and gender non-conformity in schools.[7] So-called 'progressive havens' for LGBTIQA+ people like the UK and some USA states treat the existence of trans and non-binary people as a threat to the social order, and these groups find their access to public spaces and healthcare is rendered a topic of hostile public scrutiny.[8] Countries like Uganda have further strengthened laws criminalizing homosexuality, including the death penalty for certain gay sex offences.[9] The scale and intensity of what we might colloquially describe here as a 'backlash' to LGBTIQA+ rights highlight that our rights do not emerge transnationally as a simple story of progress. Our existence, visibility, safety, and freedom remain deeply contested across the world. And legal progress is haphazard, insecure, and contingent.

In this context of flux and contradiction, we offer *Queer Judgments* as a space to reflect on the desirability and possibilities of law while holding space to cultivate friendship and solidarity between communities fighting for justice. This is not a new conversation. Many queer legal scholars have written extensively about how legal systems perpetrate systemic inequalities and are sceptical about the role

---

4. *Gender Identity, Gender Expression and Sex Characteristics Act 2015* (Malta).
5. Mauro Cabral Grinspan, Morgan Carpenter, Julia Ehrt, Sheherezade Kara, Arvind Narrain, Pooja Patel, Chris Sidoti, and Monica Tabengwa, 'Yogyakarta Principles Plus 10,' accessed 26 January 2024, https://yogyakartaprinciples.org.
6. This is part of a global trend involving state and non-state actors, which academics and activists are documenting. See LSE Gender Institute, 'Transnational Anti-Gender Movements,' accessed 26 January 2024, https://www.lse.ac.uk/gender/research/AHRC/AHRC-home.
7. Catherine Jean Nash and Kath Browne, *Heteroactivism: Resisting Lesbian, Gay, Bisexual and Trans Rights and Equalities* (London: Zed Books, 2020).
8. David Remnick and Masha Gessen, 'What We Talk About When We Talk About Trans Rights,' The New Yorker, 11 March 2023, accessed 26 January 2024, https://www.newyorker.com/news/the-new-yorker-interview/what-we-talk-about-when-we-talk-about-trans-rights.
9. Reuters, 'Uganda passes a law making it a crime to identify as LGBTQ,' Reuters, 22 March 2023, accessed 26 January 2024, https://www.reuters.com/world/africa/uganda-passes-bill-banning-identifying-lgbtq-2023-03-21/.

of law in remedying the harms faced by people minoritized because of their sexual or gendered identities and behaviours.[10] Such scholarship detail the way legal and administrative institutions police non-normative sexual identities and expressions (criminalizing homosexuality, denying family recognition, banning Pride) and how public policies and social norms inhibit gender diversity (fixing legal sex/gender to what is assigned at birth, blocking gender affirming healthcare).[11] We have each written separately about the problematic way law deals with LGBTIQA+ people, including in the areas of asylum law, family law, criminal law, and public law.[12] While we are deeply critical of law, we also do not disavow it entirely. We position ourselves as individuals who are speaking to, with, and against the law in different spaces. This resonates with what some scholars describe as 'queer lawfare,' where we seek to resist legal and political discrimination by turning to courts where it is practical or useful to do so.[13] By taking this position, we recognize the structural limits of using law to address homophobia, biphobia, transphobia, misogyny, racism, colonialism, capitalism, and ableism. Yet, we also recognize the utility of minimizing some of these structural harms by using legal remedies to make life easier and fairer for queer people.

Crafting our Queer Project

Queer Judgments builds upon these critical and ethical commitments. Before detailing the scope of the edited collection and unpacking the contributions we have gathered, we want to take a moment to explain how this project came to life. The Queer Judgments Project is an initiative that evolved from disparate conversations between the current co-editors about how legal judgments related to sexual orientation, gender identity and expression and sex characteristics (SOGIESC) could have been written in more appropriate terms in light of the legal framework at the time. We wanted to cultivate a project that brought together friends, colleagues, and activists who were interested in improving and challenging the law and its application to make life better for LGBTIQA+ people and communities. The main aim of the project (beyond just this edited collection) is to re-imagine, re-write and re-invent, from queer

---

10. Including some of this volume's contributors: see, for example, Diane Otto, ed., *Queering International Law: Possibilities, Alliances, Complicities, Risks* (London / New York: Routledge, 2018).

11. See, for example, Martha Albertson Fineman, Jack E. Jackson, and Adam P. Romero, eds., *Feminist and Queer Legal Theory: Intimate Encounters, Uncomfortable Conversations* (Farnham: Ashgate, 2009); Robert Leckey and Kim Brookes, eds., *Queer Theory: Law, Culture, Empire* (Abingdon: Routledge, 2010); Libby Adler, *Gay Priori: A Queer Critical Legal Studies Approach to Law Reform* (Durham: Duke University Press, 2018); Dean Spade, *Normal Life: Administrative Violence, Critical Trans Politics and the Limits of Law* (Boston: South End Press, 2011).

12. See some of our most recent scholarship: Nuno Ferreira, 'Utterly Unbelievable: The Discourse of "Fake" SOGI Asylum Claims as a Form of Epistemic Injustice,' *International Journal of Refugee Law* 34 (2022), 303-326; Francesca Romana Ammaturo and Maria Federica Moscati, 'Children's Rights and Gender Identity: A New Frontier of Children's Protagonism,' *Nordic Journal of Human Rights* 39 (2021), 146-162; Senthorun Raj, 'Legally Affective: Mapping the Emotional Grammar of LGBT Rights in Law School,' *Feminist Legal Studies* 31 (2023), 191-215.

13. Adrian Jjuuko, Siri Gloppen, Alan Msosa, and Frans Viljoen, eds., *Queer lawfare in Africa: Legal Strategies in Contexts of LGBTIQ+ Criminalisation and Politicisation* (Pretoria: University of Pretoria Press, 2022).

and other complementing perspectives, judgments that have considered SOGIESC issues. The project has an international reach and multi-disciplinary scope. Individual contributors were free to choose which judgment they wanted to focus on, featuring voices from across the globe. Similarly, the audiences for the outputs of our project include people outside of academia, especially marginalized communities and young people.

In July 2021, in the midst of the COVID-19 pandemic and related public-health 'lockdowns' at home, we held two scoping workshops to bring together queer scholars and activists to reflect on jurisprudential challenges related to SOGIESC matters. In framing this conversation, we were not tied to specific SOGIESC-related rights issues or subdisciplines of law or styles of jurisprudence. We wanted to create an open space which gave people the opportunity to identify some of the pressing legal, scholarly, and activist concerns relating to SOGIESC-related rights and to work out what a 'queer judgments project' might offer to our collective work to improve SOGIESC-related rights globally. To that end, we asked those interested in the conversation to reflect on the following questions:

1. How might queer judgments be relevant to your work (as a lawyer, scholar, activist, etc)?
2. What jurisdictional and jurisprudential scope should the project have?
3. What theoretical perspectives should inform such a project?
4. What form should 'queer judgments' take?
5. What (scholarly, political, artistic) outputs could we develop together?
6. How might we resource this work?

We had over 30 people from different parts of the world join the initial (virtual) dinner-table conversation to discuss these questions. The discussions that took place online were enormously rich. Some participants spoke about more conventional legal issues like improving the family law system for queer families or removing sex/gender markers from legal documents. Others reflected on the role of queer thinking for less obvious topics like cultural heritage and environmental noise. What became clear as the conversations progressed was that the Queer Judgments Project would not just be limited to an academic edited collection. Rather, people were interested in offering critical commentaries through writing and podcasts, re-writing judgments, experimenting with legal form, queering legal interventions by theatricalizing them or turning them into comics, and collaborating with activists and artists to rethink the limits and possibilities of law when it comes to SOGIESC issues or the lives of LGBTIQA+ people. The possibilities were, quite literally, endless.

We held further workshops with more participants (following an open call) in October 2021 to explore this further. At these workshops, we invited people to address several theoretical questions:

1. How does legality reflect colonial power structures?
2. What kind of queer subjects does the law imagine?
3. Are we seeking legality?

4. Is there value in being stigmatized?
5. In what ways does the law think about the queer subject and how queer subjects position themselves in relation to the law?

We also addressed some methodological questions:

1. How deep does our knowledge of the judgment have to be?
2. How can evidence be queered to become accessible?
3. How can we queer the files that judges have access to?

At these workshops, fellow queer scholars and activists spoke passionately about issues ranging from reimagining the decriminalization of homosexuality to making room for the experiences of LGBTIQA+ people who seek asylum, to rethinking modes of legal gender recognition, to dismantling carceral systems harming socially marginalized populations, etc. The various topics discussed spanned jurisdictions, court hierarchies, and subdisciplines of law. In order to capture all potential contributions, the editors collated the preferences of about 70 people interested in contributing to the project. Based on the responses, we decided that our first output would be an edited collection. But we did not want this to be an expensive output that would only be read by a few academics with access to a library budget. We wanted this collection to be open access and identified Counterpress as our preferred publisher because of their commitment to publishing accessible critical legal scholarship.

After documenting the conversations from these workshops and fiddling with spreadsheets, we identified a group of about 40 people who wished to contribute a critical judgment and/or commentary to the edited collection. While we have assembled an excellent range of scholars and topics in this volume, we also recognize the limitations of this volume in regional spread (we lack contributors based in the Middle East, North Africa, and Latin America) and legal focus (we lack topics relating to private law including contract law, equity, and tort law).

Writing Queer Judgments

The workshops we organized were energizing, emotional, and thought-provoking. We were immersed in a space of queer intimacy, critique, and solidarity. Rather than pre-determine the scope of a 'normal' academic output or set theoretical or institutional parameters, we held space to provoke conversation and creativity around activism, community, law, scholarship, and queerness. Our conversations were queer in the sense that they were about exploring:

> the open mesh of possibilities, gaps, overlaps, dissonances and resonances, lapses and excesses of meaning when the constituent elements of anyone's gender, of anyone's sexuality aren't made (or can't be made) to signify monolithically.[14]

---

14. Eve Sedgwick, *Tendencies* (Durham: Duke University Press, 1993), 8.

In thinking about the intimacies and emotions constituted through the workshops, we were reminded that we were not simply a group of academics approaching a subject to analyse in a dispassionate or objective sense. We were also not simply a collection of LGBTIQA+ people talking about our lives. We were instead activist-scholar-friends motivated by feelings of responsibility towards minoritized communities (to which we belonged) as well as our desires for scholarly camaraderie that might be used in service of our communities. This meant we had to attend to the 'gaps and overlaps' caused by law, 'dissonances and resonances' of language to describe identity, and 'lapses and excesses' when considering how judgments intervene in the lives of LGBTIQA+ people.

We take 'queer' as a term to express our methodology in putting this collection together. Critical judgment writing—much like the concept of queer—is freighted with tensions, contradictions, and possibilities. Fortunately, we are not new to navigating this terrain. Our labour in putting this edited collection together draws energy from the rich sources of existing critical judgments, including Feminist Judgments, Indigenous Judgments, Children's Rights Judgments, African Judgments, and Earth Law Judgments.[15] As Rosemary Hunter, Clare McGlynn, and Erica Rackley note in relation to feminist judgment writing, 'by intervening in law from a feminist perspective, one of the aims of the Feminist Judgments Project was to disrupt the process of gender construction, and to introduce different accounts of gender that might be less limiting for women.'[16] We recognize the normative importance of this feminist approach because re-writing judgments has the potential to challenge gendered and sexualized power dynamics and make new identities legible in law. In thinking of how to undertake a queer re-imagining of critical judgment writing, we also turned to Alex Sharpe's important article, 'Queering Judgment.' Sharpe describes the process of queer judgment writing as an ethical process that involves foregrounding the voices/stories of those who are marginalized in law, accommodating non-normative identities and relationships, and redressing social disadvantage while recognizing the limitations of law.[17] In doing so, the feminist and queer approaches to critical judgment writing function as both critique and law reform. We embrace critique and normativity in the pursuit of justice.[18] Drawing from the Feminist Judgments Project, Sharpe locates queer judgment writing within parameters that would be easily recognisable as 'judicial' in character. That is,

---

15. For more detail on the various projects, see 'Critical Judgments,' accessed 26 January 2024, https://criticaljudgments.com/, and 'Queer Judgments,' accessed 26 January 2024, https://www.queerjudgments.org/project. The Feminist Judgments projects have, themselves, been inspired by previous Canadian and USA scholarship: Jack M. Balkin, ed., *What Brown v Board of Education Should have Said: The Nation's Top Legal Experts Rewrite America's Landmark Civil Rights Decisions* (New York: New York University Press, 2002); Jack M. Balkin, ed., *What Roe v Wade Should have Said: The Nation's Top Legal Experts Rewrite America's most Controversial Decision* (New York: New York University Press, 2005); Special Issue, 'The Women's Court of Canada,' *Canadian Journal of Women and the Law* 18(1) (2006).

16. Rosemary Hunter, Clare McGlynn, and Erika Rackley, 'Introduction,' in *Feminist Judgments: From Theory to Practice*, eds. Rosemary Hunter, Clare McGlynn, and Erika Rackley (Oxford: Hart, 2010), 7.

17. Alex Sharpe, 'Queering Judgment: The Case of Gender Identity Fraud,' *Journal of Criminal Law* 81 (2017), 417-435. Sharpe's work has been key in inspiring other scholars to undertake 'queer' re-writing of judgments. See, for example, Damian Gonzalez-Salzberg, *Sexuality and Transsexuality Under the European Convention of Human Rights: A Queer Reading of Human Rights Law* (Oxford: Hart, 2019).

18. See Aleardo Zanghellini, 'Queer, Anti-Normativity, Counter-Normativity and Abjection,' *Griffith Law Review* 18 (2009), 1-16.

her queer judgment (she writes of a case relating to 'gender fraud' in the context of a sexual assault prosecution in England) is one that shows 'fidelity to precedent, to judicial custom and to the practices of judges in the English appellate courts.'[19] In each of these projects, a judgment can be queered in relation to how it approaches issues of sexual and gender non-normativity but the form or genre of judgment remains largely the same in order to make the judgment useful for judges who are constrained by the institutional realities of being a judge. This emphasizes the point that judges, like authors, have to make 'strategic choices about how to tell a story,' because 'the way in which the judge tells the story, alongside the form and language of their opinion, plays a role in determining how the judgment is received and whether it gains acceptance.'[20]

What does it mean to be 'strategic' with law in a queer sense? How do we express a 'useful' judgment in queer terms? While we share the commitments expressed by those feminist and queer scholars who have engaged in counter-judgment writing, we expand on them in this volume by providing greater flexibility to 'play' with the genre of judgment. We nurtured a 'queer methodology' by asking our contributors to challenge legal conventions of what a 'correct judgment' ought to look/sound like, inviting them to think with/about other (non-legal) disciplines, and encouraging them to locate themselves more self-reflexively within the terms of their judgments.[21]

We invited ourselves to play. We riff from Davina Cooper's recent scholarship which explores playing as a provisional and pleasurable strategy of governance that can enable us to realize progressive social agendas.[22] While Cooper focuses on extralegal or nonlegal avenues or subjects to explore new modes of governing, we look to play within judgments (as a form of governance) by troubling judicial form and making room to express legal decisions in unexpected ways. In the collection, we make room for our contributors to role play being a judge and engage in 'judicial drag.'[23] In some chapters, this means contributors play politely with law—making decisions that toy with discrete legal concepts or identities without overhauling normative ways of writing a judgment. Others in our collection are more rambunctious, seeking to disrupt the form of legal judgment as well as troubling the subjects that form the basis of a judgment.

We anchor this collection around specific themes, and in this introductory chapter we use the acronyms 'LGBTIQA+' and 'SOGIESC.' We do so ambivalently, noting the limitations of finding a term that does justice to the heterogeneity of people who are minoritized because of their sex characteristics, sexual orientations, gender identities and expressions. De- and postcolonial scholars caution us to attend carefully

---

19. Sharpe, 'Queering Judgment,' 420.
20. Erika Rackley, 'The Art and Craft of Writing Judgments: Notes on the Feminist Judgments Project,' in *Feminist Judgments: From Theory to Practice*, eds. Rosemary Hunter, Clare McGlynn, and Erika Rackley (Oxford: Hart, 2010), 46.
21. For a more detailed explanation of what queer methodologies involve, and the importance of self-critique and positionality, see Kath Browne and Catherine J. Nash, eds., *Queer Methods and Methodologies: Intersecting Queer Theories and Social Science Research* (Farnham: Ashgate, 2010).
22. Davina Cooper, *Feeling Like a State: Desire, Denial, and the Recasting of Authority* (Durham: Duke University Press, 2019), 116.
23. Judith Butler describes 'drag' as a performance that draws attention to, and denaturalizes, the construction of categories (like sex/gender) that are presumed to be 'normal' or 'natural.' Judith Butler, *Gender Trouble: Feminism and the Subversion of Identity* (London: Routledge, 1990), 145.

to the precarity and porosity of terms relating to sexual and gender diversity in non-Western societies.[24] Identities and behaviours that we might describe in English language academic discourses as 'queer' or 'trans,' have unique cultural and linguistic formulations in different parts of the world. Even the very terms 'sexual orientation' and 'gender identity' have been critiqued for having entered human rights discourses in a way that privileges a binary model of gender.[25] In using the terms LGBTIQA+ or SOGIESC we do not seek to erase these complexities and the contributors in this collection use different terminologies. We invite readers to critically reflect on terminology and recognize that terms evolve.

Dance with Us

Now, dear reader, you must remember that our project is legally artistic, meaning that it aims at stimulating further questions on queer law by unleashing bravery, grace, sensitivity to others, and creativity. Thus, we wish to share with you some moments of our journey that symbolize our legally artistic project: our flower, our relations, the creation of a queer norm, and the queer judge.

The Flower: Visualizing our Proud Authenticity

We, contributors and editors, all pledged to celebrate and not to assimilate—paraphrasing Joseph Sissens, we all turned up authentically as ourselves.[26] Authenticity, passion, beauty, rigour, activism and curiosity drew people together in this project. As editors, we wanted to visually aid the reader to follow our creative and proud journey. Thus, the flower is our logo.

Of course, we are aware that it is nothing new to use a logo for research projects, and it is not new to use flowers as symbols. So, we did not really bring in any innovative marketing tool here! But we tried to bring in some queerness. Conversations about the logo started among the three editors and then involved Rose Gordon-Orr and Gabriel Purvis. The aim was to create a big, wide flower proudly open towards those who look at it. We also wanted to include the new Progress Pride Flag colours for each petal.[27]

After a first enthusiastic brain-storming meeting, creating the flower appeared a bigger task than we had initially thought, and using basic PhotoShop tools only allowed using pre-existing templates of quite rigid flowers and not the more open/queer flower

24. For a more detailed exploration of this point on language and culture, see Sita Balani, *Slick and Deadly: Sexual Modernity and the Making of Race* (London: Verso, 2023); Ratna Kapur, *Erotic Justice: Law and the New Politics of Postcolonialism* (London: Glasshouse Press, 2005); Sandy O'Sullivan, 'The Colonial Project of Gender (and Everything Else),' *genealogy* 5 (2021), 67-75; Ryan Thoreson, *Transnational LGBT Activism: Working for Sexual Rights Worldwide* (Minneapolis: Minnesota University Press, 2014).
25. Matthew Waites, 'Critique of "Sexual Orientation" and "Gender Identity" in Human Rights Discourse: Global Queer Politics beyond the Yogyakarta Principles,' *Contemporary Politics* 15(1) (2009), 137.
26. Royal Opera House, 'Insights: Ballet and the Black Experience,' accessed 26 January 2024, https://www.youtube.com/watch?v=a4Q8cm9g4fo.
27. Victoria and Albert Museum, 'The Progress Pride flag,' accessed 26 January 2024, https://www.vam.ac.uk/articles/the-progress-pride-flag.

Fig. 1: Queer Judgments Project logo

we had discussed. Thus, in a typical collaborative queer creative style that nurtures the talent and the beauty of those involved, Rose and Gabriel played with colours and edited them into a logo. As a result, the flower of the Queer Judgments Project is a queer flower (Fig. 1)!

Although, like all flowers, it brings psychological and physiological advantages to those who look at it,[28] the Queer Judgments Project Flower—with its colours— celebrates all queer people, and inspires you (the reader) to smile, joyfully act, and cultivate 'an emotional spark, social engagement, novelty-seeking, creative exploration—ESSENCE.'[29]

Moreover, our flower wants to remind you of—and respect—what queer people are teaching all of us around the world: braveness, dignity, and pride to be our real self.

---

28. For a review on the literature on the effects of looking at flowers, see: Junfang Xie, Binyi Liu, Mohamed Elsadek, 'How Can Flowers and Their Colors Promote Individuals' Physiological and Psychological States during the COVID-19 Lockdown?' *International Journal of Environmental Research and Public Health* 18/19 (2021), 10258.
29. Daniel Siegel, *Brainstorm.The Power and Purpose of the Teenage Brain* (London: Scribe UK, 2013), 16.

Relations

What became apparent from the conception of this endeavour was the centrality that relations—as social relations and knowledge-making—played and play in this project and in our queer approach to law (its production, reproduction, transgression, and re-writing).

Friendship, collegiality, collaborations, writing together with the protagonists of some cases, dedication to friends, all characterize this project. We believe that 'freedom is participation,'[30] and encouraged a participative and collaborative approach through-out all the creative process of writing, re-drafting, and reviewing the papers. Editors and contributors met for group and one-to-one meetings to better define the focus of chapters; similarly, editors and contributors reviewed the chapters. We wish to thank all contributors for reviewing each other's chapters with thorough kindness and curiosity.

Relationality, connections, and collaboration speak also to the future steps of this project to accommodate the voices of those that for various reasons have not contributed to this edited collection. For instance, although the workshops saw the participation of friends from South America, Africa, and Middle East, most of their contributions will be eventually included in the future outputs of this project.

Our relations (some already consolidated, others created during the project) became a tool for knowledge-making. Using dancing as metaphor, we were at the same time choreographers and dancers. We created starting from the basic steps, slowly adding details that would highlight our potential, while ensuring coordination.[31] Like dancers, we learned from each other, sometimes through a process of unlearning our individ-ual knowledge and relearning from interacting with each other; we did not avoid divergences, instead we worked together to resolve them, and dance in harmony. We used our social relations as tool to produce knowledge too. Thus, our endeavour—to use Strathern's reflections—'does not simply seek out associations and dissociations across phenomena, but imagines and describes them as relations, and indeed may use the epithet "relational" to claim a distinctive quality of analysis.'[32] But like Les Ballets Trocadero de Monte Carlo, Alvin Ailey or Maurice Bejart,[33] the knowledge we produce in our Queer Judgments Project dance, wishes to enable you—a dancing reader—to reflect on your own (biased) knowledge about the other, and change it. Indeed, we created a new norm!

---

30. Giorgio Gaber, 'La Libertà,' 1972 (original text in Italian: 'La Libertà è Partecipazione'). To listen to the song: accessed 26 January 2024, https://www.youtube.com/watch?v=j3vowbyQBiQ.

31. For some reading on creating choreography, see, for instance, Validimir Angelov, *You, the Choreographer. Creating and Crafting Dance* (London: Routledge, 2023); Jo Butterworth and Liesbeth Wildschut, eds., *Contemporary Choreography. A Critical Reader,* 2nd ed. (London: Routledge, 2017). On legal dancing, see, Sean Mulcahy, 'Dances with Laws: From Metaphor to Methodology,' *Law and Humanities* 15/1 (2021), 106.

32. Marilyn Strathern, *Relations: An Anthropological Account* (Durham and London: Duke University Press, 2020), 1.

33. If you do not know them, that is a shame. However, you can always learn about them: accessed 26 January 2024, https://trockadero.org/; https://www.alvinailey.org/; https://www.bejart.ch/en/company/maurice-bejart/.

Queer is the Norm

Tom Boellstorff has suggested that queer might be a method to be adopted to queer aspects of life that do not appear to be queer at first sight. He poses questions like:

> How might a shift to method, 'a word [queer studies] rarely uses,' open conceptual space for interpreting queer studies as a modality of inquiry potentially applied to any topic? How might the 'studies' of 'queer studies' thereby act less like a noun and more like a verb, a 'queer studying' even of things not self-evidently queer?[34]

Similarly, in this project, we all reflected on whether and how we could queer a judgment. We discussed whether to write a queer judgment, who is the queer judge, and how to write a queer judgment. Without giving away any spoilers about personal choices that each contributor explained in their commentary (because for you to read the whole book is indeed a queer act), three main common facets are apparent.

First, deciding to write a queer judgment came up through personal negotiations balancing conflicting emotions, resistance to the oppressive hetero-cis-normativity of the law, our personal experience of acceptance and oppression, and queer innate tensions to innovate. Motivations were several. For some of us, writing for this project has been an exercise in resilience—as Kseniya Kirichenko in this volume suggests, '[t]o find the source of support within myself'—to overcome brutal judgments against queer people. For others, writing for this project represented one of the numerous occasions to raise awareness and educate to respect. For others, it was a further step towards decolonizing knowledge, law, and academic writing. For others yet, it has been a way to conclude an intense journey of ethnographic activism.[35] But at the end, to put it joyfully and using Raffaella Carrà's words, we thought that '[m]any times, unconsciousness is the path to virtue. Arguing, arguing to love each other more and more.'[36] And so, we argued—and wrote!

Next, how did we queer our writing, you might ask? In a queer way of course! Let us explain. At the outset, the contributors to this edited collection have precisely shown how a queer approach creates new understanding and practice of drafting, writing, and publishing in law. We welcomed what Mario Mieli once pointed out, in that '[w]e should stop to be the exception that proves the norm given that this norm oppresses us.'[37] Proudly, the voices of the Queer Judgments Project have not only revised,

---

34. Tom Boellstorff, 'Queer Techne: Two Theses on Methodology and Queer Studies,' in *Queer Methods and Methodologies: Intersecting Queer Theories and Social Science Research*, eds. Kath Browne and Catherine J. Nash (Farnham: Ashgate, 2010), 215-216 (citations omitted).

35. Claire Jin Deschner and Léa Dorion, 'A Feminist and Decolonial Perspective on Passing the Test in Activist Ethnography: Dealing with Embeddedness through Prefigurative Methodology,' *Journal of Organizational Ethnography* 9/2 (2020), 205.

36. Raffaella Carrà, 'Tanti Auguri,' 1978 (original text in Italian: 'Tante Volte l'Incoscienza è la Strada della Virtù, Litigare, Litigare per Amarsi Sempre di Più"). To dance and sing with us you can look at: accessed 26 January 2024, https://www.youtube.com/watch?v=nFvrARdJuAU.

37. Mario Mieli, 'Dirompenza della Questione Omosessuale,' in *La Gaia Critica. Politica e liberazione sessuale degli anni Settanta. Scritti (1972-1983)*, eds. Paola Mieli and Massimo Prearo (Venezia: MarsilioEditori, 2019), 99. For an English account of Mario Mieli's work, see *Towards a Gay Communism. Elements of a Homosexual Critique*. Translated by David Fernbach and Evan Calder Williams (London: Pluto Press, 2018).

but proposed new ways to create, interpret and apply the law. Our contributors have shown that queering judgments is not only a process of rewriting but is also a process of deconstructing the oppressive norm and creating a queer norm.

The process of creating a queer norm goes beyond the subversion of the hetero-cis-norm, beyond acknowledging that law is oppressive, and beyond trying to re-shape the hetero-cis-norm to accommodate queer experiences. Surely, a queer approach is subversive, but this collection suggests a new starting point which is queer and not only resistance or opposition to the hetero-cis-normative. As Alex Powell explains in his chapter, queer writing is not only anti-normative but also, welcoming Aleardo Zanghellini's call, queer can be counter-normative. As Joanne Stagg also suggests in her chapter, '[t]he queer judge would not assume that cis-heteronormativity signifies a monolithic "norm" from which noncisgendered people or nonheterosexuals depart, nor a norm to which queer individuals should aspire. ... They may make the queer ordinary and the ordinary queer.'

This project goes even further than counter-normative—it creates a new norm. This does not mean overlooking or even replicating power structures that have created oppression for queer people. Instead, it means asserting queerness as new norm and to believe that:

> A gay moralisation of life, which combats misery, egoism, hypocrisy, and the repressive character and immorality of customary morality, cannot take place unless we uproot the sense of guilt, that false guilt which still ties so many of us to the status quo, to its ideology and its deathly principles, preventing us from moving with gay seriousness in the direction of a totalising revolutionary project.[38]

We all have struggled, at least once in life, deciding whether to position ourselves within a pseudo-comfortable adherence to what is hetero-cis-morally acceptable—the good gay, good lesbian, the 'it's just a phase bisexual,' the 'she looks like a real woman' trans—or within a tumultuous and liberating subjectivity of who we really are. When adhering to the norm, some of us have faced shame that has immobilized us. Not anymore! We all bring along our personal experiences of exclusion, but we have queerly transformed those experiences into a dynamic force for change. Thus, the 'queer norm' we embrace is one that encourages humility, relationality, care, and courage. As such, it responds to the hierarchical and dominating norms that currently govern queer life.

By creating a queer norm, this collection has taken original shapes and paths. For instance, this novelty is evident in the formats adopted to express our voices in the judgments and in the commentaries that do not always conform to the typical, formal judgment. In this volume, there are counter-judgments, re-written judgments, fiction-alized judgments, and even theatre plays and poems (see the contribution by Sanna Elfving, Katie Jukes, Miriam Schwarz and Surabhi Shukla). Although each chapter has a commentary and a judgment, the commentaries take different shapes such as essays, conversations and poems; some commentaries introduce the judgments, and others follow the judgments. Some of us, to celebrate queer people, have used rainbow colours in their text or added pictures (see, for instance, the contributions by Odette Mazel,

---

38. Mieli, *Towards a Gay Communism*, 105.

Claerwen O'Hara and Dianne Otto, and by Yàdad De Guerre and Marica Moscati). Further, the judgment writing carried out by contributors to this volume has drawn upon an interdisciplinary variety of sources ranging from ethnographic accounts to poetry.

Even when the format of the re-written judgment has been the same as the original judgment in the case in question, something queerly new and original has been added. For instance, conscious of how language can be used politically, some of us have played with words, sometimes making them more respectful (see, for instance, the chapter by Carmelo Danisi and Nuno Ferreira), but other times claiming the ownership of words like dyke/faggot/homosexual. To some readers the use of words such as 'dyke' or 'faggot' or 'homosexual' can sound offensive. However, using them, as in this collection, as Rafael Carrano Lelis and Paula Gerber point out in their chapter:

> is not intended to establish these as the identities of the authors (or anyone else). Rather, they are used as discursive positions that resignify injury, so as to allow collective agency. In this sense … these categories should not be viewed as gendered or binary. Rather, they are introduced as a new linguistical framework that should not be reduced to the heteronormative interpretation of language.

Others have used the text of the original judgment and then queered words, grammar, and punctuation.

Our pride in creating a queer norm has stretched the limits of what queer judgment writing can mean by adding another layer of queer approach to judgments that were originally favourable to the applicants (see, for instance, contributions by Daryl Yang and by Joanne Stagg). Furthermore, contributors extended a queer approach to topics not directly related to sexuality and gender, like noise pollution from airplanes at Heathrow Airport constituting a violation of private and family life, as Kay Lalor does, or the destruction of cultural heritage as an international crime as Lucas Lixinski does. Creating a queer norm and stretching queer judgment writing has not meant lack of rigour and impartiality of judges, though (see, for instance, Liam Davis considering the limits of a queer approach in addressing the request of the party as well). As suggested at the beginning of this introductory chapter, we are dancers, and like dancers we innovate by bringing together different styles, pushing our minds, and expressing emotions, while committed to rigour and clarity.[39]

Like dancers that know how to manage and liberate the body in time and space— respecting the body although pushing it to its limits—in this collection queer bodies are catalysts and a common theme. Overall, court proceedings transform the body

---

39. For a beautiful visual account of what dance is, you must see and listen to Maurice Bejart, accessed 26 January 2024, https://www.youtube.com/watch?v=2IsUmj6fTj4. For an overall overview on dance studies, see: Jens Richard Giersdorf and Yutian Wong, eds., *The Routledge Dance Studies Reader, 3rd ed.* (London: Routledge, 2019); and visit the website of the Dance Studies Association, accessed 26 January 2024, https://www.dancestudiesassociation.org/. For a critical analysis of dance ontology, see Anna Pakes, *Choreography Invisible. The Disappearing Work of Dance* (Oxford: Oxford University Press, 2020). On queer studies and dance, see: Claire Croft, ed., *Queer Dance. Meaning and Making* (Oxford: Oxford University Press, 2020); Penny Farfan, *Performing Queer Modernism* (Oxford: Oxford University Press, 2017). See, also, *Queer the Ballet*, accessed 22 April 2024, https://www.queertheballet.com/.

of the litigants involved in them; the psychophysical effects of stress, emotions and expectations impact the parties' bodies. If the hetero-cis-normative law often shapes queer bodies by limiting, castrating, invisibilizing, blaming, sterilizing, repressing and (only rarely) slightly supporting queer bodies, our queer norm celebrates all queer bodies by conceptualizing queer bodies as forces for change, by centring the voices of the queer people who challenged the law (Odette Mazel, Claerwen O'Hara and Dianne Otto), by emphasizing the emotions of queer people (Senthorun Raj), by opening up spaces for queer bodies (see chapters in Part 5), by decriminalizing sexual acts between people of the same sex (see chapters in Part 1), and by recognizing queer reproduction and health (see chapters in Part 4). However, we are aware that this collection does not include judgments addressing the issues that, for example, intersex people face. Given the spontaneous nature of this project, we did not impose any topics on contributors, and topics that have not been covered here will hopefully be included in other, future outputs of the project.

Who is the Queer Judge?

In queering this introductory chapter, we, the editors, have played, experimented, performed, and joyfully pushed our boundaries; so, why not convey our reflections on the identity of the queer judge through a poem? Thus, with the help of a dear and precious friend, Barney Ashton-Bullock, here you are, dear reader, we introduce you our queer judge:[40]

THE QUEER JUDGE...

The queer judge provokes, as and when 'needs must.'

The queer judge is rigorous, impartial, a builder of trust.

The queer judge is often droll, employs wit, can humour us.

The queer judge elevates the parties/claimants
both in their reveal and their vent.

The queer judge wields spirited sensibility, applies it to other sensitivities; is well
intentioned, well meant.
Changes hearts and minds bit by bit.

The queer judge doesn't compromise, broker the irrelevant
or inopportune; can revise a perjurer's hateful tune.

---

40. Maria Federica (Marica) and Barney are the authors of this poem. Marica wrote a list poem condensing in it what emerged from the contributors' work, and then Barney embellished it to accentuate a playful rhyme structure, so that it could almost be performative / spoken word.

The queer judge utters words like dyke/homo/faggot to show that queer ownership
of such words matters.

The queer judge is attentive, alert; listens to the meanings beyond the words.

The queer judge slaloms through archaic laws that produce
the 'same old, same old' outcomes as before.

The queer judge makes sure the oppressed and marginalized
are seen and heard in the eyes of the law.

The queer judge aims to aid the cause against the hetero-cis-normative, the racist, the
classist, the ableist, the colonialist. Prejudice? The queer judge will not stand for it!

The queer judge is empathetic to the charge
and course of emotions.

The queer judge is a visionary for what justice could
and should be.

The queer judge is a choreographer of curiosity,
respects and reads the signs of prosecuting,
and defends minds and bodies.

The queer judge makes resilient, informed judgment
to mitigate past injustices against all of us 'othered.'

*So that we are no more smothered in **prejudice** and **ignorance**, intended or
otherwise, and in this way **the queer judge**
opens all of our eyes!*

Dear Reader, this brings our dance to the end of the second Act. Take a break and come
back to us for the final Act.

The Structure of the Book

The book is structured in five main parts. Part 1 focuses on crime and sodomy cases,
Part 2 on privacy and discrimination cases, Part 3 on family and parenthood cases,
Part 4 on health and reproduction cases, and Part 5 on asylum and migration cases.
Although this structure was adopted for reasons of clarity and logic of the organization
of contributions, there is unavoidably some overlap between the five parts of the book
owing to the richness and complexity of the cases. Contributions within each Part
of the book were ordered chronologically, thus avoiding any other ordering criteria
that could prioritize any region, jurisdiction or theme. A chronological order can also

help us unearth influences some case law may have had on subsequent cases in other jurisdictions and even on seemingly unrelated topics.

Part 1—on crime and sodomy cases—starts off with Thomas Crofts, who worked on the 1953 Australian case of *Re Humpris*.[41] Crofts' interest in the case stems in part from the importance of the case in the role it played in the partial and subsequently full decriminalization of male same-sex sexual acts in the UK and afterwards across Australia. The case related to cruising in a park in Sydney, in what was seen according to the law at the time as soliciting for an immoral purpose. Although the man in question won the case on appeal, Crofts re-imagines a positive decision from a queer perspective, within the temporal limits of the case. Senthorun Raj's contribution follows, with a queer dissenting judgment in the 1997 Australian *R v Green* case.[42] The case had to do with a man who killed another man following sexual advances by the latter, where the accused made use of the Homosexual Advance Defence (HAD) to see his crime reduced from murder to manslaughter. Raj puts forward a dissenting judgment focusing on the role of disgust to contest the outcome of the original judgment. Yerram Raju Behara, Malhar Satav and Sal then offer a queer re-working of the judgment in the 2018 Indian case of *Navtej Singh Johar v Union of India*.[43] The case related to the criminalization of sexual acts between people of the same sex, and the Supreme Court of India finally agreed on the unconstitutionality of Section 377 of the Indian Penal Code. Behara, Satav and Sal offer an analysis of the impact of this case on the lived experiences of queer people in India through the form of a belated opinion written after the original judgment. Kseniya Kirichenko follows with a contribution exploring the 2018 decision in *KK v Russian Federation*.[44] This decision from the United Nations Committee on the Elimination of Discrimination against Women (CEDAW) concerned the offensive and discriminatory language used by a member of a Russian regional parliament against the author herself. Kirichenko offers a very personal, queer and intersectional therapeutic dissenting opinion to CEDAW's original decision. Finally, Part 1 closes with the contribution from Waruguru Gaitho, who considers the 2019 Kenyan decision of the High Court of Nairobi on Petition 150 and 234 of 2016.[45] Gaitho re-imagines from a queer and decolonial perspective the upholding of the constitutionality of the criminalization of same-sex relations, by offering a dissenting opinion to the original decision.

Part 2 of the book—on privacy and discrimination cases—is opened with the contribution from Alexandra Grolimund and Alexander Maine, on the 1997 European Court of Human Rights (ECtHR) judgment in *Laskey, Jaggard and Brown v The United Kingdom*.[46] The case concerned the Bondage-Domination-Sadism-Masochism (BDSM) activities of a group of queer men, who were eventually found guilty of

---

41. *Ex parte Langley; Re Humphris* (1953) 53 SR (NSW) 324.
42. *R v Green* (1997) 191 CLR 334.
43. *Navtej Singh Johar v Union of India* (2018) 10 SCC 1.
44. *K.K. v Russian Federation* (25 February 2019) U.N. Doc. CEDAW/C/72/D/98/2016.
45. *Petition 150 & 234 of 2016* (High Court of Nairobi: Constitutional and Human Rights Division).
46. *Laskey and Others v The United Kingdom* (Applications no. 21627/93; 21628/93; 21974/93) [1997] 24 EHRR 39.

assault occasioning actual bodily harm and sentenced to prison. Grolimund and Maine re-imagine the original judgment from a queer perspective, finding that there was indeed a violation of the applicants' right to private life. Kay Lalor follows with a contribution on the *Hatton v UK* case, another ECtHR judgment, this time from 2003.[47] The case related to the noise pollution caused by airplanes at Heathrow Airport, and the ECtHR found that those living in the airport's flight path did not have their right to private and family life violated. Although not an obvious choice of topic for a contribution to this book, Lalor effectively puts forward a queer ecological re-imagining of the original judgment and finds in favour of the applicants. The next contribution is by Andrew Gilden, who explores the decision in *Reliable Consultants, Inc. v Earle*, concerning a 2008 decision by the USA Fifth Circuit Court of Appeals decision to strike down the ban on the sale of sexual devices in Texas.[48] Although the original decision was positive, Gilden argues for greater constitutional protection for the use and purchase of sex toys in his imagined concurring opinion, thus achieving a more transparent, sex-positive, and queerer consideration of sexual technology. Odette Mazel, Claerwen O'Hara and Dianne Otto then offer a poignant analysis of the 2014 Australian High Court decision in *NSW Registrar of Births, Deaths and Marriages v Norrie*.[49] Through this decision, Norrie was successful in changing her sex/gender descriptor on their birth certificate to 'non-specific.' Mazel, O'Hara and Otto re-imagine the case through the lens of the queer figure of tricksters, who unsettle and transgress the limits of the law. Although the original judgment was positive to Norrie, the authors offer an even more positive—and queer—decision, centring Norrie's voice and challenging colonial and heterocisnormative thinking by celebrating self-determination and difference. After this, Flick (Felicity) Adams and Fabienne Emmerich re-imagine the 2016 UK High Court decision in *Hopkins and Sodexo*.[50] The case concerned a lesbian couple in prison, who wished to remain in the same cell and offer each other emotional and physical support, particularly on account of the disability of one of them. Adams and Emmerich put forward a counter-judgment informed by queer, disability and abolitionist perspectives, in the form of a decision by the Court of Appeal on a fictional appeal against the original High Court decision, and find that the appellants did see their rights to private life and equality violated by the prison authorities. Lucas Lixinski offers another contribution that may not seem the most obvious option for a queer judgments volume, but that can effectively be read from a queer perspective: the 2017 International Criminal Court decision in *Prosecutor v Ahmad Al Faqi Al Mahdi (Reparations)*.[51] The case concerned the destruction of parts of the World Heritage Site of Timbuktu in Mali by Islamic extremists, and the reparations order that followed. Lixinski makes a valuable contribution to a developing queer international cultural

---

47. *Hatton v UK* (2003) 37 EHRR 28.

48. *Reliable Consultants, Inc. v Earle*, 517 F. 3d 738 (5th Cir. 2008).

49. *NSW Registrar of Births, Deaths and Marriages v Norrie* [2014] HCA 11.

50. *R (on the application of Hopkins) v Sodexo / HMP Bronzefield QB* (Administrative Court) [2016] EWHC 606 (Admin).

51. *Prosecutor v Al Mahdi (Reparations Order)* (International Criminal Court Trial Chamber VIII, ICC-01/12-01/15), judgment of 17 August 2017.

heritage law, by queering the binaries and other premises subjacent to the original decision, all in the shape of a re-written reparations order. Mariza Avgeri follows with a re-imagined judgment in the 2018 judgment of the Court of Justice of the European Union (CJEU) in *MB v Secretary of State for Work and Pensions*.[52] The case related to the refusal by the UK authorities to grant an earlier retirement pension to the applicant due to her refusal to annul her marriage to obtain official recognition of her gender. The original decision was favourable to the applicant, but by looking at UK, European Union (EU) and European Convention on Human Rights (ECHR) legal elements from a queer and transgender studies perspective, Avgeri puts forward an even more favourable re-written judgment. Avgeri offers a decision which is much more respectful of the rights and needs of trans, non-binary or genderqueer people, especially those who do not wish to undergo surgical interventions or fulfil other legal requirements not compatible with individuals' self-determination. Finally, Carolynn Gray concludes this Part by looking at the 2021 UK Supreme Court judgment in the *Elan-Cane* case.[53] The case concerned the legal recognition of the applicant's non-binary identity in their passport by using X as gender marker. Gray offers a cogent and positive dissenting judgment to the original negative decision of the Supreme Court, built on a critique of the cisgenderism and bigenderism subjacent to the original decision, and a queer interpretation of the human rights of the applicant.

Part 3—on family and parenthood cases—starts off with the contribution from Rafael Carrano Lelis and Paula Gerber, on the 2002 View of the United Nations Human Rights Committee (HRC) in *Joslin et al. v New Zealand*.[54] The case related to the right to marry of two lesbian couples in New Zealand. Lelis and Gerber queer the jurisprudence of the HRC, by offering a re-written View that finds in favour of the applicants, on account of a violation of their right to marry in conjunction with the right to non-discrimination and equal protection of the law. Sanna Elfving, Katie Jukes, Miriam Schwarz and Surabhi Shukla follow with a creative exploration of the 2008 ECtHR judgment in *EB v France*.[55] The case concerned a lesbian adoption applicant who was refused by French authorities. By deploying drama and poetry techniques, the authors explore notions of family, gender, motherhood, parenting and childhood. Although the original decision of the ECtHR was positive to the claimant and found that her right to non-discrimination in conjunction with her right to private and family life had been violated, the authors powerfully unpack the stereotypes and stigma judges still associate with queer parents. The next chapter—authored by Claire O'Connell and James Rooney—re-work the Irish Supreme Court decision in *McD v L and M*.[56] The case consisted of a guardianship dispute between a lesbian couple and a gay man who had acted as sperm donor in the conception of the couple's child. The authors offer a re-imagined dissent against the Supreme Court's original decision,

---

52. Case C-451/16, *MB v Secretary of State for Work and Pensions* [2016] ECLI:EU:C:2018:492.
53. [2021] UKSC 56; [2023] A.C. 559.
54. *Joslin et al. v New Zealand* [2002] United Nations Human Rights Committee (UN HRC), Communication No. 902/1999, U.N. Doc. CCPR/C/75/D/902/1999.
55. *EB v France*, Application no 43546/02 (ECtHR, 22 January 2008).
56. *McD v L* [2010] 2 IR 199.

by critiquing the notions of marital and de facto families, supported by a queer creation of a constitutional right to procreative liberty. Yàdad De Guerre and Marica Moscati then offer a creative contribution related to the Italian Constitutional Court judgment no. 138/2010, which explored the right of same-sex couples to marry under the Italian Constitution.[57] In an intensely personal dialogue, the authors explore the legal and social developments up until the Court's judgment and subsequent events as well. De Guerre and Moscati also put forward a re-imagined judgment which concludes that the civil code rules concerning marriage that are interpreted as prohibiting same-sex marriages are unconstitutional for violating the parties' rights to marry, constitute a family and equality. Daryl Yang concludes Part 3 by offering a rich discussion of the 2018 Singapore High Court decision in *UKM v Attorney-General*.[58] The case related to an adoption application by a father to legally establish a parental relationship with his biological child gestated through surrogacy, with the aim of obtaining Singaporean citizenship for the child. Although the Court granted the adoption order, Yang argues in favour of a queerer, liberating approach to the case, in the form of a concurring opinion.

Part 4—on health and reproduction cases—opens with Lynsey Mitchell's contribution on the 2017 judgment of the UK Supreme Court in *R (on the application of A and B) v Secretary of State for Health*.[59] The case related to the right to abortion, more specifically having access to abortion in England through the National Health Service (NHS) despite being normally resident in Northern Ireland. Mitchell uses a queer lens to frame this case as being about reproductive rights and, more essentially, about bodily autonomy, rather than a competence devolution issue. This allows Mitchell to re-write the original judgment to find that there had been a violation of the applicants' right to non-discrimination in conjunction with the right to private and family life, as well as a violation of the prohibition on torture and inhuman or degrading treatment. Liam Davis then offers a contribution on the 2020 Court of Appeal judgment in *McConnell and YY v The Registrar General for England and Wales*.[60] The case dealt with the request of a trans man who had given birth to be named as father or parent (but not as mother) in the child's birth certificate. Despite concluding that not even a queer approach to the case could give the applicant the desired outcome, Davis reaches a re-written judgment that considers queer parenthood more carefully and declares the applicable legal norms incompatible with the ECHR. Joanne Stagg follows with an analysis of the 2020 decision of an Australian Family Court in the case *Re Imogen (No. 6)*.[61] The case—relating to a 16-year-old transgender girl—hinged on issues such as medical age of consent, parental authority, and witness expertise. Although the original decision was positive and allowed the girl to access medical transition, Stagg offers an anti-cisnormative and anti-transphobic discussion of the matter in the form of a fictional decision on an appeal against the original decision. The next contribution—authored

---

57. Constitutional Court, judgment no. 138, 14 April 2010.
58. [2018] SGHCF 18.
59. *R (on the application of A and B) v Secretary of State for Health* [2017] UKSC 41 (UK).
60. *R (on the application of McConnell) v The Registrar General for England and Wales* [2020] EWCA Civ 559.
61. *Re Imogen (No 6)*, No. 761 (FamCA 10 September 2020). [2020] FamCA 761.

by Po-Han Lee, Tsung-Han Yu, Titan Deng and Tzu-Wei Lin—considers the Taiwan High Court's 2022 judgment in Appeal-Review-(1)-Zi No. 162 (2021). The case concerned the criminalization of HIV transmission in the context of chemsex. By offering a queer reading of the 'undetectable equals untransmittable' (U=U) discourse, problematizing the exceptional status of HIV amongst other infectious diseases, and focussing on the agency and shared responsibility of people who engage in sex, the authors re-write the original decision and acquit the defendant. Frank Nasca closes this Part of the volume by proposing a 2023 decision by the Health Services Appeal and Review Board in the *Nathaniel Le May v The General Manager, Ontario Health Insurance Plan* case. The case involved the refusal by the Ontario Health Insurance Plan (OHIP) to fund a phalloplasty surgery for a non-binary transmasculine applicant, on the basis of his need for non-normative surgical outcomes. Before the Board could reach a decision, OHIP chose to fund the surgery and moved to dismiss the case as moot, meaning that the other legal issues raised in the case went undecided. Nasca therefore puts forward the decision the Board should have nonetheless taken to promote systemic policy change, by asserting a queer reading of the applicant's right to transgender healthcare under the constitutional protection of his rights to equality and security of the person.

Finally, Part 5—on asylum and migration cases—contains three contributions. The first one is authored by Alex Powell and it relates to the 2010 UK Supreme Court's decision in *HJ(Iran) & HT(Cameroon) v Secretary of State for the Home Department*.[62] The case concerned two gay men seeking asylum in the UK, and the main point revolved around whether authorities could legitimately expect asylum claimants seeking protection on grounds of their sexual orientation to return to their countries of origin and conceal their sexual orientation to avoid the risk of persecution. Although this judgment has been considered a significant victory for such claimants for reducing the scope of such discretion reasoning, Powell argues for a queer counter-judgment that completely precludes any expectation of discretion and puts forward an alternative that is less homonormative, homonationalist, and restrictive of sexual diversity. This contribution is followed by that of Carmelo Danisi and Nuno Ferreira, who explore the 2013 CJEU judgment in *X, Y and Z v Minister voor Immigratie en Asiel*.[63] The case related to three gay men—from Sierra Leone, Uganda and Senegal—who saw their asylum claims refused by the Dutch authorities. The authors offer a re-written judgment that is informed by a queer reading of the legislation and fundamental rights in question, as well as a human rights-based approach to refugee law, thus not only precluding any expectation of discretion, but also adopting a less restrictive approach to determine that claimants belong to a particular social group, and considering that criminalization of same-sex sexual acts should be presumed to be persecution. Alina Tryfonidou concludes this book by reimagining the 2018 CJEU judgment in the *Coman* case.[64] In this case, the Court considered the situation of a same-sex male couple who

---

62. *HJ(Iran) & HT(Cameroon) v Secretary of State for the Home Department* [2010] UKSC 31.
63. Joined Cases C-199/12, C-200/12 and C-201/12, *X, Y and Z v Minister voor Immigratie en Asiel*, 7 November 2013, ECLI:EU:C:2013:720.
64. Case C-673/16, *Coman and Others v Inspectoratul General Pentru Imigrari and Ministerul Afacerilor Interne*, ECLI:EU:C:2018:385.

had made use of EU free movement of persons, and wished to see their marriage recognized in Romania—the home country of one of the members of the couple. Although the Court produced a decision that was positive for the applicants by recognizing that their right to free movement under EU law required the recognition of their marriage in Romania, Tryfonidou proposes a re-written judgment that adds to the original by also considering a fundamental rights line of argumentation and queering the terminology and overall approach of the Court.

While most commentaries followed the Counterpress style guide, contributors were given the freedom to vary from that style if for some substantive or stylistic reason they believed a certain variation was required. In relation to the judgments, contributors were also given the option to either follow the publisher's style guide or the original decision's own style.

What Lays on the Horizon

Although we are immensely proud of the substantive piece of work that we—editors and contributors—have put together, and are convinced of the generative nature of this project, we are also undoubtedly aware of the limitations of this volume. We have been unable to include contributions relating to certain regions, such as Latin America and Middle East. The selection of topics considered by the contributions that follow are necessarily limited, and do not cover so many other SOGIESC-related topics such as polygamy, open relationships, cohabitation, political representation, intersex people,[65] asexual people, tensions between SOGIESC-related rights and freedom of religion and other rights, and so on. Moreover, we believe any topic can be 'queered' and 'queer' does not necessarily need to be indexed to SOGIESC issues. Consequently, issues like climate change, Indigenous sovereignty, disability liberation, self-determination, borders, militarization, poverty, etc. can all be analyzed from queer perspectives and judgments pertaining to those issues can be re-written by adopting queer methodologies. We trust future initiatives will gradually cover the space still left uncovered by this volume.

We are also conscious of the limitations of the written medium. Although we have given contributors plenty of freedom to experiment with the form of their contributions, and many have been deliciously creative and inspiring, all contributions remain for the most part constrained by the written format. We will pursue other modes of expression in the future steps of the Queer Judgments Project, including live drama, photography, comic strips, and so on. We invite fellow scholars, activists and artists to join us in this effort to queer the law through non-written and other creative means.

Similarly, we have given much freedom to contributors in terms of terminology. Some preferred shorter acronyms, others longer ones; some preferred to concentrate on characteristics, others on identities; some on collective dimensions, others on individual ones; some on widely accepted terms, others on challenging historically offensive terms

---

65. Mazel, O'Hara and Otto's commentary makes reference to an amicus curiae submission from Organisation Intersex International Australia, which raised a number of concerns although the *Norrie* case did not involve an intersex person.

that are now being reclaimed but still come across as hurtful to most. As it is commonly recognized in academia and across community groups and organizations, terminology is a minefield. Rather than pretending that there is clearly right and wrong terminology, we accepted the need to embrace a variety of stances about terminology, and embraced the queering of words as well. Can the respectful and well-informed approach to terminology of this volume's contributors serve as an example for future efforts in the field of queer studies and beyond?

More fundamentally, we realize the somewhat naïve idea that we can queer a system that—both historically and presently—has caused so much harm to queer people and resists any urgent change. Even more deeply, as some of our contributors have rightly pointed out, there may not be any point in trying to queer the law, as it will always remain a repressive tool. As true as that may be, we are still of the opinion that there is merit in attempting to queer the judgments below. No matter how slow and partial this process may be, if it translates in some improvement, then this effort will have been worth it. How much this sort of enterprise translates into any practical change is of course extremely difficult to measure and requires a complex mixture of consistent effort, changing of teaching practices,[66] targeted dissemination, continuous awareness raising, and—let us admit it—luck. Still, much beyond any current neo-liberal pressure to translate academic research into practical changes to law and policy (framed as research impact in many jurisdictions), we do hope that this volume will produce positive change to legal frameworks and practices around the globe.

We also wonder how much more queering the law may be stretched and wait expectantly for works that will push those boundaries even further. As contributions below combine queer approaches with feminist, trans, critical race, decolonial, heritage, reproductive, decarceration, disability and ecological approaches, we hope these contributions will inspire others to consider—often unexpected—queer angles to their own work, and nurture combinations of theoretical frameworks that join efforts in broader social justice issues and movements.

This volume is but a seed of many more queer judgments initiatives that may follow. Besides other initiatives still to come within the framework of the Queer Judgments Project itself, we hope that this volume will work as a stepping stone for other volumes and initiatives, perhaps focused on specific jurisdictions, regions, themes, identities, characteristics, and so on. We look forward to seeing those come to fruition and supporting them the best we can along the way. As we do, read our chapters and dance with us!

---

66. In line with the principles developed by Paula Gerber and Claerwen O'Hara: Paula Gerber and Claerwen O'Hara, 'Teaching Law Students about Sexual Orientation, Gender Identity and Intersex Status within Human Rights Law: Seven Principles for Curriculum Design and Pedagogy,' *Journal of Legal Education* 68(2) (2019), 416.

PART 1

CRIME AND SODOMY

2

Ex parte Langley; Re Humphris (Australia):
Cruising, Crime and the Path to Decriminalization

Thomas Crofts

Introduction

This rewritten judgment concerns the New South Wales (NSW), Australian case of *Ex parte Langley; Re Humphris* (1953) 53 SR (NSW) 324 (*Re Humphris*). It was chosen because it highlights a number of issues in relation to how homosexuality[1] has been conceptualized and regulated throughout history. It is valuable to explore *Re Humphris*, in its historical context, because it takes place at a turning point in the long and complicated relationship between the criminal law and homosexuality. Indeed, the original judgment in this case may be seen as representing a[2] high-water mark in the punitive treatment of male same-sex desire. Soon after this case was decided, and perhaps exactly because of this punitive drive, efforts to decriminalize homosexuality gained momentum. Only one year after the case was decided, Sir John Wolfenden, then Vice-Chancellor of the University of Reading, was commissioned by the United Kingdom (UK) Government to examine the criminal law's approach to prostitution[3] and male homosexuality. The Report of this Committee, published in 1957, paved the way

---

1. While it is acknowledged that the term 'homosexual' can convey problematic labelling connotations, it is used here because it is 'a formal term of significance within the law,': Les Moran, *The Homosexual(ity) of Law* (Abingdon: Routledge, 1996), 2.
2. This is not intended to indicate that this was 'the' high water mark but was 'a' high water mark in a series of waves of repression throughout history.
3. 'Prostitution' is the term used by the Wolfenden Committee, the legislation and the case law of that time and is therefore used throughout this chapter. It should be noted, however, that the term is problematic because the word prostitution does more than merely describe, it condemns and carries derogatory connotations, and it 'conflates work and identity,': see Sylvia Law, 'Commercial Sex: Beyond Decriminalization,' *Southern Californian Law Review* 73 (2000), 525; see, also, Karen McMillan, Heather Worth and Patrick Rawstorne, 'Usage of the Terms Prostitution, Sex Work, Transactional Sex, and Survival Sex: Their Utility in HIV Prevention Research,' *Archives Sexual Behaviour* 47 (2018), 1517–1527. Furthermore, the terms 'prostitution' and 'prostitute' may not reflect the opportunistic and transient nature of sex work for some workers, which means that there are workers who do not identify themselves with this label and define themselves differently: see Aimee Wodda and Vanessa R Panfil, *Sex Positive Criminology* (Abingdon: Routledge, 2021), 21.

for the partial (and later full) decriminalization of male homosexuality in the UK in 1967 and later throughout Australia.

Facts and Original Decision

The appellant was observed by police officers in the evening of 24 November 1952 loitering near the Archibald Monument in Hyde Park, Sydney, dressed in clerical clothes. He approached C and engaged in conversation, during which he made lewd remarks and invited C to become an accomplice in the commission of an 'unnatural sex offence.' He placed his hand on C's leg and genitals, at which point C stood up and walked away. The appellant then approached another man in the park, whereupon he was apprehended by police officers.

The appellant was convicted in the Court of Petty Sessions under s 4(2)(o)(ii) of the *Vagrancy Act 1902* of being a male person soliciting for an immoral purpose. This appeal concerned a motion to make absolute a rule nisi for a writ of prohibition regarding the appellant's conviction under s 4(2)(o)(ii) of the *Vagrancy Act 1902* in the Court of Petty Sessions. This meant that it would be confirmed that the appellant should not have been charged with the offence contained in the *Vagrancy Act 1902*. The NSW Court was being asked to determine whether the behaviour of the appellant was an offence of the kind that had been contemplated by the subsection of the *Vagrancy Act 1902* under which the charge was laid. It was conceded that there was sufficient evidence to establish a prima facie case against the accused under other offences in the *Crimes Act 1900* and at common law. These were the offences of indecent or offensive behaviour in a public place under s 8, indecent assault on a male person under s 81, and the common law misdemeanor of inciting another person to commit the 'abominable crime' contained in s 79.

Counsel for the appellant argued that the mischief that s 4(2)(o)(ii) of the *Vagrancy Act 1900,* was designed to address was that of trading in prostitution. It was not the purpose of the provision to address behaviour such as that engaged in by the appellant, who was not acting for purposes of prostitution. Furthermore, the intention of the legislature was not to add a further penalty for the type of conduct engaged in by the appellant, i.e. seeking to engage in 'abnormal sexual relations,' but rather to address a man in a public place soliciting clients for a female prostitute.

Counsel for the respondent argued that the intention of the legislature in introducing s 4(2)(o)(ii) of the *Vagrancy Act 1902* was to provide an alternative to laying charges under offences in the *Crimes Act 1900* or common law relating to 'unnatural sexual behaviour between men.'

Street CJ, Owen J and Clancy J all agreed in separate judgments that the rule nisi should be made absolute. It was held that the appellant should not have been convicted under s 4(2)(o)(ii) of the *Vagrancy Act 1902*.

Both Owen J and Clancy J related that the court had been told that it had been long-standing practice in NSW and in the UK to charge men who, in a public place, sought to engage in sexual relations with other men under s 4(2)(o)(ii) of the *Vagrancy Act 1902* rather than to charge them with more serious offences under the *Crimes Act 1900* or common law. Taking a literal view, Clancy J found that there was no doubt that the words of the subsection of the *Vagrancy Act 1902* could be interpreted as referring to the appellant's behaviour if looked at on their own without reference to their context in the Act as a whole. Support for this interpretation was found in the English case of *Horton v Mead* (*Mead*)[4] where it was assumed that the equivalent provision of the *Vagrancy Act 1898* (UK) applied to the type of behaviour engaged in by the appellant.

Despite this apparent longstanding approach, Clancy J noted that the answer to the question of whether it was correct for a person to be charged under that subsection of the *Vagrancy Act 1902* could not simply be answered by referring to what had been assumed to be the correct practice in the past. Now that the question had been specifically asked of the Court, it needed answering directly. His Honour cautioned against the Court simply considering the words in the subsection as if they stood alone. Rather, the rule of legal interpretation required that the Court considered the words in their setting and the Act as a whole.

In viewing the provision in the context of the whole Act, his Honour noted that s 4 of the *Vagrancy Act 1902* groups together offences relating to a person who does not have a visible means of support, or who is the owner of a house frequented by reputed thieves or persons who have no visible lawful means of support, or who is a 'common prostitute' wandering in the street, as well as other similar offences. It was then noted that the nature and gravity of these offences stood in sharp contrast to the offences in the *Crimes Act 1900* and common law relating to sexual behaviour between men. The penalty under the relevant subsection of the *Vagrancy Act 1902* was imprisonment with hard labour for a term not exceeding six months. In contrast, for example, the maximum penalty for a conviction under the common law offence of inciting another person to commit the 'abominable crime' in s 79 of the *Crimes Act 1900* was fourteen years of penal servitude. Clancy J opined that the substantial difference between the penalty provided for these 'unnatural offences' in the *Crimes Act 1900* and common law and that which could be imposed under the *Vagrancy Act 1902* was significant. It indicated that the provision in the *Vagrancy Act 1902* was not designed to be an alternative to prosecution under the offences in the *Crimes Act 1900* or common law. If it were otherwise, it would expose the acts of homosexual men to the same penalty 'as those who engage in practices such as fortune telling, playing or betting at an unlawful game,' etc.

Clancy J found that, rather than providing an alternative charge to the offences in the *Crimes Act 1900* or common law for sexual relations between men, the prohibition on soliciting by male persons in the *Vagrancy Act 1902* was designed to address the actions of a male who solicits another male to have intercourse with a female prostitute. Support for this reading was found in the fact that the offence in s 4(2)(o)(ii) is preceded by an offence relating to a male person knowingly living wholly or in part on the earnings of prostitution and is followed by offences of a similar type. Clancy J made reference to *Skinner v King*,[5] which confirmed that a prostitute is a 'woman

---

4. (1913) 1 KB 154.
5. (1913) 16 CLR 336.

who indiscriminately consorts with men for hire,'[6] and noted that the subsection should be read in light of that definition. Accordingly, in the view of Clancy J, Parliament designed the relevant legislative provision to deal only with the subject matter of female prostitution.

Thus, when considering the Act as a whole and the setting of the subsection, Clancy J took the view that the mischief that the subsection was designed to address was touting for the immoral purpose of (female) prostitution. There was no evidence that the appellant had engaged in this behaviour and therefore he should not have been convicted under that subsection. His Honour then noted that depending on the extent to which there was proof of the allegations made about the behaviour of the appellant, he could be convicted under the *Crimes Act 1900*, s 8A, for indecent or offensive behaviour in a public place, or upon indictment for indecent assault on a male person under the *Crimes Act 1900*, s 81, or for the common law offence of inciting another to commit the 'abominable crime of buggery' under the *Crimes Act 1900*, s 79.

Owen J similarly held that the subsection of the *Vagrancy Act 1902* was not designed to address conduct such as that engaged in by the appellant, but rather to deal with men involved in the prostitution of women. In the words of Owen CJ, the *Vagrancy Act 1902* provision applied to 'minor pests, not inaptly described as rogues and vagabonds,' that is men who live off the earnings of prostitutes, such as souteneurs and runners. His Honour found support for this view in the fact that in legal commentaries on crime and procedure, such as Archbold and Russell, the provision, or its counterpart in England, appeared under the heading 'Trading in Prostitution' and was found together with other offences relating to women and young girls.

Street CJ agreed with the reasoning of Owen and Clancy JJ and added no further comments. The decision was therefore unanimous that the appellant should not have been convicted under s 4(2)(o)(ii) of the *Vagrancy Act 1902* and that the rule nisi should be made absolute.

Social, Political and Legal Context

The particular challenge, but also the opportunity, in re-imagining this case from a queer[7] perspective is that it took place at a turning point in the conceptualization and legal treatment of male homosexuality. This re-written judgment is not a contemporary academic critique of how male same-sex desire was regulated and treated by the apparatus of the criminal justice system. It is a re-imagining of how a queer-friendly judge could have interpreted the law and decided the case in NSW in 1953. This means that there were limits on how far the judgment could go. As noted by Hunter, McGlynn and Rackley in relation to the Feminist Judgments Project, writing a judgment subjects

---

6. (1913) 16 CLR 336, 343.
7. While the term 'queer' is used here, it is often used to denote 'almost simply, same-sex sexuality' and it is noted that it would not have been familiar to a judge in 1953 as a term referring to 'the open mesh of possibilities, gaps, overlaps, dissonances and resonances, lapses and excesses of meaning when the constituent elements of anyone's gender, or anyone's sexuality aren't made (or can't be made) to signify monolithically': Eve Sedgwick, *The Weather in Proust* (Durham: Duke University Press, 2011), 200.

the writer to various constraints that a judge would feel, such as 'fidelity to the judicial oath, respect for existing legal principles, and consciousness of the impact of decisions on the particular and the broader community.'[8] With this in mind, I aimed in writing my judgment to adopt a style that is appropriate for that time period, reflecting an approach that could feasibly be held by a judge in NSW in 1953 and relying on materials and attitudes that the judiciary might realistically have been familiar with. A judge of that period almost certainly would not have felt able to radically change the legal position on homosexuality, regardless of how queer friendly they may have been. Indeed, as Lord Salmon noted in *Abbott v The Queen,* judges do not have the power to fundamentally change the criminal law and any policy changes of a fundamental nature can only be made by Parliament.[9]

However, judges can 'push existing rules a bit further in a desired direction'[10] and they can also recommend that Parliament explore the need for reform of the law in a certain area.[11] This is what I have aimed to do in the rewritten judgment, acknowledging that law and its enforcement reflects culture but can also be used to shape it. I drew on the historical context of how male homosexuality has been treated by society, the law and apparatus of the criminal justice system. I gently criticized practices of the criminal justice apparatus (for example, police entrapment practices) and urged for a rolling back of punitive approaches. I also drew on documents, attitudes and material available at the time, such as the research of the Kinsey Institute and John Stuart Mill's *On Liberty,* to push this decision in a more queer-friendly direction. Developments that followed this case, particularly the commissioning of the Wolfenden Committee, show that this was a period of social and legal change and that, against this background, a bold judge might have felt able to urge for reform to decriminalize homosexuality.

To better understand the constraints that a judge in 1953 may have felt, even while aiming to provide a more queer friendly judgment, it is useful to briefly trace the long and complicated relationship between the criminal law and male same-sex desire. This not only gives context to the original and rewritten judgments, but it also helps expose how queer people have historically been denied justice and what methods could be, and were, used to push for equality. While it is tempting to think that there has been a linear progression towards the decriminalization of male homosexuality and a steady move towards a less punitive approach to the policing of male same-sex desire, the reality is more complex. At certain points in history, there have been sometimes more and sometimes fewer punitive approaches, which have not always been driven by legal developments. Changes in official priorities, policing approaches, judicial opinions, shifting societal norms and expectations, and academic/scientific research, have also impacted upon the way that male same-sex desire has been conceptualized and regulated.

---

8. Rosemary Hunter, Clare McGlynn and Erika Rackley, 'Feminist Judgments: An Introduction,' in *Feminist Judgments: From Theory to Practice*, eds. Rosemary Hunter, Clare McGlynn and Erika Rackley (Oxford: Hart, 2010), 3.

9. *Abbott v The Queen* [1977] AC 755, 767.

10. Hunter, McGlynn and Rackley, 'Introduction,' 6.

11. For an example of this, see *Re C (A Minor)* [1995] UKHL 15 (Lord Jauncey of Tullichettle, Lord Bridge of Harwich, Lord Ackner and Lord Lowry).

The first piece of secular legislation criminalizing sodomy was the *Buggery Act 1533* in England.[12] While other sexual acts between men could be prosecuted as an incitement or attempt to commit sodomy, it was not until the late nineteenth century that the concept of *the homosexual* arose, and with it the drive to combat homosexuality.[13] Thus, until this time the law was directed at certain sexual acts rather than at 'a particular type of person.'[14] In response to concerns about an apparent increase in homosexual activity and rising concerns about public displays of immorality, the Liberal MP Henry Labouchere proposed that an offence of outraging decency be included in the *Criminal Law Amendment Act 1885* in the UK.[15] According to s 11 of that Act, '[a]ny male person who, in public or in private, commits, or is a party to the commission of, or procures or attempts to procure the commission by any male person of, any act of gross indecency with another male person' could be punished by up to two years imprisonment. Only a few years later the *Vagrancy Act 1898* amended the *Vagrancy Act 1824* to criminalize men who persistently solicited or importuned for an immoral purpose in a public place.[16] This latter offence was replicated in the *Vagrancy Act 1902* in NSW. This means that by the beginning of the twentieth century, there were a range of offences differing in severity in the UK and NSW which could be used to prosecute men seeking or engaging in sexual activity with other men. Weeks notes that these new offences, while not radical, did have important effects in being capable of more flexible interpretation and being more likely to lead to conviction because they were less serious than the sodomy offence.[17] According to Cook, these offences also gave 'powerful messages about expectations of private conduct and public behaviour.'[18]

Of these offences, it seems that there was a greater use of the offence found in the Vagrancy Acts of the UK and NSW, as noted in *Re Humphris* and *Mead*. Both these cases are illuminating in revealing the sort of behaviours that were thought to be indicators of homosexuality at that time. As was commented in *Mead*, frequently visiting urinals, smiling in the faces of men, pursing the lips, wiggling the body, and wearing make-up were the tell-tale signs. Another interesting feature of *Mead* and *Re Humphris* is that they show that legally there was a lack of nuance and understanding about male same-sex desire up to the twentieth century. Until this time, no real distinction

---

12. Before that time, the offence of sodomy (any non-procreative sex) was a matter for the ecclesiastical courts. For further discussion of the early history of the regulation of sodomy, see, for example, Michael Kirby, 'The Sodomy Offence: England's Least Lovely Criminal Export,' *Journal of Commonwealth Criminal Law* (2011) 1, 23–24; Montgomery Hyde, *The Other Love: A Historical and Contemporary Survey of Homosexuality in Britain* (London: Heinemann, 1970), 29–56; A. D. Harvey, 'Prosecutions for Sodomy in England at the Beginning of the Nineteenth Century,' *Historical Journal* 21 (1978), 939–948.

13. Jeffrey Weeks, *Against Nature: Essays on History, Sexuality and Identity* (London: Rivers Oram Press, 1991), 16–20.

14. Jeffrey Weeks, *Sex Politics and Society, The Regulation of Sexuality Since 1800* , 4th ed. (Abingdon: Routledge, 2018) 104.

15. For a critical account of the reasoning behind Labouchere's amendment, see Francis Smith, 'Labouchere's Amendment to the Criminal Law Amendment Bill,' *Australian Historical Studies* (1976) 17, 165–173.

16. Section 1(1)(b). This was alongside criminalizing a male person knowingly living off the earning of prostitution: s 1(1)(a).

17. Weeks, *Sex, Politics and Society*, 108.

18. Matt Cook, *London and the Culture of Homosexuality, 1885–1914* (Cambridge: Cambridge University Press, 2008), 44.

was made between men seeking and engaging in sex with men and those doing so for the purposes of sex work; both were 'conflated and assumed indistinguishable.'[19]

Another reason why *Re Humphris* is a useful case to examine is because it reveals that often more punitive approaches in history were not due to legislative change but rather due to changes in the public's perceptions of male homosexuality, prosecutorial priorities, shifting police practices, as well as modifications in how judicial officers have interpreted and applied criminal laws. It has been commented that before the mid-twentieth century, police had turned a blind eye to male vice, only prosecuting men where particular complaints had been made.[20] Police sporadically raided areas where men would meet for sex, such as public lavatories, bars, clubs and *molly houses*, and such raids were performed openly by police in uniform.[21] However, changes in personnel at high levels within the criminal justice system towards the middle of the twentieth century led to a significant change in policing practices, with the adoption of more insidious methods of rooting out and prosecuting homosexual men.

In 1944, Sir Theobald Mathew was appointed as Director of Public Prosecutions and led a charge against homosexual men.[22] Further fuel was added with the appointment of Sir David Maxwell Fyfe as Home Secretary in 1951. Fyfe proclaimed the aim of ridding England of homosexuality and indicated that homosexuals should expect no mercy. He directed magistrates to make sentences stiffer and more consistent.[23] He also backed police tactics to increase the arrest of homosexual men through greater police surveillance and the use of agent provocateurs. In 1953, things became even more dire with the appointment of Sir John Nott-Bower as Commissioner of the Metropolitan Police.[24] Nott-Bower swore to institute a new drive by police against male vice and directed Police to prioritize increasing the arrests of homosexual men.[25]

These changes took place during a period, and no doubt as a result, of 'heightened anxiety around dangerous sexualities in the context of profound social changes in post-war Britain,' that 'was further exacerbated by the publication of criminal statistics, which appeared to indicate a marked increase in sexual offences.'[26] Indeed, Weeks notes that: 'The real change in the 1950s was the growth of official concern and public anxiety to which the police zeal was a response.'[27] Adding to this punitive drive was pressure from the US government, which advised that there was a need to weed out homosexuals from important government jobs because of the security risks

---

19.   John Scott, 'A Prostitute's Progress: Male Prostitution in Scientific Discourse,' *Social Semiotics* 13 (2003), 181. For further discussion, see Thomas Crofts, 'Male Sex Work – A Gendered, (Hetro)Sexist Approach to Regulation,' in *Research Handbook on Gender, Sexuality and the Law,* eds. Chris Ashford and Alex Maine (Cheltenham: Edward Elgar, 2020), 379–395.
20.   Hyde, *The Other Love,* 201.
21.   Hyde, *The Other Love,* 209.
22.   Hyde, *The Other Love,* 209; Weeks, *Sex, Politics and Society,* 261.
23.   Hyde, *The Other Love,* 215.
24.   Weeks, *Sex, Politics and Society,* 261.
25.   Hyde, *The Other Love,* 214.
26.   Julia Maclachlan, 'Male Homosexuality 1945-70: Transnational Scientific and Social Knowledge in British and West European Contexts' (PhD, University of Manchester, Manchester, 2020), 46.
27.   Weeks, *Sex, Politics and Society,* 261.

they posed.[28] The case of Guy Burgess and Donald Maclean highlighted the security risk that homosexual men were perceived to present. It was believed that one of them, who held a position in the British embassy in Washington, had blackmailed the other into handing top-secret information to the Russians.[29] As Maclachlan comments:

> British spy cases mirrored US rhetoric during the 'Lavender Scare,' which had linked American anti-homosexual sentiment to the fight against communism, and marked homosexuals as unpatriotic and subversive elements in society, with the mass removal of homosexual men from government positions.[30]

The effect of this campaign against homosexual men was a massive increase in arrests and prosecutions. In England and Wales, from 1938 to 1952, prosecution of cases of sodomy rose from 134 to 670 and cases of gross indecency between males rose from 320 to 1686.[31] Issues of social significance in the UK were of course carefully watched and interpolated in Australia at this point in history, and this increase in arrests and directions to courts to show no leniency towards homosexual men was the contemporary context in which *Re Humphris* was decided.

A judge in NSW, Australia, would have been aware of this escalation in punitiveness both in the UK and throughout Australia and interpolated this into their judgments. It no doubt shaped the original judgments in *Re Humphris* which put an end to taking a more lenient approach by charging men seeking other men for sex under the *Vagrancy Act 1902* rather than under more serious offences. Where a person was caught cruising, but no sexual activity had yet taken place, the more serious offences applicable were indecent or offensive behaviour in a public place under *Crimes Act 1900*, s 8A, which like the charge under the *Vagrancy Act* could be tried summarily. The other two potential offences of indecent assault on a male person under s 81 of the *Crimes Act 1900*, or the common law offence of inciting another to commit an 'abominable crime of buggery' under s 79 of the *Crimes Act 1900* were tried on indictment. Presumably, the latter offences, being more serious and charged on indictment, would have been more time consuming and difficult to prosecute. Thus, the choice of prosecuting under the *Vagrancy Act 1902* may not actually have been the result of feelings of leniency towards homosexual men by police and prosecutors, but rather may have been due to police choosing the easiest route to conviction. As Hyde notes:

> Promotion in the junior ranks of the force has always depended to a considerable extent upon the number of convictions a particular officer has been able to secure, and when the news filtered down to the lower ranks that the authorities are interested in a particular type of offender the inference is obvious, especially as in this instance it was easier and incidentally safer to catch a homosexual than a burglar.[32]

---

28. Maclachlan, 'Male Homosexuality 1945-70,' 46.
29. Maclachlan, Male Homosexuality 1945-70,' 46; Weeks, *Sex, Politics and Society*, 262.
30. Maclachlan, 'Male Homosexuality 1945-70,' 15.
31. Hyde, *The Other Love*, 212.
32. Hyde, *The Other Love*, 213.

An article by Detective Constable Hamilton of Glasgow Police, in the *Police Journal* in 1949,[33] reveals the particular lengths that the police went to prosecute homosexual men. Hamilton notes that officers would have a good knowledge of the places men would frequent and they could base suspicion of soliciting on observing men repeatedly visiting public toilets in a short space of time and talking to various men. He then explained how evidence could be gathered in terms that indicate the 'full-scale harrying of male homosexuals' committed by police.[34] Police officers were cautioned not to engage in practices that could raise 'the suspicion or suggestion that they were out to get a case of importuning, nor must they act as agents provocateurs.'[35] Yet, police zealously prosecuted homosexual men, driven by directives from senior officials. I incorporated knowledge of these practices into this judgment, being mindful that a judge of this time may not have wanted to publicly challenge or criticize the police. I therefore aimed to veil such criticism as concern for the effect that such excessive prosecutory zeal could have on the reputation of the police.

Blackmail was also a particular concern that judges both in the UK and throughout Australia would have been aware of. During the passage of the Labouchere amendment, concerns were expressed that this would become a blackmailer's charter;[36] a concern that turned out to be well founded. In a later review of the laws relating to homosexuality in the UK, Abse noted that:

> On the last occasion when we had a debate, it was said that a former Attorney-General, Sir William Jowitt, had estimated that 90 per cent of the cases of blackmail which came to his attention contained an element of homosexual conduct ... We know that this can only be the tip of the iceberg, for any man who reports that he is being blackmailed as a consequence of a homosexual act knows that he is placing himself in jeopardy with the possibility of a prosecution.[37]

It is clear that the scandals caused by cases of blackmail, the notoriety caused by the enormous increase in the prosecution of homosexual men, and the sensational prosecutions of public figures,[38] were making homosexuality more visible and also creating an impetus for legal change. This was a period of 'moral panic' about publicly visible incidences of 'sexual deviance,' which were perceived to have sharply risen

---

33. Douglas Hamilton, 'Traces of Footwear, Tyres and Tools, etc. in Criminal Investigation,' *Police J* 22 (1949), 42–49.

34. Hyde, *The Other Love*, 214.

35. Hamilton, 'Traces of Footwear,' 42.

36. Smith, 'Labouchere's Amendment,' 171. NSW had not enacted a prohibition on gross indecency between males in private as in the British *Criminal Law Amendment Act 1885*, but immediately following the case of *Re Humphris* the *Crimes (Amendment) Act 1955* (NSW) was passed to introduce new offences of outraging public decency and soliciting, inciting or attempting to solicit or incite a male to commit an indecent act, indecent assault or to commit buggery. To avoid the problems of blackmail associated with the British Act, the following was added to the NSW provision: 'A person shall not be convicted of an offence under this section upon the testimony of one witness only, unless such testimony is corroborated by some other material evidence implicating the accused in the commission of the offence.'

37. Leo Abse, UK HC Deb, 19 December 1966, vol 738 c1073.

38. For example, the trial of Lord Montagu of Beaulieu and Peter Wildeblood, Diplomatic Editor of the *Daily Mail*, in 1954: see Weeks, *Sex, Politics and Society*, 262.

in the post-war period, and the social dangers that this was thought to present.[39] Against this background, Sir Wolfenden was commissioned in 1954 to review the criminal laws relating to prostitution and homosexuality. The conjoining of these two social issues was not surprising, given that 'not only had they been historically intertwined in legal practice but both were seen as evidence of a common problem: a decline in moral standards.'[40] As Weeks notes, in the post-war period great emphasis was placed on 'the importance of monogamous heterosexual love, which threw into greater relief than ever before the "deviant"' nature of both prostitution and homosexuality.[41]

Naturally, in writing the judgment I had the benefit of knowing what came after *Re Humphris*. I was therefore plausibly able to rely on materials and ideas that were circulating during this period and which were examined by the Wolfenden Committee. The Committee's Report led to a significant change in the legal positioning of male homosexuality, based largely on scientific research into male same-sex desire.[42] As Weeks notes:

> [I]n part, a new climate in discussing sexuality had been generated by the Kinsey reports on Sexual Behaviour in the Human Male, published with much éclat in 1948, and Sexual Behaviour in the Human Female, published in 1953, and Alfred Kinsey himself gave key evidence in person to the Wolfenden Committee.[43]

Despite seeking advice from a range of sources, including scientific experts, the legal profession and religious groups, the Wolfenden Committee largely took an approach based on legal utilitarianism.[44] The Committee's starting point in making its recommendations was Jeremy Bentham's argument that homosexuality may be viewed as an 'imaginary offence,' because it was subject to criminalization based on 'changing concepts of taste and morality,' and John Stuart Mill's argument, in *On Liberty*, that the only justification for using law to intervene in matters of a person's private life was to prevent harm to others.[45] In determining the appropriate role of criminal law, the Committee stated that:

> [I]t is not, in our view, the function of the law to intervene in the private lives of citizens, or to seek to enforce any particular pattern of behaviour, further than is necessary to carry out the purposes we have outlined.[46]

The purposes outlined were: 'to preserve public order and decency, to protect the citizen from what is offensive or injurious and to provide sufficient safeguards against

39.   Stuart Hall, 'Reformism and the Legislation of Consent,' in *Permissiveness and Control: The Fate of the Sixties Legislation*, ed. National Deviancy Conference (London: Macmillan, 1980), 12–15; see also Weeks, *Sex, Politics and Society*, 260.
40.   Weeks, *Sex, Politics and Society*, 260.
41.   Weeks, *Sex, Politics and Society*, 260.
42.   Maclachlan, 'Male Homosexuality 1945-70,' 35.
43.   Weeks, *Sex, Politics and Society*, 263–264.
44.   Maclachlan, 'Male Homosexuality 1945-70,' 16.
45.   Weeks, *Sex, Politics and Society*, 264.
46.   Home Office, *Report of the Committee on Homosexual Offences and Prostitution*, Cmnd 247 (HMSO 1957), [14].

exploitation and corruption of others.'[47] Adopting this approach, the Committee recommended that private adult consensual acts should not be subject to criminalization. As such, the Committee's Report created a 'new moral economy' by providing a template for the permissive legislation of the 1960s, which redefined the relationship between public morality and individual freedom by privatizing selective aspects of sexual conduct.[48] I followed such arguments and drew on similar materials in my judgment to present the case for reform of the law relating to male homosexuality. Expressing the view in my judgment that Parliament should review whether male homosexuality should continue to be subject to the criminal law on the basis of such materials would hopefully not stretch too much the constraints a judge of that time in NSW would feel.

---

47. Home Office, *Homosexual Offences*, [14].
48. Maclachlan, Male Homosexuality 1945-70,' 39–40; Weeks, *Sex, Politics and Society*, 264.

EX PARTE LANGLEY; RE HUMPHRIS (1953)

53 SR (NSW) 324

[1] CROFTS J: I agree with my brothers[49] that the provision in the *Vagrancy Act 1902* was not designed to deal with behaviour such as that engaged in by the appellant, and that the rule nisi for a writ of prohibition in relation to the conviction of the appellant under the *Vagrancy Act 1902* should be made absolute. I reach this conclusion, however, for different reasons, which I will now explain more fully.

[2] This Court is asked to determine whether it is correct to charge a man who solicits in a public place another man for sexual relations under s 4(2)(o)(ii) of the *Vagrancy Act 1902*. As my brothers have noted, the Court has been informed by counsel for the respondent that it has been common practice both in this State and in England to charge men who behave in this way under the relevant subsection of the *Vagrancy Act 1902* (or the English equivalent) as an alternative to more serious charges for offences relating to unnatural sexual relations between men. In support of this approach, we have been referred to the English case of *Horton v Mead*, where it was assumed that it was correct to charge a man under the equivalent provision in the *Vagrancy Act 1898* (UK) for similar behaviour to that engaged in by the appellant. In *Horton*, the accused had been observed by police officers soliciting other men for an immoral purpose by visiting urinals, where he had engaged in behaviour such as smiling in the faces of gentlemen, pursing his lips, and wiggling his body. Further evidence of solicitation was found in the fact that the lips and face of the accused were artificially reddened and that he possessed pink powder and a powder puff. It was found that the immoral purpose could be inferred from the nature of this behaviour and the systemic conduct of the accused.

[3] While *Horton* was not decided in this State, it would ordinarily be persuasive in assisting this Court to interpret a provision that is clearly very similar to that in the English Act. However, *Horton* proceeded on an assumption that it was correct to charge the accused under the *Vagrancy Act 1898*. The direct question of whether this was the type of behaviour contemplated by that Act was not asked in *Horton*. I agree with my brother Clancy J that now that this question has been specifically raised for the first time in this Court, we cannot simply answer it by making reference to what has been assumed to be an acceptable approach in the past.

---

49. Australian judges at this time referred to one another as 'brothers,' a practice abandoned with the appointment of female judges.

[4] In making a determination, I agree with Clancy J that we must have regard to the words in their setting and in the context of the whole *Vagrancy Act 1902*. As noted by my brothers Owen and Clancy JJ, s 4(2)(o)(ii) of the *Vagrancy Act 1902* is found among other provisions dealing with prostitution and like activities. Indeed, the equivalent provision in England is dealt with in legal commentaries, such as Archbold, under the heading "Trading in Prostitution." It seems clear, then, that s 4(2)(o)(ii) of the *Vagrancy Act 1902* is designed to deal with matters relating to prostitution.

[5] An ordinary reading of the words in their context indicates that s 4(2)(o)(ii) of the *Vagrancy Act 1902* was designed to deal with the mischief of men soliciting, in a public place, other men for the purposes of prostitution. I find support for this view in the fact that the NSW legislature inserted through the *Vagrancy Act 1908* not only this subsection, but also an equivalent provision worded in the same way directed only at female prostitutes. That subsection, s 4(1)(h)(i), states that a person "(i) Being a common prostitute, solicits or importunes for immoral purposes, any person who is in any public street, thorough fare, or place" is liable to six months hard labour. It is common understanding that the word "common prostitute" refers only to a "woman who indiscriminately consorts with men for hire," as was confirmed in *Skinner v King* (1913) 16 CLR 226.

[6] Reading these two insertions into the *Vagrancy Act 1902* through the *Vagrancy Act 1908* together, it is clear that they are addressing the same mischief – that is, solicitation in a public place for the purposes of prostitution. This is indicated in part of the long title of the *Vagrancy Act 1908* – "An Act to prevent soliciting for the purpose of prostitution …." The only difference between the provisions is that s 4(1)(h)(i) applies to a "common prostitute," that is, a female prostitute, and s 4(2)(o)(ii) applies to "male persons." A question, then, arises as to whether there is significance in the lack of reference to prostitute in s 4(2)(o)(ii). One reading of the words of s 4(2)(o)(ii) is that it is intended to address only men who solicit men on behalf of female prostitutes, but not men who are themselves acting as prostitutes and soliciting their own clients.

[7] My brother, Clancy J, has formed the view that this subsection applies only to men seeking men for the purposes of prostitution on behalf of female prostitutes. However, I see nothing in this subsection that indicates that it should be read only in this way. I note that the term male person is used in that subsection rather than prostitute. I consider that the choice of the words "male person" rather than prostitute was a deliberate one by the legislature to avoid any confusion on the application of s 4(2)(o)(ii). The term prostitute is associated only with female persons; it is not a term that has been used to refer to men who act as prostitutes. This may be because in the past no distinction has been made between men who have sex with other men for remuneration and those who do so without seeking remuneration; both were considered to be performing unnatural acts deserving of punishment regardless of the motivation.

[8] Furthermore, I take the view that the term "male person" was chosen to allow the subsection to be applied more broadly at the mischief of persons soliciting for the purpose of prostitution. Use of this term means that it can apply not only to a man who solicits other men for the purposes of his own prostitution, but also to a man who solicits men for female prostitutes or other men acting as prostitutes. It is a well-known mischief that men, known as "pimps," may be involved in the solicitation of clients for prostitutes. There is no suggestion that there is an equivalent mischief of women engaging in that behaviour, that is, soliciting men on behalf of other prostitutes (whether male or female). Therefore, there was no necessity to use a broader term in s 4(1)(h)(i) when referring to "common prostitutes."

[9] Accordingly, I find that it was the intention of Parliament to introduce new provisions into the *Vagrancy Act 1902* to equally address women and men who solicit for the purposes of prostitution. Our nation has led the world in recognizing that the sexes should be treated equally. South Australia was the first colony in the world to grant most women the right to vote in 1895 and this was followed by the Commonwealth in 1902. I therefore presume that the New South Wales Parliament intended to continue this trajectory of ensuring equal treatment of men and women, as far as possible, also in relation to criminal offences.

[10] Equality of the sexes may have seemed a radical notion to some in 1902, but there is no reason that this Court should not embrace this principle today, in 1953, unless it would lead to an absurd result. The interpretation that there is no reason to distinguish the treatment of prostitutes based on whether they are women or men is to be preferred. In the words of Justice Holmes, in *Towne v Eisner*, 245 U.S. 418 (1918): "A word is not a crystal, transparent and unchanged; it is the skin of a living thought and may vary greatly in color and content according to the circumstances and the time in which it is used."

[11] I note in passing that such a conclusion is consistent with the Universal Declaration of Human Rights, which was adopted by the UN General Assembly only five years ago. This Declaration states that "everyone is entitled to all the rights and freedoms set forth in this Declaration, without distinction of any kind, such as race, colour, sex, … birth or other status." The *Vagrancy Act 1902* was enacted quite some time before this Declaration and the Declaration has no binding status on my judgment. However, it is a sign that societies are moving to accept the principle of equality of the sexes.

[12] The conclusion that I have reached, that s 4(2)(o)(ii) of the *Vagrancy Act 1902* is intended to be directed at men who solicit men for the purposes of prostitution, leads to the unsatisfactory result that where a man solicits or importunes another man in a public place for sexual relations without this being for remuneration, that is, not for the purposes of prostitution, he is exposed to prosecution under the more serious offences contained in the *Crimes Act 1900* and at common law. I cannot accept that Parliament intended a man acting as a prostitute should be considered deserving

of considerably more lenient treatment than a man who is not acting as a prostitute. It is surely the commercial aspect of prostitution and the nuisance that solicitation for the purposes of prostitution may cause that mark it as behaviour needing to be controlled by the criminal law.

[13] I am of the opinion that it has been common practice to lay charges under s 4(2)(o)(ii) of the *Vagrancy Act 1902* for behaviour such as that engaged in by the appellant because it has been thought that these unfortunate men are deserving of a degree of leniency rather than punishment under the more serious offences in the *Crimes Act 1900*. Unfortunately, the decision which myself and my learned brothers have reached in this case would prevent that such a charge is open in the future. While my brother Clancy J notes that behaviour such as that engaged in by the appellant may be charged under one of the more serious offences in the *Crimes Act 1900* or the common law depending on the available evidence, I find it hard to accept that behaviour that was previously, even if incorrectly, dealt with under the *Vagrancy Act 1902* should now be charged under the *Crimes Act 1900* or common law. This means that behaviour that had previously been punished with up to six months hard labour would now be subjected to much more severe punishment, depending on the charge laid.

[14] While in the past we have not recognised that there can be different motivations and reasons for a male to seek another male for immoral purposes, we now have a better understanding of the circumstance of homosexuality. Counsel for the appellant has directed me to research that is being done by the Kinsey Institute for Research in Sex, Gender, and Reproduction. I expect that the findings of this Institute, that around 10% of men are homosexual, might surprise many. These findings suggest that there may be greater prevalence of homosexual men than we may previously have thought. It also appears that homosexuality does not merely refer to sexual acts but is part of the character of these men.

[15] This minority of men, because of their tendencies, live in fear of the law. It is a fear that is well founded, as we are seeing an increasing number of men coming before the court on charges relating to homosexual acts. This may be due to greater numbers of men forming, or giving in to their, sexual attraction to other men as reported by the Kinsey Institute. I cannot, nor do I wish to, comment on the accuracy of this observation. It has also been commented that the Second World War and ensuing societal changes are responsible for an increase in homosexual behaviour. It is true that in this post-war period we have seen a certain relaxation of moral attitudes towards matters of sexuality, especially among the younger generation.

[16] A further possible explanation for the rise in prosecutions of homosexual men is that police officers are increasingly adopting tactics to capture homosexual men. I have been referred to an article by Detective Constable Hamilton of the Glasgow Police in the Police Journal from 1949, which explains the strategies that the police may use to obtain evidence to support criminal charges. This involves officers entering public

lavatories in plain clothes and attempting to entice the homosexual man to make lewd advances. I agree with Hamilton that police must be cautious not to do anything that could raise the suspicion that they are solely out to get arrests and acting as agents provocateur. Police officers should be wary of engaging in tactics that could tarnish the reputation of the police and the apparatus of the criminal justice system.

[17] Furthermore, continuing to subject men who engage in homosexual behaviour, the appellant to the criminal law may be harmful to the public good. Counsel for the appellant has submitted that it is not uncommon for homosexual men to be subjected to blackmail. Indeed, there is some evidence that the majority of blackmail cases that come before the court concern matters of homosexuality. This not only threatens the security of blackmail victims but also our national security. Only last year, two British diplomats, Guy Burgess and Donald Maclean, defected from the United Kingdom to the Soviet Union. Both men were homosexuals and there is reason to believe that one of them, who held a position in the British embassy in Washington, was blackmailed by the other into handing top-secret information to the Russians.

[18] It seems to me that in this post-war age we should carefully consider the circumstances in which it is right to impose criminal law on the private lives of individuals. There is a view, most famously expounded by John Stuart Mill in his seminal work *On Liberty*, that citizens should be permitted to make their own determinations about what amounts to a good life and that criminal law should be reserved for behaviour that is harmful to others or injurious to the public good. According to this view, the function of the criminal law is to preserve public order and decency, but not to enforce any type of private behaviour that does not harm the public. The type of behaviour engaged in by the appellant in this case occurred in a public place and may, therefore, be a matter of public nuisance. There are, however, criminal laws in place to address indecency in public and it does not seem to me that there is need for an offence to specifically address men who behave indecently with other men in a public place. Whether homosexual behaviour should continue to be subjected to the criminal law is a matter of great public concern and within the province of Parliament to address. I am not qualified or asked to give an answer to this question; however, I hope that my survey of this matter provides an incentive for Parliament to review these offences and consider whether and upon what basis homosexual conduct should continue to be subject to the criminal law.

3

R v Green (Australia):

Affective Judging—An Australian Case of Disgust

Senthorun Raj

Feeling Queer About Law

I first encountered *R v Green* (1997) 191 CLR 334 as a naive undergraduate student in Criminal Law in 2007. Crudely speaking, this case was about a young man who viciously killed a friend because his friend had made a sexual advance towards him. I remember reading the case and feeling angry, disgusted, and upset, as a newly out gay man, at how the highest court in Australia could endorse homophobic sentiments to excuse homophobic violence, to the point of reducing the punishment for murder. We had a lively and passionate discussion about the case in class when exploring defences to murder, with most of my peers at the time expressing similar concerns to me about the normalisation of homophobia in society and the legal system. The emotional discomfort in the classroom was palpable. Yet, rather than give space to our emotions, we channelled our objections to, and critiques of, the case through conventional legal paths like Australian common law precedent and doctrine. In pedagogical texts discussing the majority and minority judgments in *R v Green*, it has been noted that few differences exist in terms of relevant legal principles.[1] The majority held that the issue of provocation should have been left open to the jury, while the minority disagreed. The distinguishing features of these two positions were ascribed to evidentiary interpretations rather than legal propositions.

The affective scene I describe above provides the backdrop to how I approached re-imagining and re-writing one of the judgments of the dissenters in *R v Green* for this collection. Rather than turn away from feelings, I wanted to foreground how emotions shape the individual defendant, the defence of provocation, and the differing opinions of the Court in relation to the evidentiary questions on appeal. In my monograph, *Feeling Queer Jurisprudence: Injury, Intimacy, Identity*, I use emotion analytically

---

1. David Brown, David Farrier, Sandra Egger, Luke McNamara, and Alex Steel, *Criminal Laws: Materials and Commentary on Criminal Law and Process of New South Wales*, 4th ed. (Sydney: The Federation Press, 2006), 619.

to track how cases like *R v Green* crystallise and refract specific emotional enactments that obscure the structural conditions of homophobic injury and limit legal perceptions of queer intimacy and identity.[2] While my existing scholarship discussing the case was descriptive and analytical, the work of re-imagining and re-writing a judgment like *R v Green* from a *pro-queer* perspective took me to a more normative intellectual space. I had to think prescriptively about how I might have given a judgment differently to the High Court judges I critiqued in my book. To talk about queer alongside the normative and prescriptive is to invite a conceptual contradiction, especially as queer scholarship is usually associated with an anti-foundationalist impulse and refusal of norms.[3] For the purposes of re-thinking my judgment in queer terms, I followed Eve Kosofsky Sedgwick, who describes queer as 'the open mesh of possibilities, gaps, overlaps, dissonances and resonances, lapses and excesses of meaning when the constituent elements of anyone's gender, of anyone's sexuality aren't made (or can't be made) to signify monolithically.'[4]

In Sedgwick's outline, queer is more than a personalised statement of one's identity or being in the world. Queer is an analytic position from which scholars can expose and critique how social norms organise subjects, issues, politics, and relationships that do not conform to (hetero)normative ideas of reproduction, nationhood, productivity, and domesticity.[5] In bringing queer to law, I drew on work by queer legal scholars like Aleardo Zanghellini and Libby Adler, who note the merging of queer with law enables a critical legal politics that can affirm the lives of sexual and gender minorities while challenging institutions that inhibit their flourishing.[6] To write about emotion in law is also a queer exercise, as it involves writing against law's 'proper objects' that conventionally organise around dispassionate rules and norms.[7]

What is distinctively queer about my judgment in *R v Green*, then, is that it deviates

---

2. Senthorun Raj, *Feeling Queer Jurisprudence: Injury, Intimacy, Identity* (Abingdon: Routledge, 2020), Chapter 2.

3. Robyn Wiegman and Elizabeth Wilson, 'Introduction: Antinormativity's Queer Conventions,' *differences* 26 (2015), 1–25. Queer theory is not monolithic and has varied theoretical and political commitments to norms. For a brief but insightful discussion of this debate in queer theory, see Robyn Wiegman, 'Sex and Negativity; Or What Queer Theory Has for You,' *Cultural Critique* 95 (2017), 219–243.

4. Eve Kosofsky Sedgwick, *Tendencies* (Durham: Duke University Press, 1993), 8. I have explored the utility of 'queer' for normative LGBTIQ+ legal projects elsewhere. See Senthorun Raj and Peter Dunne, 'Queering Outside the (Legal) Box: LGBTIQ People in the United Kingdom,' in *The Queer Outside in Law: Recognising LGBTIQ People in the United Kingdom*, eds. Senthorun Raj and Peter Dunne (Cham: Palgrave Macmillan, 2020), 1-19.

5. See Ian Barnard, *Queer Race: Cultural Interventions in the Racial Politics of Queer Theory* (New York: Peter Lang, 2004); Lauren Berlant, 'Starved,' in *After Sex? On Writing since Queer Theory*, eds. Janet Halley and Andrew Parker (Durham: Duke University Press, 2011), 79-90; Richard Collier, 'Straight Families, Queer Lives? Heterosexual(izing) Family Law,' in *Sexuality in the Legal Arena*, eds. Carl Stychin and Didi Herman (London: The Althone Press, 2000), 164-179; David Eng, *The Feeling of Kinship: Queer Liberalism and the Racialization of Intimacy* (Durham: Duke University Press, 2010); Judith Halberstam, *The Queer Art of Failure* (Durham: Duke University Press, 2011); Elizabeth Povinelli, 'Disturbing Sexuality,' in *After Sex? On Writing since Queer Theory*, eds. Janet Halley and Andrew Parker (Durham: Duke University Press, 2011), 257-269.

6. Aleardo Zanghellini, 'Queer, Antinormativity, Counter-Normativity and Abjection,' *Griffith Law Review* 18 (2008), 1–16, and Libby Adler, *Gay Priori: A Queer Critical Legal Studies Approach to Law Reform* (Durham: Duke University Press, 2018).

7. Judith Butler, 'Against Proper Objects,' *differences* 6 (1994), 4, and Kathryn Abrams and Hila Keren, 'Who's Afraid of Law and the Emotions?,' *Minnesota Law Review* 94 (2008), 1997–2074.

from norms of traditional judgment writing by: (1) anchoring jurisprudence in terms of emotion (disgust) rather than doctrine, and (2) using that emotion self-reflexively to pursue an anti-homophobic jurisprudence that affirms the lives of queer people. This focus on emotion draws inspiration from Sara Ahmed's theorisation of the cultural politics of emotion and Eve Kosofsky Sedgwick's concept of reparative reading. For Sedgwick, a reparative reading is one that scans and amplifies the emotions in texts, with a view to following the surprise and pleasures such attentiveness might generate.[8] Reparative analysis aspires for possibility rather than closure. In re-imagining the judgment, I have scanned and amplified disgust in order to follow the disparate ways disgust organises gay intimacy, identity, and injury. While I take Sedgwick's invitation to engage in a reparative reading of disgust when approaching homophobic violence in *R v Green*, I do not allow my re-imagined judgment to roam free of critical anchors. To assist in crafting a critical framework for exploring the emotional grammar of disgust, I think with Sara Ahmed, who writes about reckoning with the politics of emotion in texts.[9] Specifically, I observe how emotion materialises as a textual enactment of jurisprudence in order to map the ways those affective textual enactments (of disgust) reproduce specific relations of gendered/sexualised power and privilege that cohere the ways judges recognise, and might excuse, homophobic violence.

Forming Queer Judgment

The form of my judgment is conversational and this dialogue format might be described as 'jurisprudential drag,' as it centre stages conventional doctrinal ideas of provocation only to then use emotion to expose the legal fiction that norms relating to the 'ordinary person' are objective and to denaturalise their purchase on law.[10] In crafting this judgment, I took inspiration from the *Feminist Judgments Project*, which seeks to 'disrupt the process of gender construction, and introduce different accounts of gender that might be less limiting for women.'[11] As Raj J, I sought to disrupt the ways heteropatriarchal norms of gender and sexuality construct a susceptible straight man and an aggressive gay man, where the former can only relate to the latter through repressed desires and overt violence. My focus on the way in which homosexuality or homophobia is exceptionalized through logics of disgust was deliberate to show how this can undermine the prospect of recognizing homophobic violence and inhibiting gay intimacy and identity.

The content of my re-written judgment is indebted to critical queer and feminist socio-legal scholarship that deconstructs the homophobia in the original case.[12] Much

---

8. Eve Kosofsky Sedgwick, *Touching Feeling: Affect, Pedagogy, Performativity* (Durham, Duke University Press: 2003), 135–136.

9. Sara Ahmed, *The Cultural Politics of Emotion* (Edinburgh: Edinburgh University Press, 2004), 5.

10. Rosemary Hunter, Clare McGlynn and Erika Rackley, 'Feminist Judgments: An Introduction,' in *Feminist Judgments Project: From Theory to Practice*, eds. Rosemary Hunter, Clare McGlynn and Erika Rackley (Oxford: Hart, 2010), 8.

11. Hunter, McGlynn and Rackley, 'Feminist Judgments,' 7.

12. See Adrian Howe, 'More Folk Provoke Their Own Demise (Homophobic Violence and Sexed Excuses – Rejoining the Provocation Law Debate, Courtesy of the Homosexual Advance Defence),' *Sydney Law*

of the public admonition directed towards the outcome in *R v Green* was provoked by the chilling words Green spoke after he was charged with the murder of Gillies. In his statement to the police, Green said, 'Yeah, I killed him, but he did worse to me … he tried to root me.'[13] His statement sought to suggest that his violence should be considered less morally reprehensible than Gillies' attempt to solicit homosexual intercourse from Green. As Adrian Howe and Robert Mison argue, the success of pleading provocation depends on the extent to which social stigmas can engender emotions of hatred and revulsion towards the victim to which the judge(s) and/or jurors can relate.[14] Such emotions are recognised and reproduced by the law.[15] Howe notes that the inability to see the homophobic sentiments that are embedded in law reveals the 'privilege of unknowing,' an ignorance that uncritically accepts the assumption that gay men are dangerous and predatory.[16] Even where reforms have been introduced to remove non-violent sexual advances as the basis for provocation, the fact the Homosexual Advance Defence (HAD as it is referred to in critical scholarship) is underpinned by strong emotional sentiments such as outrage and disgust, suggests that it can be reformulated in self-defence claims or even as 'gross provocation.'[17] Alternatively, Joshua Dressler, who shares Howe's assessment of how emotion is transmitted, argues contra Howe for the retention of provocation. In refuting the justification rationale, Dressler argues for provocation as an excuse because it takes account of the limits of human rationality.[18]

While Dressler has been criticized for condoning heterocentric criminal law defences, his broader argument invites us to ask a vitally important question about how the law remedies injury against sexual minorities: should an individual perpetrator be held responsible for a culturally condoned homophobia that makes individuals susceptible to disgust in the first place? To pursue this question, my queer judgment confronts how disgust was used in *R v Green*. Specifically, I refute that disgust should be used to partially excuse the murder of Gillies and challenge how other justices use it to legitimize the idea that ordinary individuals (read: heterosexual men) have susceptibilities to unwanted same-sex advances.

The critical legal exploration of HAD in my queer judgment raises another important question: if movements of disgust in the law can harm sexual minorities, is their formal

Review 19 (2002), 338; Kara Suffredini, 'Pride and Prejudice: The Homosexual Panic Defense,' *Boston College Third World Law Journal* 21 (2001), 287–301.

13. *R v Green* (1997) 191 CLR 334, 391 (Kirby J). The term 'root' is an Australian expression for casual sex.

14. Howe, 'More Folk Provoke Their Own Demise,' 344, and Robert Mison, 'Homophobia in Manslaughter: The Homosexual Advance as Insufficient Provocation,' *California Law Review* 80 (1992), 135.

15. Disgust is not limited to homophobic violence. Other areas of criminal law, such as those dealing with lethal and non-lethal violence, engender disgust. See Dan Kahan, 'The Progressive Appropriation of Disgust,' in *The Passions of Law*, ed. Susan A Bandes. (New York: NYU Press, 1999), 63-79.

16. Adrian Howe, 'Homosexual Advances in Law: Murderous Excuse, Pluralized Ignorance and the Privilege of Unknowing,' in *Sexuality in the Legal Arena*, eds. Carl Stychin and Didi Herman (London: The Althone Press, 2000), 98.

17. See Crimes Amendment (Provocation) Act 2014 (NSW) and *R v CR* [2008] NSWSC 1208, for an example of how HAD can re-emerge in other defences or even through 'loss of control' caused by a 'serious indictable offence.'

18. Joshua Dressler, 'When "Heterosexual" Men Kill "Homosexual" Men: Reflections on Provocation Law, Sexual Advances, and the "Reasonable Man" Standard,' *Journal of Criminal Law and Criminology* 85 (1995), 755.

abolition the key to ending its homophobic a/effects? Formal abolition has been widely touted as key to eliminating the use of disgust and homophobia in the law. However, in crafting a pro-queer judgment, I observed a cautionary note offered by Cynthia Lee in relation to the progressive demands to abolish HAD: a statutory exclusion of HAD will enable homophobia to persist in other, less visible, ways. Lee notes that the only way to contest the stereotypes of gay men as deviants or predators is to draw attention to the cultural (as well as legal) currency that enables such investments.[19] For Lee, the focus on the more formal or technical aspects of HAD (and their abolition) covers the broader concern about how homophobia is articulated in legal defences. Statutory abolition risks covering over institutional forms of homophobia that contribute to violence faced by sexual minorities and impede the flourishing of their intimacies and identities. If HAD derives its judicial force from disgust, then detaching from it will require more than a doctrinal shift in statutory interpretation. In using disgust self-reflexively, my queer judgment outlines how justices might confront the homophobic articulation of provocation through disgust by first recognizing the emotional life of the defendant and then challenging how their individual disgust is recognised, and refracted, institutionally through the Court.

My queer judgment responds to the articulation of touch in the original judgment. For Brennan CJ, McHugh and Toohey JJ, writing the majority opinion in *R v Green*, disgust worked to differentiate between Green and Gillies. Gillies' unwanted queer touching of Green was rendered more disgusting than an advance of a similar heterosexual kind done by men to women. The latter consideration was erased from the majority's discussion. The majority's heightened focus on *queer* touching was developed alongside Green's purported vicarious trauma (having witnessed abuse perpetrated against his sisters) and Gillies' position of trust. Abuse of intimacy (in parental and homosocial relationships) framed the majority accepting Green's claim that Gillies' same-sex advance triggered lethal violence. These facts combined in the majority judgments to form the basis of Green's 'special sensitivity' to an unwanted advance – that is, disgust pointed to queer intimacies and identities that deviate from, or seek to disturb, a fixed heterosexual line.[20] HAD revealed the way in which 'projective disgust' worked to repudiate that which is perceived to contaminate boundaries and bodies.[21] In *R v Green*, the majority's disgust pointed to Gillies' conduct as a violation of Green's heteromasculine bodily and emotional integrity. The judicial reasoning stigmatized and separated the ordinary (heterosexual body) from the monstrous (gay body). Disgust worked in the majority's reasoning to enable the majority to qualitatively differentiate between the gay grope that pressed upon Green and the violent assault that ended Gillies' life. The majority's judicial touch worked to condemn Gillies, while it acted as a (partially) saving grace for Green.

---

19. Cynthia Lee, *Murder and the Reasonable Man: Passion and Fear in the Criminal Courtroom* (New York: NYU Press, 2003), 247–59.

20. Sara Ahmed, *Queer Phenomenology: Orientations, Objects, Others* (Durham: Duke University Press, 2006), 145–6.

21. Martha Nussbaum, *Hiding from Humanity: Disgust, Shame and the Law* (Princeton: Princeton University Press, 2004), 88.

Feeling Queer Jurisprudence

Writing a queer judgment in a register of emotion exposes the paradox and ubiquity of disgust when it comes to homophobia. On the one hand, homophobic disgust is cast as banal. In *R v Green*, Gillies' advance became aggressive precisely because the 'ordinary person' could find such an act 'revolting.' Brennan CJ and McHugh J inhabited a judicial space that took comfort in the bodily integrity and normality of heterosexuality. Rhetorical oscillation from the 'aggressive' to the 'revolting' response positioned queerness as a dis-ease. On the other hand, the use of a richly evocative description to define Gillies' conduct created a rather visceral spectacle (of disgust). Even if we focused specifically on Green's familial circumstances as the basis to understand the provocative gravity of Gillies' sexual touch, the majority referenced the fact that the appellant's sisters were allegedly subject to (heterosexual) sexual abuse. The Court justified the injurious gravity of the same-sex advances and, in doing so, revealed how queer intimacies could easily be conflated with violence.

In re-imagining the judgment through disgust, I refused to legitimize violence against those who were cast (by the judges writing in the majority) as socially transgressive. Kirby J's dissent typified a counterpoint to the disgust rhetoric relied on by the majority. Specifically, Kirby J's dissent directed disgust towards the majority's belief that a homosexual advance alone could ever be enough to constitute legal provocation. While that approach sought to work against homophobia, Kirby J's judgment exposed how the problematic mobilization of disgust worked by sticking disgust to some objects, while leaving other (possibly harmful) objects—such as laws denying equality to same-sex couples—without its visceral taint. By localizing Gillies' sexual advance, Kirby J attempted to excise the revulsion that underpinned Green's violence from the rest of society. Both Green's homophobia and the homophobia legitimated by the majority were alien to Kirby J precisely because they sat 'ill' or at odds with other social changes. By seeking to break the coupling of a homosexual advance with the objective requirement for the defence of provocation, Kirby J found that a reasonable jury, properly instructed, could not make a finding that Green was guilty of manslaughter rather than murder. After all, the revulsion that sparked Green's violence was exceptional —not ordinary. While sympathetic to Kirby's moralized use of disgust to challenge homophobia, my queer judgment thinks with disgust to refuse a construction of the ordinary person as being not homophobic. While still upholding the primary judge's refusal to make certain evidence available to the jury, my judgment does not seek to isolate Green and his homophobic violence.[22]

By returning to feelings, I conclude my queer judgment with an invitation for courts to grapple with emotions critically and reflexively. Making (queer) judge—as well as lawyers, scholars, and activists—sensitive to the work of emotion will allow us to better address homophobic violence across individual, interpersonal, and institutional levels.

---

22. I am indebted to abolitionist literature for emphasizing this point. See Angela Davis, *Are Prisons Obsolete?* (New York: Seven Stories Press, 2003).

R v Green (1997) 191 CLR 334

Raj J

[1] This case is about individual and institutional sensitivities. Broadly speaking, this case is about how socialised homophobic sensitivities, like disgust towards same-sex intimacy, institutionalize lethal violence against gay men in society. Narrowly construed, however, this case is about the extent to which Section 23 of the *Crimes Act 1900* (NSW) is applicable to an individual situation where a heterosexual man claims that he was provoked into perpetrating homicide as a result of his 'special sensitivity' to a gay man who made sexual advances towards him.

[2] The institutional and individual sensitivities raised by this case are not mutually exclusive. In order to determine the applicability of Section 23 to the circumstances of this case, it is necessary to understand the emotional life of the defendant in terms of his familial, social, and cultural environment, and how this emotional life might be legally relevant to his criminal responsibility in the context of homicide. My colleagues who write in the majority have, in different ways, expressed their disgust towards some of Donald (Don) Gillies' (the victim) conduct to understand it as provocative to the ordinary person. My colleague, Kirby J, on the other hand, feels disgusted at the normalization of homophobia.

[3] In my dissenting opinion, I feel the need to sensitively engage with the emotional content of what my colleagues have said and outline what I see as anti-homophobic jurisprudence. I start by addressing Malcom Green's (the defendant) hostile emotional reactions towards Gillies. I then trace how his reactions shape the jurisprudential terms through which provocation defences gain meaning and why we, as a Court, must confront our emotions.

Feeling Facts

[4] The facts of the case are painful. On 19th May 1993, Donald Gillies, 36, was brutalized by Malcolm Green, 22, in Mudgee, New South Wales. The two could be described as acquaintances, though I would caution that this description might not be accurate. Without Gillies' testimony, we can only glimpse the nature of their relationship through Green's account of it. Gillies invited Green to stay over at his home. According to Green, at some point during the night, Gillies left his room and got into bed with Green. Gillies lightly rubbed Green's shoulders and back. Gillies tried to touch Green's groin. Green responded to this unwanted touching with violence. According to the medical evidence, Gillies was punched 35 times and then stabbed in the face with a pair of scissors at least 10 times.

[5] It is worth extracting parts of Green's emotional and confusing interview with the police to contextualise his account of what happened:

> Then he started touching me. I pushed him away. He asked what was wrong. I said, 'What do you think is wrong? I'm not like this.' He started grabbing me with both hands around my lower back. I pushed him away. He started grabbing me harder. I tried and forced him to the lower side of me. He still tried to grab me. I hit him again and again on top of the bed until he didn't look like Don to me. He still tried to grope and talk to me that's when I hit him again and saw the scissors on the floor on the right hand side of the bed. When I saw the scissors he touched me around the waist shoulders area and said, 'Why?' I said to him, 'Why, I didn't ask for this.' I grabbed the scissors and hit him again. He rolled off the bed as I struck him with the scissors. By the time I stopped I realised what had happened. I just stood at the foot of the bed with Don on the floor laying face down in blood. I thought to myself how other people can do something like this and enjoy what they do.

[6] Green pleaded that Gillies made unwanted sexual advances towards him. He claimed these advances triggered his latent rage towards his father who had allegedly sexually assaulted his sisters. Green confessed to killing Gillies, but he argued that his act was manslaughter, not murder, on the basis that Gillies' attempt to solicit sexual contact with Green constituted provocation as defined by Section 23 of the *Crimes Act 1900* (NSW), as Brennan CJ has so clearly articulated at 339.

[7] During the trial, the primary judge refused to direct the jury to consider the question of provocation in respect to Green's alleged history of family violence. He was convicted of murder. Green appealed on a number of procedural and evidentiary points relating to the judge's exclusion of evidence and failure to direct properly on the issue of provocation. The NSW Supreme Court of Criminal Appeal dismissed Green's claim that the judge's refusal to allow the jury to consider evidence of family abuse amounted to a substantial miscarriage of justice (with Smart J in dissent).

[8] The case now arrives before the High Court. This Court has to consider whether the trial judge's refusal to allow the jury to consider evidence of the defendant's father's sexual abuse of his sisters, when determining provocation, constitutes a 'substantial miscarriage of justice' per *House v King* (1936) 55 CLR 499. We have to consider the scope of a provocation defence by clarifying the objective character of questions relating to self-control and gravity that are statutorily required per Section 23(2)(b) *Crimes Act 1900* (NSW).

Emotions in the Defence of Provocation

[9] Chief Justice Brennan, in his comprehensive judgment, has offered a more detailed examination of the defence of provocation through its contextualisation in Australian common law. Provocation can reduce a charge of murder to manslaughter (Section 23(1) of the *Crimes Act 1900* (NSW)). The elements of provocation are both subjective and objective in character. To appreciate whether a person 'lost control,' the jury

has to consider the subjective background of the defendant in relation to the provoc-ative conduct in question (Section 23(2)(a)) and then weigh that provocation against such a background to determine, objectively, if it could cause an ordinary person in the position of the accused to have lost self-control and form an intent to kill or inflict grievous bodily harm (GBH) (Section 23(2)(b)).

[10] This Court must determine whether an 'ordinary person in the position of the accused' could have been induced to form an intent to kill or inflict GBH when consid-ering the gravity of Gillies' *homosexual advances* towards Green given his sensitivities.

[11] I depart from Brennan CJ's doctrinal reasoning to further explore how emotions manifest in the pleading of provocation and its subsequent adjudication. The defence of provocation has legal currency because it gains value from emotions such as rage, hatred, and disgust. That is, the defendant must establish an emotional trigger that prompts an unlawful killing, and this emotion must be translated for the judge or jury in order for them to determine if the defendant can be (partially) exculpated for the crime.

[12] In common law jurisdictions, the doctrinal foundations of what some commen-tators refer to as the 'Homosexual Advance Defence' (HAD) are drawn from insanity, diminished responsibility, provocation, and self-defence. Some academic commentary has been written on this topic.[23]

[13] The most important thing for this Court to note is the subtle doctrinal changes over the decades. Prominent legal academics outline that the legal genealogy of the HAD can be traced back to the 1960s in cases where defendants could seek to mitigate the charge of murder by arguing that the victim's unwanted same-sex sexual advance triggered a psychiatric *panic* by revealing their latent homosexuality. In the 1980s, the declassification of homosexuality as a mental illness precipitated a shift away from defining the defence in terms of a defendant's mental incapacity. If homosexuality could no longer be considered a mental disorder, then the emotional responses that were elicited when people are confronted with their own same-sex attraction could no longer be referred to as a mental defect. Instead, the pathological panic used to legitimate the defence for a number of years gave way to passionate provocation.

[14] Coupling the HAD with provocation rather than insanity crystallized the way emotions could mitigate legal responsibility for murder. Provocation developed from the premise that criminal responsibility must be countenanced with a recognition of human frailty. Such frailties came to be understood in terms of emotions that people (historically referring only to men) were ordinarily susceptible to in various circum-stances. These emotions typically included outrage, fear, humiliation, and disgust from a breach of social mores.

---

23. For example, Robert Mison, 'Homophobia in Manslaughter: The Homosexual Advance as Insufficient Provocation,' *California Law Review*, vol 80 (1992), 133.

[15] The HAD, as a form of provocation, allows a defendant to be convicted of manslaughter instead of murder where they can demonstrate that the gravity of the same-sex advance constituted sufficiently provocative conduct that could cause an ordinary person in the circumstances of the accused to lose control.

[16] Homophobic violence (which manifests as physical attacks and verbal insults against sexually minoritized people) is attributed to the human sensitivities or frailties of ordinary people. By refracting the focus from the culpability of the perpetrator to the threat posed by the victim, this Court must be wary of how the HAD advances stereotypes of gay men as sick, effeminate, and predatory. We only need to consider the ways broadsheets and tabloids refer to gay men, particularly in the context of the Human Immunodeficiency Virus (HIV), to observe how these tropes emotionally materialize. Professor Robert Mison elaborates that the success of the defence depends on the extent to which these stereotypes can engender feelings of hatred and revulsion towards the victim that the judge(s) and/or jurors can relate to.[24] As judges, we must be careful to avoid reproducing such homophobic stereotypes.

Appeals on/to Emotion

[17] In the appeal before this Court, my colleagues have succumbed to uncritically embracing homophobic stereotypes about how gay intimacy manifests. Smart J's dissent in the Court of Appeal is echoed in this Court's discussion of their disgust towards unwanted same-sex sexual advances as provocative. Smart J notes:

> Some ordinary men would feel great revulsion at the homosexual advances being persisted with... They would regard it as a serious and gross violation of their body and their person... Some ordinary men could become enraged and feel that a strong physical re-action was called for. The deceased's actions had to be stopped.[25]

Smart J's reasoning reveals how provocation tears at the bounded rationality of the male subject through a violation of bodily or sexual integrity. By conflating same-sex advances with 'revulsion' and 'ordinariness,' Smart J transforms unwanted touching into an overtly disgusting gesture. In his words, the approaching intimacy 'had to be stopped.' His reasoning here relies on depersonalizing Green's statement by invoking 'some ordinary [read: heterosexual] men.' However, this becomes more than a simple statement of facts. Smart J's revulsion brings the *queer* body into view as a threat. Smart J focuses on 'ordinary men' in order to justify the fact that such 'feeling' could call for a 'strong physical reaction.' Same-sex touching is presented here as a 'violation of their body.' Yet, Smart J's movement from a more distanced account of 'ordinary men' to a more forceful personalised statement that 'the deceased's actions had to be stopped' reveals something much more troubling: the movement of disgust from the defendant to the judge hearing the case. By construing the ordinary man as disgusted

---

24. *Id*, at 136.
25. *R v Green* unreported, Court of Criminal Appeal of New South Wales, 8 November 1995 at 24 (Smart J).

by homosexuality, Gillies' physical touches were not only a threat to Green, but they also become affective threats that impress quite forcefully in Smart J's understanding of provocation as per Section 23(2)(b) of the *Crimes Act 1900* (NSW). The HAD, therefore, gets articulated here as something much more than a personal defence of provocation. Smart J's evocative dissent in the NSW Court of Criminal Appeal designates gay sexual advances as ordinarily gross.

[18] My view is that using disgust to tether homosexuality to provocation, in the way Smart J does, is not only homophobic, but it also undermines our responsibilities as judicial officers to separate our emotional biases from the cases we are asked to consider. My attention to emotion, particularly disgust in this case, is not just to challenge some of my colleagues who see the relevance of provocation uncritically because they view gay people in abject terms. Rather, I take a reparative approach in my understanding of the circumstances of this case and the relevant law to show how judges might approach appeals of this nature. Specifically, I outline how judges can: (1) recognise the emotional life of a homophobic defendant for the purposes of law relating to provocation, while (2) reflexively attending to how our emotions might provoke the homophobic terms through which we judge the applicability of provocation to situations involving homophobic violence.

[19] Divergent judicial opinions in this case can be ascribed to emotionally divergent understandings of 'ordinariness' and whether what was recurringly described as the 'sexual interference' by Gillies towards Green could lead a reasonable jury, properly instructed, to make a finding of provocation.[26] In my opinion, the concurring judgments of Brennan CJ, Toohey and McHugh JJ narrate Gillies' advances as 'persistent' as part of a broader jurisprudence defending against the threat of gay intimacy. That is, Gillies' non-violent sexual advance is seen as a microcosm for how same-sex intimacy can demean the integrity of the person. In this particular case, same-sex advances are judicially claimed as 'sexual interferences' when read against Green's personal background of alleged third-party family sexual abuse.[27] Brennan CJ's judgment holds:

> It was essentially a jury question, a question the answer to which depended on the jury's evaluation of the degree of outrage which the appellant might have experienced. It was not for the Court to determine questions of that kind, especially when reactions to sexual advances are critical to the evaluation. A juryman or woman would not be unreasonable because he or she might accept that the appellant found the deceased's conduct 'revolting' rather than 'amorous.'[28]

Provocation is referable to disgust and outrage—an issue that Brennan CJ believes should have been left to the jury to decide in this case. While there is an explicit claim about deferring assessments on anger to juries, the qualifying sentences shape the evaluation of outrage through judicial invocation of disgust. Observing that the conduct of the deceased could reasonably be seen as 'revolting' rather than 'amorous'

---

26. *R v Green* (1997) 191 CLR 334 at 341–2 (Brennan CJ).
27. *Id*, at 342 (Brennan CJ).
28. *Id*, at 346 (Brennan CJ).

exposes the emotional threat posed by any same-sex advance, regardless of context. Brennan CJ's movement from attraction to disgust in his judgment constructs a scene that foregrounds same-sex intimacy as negative. This jurisprudence suggests we can view unwanted same-sex sexual advances as reasonably capable of disgusting the ordinary person and provoking them to understandable outrage. Through this emotional parameter setting, violently rebuking such touching may not be a reasonable response but it is still, at the very least, an excusable act.

[20] Brennan CJ relies on Green's testimony to frame Gillies' non-violent touching as innately intrusive or aggressive: 'Here, the deceased was the sexual aggressor of the appellant.'[29] Gillies' flirtatious gestures become assaulting ones. Even if I were to accept Green's testimony and see these unwanted advances in such aggressive terms, the fact that Brennan CJ seems to ignore comparable scenarios involving women (Brennan CJ distinguishes *Stingel v The Queen*) who are groped by men, is telling of the way disgust renders a 'sexual advance' in terms that capture the interpersonal dynamics between straight men and gay men.[30] As Brennan CJ points out: 'the real sting of provocation could be found not in the force used by the deceased but in his attempt to violate the sexual integrity of a man who had trusted him.'[31] The physically non-aggressive nature of the touching becomes obscured against the anxious figuration of the same-sex advances as an act of sexual violation. Despite Brennan CJ's attempt to distinguish force from violation, the two terms bleed together when considering Brennan CJ's earlier use of the term 'aggression' to qualify the same-sex advances made to Green.

[21] Moreover, little effort is made in Brennan CJ's judgment to distinguish between wanted and unwanted same-sex intimate activity. Much of his judicial narrative uses his disgust as a means of recoiling from, and pushing back, these purportedly aggressive queer sexual advances. Gillies' advances not only touch Green both literally and emotionally, but they also touch upon our jurisprudence. It becomes a gesture that solidifies legal disgust in this case—an emotive aberration that now justifies the advance of provocation as a defence.

[22] Furthermore, McHugh J's reasoning builds on a similar emotional grammar articulated by Brennan CJ. Despite his attempts to emphasise the sexual nature of Gilles' conduct, rather than its gay sexual character specifically, his judgment obscures the way same-sex sexual contact in this case is rendered public or (hyper)visible. Same-sex advances are impugned, while heterofamilial sexual relationships do not attract such emotional scrutiny. The latter point is particularly important to emphasise, because in this case the alleged sexual violence that made Green 'especially sensitive' arose from a violent heteropatriarchal dynamic, where Green claimed his father consistently sexually abused his sisters. McHugh J tries to decouple private sexuality from public violence:

---

29. *Ibid.*
30. (1990) 171 CLR 312.
31. *Green*, at 245 (Brennan CJ).

[T]he fact that the advance was of a homosexual nature was only one factor in the case. What was more important from the accused's point of view was that a sexual advance, accompanied with some force, was made by a person whom the accused looked up to and trusted.[32]

The act of touching becomes a glaring problem of a 'persistent' sexual character. Specifically, Gillies unwanted advances are marked outside the legitimate space of reproductive heterosexual relations. In this case, the 'force' of the touch is considered in terms of the 'special sensitivity' Green had on the basis of alleged child abuse perpetrated against his sisters. Even though McHugh J follows the issues relating to Green's alleged history of abuse more closely, he renders homoerotic touching as a socially unacceptable breach of socially acceptable homosociality. That is, despite the importance of family abuse to underscoring the gravity of the provocation, McHugh J's reasoning focuses mostly on how touching becomes stigmatized as something perverse insofar as it relates to (unacceptable) homoeroticism rather than (acceptable) homosociality.

[23] Rather than categorizing the physicality of the act, the reference to 'some force' reflects a broader discursive and affective problematic that I want to contextualise. The 'force' of Gillies' conduct (touching on the shoulders and back) is jarringly felt in McHugh J's judgment. The literal (sexual advance) and metaphorical (legal response) 'touch' are intimately tied to the overdetermined sexual meaning ascribed to Gillies' same-sex attraction. Gilles was a 'trusted friend' whose non-platonic conduct breached the acceptable (homosocial) integrity of their relationship. Gillies had abused his position of being 'looked up to' by seeking to express his same-sex desire towards Green.

[24] McHugh J articulates the violation differently to Smart J: it is a threat to homosocial friendship rather than heterosexual masculinity. Yet, despite McHugh J's different rhetorical maneuvers, his disgust reinscribes the privileged position of homosocial friendship while recoiling from Gillies' homoerotic act which seeks to abuse that privilege. Gillies' provocative conduct is condemned as an act of violating trust. His articulation of the provocation defence exposes an unusual relationship between the conceptions of dominant (static) masculinity and the 'special sensitivities' towards heterosexual male identity that give rise to provoked homophobic violence. Such sensitivities are understood against a background of same-sex advances along with alleged sexual abuse perpetrated against siblings.

[25] Taken together, Brennan CJ and McHugh J's concurring judgments problematise the coherence of criminal law doctrines relating to personal responsibility and the 'objective' way the ordinary person is understood.[33] Indeed, the ordinary person is not simply some abstract rational or atomistic actor. Rather, in giving emotional force to the HAD, the majority accepts, unproblematically, the 'unusual' sexuality of the victim in the case, and in doing so suggests that ordinary persons are susceptible to homophobic

---

32. *Id*, at 370 (McHugh J).
33. *Id*, at 346–7 (Brennan CJ) and 372 (McHugh J).

prejudices. While 'special sensitivities' are used to mitigate (or at least understand) the conduct of the perpetrator, my colleagues reveal their own disgusted sensitivities or feelings relating to gay intimacy. By conflating terms like 'advance' and 'aggression' and coupling them with revulsion, the concurring judgments reveal an emotional inability to separate non-violent and violent gestures in relation to gay intimacy.

[26] In refusing the abjecting rhetoric of my colleagues, I find myself drawn in sympathy to Kirby J's dissent. He notes: 'In my view, the "ordinary person" in Australian society today is not so homophobic as to respond to a non-violent sexual advance by a homosexual person as to form an intent to kill or to inflict grievous bodily harm.'[34] Kirby J's judgment seeks to move against the overtures of disgust articulated by the majority by suggesting that a non-violent sexual advance—even given the appellant's specific circumstances—cannot create an excusable intent to kill or inflict grievous bodily harm. The ordinary person is not homophobic. Coupled with Kirby J's previous comments about the role of law in remedying violence against gay men, the common law is recuperated in his judgment as a place for eliminating homophobia. It is not supposed to entrench it, but should safeguard against such harms.

[27] I find Kirby J's dissent appealing because his judgment rejects the disgust of my colleagues and movingly disclaims homophobia. He refuses to accept homophobic disgust as ordinary in the terms required by Section 23 of the *Crimes Act 1900* (NSW). However, I must also note that his words come with emotional erasures of a different kind. Firstly, Kirby J seeks to equate the potential offensiveness of heterosexual and homosexual advances. He says:

> Any unwanted sexual advance, heterosexual or homosexual, can be offensive. It may intrude on sexual integrity in an objectionable way. But this Court should not send the message that, in Australia today, such conduct is objectively capable of being found by a jury to be sufficient to provoke the intent to kill or inflict grievous bodily harm.[35]

By reading the same-sex advance alongside the heterosexual kind, Kirby J's dissent obscures the way disgust has enabled the majority to reason the existence of the HAD in the first place. These affective differences arise due to the largely invisible positioning of heterosexuality (as a norm), while repudiating 'unusual' homosexuality (as other). Moreover, it is unclear to me whether making room to reject homophobia from a structural point of view (as a Court) means we need to eliminate consideration of how it might manifest in interpersonal relationships. In fact, recognizing that homophobia is structural necessitates careful consideration of how it manifests in social interactions. The extent to which this Court ought to take account of these structural factors when making judgments about individual criminal culpability is not fully explicated by Kirby J in his moving judgment.

---

34. *Id*, at 409 (Kirby J).
35. *Id* at 416 (Kirby J).

Affecting an Anti-Homophobic Jurisprudence

[28] I have gone to great pains to explore the emotional (homophobic) underpinnings of Green's lethal act, the statutory relevance of provocation to Green's pleadings about his traumatic family history, and the affective jurisprudence of this Court in connecting the two. I have done this in order to understand to what extent the provocation defence allows for homophobic disgust, and how this disgust has taken shape for both Green and this Court.

[29] However, while I recognise the relevance of homophobic disgust to the ordinary person acting homicidally, I also recognise the importance of pursuing an anti-homophobic jurisprudence that critically confronts, rather than casually accepts, homophobic disgust in jurisprudence. It is important to ask then: what are the conditions under which the HAD should be accepted in criminal law and are those conditions made out in this case?

[30] Provocation was designed as a concession to human frailty. It is unsurprising that emotion is central to its exercise. Criminal law recognises that there are circumstances where people react in lethal ways that are not compatible with their character as a result of others' behaviour beyond their control. It is clear that homophobia is a persistent social problem. Homophobic beliefs do not automatically result in violent behaviour, but we cannot underestimate that homophobic disgust in particular has visceral consequences. We must account for this.

[31] Green uses his disgust of Gillies' advance in order to mitigate the heinous nature of killing. My colleagues in writing the majority judgment entertain this homophobic disgust in order to assess the gravity of Gillies' unwanted conduct and whether it amounted to provocation. Gillies' unwanted 'queer' touching of Green is rendered more disgusting than an advance of a similar heterosexual kind done by men to women. The latter consideration is erased from the majority's discussion.

[32] I am willing to accept that Green's anxiety over unwanted same-sex advances might be tied to a history of child sexual abuse in relation to his siblings. Green may have suffered vicarious trauma having witnessed abuse perpetrated against his sisters. However, even accepting these propositions, I am not convinced there was evidence to suggest Gillies' unwanted advances triggered rage towards his father that was subsequently projected upon Gillies. This Court must take care to distinguish angry reactions to parental abuses of kinship from disgusted responses to unwanted same-sex sexual encounters. For the majority, homophobic conflation of unexpected same-sex interactions between friends with patriarchal sexual abuse anchors Green's 'special sensitivity' to provocation. I reject that emotional framing of provocation because it abstracts same-sex intimacy through framings of violation.

[33] It is also important for this Court to recognise that Green's violent reactions are culturally contingent. No argument was made to suggest Green's violence was due to a substantial impairment by abnormality of mind or disease of the mind. Homophobia is, after all, not a mental illness. Homophobia is not unique to Green. Making Green solely responsible for the killing of Gillies may satisfy Kirby J's emotional call to challenge individual a/effects of homophobia, but, in doing so, this Court would obscure the social norms that gave rise to Green's hostilities towards gay intimacy.

[34] While challenging the majority's abject framing of the case, I am wary of turning Green into a *bad apple* to absorb our disgust. Recognizing the institutionalization of homophobia becomes difficult if we uncritically redirect our disgust to individuals like Green. This Court should rightly feel disgusted by homophobic violence, but it should also be cautious about what it does with that disgust. Disgust is institutionally ordinary (in how the majority recognise the recoil Green felt towards Gillies) and individually spectacular (in how Kirby J recognises the brutality of homophobic violence perpetrated by individuals).

[35] Even if we accept, as Kirby J does, that homophobia should no longer be referable to the 'ordinary person,' that does not mean it has simply been expunged from legal circulation. Even legislative reform to explicitly exclude the HAD from the remit of provocation would not affect this. In fact, by suggesting violent homophobia is a non-issue in the broader community, cases that follow a similar emotional tread to this one will only continue to cloud judicial perceptions of just how pernicious and pervasive homophobia (in the forms of physical attacks, sexual abuse, vilification, harassment, discrimination, etc.) is in society.

[36] A cursory examination of the rates of homophobic violence, vilification, and harassment around the time the case was first heard in NSW reveals homophobia persists at terrifyingly common (or even 'ordinary') levels.[36] Homophobia is far from exceptional. In both the majority and minority judgments, my colleagues' respective judgments reveal the problematic way expressions of disgust are invoked to deal with lethal violence perpetrated against sexual minorities.

[37] With these tensions in mind, I am left in the unenviable position of stating whether to accept the appeal or refuse it. In order to arrive at my conclusion, I want to use the disgust present in this case to distinguish between individual and institutional realities. The institutional reality of homophobia and associated homophobic disgust are not grave enough to warrant an individual claim of murder being reduced to manslaughter. To conflate institutional abjection of same-sex attraction with Green's lethal homophobic acts would be to assume too much about the causes of such violent behaviour. Moreover, it would ignore the restraint which Section 23(2)(b) requires ordinary people to possess.

---

36.   NSW Police Service, 'Out of the Blue' (February 1995).

[38] Essentially, the emotional susceptibilities of Green, and those exposed by the jurisprudence of my colleagues in this case, speak to the importance of holding individuals accountable for their actions while recognizing the broader social context of homophobia. Exceptionalising queer intimacies or homophobia through the rubric of disgust risks undermining attempts to protect the former or remedying the latter.

Conclusion

[39] This is an emotional case and rendering a judgment has been an emotional exercise. The case reflects homophobic disgust across varied individual and institutional contexts. Malcolm Green's killing of Donald Gillies is inexcusable, but it is understandable. Green is not evil. He is a product of a homophobic environment. Homophobia is a corrosive social malaise that inhibits our capacity to love and relate to each other. Criminal law is ill-suited to address its deleterious dynamics. We need more than just legal interventions to institutionally dismantle homophobia. So, what can this Court do? I implore my colleagues to think critically with their emotions and not to allow disgust to obscure their views of relevant legal and social issues. As judicial officers, we should take seriously the claims presented before us and approach them with a sensitive, self-reflexive, and anti-homophobic ethic.

[40] I would refuse the appeal and affirm the decision of the trial judge.

4

Navtej Singh Johar & Ors. v Union of India thr. Secretary Ministry of Law and Justice (India):

Queering Section 377 Litigation

in the Indian Higher Courts through Bringing in

Multiple Marginalized and Intersectional Narratives

Yerram Raju Behara, Malhar Satav and Sal

Introduction[1]

In the verdict delivered on 6 September 2018 in *Navtej Singh Johar v Union of India*[2] (hereinafter *Navtej*), there was an emphatic and unequivocal articulation of fundamental rights of equality, non–discrimination, privacy, dignity, autonomy and health guaranteed under Articles 14, 15, 19(1), and 21 of the Indian Constitution in the judgment by four judges, led by Justice D.Y. Chandrachud (as he then was).

The Section 377 of the Indian Penal Code 1860 which criminalized sexual acts between consenting adult queer persons, was read down after a long period of struggle. The entire queer community had rallied around to repeal the law and to claim their fundamental rights to dignity, freedom and non–discrimination, while navigating their sexual identity in family, schools, colleges, workplaces, and in public spaces, for over two decades in this long protracted legal struggle.

The community seemed to have finally triumphed. However, was this victory actually *lived* by the queer–trans communities? Did the decriminalization of same–sex relations between consenting adults in *Navtej* inform and animate the lived experiences of the queer–trans community? Did the community have any freedom to celebrate the *freedom* granted to them?

1. Research funded partly by EQUAL Fellowship, TheYP Foundation. Research assistance provided by Pranjal Agarwal, II Year, MNLU, Nagpur, and Pratham T, II Year, NLSIU, Bangalore. Editorial support by Ria De, PhD, Film Studies. The authors would like to thank Abigail and all other artists for permissions to use their poems/art stemming from the workshops, and Koonal Duggal, Kunal Dongre, Ikshaku Bezbaroa, Praveen Kumar T, Santanu Mondal, Koustubh RoyChoudhari for their steadfast emotional support, peer-feedback during the ideation and execution of the workshops.
2. (2018) 10 SCC 1.

It is pertinent to draw upon Rukmini Banerjee, from her work 'If Resistance Could Be Tender,'[3] insofar as they observe:

The day I heard 'gone are the days when we were told that to love was a crime'—

I rejoiced with my friends,

We sang and we danced,

I stepped outside of the gates of familiarity and I held my lover's hand as a symbol of resistance,

Instead of a declaration of love.

Our mouths were cannons spitting slogans of victory

But my mind was weary of this feeble triumph

Because I still made a weapon of something as tender as loving.

Almost ten months since our short lived joy,

My trans friend asked me if she should dress more conservatively because

'My celebration shouldn't land me in a hospital, now that would be terrible.'

'Provided you are not alone or out at night, you should declare your love for your body'—

And so her friends, including me, helped her make up her mind

To love her body

As a symbol of resistance.

I don't know if we were meant to love as a symbol of resistance all our lives

…… maybe my affection will always be a symbol of resistance

And my biggest weapon

Something as tender as loving.

Against the backdrop of the freedom to exercise the judicially granted freedom by *Navtej*, it becomes imperative to question how the judgment has impacted the community. What meaning does it hold for our quotidian lives, individually as well as a community? What freedoms does *Navtej* enable and which still elude its ambit?

3. Rukmini Banerjee, 'If Resistance Could Be Tender,' in *Criminal No More*, ed. The YP Foundation (Noida: The YP Foundation, 2019)

To be better placed to address this inquiry, we seek to revisit the verdict to probe the lacunae between the judicial declaration in *Navtej* and its demonstrable impact on the lived realities of the queer-trans communities.

In this endeavour, we attempt to rewrite the judgment, as a belated opinion written after the original judgment to take stock of the material and social consequences of the original decision. We did this in a form which would enable all parts of the community with the rights which the original verdict intended. This included poetry that would also encompass the unheard, unseen and often invisibilized narratives through the languages of the tongue alien to the colonizer yet translated to English.

To understand the consequences of the judgment, we organized a workshop as a judicial initiative, which helped us understand the implications of the 2018 judgment. Material and data from that workshop has been used in this judgment.

IN THE SUPREME COURT OF INDIA

Writ Petition (Criminal) No. 76 of 2016, Writ Petition (Civil) No. 572 of 2016, Writ Petition (Criminal) Nos. 88, 100, 101 and 121 of 2018 (Under Article 32 of the Constitution of India)

Decided On: 06 September 2018

Appellants: **Navtej Singh Johar and Ors.**
vs.
Respondent: **Union of India (UOI) and Ors.**

Hon'ble Judges/Coram:
Anonymous, J.
Navtej Singh Johar and Ors. v Union of India (UOI) and Ors. (06.09.2018 – SC): MANU/SC/0947/2018

JUDGMENT
ANONYMOUS, J. (for themself)

[1] The case before this Court presents us with the issues relating to rights such as those of equality, privacy, dignity, and autonomy guaranteed under the Constitution that a class of people have been deprived of by the verdict of *Suresh Kumar Kaushal v Naz Foundation.*[4] The issues that would be addressed are:
1. Whether Section 377 of the Indian Penal Code 1860 is constitutionally valid and the judgment given in the case of *Suresh Kumar Koushal v Naz Foundation*[5] is to be upheld?
2. In the case that the consensual sexual acts of adults under Section 377 is decriminalized, how would the verdict affect the working class and marginalized groups of society?

[2] In the context of the first issue, I stand by the ratio being given by my fellow justices, who, challenging the constitutionality of the 2013 judgment, hold that insofar as Section 377 criminalizes consensual sexual acts of adults (i.e. persons above the age of 18 years who are competent to consent) in private, it violates Articles 14, 15, 19, and 21 of the Constitution.

---

4. (2014) 1 SCC 1.
5. ibid.

[3] However, I believe it would be critical to reflect on the work of queer theorists, whose work around sex, sexuality and desire can help us understand and work through the deeply entrenched nuances of cis–heteronormative views, and the binary construct of sex/gender, which are expressed for the purpose of the case before us.

[4] The depravity of sex, or good versus bad sex, has been well defined in Gayle Rubin's essay, through the introduction of the Charmed Circle under the ambit of which 'peno–vaginal sex for procreation' occupies a higher position in comparison to sexual acts for pleasure.[6] This cis–heteronormative construct looks at majoritarian morality as one of its guiding principles.

[5] As Justice D.Y. Chandrachud says in his opinion:

> The order of nature that Section 377 speaks of is not just about non-procreative sex but is about forms of intimacy which the social order finds 'disturbing.' This includes various forms of transgression such as inter-caste and inter-community relationships which are sought to be curbed by society. *What links LGBT individuals to couples who love across caste and community lines is the fact that both are exercising their right to love at enormous personal risk and in the process disrupting existing lines of social authority.* Thus, a re-imagination of the order of nature as being not only about the prohibition of non-procreative sex but instead about the limits imposed by structures such as gender, caste, class, religion and community makes the right to love not just a separate battle for LGBT individuals, but a battle for all. (footnotes omitted and emphasis added)

[6] I find it imperative to highlight how the limits imposed by such structures, could continue anti-trans repression even after consensual sexual acts in private spaces are decriminalized. Homosexuality, when coupled with repressive structures like caste, religion, class, gender norms and heteronormative spaces of society, continues facing stigmatization. This brings us to review the extent to which this verdict would affect people in different spaces and different communities of people even in public spaces, where queer bodies are *museumised* or memorialised for vicarious viewing, in health-care institutions, in the streets for sex work, and when detained in prisons, or when confined in their homes through incarceration.

[7] THE DISCOURSE OF DECRIMINALISATION VERSUS LIBERALISATION

[7.1] Extending the scope of the judgments by fellow justices, by attempting to paint a picture of the societal conditions post decriminalisation, we must recollect instances of violations to the rights to dignity, privacy, equality of queer individuals from rural or suburban locations, those from religious or caste minorities, individuals in housing, at workplaces and in healthcare, and those who, in public spaces, feel caged owing to societal hatred.

---

6. Gayle S. Rubin, 'Thinking Sex: Notes for a Radical Theory of the Politics of Sexuality,' in *Culture, Society and Sexuality*, eds. Richard Parker and Peter Aggleton (New York: Routledge, 2006), 38.

[7.2] To put the tangible impacts of *Navtej* in perspective, I look at chronicling missing social histories, and document workplace, housing, and healthcare harassment as a pilot, with the aid of an ethnographic study centred around Andhra Pradesh and Karnataka, which culminated in a virtual workshop with legal bodies, NGOs, and policy think-tanks to understand the gaps in the implementation of the verdicts.

[7.3] As an initiative from the judicial side, I, as a judge in my personal capacity, initiated myself into a systematic process of sensitization of queer rights and the lived experiences of the queer community as a whole. Redefining Queerscapes, was one such holistic and wholesome sensitization that involved three pilot poetry workshops (two at Uru, a queer camping festival in Wayanad, Kerala, and one at Namma Pride in Bengaluru, Karnataka) that explored poetry and art to envision what safe spaces mean to queer–trans individuals. In the workshop, each participant explored a narrative of workplace/healthcare/housing discrimination, with poetry (blackout/redacted/any form of poetry) of their choice, to rewrite the definition of safe spaces—I also used these workshops as spaces to drive awareness around legal entitlements available to the community. In these poetry workshops, queer–trans participants examined what an ideal safe space means to them; using blackout poetry and/or erasure poetry, redacted poetry, and found poetry. Queer participants have attempted writing poems that redefine and reimagine the first–hand narratives of queer–trans experiences of physical/psychosocial/emotional violence encountered in housing, workplace, and healthcare spaces.

[7.4] Pursuant to my sensitisation, I was able to view how my decision making was guided through the cis-heteronormative lens in which we all grow up, and therefore erased the needs of the communities whose rights I seek to address through the verdict. I would seek to understand, examine, amplify, and ponder over the profound impact of decriminalisation on the mental health of queer individuals, communities and movements visualizing them through time, travel, urban aspirations, and anxieties thereby reimagining queerscapes.

[7.5] Undergirding this inquiry is the intuitive recognition that mere decriminalisation is not enough unless *liberalisation* eliminates the consequences of discrimination in lived experiences. Decriminalisation is a consequence of a judicial scrutiny of the fact that a provision in the statute books does not pass muster of vested Constitutional guarantees. In other words, it is an act of *expunging* and *eclipsing* that which infracts our Constitutional ethos. Therefore, an act of *expunging* Section 377 from the statute book with the rationale of safeguarding the rights enshrined in Articles 14 and 21 read in conjunction with Article 19, does not, in and of itself, guarantee that the consequences of decriminalisation would necessarily further the ethos of Articles 21, 14 read in conjunction with 19 of the Constitution of India. On the other hand, *liberalisation* entails a proactive and positive furtherance of the dictum in *Navtej* both infrastructurally and psychosocially. It refers to the positive endeavours by the State to implement the equality dicta of *Navtej* in the grassroots insofar as there is an infrastructural reimagining of queer-trans individuals in public spaces along with a psychosocial transformation shift. This is the meta–concept of *equity* that this Hon'ble Court would like to sanctify and cement in the jurisprudence of queer rights.

[7.6] Hence, in order to ensure that the exercise of decriminalisation is actually consequential and beneficial in ethos, one must examine whether it has led to a process of liberalisation insofar as the queer community has the wherewithal to enjoy and fructify their ordained freedoms. I put this proposition to scrutiny in the subsequent sections.

[8] QUEERNESS AND HOUSING

[8.1] Homes for queer–trans people are closely linked to their aspirations and akin to their survival. For some it may be an escape from the violence faced in their natal homes, which may include wrongful confinement in family homes and involuntary institutionalization. For many others, it could be one of the first places where they feel safe to explore their queer non–binary selves.

[8.2] The workshops have had candid sharing, which offered instances of people being subject to harassment in homes, apartments, being denied spaces owing to their queerness or being thrown away from them owing to the same.

[8.3] Against this backdrop, it is pertinent to reproduce the poignant reflection of social ostracisation of queer individuals owing to their sexuality, in the incisive words of Shals Mahajan in 'The word is red'[7]:

> When he was refused a house on rent once again,
>
> his professor credentials making no dent,
>
> nor the university lifting a finger to help,
>
> he went back home to Srinagar carrying with him the
>
> "no more a criminal" tag his gay self had in Mumbai.
>
> The city gave him that, no more.

[8.4] It would be remiss to aver that the aforementioned is particular to India, since it is founded by dogmatic conservative thought, knowing no national boundaries.

[8.5] The House of Lords case *Ghaidan v Godin–Mendoza*[8] reflected the problems faced by the community in the housing sector in England, observing discrimination against tenants based on their sexuality. A same-sex couple was staying as tenants, and upon

---

7.   Shals Mahajan, 'The Word Is Red,'in *Criminal No More*, ed. The YP Foundation (Noida: The YP Foundation, 2019), 15.
8.   [2004] UKHL 30.

the death of the partner of Godin, Mendoza, the landlord claimed possession of the flat. The judgment was in favour of the tenant's partner, and it was held that discrimination because of sexual orientation was impermissible.

[8.6] Maya, a non–binary professional, spoke about how they had to hide the queer markers in their home in Delhi to avoid unfair eviction in an interview to *The Caravan* magazine.[9]

As a precursor to the workshops, I facilitated an ethnographic study with the intent to chronicle the experiences of violations in housing, healthcare and workplaces meted out to trans folks. Two trans participants from Andhra Pradesh also shared narratives of similar experiences:

> There are obstacles right from the moment we start looking out for homes through brokers with landlords refusing to show homes. This continues in the form of unfair increase in rents, in violation of existing rental agreements upon discovering our trans identity. This also comes with added anxiety of never knowing how long the agreement or the tenancy of homes will stay under our names.

[8.7] During a panel discussion, to which I was invited, towards the culmination of my sensitisation framework, Shubha Chacko, the Executive Director of Solidarity Foundation, stated emphatically that even organisations working with the community face difficulty in finding spaces to rent for running their respective offices, though this refusal to sublet/rent properties is often masked with other semi–plausible reasons to deny direct transphobia.[10]

[8.8] I concede that certain governmental protections have been granted. For instance, the Social Welfare Department of the Government of Maharashtra rolled out an affordable housing scheme for the trans community, with plans of offering around 150 flats of 450 square feet each in a dedicated housing complex in Nagpur city. Garima Griha is a scheme launched by the Ministry of Social Justice that introduced shelter homes for trans people in need. However, there have been instances where the same safeguards have led to greater oppression, such as violence faced by the queer community as a consequence of the protection granted, which exposed their identity and made them more visible.

[8.9] In July, a trans person was forcibly picked up from Garima Greh along with Shaman and Gautam, board members of TWEET[11] who work closely with the community,

---

9. Vinayak Dewan, 'Open House: Finding Discrimination-Free Housing for Queer Communities in Delhi,' *The Caravan*, 1 March 2022, accessed on 10 December 2022, https://caravanmagazine.in/gender/housing-discrimination-against-queer-communities-delhi-article377.

10. An NGO that supports grassroots level organisations of gender/sexual minorities (LGBTIAQ+) and sex workers by building collectives and capacities.

11. Transgender Welfare Equity and Empowerment Trust (TWEET) Foundation is a registered body under the Mumbai Charity Commissioner led by seven trans activists, whose mission is to build an empowered, self-sufficient, and vibrant Trans movement in India by wholly caring for the welfare of trans persons through

and were beaten by police.[12] This brings us back to the questions of right to privacy and right to dignity, as enshrined in our Constitution, and emphasised during the Section 377 verdicts. Meanwhile, officials at the Ministry of Social Justice and Empowerment and at the National Institute of Social Defence who were earlier working with the organisations running the shelter homes, have not been responding to the desperate pleas of the organisations for funds. Despite making the risk of closure clear, the government has failed to make the payments for over 10 months, in 2022.

[8.10] It is rather a cruel irony that 'Garima' in Hindi means dignity, but the Central government has failed to act in a dignified manner, due to which several organisations have now been forced to initiate fundraisers to ensure the survival of the shelter homes and the safety and well–being of the residents.[13]

[8.11] This buttresses the above question of decriminalisation versus liberalisation: it is debatable as to who among the community can afford to have the wherewithal to actualise seemingly haughty promises like privacy and dignity accorded by the verdict. The members of the community are forcefully evicted from safe houses without due cause or process and subjected to police violence, treated as criminals, when they are not legally or otherwise culpable for anything other than their informed and intuitive internalisation of sexuality. If wearing one's sexuality as a badge of honour were an offence, then the aforementioned instances of atavistic vigilantism would have attracted a kernel of legitimacy, if not nothing more. Fortunately, this is not the law of the land in India—rather far from it, our laws *abhor, repel* and *penalise* such kangaroo acts of vigilantism, but evidently not adequately so.

The Transgender Persons (Protection of Rights) Act, 2019 is a case in point since it is normative in spirit and not consequential in its framework, insofar as it does not prescribe penalties for contravening the postulates of the Act. The Prohibition Against Discrimination enshrined under Section 3 entails no penalties if the section is not complied with.

[8.12] An essay, from the same report, titled 'Till Death do us Part,' which captured the painful narrative of two lesbian women who, following abuse from their home, attempted suicide, helped us unlock conversations around safe spaces, leaving home and the legal rights of queer members when they leave home as adults. The participants from the queerscapes workshops also brought in the narrative of two women marrying and living together in India in their utopian poem, thereby opening us to an active conversation on same–sex marriage and living rights in India. There were conversations

---

their education, medical treatment, legal standing, and culture and social upliftment.

12. Aditya Tiwari, '4 Years After Section 377, The Duality In India's Current LGBTQIA+ Momentum,' *Feminism in India*, 9 September 2022, accessed 9 December 2022, https://feminisminindia.com/2022/09/09/4-years-after-section-377-the-duality-in-indias-current-lgbtqia-momentum/.

13. 'Multiple Government-Funded Shelter Homes for Transgender People Face Risk of Closure,' *Yes We Exist India*, 26 November 2022, accessed 9 December 2022, https://www.instagram.com/p/ClbvM_QucuB/.

around the case of Jothi and her partner's suicide from Tamil Nadu in 2021,[14] and another lesbian couple's suicidal note in 2018. This brings us back to the conversation: 'Whose decriminalisation were we celebrating in and after 2018?'[15] Has there been a change in the lives of the queer communities from rural and suburban Tier–2 cities?

[9] QUEERNESS AND WORKPLACES

[9.1] The decriminalisation of Section 377 guaranteed members of the queer community the benefit of equal citizenship without discrimination and equal protection of law. During the hearing, it was noted that Section 377 forces queer individuals to hide their identities in workplaces and this impacts their self–esteem and affects their rights under Article 19(1)(g) of the Constitution, an impediment to their right to practice any profession or to carry on any occupation, trade, or business. This Court explicitly recognised in *Navtej* that the Indian Constitution's guarantees of equality of opportunity and non–discrimination 'in matters of employment or appointment to office under the State' apply to queer persons, who have a right to non–discrimination in access and enjoyment of the right to work.

[9.2] Queer individuals who are able to access workplaces are often vulnerable to sexual harassment, assault, verbal harassment and other forms of workplace harassment and discrimination. Most workspaces are gendered, in particular restrooms, which creates additional difficulties including placing queer and gender-non-conforming persons at risk of assault. Queer employees also report being forced, as a consequence of persistent discrimination and abuse, into leaving their jobs or having their employment arbitrarily terminated. Transgender persons and gender non–conforming persons face an additional hurdle in accessing employment, as they lack identity documents in their preferred or expressed gender.

[9.3] At this juncture, my judicial mind cannot render a judgment so intimately connected to the lived experiences of the queer community without alluding to literature animating their lived experiences.
    Audre Lorde, in 'A Litany for Survival'[16], writes:

For those of us who live at the shoreline

standing upon the constant edges of decision

---

14. Annie Banerji, 'Lesbian Couple's Suicide Notes Reveal Stigma They Face in India,' *Reuters*, 13 June 2018, accessed 8 December 2022, https://www.reuters.com/article/india-women-lesbian-idINKBN1J90VE.
15. Nishant Ranjan, 'Fearing Separation, Lesbian Couple Commits Suicide in Tamil Nadu,' *The Logical Indian*, 21 May 2020, accessed 8 December 2022, https://thelogicalindian.com/news/fearing-separation-lesbian-couple-commits-suicide-in-tamil-nadu-21206.
16. Audre Lorde, 'A Litany for Survival,' Poetry Foundation, accessed on 9 December 2022, https://www.poetryfoundation.org/poems/147275/a-litany-for-survival.

crucial and alone

for those of us who cannot indulge

the passing dreams of choice

who love in doorways coming and going

in the hours between dawns

looking inward and outward

at once before and after

seeking a now that can breed

futures

like bread in our children's mouths

so their dreams will not reflect

the death of ours.

[9.4] An anonymous story shared at Gaysi, titled '6th September 2018,' reads:

> I remember hating that while the televisions in my workplace were announcing the fact that I wasn't a criminal anymore, I was listening to homophobic jokes and comments made by colleagues sitting nearby. I remember hating not getting up and asking them to shut the fu*k up.

[9.5] During the ethnographic study, a trans woman from Bangalore stated her experiences of working as a teacher:

> I realised that nothing had really changed after the verdicts. Yes, I could no longer be branded as a criminal and put behind bars for my sexuality or my gender identity. But the shame and fear prevailed. In the eyes of society, nothing had changed. I could hear whispers across the corridor when I walked past a particular class. A judgment cannot grant us societal acceptance or alter the societal perception. If you are not marginalised for your sexual identity, you continue to be marginalised for identifying as a woman, or for being a Muslim. As a trans person, who is still closeted, it becomes extremely difficult to navigate the conversations of sexuality and gender with colleagues or senior teachers, or to seek resources to implement trans–friendly workplace policies in an understaffed school.

[9.6] Meanwhile, a trans woman who was working in the healthcare industry shared:

> I was hired with no formal work contract, despite having an MSc. Most times, the wages were always variable with no sense of job–security, despite being in bulk pharmaceuticals. There was an additional risk of the chemicals interacting with my transitioning, and HIV medication,

which I had to endure. They chose to suddenly terminate my work, with no formal experience letter either.

[9.7] In another conversation with a Dalit gay man, working in the Information Technology (IT) and Information Technology Enabled Services (ITeS) sector from Bengaluru, who spoke candidly about workplace harassment faced by him before and after the reading down of Section 377, shared that despite legal frameworks, workplace hierarchy and institutional savarna[17] entitlements make it structurally impossible to seek a legal recourse without facing pushback, especially when the complainant is relatively new to the workplace or industry:

> After I chose to report homophobia at work, the HR actively discouraged me from reporting the incident, while my manager also shared similar thoughts. I was performing well in my organisation, so I could change teams, but I had to work through the psychological impact of harassment in my own time, through my resources.

[9.8] In this context, it is important to note that the Queer Tech Workers' Demand Charter,[18] specifically sought to extend legal protections as follows:

> 1. Existing laws such as the Industrial Disputes Act and Shops and Establishments Act prevent discrimination among workers on the basis of sex. This anti–discrimination protection should be extended to other categories such as sexual orientation and gender identity.

> 2. Currently, Indian law recognises sexual harassment at the workplace as punishable only against women. Harassment, and sexual harassment, in the workplace against trans women and other sexual and gender minorities should be specifically covered by the law.

> 3. In addition, State and Central governments must effect laws and regulations that legally protect queer workers and provide them with proper recourse against workplace discrimination.

[9.9] The Charter also demands multiple policy changes to drive institutional reform. I must however also note that in a landmark decision, the High Court of Calcutta ruled that same–gender allegations could be upheld under the Sexual Abuse of Women at Workplace (Prevention, Prohibition and Redressal) Act, 2013, commonly referred to as the POSH Act. This judgment was handed down by the High Court of Calcutta in the case of *Dr Malabika Bhattacharjee v Internal Complaints Committee, Vivekananda College,* by a sole tribunal of Hon'ble Justice Sabyasachi Bhattacharyya.[19]

[9.10] During the panel discussion, both the panellists, Mansi Singh from Centre for Law and Policy Research (CLPR) and Shubha from Solidarity Foundation, commented that while workplaces have started actively practising allyship, despite having the right intentions, misinformed allies may practice performative allyship without making

17. This refers to caste lineage and hierarchy.
18. Queer Tech Workers' Demand Charter, 15 August 2022, accessed on 9 December 2022, https://www. aiiteu.org/letters/queer-tech-workers-demand-charter/. Queer Tech Workers' Demand Charter was built through the organised consultations held by All India IT and ITeS Employees' Union with queer IT workers.
19. *Dr Malabika Bhattacharjee v Internal Complaints Committee, Vivekananda College & Ors.* W.P.A. 9141 of 2020.

the necessary structural changes to drive queer and trans–inclusive workplaces, reducing these gestures to tokenistic *pink capitalism*.

[9.11] However, there have also been instances where the trans community has questioned the legal entitlements not being made available. Adam Harry became the first trans–masculine pilot in India to question the Directorate General of Civil Aviation (DCGA) over its transphobic guidelines, while calling out DGCA's unwillingness to make changes in guidelines for the employment of trans community members and also denial of the constitutional right not to be discriminated on the basis of gender, bringing much needed changes to the aviation industry.[20] Meanwhile, teachers such as Jane Kaushik are fighting the long battle of accessing their legal entitlements, as she was forced to resign by a Uttar Pradesh private school, with The National Commission for Women (NCW) stepping in to initiate an independent enquiry.[21]

[9.12] Furthermore, engaging with queer–trans rights in workplaces is a constant act of learning and unlearning. Being a queer ally would require them to also actively listen and question their preconceived savarna and colonial notions of morality, whilst unlearning their biases entrenched in a patriarchal mindset. That is precisely when meaningful allyship contributing to structural long–term changes would be noted. It would also need to address the critical question of psychological safety of formalised Indian workplaces through these active engagements.

[9.13] Furthermore, CLPR, in its report 'Intersectionality: A Report on Discrimination Based on Caste with the Intersections of Sex, Gender Identity and Disability in Karnataka, Andhra Pradesh, Tamil Nadu and Kerala,' identified a few key concerns:

> Dalit transgender persons were especially vulnerable to sexual violence at work and 33% reported sexual assault and harassment at work. Dalit women in particular faced blatant casteism and sexism from their employers and co–workers and over 30% Dalit women reported verbal harassment. 63% of Dalit respondents who faced discrimination did not choose to report the incident as the avenues for grievance redressal were limited.[22]

[10] QUEERNESS AND HEALTHCARE

[10.1] My brother judge, Justice Chandrachud, in his judgment in *Navtej,* highlights how 'individuals belonging to sexual and gender minorities experience discrimination,

20.   Imran Qureshi, 'Adam Harry: India Transgender Pilot's Long Fight to Fly,' *BBC News*, 16 July 2022, accessed on 10 December 2022, https://www.bbc.com/news/world-asia-india-62160024.
21.   'NCW Asks U.P. Chief Secretary to Probe Firing of Transwoman Teacher by Private School,' *The Hindu*, 9 December 2022, accessed on 10 December 2022, https://www.thehindu.com/news/national/other-states/ncw-asks-up-chief-secretary-to-probe-firing-of-transwoman-teacher-by-private-school/article66238782.ece.
22.   Jayna Kothari et al, 'Centre for Law and Policy Research, Intersectionality: A Report on Discrimination Based on Caste with the Intersections of Sex, Gender Identity and Disability in Karnataka, Andhra Pradesh, Tamil Nadu and Kerala,' Centre for Law & Policy Research, accessed on 10 December 2022, https://translaw.clpr.org.in/wp-content/uploads/2022/11/Intersectionality-A-Report-on-Discrimination-based-on-Caste-with-the-intersections-of-Sex-Gender-Identity-and-Disability-in-Karnataka-Andhra-Pradesh-Tamil-Nadu-and-Kerala.pdf.

stigmatisation, and in some cases, denial of healthcare on account of their sexual orientation and gender identity.'

[10.2] It is interesting to note how the verdicts came full circle, considering the first petition being filed by social workers working closely with people living with HIV AIDS Bhedbhav Virodhi Andola, ABVA, or in English, AIDS Anti-Discrimination Movement.

However, it goes without saying that there is persistent and systemic exclusion of the queer community from healthcare and in health-care decision making. Due to the huge geography and widespread communities, access to healthcare and its barriers also differ widely when we look at several subsections of the queer community. Recently, the National Medical Commission, the apex regulatory body of medical professionals in India, has banned conversion therapy, calling it 'professional misconduct.'[23]

[10.3] With so many positive developments and a definitive Supreme Court judgment, it would seem that all problems have been addressed. But is that really the case? While the law has conferred rights to the queer community, its members continue being stigmatised and ostracised by society. Even today, a majority of mental health professionals in the country do not accept the fact that non-heterosexuality is not the equivalent of a mental illness. Mental health professionals continue operating within the confines of their prejudiced environments, with the result that the queer community's mental health needs continue to suffer.

[10.4] A trans woman participant from Andhra Pradesh spoke in the ethnographic study:

> It is impossible for those who are unaware of HIV medication to get access to the same. For those who already have access and are receiving the medication, it becomes difficult to continue accessing if they wish to change cities or districts. Similarly, it is also difficult to change one medication to another. Almost always, the diagnostic tests (Kidney and Liver Function Tests) are never conducted in public healthcare settings, to check if we are developing adverse effects… For those of us who are unaware of the medical terminology, and do not speak refined English, healthcare experiences are harrowing, from entry at the hospitals till we exit the system. The security personnel are untrained at how to check trans people and the receptionists are always misgendering us; the worst experiences would be from physicians and paramedical staff who even refuse to touch us while treating us. There is a general unease while doing full body check–ups or any pre–surgical diagnostic procedures. Casual cruel remarks are often commonplace, with all our saline, IV fluids, medical equipment kept in a corner, near the garbage, almost discarded, and us being treated inhumanely.

[10.5] My brother, Justice Chandrachud, spoke about queer–affirmative counselling and the recognition of the Yogyakarta Principles in his judgment. While queer–affirmative counselling is still at its nascency in India, it is a known fact that most queer persons

---

23. Sudipta Datta, 'Explained: The Ban on Conversion Therapy for the LGBTQIA+ Community,' *The Hindu*, 6 September 2022, accessed 10 December 2022, https://www.thehindu.com/news/national/explained-the-ban-on-conversion-therapy-for-the-lgbtqia-community/article65853083.ece.

spend a majority of their healthcare experiences being medicalised by the healthcare community, especially in the mental healthcare services.

[10.6] Perhaps it is time to reflect on the words of Arvind Narain and Vinay Chandran, written much before the Section 377 litigations, and understand why societal change goes a long way towards healing, as well as having medical texts that are updated.

[10.7] The fabric of our society is hemmed to the edge with anachronistic notions of binaries—of perfect versus flawed, man versus woman, heterosexual love and monogamous relationships, that anything outside of health is sickness and everyone outside this neat definition is pathological. Transness has been pathologized for far too long. Medical manuals and outdated psychology textbooks continue to propagate this pathologisation.[24]

[10.8] Dr Aqsa has been breaking barriers and widening the medical narratives by being a vocal advocate for trans-inclusion, not just through her regular work but by being the first trans-physician of India in several areas and also by chairing and facilitating the international conference on transgender healthcare IPATHCON. Spaces such as these bring in the much–needed conversations among professionals working in the field of transgender healthcare, researchers from both medical and social sciences streams, students, allies, support groups and officials from government and non–government organisations entrusted with provisioning of welfare to the transgender and gender diverse individuals.[25]

[10.9] Despite such landmark work being undertaken, very little is spoken about the medical negligence and babies with intersex traits continue being abandoned at birth. Gross medical negligence due to poor existing support frameworks and lack of medical awareness becomes a big part of their life.

[10.10] Dr Aqsa, a trans activist, a medical educator, and a healthcare practitioner, in one of her interviews opines:

> What is 'normal'? The endeavour to identify the 'normal body' in medical science often becomes exclusionary and inhibits access to correct healthcare for marginalised groups. I always ask medicos, in the anatomy class of MBBS college, if they ever come across a cadaver of a trans person? Or a person with disability?[26]

---

24. Arvind Narain and Tarunabh Khaitan, 'Medicalisation of Homosexuality: A Human Rights Approach,' in *Humjinsi: A Resource Book on Lesbian, Gay and Bisexual Rights in India*, ed. Bina Fernandez (Bombay: Combat Law Publications, 2002), 29; Vinay Chandran, 'Ain't No Cure for Love,' *India Together*, 6 April 2006, accessed on 10 November 2022, http://www.indiatogether.org/2006/apr/hrt-nocure.htm.
25. Association for Transgender Health in India, iPath 3rd International Conference on Transgender healthcare 'Building Foundations for the Delivery of Transgender Healthcare in the Indian Subcontinent' IPATHCON 2022, accessed 9 December 2022, https://www.athionline.com/2022ipathcon.
26. Divyadarshan C, 'How a Trans Doctor Is Fighting to Make Healthcare in India Inclusive,' *Yourstory*, 6 October 2022, accessed on 9 December 2022, https://yourstory.com/socialstory/2022/10/

Unsurprisingly, she is yet to find a doctor or medical student who has worked with the cadaver of a trans person. 'Since trans and disabled bodies are not considered "normal", students end up not learning about them,' she adds.

[10.11] *S. Sushma and Ors. v Commissioner of Police*, WP 7284 of 2021, banned conversion therapy and the Court there spoke extensively on the role of chosen families in the state of Tamil Nadu.[27] Conversations took place around the provisions of healthcare guaranteed through the Transgender Act 2019, and also the petitions filed by Rachna and Grace Banu, trans activists.[28]

[10.12] Desire—sexual, physical or emotional desire—has often been viewed through the lens of the normal. A poet in the pilot workshop at Uru re–examined her relationship with desire, through found poetry. She referred to Rushati Mukherjee's work:

lick the smoke that

curls out

from your languid

mouth

trace the

     dip

        of your navel

       lipstick–stained

       orgasm–bubbled

Cigarettes.[29]

[10.13] The act of love, the act of being desired by the same sex, has historically been medicalised as an illness, and hence poems such as these, which focus exquisitely and exclusively on desire, normalise what queerness and queerifying desire means, instead of simply observing the poems that embody cis–heteronormative constructs of desire. While sharing their story, tedagadu questions:

If you prick us, do we not bleed?

If you tickle us, do we not laugh?

If you poison us, do we not die?

And if you wrong us, do we not seek revenge? [30]

queer-changemakers-trans-doctor-fighting-healthcare-inclusive.
27. *S. Sushma and Ors. v Commissioner of Police*, WP 7284 of 2021.
28. *Grace Banu Ganesan v State of Tamil Nadu*, WP 6052 of 2019 (PIL).
29. Rushati Mukherjee, 'Rushati Mukherjee,' in *The World That Belongs to Us: An Anthology of Queer Poetry from South Asia*, eds. Aditi Angiras and Akhil Katyal (Noida: Harper Collins, 2020), 54–56.
30. tedagadu, 'Accessing Gender-Affirming Healthcare Services in India: A Lived Experience,' *Gaysi*, 6 October 2021, accessed on 10 December 2022, https://gaysifamily.com/lifestyle/accessing-

[10.14] Misgendering in healthcare and using deadnames is commonplace; and this is such cruel mistreatment, when the patient comes seeking treatment for all the psycho-social trauma that they have to endure. In an article speaking about lived experiences, of accessing gender–affirming healthcare services in India, a trans person shared the below narrative:

> How am I supposed to feel safe in a space that fails to address me by my name? Doesn't that mean that they are refusing to see me for me? By way of explanation, I was told that the reason the hospital has such a policy is not for people 'like me,' but because they can't trust the 'uneducated, trans–women' who come there... seeking help, might I add. The audacity of cis–people to talk down to a trans person about other trans people! I was neither shocked nor saddened, given that I'm used to hearing ignoramuses spew such venom on the daily. I need a healthcare system that centres my needs. Providing healthcare is not just limited to medical interventions such as testosterone injections and mandatory counselling sessions. It is about the all–important little things that go a long way in making us feel seen and heard.[31]

In this blackout poem, addressed to the Mental Health Department, Abigail Silversmith, a trans person, asserts her lived experiences (Fig. 1):

> Mental Health Department
>
> give it to me
>
> till I get
>
> my physical transition.
>
>
> The courage and conviction
>
> it takes to assert yourself
>
> is
>
> Healthcare.

[11] INTERSECTIONALITY – QUEER-TRANS COMMUNITIES WITH MULTIPLE MARGINALISATIONS

[11.1] Has the reading down of Section 377 truly impacted the most vulnerable communities at the intersection? While striving towards equality for the queer community, did the judgment bring those under double forms of oppressions such as caste, disability, religion or region, to avail the same rights as those free from any secondary oppression? To answer this, I must consider the violations inflicted on the trans community members in Assam, during the NRC Process,[32] or in the strife regions of Kashmir around abrogation of Section 370,[33] or the countless systemic caste–based

---

gender-affirming-healthcare-services-in-india-a-lived-experience/.
31. tedagadu, 'Accessing Gender-Affirming Healthcare.'
32. Shivalal Gautam, 'Multi-Layered Exclusions for Trans Persons in Assam NRC Process,' *Varta*, 14 July 2019, accessed on 10 December 2022, https://vartagensex.org/2019/07/14/multi-layered-exclusions-for-trans-persons-in-assam-nrc-process/.
33. Surbhi Dewan, S.A. Hanan (dir.), 'Trans Kashmir,' screened at Bangalore Queer Film Festival 2022.

*Fig. 1: Accessing gender-affirming healthcare in India
—a blackout poem by Abigail Silversmith.*

violences inflicted upon trans communities at the intersection. While the verdict linked the sisterhood of struggles inflicted on queer–trans communities with communities from other marginalisations, it fails to consider the struggles borne by the members living at intersections. Do these citizens also enjoy their fundamental rights of equality, non–discrimination, privacy, dignity, autonomy, and health?

[11.2] When I seek to create a dialogue between the State or its actors, the law and its subjects, and while looking at how the law impacts a historically marginalized community, it is equally important to trace the historical origins of the litigations. I do this while in parallel examining any art, especially poetry that could also be parroting the language of the oppressor, when the said art is being considered to disseminate the law.

[11.3] The Section 377 litigations were inspired by the 2017 verdict in which Right to Privacy officially became a part of the Fundamental Rights of Indian citizens. This was read within the ambit of Section 377, emphasizing the privilege of privacy in connection with sexual orientation. However, as Esvi Anbu Kothazam categorically states in their essay 'Whose Decriminalization Are You Drumming on About' from the anthology *Criminal No More*,[34] the ciscentric queer movement through their savarna liberal posturing, and Manuwadi[35] status–quo has never looked at recognizing the deeply entrenched inequalities borne by the ones without the claim to privacy– the Dalit Bahujan Adivasi[36] Trans/gender diverse communities.

In this light, will the queer art disseminated through savarna posturing, not work towards the marginalisation by erasing, occupying, and misrepresenting the Bahujan and Dravidian ideologies[37] of queerness.

[11.4] In this context, let us observe Chand's poem from *The World That Belongs to Us*:

Queer is the Tedagadu

the strange gender/sexual variant

who brings destruction to the family

who every Telugu parent warns their child not to be

Queer is the end of the structure

and the resistance to the epistemological violence.[38]

---

34. Esvi Anbu Kothazam, 'Whose Decriminalization Are You Drumming on About,' in *Criminal No More*, ed. The YP Foundation (Noida: The YP Foundation, 2019)
35. Manuwadi refers to those who follow the text of Manusmriti, which established the caste hierarchy.
36. Dalit refers to those belonging to the social group which has been considered as the lowest in the traditional caste divide. Bahujan refers to the people belonging to all the different marginalized groups and together forming a majority population, still being subject to oppression owing to the divide. Adivasi refers to the indigenous groups of India.
37. Bahujan and Dravidian ideologies advocate against caste-based hierarchy and oppression.
38. Chand, 'What is Queer?,' in *The World That Belongs to Us: An Anthology of Queer Poetry from South*

Through this poem, Chanc, an agender trans research scholar, reclaims the word *tedagadu*, a slur used in Telugu, in close parlance to the etymological origins of the word *queer* in English.

[11.5] Now, I switch to one of the historic moments in Indian queer history: The AIDS Bhedbhav Virodhi Andolan's (ABVA) report.[39] ABVA's 1991 report *Less than Gay* was one of the first documents to locate the violence faced by sexual minorities within a larger circle of intolerance. This was one of the texts used in the workshops for erasure or blackout poetry that turned the wheels of times to reimagine what safe spaces could mean. The report had personal narratives such as 'The Love That Dare Not Speak Its Name' that helped workshop participants unlock urban aspirations and passing privilege as a component in their poems. This report is essential, as it also happens to chronicle the queer-trans narratives that were left undocumented until these narratives by Humjinsi spoke of the larger discourse that was often left out of cis-heteronormative imaginations, which led to the re-criminalisation of Section 377, a grave error, I intend to address.

[11.6] It is pertinent to note that in 2018, while the Court decriminalised consensual sex in private spaces, it failed to address sex work, which, then, was a crime. Similar was the case with regional legislations such as the Telangana Eunuchs Act of 1919, Section 36A in the Karnataka Police Act 1963, which criminalised the entire trans-community. This left the most vulnerable in the community still without any protection.

[11.7] It is important to observe that there are no linear queer issues, but that inter-sectionality lies at the core of queer issues, especially in the lived realities of many vulnerable groups who are not covered under equality and non–discrimination legisla-tion, and there is no recognition of and protection against intersectional discrimination in such cases.

[12] CONCLUSION AND DIRECTIONS

[12.1] Owing to the demonstrable systemic and draconian social ostracisation of queer individuals owing to their identity, I find it just and proper to pass the following orders:

[12.2] *Firstly*, the right to love and its incidental right to engage in consensual same-sex intercourse is sanctified by the law by not just expunging the impugned part of Section 377 of the Indian Penal Code 1860, but also by directing positive obligations to be undertaken for a systematic actualisation of queer rights at least insofar as they are now mandated to be treated at parity with cis–gender individuals.

Asia, eds. Aditi Angiras and Akhil Katyal (Noida: Harper Collins, 2020), 212-214.
39. The AIDS Bhedbhav Virodhi Andolan (AIDS Anti-discrimination Movement), founded in 1988 in New Delhi, was the first HIV/AIDS activist movement in India.

[12.3] In pursuance of the above, this Court directs the government to engage with the queer community to *beneficially* amend the Transgender Persons Act, 2019 insofar as insertion of penalties is concerned, if statutory provisions of the 2019 Act are contravened.

[12.4] *Secondly,* the Government is directed to expeditiously implement the reservation structure in *NALSA v Union of India*[40] in favour of transgender individuals to accrue deserved entitlements to the transgender community. The Government is actively encouraged to deliberate upon a statute benefiting the queer community as a whole.

[12.5] *Thirdly,* this Court directs an institutional sensitisation of all relevant stakeholders including policymakers, lawyers, judges and doctors in the domain of queer rights as to enable a departure of the discourse of *mere* decriminalisation to proactive liberalisation of queer rights—both spatially and psychologically. The key to unlock the fountainhead of queer rights in practice is a top–down sensitisation of stakeholders, so that the adjudication and lawmaking for queer individuals is seen not as granting 'doles' or 'freebies' but rather as an institutional recognition of deserved entitlements. To this effect, this Court directs the revamping of the medical and the legal profession's curricula to include a systemic queer sensitisation.

[12.6] The Court also observes that there are several regional laws/legal statutes such as the Telangana Eunuchs Act of 1919, Section 36A in the Karnataka Police Act 1963, which should be rendered unconstitutional and an intrusion into the private sphere of transgender people, as well as an assault on their dignity. IPC's Section 294 talks about punishment for obscene acts, and Section 65 of the Karnataka Police Act empowers officers to take preventive action. I observe that moral policing through obscenity laws have been used to harass trans communities at the margins, and while affirming the fundamental rights of transgender persons, I note that transgender persons face extreme violence and discrimination at every stage of their lives and are pushed to the fringes of society where begging and sex work are the only ways to make ends meet. Therefore, I deem the use of such laws to further marginalize trans communities as unconstitutional and would encourage legislators to consolidate data within their constituencies, the instances of such violations and drive trans inclusive laws that would enable policy changes at different levels. To this effect, I suggest the local, state, and central government bodies to organise ongoing spaces inviting dialogue from queer-trans leaders at annual intervals to empower and enable inclusive decision making. These leaders could be identified through nominations submitted to queer-trans welfare boards, chaired by the respective local and state governments and ongoing assessments of queer-trans upskilling initiatives led by these bodies.

[12.7] This Court also highlights *mental justice*, positioning mental health as a justice issue with a focus on community healing. Mental justice extends beyond

---

40. (2014) SCC 438.

individual treatment, asserting that mental health issues within vulnerable social identities stem from injustice, discrimination, or violence against these minority communities. It emphasises that mental health cannot be viewed solely on an individual basis; persistent violations of justice impact both communal and individual mental health. Achieving mental justice involves individuals and communities accessing their rights in a dignified, non-discriminatory manner, aligning with constitutional principles, specifically, as enshrined in Article 21 of the Constitution of India. In light of this, the Court recommends setting up state and local government LGBTIQA+ bodies in all private and public mental health and healthcare institutions to drive conversations on mental health and enable policy-level changes, and authorises these institutions to chronicle and build epidemiological datasets to enable rational decision making in medical institutions.

[12.8] This Court, therefore, reads down Section 377 of the IPC, to the extent that consensual sexual acts between adults is criminalised. I acknowledge that mere decriminalisation is not enough to remedy the historical wrongs meted out to the queer community; there must be active legislation protecting the rights of queer persons in matters like housing, employment, healthcare, and society. I also acknowledge that decriminalisation does not adequately address the real-world issues faced by working class, bahujan and other marginalized queers. The provisions of Section 377 shall continue governing non–consensual acts between adults, and all acts of carnal intercourse against minors, and acts of bestiality. The judgment in *Suresh Kumar Koushal*[41] shall be overruled and the writ petitions are allowed.

---

41. (2014) 1 SCC 1.

5

KK v Russian Federation (United Nations Committee on the Elimination of Discrimination against Women):

Rewriting Judgment as Queer Therapeutic Autoethnography

Kseniya Kirichenko

I do more translating

Than the Gawdamn UN

Forget it

I'm sick of it

—Kate Rushin, *The Bridge Poem*

It's only a story, you say. So it is, and the rest of life with it …

The alphabet of my DNA shapes certain words, but the story is not told. I have to tell it myself.

What is it that I have to tell myself again and again?

That there is always a new beginning, a different end.

I can change the story. I am the story.

Begin.

—Jeanette Winterson, *The Powerbook*

Prologue: The (Her)story

This story begins on 25 February 2019, the day when the United Nations Committee on the Elimination of Discrimination against Women (hereinafter 'CEDAW Committee' or 'Committee') adopted a decision in my case, the case *KK v Russian Federation* (*KK*).[1] Or should I say it begins on 7 December 2015, when I submitted my communication

---

1. *K.K. v Russian Federation* (25 February 2019) UN Doc CEDAW/C/72/D/98/2016.

to the Petitions Team of the Office of the High Commissioner for Human Rights?[2] Perhaps it begins on 19 September 2013, when I was harassed and insulted by the then Member of the Legislative Assembly of Saint Petersburg, the author of the infamous law prohibiting so-called 'propaganda of sodomy, lesbianism, bisexualism and trans-genderness among minors.'[3] It may be, however, that this story begins even earlier, with me deciding to work on LGBT human rights in Russia or entering a law school. Or long before, when I heard, for the first time, the ugly, disgusting words referring to lesbian women, including myself, as I will realize later.

Gaslighting: 'Are You Trying to Tell Me I Am Insane?'

On 19 September 2013, while I was supporting my fellow activists in launching a queer culture festival in Saint Petersburg, Russia, a regional parliamentarian, VM, infamous for his anti-LGBT[4] actions, verbally harassed me and called me *kovyryalka*—a word which, together with several other words used by VM that day and on multiple other occasions, is part of a very particular vocabulary rooted in the prison jargon used in the Russian language to insult LGBT people. That specific word refers to lesbian women.

My request to open a case on discrimination and insults under the Code of Administrative Offences was denied because there was no procedure to lift the regional parliamentarian's immunity. My civil lawsuit was also dismissed. VM has never appeared in a courtroom, and his representatives suggested I misinterpreted his state-ments. The court dismissed my claims, stating that I failed to prove that VM insulted me in connection with my sexual orientation and human rights activities. Having exhausted domestic remedies, I submitted a complaint to the CEDAW Committee. Five and a half years after the incident, the Committee declared my communication inadmissible, considering that nothing in the case showed that the national authorities' examination had been biased or based on gender stereotypes, clearly arbitrary, or amounted to a denial of justice.[5]

Contrary to the CEDAW Committee's conclusion, I see my case as an example of epistemic injustice, testimonial injustice, hermeneutical injustice, and gaslighting— perhaps enough to believe that the national evaluation of the case was biased and based on harmful intersecting stereotypes.

The concept of epistemic injustice examines how practices and institutions are struc-tured so that particular knowers are silenced, remain unintelligible, or otherwise experience injustice.[6] Testimonial injustice occurs when a speaker from a marginalized background

---

2. Copies of the communication and other materials on the case are in possession of the author.
3. Law of Saint Petersburg of 7 March 2012, No. 108–118.
4. 'LGBT' refers to 'lesbian, gay, bisexual and trans.' Throughout the commentary, I also use different abbreviations when following the language of the source (with 'Q' referring to 'queer' and 'I' referring to 'intersex,' and 'LBTI' frequently used by the CEDAW Committee as a committee focusing on women and therefore not addressing, as a rule, the situations of gay men).
5. *KK*, para. 8.6.
6. Gaile Pohlhaus Jr, 'Varieties of Epistemic Injustice,' in *The Routledge Handbook of Epistemic Injustice*, eds. Ian James Kidd, José Medina and Gaile Pohlhaus Jr (London: Routledge, 2017), 13.

is given less credibility because of a hearer's stereotypes about the speaker's group.[7] Hermeneutical injustice is caused by structural prejudice. It occurs 'when a gap in collective interpretive resources puts someone at an unfair disadvantage when it comes to making sense of their social experiences.'[8] Gaslighting is an example of epistemic injustice, as it wrongs its targets in relation to their status as knowers.[9]

Hermeneutic injustice occurred both in the national adjudication process and in the CEDAW Committee's consideration. National judges—by the way, women—could not understand the meaning of the insults because they had the privilege of not being targeted by anti-LGBT discourses. This made the marginalized queer subject's claims unintelligible to the courts. Notably, during the preparation for the hearing, a judge told us that 'the court does not know the jargon,' referring to the words in question.[10] Later, the CEDAW Committee's members deferred to the national courts' assessment of the facts. One of the reasons was probably their incapacity to understand the real meaning of the insulting words. At that time, none of the Committee members were native Russian speakers, and even those with Russian as their working language could not be expected to know the specific jargon used in anti-LGBT speeches in Russia. The queer subject remained unintelligible.

Testimonial injustice is particularly visible in how the national courts treated the evidence provided by the parties. One of the inventories of international LGBT case law identified 'the tendency to find queer witnesses unreliable.'[11] All the three witnesses supporting my position in the national court were queer; the judge questioned the credibility of all three of them.[12] Further, the courts did not explain why they relied on the opinion of VM's specialist (who was not even an expert in the Russian language) and disregarded another specialist's conclusions supporting my position.

I also consider VM's position in the courts, including the specialist's opinion provided by his side, as an illustrative example of gaslighting—something the CEDAW Committee ignored completely.

The concept of gaslighting, initially developed in psychology and first considered in relation to domestic violence, has since then been applied to other power dynamics, including racism, patriarchy, heteronormativity, and transphobia.[13]

In the context of the CEDAW Convention, the entry point for introducing the concept of gaslighting is Article 5(a), establishing State obligations to modify gender stereotypes

---

7. Miranda Fricker, *Epistemic Injustice: Power and the Ethics of Knowing* (Oxford: Oxford University Press, 2007), 1, 4, 7.

8. Fricker, *Epistemic Injustice*, 1, 6–7.

9. Kelly Oliver, 'Gaslighting: Pathologies of Recognition and the Colonization of Psychic Space,' in *Epistemic Injustice and the Philosophy of Recognition*, eds. Paul Giladi and Nicola McMillan (London: Routledge, 2023), 114.

10. This phrase was not, however, included in the subsequent judgment.

11. Tamsin Phillipa Paige and Joanne Stagg, 'Queer Approaches to International Adjudication,' (last updated September 2021) in *The Max Planck Encyclopedia of International Procedural Law*, ed. H. Ruiz Fabri (Oxford: University Press, 2019), accessed 28 December 2022, www.opil.ouplaw.com/home/mpil.

12. The judge did not indicate explicitly that the witnesses were not considered credible because they were queer. However, taking into account all the circumstances of the case, this could be the case.

13. For example, Angelique M. Davis and Rose Ernst, 'Racial Gaslighting,' *Politics, Groups and Identities* 7/4 (2017), 761–774; Elena Ruiz, 'Cultural Gaslighting,' *Hypatia* 35 (2020), 687–713.

and eliminate gender-based prejudices. Gaslighting is based on the perpetrator's usage of gender stereotypes, intersecting inequalities, and institutional vulnerabilities against their target.[14] Examples of institutional settings include police, courts, and legal systems, particularly when perpetrators 'gain control of the narrative and "flip" stories and events, drawing on stereotypes about women as irrational … In this way, institutional authorities sometimes become unknown colluders in gaslighting tactics, setting women up for further violence and loss of credibility.'[15] Gaslighting intends to 'undermine women by denying their testimony about harms done to them by men,'[16] through 'sidestepping' (ignoring supporting evidence) and 'displacing' (explaining the harm by the target's own defects).[17]

The very position of VM was built on gaslighting tactics: supposedly, he did not say the insulting words, and even if he did, I misinterpreted their meaning. The specialist engaged by VM used several gaslighting tactics: characterizing the Queerfest as a 'scandalous event'[18] and insinuating that it was easy for me 'to assign such a far-stretched vivid meaning as "active lesbian" or "the rudest insult in prison in the context of the event's theme."'[19] The VM's side also claimed that his statement denying me of national belonging was based on our alleged violations of laws on 'gay propaganda' and 'foreign agents.'[20] The idea here was that it was not VM who used the insults but we—'scandalous'[21] LGBT activists—who saw insults everywhere. Moreover, due to his high social status and intelligence, VM would not have even known the insulting meaning of the words in question.

Gaslighting is aimed at making the target doubt herself, her reality, and her sanity.[22] I have never really questioned whether or not VM intended to insult me—as a woman human rights defender who dared to stand in his way literally and figuratively. Of course, he had. At one point, however, I started questioning my perception of what happened to me, as almost everyone around me—the other side of the legal dispute and all the authorities all the way up to the CEDAW Committee—denied my experience. My doubts led me to a group of Russian-speaking LBQ women on social media, where I made a post asking the group members if they knew the word *kovyryalka*. While a few women said they did not know the word, all those who had heard it confirmed that it was offensive for a lesbian woman. One of them even wrote, 'Why discuss this? It's disgusting.' At least it was not just me making things up.

---

14. Paige L. Sweet, 'The Sociology of Gaslighting,' *American Sociological Review* 84/5 (2019), 852, 856.

15. Sweet, 'The Sociology of Gaslighting,' 867.

16. Cynthia A. Stark, 'Gaslighting, Misogyny, and Psychological Oppression,' *The Monist* 102 (2019), 221.

17. Stark, 'Gaslighting, Misogyny, and Psychological Oppression,' 221.

18. Opinion of the Linguist Expert with Regard to Materials Contained in the Opinion of [The Specialist's Name] of 28 April 2014, 1 (on file with author).

19. Opinion of the Linguist Expert of 28 April 2014, 2.

20. Written Statement for the Judicial Debate by [my representative], Kirovsky District Court of Saint Petersburg, Case no. 2-1617/2014 (on file with author).

21. Opinion of the Linguist Expert of 28 April 2014, 1.

22. For example, Veronica E. Johnson et al, '"It's Not in Your Head": Gaslighting, 'Splaining, Victim Blaming, and Other Harmful Reactions to Microaggressions,' *Perspectives on Psychological Science* 16/5 (2021), 1024.

Epilogue

Much water has flowed since the CEDAW Committee adopted its decision in the case of *KK*.

At the beginning of 2020, just a year after declaring my communication inadmissible, the CEDAW Committee adopted its first-ever decision recognizing the violation of lesbian women's rights. In ON and *DP v Russian Federation*, the Committee found that the State's failure to properly investigate a lesbophobic attack violated the CEDAW Convention and acknowledged that the authorities' actions were influenced by negative stereotypes against lesbian women.[23]

In November 2021, the Committee expressed its concerns about the worsening situation of LBTI women in Russia and called for public campaigns to address hate speech and stigmatization of LBTI women, capacity-building for law enforcement officials on their duty to protect LBTI women's rights, as well as investigation, prosecution and punishment of all acts of gender-based violence and hate crimes against LBTI women.[24] The Committee highlighted specifically the anti-LBTI hate speech in the context of discriminatory stereotypes.[25]

VM continued to spread hateful messages and insult those from different marginalized groups. On several instances, he publicly used the word *kovyryalka* directed at LBQ women, among them: participants of the Rainbow Column of the May Day demonstration in Saint Petersburg in 2015; Olga Seryabkina, one of the very few openly bisexual celebrities in Russia; and Brittney Griner, an African American basketball star and an open lesbian. VM also continued his career growth and became a member of the Russian State Duma from the ruling party 'United Russia' in 2016. In February 2022, he was included in the European Union's blacklist for 'support[ing] and implement[ing] actions and policies which undermine the territorial integrity, sovereignty and independence of Ukraine, and further destabilized Ukraine.'[26]

In late 2022, a new anti-LGBT law was adopted in Russia punishing by significant fines the so-called 'propaganda of non-traditional sexual relations, pedophilia, and change of sex' among any age group. 'Just as the original law resulted in significant stigma and harm toward LGBT people in Russia, this updated version will have an even more stifling effect on freedom of expression, well-being and security,' commented Tanya Lokshina of the Human Rights Watch.[27]

In November 2023, the Russian Supreme Court designated the 'international LGBT movement' as extremist and prohibited it fully in Russia. The Supreme Court's ruling referred to, among other activities, reporting human rights violations to the UN treaty

---

23. ON. and DP v Russian Federation (24 February 2020) UN Doc CEDAW/C/75/D/119/2017, paras. 7.8 and 7.11.

24. CEDAW Committee, 'Concluding Observations on the Ninth Periodic Report of the Russian Federation' (30 November 2021), UN Doc CEDAW/C/RUS/CO/9, paras. 46–47.

25. CEDAW/C/RUS/CO/9, para. 23.

26. Official Journal of the European Union 65, 23 February 2022, accessed 16 February 2023, https://eur-lex.europa.eu/legal-content/EN/TXT/PDF/?uri=OJ:L:2022:042I:FULL&from=EN.

27. Human Rights Watch, 'Russia: Expanded "Gay Propaganda" Ban Progresses Toward Law: Another Blow to LGBT Rights,' 25 November 2022, accessed 16 January 2023, https://www.hrw.org/news/2022/11/25/russia-expanded-gay-propaganda-ban-progresses-toward-law.

bodies by Russian LGBT activists.[28] The ruling has been followed by a number of police raids and prosecutions against LGBT individuals in the country.[29]

Afterword

I am the author of the communication number 98/2016 and of this text; an imaginable queer CEDAW member who wrote an imaginable queer dissenting opinion; a woman; a lesbian; a migrant; an activist; an intersectional feminist; a daughter of my mother; a lawyer; a former university teacher; a PhD researcher extremely passionate about my project; a UN Programme Manager; a survivor.

Those who have been in therapy may be aware of this 'reparenting' exercise—writing a letter to your younger self from your parent as you needed them to be. My dissenting opinion is, in a way, this type of a letter to myself. The letter with long-awaited messages I wanted to find, and I did not when I received the Committee's decision. I was prepared, to some extent, for the majority decision to be disappointing—after all, I had been observing the Committee's work for years as part of my current job; but finding nothing else scrolling down the document, no one dissenting—that was the dark silence.

To make sense of my experience, I decided to participate in the Queer Judgments Project and to rewrite the decision on my own case. I did not find justice in national courts, and this was by no means a surprise. However, I still had some hope in the CEDAW Committee—whose tasks, in the words of Loveday Hodson, 'is to use its voyages to the periphery in order to expand its frame of reference' and to ensure 'that women's rights law may be appropriately connected to a wider understanding of women's rights, not only as legal expectations but as expressions of empathy with and compassion for the suffering of the powerless.'[30] My decision to apply to this international body—as opposed to, for instance, the European Court of Human Rights or the Human Rights Committee—was because I saw it as my (intersectional) feminist ally, the one holding some formal power to confront the power of the Russian Federation on my behalf. Ironically, in the same way the women judges of the Russian courts denied my claims, the (mostly) women members of the CEDAW Committee found my communication inadmissible. We are all women, but our experiences are different. Perhaps, by applying to a body of the United Nations, I was trying to dismantle the master's house with the master's tools. Following Audre Lorde:

> They may allow us temporarily to beat him at his own game, but they will never enable us to bring about genuine change. And this fact is only threatening to those women who still define the master's house as their only source of support.[31]

---

28. Ruling of the Supreme Court of the Russian Federation of 30 November 2023, case No. АКПИ23-990с, 12, accessed 29 April 2024, https://fn-volga.ru/news/view/id/219533 (unofficial publication).
29. For example, Human Rights Watch, 'Russia: First Convictions Under LGBT "Extremist" Ruling: Thousands More at Risk After Top Court's Decision,' 15 February 2024, accessed 29 April 2024, https://www.hrw.org/news/2024/02/15/russia-first-convictions-under-lgbt-extremist-ruling.
30. Loveday Hodson, 'Women's Rights and the Periphery: CEDAW's Optional Protocol,' *The European Journal of International Law* 25/2 (2014), 577.
31. Audre Lorde, 'The Master's Tools Will Never Dismantle the Master's House,' in *Your Silence Will Not*

To find the source of support within myself, I decided to rewrite the judgment and thus contribute to the creation of Sara Ahmed's feminist (and, I would add, also queer) catalogue of documented violence,[32] and to make the intersecting forms of oppression I experienced tangible as 'a way of making them appear outside of oneself; something that can be spoken of and addressed by and with others.'[33] This experience remained unintelligible for the women judges and CEDAW members; however, I created a figure of a dissenting Committee member and named her Intersectional Queer. She expressed what I wanted and needed to find. That I was denied justice. That I was subjected to insults and gaslighting. That gender-based and intersecting stereotypes played out in the case from its very inception.

It has been more than four years since the Committee adopted its decision and more than seven since I moved to another country. I thought I made peace with my experience of being in close proximity to or a target of never-ending oppression, violence, and humiliation. Unlike many of my friends, fellow activists, and former colleagues, I have never been physically beaten up for being a lesbian or an activist, formally prosecuted as an individual, or even detained by police—I was lucky. That is what I was telling myself before starting this writing. I do not have any visible scars. The writing process included hours of rereading written documents, relistening and rewatching recordings—those made on 19 September 2013 near the entrance to the venue of the Queerfest, as well as those made in courts. My rational self was fine with this time-travelling, but the dreams I had for several nights showed me that this herstory had not ended yet and that I was still in need of something.

Neither pity, nor admiration. That experience was objectively hard, sometimes almost unbearable, but that was, and still is, part of my herstory. What I was looking for, and what I am probably still seeking, is respect, validation, and justice. I want to be seen and recognised. I do not want my experience to be denied again. And I want to make sense of that painful experience.

This gives me the power to write.

The bridge I must be

Is the bridge to my own power

I must translate

My own fears

Mediate

My own weaknesses

I must be the bridge to nowhere

But my true self

And then

I will be useful[34]

Protect You: Essays and Poems (London: Silver Press, 2017), 91-92.

32. Sara Ahmed, *Living a Feminist Life* (Durham: Duke University Press, 2017), 26, 30.

33. Ahmed, *Living a Feminist Life*, 34.

34. Kate Rushin, 'The Bridge Poem,' in *This Bridge Called My Back: Writings by Radical Women of Color*,

Committee on the Elimination of Discrimination against Women

DECISION ADOPTED BY THE COMMITTEE UNDER ARTICLE 4 (2) (C) OF THE OPTIONAL PROTOCOL, CONCERNING COMMUNICATION NO. 98/2016

Communication submitted by:	K.K.
Alleged victim:	The author
State party:	Russian Federation
Date of adoption of decision:	25 February 2019

Background

1. The author is K.K., a Russian national ... She claims a violation of her rights guaranteed by articles 2 (b), (d) and (e), 5 (a) and 7 (c) of the Convention. ...

Facts as submitted by the author

2.1 The author, who is an activist for [lesbian, gay, bisexual and transgender (LGBT)] rights and a ... legal counsel for the organization ["Coming Out"], was invited to assist with running the QueerFest festival ... On 19 September 2013, at the entrance of the building in which the event was held, she saw a deputy of the Saint Petersburg Legislative Assembly, [M.], with representatives of the police and several other men, whom she recognized as perpetrators of previous assaults against [LGBT] activists ... Under instructions from Mr. [M.], the police requested that the organizers of the event provide them with the lease documents for the venue. The author intervened to clarify the legal aspects of the request. At that moment, Mr. [M.] interrupted the conversation, saying that the author and other participants of the event were not Russians and that

eds. Cherríe L. Moraga and Gloria E. Anzaldúa (Albany: SUNY Press, 2021), xlii.

they bowed to foreign diplomats and begged them for money. Subsequently, he and his party continued to threaten and insult visitors and volunteers at the festival. In particular, he used such words as "*spidozny*", "*petukh*" and "*petushatnik*". Regarding women, he used the phrases "cut your hair, animal" and "beast", and he called one woman the "husband" of another woman. He called the author "*stukachka*" and "*kovyryalka*", when, seeing one of Mr. [M.]'s men trying to use violence against an event participant, she had asked police officers to intervene. However, the police officers took no action in response to the offensive conduct against the author.

2.2 On 30 September 2013, the author filed a request to initiate proceedings against Mr. [M.] with the Office of the Prosecutor ... under articles 5.61 (insult) and 5.62 (discrimination) of the Code of Administrative Offences of the Russian Federation. The Office ... rejected the request ... on the grounds that the Code of Administrative Offences did not contain any regulations regarding the administrative liability of deputies, because deputies of the Legislative Assembly had immunity and any prosecution against them must be regulated by a special federal law, but such a law had not been adopted. The author appealed to the ... District Court ... requesting that the decision of the Office ... be quashed. ... [T]he ... District Court ... rejected the appeal.

2.3 On 9 November 2013, the author filed a civil lawsuit against Mr. [M.] with the ... District Court ... asking the court to protect her honour and dignity and to recognize a violation of her moral rights. ... [T]he lawsuit was rejected, in a decision stating that there was no evidence proving that [M.] had made offensive statements.

2.4 ... [T]he author appealed to the ... City Court against the decision of the ... District Court. ... [T]he ... City Court denied the appeal.

2.5 ... [T]he author filed a cassation appeal to the Presidium of the ... City Court. ... [T]he Presidium denied the appeal.
...

Issues and proceedings before the Committee

...
9. The Committee ... decides that:
   (a) The communication is inadmissible under article 4 (2) (c) of the Optional Protocol; ....

Appendix

Individual opinion by Committee member Intersectional Queer (dissenting)

1. The Committee decided that the communication was inadmissible as insufficiently substantiated under article 4 (2) (c) of the Optional Protocol.[35]

---

35. The majority decision, paras. 8.6 and 9(a).

2. I disagree with the majority and hold the view that this communication is admissible and that the author's rights have been violated.

Consideration of admissibility

3. I join the majority in considering that it is generally for the courts of the States parties to evaluate the facts and evidence in a particular case unless it can be established that such evaluation was biased or based on harmful gender stereotypes constituting discrimination against women, was clearly arbitrary or amounted to a denial of justice.[36] I disagree, however, that nothing in the material before us suggests elements likely to demonstrate that the examination of the author's case by the courts suffered from any such defects.

4. The majority observed that both sides of the lawsuit were able to put forward their specialists' opinions on the meaning of the words used towards the author, some of which had several meanings, including offensive ones, and that the courts determined that the author's claims were not corroborated by sufficient evidence.[37] I note, however, that there were several other factors—ignored by the majority—related to the consideration of the case by national authorities, demonstrating that the author may have faced obstacles impeding her access to justice on the basis of equality.

5. It has been noted by this Committee that intersecting factors, such as identity as a lesbian woman and stigmatization of women human rights defenders, make it more difficult to gain access to justice.[38] The Committee has also recommended that States parties revise the rules on the burden of proof to ensure equality between the parties in all fields where power relationships deprive women of fair treatment of their cases,[39] and ensure that women human rights defenders are able to gain access to justice and receive protection.[40]

6. I notice that the author attempted to protect her rights through two different mechanisms. First, she requested to initiate proceedings against Mr. M. under the Code of Administrative Offences of the Russian Federation. Her request was rejected because deputies of the Legislative Assembly had immunity, and any prosecution against them must be regulated by a special federal law. Still, such a law had not been adopted.[41] This deprived the author of protection against alleged discrimination and harassment as part of public proceedings by State authorities that could have led to investigation, prosecution, and punishment.

7. The only other mechanism still available to the author—to which she applied—was a civil lawsuit. This procedure implies formal equality of the parties, and the burden

---

36. *M.S. v Philippines* (CEDAW/C/58/D/30/2011), para. 6.4.
37. The majority decision, para. 8.6.
38. General recommendation No. 33, paras. 3, 8 and 9.
39. Ibid., para. 15 (g).
40. Ibid., para. 15 (i).
41. The majority decision, paras. 2.2.

of proof is mainly on the plaintiff. Both sides of the lawsuit, indeed, were able to put forward their specialists' opinions on the meaning of the words used towards the author. At the same time, the author provided other evidence supporting her claims, including audio and video recordings, witnesses' testimonies and a psychologist's letter confirming the psychological harm inflicted on the author by Mr. M.'s actions.

8. The specialist's opinion provided by K.K. concluded that the words of Mr. M., considering the context of the event, were extremely insulting. These words were used to negatively characterize K.K. based on her alleged relation to LGBT, with an intent to humiliate her dignity and in a form contrary not only to public morals but also to the Law on the Russian Language. In addition, Mr. M.'s expressions clearly attempted to discriminate against people attending the event, including K.K., based on their nationality. The courts did not explain why one specialist's opinion (presented by Mr. M.) prevailed over the other (provided by K.K.) in its assessment of evidence.

9. I note that, as explained by the author and not contested by Mr. M., he was not a random passerby present near the venue of the queer culture festival by coincidence. Instead, according to the available reports, he had repeatedly attacked LGBT human rights defenders. He was also an initiator of one of the first regional laws aimed at prohibiting so-called "propaganda of non-traditional sexual orientation."[42] This Committee have stated elsewhere that such laws may reinforce homophobia.[43] According to other international human rights bodies, these laws promote stigma and prejudice against LGBT persons,[44] could result in discrimination, prosecution and punishment of people because of their sexual orientation or gender identity,[45] exacerbate the negative stereotypes against LGBT individuals and represent a disproportionate restriction of their rights,[46] and encourage the stigmatization of and discrimination against LGBT persons, including children, and children from LGBT families.[47] Moreover, as reported by the author, there had been multiple cases where Mr. M. insulted LGBT persons and activists, including using the very same words whose meaning was contested by him in the author's case. In another case on a lawsuit against Mr. M., a forensic expert testified that the word "*kovyryalka*", when directed at a particular individual, is used as an insult and maintains its insulting meaning in practically any context.[48]

10. In light of the above and taking into account the prevalent climate of stigmatization, discrimination and violence experienced by LGBT persons and lesbian women in particular, as well as LGBT human rights defenders in the State party,[49] social hierarchies

---

42. Law of Saint Petersburg of 7 March 2012. No. 108-18.
43. CEDAW/C/RUS/CO/8, para. 41.
44. CAT/C/RUS/CO/6, para. 33 (b).
45. E/C.12/RUS/CO/6, para. 23 (a).
46. CCPR/C/RUS/CO/7, para. 10 (d).
47. CRC/C/RUS/CO/4-5, para. 24.
48. The majority decision, para. 5.6.
49. See, for example, CAT/C/RUS/CO/6, paras. 32–33, CCPR/C/RUS/CO/7, para. 10, CRC/C/RUS/CO/4-5, paras. 24–25, CEDAW/C/RUS/CO/8, paras. 41–42, E/C.12/RUS/CO/6, paras. 22–23, *Irina*

and power relations between the author and Mr. M., I am of the view that the author's claims cannot be regarded as manifestly ill-founded, but that the admissibility and the level of substantiation of the claims in the communication are so closely linked to the merits of the case that it would be more appropriate to determine them during the consideration of the merits.

Consideration of the merits

11. The author claims that she was insulted, discriminated, and humiliated by Mr. M., a regional legislature member, on the basis of her sexual orientation and gender identity, connection to the LGBT community and human rights activities, and that the State party failed to provide her with a remedy and access to justice.

Gender-based stereotypes, hate speech, verbal and psychological forms of gender-based violence under the Convention

12. Discrimination within the meaning of article 1 of the Convention encompasses gender-based violence against women,[50] which takes multiple forms, including, inter alia, acts or omissions intended or likely to cause or result in psychological harm or suffering to women.[51] Gender-based violence may take the form of psychological[52] or verbal[53] violence. Verbal violence may be classified as hate speech, and hate speech, in turn, can be understood as entailing the use of one or more particular forms of expression—advocacy, promotion or incitement of the denigration, hatred or vilification of a person or group of persons, as well as any harassment, insult, negative stereotyping, stigmatization or threat of such person and any justification of all these forms of expression—and is based on a non-exhaustive list of personal characteristics or status that includes, for example, age, sex, gender, gender identity and sexual orientation.[54]

13. Article 5 (a) of the Convention establishes States parties' obligations in relation to modification or elimination of social and cultural patterns, prejudices and customary and all other practices based on the idea of the inferiority or the superiority of either of the sexes or on stereotyped gender roles. This Committee have considered hate speech against women and their certain groups as constituting a form of discriminatory stereotypes or attitudes, or as a phenomenon based on negative stereotypes.[55]

Fedotova v Russian Federation (CCPR/C/106/D/1932/2010), *Kirill Nepomnyaschiy v Russian Federation* (CCPR/C/123/D/2318/2013), and *Nikolai Alekseev v Russian Federation* (CCPR/C/109/D/1873/2009).

50. General recommendation No. 35, para. 21; general recommendation No. 19, paras. 6–7.

51. General recommendation No. 35, para. 14.

52. Council of Europe Convention on preventing and combating violence against women and domestic violence (Istanbul Convention), article 33.

53. Protocol to the African Charter on Human and People's Rights on the Rights of Women in Africa (Maputo Protocol), article 3 (4).

54. European Commission against Racism and Intolerance, General policy recommendation No. 15 on combatting hate speech, CRI(2016)15, Explanatory memorandum, para. 9.

55. CEDAW/C/MKD/CO/6, para. 21 (d), CEDAW/C/NLD/CO/6, para. 21 (c), CEDAW/C/RUS/CO/8, para.

The Committee expressed its particular concerns about hate speech by politicians and political leaders.[56]

14. Therefore, the author's claims of being subjected to discriminatory insults, harassment and hate speech by Mr. M., a regional parliamentarian, can be considered from the perspective of discrimination and stereotypes under articles 1 and 5 of the Convention.

States parties' obligations to prevent, investigate and punish gender-based discrimination and violence, and to ensure access to justice and effective remedy

15. Gender-based violence covered by the notion of discrimination under the Convention is not restricted to action by or on behalf of States parties. States parties may also be responsible for private acts if they fail to act with due diligence to prevent violations of rights or to investigate and punish acts of violence, and for providing compensation.[57] States parties should ensure that all legal systems protect victims/ survivors of gender-based violence and that they have access to justice and to an effective remedy.[58]

16. In relation to hate speech, the Committee called on States parties to combat, modify and eliminate stereotypes against women targeted by hate speech, including by adopting comprehensive strategies,[59] preventing[60] and publicly condemning[61] hate speech and monitoring them.[62] The Committee also recommended States parties to criminalize hate speech, including directed against women from minority groups, as a separate form of crime in law;[63] enforce these laws strictly and effectively, through prosecutions of perpetrators with timely and commensurate punishment;[64] avoid prosecution of hate speech under misdemeanour law rather than hate crime provisions;[65] provide victims of hate speech with effective access to justice;[66] and adequately train judges, prosecutors and law enforcement officials to recognise and effectively address hate speech.[67]

41, and CEDAW/C/UKR/CO/8, para. 45.

56. CEDAW/C/ROU/CO/7-8, para. 36 (d), and CEDAW/C/SVK/CO/5-6, para. 39.

57. General recommendation No. 35, para. 24.

58. Ibid., para. 29 (b).

59. CEDAW/C/ITA/CO/7, para. 26 (a), CEDAW/C/NLD/CO/6, para. 22 (d), and CEDAW/C/SWE/CO/8-9, para. 25 (a).

60. CEDAW/C/MKD/CO/6, para. 22 (d).

61. CEDAW/C/SVK/CO/5-6, para. 40 (c).

62. CEDAW/C/LUX/CO/6-7, para. 50 (d), CEDAW/C/MKD/CO/6, para. 22 (d), and CEDAW/C/ROU/CO/7-8, para. 37(c).

63. CEDAW/C/ARM/CO/5-6, para. 45, CEDAW/C/JPN/Q/7-8, para. 4, and CEDAW/C/SVK/CO/5-6, para. 40 (c).

64. CEDAW/C/FJI/CO/5, para. 52 (a), CEDAW/C/HRV/CO/4-5, para. 39, CEDAW/C/MKD/CO/6, para. 22 (d), and CEDAW/C/SVK/CO/5-6, para. 40 (b).

65. CEDAW/C/HRV/CO/4-5, para. 38.

66. CEDAW/C/ARM/CO/5-6, para. 45.

67. CEDAW/C/ROU/CO/7-8, para. 37 (c), and CEDAW/C/SVK/CO/5-6, para. 40 (b).

17. The Committee has observed several obstacles and restrictions that impede women from realizing their right to access to justice on the basis of equality. These obstacles occur in a structural context of discrimination and inequality owing to factors such as gender stereotyping, intersecting discrimination, procedural and evidentiary requirements and practices, and a failure to systematically ensure that judicial mechanisms are accessible to all women.[68]

18. As previously acknowledged by the Committee, gender-based violence may affect some women to different degrees or in different ways, and intersecting forms of discrimination have an aggravating negative impact. This implies the need for appropriate legal and policy responses.[69] Grounds for intersecting discrimination, such as socioeconomic status, political opinion, national origin, age or being a lesbian, bisexual or transgender woman, as well as being a human rights defender, make it more difficult for women from these groups to gain access to justice.[70] The Committee has documented many examples of the negative impact of intersecting discrimination on access to justice, including ineffective remedies. When women from such groups lodge complaints, the authorities frequently fail to act with due diligence to investigate, prosecute and punish perpetrators and/or provide remedies.[71]

19. One of the core components necessary to ensure women's access to justice is justiciability—the women's unhindered access to justice and their ability and empowerment to claim their rights as legal entitlements under the Convention.[72] In this regard, States parties should revise the rules on the burden of proof in order to ensure equality between the parties in all fields where power relationships deprive women of fair treatment of their cases by the judiciary,[73] to implement mechanisms to ensure that evidentiary rules and investigations are impartial and not influenced by gender stereotypes or prejudice,[74] and to ensure that women human rights defenders are able to gain access to justice and receive protection from harassment, threats, retaliation and violence.[75]

20. States parties should also provide mandatory, recurrent, and effective education and training for members of the judiciary, lawyers, law enforcement officers and legislators, to equip them to prevent and address gender-based violence against women. Such education and training should promote understanding of how gender stereotypes lead to gender-based violence against women and inadequate responses to it, as well as the varying situations of women experiencing diverse forms of gender-based violence,

---

68. General recommendation No. 33, para. 3.
69. General recommendation No. 28, para. 18, general recommendation No. 35, para. 12, and report of the inquiry concerning Canada (CEDAW/C/OP.8/CAN/1), para. 197
70. Ibid., paras. 8–9.
71. Ibid., para. 10.
72. Ibid., para. 14.
73. Ibid., para. 15 (g).
74. Ibid., para. 18 (e).
75. Ibid., para. 15 (i).

which should include intersecting forms of discrimination.[76]

Proceedings under the Code of Administrative Offences

21. The author attempted to protect her rights by requesting the General Prosecutor's office to initiate proceedings against Mr. M. under articles 5.61 (insult) and 5.62 (discrimination) of the Russian Code of Administrative Offences. Her claim was, however, rejected because a law regulating the lifting of parliamentary immunity and prosecution against parliamentarians had never been adopted. The author's appeal against the decision of the General Prosecutor's office was unsuccessful.

22. This left the author without protection against the alleged violation in the form of public proceedings led by State authorities that could have resulted in investigation, prosecution and punishment of Mr. M. Because the only reason provided by the General Prosecutor's office was the lack of a law establishing the procedure for lifting the parliamentary immunity, these actions should be directly attributed to the State party. Consequently, even though the State party's laws recognize discrimination and insults as administrative offences, the State party failed to ensure the author's access to justice and to protect her from discrimination through an administrative procedure. In addition, by failing to adopt a procedure for lifting the immunity, the State party contributed to the impunity of insults and discrimination, including based on gender, conducted by parliamentarians, thus also failing to prevent gender-based violence and discrimination.

Proceedings under the Civil Code

23. The author also submitted a lawsuit against Mr. M., requesting the court to recognize the violation of her moral rights protected under the Russian Civil Code, to publish the decision establishing the violation, to prohibit Mr. M. from using offensive expressions in the future, and to award her compensation.

24. I note the State party's comments that the courts have carried out justice based on an adversarial approach and the principle of equality of the parties.[77] I am not convinced, however, that a civil procedure can provide an effective remedy to victims/survivors of gender-based discrimination and violence, especially when gender intersects with other factors and the unequal power dynamics are particularly pronounced. As I observed earlier, States parties' obligations in relation to hate speech against women may include criminalizing hate speech, including directed against minority women, and avoiding prosecution of hate speech under misdemeanour law rather than hate crime provisions. I also note the author's comments that, because of the nature of the case and positionality of its parties, not only formal but also substantive equality and an intersectional approach should have been applied.[78]

---

76. General recommendation No. 35, para. 30 (e).
77. The majority decision, para. 4.3.
78. Ibid., para. 7.2.

25. The material before the Committee shows that the only evidence put forward by Mr. M. in the courts was an opinion by a linguist chosen by him. I note the author's comment that the court did not ascertain the identity of this linguist and his qualifications, and from the photocopies provided, it is evident that the linguist is a specialist in English and not the Russian language. By contrast, the evidence provided to the courts by the author included audio and video recordings with transcriptions, a psychologist's certificate confirming the psychological damage experienced by the author as a result of Mr. M.'s actions, testimonies by three witnesses and another specialist's opinion by a linguist.

26. The majority observed that both sides of the lawsuit were able to put forward their specialists' opinions on the meaning of the words used towards the author, some of which had several meanings, including offensive, and that the courts determined that the author's claims were not corroborated by sufficient evidence.[79] I notice, however, that neither the courts nor the State party, in its comments to the Committee, elaborated on any reasons why one specialist's opinion (provided by Mr. M.) prevailed over the other (put forward by the author) in the assessment of evidence, ultimately leading the court to reject the author's claims.

27. I observe that the specialist's opinion submitted by the author to the court and provided to the Committee concludes with the following:

> 1. The word 'kovyryalka' is used in the given context in its meaning of 'lesbian.' This word is extremely insulting and characterizes the person negatively.
>
> 2. Statements are addressed to [K.K.] personally and characterize her personality and not her particular actions or skills.
>
> 3. The negative judgment of the person is expressed in a form that contradicts not only the norms of public morals but also the Law on the Russian Language.
>
> 4. The statement of [Mr. M.] characterizes [K.K.] negatively based on her assumed connection to LGBT. The statements of [Mr. M.] also clearly attempt to discriminate against those attending the event, including [K.K.], based on [their] nationality.[80]

28. I further observe that neither the courts nor the State party, in its comments to the Committee, assessed or even commented on these conclusions. The only reason why the court did not find this opinion sufficient to establish the alleged violations was that Mr. M. provided another specialist's opinion with different conclusions.

29. At the same time, having considered the specialist's opinion provided by Mr. M. to the court and submitted by the author to the Committee,[81] I conclude that the very

---

79. Ibid., para. 8.6.

80. Opinion of the linguist expert concerning evidence of insult and humiliation of human dignity in the statement of [Mr. M.] video recorded on 19 September 2013.

81. Opinion of the linguist expert with regard to materials contained in the opinion of [the specialist's name] of 28 April 2014.

text of this opinion—which became virtually the only reason for the courts to reject the author's claims—demonstrates stereotypes and expresses ideas of inferiority and superiority based on gender, age, social status, involvement in LGBT activism, sexual orientation and gender identity. The courts did not provide any assessment of these parts of the opinion, thus only contributing to the reinforcement of stereotypes. In particular:

a. The specialist described the context of the incident as follows: "The participants of the dialogue were a man [Mr. M.] ... of quite a high social status, a well-known public figure, well-educated, middle-aged, and a woman [the author] ... also educated but of a lower social status ... and looking obviously younger than him."[82] Further, the specialist explained that some of Mr. M.'s statements addressed to the author were not polite because of the differences based on these characteristics, and that these characteristics explain why Mr. M. identified himself with Russia, saying that the author and other participants of the event cannot be identified with it.

b. Regarding the word "*kovyryalka*", the specialist stated that: "Most likely, this was a sporadic word, meaning a spontaneous nomination invented on the fly, a neologism derived from the ... verb 'kovyryat'sya'—'doing something very slowly'—that came out of [Mr. M.'s] mouth in an emotional impulse ... Apparently, [the author], being the addressee of this, frankly, not very proper epithet to a lady, did not want to pass [Mr. M.], was moving very slowly or did not want to move at all. For this, [the author] received such an emotionally charged verbal assessment of her actions/inactions."[83]

c. Describing the event during which the incident happened—the Queerfest— the specialist characterized it as "having a somewhat scandalous undertone."[84] He then continued: "Of course, in the context of the event's theme ... it is very easy to assign such a far-stretched vivid meaning as 'active lesbian' or 'the rudest insult in prison.' However, this contradicts [two other statements by Mr. M. addressed to the author, 'I have Russia, you have a different country' and 'Report me to the police, you can report me directly to the police of your country'] which we consider as having a deep philosophical meaning. It is unlikely that their author used the word 'kovyryalka' in such a meaning."[85]

d. The specialist also assessed the two statements by Mr. M. addressed to the author: "No, we have... I have Russia, you have a different country" and "Report me to the police, you can report me directly to the police of your country." In relation to both statements, the specialist indicated that Mr. M., "being an important public figure, identifies himself with his country and contrasting it with [K.K.]."[86] The second statement, according to the specialist, was a response by Mr. M. to the author's "provocative proposition to report

---

82. Ibid., p. 1.
83. Ibid., p. 2.
84. Ibid., p. 1.
85. Ibid., p. 2.
86. Ibid.

him to the police," was transcribed by the author incorrectly and should be read as "Report me to the police, you can report your country directly to the police."[87] According to the specialist, Mr. M. meant the following: "I am not hiding my actions, my views, and there is nothing reprehensible in them; the majority of people living in our country think and believe as I do; reporting me to the police would amount to reporting to the police the majority of the citizens of our country."[88]

30. Rejecting the author's claims, the courts stated that the words used by Mr. M. were not commonly known in their jargon meaning of "lesbian" and "the most offensive insult in a women's prison," and there was no reason to suggest that Mr. M. was aware of this meaning of the words. In my opinion, hate speech and discriminatory insults do not have to be well-known; they are frequently part of a specific vocabulary of which both the perpetrator and the victim/survivor are aware because of their positionalities. This is the reason why, as stated by this Committee in its previous practice, States parties need to train judiciary and law enforcement on how to identify and recognize hate speech, hate crimes and discrimination.

31. I also believe that the courts' conclusion that Mr. M. could not know the offensive meaning of the words used by him is based on either stereotypical ideas related to his positionality or complete ignorance of the context in which the case happened. In this regard, I observe the author's multiple appeals—left unacknowledged by the courts—to the context of the case, particularly the nature of the event during which the incident in question happened and reports on Mr. M.'s actions targeting LGBT activists, among other marginalized groups, including through the use of the very same words that the courts considered likely to be unknown to Mr. M.

32. In the light of the foregoing, I conclude that there are enough reasons to believe that Mr. M.'s acts amounted to insults, harassment and hate speech based on the author's gender, sexual orientation and her human rights work, and this inflicted phycological injury on the author. She was denied entirely access to proceedings based on the Russian Code of Administrative Offences because of the State party's failure to adopt a procedure for lifting the parliamentary immunity, and Mr. M. avoided investigation, prosecution and punishment for holding a special status as a parliamentarian. The author was only left with a civil procedure, which put a higher burden of proof on her and, in any case, could only lead to limited reparation. Mr. M.'s position in the civil proceedings continued to reflect gender-based and intersecting stereotypes, particularly gaslighting techniques, which the courts failed to assess and thus contributed to their reinforcement. The courts denied all the author's claims, specifically noting that the words considered insulting and stereotyping by the author and a specialist were not well-known. The State party reiterated this argument in the communication with us. The State party did not provide any information on training judges to allow them

87. Ibid., pp. 1-3.
88. Ibid., pp. 2-3.

to recognize hate speech and discrimination based on gender, sexual orientation, gender identity and human rights activism, among other grounds, including intersectional discrimination. The courts completely ignored the author's multiple appeals to the context of the case, particularly the nature of the event during which the incident happened and the systematic actions of Mr. M. targeting LGBT activists, among other marginalized groups, including through the use of the very same words that the courts considered likely to be unknown to Mr. M.

33. Consequently, I find that the State party has breached the author's rights under articles 2 (b) and (d)–(f), 5 (a), 7 (c) and 15 (1) of the Convention, read in the light of general recommendations Nos. 19, 33 and 35.

6

Petition 150 & 234 of 2016 (consolidated) [2019] High Court of Kenya (Kenya):

The Potent Possibilities of Dissent —Towards a Renegade Judicial Praxis

Waruguru Gaitho

Introduction

In the words of Sylvia Wynter, the human is '*homo narans*'—a story telling species.[1] Intimately bound up with our evolution, and distinct from other primates, is our capacity for storytelling.[2] Therein, we construct ourselves, and fashion bodies, lives, and worlds of our desire into reality. Law is a story unto itself and it is also, I argue, a powerful storytelling device. That the law has helped to create the world we live in is unassailable; that it shapes our everyday realities is apparent. Somewhat axiomatic then, the stories we tell of, and using the law, are therefore critical. The Constitution of Kenya itself expressly acknowledges this *story-telling* role of law in stating that 'every provision of this Constitution shall be construed according to the doctrine of interpretation that *the law is always speaking*'[3] As officers of the court—whether on the bar or the bench—we would be remiss if we failed to ask ourselves daily, then, what stories we want to tell.

With this as my opening gambit, the piece sets out to [re]imagine, [re]interpret, and [re]present the story of the decriminalization of same-sex relations in Kenya, in the Constitutional and Human Rights Division of the High Court of Kenya. On 24 May 2019, the court rendered a judgment on *Petition 150 and 234 of 2016*.[4] The case sought to challenge the constitutionality of sections 162(a) and (c) and 165 of *The Penal Code of Kenya 1930* which criminalize same-sex conduct. The Penal Code, which first came into force as part of the British colonial legal order in 1930,[5] prescribes

---

1. Sylvia Wynter and Katherine McKittrick, 'Unparalleled Catastrophe for Our Species?: Or, to Give Humanness a Different Future: Conversations,' in *Sylvia Wynter*, ed. Katherine McKittrick (Durham: Duke University Press, 2015), 25.

2. Wynter and McKittrick, 'Unparalleled Catastrophe,' 25.

3. The Constitution of Kenya 2010, art 259(3) (emphasis added).

4. *Petition 150 & 234 of 2016* (High Court of Nairobi: Constitutional and Human Rights Division), [1].

5. 'CAP. 63,' accessed 27 July 2022, http://www.kenyalaw.org/lex/actview.xql?actid=CAP.%2063.

a 14-year prison sentence for anyone found guilty of 'carnal knowledge against the order of nature,'[6] and a 5-year sentence for 'indecent practices between males.'[7] The petitioners argued that the impugned provisions were unconstitutional on grounds of vagueness and ambiguity, as well as a violation of several fundamental human rights clauses in the Bill of Rights, *inter alia*, Articles 27(4), 28, 29, 31, 32, 43 and 50 of the Constitution.[8] In a resounding rejection of these claims of unconstitutionality, the three-judge bench unanimously ruled to uphold the criminalization of same-sex relations in Kenya.

The narrativization unfolds along two arcs: the first explores, by way of a short commentary, what I call a *renegade judicial praxis*, in particular, its theoretical underpinnings and its offerings to us in terms of possibilities for effectively mobilizing the law. The second arc animates this modality, through the crafting of a dissenting judgment in response to the High Court's decree on *Petition 150 & 234 of 2016*. This chapter engages with judicial dissent as a mode of queering judgment. Queering in the literal sense of making visible the terrain that lies beyond cis-patriarchal heteronormativity, but more broadly, queering as in troubling, deconstructing, and critically analyzing; making strange that which appears unquestionable, and unquestioning. In doing so, it explores the contours of a legal praxis rooted in the interrogation and disruption of coloniality (with its attendant logics of gender and sexuality), and in confronting the uncomfortable paradox of the law as both a colonial institution and emancipatory paradigm.

On Renegade Judicial Praxis: Assembling the Constituents

The word *renegade* evokes various notions: shifting allegiance, desertion, ideological rebellion, deviation, resistance, and so forth. To *choose otherwise*. The law has long been recognized as a complex site of contestation, tasked with the rather arduous undertaking of regulating norms, bodies, values and behaviour. In this arena of regulation, what does it mean to shift allegiance? If norms are interpreted as giving residence to bodies, what does it mean to criminalize certain bodies?[9] And in turn, what does it then mean to use the law to transform bodies from 'misfits into fits?'[10] At the core of these questions lies a reckoning with power; the power relations that shape and define the world, and law's place in it. Decoloniality, a school of thought premised on the disinterment of global power relations, describes the current world order as 'coloniality': a 'Euro-America-centric, Christian-centric, patriarchal, capitalist, hetero-normative, racially hierarchised, and modern world system that came into being in the 15th century.'[11] This moment of birth was brought about by the discovery,

---

6. *The Penal Code of Kenya 1930*, sec 162(a).
7. *The Penal Code of Kenya 1930*, sec 165.
8. The Constitution of Kenya, chap 4.
9. Sara Ahmed, *Living a Feminist Life* (Durham, NC: Duke University Press, 2017), 115.
10. Rosemarie Garland-Thomson, 'Misfits: A Feminist Materialist Disability Concept,' *Hypatia* 26/3 (2011), 601.
11. Sabelo J. Ndlovu-Gatsheni, 'Decoloniality as the Future of Africa,' *History Compass* 13/10 (2015), 489.

and conquest of the Americas, a watershed moment that marked the largest and most ambitious colonial conquest by mankind yet.[12] It is through this project that capitalism and racism came to be entwined, and form the basis of modernity, which was 'inescapably framed by world capitalism, and a system of domination structured around the idea of race.'[13] Premised on the realisation of this asymmetrical world order, decoloniality thus 'implies the recognition and undoing of the hierarchical structures of race, gender, heteropatriarchy, and class that continue to control life, knowledge, spirituality, and thought.'[14] Decoloniality, as Ndlovu-Gatsheni argues, 'pushes for transcendence over narrow conceptions of being decolonized, and consistently gestures towards liberation from coloniality as a complex matrix of knowledge, power, and being.'[15] It recognizes the longue durée of coloniality relative to shorter-lived colonialism, and seeks to unmake the fabric of the world as we know it. In relation to the law, decoloniality unveils the nature, content and institution of law as intrinsic to modernity, and therefore, coloniality. This uncomfortable intimacy demands sitting with whether and how we invest in the law, and its concomitant projects of justice and morality. A shifting allegiance to the law could take on myriad forms, including complete divestment from the overarching normative and political project of law itself. I am, however, interested in exploring what it means to *desert* conventional judicial praxis, what it means to be *disloyal* to the coloniality of law. In these interstices, the first stake of rebellion is planted: a judicial praxis that is driven by a decolonial impetus in its perception, interpretation, and application of the law.

Various scholars have articulated radical visions for the law which transcend a disciplining role that re-entrenches extant power dynamics. For example, in 1998, against the backdrop of a post-apartheid South Africa, Klare introduced the concept of transformative constitutionalism, defining it as the 'long-term project of constitutional enactment, interpretation, and enforcement committed to transforming a country's political and social institutions and power relationships in a democratic, participatory and egalitarian direction.'[16] Focusing on judges, he imagined it as a 'large-scale, egalitarian, social transformation,'[17] further arguing that transformative constitutionalism was not, in principle, inconsistent with a court's duties of interpretive fidelity.[18]

He framed this in response to traditional legal theory, whose sharp insistence on the law/politics divide he viewed as a considerable weakness to adjudication, a yoke that transformative constitutionalism readily cast away.[19] By doing away with the denial of the porousness of law and politics, judges could be honest about the politics of adjudication, and commit to practices aimed at constructing a new world order

---

12. Nelson Maldonado-Torres, 'On the Coloniality of Being,' *Cultural Studies* 21/2–3 (2007), 243.

13. Maldonado-Torres, 'Coloniality,' 244.

14. Walter D. Mignolo and Catherine E. Walsh, *On Decoloniality: Concepts, Analytics, Praxis* (Durham: Duke University Press, 2018), 17.

15. Ndlovu-Gatsheni, 'Decoloniality,' 490.

16. Karl E Klare, 'Legal Culture and Transformative Constitutionalism,' *South African Journal on Human Rights* 14/1 (1998), 150.

17. Klare, 'Legal Culture,' 150.

18. Klare, 'Legal Culture,' 151.

19. Klare, 'Legal Culture,' 158.

anchored in the egalitarian promises of the Constitution. In response to Klare's theorisation, Van Marle reformulated transformative constitutionalism 'as/and critique' which she explained as 'an approach to the Constitution and law in general that is committed to transforming political, social, socio-economic and legal practices in such a way that it will radically alter existing assumptions about law, politics, economics, and society in general.'[20] Van Marle's formulation is divorced from liberal approaches to law, and is not bound solely to law as its only site of intervention.[21] What makes this formulation appealing is that it contends with the ontological paradox of the law as inherently incapable of transforming the world order, and interrogates how we might generatively sit in that tension. Of particular use is her deployment of the metaphors of 'weaving and walking' as ways of thinking about the irresolvable nature of these tensions, but nevertheless engaging them continuously.[22] It is in this liminal space, this 'broken middle,'[23] that decoloniality might be deployed as a set of analytics and practices aimed at undoing the matrix of coloniality in the courtroom and beyond. In this 'precarious and uncomfortable space and time,'[24] renegade judicialism weaves together these modes of choosing otherwise, and proffers a pathway to staking our allegiances elsewhere.

As regards the specific question that this chapter addresses—the decriminalisation of same-sex relations in Kenya—I turn to critical insights on the coloniality of gender. Quijano incisively linked gender to race in the operations of colonial power, arguing that the hierarchicalizing systems of racism and sexism were inseparable and therefore mutually constitutive of the colonial matrix of power.[25] Building off of Quijano's theorization, Lugones posited that, in fact, gender itself was a colonial production; that colonialism did not impose European conceptions and protocols of gender, but rather produced a new gender order, which created different expectations for the colonised male and female body, than for the colonizing white male and female body.[26] She succinctly called this the 'coloniality of gender.'[27] This gender system not only created myriad genders, but also *gendered* the entirety of social organizing to begin with. Its scope was therefore never just centred on the control of sex, its products and resources, but is instead always reaching, wrapping around and warping all parts of collective existence, including the organisation of labour, collective authority, subjectivity, spirituality and so forth.[28] The imbrication of class (labour), race, gender, sexuality and other categories of being has long been illuminated by women of colour. By the 1980s, for instance, Black feminists had already called attention to the intricate permutations

---

20. Karin Van Marle, 'Transformative Constitutionalism as / and Critique,' *Stellenbosch Law Review* 20/2 (2009), 288.
21. Van Marle, 'Transformative Constitutionalism,' 288.
22. Van Marle 'Transformative Constitutionalism,' 298.
23. Van Marle, 'Transformative Constitutionalism,' 298.
24. Van Marle, 'Transformative Constitutionalism,' 297.
25. Mignolo and Walsh, *On Decoloniality*, 158.
26. María Lugones, 'Heterosexualism and the Colonial / Modern Gender System,' *Hypatia* 22/1 (2007), 188.
27. Lugones, 'Heterosexualism,' 201.
28. María Lugones, 'The Coloniality of Gender,' in *Globalization and the Decolonial Option*, eds. Walter D. Mignolo and Arturo Escobar (Abingdon: Routledge, 2010), 12.

of oppression that arose out of the inseparability, interconnectedness and productions of and within these axes of domination.[29] Collins named these interlocking systems of oppression the 'matrix of domination.'[30] The term 'intersectionality' was specifically coined to explain how systems of oppression interlock to create new, synergistic forms of oppression within multiply marginalized bodies, and Crenshaw defined it as 'a lens through which you can see where power comes and collides, where it interlocks and intersects.'[31]

To employ a renegade judicial praxis, then, would mean to choose to see differently, or rather, *unsee*, gender in its modern construction. Unseeing as method opens up possibilities for the configuration of new liberatory realities. It would mean to interrogate the underlying presumptions of laws that order gender relations, including those that regulate desire. To pay attention to collisions of power in law, and to unpick the enmeshments and entanglements entrenched in these provisions of law. As Okech notes, the purpose of sodomy laws was to 'simultaneously racialize, sexualize and gender the population.'[32] To unsee gender and sexuality as prescribed by law, would thus require judges to recognize and engage with the inherent civilizing mission of law in modernity, to reckon with it as always concurrently a racial project, a class project and so on. Beyond this, it would require them to employ decriminalization as a larger project of decoloniality and transformative constitutionalism; to insistently pull at the seams of a socio-political oppressive project we have long claimed ownership to, as so-called formerly colonised nations. Ultimately, to choose to shift judicial allegiance towards liberation and commit to the transformation of the social, economic, legal, and political fabric of society.

The next section applies this praxis to the High Court judgment in *Petition 150 & 234 of 2016*, by way of a dissenting opinion. In particular, the 'framework for determination' contends with weaving theory together with the practical task of adjudication, within the bounds of legal rationale. The exercise reflects the tensions discussed extensively in this section, but also aims to showcase the potent possibilities of dissent as renegade judicial praxis.

---

29. See Akasha Hull, Patricia Bell-Scott, and Barbara Smith, eds., *But Some Of Us Are Brave: All the Women Are White, All the Blacks Are Men: Black Women's Studies* (Old Westbury: The Feminist Press at CUNY, 1993).

30. Patricia Hill Collins, *Black Feminist Thought: Knowledge, Consciousness, and the Politics of Empowerment* (Abingdon: Routledge, 2002), 23.

31. Kimberlé Crenshaw, 'Demarginalizing the Intersection of Race and Sex: A Black Feminist Critique of Anti-Discrimination Doctrine, Feminist Theory, and Anti-Racist Politics,' *University of Chicago Legal Forum* 140 (1989), 139.

32. Awino Okech, 'Queer Movements and Disciplinary Laws in Africa,' in *Law on the Move: Technical, Political, and Social Developments and Theoretical Challenges for Legal Gender Studies*, eds. Sandra Hotz, Nils Kapferer, and Michelle Cottier (Zurich: DIKE, 2022), 2.

REPUBLIC OF KENYA

IN THE HIGH COURT OF KENYA AT NAIROBI
MILIMANI LAW COURTS
CONSTITUTIONAL AND HUMAN RIGHTS DIVISION

PETITION NO. 150 & 234 OF 2016

DISSENTING OPINION

Introduction

1. This dissenting opinion is framed in response to the judgment signed and delivered by the Honourable Justices Aburili, Mwita and Mativo on the 24th of May, 2019 at the High Court of Kenya at Nairobi in the Constitutional and Human Rights Division. The petition at hand seeks to challenge the constitutionality of sections 162(a), (c) and 165 of the Penal Code, on the basis of vagueness and uncertainty of the sections on the one hand, and the violation of fundamental rights outlined in the Bill of Rights of the Constitution of Kenya on the other. This judgment dispenses with the former, having found the High Court to have sufficiently dealt with the questions arising therein, and focuses on the latter.

2. The role played by dissenting judgments is decidedly critical, as persuasively elucidated by the honourable Nyamu JA:

> [D]issenting judgments may provide a firm base for future generations not to contain themselves in straight jackets, but to always remember that at the end of the day, that much sought justice might after all not be in the thunder of the majority judgment, but in the silent breeze of the minority judgment! Dissenting opinions constitute an appeal to the brooding spirit of the law, to the intelligence of a future day, when a later decision may possibly correct the error into which the dissenting judge believe the Court to have betrayed.[33]

3. In examining the facts and legal basis of *Petition 150 & 234 of 2016*, I find that the bench gravely erred in its interpretation of law and fact; it is my aversion that in so doing, the court compromised its constitutional duty to 'observe, respect, protect, promote, and fulfil the rights, and fundamental freedoms in the Bill of Rights.'[34] As such, this judgment aspires to embody the brooding spirit of the law.

The Parties

4. The Petitioners' side is comprised of a gay human rights lawyer, two other gay men and a lesbian, all of whom claim to have been subjected to attacks, stigma and discrimination

---

33. *Stanbic Bank Kenya Limited v Kenya Revenue Authority* [2009] The Court of Appeal at Nairobi Civil Appeal 77 of 2008 [20].
34. The Constitution of Kenya art 21(1).

on the basis of their sexual orientation. Additionally, it is comprised of the mother of a gay man and a priest, who claim they have witnessed discriminatory acts committed against members of the LGBTIQ+ community. Three organisations working on human rights and the welfare of LGBTIQ+ persons specifically or human rights more generally also joined the suit as petitioners.[35]

5. The Respondent's side is comprised of the Attorney General as the representative of the State, pursuant to Article 156 of the Constitution.[36]

6. There are 10 interested parties to the lawsuit: the first to sixth interested parties swore an affidavit in support of the suit, having described themselves as individuals who had been advocating for the protection of lesbian, gay, and bisexual individuals as well as men who have sex with men (MSMs). The eighth interested party is the Kenya Legal & Ethical Issues Network on HIV & Aids, whose interest in the petition lies in access to healthcare for MSMs, and the impact of criminalization of same-sex relations on the right to health.

7. The seventh, ninth and tenth interested parties are, respectively, the Kenya Christian Professional Forum, self-described as an organization whose object is, *inter alia*, to campaign for the 'consideration of the perspectives and ideals' held by Christians in Kenya,[37] Irun'gu Kang'ata, the Senator of Murang'a County, whose interest in the petition is to 'secure the diversity of Kenyan Cultures in their common rejection of homosexuality,'[38] and registered trustees of two foundations linked to the largest Mosque in Kenya, Jamia Mosque, standing in to represent the interests of Kenyan Muslims and Islamic values.[39]

8. Finally, two *Amicus Curiae* joined the suit: Katiba Institute, a 'non-profit, non-governmental NGO with expertise in constitutional law and international human rights law,'[40] and the Kenya National Commission on Human Rights, an independent, constitutional commission established to promote respect for human rights.[41]

Facts of the Case & Relevant Law

9. The current Petition was consolidated from two separately filed cases: *EG & 7 others v Attorney General (Petition 150)* and *DKM & 9 others v Attorney General (Petition 234)*. The court anchored the decision to consolidate the two matters on the basis of their similarity, as they both challenged the constitutionality of sections 162 and 165 of the Penal code. The impugned provisions prescribe a 14-year prison sentence for anyone found guilty of 'carnal knowledge against the order of nature,'[42] or permitting

---

35. *Petition 150 & 234 of 2016* paras. 3–12 & 16.
36. The Constitution of Kenya art 156(4).
37. *Petition 150 & 234 of 2016* (n 4) para. 15.
38. *Petition 150 & 234 of 2016* (n 4) para. 17.
39. *Petition 150 & 234 of 2016* (n 4) para. 103.
40. *Petition 150 & 234 of 2016* (n 4) para. 19.
41. The Constitution of Kenya art 59.
42. The Penal Code of Kenya sec 162(a).

'a male person to have carnal knowledge of him or her against the order of nature.'[43] Further, the Code imposes a 5-year sentence for 'indecent practices between males.'[44]

10. The Petitioners contended that 'the provisions have in effect, or are in practice applied to criminalise private consensual sexual conduct between adult persons of the same-sex.'[45] Further, they argued that to the extent to which the provisions purport to criminalise the relevant conduct, they are unconstitutional because, *inter alia*, they violate Articles 27 (Equality and freedom from discrimination), Article 28 (Human dignity), Article 29 (Freedom and security of the person), Article 31 (Privacy), 32 (Freedom of conscience, religion, belief and opinion) and Article 43 (Economic and social rights—specifically health) of the Constitution.[46]

11. The Petitioners further relied on regional law, in particular, the African Charter on Human and People's Rights,[47] and Resolution 275 on the protection against violence and other human rights violations against persons on the basis of their real or imputed sexual orientation or gender identity.[48] Further, they cited international law, principally, relevant provisions of the Universal Declaration of Human Rights (UDHR),[49] International Covenant on Civil and Political Rights (ICCPR)[50] and the International Covenant on Economic, Social and Cultural Rights (ICESCR).[51]

12. Moreover, the Petitioners made it clear that the Petition did not concern same-sex marriage, nor did it seek to legalise same-sex marriage; that indeed, if successful, the Petition 'would not have the effect of mandating or requiring Kenya to recognise same-sex marriage.'[52]

13. On these grounds, they sought to have the impugned provisions struck out, and the second Petition specifically sought an additional declaration that 'sexual and gender minorities are entitled to the right to the highest attainable standards including the right to health care services as guaranteed in Article 43 of the Constitution.'[53]

---

43. The Penal Code of Kenya sec 162(c).
44. The Penal Code of Kenya sec 165.
45. *Petition 150 & 234 of 2016* (n 4) para. 58.
46. *Petition 150 & 234 of 2016* (n 4) para. 59.
47. African Charter on Human and Peoples' Rights ('Banjul Charter') 1981 (CAB/LEG/67/3 rev 5, 21 ILM 58 (1982)) arts. 2, 3, 4, 6, 10, 19 & 28.
48. 275 Resolution on Protection against Violence and other Human Rights Violations against Persons on the basis of their real or imputed Sexual Orientation or Gender Identity 2014 (ACHPR/Res275(LV)2014).
49. Universal Declaration of Human Rights 1948 (General Assembly Resolution 217 A (III)) art 1, 2, 3, 7, 9, 12 & 28.
50. International Covenant on Civil and Political Rights 1966 (999 UNTS 171) arts. 2(1), 6(1), 7, 9(1), 17(1) & 26.
51. International Covenant on Economic, Social and Cultural Rights 1966 arts. 2(2) & 12(1).
52. *Petition 150 & 234 of 2016* (n 4) para. 64.
53. *Petition 150 & 234 of 2016* (n 4) para. 2.

14. In turn, the Respondent argued that the Constitution acknowledged the suprem-acy of the almighty God as the 'objective moral law giver'[54] and that this propelled their insistence at the retention of the provisions in question. They maintained that 'the Constitution recognises marriage as a union of two consenting adults, male and female,[55] and, that the legislative function of the State is exercised by Parliament, hence, the court cannot compel the government to legalise homosexuality by amending the impugned provisions.'[56]

15. The 7th interested party, the Kenya Christian Professional Forum, contended that the Petitioners were using 'judicial craft to legitimise gay liaisons and such other inde-cent offences and create a new breed of rights which do not exist in the Constitution.'[57] They further reasoned that 'no right confers a cover to an individual to engage in illegal criminal conduct;'[58] and that, resultantly, the alleged violation of constitutional rights could not have taken place as the conduct in question is illegal.[59] Agreeing with the Respondent, the 7th interested party described the petition as 'an assault on Article 45 of the Constitution' and stated that, in any case, Article 24 of the Constitution provided for the limitation of rights where justifiable 'on the basis of public interest and public policy.'[60]

16. The 9th interested party, Senator Irungu Kang'ata, argued that 'none of the Kenyan communities or culture embraces homosexuality and that historically, homosexuality was punished through ostracisation or death.'[61] Therefore, in his view, decriminalizing homosexuality would be 'tantamount to compelling communities to embrace the prac-tice in breach of their right to preservation of their culture.'[62] Moreover, in comparison to 'other jurisdictions where homosexuality had been accepted, Kenya had a "socially conservative' Constitution that detest[ed] the practice."[63]

17. The 10th interested party, representatives of Jamia Mosque, the largest Mosque in Kenya, stated that 'the Holy Quran and Hadith abhor homosexuality, which echoes Kenyan cultural values, which the people of Kenya desired in the Constitution.'[64]

Issues

18. Having fastidiously assessed the pleadings, submissions and authorities, it is my view that the following issues present themselves for determination:

---

54. *Petition 150 & 234 of 2016* (n 4) para. 66.
55. The Constitution of Kenya art 45(2).
56. *Petition 150 & 234 of 2016* (n 4) para. 66.
57. *Petition 150 & 234 of 2016* (n 4) para. 71.
58. *Petition 150 & 234 of 2016* (n 4) para. 71.
59. *Petition 150 & 234 of 2016* (n 4) para. 73.
60. *Petition 150 & 234 of 2016* (n 4) para. 76.
61. *Petition 150 & 234 of 2016* (n 4) para. 100.
62. *Petition 150 & 234 of 2016* (n 4) para. 101.
63. *Petition 150 & 234 of 2016* (n 4) para. 200.
64. *Petition 150 & 234 of 2016* (n 4) para. 103.

(a) Whether the impugned provisions are unconstitutional for violating Articles 27, 28, 29, 31, 32 and 43 of the Constitution.

(b) Whether the existence of Article 45 serves as a bar to the realisation of the fundamental rights enshrined in the Bill of Rights.

19. Before addressing these issues, it is important to highlight the fundamental tenets governing this process, and ultimately, its outcome. These tenets form a guiding framework for the determination of the issues set forth.

Framework for Determination

20. To begin with, the question of how to interpret the law strikes at the very heart of the judicial process, and remains an intricate and formidable undertaking, subject to perpetual reflection by all judicial officers. This exercise is strongly buttressed by the Supreme law of the land, per Article 259, which sets out the principles of interpretation of the Constitution as follows:

(1) This Constitution shall be interpreted in a manner that—

(a) promotes its purposes, values and principles;

(b) advances the rule of law, and the human rights and fundamental freedoms in the Bill of Rights;

(c) permits the development of the law; and

(d) contributes to good governance.[65]

21. With these principles as a sturdy foundation on which this matter shall be assessed, we turn to the rules of statutory interpretation. It is generally accepted that statutes may be interpreted using the literal rule, the golden rule or the mischief rule. In *Duport Steel v Sirs*, Lord Diplock defined the literal rule, acknowledging that it was not for judges to 'invent fancied ambiguities' to words, however, in doing so also, he made it clear that the application of this rule might result in 'manifest absurdities.'[66] The golden rule acts as a shield to these 'manifest absurdities' and prioritises the will of Parliament as law makers. The mischief rule, as laid out in the landmark *Heydon's Case*,[67] sets out to determine the specific defect which the law seeks to cure, allowing for an interpretation that most effectively does so, and is thus seen as giving the widest interpretive berth to judges.

22. This rule, contemporaneously construed as the purposive approach, is frequently favoured in recognition of its inherent ability to bring to life the essence of the law as it was intended by the people. In *Nicholas Kiptoo Arap Korir Salat v Independent Electoral and Boundaries Commission & 6 others*, Ouko J.A. stated that 'in modern

---

65. The Constitution of Kenya art 259(1).
66. *Duport Steels Ltd and Others v Sirs and Others* [1980] House of Lords 1 WLR 142.
67. *Heydon's Case* [1584] Exchequer of Pleas 76 ER 637.

times the courts do not apply or enforce the words of statute or rules but their objects, purposes and spirit or core values. The mischief rule of construction is much the same as the spirit of a statute or rules of procedure.'[68]

23. Similarly, Justice Ringera, in speaking of the Constitution, declared that 'it is the supreme law of the land, and it ought to be regarded as a living instrument with a consciousness and a soul that contains particular basic principles and values that ought to be construed purposely, broadly, liberally, or teleologically with the aim of according effect to those principles and values.'[69]

24. These sentiments were echoed by Justice Emukule in his ratio decidendi in *Dileep Manibhai Patel & 3 others v Municipal Council of Nakuru & another,* where he referenced Bello JSC of the Nigerian Supreme Court's decision in *Ifezu v Mbadugha*:

> The fundamental principle is that such interpretation as would serve the interests of the constitution and would best carry out its object and purpose should be preferred. To achieve this goal its relevant provisions must be read together and not disjointly ... where the provisions of the constitution are capable of two meanings the court must choose the meaning that would give effect to the Constitution and promote its purpose.[70]

25. Per Bello JSC's rationale, in addition to a purposive, living-instrument framework, a holistic approach to reading and interpreting the Constitution is critical. Justice Mwita referred to this as the 'rule of harmony' in *Josephat Musila Mutua & 9 others v Attorney General & 3 others,* in a cogent articulation set forth thus:

> The entire Constitution should be read as an integrated whole and no particular provision destroying the other but each sustaining the other. This is the rule of harmony, the rule of completeness and exhaustiveness and not one provision destroying another.[71]

26. Along this vein, I contend that a holistic, purposive, living-instrument approach would be remiss without an appreciation of the legal-political-historical context and aims that informed the promulgation of the Constitution, in particular, the decolonizing drive behind doing away with the 1969 and colonial constitutions and embracing a new, transformative Constitution. As former Chief Justice and President of the Supreme Court of Kenya, Dr. Willy Mutunga, reflected, the new constitution 'is a radical document that looks to a future that is very different from our past, in its values and practices. It seeks to make a fundamental change from the 68 years of colonialism and 50 years of independence.'[72] He further commented that he saw in the Constitution,

---

68. *Nicholas Kiptoo Arap Korir Salat v Independent Electoral and Boundaries Commission & 6 others* [2013] Court of Appeal at Nairobi Civil Appeal (Application) 228 of 2013.

69. *Njoya and others v Attorney-General and others* [2004] High Court of Kenya at Nairobi LLR 4788 (HCK).

70. *Dileep Manibhai Patel & 3 others v Municipal Council of Nakuru & another* [2014] High Court of Kenya at Nakuru Petition No. 6 of 2009 [50(2)].

71. *Josephat Musila Mutua & 9 others v Attorney General & 3 others* [2018] High Court of Kenya at Nairobi Petition 120 of 2017 [19].

72. Willy Mutunga, 'The 2010 Constitution of Kenya and Its Interpretation: Reflections from the Supreme

'a mandate to carry out reforms tailored to Kenya's needs, and aimed at doing away with colonial and neo-colonial inefficiencies and injustices.'[73]

27. Law Professor Karl Klare introduced the term 'transformative constitutionalism,' defining it as 'a long-term project of constitutional enactment, interpretation, and enforcement committed ... to transforming a country's political and social institutions and power relationships in a democratic, participatory and egalitarian direction.'[74] In doing so, he proposed a post-liberal reading of the South African Constitution, categorizing it as 'social, redistributive, caring, positive, at least partly horizontal, participatory, multicultural, and self-conscious about its historical setting and transformative role and mission.'[75] Whilst we can appreciate that South Africa and Kenya are materially different contexts, given Kenya's colonial history, and indeed the perception of our new Constitution as a 'second independence,'[76] it would not be too far reaching to transpose these qualities, these ambitions, to the judicial interpretive and adjudicative project. The reigning question then would be: what would a social, redistributive, caring, positive, multicultural, participatory, *decolonial* interpretation of the Constitution look like? Arguably, an anti-colonial, purposive, living-instrument, holistic, transformative interpretation begins to answer this complex question.

28. The following diagram illustrates the iterative, integrated, symbiotic nature of the ideas and rationale elucidated above; the framework serves as a visual representation of the schema that will guide the subsequent reflexive process of determination.

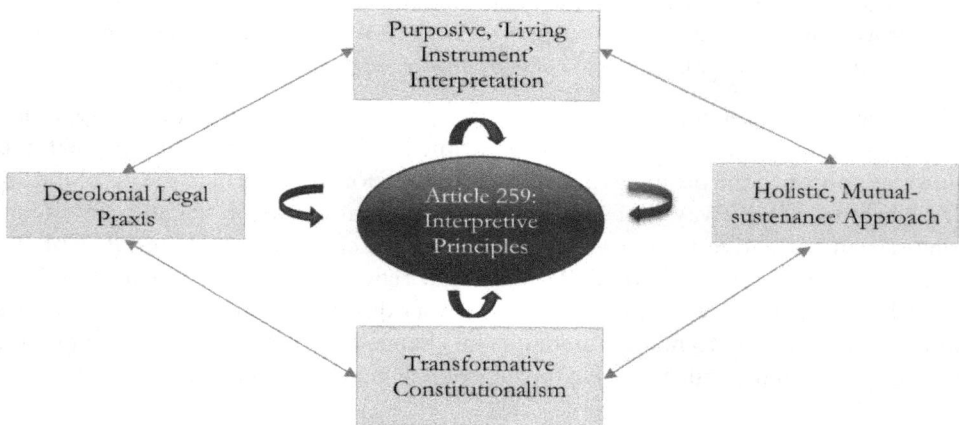

Fig. 1

Court's Decisions,' *Speculum Juris* 1 (2015), 2.
73. Mutunga, 'The 2010 Constitution,' 5.
74. Klare, 'Legal Culture,' 150.
75. Klare, 'Legal Culture,' 153.
76. Mutunga, 'The 2010 Constitution,' 1.

Determination

A. Whether the impugned provisions are unconstitutional for violating Articles 27, 28, 29, 31, 32 and 43 of the Constitution

    i.   The Right to Equality and Freedom from Discrimination, as read together with the Right to Human Dignity (Articles 27 & 28)

29. The Petitioners' case was that as a result of the existence of the impugned provisions, they had been subjected to discrimination on the grounds of their real or imputed sexual orientation. To support their claim, they swore affidavits to that effect, providing numerous accounts of violence, blackmail and extortion, harassment, arbitrary arrest, detention, and eviction; they produced authoritative reports, as well as expert witness accounts on the lived experiences of LGBTIQ+ persons in Kenya, evidencing the subjugation they face. They also cited relevant case law, including Kenyan case law wherein the Court of Appeal had read 'sexual orientation' into Article 27.[77]

30. My esteemed colleagues rejected their arguments on two grounds: a textual 'ordinary meaning' interpretation of the words used to construct the impugned provisions, and a failure to sufficiently bear the evidentiary burden of proof. I reiterate their central *ratio decidendi* here below:

> 295. The substance of the Petitioners' complaint is that the impugned provisions target the LGBTIQ community only. If we understood them correctly, their contestation is that the impugned provisions do not apply against heterosexuals.
>
> 296. Our reading of the challenged provisions suggests otherwise. The language of section 162 is clear. It uses the words 'Any person.' A natural and literal construction of these words leaves us with no doubt that the section does not target any particular group of persons.
>
> 297. Similarly, section 165 uses the words 'Any male person.' A plain reading of the section reveals that it targets male persons and not a particular group with a particular sexual orientation. The wording of this section leaves no doubt that in enacting this provision, Parliament appreciated that the offence under this section can only be committed by a male person. In fact, the short title to the section reads 'indecent practices between males.' The operative words here are 'Any male person' which clearly does not target male persons of a particular sexual orientation...
>
> 299. No iota of evidence was tendered to establish any of the cited acts of discrimination. It is our finding that there is no basis at all upon which the court can uphold any of the alleged violations. In the end, we find that the Petitioners have failed to establish that the impugned provisions are discriminatory.[78]

---

77. *Eric Gitari v NGO Coordination Board & 4 others* [2015] High Court of Kenya, Constitutional and Judicial Review Division Petition No. 440 of 2013.
78. *Petition 150 & 234 of 2016* (n 4) paras. 295, 296, 297 & 299.

31. In adopting this 'plain reading' interpretive methodology, the bench clearly favoured a formal equality reading of the law, a specious position I cannot subscribe to as it is fundamentally flawed. To begin with, whilst I readily accept that the word 'any' is used to mean 'all' or 'without distinction,' I reject the judges' extrapolation of the implication of the law's framing. By their rationale, the law was not discriminatory because it equally targeted all individuals, or per section 165, 'any male person.' Putting aside the indisputably gendered boundaries of the framing, it is glaringly obvious that the law, by dint of criminalizing consensual same-sex acts of desire, creates a specific second-class tier of citizens, who are rendered criminals on the basis of their sexuality, thereby entrenching an axis of marginalisation. The purpose and effect of the law is in fact to single out, ergo, target, a particular group of persons whose sexuality is prescribed as deviant. That the net casts wide, is not proof of the lack of discrimination against a subset of society. As presented by the Petitioners, the impugned provisions produce a very different, indeed chilling, effect on sexual and gender minorities compared to their heterosexual counterparts.

32. Article 260 of the Constitution defines a 'marginalized group' as 'a group of people who, because of *laws and practices* before, on or after the effective date, were or are disadvantaged by discrimination on one or more of the grounds in Article 27(4)'[79] (emphasis added). In *COI & GMN v Chief Magistrate Ukunda Law Courts & 4 others,* for example, the appellate court decried the inhumane practice of forced anal examinations, having accepted evidence that the tests were done under the presumption that the appellants were gay men, i.e., specifically targeted for their sexuality, with a view to prove their homosexuality.[80]

33. Further, the Respondents themselves openly admitted that the issue at hand concerned the acceptance (or rather the lack thereof) of homosexuality in the Kenyan context. That the impugned provisions render a legal proscription to sexual and gender minorities in Kenya therefore cannot be swept under the rug under the guise of 'neutral' and universalizing language. Delivering his judgment in the decriminalisation of same-sex relations case of *Caleb Orozco v Attorney General of Belize*, Chief Justice Benjamin acknowledged the value of going beyond a plain reading of the Belize Criminal Code stating that 'in as much as section 53 is framed in gender neutral language, the evidence demonstrates that it is discriminatory in its effect. The Claimant has shown that he has been rendered a criminal by virtue of his homosexuality.'[81]

34. Furthermore, transformative constitutionalism and the living instrument principle demand an ongoing assessment of relations of power that define a society, with the view to not only provide redress to those marginalized, but to also begin to create

---

79. The Constitution of Kenya art 260.
80. *COI & another v Chief Magistrate Ukunda Law Courts & 4 others* [2018] Court of Appeal at Mombasa Civil Appeal 56 of 2016 [32].
81. *Caleb Orozco v Attorney General of Belize* [2016] Supreme Court of Belize Claim 668 of 2010 [92].

conditions necessary for equality. Chief Justice Willy Mutunga stated *In the Matter of the Principle of Gender Representation in the National Assembly and the Senate* that:

> [T]he Constitution's view of equality, as one of the values provided under the Constitution, in this case is not the traditional view of providing equality before the law. Equality here is substantive, and involves undertaking certain measures, including affirmative action, to reverse negative positions that have been taken by society. Where such negative exclusions pertain to political and civil rights, the measures undertaken are immediate and not progressive. [82]

35. With regard to failing to tender sufficient—nay, any—evidence, I find that the bench was misguided and negligent in its conscious choice to overlook the probative value of the copious amounts of both oral and written evidence that was presented by Counsel for the Petitioners. It is my assertion that this oversight amounts to a grave miscarriage of justice.

36. In light of all of the above, I am therefore compelled by the Petitioners' case and find a violation of Articles 27 & 28 of the Constitution.

    ii.   The Right to Freedom and Security of the Person, The Right to Privacy, The Right to Freedom of conscience, religion, belief and opinion and The Right to the highest attainable Standard of Health (Articles 29, 31, 32 & 43)

37. Having assessed Articles 27 and 28 and found that the impugned provisions were indeed in breach of the right to equality and non-discrimination as well as human dignity, I find it unnecessary to engage in an in-depth analysis of Articles 29, 31, 32 & 43 vis-à-vis the impugned provisions. The reason for this two-fold:

    a.   The finding of a violation on the grounds of Articles 27 and 28 effectively answers the general question arising out of the issue for determination. Furthermore, given that they underpin the rest of the fundamental rights implicated in this matter, this answer in the affirmative cascades down to Articles 29, 31, 32 & 43.

    b.   The central objections raised in the examination of Articles 27 and 28 by the bench are largely similar to those raised in the aforementioned Articles, with the obvious exception of particularities inherent in the substantive value of each Article.[83] Thus, in my opinion, pulling at this common thread is largely superfluous, in the sense that the issue at hand is overdetermined.

38. Bearing in mind the weighty nature of these provisions, the rationale outlined above and the integrated *ratio decidendi* of the issue for determination, I thus answer the whole question in the affirmative, finding a violation of Articles 27, 28, 29, 31 & 43.

---

82. *Njoya and others v Attorney-General and others* (n 70) pt D.
83. See *Petition 150 & 234 of 2016* (n 4) paras. 304, 305, 321, 322 & 347.

B. Whether the existence of Article 45 functions as a sufficient limitation to the realisation of the fundamental rights enshrined in the Bill of Rights

39. In their deliberations on whether the impugned provisions were in violation of the fundamental rights enshrined in the Constitution, the bench honed in on Article 45, which reads as follows:

> Every adult has the right to marry a person of the opposite sex, based on the free consent of the parties.[84]

In their own words, my esteemed colleagues were satisfied that the presence of this provision acted as an ineluctable bar to finding a violation of fundamental rights as claimed by the Petitioners:

> 395. We have carefully examined the purport and import of sections 162 and 165 of the Penal Code vis-a-vis Articles 28 and 31 of the Constitution; we have also read the Constitution holistically. We are unable to agree with the Petitioners that the impugned provisions violate the Constitution or their rights to dignity and privacy. If we were to be persuaded that the Petitioners' rights are violated or threatened on grounds of sexual orientation, we find it difficult to rationalise this argument with the spirit, purpose and intention of Article 45(2) of Constitution.[85]

> 396. Article 45(2) only recognises marriage between adult persons of the opposite sex. In our view, decriminalising same-sex sex on grounds that it is consensual and is done in private between adults, would contradict the express provisions of Article 45 (2). The Petitioners' argument that they are not seeking to be allowed to enter into same-sex marriage is in our view, immaterial given that if allowed, it will lead to same-sex persons living together as couples. Such relationships, whether in private or not, formal or not would be in violation of the tenor and spirit of the Constitution.[86]

40. I find it untenable to agree with the assertions of the bench that their assessment was holistic, given the emphasis they placed on Article 45 to define the 'tenor and spirit of the Constitution.' To my mind, as a living instrument 'having a soul and consciousness of its own' as articulated by the Tanzanian Court of Appeal in *Ndyanabo v Attorney-General,*[87] no one clause could be read as defining the entirety of its consciousness. Instead, a holistic reading would call for the consideration of a myriad clauses to determine its object and purpose. I readily accept that Article 45 implies a rejection, as at the current moment, of the singular act of same-sex marriage. But a rejection of same-sex marriage is not mutually exclusive to the protection of the general corpus of fundamental rights granted to all individuals, including those who would not enter into such unions as a matter of personal choice, life circumstances or sexual orientation.

---

84. The Constitution of Kenya art 45(2).
85. *Petition 150 & 234 of 2016* (n 4) para. 395.
86. *Petition 150 & 234 of 2016* (n 4) para. 396.
87. *Ndyanabo v Attorney-General* [2002] Court of Appeal of Tanzania at Dar es Salaam AHRLR 243 (TzCA) [57].

41. This position is easily defensible, as evidenced below:

1. The Preamble, a declaration of the constitutive will of the people, recognises the 'aspirations of all Kenyans for a government based on the essential values of human rights, equality, freedom, democracy, social justice and the rule of law.'[88]

2. Article 10 outlines the National values and principles of governance and expressly includes the following cluster of values: 'human dignity, equity, social justice, inclusiveness, equality, human rights, non-discrimination and protection of the marginalised.'[89]

3. Article 19 which introduces the Bill of Rights states that, *'the purpose of recognising and protecting human rights and fundamental freedoms is to preserve the dignity of individuals and communities and to promote social justice and the realisation of the potential of* **all** *human beings'*[90] (emphasis added).

4. Article 21 on the implementation of rights and fundamental freedoms bestows a duty on all State organs and public officers *'to address the needs of vulnerable groups within society, including women, older members of society, persons with disabilities, children, youth, members of minority or marginalised communities, and members of particular ethnic, religious or cultural communities.'*[91] Additionally, it tasks the State with *'enact[ing] and implement[ing] legislation to fulfil its international obligations in respect of human rights and fundamental freedoms'*[92] (emphasis added).

5. Article 259, as cited earlier, mandates interpretation of the Constitution in a manner that, *inter alia*, 'advances the rule of law, and the human rights and fundamental freedoms in the Bill of Rights.'[93]

6. Overall, the words 'human rights' are used thirty-two times in the text of the Constitution, 'fundamental freedoms' twenty-three times, 'equality' twenty times, 'marginalised' fifteen times, 'dignity' fourteen times, and (the elimination of/intolerance towards/freedom from) discrimination seven times. That these ideals carry immense weight in the Supreme Law of the land is patently irrefutable. By contrast, 'opposite-sex marriage' is mentioned once.

42 Another point of emphasis for the bench lay in the fact that regardless of multiple jurisdictions having decriminalised their own provisions similar to Section 162, they had not come across a country with an opposite sex marriage clause that had decriminalised its laws on same-sex relations.[94] To this, I turn to the wisdom of the court in *Navtej Singh Johar & Ors v Union of India thr. Secretary ministry of Law and Justice*, which stated:

---

88. The Constitution of Kenya Preamble.
89. The Constitution of Kenya art 10(2)(b).
90. The Constitution of Kenya art 19(2).
91. The Constitution of Kenya art 21(3).
92. The Constitution of Kenya art 21(4).
93. The Constitution of Kenya art 259(1)(b).
94. *Petition 150 & 234 of 2016* (n 4) para. 398.

The Court, as the final arbiter of the Constitution, has to keep in view the necessities of the needy and the weaker sections. The role of the Court assumes further importance when the class or community whose rights are in question are those who have been the object of humiliation, discrimination, separation and violence by not only the State and the society at large but also at the hands of their very own family members. The development of law cannot be a mute spectator to the struggle for the realisation and attainment of the rights of such members of the society.[95]

43. The force and logic of this statement is wholly persuasive, and serves as a clarion call to the bench not to shirk its duties for the mere reason that 'it has not been done before.' In the spirit of this sacred duty, I find Article 45(2) to be an insufficient bar to the realisation of the fundamental rights outlined in the Constitution.

44. In conclusion, I return to our schema, to the question at the heart of the interpretive framework: what does an analysis of Articles 27, 28, 29, 31, 43, & 45 of the Constitution in juxtaposition with the impugned provisions generate? In my opinion it directs our gaze to the historical-political context of both laws, the former a reflection of a 'second independence' and the latter a British colonial law dating back to 1930. In disinterring the object and purpose of the Constitution, I hear loud and clear, an enduring commitment to protecting the fundamental rights of all citizens of Kenya, regardless of difference.

45. The upshot of the foregoing is that I would allow the Petitioners' case and move to strike out the impugned provisions with immediate effect, and grant the declarations sought in the Petition.

Dated, signed and delivered at Nairobi this 13th day of December, 2022

....

W. GAITHO

---

95. *Navtej Singh Johar & Ors v Union of India thr Secretary ministry of Law and Justice* [2018] Supreme Court of India Writ Petition (Criminal) No. 76 of 2016 [89].

PART 2

PRIVACY AND DISCRIMINATION

7

Laskey, Jaggard and Brown v United Kingdom (European Court of Human Rights):

A Queer Judgment

Alexandra Grolimund and Alexander Maine

Introduction

Laskey, Jaggard and Brown v The United Kingdom, decided by the European Court of Human Rights (ECtHR),[1] is the consequence of 'Operation Spanner,' an infamous investigation of the London Metropolitan Police into the activities of Bondage-Domination-Sado-Masochism (BDSM) between a group of men in the late 1980s and 1990s in Greater Manchester. Convicted of assault occasioning actual bodily harm and sentenced to prison in *R v Brown*,[2] three of the men lodged an application with the ECtHR in 1997. Ultimately, they were unsuccessful, as the Court unanimously rejected their appeal.

The practice of BDSM can accommodate varied sexual and non-sexual behaviours and activities between consenting adults of all genders and sexualities. The recreational infliction, enjoyment, and anticipation of pain and control are widely misunderstood. Society struggles to comprehend the sexual pleasure often related to acts that may not appear pleasurable. The use of artifice and performance reaffirms BDSM as an othered act that is stigmatised and practised by a minority. As Rubin states, 'the most despised sexual castes currently include transsexuals, transvestites, fetishists, sadomasochists, [and] sex workers such as prostitutes and porn models.'[3] Khan has written that 'BDSM disrupts social categories because it appropriates roles and activities not recognized as erotic or pleasurable in mainstream consciousness,'[4] while Ferris describes the implications of *Laskey* as a 'global legal blind spot facing the BDSM community concerning

---

1. *Laskey and Others v The United Kingdom* (Applications no. 21627/93; 21628/93; 21974/93) [1997] 24 EHRR 39.
2. [1993] UKHL 19, [1994] 1 AC 212.
3. Gayle Rubin, 'Thinking Sex: Notes for a Radical Theory of the Politics of Sexuality,' in *Pleasure and Danger: Exploring Female Sexuality*, ed. Carol Vance (New York: Routledge, 1984), 151.
4. Ummni Khan, 'Kinky Identity and Practice in Relation to the Law,' in *Research Handbook on Gender, Sexuality and Law,* ed. Chris Ashford and Alexander Maine (London: Edward Elgar, 2020), 362.

the affirmative defence of consent.'[5] Therefore, in using queer legal theory to rewrite the case, the normative underpinnings of the law can be revealed and critiqued.

The case designates a curiously wide margin of appreciation afforded to States by the Court for cases of sadomasochism, in an area of the law (the 'intimate area of an individual's sexual life') where this margin is usually narrow.[6] The right to privacy enshrined in Article 8 of the European Convention on Human Rights (ECHR) incorporates physical, psychological and moral integrity, extending to sexual orientation and sexual life, in the protected sphere of 'private life.'[7] In its contemporary Guide on Article 8, the Court references *Laskey* twice: once in reference the Court's holding that the elements of 'sexual life' are an important part of the protected 'personal sphere,' and secondly to underscore that 'Article 8 does not prohibit criminalisation of all private sexual activity.'[8] It is the latter exclusionary reference to the case that cements it, alongside incest, as an exception to the protected area of sexual life. The topic of sadomasochism, owing to the precedent set in *Laskey*, maintains an awkward space in human rights law.

Perhaps most importantly, the decision signifies the Court's affirmation of *R v Brown*, and the underlying sentiment that BDSM, in the view of the law, is a morally distasteful form of sexuality that borders on the edge of legal acceptability. Scholars have long noted this tension, and its incongruous equivalency between sexual violence and sexual pleasure that is evidenced in lived experiences of sadomasochism (SM) practitioners.[9] Furthermore, SM as a 'threat' of violence is, in the view of the Court, not only one to the individual but society at large.[10] Criticism of *Laskey* echoes the calls made immediately following *Brown*, that the Court merely adds a 'gloss of legitimacy' to what is ultimately untenable legal reasoning.[11]

The consistently negative decisions handed down by the ECtHR against SM practitioners (also involving 'heterosexual' encounters), including *K.A. and A.D. v Belgium*,[12]

---

5. Stephan Ferris 'Red, White, and BLACK AND BLUE: the American Criminalization of BDSM,' in *Research Handbook on Gender, Sexuality and Law*, ed. Chris Ashford and Alexander Maine (London: Edward Elgar, 2020), 495.

6. European Court of Human Rights, 'Guide on Article 8 of the European Convention on Human Rights: Right to Respect for Private and Family Life, Home and Correspondence,' 47 at 169, accessed 11 December 2023, https://www.echr.coe.int/documents/guide_art_8_eng.pdf.

7. Article 8 protects against arbitrary interferences with private and family life, home, and correspondence by public authorities (*Libert v France*, paras. 40–42). The concept of 'private life' is broad and incapable of exhaustive definition (*Niemietz v Germany*, para. 29; *Pretty v the United Kingdom*, para. 61; *Peck v the United Kingdom*, para. 57).

8. European Court of Human Rights, 'Guide on Article 8 of the European Convention on Human Rights: Right to Respect for Private and Family Life, Home and Correspondence,' 47 at 169 and 171.

9. Carl Stychin, *Law's Desire Sexuality and the Limits of Justice* (London: Routledge 2013); Ummni Khan, *Vicarious Kinks: S/M in the Socio-Legal Imaginary* (Toronto: University of Toronto Press 2014); Rubin, 'Thinking Sex: Notes for a Radical Theory of the Politics of Sexuality,' 3; Darren Langdridge and Meg Barker, 'Situating Sadomasochism,' in *Safe, sane and consensual: Contemporary perspectives on sadomasochism*, ed. Darren Langdridge and Meg Barker (London: Palgrave Macmillan 2007); Sarah Beresford, 'Lesbian Spanners: A Re-Appraisal of UK Consensual Sadomasochism Laws,' *Liverpool Law Review* 37 (2016), 63.

10. Leslie J Moran, '*Laskey v The United Kingdom*: Learning the Limits of Privacy,' *The Modern Law Review* 61 (1998) 77, 81.

11. Moran, '*Laskey v The United Kingdom*.'

12. [2005] ECHR 110, [2005] ECHR 110.

Pay v UK,[13] and *Mosley v UK*,[14] point to the notion that the Court generally 'may be uncomfortable with the very concept of appraising, evaluating and adjudicating on so-called "non-traditional" sexualities.'[15] Though the decision in Laskey was premised on the 'protection of health,' this suggests a more engrained moralistic unease at non-normative sexuality. In turn, SM is deprived of identity-based protections of sexual orientation.

Background

The case came at a time when queer people, especially given the ongoing HIV/AIDS epidemic, faced rampant discrimination under Thatcher's Conservative government. Though the Sexual Offences Act 1967 partially decriminalised homosexual acts between men, legally sanctioned homophobia and discrimination were widespread. In 1987, the Metropolitan Police's Obscene Publications Squad launched 'Operation Spanner' at the tail-end of a larger 10-year investigation into men involved in sadomasochistic sex 'rings.'[16] In the course of 'routine' investigations, the police had been passed videotapes of men engaged in consensual sadomasochistic activities that were purported to be 'snuff' films.[17] The police dug up gardens in search of dead bodies and carried out dozens of interviews (some reports claim more than 100) with prospective defendants.[18]

Colin Laskey, Roland Jaggard, and Tony Brown were among a group of 16 in total, charged and convicted for various offences, namely assault, as a result. In December 1990, at the Central Criminal Court in London, the men pleaded guilty on advice of their lawyers, and no jury was involved; their guilty plea followed Judge James Rant's decision that consent would not provide a defence to the charges of assault against the men. Judge Rant accepted that all the men had consented, no money had been exchanged for the videos, and that the videos were not meant for wider circulation. The acts in question were described as 'degrading and vicious.' Recognizing the decision's restrictions on private sexual acts, he underscored the court's edifying duties, stating at the sentencing:

> Much has been said about individual liberty and the rights people have to do what they want with their own bodies, but the courts must draw the line between what is acceptable in a civilised society and what is not.[19]

---

13. [2009] IRLR 139.

14. [2011] 53 E.H.R.R. 30.

15. Francesca Romana Ammaturo, 'The Council of Europe and the Creation of LGBT Identities through Language and Discourse: A Critical Analysis of Case Law and Institutional Practices,' *The International Journal of Human Rights* 23 (2019), 575, 583.

16. Michael Hames, 'Operation Spanner,' in *Dirty squad: the story of the Obscene Publications Branch* (London: Little Brown and Company, 2000).

17. Snuff films refer to films which claim to depict scenes of bona fide, in contrast to fictional, homicide. There is often a sexual overtone involved in references to the purported existence of snuff films: Hames, 'Operation Spanner,' 16, 158, 162.

18. Colin Richardson, 'Myths, Half-Truths and Fantasies,' *Gay Times* (1992).

19. 'Jail for the Men Who Ran Sex and Torture Group,' *Daily Mail*, 20 December 1990.

Doing away with any question of prejudice, he said: 'This is not a witch-hunt against homosexuals. The unlawful conduct before the court would result equally in the prosecution of heterosexuals or bisexuals.'[20]

Although their appeal was dismissed, their sentences were shortened and leave was granted to appeal to the House of Lords.[21] The question before the Lords centred on charges under the Offences Against the Person Act 1861 (OAPA), of assault occasioning actual bodily harm (ABH) and more serious wounding/ grievous bodily harm (GBH). The question before the Lords was whether consent could be used as a defence for harm amounting to ABH or greater. Notably, given past case law, the Court's answer in the negative would indicate that a victim's consent is legally irrelevant, if the harm caused was more than 'transient and trifling' (rather than serious injury).[22]

The House of Lords dismissed the men's final appeals in a narrow 3:2 decision. *R v Brown* affirmed—and established the precedent—that consent is no defence to bodily harm. Through the Lords' detangling of acceptable versus non-acceptable exemptions of consensual harm, the Brown judgment also established, or in a sense summarized, the 'lawful' activities constituting a 'good reason' for which consent can defend harm, including surgery, ritual circumcision, tattooing, ear-piercing, parental chastisement and violent sports and games.[23] Consent for the purposes of sexual gratification was, therefore, deemed no good reason for harm. The judgment is best summarized by Lord Templeman's words: 'Society is entitled and bound to protect itself against a cult of violence. Pleasure derived from the infliction of pain is an evil thing. Cruelty is uncivilised.'[24]

The impact of the case was unquestionably detrimental to the men's lives and resulted in an outpouring of protest. The men's personal lives and reputations were irrevocably tarnished, some losing their jobs, as the press named and shamed them.[25] Eight of the fifteen defendants received prison sentences, some to over four years.[26] But the men had gained international support in the form of coordinated organisations such as the Spanner Trust, which was set up to support the men in their appeal and lobby for a change in the law.[27] 'Countdown on Spanner' formed as the political activist group in defence of the men and sadomasochism, holding public demonstrations for

20. John Steele, 'Torture Vice Gang Sentenced,' *The Daily Telegraph*, 20 December 1990.

21. It asked the Lords to ascertain the resulting point of law: 'Where A wounds or assaults B occasioning him actual bodily harm in the course of a sado-masochistic encounter, does the prosecution have to prove lack of consent on the part of B before they can establish A's guilt under section 20 or section 47 of the Offences against the Person Act 1861?' Section 47 refers to assault occasioning actual bodily harm (ABH), and Section 20 to the more serious offence of wounding or grievous bodily harm (GBH).

22. *R v Donovan* [1934] 2 KB 498.

23. *R v Brown* [1993] 2 WLR 556, [1994] 1 A.C. 212; Templeman at 231, Jauncey at 245.

24.   *R v Brown* at 237.

25. *Operation Spanner—The Roland Jaggard Interview (Part 2)* (Directed by Douglas O'Keeffe, 2020), accessed 11 December 2023, https://www.youtube.com/watch?v=nzCiJVXJbiY.

26. On appeal by five of the men, the sentences were commuted: Stephen Ward, 'Masochists Win Right to Appeal over Convictions,' *The Independent*, 19 January 1995, accessed 11 December 2023, https://www.independent.co.uk/news/masochists-win-right-to-appeal-over-convictions-1568640.html; 'The Guilty Men and Their Sentences,' *The Times*, 20 December 1990.

27. 'About The Spanner Trust,' The Spanner Trust, accessed 11 December 2023, http://www.spannertrust.org/.

'SM rights' in addition to educational events; their annual 'S&M Pride' took place with reports of 1,000 protesters marching through London.[28]

At the time of *Brown*, the UK had not yet passed the Human Rights Act 1998, and commentators pointed to the lack of serious consideration for human rights by the Lords as also underpinning their views.[29] So, the prospect of challenging the case in Strasbourg was hopeful. The European Commission of Human Rights held consecutive hearings on 18 January 1995 to deliberate whether to declare the men's applications admissible. The three complainants filed alleged violations of Articles 7 (their convictions were the result of an unforeseen application of a pro-vision of the criminal law), 8 (these convictions violated their right to respect for private life) and 14 (discrimination in the enjoyment of rights and freedoms), of the Convention,[30] the Court only deeming the Article 8 claim admissible.[31] In their application, with reference to Article 8, the men alleged that the acts themselves were discriminated against, compared to others involving more serious forms of injury (e.g. boxing), and the Court accepted this, noting the case raised 'serious issues of fact and law.'[32] The men had finally won the right to challenge their convictions at the ECtHR.

Queering *Laskey, Jaggard and Brown*

What makes this case so vital is that it is obvious that while the Court's argumentation is based on the cover of health, it is steeped in broader concerns about morality and sexuality. Moran explains that the politics of exclusion are masked by the 'medical-isation of the practitioners by a rhetoric of 'public health.'[33] The case equates sexual pleasure with violence—this necessitates a detangling of these ideas via a queer lens. This is especially timely, given the case's positionality as the leading authority on the question of sadomasochism more than a quarter of a century on from *Laskey*.

As Moran points out, there is 'little doubt' that the Court's interpretation is rooted in its view that the men's actions were ones of extreme violence and even torture,

---

28. Nick Cohen, '"Perverts" on Parade for the Right to Practise Safe Sadism,' *The Independent*, 2 September 1995, accessed 11 December 2023, https://www.independent.co.uk/news/uk/home-news/perverts-on-parade-for-the-right-to-practise-safe-sadism-1599215.html.

29. Steve Hedley, 'Sado-Masochism, Human Rights and the House of Lords,' *The Cambridge Law Journal* 52 (1993), 194, 194.

30. Applications No. 21627/93, 21826/93 and 21974/93.

31. The Article 14 claim was rejected as having been requested out of time; the Commission noted it was introduced to it outside of the 6-month time-limit (after the House of Lords' decision) within which a filing is to be made. It dismissed the Article 7 complaint, finding that, given appropriate legal advice, the applicants should have reasonably foreseen their conduct as offences, which were in their view already established by past case law as argued in *Brown*. See *Laskey, Jaggard and Brown v U.K.*, Hum Rts Case Dig 6 (1995) 54.

32. Interestingly, alongside Laskey, Jaggard and Brown's applications, a separate submission was made on behalf of five other applicants who were practicing sadomasochists involved in the activist campaigns following *Brown* (Application No. 22170/93). They claimed that as a direct result of *Brown*, their freedom had been impacted and that their sexual, sadomasochistic behaviours were under threat. Their submission invokes not only Article 8 but also Article 14 of the Convention in conjunction with the former. It was declared inadmissible.

33. Moran, '*Laskey v The United Kingdom*,' 10, 83.

as analogous also to rape and sexual abuse.[34] It is a clear demonstration of how the Court misconstrues sexual practice as the threat of sexual violence.[35] Historically speaking, we can see this mirroring scepticism towards queer men as laws criminalizing homosexuality focused on conduct-based sexual activity. Yet, the Court's debate is an odd reconfiguration as the case goes beyond same-sex physical intimacy in compounding this with the element of sadomasochistic actions. This poses a particular conundrum for the Court. The case is a significant examination of queer sexuality and allows for a more inclusive consideration of the European Convention on Human Rights.

In using queer legal theory to reinterpret *Laskey, Jaggard and Brown*, we can challenge and resist the heteronormative nature of the law, interrogate the 'majority's story and weaken its hold on our collective imagination.'[36] A queer approach assumes that judgment-writing is guided by certain queer principles; these centre on deconstructing dominant notions of what is 'normal' and deviant, by challenging binary categories of sex, gender and sexuality, and in turn centering those marginalized by such categories.[37] We align with these principles in re-writing this judgment.

Ultimately, the case demonstrates an articulation of Rubin's sexual hierarchy, in which the 'despised sexual castes of fetishists, sadomasochists, and porn models'[38] are criminally sanctioned. *Laskey* reinforces 'institutionalism of an ontological order as a moral order,'[39] based on preferential sex and sexuality, to which sadomasochism acts as a queer challenge to the law, particularly highlighted by the *unmanliness* of the activities. This is perhaps most evident in Judge Petitti's concurring decision, where he blatantly dissociates 'intimacy and dignity as a protected facet of [a person's] privacy' from 'his baseness or the promotion of criminal immorality'—the appellants' actions apparently being re-characterised. Further, this hierarchical organisation of sexuality is manifest in the gendered need to protect the 'vulnerable.' This pollution management assumes the supposed contagion[40] that gay and bisexual men are guilty of spreading through conducting deviant sexual acts. Stychin described the case as symbolic, in that it reaffirmed 'definitions of normalcy, [...] designed to expurgate the gay man from the realm of the social to a pathologised sphere of decay, illness, and to an avoidably brutal, and, ironically, seductive death.'[41] Finally, this protection of the vulnerable is also hypocritical, an obvious reinforcement of homophobia in its comparison with, and support of the House of Lords' decision in *Wilson*, in which a husband branded his initials on his wife's buttocks (which did require medical treatment). The court justified exonerating Wilson because the participants were a wedded couple, and the incident

---

34. Moran, '*Laskey v The United Kingdom*,' 10, 80.
35. Moran, '*Laskey v The United Kingdom*,' 10, 82.
36. Ericka Rackley, 'The Art and Craft of Writing Judgments: Notes on the Feminist Judgments Project,' in *Feminist Judgments: From Theory to Practice,* ed. Rosemary Hunter, Clare McGlynn and Erika Rackley (London: Hart, 2010), 33.
37. Alex Sharpe, 'Queering Judgment: The Case of Gender Identity Fraud,' *Journal of Criminal Law* 81(5) (2017), 417–435.
38. Rubin, *Thinking Sex*, 3.
39. Moran, '*Laskey v The United Kingdom*,' 10, 83.
40. Stychin, *Law's Desire*, 9, 126.
41. Stychin, *Law's Desire*, 117.

took place in the sanctified space of the 'marital home.'[42] Therefore, this case was chosen as a significant symbolic rejection of queer sexuality by the Court, reliant on homophobia, prejudice, and a deliberate misunderstanding of the lives of the queer men involved and their consent. In this queer judgment, we seek to provide a more nuanced and inclusive adjudication.

---

42. *R v Wilson* (1996) 2 Cr App Rep 241; Khan, *Kinky identity and practice in relation to the law*, 4, 364.

LASKEY, JAGGARD AND BROWN V THE UNITED KINGDOM

JUDGMENT

19 February 1997

I. AS TO THE FACTS

[1] The case originated in three applications by Colin Laskey, Roland Jaggard and Anthony Brown against the United Kingdom. The case was referred to the Court by the European Commission of Human Rights; their request was to obtain a decision as to whether the facts of the case disclosed a breach of Article 8 of the Convention.

[2] In 1987, in the course of routine investigations into other matters, the police came into possession of a number of videos made during sadomasochistic encounters involving the applicants and other men. As a result, the applicants, and several other of the men, were charged with offences including assault and wounding, relating to sadomasochistic activities that had taken place over a ten-year period.

[3] The activities took place at several locations. Video cameras were used to record events and the tapes copied and distributed amongst members of the group. The prosecution was largely based on the contents of those videotapes.

[4] The acts consisted of hot wax, sandpaper, fishhooks, and needles placed in or on the genitalia and ritualistic beatings with the hands, stinging nettles, spiked belts and a cat-o'-nine tails. These activities were consensual and conducted in private for the achievement of sexual gratification. The infliction of pain did not lead to any instances of infection, permanent injury or the need for medical attention. The video tapes had not been sold or distributed outside the group.

[5] The applicants pleaded guilty to the assault charges after the trial judge ruled that they could not rely on the consent of the "victims" as an answer to the prosecution case, the judge noting "... the unlawful conduct now before the court would be dealt with equally in the prosecution of heterosexuals or bisexuals if carried out by them. The homosexuality of the defendants is only the background against which the case must be viewed."

[6] The men were sentenced to terms of imprisonment up to 4.5 years, for various counts of assault occasioning actual bodily harm and wounding and aiding and abetting these offences, under sections 47 and 20 of the Offences against the Person Act 1861 (OAPA). Mr. Laskey was also charged with aiding and abetting keeping a disorderly house and possession of an indecent photograph of a child.

[7] The applicants appealed against the conviction and sentence. In February 1992, the Court of Appeal, Criminal Division, dismissed the appeal but reduced the sentences, since the applicants did not appreciate their actions were criminal. They appealed to the House of Lords, the certified point of law of public importance to be considered:

> "Where A wounds or assaults B occasioning him actual bodily harm in the course of a sado-masochistic encounter, does the prosecution have to prove lack of consent on the part of B before they can establish A's guilt under section 20 or section 47 of the 1861 Act?"

On 11 March 1993, the appeal, known as the case of *R. v Brown* ([1993] 2 All England Law Reports 75), was dismissed by a majority of the House of Lords in a 3:2 decision. Lord Templeman, in the majority, held that the question is whether consent as a defence to the infliction of bodily harm should be extended to said harm in the course of sadomasochistic encounters. Lord Templeman, summarizing the majority opinion, held:

> "... In principle there is a difference between violence which is incidental and violence which is inflicted for the indulgence of cruelty. The violence of sado-masochistic encounters involves the indulgence of cruelty by sadists and the degradation of victims. Such violence is injurious to the participants and unpredictably dangerous. I am not prepared to invent a defence of consent for sado-masochistic encounters which breed and glorify cruelty ... Society is entitled and bound to protect itself against a cult of violence. Pleasure derived from the infliction of pain is an evil thing. Cruelty is uncivilised."

Lord Jauncey of Tullichettle, also in the majority, found that:

> "Considerable emphasis was placed by the appellants on the well-ordered and secret manner in which their activities were conducted and upon the fact that these activities had resulted in no injuries which required medical attention. There was, it was said, no question of proselytising by the appellants..."

Be that as it may, in considering the public interest it would be wrong to look only at the activities of the appellants alone, there being no suggestion that they and their associates are the only practitioners of homosexual sado-masochism in England and Wales. The Court must therefore consider the possibility that these activities are practised by others and by others who are not so controlled or responsible as the appellants are claiming to be. Without going into details of all the rather curious activities in which the appellants engaged it would appear to be good luck rather than good judgment which has prevented serious injury from occurring. Wounds can easily become septic if not properly treated, the free flow of blood from a person who is HIV-positive or who has AIDS can infect another and an inflicter who is carried away by sexual excitement or by drink or drugs could very easily inflict pain and injury beyond the level to which the receiver had consented.

Lord Slynn of Hadley, dissenting, found the current law as allowing consenting adults in private to carry out sadomasochistic acts, so long as said acts did not result in serious bodily harm. Ultimately, the question is a matter of policy involving extremely important social and moral factors, and regulated by changing attitudes; the legislature, rather than the paternalism of the courts, is best poised to regulate such conduct and its place within the criminal law.

[8] The applicants contested their convictions amounted to an unlawful and unjustifiable interference with their right to respect for their private life. They asked the Court to find a violation of their right to respect for their private lives through the expression of their sexual personality, as guaranteed by Article 8 of the Convention.

[9] Widespread press coverage detailed the proceedings. All the applicants lost their jobs and some required extensive psychiatric treatment.

II. RELEVANT DOMESTIC LAW

Offences against the person
The Offences against the Person Act 1861

[10] Section 20 of the OAPA provides:

> "Whosoever shall unlawfully and maliciously wound or inflict any grievous bodily harm upon any other person, either with or without any weapon or instrument, ... shall be liable ... to [imprisonment] ... for not more than five years."

Case-law defines a wound as the breaking of the whole skin, not merely the outer layer or epidermis.

[11] Section 47 of the OAPA provides:

> "Whosoever shall be convicted on indictment of any assault occasioning actual bodily harm shall be liable ... to imprisonment for not more than five years."

Actual bodily harm is defined as "any hurt or injury calculated to interfere with health or comfort" (*Liksey J, in R. v Miller* [1954] 2 Queen's Bench Reports 282, at 292).

Case-law prior to R. v Brown

[12] In *R v Donovan* ([1934] 2 King's Bench Reports, at 498), the accused had caned a girl for the purposes of sexual gratification, with her consent. Swift J held:

> "It is an unlawful act to beat another person with such a degree of violence that the infliction of actual bodily harm is a probable consequence, and when such an act is proved, consent is immaterial."

[13] In Attorney-General's Reference (No. 6 of 1980) ([1980] Queen's Bench Reports, at 715) two men publicly settled a quarrel with a consensual fist fight. Lord Lane CJ held:

> "It is not in the public interest that people should try to cause or should cause each other actual bodily harm for no good reason. Minor struggles are another matter. So, in our judgment, it is immaterial whether the act occurs in private or in public; it is an assault if actual bodily harm is intended and/or caused. This means that most fights will be unlawful regardless of consent. Nothing which we have said is intended to cast doubt upon the accepted legality of properly conducted games and sports, lawful chastisement or correction, reasonable surgical interference, dangerous exhibitions, etc. These apparent exceptions can be justified as involving the exercise of a legal right, in the case of chastisement or correction, or as needed in the public interest, in the other cases."

Case-law prior subsequent to R. v Brown

[14] In *R v Wilson* ([1996] 3 Weekly Law Reports, at 125) the Court of Appeal, Criminal Division, allowed the appeal of a man convicted of assault occasioning actual bodily harm for branding his wife's buttocks with her consent, using a hot knife. Lord Justice Russell stated:

> "... there is no factual comparison to be made between the instant case and the facts of either *Donovan* or *Brown*: Mrs Wilson not only consented to that which the appellant did, she instigated it. There was no aggressive intent on the part of the appellant ...
>
> We do not think that we are entitled to assume that the method adopted by the appellant and his wife was any more dangerous or painful than tattooing ...
>
> Consensual activity between husband and wife, in the privacy of the matrimonial home, is not, in our judgment, a proper matter for criminal investigation, let alone criminal prosecution."

III. AS TO THE LAW

ALLEGED VIOLATION OF ARTICLE 8 OF THE CONVENTION

[15] The applicants contended that their prosecution and convictions for assault and wounding in the course of consensual sado-masochistic activities between adults was in breach of Article 8 of the Convention, which provides:

> "1. Everyone has the right to respect for his private and family life, his home and his correspondence.
>
> 2. There shall be no interference by a public authority with the exercise of this right except such as is in accordance with the law and is necessary in a democratic society in the interests of national security, public safety or the economic well-being of the country, for the prevention of disorder or crime, for the protection of health or morals, or for the protection of the rights and freedoms of others."

It was common ground among those appearing before the Court that the criminal proceedings against the applicants which resulted in their conviction constituted an "interference by a public authority" with the applicants' right to respect for their private life. It was similarly undisputed that the interference had been "in accordance with the law." Furthermore, the Commission and the applicants accepted the Government's assertion that the interference pursued the legitimate aim of the "protection of health or morals," within the meaning of the second paragraph of Article 8, however contended the conclusions drawn by the Government.

[16] The Court observes that not every sexual activity carried out behind closed doors necessarily falls within the scope of Article 8. That is, activities that are non-consensual, forced, or harmful to others, in particularly children, cannot be deemed to be wholly private. These activities demonstrate a disregard for privacy and invite scrutiny due to the fact that non-consensual sexual activity, by its nature, is a harmful and unwanted act, criminalised in all European jurisdictions. However, in the present case, the applicants were involved in *consensual* sado-masochistic activities for purposes of sexual gratification. There can be no doubt that sexual orientation and activity concern an intimate and important aspect of private life (see, mutatis mutandis, the *Dudgeon v the United Kingdom* judgment of 22 October 1981, Series A no. 45, p. 21, para. 52). Further, it is contended that a matter of consensual BDSM sexual activity is to be interpreted as a manifestation of personality, therefore falling within Article 8 as same-sex sexual activity did within Dudgeon. Therefore, it should not be interfered with by a public authority.

[17] This point is made despite the fact that a considerable number of people were involved in the activities in question, which included, inter alia, the provision of several specially equipped "chambers" to engage in sexual activities, the filming of many videotapes which were distributed among the members, and the invitation of new participants (see paragraph 3 above). Assuming, therefore, that the prosecution and conviction of the applicants amounted to an interference with their private life, the question arises whether such an interference was "necessary in a democratic society" within the meaning of the second paragraph of Article 8.

"Necessary in a democratic society"

[18] The applicants maintained that the interference in issue could not be regarded as "necessary in a democratic society." This submission was contested by the Government and by a majority of the Commission.

[19] In support of their submission, the applicants alleged that all those involved in the sado-masochistic encounters were willing adult participants; that participation in the acts was carefully restricted and controlled and was limited to persons with like-minded sado-masochistic proclivities who chose to participate; that the acts were not witnessed by the public at large and that there was no danger or likelihood that they would ever

be so witnessed and therefore can be considered private; that no serious or permanent injury had been sustained, no infection had been caused to the wounds, and that no medical treatment had been required. Furthermore, no complaint was ever made to the police—who learnt about the applicants' activities by chance.

The potential for severe injury or for moral corruption was regarded by the applicants as a matter of speculation. Indeed, as this did not occur, it is not for the State to interfere with Article 8 rights on the basis that serious injury *may* happen in the course of sexual activity.

[20] The applicants submitted that their case should be viewed as one involving matters of sexual expression, rather than violence. With due regard to this consideration, the line beyond which consent is no defence to physical injury should only be drawn at the level of intentional or reckless causing of serious disabling injury.

[21] The State is entitled to punish acts of violence that cause harm, particularly those that cause serious injury, and are not trifling or transient. However, it should not entertain punishing acts of consensual sexual expression that may encompass forms of sexualised or performed violence. A distinction must be made between violent criminal acts, on the one hand, and sexual acts that incorporate violence in the pursuit of pleasure, on the other hand. Sexual expression and experience that incorporates the infliction and reception of pain, also known as Bondage, Domination, and Sadomasochism (BDSM) can be a significant element of a person's private life. BDSM forms a distinct and significant sexual subculture, practised across groups of people of all sexual orientations alike and should be treated as if analogous to sexual orientation. It is true that in the present case some of these acts could well be compared to "genital torture" and a Contracting State could not be said to have an obligation to tolerate acts of torture. However, these acts must be considered in their context of BDSM sexual relationships between consenting individuals who were part of a larger group that worked together to ensure such acts were conducted safely and consensually. Therefore, they cannot be compared to acts of torture prohibited by the Convention. The Government further contended that the criminal law should seek to deter certain forms of behaviour on public health grounds but also for broader moral reasons. The State authorities' decision to prosecute should have paid regard to this; it seems it was spurred instead, as stated by Lord Jauncey of Tullichettle, by the potential for harm based on an unfavourable view of non-normative sexual activities perceived as "violence," or even more troubling, a discriminatory view of the practitioners and their sexual orientation.

The Court finds that Contracting States should enjoy a wide margin of appreciation to consider all the public policy options, however, in respect of public morals, there should be respect for consent as an important arbiter of public morals, and not seek to determine such morals from a heteronormative standpoint.

[22] The Commission noted that the injuries that were or could be caused by the applicants' activities were of a significant nature and degree, and that the conduct in

question was, on any view, of an extreme character. That being said, the "extreme" character of an individual's activities does not automatically necessitate State intervention. As noted in the national courts, other activities may also amount to such significant injuries, such as rugby and boxing, and are not treated in the same criminal manner. The "publicness" of such activities may be the distinction between such acts and BDSM, particularly significant in recognizing why they are socially acceptable, when BDSM is not. This is especially true when, as found, there was no wider "threat" of proselytization or harm; though Lord Jauncey of Tullichettle notes protection is necessary as sadomasochistic activity among the wider public is surely occurring, he himself admittedly has no evidence of this and "no information as to whether such situations have occurred in relation to other sadomasochistic practitioners." Surely such evidence would be apparent if these activities were spatially, demonstrably harmful to a wider public.

[23] According to the Court's established case-law, the notion of necessity implies that the interference corresponds to a pressing social need and, in particular, that it is proportionate to the legitimate aim pursued; in determining whether an interference is "necessary in a democratic society," the Court will take into account that a margin of appreciation is left to the national authorities (see, inter alia, the *Olsson v Sweden* (no. 1) judgment of 24 March 1988, Series A no. 130, pp. 31–32, para. 67), whose decision remains subject to review by the Court for conformity with the requirements of the Convention. The scope of this margin of appreciation is not identical in each case but will vary according to the context. Relevant factors include the nature of the Convention right in issue, its importance for the individual and the nature of the activities concerned (see the *Buckley v the United Kingdom*, judgment of 25 September 1996, Reports of Judgments and Decisions 1996–IV, pp. 1291–92, para. 74).

[24] The Court considers that one of the roles which the State is unquestionably entitled to undertake is to seek to regulate, through the operation of the criminal law, activities which involve the infliction of physical harm. However, in keeping with earlier comments regarding the *Dudgeon* outcome (*Dudgeon v the United Kingdom*, judgment of 22 October 1981), the State's interference in matters of sexual orientation amounting to BDSM relations should follow a similarly determined manner. That is, if harm occurs within a consensual BDSM sexual occasion, that harm can be deemed as being a pre-determined expectation of the activity that manifests as part of a person's sexual orientation and personality. What is at stake is related, on the one hand, to public health, and, on the other, to the personal autonomy of the individual. Where consent is demonstrated, the limitation of personal autonomy should be closely restricted. In this case, where there is no evidential consequence for public health, such a restriction is of grave concern. Though the primacy of verified consent in the law of [sexual] assault is obviously procedurally essential, and is at the core of various practitioner-created ethical models of BDSM (e.g. 'Safe, Sane, and Consensual' or SSC and 'Risk-Aware Consensual Kink' or RACK), the nuances of sexual communication require us to think beyond mere consent, especially within sexual politics. This allows us to consider sexual

experiences in context, incorporating questions of pleasure and desire, in addition to mititgation of injury.

[25] The determination of the level of harm that should be tolerated by the law in situations where the "victim" consents, is in the first instance a matter for the State concerned since what is at stake is related, on the one hand, to public health considerations and to the general deterrent effect of the criminal law, and, on the other, to the personal autonomy and right to private life of the individual.

[26] The applicants have contended that, in the circumstances of the case, the behaviour in question formed part of private morality which is not the State's business to regulate. In their submission, the matters for which they were prosecuted and convicted concerned only private sexual behaviour and sexual personality. The Court is persuaded by this submission. It is evident from the facts established by the national courts that the applicants' sado-masochistic activities involved a degree of injury or wounding that, although perceived as extreme by some, to those well-versed in BDSM practice, and the accompanying rules and language relevant to the cohesive BDSM community, can be characterised as part and parcel of the activities (frameworks and education tools are in place in this community that address such risks, for instance the 'Safe, Sane and Consensual' and 'Risk-Aware Consensual Kink' frameworks, mentioned in para. 24). Of course, the case is distinguished from those applications which have previously been examined by the Court concerning consensual same-sex sexual activities in private between adults where no such feature was present (see the *Dudgeon* judgment cited above, the *Norris v Ireland* judgment of 26 October 1988, Series A no. 142, and the *Modinos v Cyprus* judgment of 22 April 1993, Series A no. 259). However, this does not deter the Court's reasoning that such behaviour manifests itself as a part of one's sexual orientation and the private, consensual nature of the activity remains within the realms of one's right to privacy and autonomy.

[27] The Court also accepts the applicants' submission that no prosecution should have been brought against them, since their injuries were not severe and no medical treatment had been required. This, in particular, is informed by the fact that no complaint was made by the applicants in the immediate or long-term aftermath of the events in question, nor was medical advice sought. It is evident from the facts established by the national courts that the applicants' sadomasochistic activities did not beg the need for any police or medical intervention whatsoever. It is reiterated that the police would have had no knowledge of the private sexual activities, had they not stumbled upon the video tapes. Lord Templeman (see paragraph 7 above) considered the activities to be "unpredictably dangerous," however one must consider the prediction and expectation of the activities within the context of the BDSM practitioner. Certainly, State authorities are entitled to have regard not only for the actual seriousness of the harm caused but also the potential harm; however, this harm was mitigated, expected, and considered by the practitioners, while a risk of harm may have also heightened the enjoyment of such acts. Therefore, as with other activities that contain risk of or actual harm

(contact sports, piercing, and tattooing for instance), this case does not represent a valid incursion by the State.

[28] The applicants have further submitted that they were singled out partly because of the authorities' bias against same-sex sexual activity and those associated with it. They referred to the recent judgment in the *Wilson* case (see paragraph 14 above), where, in their view, similar behaviour in the context of a heterosexual couple was not considered to deserve criminal punishment. The Court finds evidence in support of the applicants' allegations in the judgment of the House of Lords, which uses prejudicial and stigmatizing language in the distinguishing of such acts against those "manly" diversions which are worthy of protection from prosecution. It seems incongruous for the trial judge when passing sentence to state that "the unlawful conduct now before the court would be dealt with equally in the prosecution of heterosexuals or bisexuals if carried out by them" when the *Wilson* judgment tells us the opposite. It is further clear that the *Wilson* judgment has a similar deal of risk of infection and permanent scarification but conducted within a heterosexual married relationship. Moreover, it is clear from the *Brown* judgment that the opinions of the majority were motivated in part by a disgust and revulsion at the actions committed by a group of men. Lord Lowry's assertion that the activities can "scarcely be regarded as a manly diversion" (page 30) appears to distinguish between those acts that are worthy and natural and those that are unmanly, dishonourable, and indeed, unnatural. Lord Templeman stated that "Society is entitled and bound to protect itself against a cult of violence. Pleasure derived from the infliction of pain is an evil thing. Cruelty is uncivilised." Such a moral distinction between civility and cruelty is surely beyond the realms of the behaviour taking place. The Court finds evidence of bias on the basis of sexual orientation, not only in support of the applicants' allegations in the conduct of the proceedings against them, but also in the judgment of the House of Lords. It is clear from the judgment that the opinions of the majority were based on a prurient interest in the practices involved only insofar as they pertain to same-sex practitioners of sadomasochism. Further, it seems this interest averts its gaze as soon as the "private sphere" concerns an opposite-sex matrimonial home, which causes us to question the privileging of the matrimonial home. Here, the Court points to the words of the trial judge in *Wilson*, decided in the UK Court of Appeal in 1996, that: "Consensual activity between husband and wife, in the privacy of the matrimonial home, is not…normally a proper matter for criminal investigation, let alone criminal prosecution". While we recognise the human right to marry under Article 12, we cannot afford all actions and activities within a marriage unbridled privilege from criminal prosecution, particularly in these circumstances where unmarried appellants are treated discriminatorily.

[29] Accordingly, the Court considers that the reasons given by the national authorities for the measures taken in respect of the applicants were relevant and sufficient for the purposes of Article 8 para. 2.

[30] However, the Court does not agree that the measures were proportionate to the legitimate aim or aims pursued. The Court notes that the charges of assault were numerous and referred to activities which had taken place over more than ten years. However, only a few charges were selected for inclusion in the prosecution case. The Court notes the plethora of charges of assault, including those that peculiarly involved the aiding and abetting of assault on oneself. It further notes the substantial prison sentences handed down to the applicants, in some cases in excess of four years in prison. Given these sentences for consensual activities that involved no lasting injuries to any of the parties involved, the Court finds the measures taken against the applicants as grossly disproportionate.

[31] The Court, unlike the Commission, finds it necessary also to determine whether the interference with the applicants' right to respect for private life could rather be justified on the ground of the protection of morals. Here, we find again, that the interference was not necessary in a democratic society for such purposes. It is not the prerogative of the State to seek to deter acts of the kind in question. Rather, it is our duty to ensure Article 8 protections, and their guarantee of sexual liberty, including sexual orientation and consensual sexual activity.

[32] In sum, the Court finds that the national authorities were entitled to consider the prosecution and conviction of the applicants, however we find that the prosecutions based on an act of private sexual orientation fall to be in breach of Article 8 and cannot be justified on the grounds of protection of health. This is not a measure of stretching privacy beyond its limits, but a matter of recognizing the importance of consent and sexual autonomy, determination and liberation.

FOR THESE REASONS, THE COURT

Holds unanimously that there has been a violation of Article 8 of the Convention.

8

Hatton v the United Kingdom (European Court of Human Rights):

Queering Environmental Protections

Kay Lalor

Queer Environments?

Hatton v UK is not an overtly queer case: it concerns the question of whether noise pollution from planes at Heathrow Airport constitutes a violation of the private and family life of those living in the airport's flight path.[1] The Chamber originally found in favour of the applicants, but the case was then referred to the Grand Chamber which found no violation of Article 8. Why re-write a case about aircraft noise in a Queer Judgments collection where the majority of contributions address issues of gender and sexuality directly? What can a queer perspective bring to a twenty-year-old European Convention on Human Rights (ECHR) judgment about planes landing in the early hours of the morning, disturbing the sleep of those who live nearby? The answer to these questions depends in part upon how one approaches queer analysis.

The re-written case adopts an approach that views queerness as attending 'to all those moments … in which the normal is achieved, produced, effected and also, therefore, exposed as contingent, constituted and open to change.'[2] Like other critical traditions, queer theory offers tools for challenging power relations and forms of epistemic domination that are too often taken for granted. As such, examining the possibilities of queering law draws attention to both the limits of our normative legal frameworks and the failure of law to question 'the gendered, raced, imperial, heteronormative, privileged, autonomous and ableist assumptions implicit in [the] "universal" subject—the human who is able to fully enjoy human rights and fundamental freedoms.'[3] This perspective

---

1. (2003) 37 EHRR 28.
2. Claire Colebrook, 'On the Very Possibility of Queer Theory,' in *Deleuze and Queer Theory*, ed. Chrysanthi Nigianni and Merl Storr (Edinburgh: Edinburgh University Press, 2009), 21.
3. Sara De Vido, 'A Quest for an Eco-centric Approach to International Law: the COVID-19 Pandemic as Game Changer,' *Jus Cogens* 3 (2021), 108. See, also, Dianne Otto, 'Queerly Troubling International Law's Vision of "Peace",' *AJIL Unbound* 116 (2022).

can be read alongside queer ecologies literatures,[4] which extend the critique of the subject to a broader recognition of the naturalized domination of humans over nature or over the earth and recognize ecological relationships as 'complex webs of relations between the human and non-human—themselves ideological, racialized, and problematic conceptual markers—and the simultaneously fraught and comforting notion of "home".'[5] Thus, a queer ecological engagement with law attends to the injustices of the present—of which gendered and sexual injustices are a part—and asks what might be different. In this way, the queering of aircraft noise draws on an established form of queer legal analysis, as well as upon many of the original Feminist Judgments projects which ranged far beyond questions of law and gender.[6]

It is important here to also recognize the limits of queering law and the way that queer thought 'frequently end[s] up reinforcing the dominant normative order of sexuality and gender rather than producing freedom from this order.'[7] In the context of environmental regulation, familiar patterns of exclusion and domination are often present, privileging and marginalizing voices unequally.[8] Moreover, a queer critique does not guarantee a queer future, and radical ideas may easily find themselves repurposed back into regimes of racialized, neoliberal cis-heteropatriarchy. This is one of the tensions that underpins the re-written judgment. Indeed, of the ironies of re-writing a judgment that is twenty years old is that some, although not all, of the positions adopted in the re-written text can be found in later cases.[9] The alignment of this imagined past queer/anti-normative position with more 'mainstream' modern positions could be interpreted in a number of ways. On one hand, it might point to a degree of prescience of queer thinking or its capacity to anticipate necessary but new perspectives. However, it could also be more pessimistically taken to demonstrate the limitations of the form through which queer ideas are expressed. The queer theoretical perspective adopted here asks how the norms, structures, powers and axioms that underpin the judgment came to be, but because the response to that investigation itself takes the form of a judgment, it must implicitly assume the inevitability and continuation of the very norms and structures that are questioned, even if in a slightly 'queered' form. As such, the form of the judgment places limits on the possibility of radical, queer, environmental or non-anthropocentric expression. This question of what a queer critique can achieve in its interactions with the formal structures of law is just one of the tensions that underpin

---

4. See e.g. 'From Queer/Nature to Queer Ecologies: Celebrating 20 Years of Scholarship and Creativity,' *UnderCurrents Journal of Critical Environmental Studies* 19 (2015).

5. Amanda Di Battista, Oded Haas and Darren Patrick, 'Conversations in Queer Ecologies: An Editorial,' *UnderCurrents Journal of Critical Environmental Studies* 19 (2015), 3.

6. Christine Chinkin, Gina Heathcote, Emily Jones and Henry Jones, '*Bozkurt Case*, aka the *Lotus Case* (*France v Turkey*): Two Ships that Go Bump in the Night,' in *Feminist Judgments in International Law*, ed. Loveday Hodson and Troy Lavers (London: Hart, 2019), 27.

7. Ratna Kapur, 'The (Im)possibility of Queering International Human Rights Law,' in *Queering International Law*, ed. Dianne Otto (London: Routledge, 2017), Chapter 7.

8. May Farrales and others, 'Queering Environmental Regulation?' *Environment and Planning E: Nature and Space* 4 (2021).

9. See e.g. Natasa Mavronicola, 'The Future is a Foreign Country: State (In)Action on Climate Change and the Right against Torture and Ill-Treatment,' *Europe of Rights & Liberties/Europe des Droits & Libertés* 6 (2022).

the re-written judgment below, and one to which I return at the end of this reflection. To some extent, these tensions are welcome: queerness does not and should not always sit easily with law.

Intimacy, Rest and Privacy

Does the fact that this is a queer judgments project imply a responsibility to attend to queer lives even in a case that barely discusses gender and sexuality? Perhaps, fortunately, the original judgment makes reference to the 1982 sodomy decriminalization case *Dudgeon v the United Kingdom*,[10] providing both a link to the wider considerations of the Queer Judgments Project and an important invitation to reflect on the nature of intimacy and privacy, as found within Article 8 ECHR jurisprudence. *Dudgeon* held that sexuality was 'a most intimate aspect of private life,'[11] setting a high threshold for State interference with the lives of sexual minorities. In *Hatton*, the Court was invited to consider whether sleep should occupy the same status: what does sleep mean to human life and livelihood? In the judgment, the Grand Chamber largely sidesteps this question, but the dissenting judgment of Judges Costa, Ress, Türmen, Zupančič, and Steiner vehemently argues for the intimacy of sleep, drawing comparisons with the right to and the protection of health.[12]

The rewritten judgment also engages with how we should understand and value sleep. The queer reading of the intimacy of sleep in the rewritten judgment was significantly influenced by calls to attend to scholarly legal writing on science fiction as 'imaginative resistance,'[13] through which we might find 'new approaches to—and directions—in law.'[14] Thus, in her 2003 short story, *Wake Island*, Ursula Le Guin writes of a society which genetically engineers a small number of people who no longer require sleep. It is thought that these people will be superior, more productive, able to access their latent genius. In fact, the opposite happens: the population of 'asomics' becomes animalistic, without speech, living in isolation on an island.[15] The story ends with a reflection on the nature of dreams. Reading the arguments of the applicants in *Hatton* through the lens of Le Guin's story forces us to reflect on questions of rest, sleep and personhood, and how often rest is deferred or interrupted in the pursuit of progress, of capital or of wealth creation. Most importantly, it reminds us how different human experiences, including those of sleep and rest, are (de)prioritized or (de)valued and how these priorities might be challenged.

---

10. (1982) 4 EHRR 149.

11. *Dudgeon v United Kingdom* (1982) 4 EHRR 149, [52].

12. *Hatton v United Kingdom* (2003), Annex: joint dissenting opinion of Mr Costa, Mr Ress, Mr Türmen, Mr Zupančič and Mrs Steine.

13. Folúkẹ́ Adébísí, 'Black/African Science Fiction and the Quest for Racial Justice through Legal Knowledge: How Can We Unsettle Euro-modern Time and Temporality in Our Teaching?' *Law, Technology and Humans* 4/2 (2022), 27. Adébísí focuses particularly on Black/African science fiction as a mode of unsettling Euro-modern law.

14. Mitchell Travis and Kieran Tranter, 'Interrogating Absence: the Lawyer in Science Fiction,' *International Journal of the Legal Profession* 21/1 (2014), 23–24.

15. Ursula Le Guin, 'Wake Island,' in *Changing Planes: Armchair Travel for the Mind* (London: Hachette, 2010), 62–67.

Beyond the question of intimacy and sleep, a wider question of the spatiality of intimacy arises in the case. Paul Johnson has argued that there is a danger in aligning sexual freedom with privacy, as this can imply a freedom that exists only *in private*.[16] Essentially, queer people are only free to be themselves within the confines of the closet. The rewritten judgment draws not just upon *Dudgeon* but also on the 2002 case of *Goodwin v the United Kingdom*,[17] to explicitly address this possibility. Inspired by activist and academic calls for queer liveable lives,[18] the rewritten judgment complicates the relationship between the public and private, highlighting the relational aspect of the public, the private and the home, to explore the idea that intimate life does not necessarily have its own separate sphere but is an integral part of our identity and our lives in all possible spaces and places. In this, the judgment perhaps anticipates later judgments of the European Court of Human Rights (ECtHR) as well as the work of queer activists who have framed their legal battles through rights of association: of the potential to be queer *together* in particular public, private and semi-private spaces.[19]

Queer Ecologies and Minority Rights

Queer analysis often seeks to unpick unchallenged binaries: male/female, human/nature, heterosexual/homosexual among many others. A key aspect of the original judgment that is retained but challenged in the rewritten judgment is the majority/minority binary. The Grand Chamber wrote extensively of the need to strike a 'fair balance' between the needs of the applicants and (it is assumed) the rest of the UK, who, the Government argued, would benefit from the economic advantages of a competitive Heathrow Airport. Queer and feminist ecological and eco-centric literatures help to challenge logics that lend themselves to a binary or zero-sum understanding of the case, pointing towards the interconnected distribution of interests, involvements, benefits, and losses in the case and to 'mutually reinforcing' systems of oppression and exclusion.[20] This point seems particularly pertinent to questions of environmental regulation and environmental collapse, and to who is included in conversations about the earth's future. With José Esteban-Muñoz, we must ask who has a right to a future and attend to how the answer to these questions is striated by race, class, and physical location.[21]

Ironically, a central 'actor' in the case is paradoxically present but unsayable. As the later parts of the rewritten judgment discuss, this is an environmental case, discussed through the lens of human experience. Such anthropocentrism is inevitable given

---

16. Paul Johnson, 'An Essentially Private Manifestation of Human Personality: Constructions of Homosexuality in the European Court of Human Rights,' *Human Rights Law Review* 10/1 (2010).

17. (2002) 35 EHRR 18

18. Niharika Banerjea and Kath Browne, 'Liveable Lives A Transnational Queer-Feminist Reflection on Sexuality, Development and Governance,' in *Routledge Handbook of Queer Development Studies*, ed. Niharika Banerjea and Kath Browne (London: Routledge, 2018).

19. See e.g. *Alekseyev v Russia* (2019) 69 EHRR 16; *Bączkowski and Others v Poland* (2009) 48 EHRR 19; *Attorney General of Botswana v Rammoge and 19 Others*, Botswana Court of Appeal, 16 March 2016, CACGB-128-14.

20. Greta Gaard, 'Toward a Queer Ecofeminism,' *Hypatia* 12/1 (1997).

21. Jose Esteban Muñoz, *Cruising Utopia: the Then and There of Queer Futurity* (Ney York: New York University Press 2009).

the structure of the court, and of rights themselves, but it necessarily occludes the extended ecological relationships that queer and feminist ecological perspectives demand. In the years since *Hatton*, a small number of courts in other jurisdictions have experimented with centring non-human actors in environmental protections.[22] Instead of fully adopting an approach that might grant rights directly to the environment, the re-written judgment seeks instead to name the tensions present without seeking to resolve them: in other words, to recognize the limits of the system. Thus, there is a fundamental and unresolved tension in the rewritten judgment between what the law can do and what might be necessary for a queerer existence.

The Limits of Law

The tension between queerness and law creates a number of questions for the writing of the judgment: what is queerness and what is just placing oneself in opposition to the original findings? How far should the re-written judgment adhere to the original framing by the Chamber in terms of finding a fair balance? There is also a question of how to anticipate the future when rewriting a twenty year old case: there have been a number of cases between 2003 and the present that would have been relevant to discussions of home,[23] vulnerability and dispossession,[24] and the full citizenship and cultural personhood of SOGI and other minorities.[25] There is a danger here of assuming linearity and progress—that there is a 'correct' time for particular cases and findings, which all build upon each other towards a more liberated future. However, queer temporal and ecological literatures contradict the narrative of linear progress and significantly, the narrative of economic development central to the court's considerations in *Hatton*.[26] So, too, does the barely mentioned ecological emergency at the centre of the case: that human actions are causing disastrous changes to the earth's atmosphere that could render the planet uninhabitable.

Equally, the decision in *Hatton* was not inevitable: the Grand Chamber's finding of no violation of Article 8 overturned that of the Chamber, which had found in favour of the applicants, and commentary at the time expressed disappointment that the Grand Chamber seemed to retreat from a developing line of case law that offered greater environmental protections that moved towards a 'special status' for the environment.[27]

---

22. Elizabeth Macpherson, 'The (Human) Rights of Nature: A Comparative Study of Emerging Legal Rights for Rivers and Lakes in the United States of America and Mexico,' *Duke Environmental Law and Policy Forum* 31 (2021). See, also, Emily Jones, 'Posthuman International Law and the Rights of Nature,' *Journal of Human Rights and the Environment* 12 (2021).

23. *Connors v United Kingdom* (2005) 40 EHRR 9.

24. *Oneryildiz v Turkey* (No.2) (2005) 41 EHRR 20.

25. See generally the ECHR Factsheet on Sexual Orientation Issues and Gender Identity Issues, accessed 21 November 2023, https://www.echr.coe.int/documents/fs_sexual_orientation_eng.pdf and https://www.echr.coe.int/Documents/FS_Gender_identity_eng.pdf.

26. Cynthia Weber, *Queer International Relations: Sovereignty, Sexuality and the Will to Knowledge* (Oxford: Oxford University Press, 2016).

27. Martha Grekos, '*Hatton v United Kingdom*: Balancing the Demands Between the Public interest and the Individual's Fundamental Rights?' ELM 15(4) (2003), 233; David Hart and Marina Wheeler, 'Night Flights and Strasbourg's Retreat from Environmental Human Rights,' *Journal of Environmental Law* 16/1 (2004);

Queer temporal thinking often looks for the transformative potential hidden within the habits of the present,[28] and it is this that animates the considerations in the final part of the rewritten judgment. Twenty years beyond *Hatton,* much of the discussion of the current environmental emergency has been of time—how little time we have to make changes, how we may already be too late, how every year counts.[29] This prompts the question: what if the Court had taken a bolder step in 2003 and had harnessed the transformative potential of a queer future hidden within the present? Would the situation we face now look different, or is law ultimately not enough to render transformative change? And what do such questions demand of us in the present? Can we further queer law in the current moment, to try to protect the environments of the future? Ultimately, and crucially, given the current climate emergency, queer judgments such as those found in the Queer Judgments Project remind us that other choices and outcomes are possible and that queer analysis is a key tool first for analysing how the normal, the linear, and the predictable are produced, and second, for making the case that different norms and different ways of living, being and doing law, are possible.

David Hart, 'Air Noise and Strasbourg's Orderly Retreat from Environmental Human Rights,' *Environmental Liability: Law, Policy and Practice* 11/4 (2003).

28. Muñoz, *Cruising utopia;* Kara Keeling, *Queer Times, Black Futures* (New York: New York University Press, 2019).

29. See e.g. Sir David Attenborough, 'Climate and Security,' Security Council Open VTC, 23 February 2021, accessed 21 November 2023, https://media.un.org/en/asset/k10/k10j8i0rt1.

CASE OF HATTON AND OTHERS v THE UNITED KINGDOM

(Application no. 36022/97)
GRAND CHAMBER
JUDGMENT
STRASBOURG

8 July 2003

The Circumstances of the Case

[1] The applicants in the case live between 4.4km and 17.3km from Heathrow Airport. They complain of disturbed and interrupted sleep caused by aircraft activity which significantly increased from 1993 onward.

[2] The Government claim the 'maximum average' sound exposure suffered by each applicant due to aircraft arriving before 6am each morning was between 83.4dBA and 94.4dBA.[30] According to the Government's own figures, these levels represent a 'very high' level of annoyance on a normal summer day. There is no widely accepted scale or standard with which to measure night-time annoyance caused by aircraft noise.

[3] Heathrow Airport is the busiest airport in Europe, and the busiest international airport in the world. Restrictions on night flights at Heathrow Airport were introduced in 1962 and have been regularly reviewed, including reports into aircraft noise and sleep disturbance.

[4] Aircraft noise is regulated by the 1982 Civil Aviation Act which provides protection to aircraft operators against action for trespass and nuisance in ordinary circumstances (s 76(1)) and empowers the Secretary of State to proscribe aircraft operations 'to limit or mitigate' noise or vibrations (s 78(3)).

[5] A 1992 study, *Report of a field study of aircraft noise and sleep disturbance* ('the 1992 sleep study'), found that approximately 80% of those living in the Heathrow area had said that they were never or only sometimes woken up for any cause. Of the 20% who were woken up, 17% gave aircraft noise as the cause, 16% blamed a partner

---
30. dBA Leq noise contour figures measure the average degree of community annoyance from aircraft noise.

or a child and another 28.5% gave a variety of different reasons. Approximately 35% of those living near Heathrow said that if awoken, for any reason, they found it difficult to get back to sleep.

[6] Following a Consultation Paper in 1993, a new scheme (the 1993 Scheme) was introduced, creating a noise quota scheme for the night period. The 1993 Scheme was subject to further consultation, reports, and research, as well as four consecutive judicial reviews brought by local authorities closest to Heathrow Airport. These resulted in some adjustments to the 1993 scheme, but the final judicial review did not find the current policy to be irrational (see *R. v Secretary of State for Transport, ex parte Richmond LBC* [1996] 1 Weekly Law Reports 1460).

The Law

[7] The applicants complained that the government policy on night flights at Heathrow introduced in 1993 violated their rights under Article 8 of the Convention, which provides:
1. Everyone has the right to respect for his private and family life, his home and his correspondence.
2. There shall be no interference by a public authority with the exercise of this right except such as is in accordance with the law and is necessary in a democratic society in the interests of national security, public safety or the economic well-being of the country, for the prevention of disorder or crime, for the protection of health or morals, or for the protection of the rights and freedoms of others.

[8] The Government denied that there had been any violation of the Convention in this case.

The General Principles

[9] This case was referred to the Grand Chamber following the finding by the Chamber that in implementing the 1993 Scheme the State failed to strike a fair balance between the United Kingdom's economic well-being and the applicants' effective enjoyment of their right to respect for their homes and their private and family lives and that there had accordingly been a violation of Article 8.

[10] The Grand Chamber notes that in previous cases the Commission has found that Article 8 is applicable to the issue of aircraft noise (*Arrondelle v the United Kingdom* no. 7889/77, Commission decision of 15 July 1980, Decisions and Reports (DR) 19; *Baggs v the United Kingdom* no. 9310/81, Commission decision of 16 October 1985, DR 44). The Court found no violation of Article 8 in *Powell and Rayner v the United Kingdom* (judgment of 21 February 1990, Series A no. 172), a case concerned with aircraft noise, but did acknowledge that Article 8 was relevant as 'the quality of [each] applicant's private life and the scope for enjoying the amenities of his home [had] been

adversely affected by the noise generated by aircraft using Heathrow Airport' (§ 40). Later judgments have affirmed the right to a healthy environment guaranteed by Article 8 of the Convention (*López Ostra v Spain*, judgment of 9 December 1994, Series A no. 303-C, and *Guerra and Others v Italy*, judgment of 19 February 1998, *Reports of Judgments and Decisions* 1998-I).

[11] In the present case as well as in previous judgments of the Court, the pollution at issue is not necessarily directly caused by the State. However, at least since *Powell and Rayner* (cited at paragraph 10), a positive obligation related to the prevention of environmental harm that affects the rights protected in paragraph 1 of Article 8 has been identified as attributable to the State (see, also, *Kyrtatos v Greece* no. 41666/98 judgment of 22 May 2003, §52). In examining this positive obligation, the Court will address both the substantive actions taken by the State to prevent harm, and the procedural processes by which the domestic regulatory regime is designed and enforced by the State

[12] The Government and the applicants all accept the engagement of Article 8 in this case. The balancing of competing factors and interests are central to the consideration of the proportionality of the application of Article 8. Previously, a wide margin of appreciation has been granted to States in cases concerning both environmental and planning decisions (see *Powell and Rayner,* paragraph 10 and *Buckley v United Kingdom* judgment of 25 September 1996, *Reports* 1996-IV, pp. 1291–93, §§ 74–77). This follows established case law in which national authorities make the initial assessment as to the necessity of an interference with a Convention right, with the Court acting in a supervisory role.

[13] The margin of appreciation granted to States may vary depending upon the facts and issues at hand. The Chamber noted that the State enjoyed a certain margin of appreciation in determining the steps to be taken to ensure compliance with the Convention. However, the Chamber underlined that in striking the required balance:

> States are required to minimise, as far as possible, the interference with these rights, by trying to find alternative solutions and by generally seeking to achieve their aims in the least onerous way as regards human rights. In order to do that, a proper and complete investigation and study with the aim of finding the best possible solution which will, in reality, strike the right balance should precede the relevant project (§ 97).

[14] This finding is supported by third party submissions from Friends of the Earth, which highlight the importance of environmental protection and the fast-developing international jurisprudence.

[15] Also arguing for a narrow margin of appreciation, the applicants highlight the importance and intimacy of the harm caused by the deprivation of sleep by exposure to excessive noise. Indeed, the applicants submit that the deprivation of sleep has been compared to inhuman and degrading treatment and must be considered in similar terms

(see *Ireland v the United Kingdom* judgment of 18 January 1978, Series A no. 25, p. 41, § 96; *Selmouni v France* [GC], no. 25803/94, ECHR 1999-V, § 97).

[16] In contrast, the Government has objected strongly to the Chamber's approach to the margin of appreciation in this case which involves difficult and complex balancing of a variety of competing interests and factors. They submit that the 1993 Scheme strikes a fair balance while maintaining the ability of Heathrow Airport to compete with other similar international airports, thus maintaining economic benefits brought by air travel into and out of the UK.

Appraisal of the Current Case in Light of the General Principles

[17] Article 8 has been recognized to protect a right to a healthy environment. However, to undertake an assessment of the different factors that must be balanced in this case, it is necessary to more closely examine the different facets of Article 8 that are relevant to privacy, intimacy and the environment. Several different but interconnected aspects of Article 8 are at issue in this case, notably Article 8 protections of intimacy and the home, minority rights and environmental protections.

Intimacy, Privacy and the Home

[18] Central to the arguments of the Government and the applicants is the margin of appreciation afforded to the Government in regulating air travel and determining the extent and impact of environmental harm. For the Government, the issues at hand are analogous to planning decisions such as the decision at stake in *Buckley* (paragraph 12) where the national authorities enjoyed a wide discretion. In contrast, the applicants emphasize the intimate nature of the right protected, relying on decisions such as *Dudgeon v the United Kingdom* (judgment of 22 October 1981, Series A no. 45). When State interference is with a particularly intimate aspect of private life, the scope of the margin of appreciation is reduced.

[19] On the surface, these two positions appear to be incommensurable. For the Government, this is a matter of bricks and mortar, planning decisions and economic development. For the applicants, at issue is a shared aspect of the human experience: sleep, and more accurately, the capacity of the applicants to fall and remain asleep within their homes. It is possible, however, to understand these two arguments as interlinked, but with a different emphasis. In both sets of arguments there is a concern with the State's intrusion into and regulation of the home. The Court has recognized that the status of 'home' is not defined or constituted simply by physical property, but by the 'sufficient and continuing links' that an individual has with a place (see *Gillow and Gillow v the United Kingdom* judgment of 24 November 1986, Series A no. 109). The homes into which the noise of aircrafts intrudes in this case are constituted by complex matrices of relationships, norms, histories, habits, practices and affects. A home is therefore a place constructed of and through relations and relationality.

[20] In arguing for the proportionality of the interference with Article 8, the Government has argued that the lack of impact upon house prices indicates the limited impact of the noise from the airport on the lives of the applicants. The implication here is that the area remains a desirable place to live and, indeed, that those who are unable to sleep through the noise might move elsewhere. The Court finds that the Government's argument that house prices have not been affected by noise from the airport is unconvincing as evidence of minimal impact. This perspective does not consider the relational concept of home, appearing to assume that one home can be easily substituted for another. It assumes that the home, be it the home of a family or an individual, is an easily moveable unit. In situations where individuals have developed continuing links with a place, this is not necessarily the case. The applicants can and may leave to escape the noise, but this is not a cost-free movement.

[21] Arguing for a narrow margin of appreciation, the applicants contend that the interference with sleep is a particularly significant interference with their private and intimate lives. In other cases, the deprivation of sleep has amounted to inhuman treatment (see *Ireland v the United Kingdom* judgment of 18 January 1978, Series A no. 25) and the applicants submit that the impact of the environmental disturbance must be understood in these terms. From this perspective, the interference experienced here is a particularly intimate aspect of private life, comparable to *Dudgeon* (paragraph 18). Accordingly, there must be particularly pressing reasons for interfering with this aspect of private life.

[22] However, a further dimension must be considered in relation to the way in which the interference is understood in relation to Article 8, privacy and home. There is a danger here in aligning intimacy with privacy and the private sphere in an unhelpful way. The division between the public and the private is not a natural and unchanging aspect of European political and legal thought but a deliberate and political divide that separates out different types of behaviours and legitimizes the operation of different power relations in different spaces. The complexity of this case is that the nature of the environmental pollution at issue means that it necessarily intrudes into, and demonstrates the artificial nature of, the barriers constructed between public and private.

[23] There is a danger here that if the constructed and relational nature of public and private is not foregrounded, the findings in *Dudgeon* (paragraph 18) might be misinterpreted to mean that the sexual freedoms protected in that case are protected *only in private*. This interpretation assumes that sexuality is a part of identity that can be easily separated out and only embodied in particular spaces that the State is prevented from touching or regulating. The more recent case of *Goodwin v the United Kingdom* (no. 28957/95, judgment of 11 July 2002) in which the Court considered transgender rights is more helpful here. The Court notes that,

> the very essence of the Convention is respect for human dignity and human freedom. Under Article 8 of the Convention in particular, where the notion of personal autonomy is an important principle underlying the interpretation of its guarantees, protection is given to the personal

sphere of each individual, including the right to establish details of their identity as individual human beings (§ 99).

Intimate lives, including sexual and gendered lives, constitute a core part of how an individual might live a life of dignity and freedom. The fact that this life is protected through the right to privacy should not be interpreted to mean that this life can only be lived in private.

[24] This clarification offers a better framework for understanding the scope of Article 8. The Grand Chamber is cognisant of the applicants' arguments about sleep deprivation and inhuman treatment, but in this case, unlike those subject to torture or ill treatment, the applicants can remove themselves from the situation causing the noise, even if their removal from that situation is not as easy as might perhaps be suggested by the Government's reference to house prices (see paragraph 20). The Court does accept, however, the importance of sleep to living a full human life: if this were not the case, then sleep deprivation would not be so severe a harm to bring it within the ambit of Article 3 when inflicted on prisoners. A lack of sleep contributes to poor health, tiredness, distraction and long-term, further severe consequences. It is a key part of a meaningful, liveable life and thus a meaningful aspect of a dignified, intimate life.

[25] In the present case, this offers an important clarification. There is a long historical distinction in Western thought between the public space of the commerce, business, and politics spheres, and the private space of the household. There is a particular danger in this case of reifying this distinction in law, first by drawing a sharp boundary between the public regulatory space of business and the private space of the home into which the airline noise is intruding, and second by assuming that particular intimate aspects of life are only relevant to the private sphere or that the relations of the private sphere are always harmonious or safe. Following *Gillow* (see paragraph 19), the Court here adopts a relational understanding of home, in which the public and the private must be understood as constructed and related rather than distinct. At issue here is not so much that the noise crosses over into a protected space of the private, but that interference from the noise prevents the applicants from living a full and meaningful life.

[26] In these circumstances, the Court finds that the arrangements of intimacies, relationships, and norms that are at issue in this case form a core part of intimate life. The applicants do have the option of moving in order to preserve their intimate lives without interference from airport noise, but there is considerable cost involved in this movement which must be taken into account when balancing the interests at play in the case.

Minority Rights

[27] Central to the arguments of the Government and the applicants is the question of the striking of a fair balance between different interests in the case. In finding a violation of Article 8, the Chamber held that in the absence of a:

serious attempt to evaluate the extent or impact of the interferences with the applicants' sleep patterns and generally in the absence of a prior specific and complete study with the aim of finding the least onerous solution as regards human rights, it is not possible to agree that in weighing the interferences against the economic interest of the country—which itself had not been quantified—the Government struck the right balance in setting up the 1993 Scheme. (§105)

[28] While accepting that night-time noise from aircraft had the capacity to disturb sleep, the Government stressed that if restrictions on night flights at Heathrow were made more stringent, UK airlines would be placed at a significant competitive disadvantage. If they were forced to operate during the day, they could provide fewer viable connections with regional services at both ends, making London a less attractive place in which to do business. Equally the respondents from the airline industry stressed the economic importance of night flights. They provided information showing that, in 1993, a typical daily night flight would generate an annual revenue between GBP 70–175 million and an annual profit of up to GBP 15 million.

[29] There are no specific figures or studies submitted that quantify the economic cost of eliminating specific night flights, however, the Government claims that some flights to London could only arrive during the daytime by departing very late at night. This inconvenient time may cause serious passenger discomfort and thus a loss of competitiveness. Both the Government and the applicants have submitted examples of airports that do and do not have night-time flight bans as evidence (for the Government) of the need to maintain the competitiveness of Heathrow and (for the applicants) of the possibility of operating a major international airport with a night flights ban.

[30] The applicants noted the limitations of the research upon which the Government relied, in that it dealt with sleep disturbance and not prevention of those disturbances, that is, the experiences of those unable to fall asleep in the first place because of noise. The applicants also pointed out that the night noise to which they are subjected is frequently far in excess of international standards, including those set by the World Health Organisation.

[31] Once again, the Court is reminded of the cases of *Dudgeon* and *Goodwin* (see paragraphs 18 and 23). These cases concerned the rights of minorities and the protection of the lives of minorities, even when those lives might be incomprehensible or distasteful to the majority of a population (see, also, *Handyside v the United Kingdom* judgment of 7 December 1976, Series A no. 24). The Court is also mindful of the unequal power relations of those subject to State interference in their intimate lives. Recalling *Dudgeon*, sexual minorities have historically faced stigma, marginalization, and shame. Historically, dispossession of home or land have been tools of State domination against those perceived as different, unimportant or as vulnerable, be this through colonisation, land enclosures or refusal of entry or residence (see *Buckley v the United Kingdom*, paragraph 12; *East African Asians v the United Kingdom* no. 4626/70 et al., Commission's report of 14 December 1973). This case cannot therefore be divorced from longer histories of oppression of those perceived as different or vulnerable by the majority, often in the name of progress or development.

[32] Thus, the striking of a fair balance here cannot discount the harm caused to applicants simply because they are numerically small, or because others in the same area may not suffer the same level of sleep disturbance. The Court acknowledges that in *Goodwin* there were no significant matters of public interest to weigh against the interests of the individual applicant. In this case, the Government highlights the loss of profits of the airlines operating from Heathrow and the economic well-being of the country at large. However, the Court recalls *López Ostra v Spain* (cited in paragraph 10) *and Berrehab v the Netherlands* (judgment of 21 June 1988, Series A no. 138), in which the economic wellbeing of a community or country could not be used as an overarching or unexamined reason for interferences with Article 8. In this case, it is notable that the statistics provided are drawn directly from the airline industry rather than an independent study, so there is limited evidence as to the details and distribution of the economic advantage provided by night flights. Moreover, the Government's arguments appear to privilege the comfort of passengers on air flights who may be required to travel at different times, over the comfort of the applicants.

[33] The Court notes that there is an underlying assumption here that either the minority must suffer for the majority's benefit, or the majority must be restrained to protect a minority. As long as the interference suffered by the minority is sufficiently small, or indeed as some of the research presented seems to imply, as long as the minority itself is sufficiently small, the interference can be justified. The nature of the dispute is framed as a zero-sum game with no consideration of how the improvement of the lives of minorities might in itself lead to a net benefit for all. At the very least, the Court notes that a more careful consideration is required of *who* is being automatically attributed to the 'minority' or 'majority' position and how harms are being distributed within these sets of relations.

[34] The Court considers that relevant interests in this case include those of:
   a. The applicants and others in similar circumstances.
   b. The airlines seeking to fly from Heathrow, including their staff and their shareholders.
   c. Travellers who use Heathrow Airport, particularly those who leave or arrive at night.
   d. The general population of the UK, including:
      i. Economic interests, tied to travel across UK borders and potential tax income from this travel and from airline profits.
      ii. Environmental interests and the harmful effects of air travel, be these noise or other forms of pollutants in the atmosphere.
   e. Non-human bodies and species, including:
      i. Non-human species in the vicinity of the airport affected by airline noise.
      ii. Economic bodies and business that might profit from air travel.
      iii. Natural and built environments that may be impacted by the proximity of air travel.

[35] At the very least, this summary of pertinent interests demands that the balancing act required be considered in terms of an ecosystem rather than a simple binary. The relationships involved here are significantly more complex than those of a simple opposition between the applicants and the rest of the United Kingdom. As such, the Court notes the profound limitations of Article 8 in this case. Paragraph two of the article holds:

> There shall be no interference by a public authority with the exercise of this right except such as is in accordance with the law and is necessary in a democratic society in the interests of national security, public safety or the economic well-being of the country, for the prevention of disorder or crime, for the protection of health or morals, or for the protection of the rights and freedoms of others.

There are no doubt questions of economy and profit at play in this case, but the way in which that economic-well-being is distributed is unclear. Equally, interference with Article 8 is permitted for protection of the rights of others, but there is a wide distribution of possible 'others' who might be affected. In particular, when considering the 'general population' of the UK, there is potential for both economic benefit—albeit with limited evidence currently provided by the Government—as well as environmental harm, with associated eventual economic harm, caused by the ongoing proliferation of air travel. There is a complex distribution of rights and harms within this case, that does not lend itself to a simplistic 'fair balance' assessment. The Grand Chamber therefore agrees with the Chamber that much greater consideration of the distribution of the costs and benefits within this complex system is required.

Environmental Harm and the Supervisory Role of the Court

[36] At the heart of this case is a distinction between day and night, and the diurnal rhythms of most human beings. Air travel and the economic demands of travel disrupt and conflict with this rhythm, leading to the consequences reported by the applicants.

[37] Paragraph 34 considers non-human bodies, natural and built environments, and thus the ecosystems of these environments, as part of the consideration of fair balance in this case. Convention rights are explicitly human rights, not the rights of environment(s). This means that the environment must be approached through a consideration of the impact of environmental degradation on humans and through rights to a clean and healthy environment, not through non-anthropocentric rights of the environment or of non-human animals. Indeed, a non-anthropocentric view of the rhythm of flight arrivals might be one in which the arrival of flights was much more evenly spread over each 24-hour period, or pushed to its extreme iteration, one where there were no flights at all.

[38] The Court recalls that the Convention is a living instrument, that must be interpreted in light of modern-day conditions (*Tyrer v the United Kingdom* judgment of 25 April 1978, Series A no. 26; *Markx v Belgium* 13 June 1979 Series A no. 31).

Yet, in this case, the considerations of the Court foreground the unanticipated consequences of the Convention's original text. The Government relies on the economic wellbeing of the country to demonstrate the proportionality of the interference, but there is no commensurate environmental wellbeing of the country that might also be considered here, even though environmental benefits may be of equal public interest to economic gains.

[39] Equally challenging is the growing international consensus on environmental harm and calls for stricter environmental protections, as captured, for example, by the United Nations Framework Convention on Climate Change, operationalized by the 1997 Kyoto Protocol, which notes that:

> human activities have been substantially increasing the atmospheric concentrations of greenhouse gases, that these increases enhance the natural greenhouse effect, and that this will result on average in an additional warming of the Earth's surface and atmosphere and may adversely affect natural ecosystems and humankind.

The Protocol further notes that nations such as the United Kingdom and other European countries have contributed most substantially to this increase.

[40] Attending to this international consensus requires the Court to consider the long-term effects of environmental harm, which is necessarily dispersed (albeit unequally) across populations and borders. This expands far beyond the relatively temporally constrained claim of the applicants. This kind of consideration might be immediately dismissed as speculation beyond the scope of the Convention, yet economic wellbeing, upon which the Government relies, requires the same kind of speculation in terms of a projection and anticipation of economic benefit unequally distributed across a large number of people. It is ironic, or perhaps tragic, that the Convention's text allows these economic but not environmental considerations of future harm and benefit.

[41] Even with the limitations of Article 8 described above, environmental cases have been found to be admissible by the Court (see paragraph 10) and arguable, including in this case, where the Chamber, in its finding of a violation of Article 8, found in favour of the applicants. The Government has objected to the test applied by the Chamber and has emphasized the supervisory role of the Court. As such, the Government is essentially arguing against developing a special status for environmental rights and the retention of the wide margin of appreciation that would be found in economic and planning decisions.

[42] The Grand Chamber notes that the growing international concern for the preservation of the environment renders the consideration of environmental rights under Article 8 different from simple planning decisions. It is generally held that because of their direct knowledge of society, needs, and resources, national authorities are better placed to judge issues of economic concern than an international tribunal (*Buckley v the United Kingdom* paragraph 12; *Lithgow v the United Kingdom* Judgment of 8 July 1986, Series A no. 102). However, this is not simply an issue that requires knowledge

of social needs and resources. It is also an issue of growing environmental catastrophe and eventual environmental collapse which will have a wide-ranging impact. This thus renders environmental concerns of significant relevance to an international tribunal.

[43] Moreover, even if growing international consensus was not of concern, the previous actions of the Court demonstrate the special relevance of environmental rights. This should be faced directly rather than obliquely. The Court has noted (paragraph 35) the profound limitations of Article 8 in relation to environmental rights, yet it has upheld environmental rights through this limited framework. Environmental rights are thus significant enough that a place has been found for them within Convention jurisprudence, even when that place is paradoxical: the environment is profoundly present, but can only be approached through civil and political human rights which tend to consider humans removed from their environmental ecosystem. If environmental rights are significant enough to sustain this paradox, they are significant enough to attain a special status and approach in Convention jurisprudence. The Court will thus continue to interpret environmental issues through the imperfect lens of Article 8 and other Convention rights, until better, more suitable, tools of interpretation emerge.

[44] In these circumstances, the Grand Chamber agrees that sleep is a core part of intimate life and that, as with other cases that have considered the value and protection of intimacy, dignity, and freedom (*Dudgeon v the United Kingdom* cited in paragraph 18; *Goodwin v the United Kingdom* cited in paragraph 23), the State must have significant reasons for justifying its ongoing and continued interference. As such, a much more careful analysis of the effects of the interference with sleep than the one undertaken by the Government is required. This need for careful analysis is further exacerbated by the special status of environmental rights.

FOR THESE REASONS, THE COURT

1. *Holds* by unanimity that there has been a violation of Article 8.
2. *Holds*
   a. that the respondent State is to pay the applicants, within three months from the date on which the judgment becomes final according to Article 44 § 2 of the Convention, the following amounts:
      i. in respect of non-pecuniary damage, 4,000 (four thousand) pounds sterling each;
      ii. for costs and expenses, 70,000 (seventy thousand) pounds sterling, including any value added tax that may be chargeable;
   c. (b) that simple interest at an annual rate of 7.5% shall be payable from the expiry of the above-mentioned three months until settlement.

Kay Lalor
President

9

Reliable Consultants, Inc. v Earle (USA):
Reimagining the Sex Toy Cases

Andrew Gilden

'You can pick up a butt plug or a dildo at Target and CVS nowadays. I don't even know how we got here.'

—US Representative Marjorie Taylor Greene[1]

'Here we go raising the price of dildos again.'

—Justice Curtiss Brown[2]

Scandalously Ordinary

Sexual technologies hold an awkward place in United States (US) law and culture. On one hand, technologies such as vibrators are scattered unremarkably throughout electronics stores, online marketplaces, and all-purposes retailers like Target and CVS. They appear prominently in pop culture on television shows like *Sex and the City* and in high-end wellness campaigns by companies like Gwyneth Paltrow's Goop. They are fun, conventionally naughty, and widely purchased objects whose mainstreamed commodification is neatly summarized by their appellation: sex toys.[3] As reflected in the Justice Brown epigraph above, it would seem silly for lawmakers to devote more than passing attention to such playthings.

On the other hand, sexual technologies *have* been the object of several waves of moral—and legal—panic during the past 150 years. The late-nineteenth century

---

1. 'Republicans Are Panicking Because They Somehow Just Found Out You Can Buy Vibrators at CVS,' Vice.com, accessed 12 December 2022, https://www.vice.com/en/article/g5v9m4/republican-gala-marjorie-taylor-greene-buttplugs-sex-toys-tucker-carlson.
2. *Regalado v State*, 872 S.W.2d 7 (Tex. Ct. App. 1994) (Brown, J., concurring).
3. e.g. Caroline Bem and Susanna Paasonen, 'Play! A Special Issue,' *Sexualities* (2021) ('[P]leasure is ... abundantly highlighted in the markets of sex toys'); Dennis Waskul and Michelle Anklan, '"Best invention, second to the dishwasher": Vibrators and sexual pleasure,' *Sexualities* 23 (2020), 849–875 ('[M]edia representations of vibrators emphasize that the technology is pleasurable, functional, and exciting').

witnessed the confluence of industrialization, urbanization, and major advances in electronics and rubber production, creating new opportunities for sexual culture and commerce.[4] Perhaps unsurprisingly, these sexual spaces became a focus of successful anti-vice campaigns launched in the late-nineteenth and early-twentieth centuries.[5] As the women's rights and gay liberation movements gained momentum in the 1960s and 70s, sexual technologies became means of exploring pleasure and intimacy outside of a heterosexual, patriarchal framework. Unsurprisingly, again, government actors ratcheted up raids and arrests of sex toy sellers.[6] As recently as the late 1990s and early 2000s, legislatures in States such as Alabama, Colorado, Kansas, Louisiana, Mississippi, and Texas have enacted laws that expressly criminalize the commercial transfer of sex toys—'obscene devices' in the Texas legislative vernacular.[7] As reflected in Marjorie Taylor Greene's dismayed remark above, sexual technologies are politically and culturally significant; they can represent major shifts in the social organization of sexuality and gender and challenge conservative moral agendas.[8]

Constitutionally Uncertain

This inconsistency in sex toy discourse—as both a plaything and a political weapon; as both unremarkable and morally repugnant—is reflected in an especially muddled sex toy jurisprudence. As conservative lawmakers enacted sex toy prohibitions in the 1970s, 80s, and 90s, sellers and consumers challenged these laws as violating the due process, equal protection, and free speech provisions of the US federal constitution. More often than not, they have failed. For example, the Eleventh Circuit Court of Appeals in 2001 rejected any fundamental constitutional right to purchase sex toys and recognized as legitimate the State of Alabama's interest in deterring 'sexual stimulation and auto-eroticism, for its own sake, unrelated to marriage, procreation, or familial relationships.'[9] Even though the court did not *endorse* the State's position, it was nonetheless rational to believe that 'commerce in the pursuit of orgasms by artificial means for their own sake is detrimental to the health and morality of the State.'[10] Even following the Supreme Court's decision in *Lawrence v Texas*, which struck down Texas's statute criminalizing same-sex sodomy, the Eleventh Circuit reaffirmed the constitutionality of Alabama's sex toy ban: 'while the statute at issue in *Lawrence* criminalized *private* sexual conduct, the statute at issue in this case forbids *public*,

---

4. Hallie Lieberman, *Buzz: A Stimulating History of the Sex Toy* (New York: Penguin, 2017), 18.
5. For a more extended discussion of the legal regulation of sex toys, see Andrew Gilden and Sarah Wasserman Rajec, 'Pleasure Patents,' *Boston College Law Review* 63 (2022), 573–621.
6. Lieberman, *Buzz*, 77–89.
7. Gilden and Rajec, 'Pleasure Patents,' 603.
8. For example, Paul Preciado writes: 'The logic of heterosexuality is the logic of the dildo, invoking the transcendental possibility of giving an arbitrary organ the power to install sexual and gender difference. "Extracting" the organ that establishes the body as "naturally male" and calling it a dildo is a decisive political act in the deconstruction of heterosexuality': Paul B. Preciado, *Countersexual Manifesto*, trans. Kevin Gerry Dunn (New York, NY: Columbia University Press, 2018), 65.
9. *Williams v Pryor*, 240 F.3d 944, 949 (11th Cir. 2001).
10. *Williams v Pryor*, at 949.

commercial activity … There is nothing "private" or "consensual" about the advertising and sale of a dildo.'[11] Before and after *Lawrence,* several States' highest courts have similarly allowed lawmakers to enforce 'public morality' against sex toy distributors, even if the laws at issue seemed silly or unwise to the presiding judges.[12]

Several constitutional challenges to sex toy bans, however, have proven successful. There have generally been two different winning strategies. First, the highest courts in the States of Colorado, Louisiana, and Kansas struck down their States' prohibition on the sale of sex toys, but notably not because they rejected the State's interest in enforcing traditional sexual morality, or because they embraced a constitutional right to pursue sexual pleasure for its own sake.[13] Instead, these courts found the statutes unconstitutional to the extent they burdened the rights of citizens to use dildos, vibrators, and other sex toys as part of *medical treatment.* Rather than challenge these statutes from the perspective of individuals who used these technologies recreationally to bring greater pleasure into their lives, the attorneys highlighted the experience of individuals who had been clinically diagnosed with sexual dysfunction, anorgasmia, pelvic inflammatory disorders, urinary incontinence, cerebral palsy, or who had sought treatment for psychological problems or marital difficulties. Drawing from extensive expert testimony about the documented medical benefits of sex toys for these populations, especially 'dildo-type vibrators,' these courts were able to reframe what most would think to be cases about sexual freedom as cases about medical privacy.[14] Within this framework, sex toy statutes invaded 'a sphere of constitutionally protected privacy which encompasses the intimate medical problems associated with sexual activity.'[15]

A second strategy, that arguably better captures the stakes at issue than do the medical privacy cases, builds upon *Lawrence v Texas* and the new protections it afforded certain forms of sexual intimacy. Most notably, in *Reliable Consultants, Inc. v Earle*, the Fifth Circuit Court of Appeals struck down Texas's ban on the sale of sexual devices. In addition to highlighting the medical benefits of vibrators, like the cases above, the court emphasized that the statute interfered with the constitutional rights of prospective purchasers to engage in 'adult sexual intimacy in the home.' Responding to the concerns raised by a dissenting judge (as well as the Eleventh Circuit in *Williams*), the majority opinion emphasized that the statute 'is not about public sex. It is not about controlling commerce in sex. It is about controlling what people do in the privacy of their own homes.' The majority opinion emphasized that, after *Lawrence,* the government cannot 'burden consensual private intimate conduct by deeming

---

11. *Williams v Morgan*, 478 F.3d 1316 (11th Cir. 2007).

12. e.g. *Yorko v State*, 690 S.W.2d 260 (Tex. Crim. App. 1985); *Morrison v State*, 526 S.E.2d 336 (Ga. 2000); *PHE, Inc. v State*, 877 So. 2d 1244 (Miss. 2004).

13. *People ex rel. Tooley v Seven Thirty-Five E. Colfax, Inc.*, 697 P.2d 348 (Colo. 1985); *State v Hughes*, 792 P.2d 1023 (Kan. 1990); *State v Brenan*, 772 So. 2d 64 (La. 2000).

14. Several legal scholars have critiqued these decisions for their medical framework, e.g. Margo Kaplan, 'Sex-positive Law,' *NYU Law Review* 89 (2014), 89; Craig Konnoth, 'Medicalization and the New Civil Rights,' *Stanford Law Review* 72 (2020), 1198; Susan Reid, 'Sex, Drugs, and American Jurisprudence: The Medicalization of Pleasure,' *Vermont Law Review* 37 (2021), 47.

15. *Hughes*, 792 P.2d at 1029 (quoting *Seven Thirty-Five E Colfax, Inc.*, 697 P.2d at 369 n.26 (citation omitted)).

it morally offensive.'[16] No State or federal court has since adopted the Fifth Circuit's reasoning, and some Texas State courts have refused to follow it.[17]

The legal status of sexual technologies within the US constitutional order is, accordingly, highly uncertain. There is a split across federal appeals circuits as to the constitutionality of sex toy bans after *Lawrence*, and even greater uncertainty following subsequent Supreme Court decisions. The Court's decisions protecting same-sex marriage expanded upon the rights to 'private, consensual intimacy,' set out in *Lawrence*, and they seem to further undermine the 'public morality' arguments used to uphold several States' sex toy prohibitions.[18] Nonetheless, other recent Supreme Court decisions suggest a gloomy future for the rights discussed in *Lawrence*. Most notably, in *Dobbs v Jackson Women's Health Organization*, the Supreme Court over-turned the right to abortion set forth in *Roe v Wade*; abortion does not appear in the Constitution's text and, according to the Court, it was neither 'deeply rooted in this Nation's history' or 'implicit in the concept of ordered liberty.'[19] The *Lawrence* Court expressly relied upon *Roe* in articulating a constitutional liberty interest in private intimacy.[20] Looking at potential future clashes between conservative lawmakers and sexual commerce, it is unclear whether sex toys will follow the pathway of LGBTIQ+ rights into greater mainstream sociolegal acceptance, or whether they will follow the pathway of abortion technologies—broadly culturally accepted, politically significant, yet constitutionally unprotected.

Purely Private

But even if US jurisprudence does eventually embrace constitutional protections for the use and purchase of sex toys, it is important to understand both how narrowly these protections have been framed and ultimately how unsatisfactory the sex toy cases are from the perspective of queer theory and politics.[21] In particular, the high-water mark of constitutional protections for sexual devices—the Fifth Circuit's majority opinion in *Reliable Consultants*—never articulates why the prohibited technologies are sought out by the vast majority of customers or acknowledges the challenges these technologies pose to dominant regimes of gender and sexuality. Both of the Fifth Circuit's framings of sex toy prohibitions—as undermining both private intimacy and access to medical interventions—obscure the social and political value of sexual technologies to feminism, queer communities, and sexual subcultures. By insisting that the sale of sex toys implicated solely sexual intimacy within the bedroom, the Court perpetuated a divide between private sex, which is outside the reach of government

---

16. *Reliable Consultants, Inc. v Earle*, 517 F.3d 738, 745 (5th Cir. 2008).
17. *See Villarreal v State*, 267 S.W.3d 204, 208 (Tex. Ct. App. 2008) ('Fifth Circuit precedent is not binding on Texas courts, and its constitutional pronouncements are highly persuasive at best.').
18. *See Flanigan's Enterprises, Inc. v City of Sandy Springs*, 831 F.3d 1342, 1348 (11th Cir. 2016) ('Although we are persuaded that *Windsor* and *Obergefell* cast serious doubt on [our decision in *Williams*], we are unable to say that they undermine our prior decision to the point of abrogation.').
19. 142 S. Ct. 2228, 597 U.S. ___ (2022).
20. 539 U.S. at 565–66.
21. Kaplan, 'Sex-positive Law,' 157–60.

intrusion, and public sex, which remains a legitimate target. This public/private divide is particularly harmful for marginalized sexual communities, which depend on 'public' contexts in which individuals can connect with others who similarly contest majoritarian heteronormative values.[22] Sexual commerce has a long history of underwriting queer politics—from consciousness-raising to political fundraising to providing physical meeting spaces—and the sex toy cases, even when striking down the prohibitions at issue, cut off the important connection between public sexual discourse and sexual activities occurring within traditionally private spaces.[23]

Moreover, by recognizing the value of sex toys primarily in terms of their medical and therapeutic benefits, the Fifth Circuit and other courts avoid discussing the role of sexual *pleasure* within US jurisprudence.[24] Implicit in the therapeutic benefits mentioned by these courts is that sex toys will enable impaired individuals to have a more enjoyable sex life, but this increased sexual enjoyment is always framed instrumentally in terms of promoting marital intimacy, facilitating procreation, or preventing the transmission of sexually transmitted infections (STIs). A queer perspective on sex toys can foreground both the intrinsic value of sexual pleasure and the connection between sexual pleasure and access to sexual technologies. In particular, sexual technologies can give rise to subjectivities that are organized around technologically-mediated sexual practices, for example, within lesbian, trans, and BDSM communities, as well as on a variety of digital platforms.[25] By focusing on sex toys solely as medical interventions for those who are unable to fulfill heteronormative sexual ideals, courts provide little space for accessing technologies in order to seek pleasure outside a heteronormative framework.

The sex toy cases may be framed specifically in terms of a set of relatively-familiar, relatively-mainstream devices such as vibrators and silicon dildos, but they impact the legal regulation of sexual technology more broadly. If the sexual privacy or medical therapy frameworks remain dominant in 'progressive' defenses of pleasure-enhancing technology, it is difficult to imagine emerging sexual technologies remaining adequately insulated from conservative backlash. Digitally-networked technologies have broadened the reach of sex toys beyond autonomous or partnered activities centered in one physical location; for example, through various forms of teledildonics— vibrators and dildos controlled remotely via the Internet—or sexual interactions via the Metaverse, sexual interactions can transcend any spatial limitations presumed by constitutional rights to 'adult sexual intimacy in the home.'[26] As increasingly realistic robots become

---

22. e.g. Lauren Berlant and Michael Warner, 'Sex in Public,' *Critical Inquiry* 24:3 (1998), 547–566; José Esteban Muñoz, *Cruising Utopia* (New York: NYU Press, 2009); Carlos A. Ball, 'Privacy, Property, and Public Sex,' *Columbia Journal of Gender & Law* 18 (2008), 1.

23. e.g. Andrew Gilden, 'The Queer Limits of Revenge Porn Laws,' *Boston College Law Review* 64 (2023), 801–866; Pat Califia, *Public Sex*, 2nd ed, (Jersey City: Cleiss Press, 2000)

24. Kaplan, 'Sex-positive Law,' 93 ('[C]ase law values sexual pleasure only to the extent that it furthers goals such as marriage, procreation, and intimate relationships.').

25. Gilden, 'The Queer Limits of Revenge Porn Laws,' 838–40.

26. See Jenny Sundén, 'Play, secrecy and consent: Theorizing privacy breaches and sensitive data in the world of networked sex toys,' *Sexualities* (2020), 12 ('Networked sex toys ground a form of intimacy and sexual play which takes place in spaces that are not private, and hence claiming rights to privacy is in a sense paradoxical. This does not, on the other hand, exclude the right to be safe, to have [one's] data kept

available for their purchaser's sexual gratification, framing sexual pleasure with robots as fundamentally either about privacy or therapy sidelines the difficult questions about how to balance new opportunities for human pleasure with legitimate questions of consent and subordination.[27] As new sexual technologies emerge, and as conservative sexual morality remains politically salient in the United States, advocates will need to be much more transparent about *why* individuals pursue pleasure through technology and the stakes of regulating (or not) the technologies in question.

The judgment below envisions a more transparent, sex-positive, and ultimately queerer judicial examination of sexual technology regulations. It takes the form of a concurring opinion in the *Reliable Consultants*. The concurrence agrees with the Fifth Circuit majority that Texas' law is contrary to the Supreme Court's decision in *Lawrence v Texas*, but it emphasizes the dangers of reinforcing a strict public/private division with respect to the regulation of sexual activity. Furthermore, the opinion does not shy away from discussing why the banned devices are important to the many individuals who do *not* suffer from the medical ailments set forth in the majority opinion—i.e. they provide enhanced opportunities for sexual pleasure, and the wide variety of individual, social, and political benefits that can accompany it. Moreover, by engaging more ingenuously with the real-world impact of the sexual devices, the concurring opinion is able to more directly engage with the real-world impacts of their legal prohibition. By prohibiting the sale of sexual technologies, lawmakers reinforce patriarchal and heteronormative expectations and limit the disruptive potential of publics that could form around the banned commerce. In order to account for case law and scholarship that post-dates the 2008 Fifth Circuit decision, the rewritten decision takes place in the context of a hypothetical 2023 lawsuit in which the Court summarily reaffirms its earlier decision in a *per curiam* opinion.[28] The rewritten decision is a concurrence to the majority's short *per curiam* opinion.

---

safe or processed safely.').
27.   See Jeannie Suk Gersen, 'Sex Lex Machina: Intimacy and Artificial Intelligence,' *Columbia Law Review* 119 (2019), 1793; Lara Karaian, 'Plastic Fantastic: Sex Robots and/as Sexual Fantasy,' *Sexualities* (2022).
28.   'A per curiam decision is a court opinion issued in the name of the Court rather than specific judges ... Per curiam decisions are given that label by the court issuing the opinion, and these opinions tend to be short. The opinions will typically deal with issues which the issuing court views as relatively non-controversial': Cornell Law School Legal Information Institute, Wex, accessed 9 November 2023, https://www.law.cornell.edu/wex/per_curiam.

UNITED STATES COURT OF APPEALS
for the Fifth Circuit

Reliable Consultants, Inc.,

Plaintiff—Appellee,

versus

JOSÉ GARZA,
TRAVIS COUNTY DISTRICT ATTORNEY,

Defendant—Appellant.
Appeal from the United States District Court
for the Western District of Texas

December 15, 2023

Per Curiam:

Reliable Consultants ('Reliable') operates several retail stores in Texas that carry a stock of sexual devices for off-premise, private use. In 2004, Reliable filed a complaint for declaratory and injunctive relief alleging, *inter alia*, that the State's 'obscene device' statute violated its customers' rights to substantive due process as protected by the Fourteenth Amendment of the United States Constitution.[29] The district court dismissed Reliable's complaint. On appeal, we reversed, holding that the 'obscene device' statute was unconstitutional in light of the United State Supreme Court's decision in *Lawrence v Texas*.[30] We held that the statute 'impermissibly burdens the individuals' substantive due process right to engage in private intimate conduct of his or her choosing … An individual who wants to legally use a safe sexual device during private intimate moments alone or with another is unable to legally purchase a device in Texas.'[31] We further observed:

> Just as in *Lawrence*, the State here wants to use its law to enforce a public moral code by restricting private intimate conduct. The case is not about public sex. It is not about controlling commerce in sex. It is about controlling what people do in the privacy of their own homes

---

29. Texas Penal Code §§ 43.21, 43.22, and 43.23 (criminalizing the promotion of an 'obscene device').
30. *Reliable Consultants, Inc. v Earle*, 517 F.3d 738 (5th Cir. 2008).
31. *Id.*

because the State is morally opposed to a certain type of private intimate conduct. This is an insufficient justification after *Lawrence*.[32]

Judge Barksdale dissented, asserting that 'the proscribed conduct is *not* private sexual conduct ... the [obscene device] statute proscribes only the sale or other promotion (such as advertizing) of those devices, including, but not limited to, a dildo or artificial vagina.'[33] In Judge Barksdale's view, after *Lawrence*, the government can still enforce public morality against conduct that is 'both public and commercial.'[34] A petition for rehearing en banc was denied, over the dissent of seven judges.[35]

Since 2008, Texas State courts have declined to follow our decision in *Reliable Consultants*.[36] Fearing future prosecution, Reliable brought the instant action seeking to enjoin defendant, the District Attorney for Garza County, Texas, from enforcing an unconstitutional statute. The district court granted summary judgment to Reliable, pursuant to our decision in *Reliable Consultants*, as that decision addressed nearly identical factual and legal issues.

We affirm. The Supreme Court has neither overturned *Lawrence* nor limited the decision in a manner that is inconsistent with our analysis in *Reliable Consultants*. Accordingly, there is no need to revisit our prior decision.

Andrew Gilden, Circuit Judge, concurring:

I join my colleagues' opinion reaffirming the unconstitutionality of the Texas 'obscene device' statute and agree that our decision in *Reliable Consultants* continues to control 15 years later. I write separately, however, to emphasize some significant shortcomings in that decision which were not addressed by any of my colleagues in 2008. In my view, despite reaching the correct outcome, the panel majority did not sufficiently appreciate—and arguably mischaracterized—the weighty liberty and equality interests raised by prohibiting the sale of vibrators, dildos, and other sexual devices. Although its reading of *Lawrence v Texas* properly led to the invalidation of the statute before it, this reading at most only weakly constrains lawmakers seeking to enforce traditional gender norms and sexuality morality in the commercial sphere.

Private vs. public conduct

Although the majority and dissenting opinions applied *Lawrence* quite differently to the facts before them, they nonetheless both interpreted that decision as imposing a binary framework for identifying sexual freedoms under the Due Process Clause. In particular, both opinions seized on the terms 'private' and 'public' in *Lawrence* to draw a bright line between those activities that take place in private locations, which

---

32. *Id.* at 746.
33. *Id.* at 748.
34. *Id.* at 749.
35. 538 F.3d 355 (5th Cir. 2008).
36. e.g. *Villarreal v State*, 267 S.W.3d 204, 208 (Tex. Ct. App. 2008) ('Fifth Circuit precedent is not binding on Texas courts.').

are constitutionally protected against majoritarian sexual morality, and those that take place in other locations, which are not.[37] The majority framed the regulated purchases as concerning 'private intimate conduct' and thus insulated from Texas criminal law. The dissent framed the same activities as 'public and commercial' and thus within criminal law's legitimate reach. The two opinions nonetheless agreed that Reliable's constitutional challenge hinged upon whether we classified the regulated activity as ontologically private or public. *Lawrence*, and the constitutional jurisprudence it builds on, certainly points to a zone of privacy protected by the Due Process Clause, but it was a mistake to reduce meaningful privacy to simply a question about whether the regulated activity took place within the homes of Reliable's customers. Unlike the majority, I think this case *is* about 'commerce in sex,' but unlike the dissent, I do not think that such classification disposes of the Reliable's constitutional claim.

Most contemporary understandings of privacy reject the notion that privacy is fundamentally about geographic location or whether some information has been kept (literally or figuratively) under lock and key. Instead, privacy is a context-specific expectation that an individual will be able to control the flow of certain information within and across different social relationships.[38] Privacy allows individuals the ability to meaningfully manage the boundaries between the very different social contexts in which they live, so that they can abide by the very different expectations that attach to those contexts.[39] For example, privacy ensures that a patient can speak to a mental health professional without fear that the conversation will be leaked to an employer. Privacy ensures that a child can make a phone call to their parent without worrying that the conversation will be shared with advertisers. And privacy ensures that sexual activity remains the concern of only those who lawfully consent to it.[40] So long as the people involved take reasonable efforts to prevent wholesale public access to sensitive information, meaningful legal privacy limits the ability of third parties—especially the government—from obtaining access to that information and using it against them.

This conception of privacy is reflected in several strands of constitutional jurisprudence. In the Fourth Amendment context, the government may not conduct a warrantless search where the object of the search retains a 'reasonable expectation of privacy.' A person may have a reasonable privacy expectation notwithstanding their physical location in a public place, such as a telephone booth.[41] They may retain a reasonable privacy expectation even as to information that has been shared with certain third parties, such as mobile phone companies.[42] The Court has recently reaffirmed

---

37. Several other courts have extracted a similar binary framework from *Lawrence* in order to exclude sexual regulations from constitutional scrutiny, e.g. *State v Pope*, 608 S.E.2d 114, 116 (2005) ('As the *Lawrence* Court expressly excluded prostitution and public conduct from its holding, the State of North Carolina may properly criminalize the solicitation of a sexual act it deems a crime against nature.'); *Williams v Morgan*, 478 F.3d 1316 (11th Cir. 2007) ('[W]hile the statute at issue in *Lawrence* criminalized private sexual conduct, the statute at issue in this case forbids public, commercial activity.').

38. Helen Nissenbaum, 'Privacy as Contextual Integrity,' *Washington Law Review* 79 (2004), 119.

39. Julie Cohen, 'What Privacy Is For,' *Harvard Law Review* 126 (2012), 1904.

40. Danielle Keats Citron, 'Sexual Privacy,' *Yale Law Journal* 128 (2018), 1870.

41. *Katz v United States*, 389 U.S. 347, 351–52 (1967) ('What [a person] seeks to preserve as private, even in an area accessible to the public, may be constitutionally protected.').

42. *Carpenter v United States*, 138 S. Ct. 2206 (2018).

that '[a] person does not surrender all Fourth Amendment protection by venturing into the public sphere.'[43]

In the Fourteenth Amendment context, liberty interests framed in terms of privacy focus much more on the sensitivity of the decision at issue, rather than whether that decision has been kept secret or secluded from view. 'Personal decisions with respect to marriage, procreation, contraception, family relationships, child rearing, and education,' fall within the ambit of privacy interests protected by the Due Process Clause, but rarely are the inputs or outputs of such decisions perfectly sequestered from public view.[44] Decisions as to contraception require interacting with retailers or medical professionals in order to receive the materials necessary to effectuate such decisions.[45] Decisions with respect to child rearing and education ultimately concern the role of the parent and child within the broader community, and these decisions will likely be known by community members.[46] And decisions with respect to same-sex sexual activity, even when taking place within the confines of the home, will often manifest in public-facing relationships.[47] Indeed, in *Obergefell* the Court ultimately struck down prohibitions on same-sex marriage in significant part because marriage often serves as an outgrowth of the private decisions it had protected in *Lawrence*.[48]

When the Court in *Lawrence* referred to sexuality as 'the most private human conduct,' we need not interpret the Court to mean that sexual privacy disappears whenever sexuality interfaces with public or commercial spheres. Much, if not most, contemporary sexual activity involves some prior commercial activity, such as purchasing condoms, lubricants, Viagra, Truvada, pornography, romantic music, or a monthly subscription to a dating app. The State of Texas cannot criminally prohibit these commercial transactions consistent with protections for personal liberty under the Fourteenth Amendment. Or at the very least, the State must have some justification beyond moral disapproval of these transactions to justify attaching criminal consequences to them. There is no principled distinction for constitutionally protecting the purchase of certain technologies that facilitate an autonomous, fulfilling sex life—e.g. condoms and certain pharmaceuticals—while excluding from protection other technologies—e.g. vibrators and dildos—that accomplish similar ends. This distinction certainly cannot be justified by classifying one group of purchases as 'private' and the other group as 'public.' Vibrators, dildos, and other 'obscene devices' may be relatively taboo compared with, say, birth control pills, but the State has failed to come forward with any plausible basis for treating them categorically differently than other sexual technologies.[49]

---

43. *Id.* at 2217.
44. *Lawrence*, 539 U.S. at 574.
45. *Carey v Population Servs. Int'l*, 431 U.S. 678 (1977).
46. *Pierce v Society of Sisters*, 268 U.S. 510 (1925).
47. *Lawrence*, 539 U.S. at 567 ('When sexuality finds overt expression in intimate conduct with another person, the conduct can be but one element in a personal bond that is more enduring.').
48. *Obergefell v Hodges*, 576 U.S. 644, 667 ('But while Lawrence confirmed a dimension of freedom that allows individuals to engage in intimate association without criminal liability, it does not follow that freedom stops there.').
49. As the majority in *Reliable Consultants* observed, Texas' proffered interests in the 'protection of minors

I acknowledge that *Lawrence* itself addressed conduct that did allegedly occur within the confines of a home, 'the most private of places,' and accordingly did not involve 'public conduct.'[50] But this does not mean that sexual activity—or communications regarding sexual activity—in a different location would be unprotected. Indeed, the Court recognized that the case touched upon *both* 'the most private of places, the home' *and* 'the most private human conduct, sexual behavior.' As the Court emphasized, 'The instant case involves liberty of the person both in spatial and in its more transcendent dimensions.'[51] The privacy stakes may have been exceptionally high due to both the location and subject matter, but this does not mean that sexual privacy ends at the front doorstep. Furthermore, *Lawrence* also said it was not addressing 'whether the government must give formal recognition to any relationship that homosexual persons seek to enter,'[52] yet the Court did go on to recognize such a constitutional requirement twelve years later in *Obergefell*.

In the fifteen years since our decision in *Reliable Consultants*, we have learned from the Supreme Court that *Lawrence* is properly understood as a floor for sexual autonomy, and not in any way as a ceiling. A strict private/public binary approach to sexual regulations, as appears to be endorsed by the majority in *Reliable Consultants*, risks unduly cabining in sexual freedoms and exposing marginalized forms of sexual expression to morally-infused criminal punishments.[53] We should not read a public or commercial setting limitation into sexual privacy rights where such settings were not presented to the *Lawrence* Court, and where doing so undermines the core autonomy and equality interests advanced by the decision.

Although it was plausible in the *Reliable Consultants* litigation to tightly connect the purchase of sexual devices to homebound sexual conduct, I must stress the dangers of limiting sexual freedoms to the confines of the home. Meaningful sexual autonomy—the ability to explore one's desires safely and consensually—requires access to material and cultural resources that are often unavailable within the walls of many households.[54] These resources include physically safe spaces for sex, a community of supporting peers, educational materials regarding sexuality, inclusive sexual healthcare, and the various physical supplies that make sexual intimacy pleasurable.[55] These resources, especially

---

and unwilling adults from exposure to sexual devices and their advertisement' is far from convincing. Minors can be shielded from 'improper sexual expression' through less heavy-handed means, and 'an adult cannot buy a sexual device without making the affirmative decision to visit a store and make the purchase': 517 F.3d 738, 746.

50. 539 U.S. at 567, 578. I note, however, that several of the factual predicates to the Court's decision appear not to have been true. The defendants were not in a relationship at the time they were arrested, and it is unlikely that they were actually engaged in sexual activity: Dale Carpenter, *Flagrant Conduct: The Story of* Lawrence v Texas (New York: W.W. Norton & Co., 2012).

51. *Lawrence*, 539 U.S. at 562.

52. *Id.* at 578.

53. Carlos A. Ball, 'Privacy, Property, and Public Sex,' *Columbia Journal of Gender & Law* 18 (2008), 1.

54. Susan F. Appleton, 'Toward a Culturally Cliterate Family Law,' *Berkeley Journal of Gender, Law & Justice* 23 (2008), 267, 326 ('Sexual activity is portrayed, in some of its most idealized descriptions, as an experience whose physicality and energy are self-sustaining and untethered, shutting out the rest of the material world ... Yet, for all the talk and imagination of "pure sex" that takes place in its own time and space, individuals often rely on a variety of external supports and interventions to facilitate sexual experiences.').

55. *Id.*

for those engaged in marginalized sexual practices, often *cannot* safely be accessed or used at home as was assumed to be true for Reliable's customers.[56] LGBTQ+ people, and especially youth, often must explore their sexuality outside the oversight of disapproving family members, and it is a cruel irony that these individuals remain vulnerable to prosecution after *Lawrence*, at least as it has been interpreted by us and our colleagues in other circuits. Our restrictive approach to sexual privacy denies the undeniably public, commercial elements of contemporary sexuality, and such denial may be impossible in future clashes between the government and sexual autonomy.

Consequently, a binary framework of sexual privacy is most likely to disadvantage those individuals whose sexual practices would benefit most from privacy protections.[57] If a person's sexual practices cannot be bracketed as fundamentally 'private,' then they remain, even under the majority opinion, vulnerable to hostile lawmaking in the name of public morals.[58] For example, the Eleventh Circuit upheld a Florida statute prohibiting adoption by a 'homosexual' person; similarly to the *Reliable Consultants* majority, the court distinguished the 'right to engage in private conduct' at issue in *Lawrence* with the 'public recognition' necessary for adopting a child.[59] Unconstrained by *Lawrence*, the court explained:

> Although social theorists from Plato to Simone de Beauvoir have proposed alternative child-rearing arrangements, none has proven as enduring as the marital family structure, nor has the accumulated wisdom of several millennia of human experience discovered a superior model.[60]

Without a more robust notion of sexual privacy, lawmakers and judges may apply the full weight of their moral disapproval against those who fail to conform to majoritarian expectations about how they should structure their intimate lives.

By allowing some degree of public or commercial activity to come within the zone of sexual privacy protected by the Constitution, the effect would *not* be to insulate all forms of sexual conduct from government oversight. If a particular conduct is nonconsensual or is demonstrably harmful, either physically or psychologically, then its location within a conceivable zone of privacy would not preclude the government from imposing criminal penalties. Nor does it even necessarily lead to 'heightened scrutiny' under the Supreme Court's 'fundamental rights' jurisprudence. What a more

---

56. Ball, 'Privacy, Property, and Public Sex,' 8; see also Derek Bambauer, 'Exposed,' *Minnesota Law Review* 98 (2014), 2025 ('[U]se of intimate media may be particularly important for people with minority sexual preferences ... Production of consensual intimate media allows people to challenge prevailing gender norms and communication patterns, and to take some control over self-representation.').

57. As Kendall Thomas wrote in the aftermath of *Bowers v Hardwick*, '[f]or heterosexuals, the concept of privacy serves to carve out a safe haven for human flourishing': Kendall Thomas, 'Beyond the Privacy Principle,' *Columbia Law Review* 92 (1992), 1431, 1454–55. By contrast, for gay men and lesbians, 'the claim of privacy always also structurally implies a claim to secrecy': Thomas, 'Beyond the Privacy Principle,' 1455.

58. Adopting the same public/private binary framework as the *Reliable Consultants* majority, several courts have interpreted *Lawrence* to permit undercover police officers to solicit and arrest gay men for consensual sex in semi-public spaces like department store bathrooms, even if no unwitting third parties were present, e.g. *Singson v Commonwealth*, 621 S.E.2d 682 (Va. Ct. App. 2005); *Tjan v Commonwealth*, 621 S.E.2d 698 (Va. Ct. App. 2005).

59. *Lofton v Dep't of Children & Family*, 358 F.3d 804, 817 (11th Cir. 2004).

60. *Id.* at 820.

robust understanding of constitutional privacy *would* preclude, however, are criminal penalties driven by nothing more than lawmakers' moral opposition.

Liberty and Equality

The *Reliable Consultants* panel downplayed an important aspect of efforts, in Texas and elsewhere, to prohibit the sale of sexual devices: these laws, like *Lawrence* and its progeny, implicate *both* liberty and equality concerns. *Lawrence* was decided under the aegis of substantive due process, i.e. as a case about liberty, but it was expressly concerned about the impact of sodomy prohibitions against sexual minorities. It acknowledged that the case involved adults 'engaged in sexual practices common to a homosexual lifestyle,' and concluded, '[t]he State cannot demean their existence or control their destiny by making their private sexual conduct a crime.'[61] In *Obergefell*, the Court observed that rights to liberty and rights to equal protection 'are connected in a profound way,' and it emphasized that denial of marriage—a liberty interest—to same-sex couples 'serves to disrespect and subordinate them.'[62]

Although Texas's 'obscene device' statute does not conspicuously discriminate against particular classes of purchasers, the majority in *Reliable Consultants* gave overly short shrift to the equality concerns before it. In response to the State's argument that *Lawrence* was inapplicable due to the Supreme Court's 'concern with how the statute targeted a specific class of people,' the *Reliable Consultants* majority simply observed that the *Lawrence* majority relied on substantive due process and not equal protection.[63] It then moved on. In doing so, it missed an opportunity to articulate the uneven impact the 'obscene device' statute has on citizens across Texas.

For example, 'obscene device' laws make it more difficult for women to access technologies through which they can explore sexual pleasure independent of the desires and demands of cisgender male partners. Most concretely, a much higher percentage of women than men utilize sexual devices during masturbation.[64] Moreover, since the 1960s, vibrators in particular have been held out within feminist circles as politically important objects and have featured prominently in decades of educational workshops focused on women's pleasure and clitoral stimulation.[65] Sexual devices can create educational, recreational, and political opportunities that especially benefit women in a still-male-dominated society.[66] By criminalizing commerce in these technologies, the State discourages women's sexual autonomy and reinforces traditional expectations of female sexual subservience.[67] The 'obscene device' statute does also prohibit commerce

---

61. *Lawrence*, 539 U.S. at 578.

62. 576 U.S. at 672, 675.

63. 517 F.3d at 744.

64. Danielle J. Lindemann, 'Pathology Full Circle: A History of Anti-Vibrator Legislation in the United States,' *Columbia Journal of Gender & Law* 15 (2006), 326, 344.

65. Appleton, 'Toward a Culturally Cliterate Family Law,'; Lieberman, *Buzz*.

66. Appleton, 'Toward a Culturally Cliterate Family Law,' 329 ('Allowing women, young and old, to become more familiar with their bodies and their capacity for pleasure not only increases sexual self-efficacy, but also fosters empowerment in other aspects of life[.]').

67. Lindemann, 'Pathology Full Circle,' 344 ('Since the majority of people who use dildos, vibrators, and

in items that may be appealing to cisgender, heterosexual men—e.g. 'artificial vaginas'—but the prohibited items are overall uniquely associated with empowering women sexually and with challenging traditional norms regarding women's sexuality.

'Obscene device' laws also disproportionately burden LGBTQ+ individuals and communities. By limiting access to dildos and other objects that might be useful for sexual stimulation, these laws make it especially difficult for transgender people to pursue their sexual desires in line with their lived gender identities. Moreover, these laws limit opportunities to experience a wide range of pleasurable activities, either alone or with others, that do not fundamentally depend on the presence of a penis or vulva. Moreover, commerce in sexual technologies have also been historically connected to LGBTQ+ activism and community.[68] It was only after the rise of the women's and LGBTQ+ rights' movements that State legislatures first singled out sexual devices for criminal prohibition, and this history should inform our understanding of the motives behind 'obscene device' laws such as Texas's.

Although I agree with the *Reliable Consultants* majority that 'obscene device' laws are most comfortably analyzed within the substantive due process framework, these laws bear many of the hallmarks of Equal Protection Clause violations. First, these laws reinforce traditional stereotypes about proper behavior with respect to gender and sexuality.[69] The relevant stereotypes here include: (1) that women's pleasure is contingent upon male sexual pleasure, (2) that self-pleasure, especially by women, is immoral, (3) that women must occupy a sexually passive role, (4) that men must occupy a sexually dominant role, and (4) that one's genitals dictate their sexual behavior. Sexual technologies can facilitate individual and societal challenges to each of these stereotypes, so long as these technologies are both accessible and culturally visible.[70] By cutting off access and visibility to certain sexual devices, Texas law insulates archaic, misogynistic, homophobic, and transphobic stereotypes from meaningful contestation.

Second, by criminalizing the sale of technologies closely associated with subordinated groups, such as women and sexual minorities, Texas brands these groups as socially inferior.[71] If someone relies on devices like dildos or vibrators to experience pleasure in sex, they risk arrest and prosecution should they attempt to obtain or replace them anywhere in the State. By contrast, if someone's sexual pleasure relies heavily on access

---

other insertable sex toys are women, making them contraband is another institutionalized form of controlling female sexuality.' (internal citation omitted)).

68. Lieberman, *Buzz*.

69. e.g. *United States v Virginia*, 518 U.S. 515, 542 (1996) ('[S]tate actors may not rely on overbroad generalizations to make judgments about people that are likely to perpetuate historical patterns of discrimination' (internal citations omitted)); *Mississippi Univ. for Women v Hogan*, 458 U.S. 718, 725 (1982) ('Care must be taken in ascertaining whether the statutory objective itself reflects archaic and stereotypic notions.').

70. Bridget Crawford, 'Toward a Third-Wave Feminist Theory: Young Women, Pornography, and the Praxis of Pleasure,' *Michigan Journal of Gender & Law* 14 (2007), 99, 122 (explaining how opening a 'sex-toy business' can 'create models of female sexual agency' and provide women opportunities to 'make their sexual desire primary').

71. *Hassan v City of New York*, 804 F.3d 277, 291 (3d Cir. 2015) (finding that New York's post-9/11 surveillance of Muslims imposed a 'badge of inferiority' on their religion even though the City did not overtly condemn it).

to condoms, or Viagra, or mainstream pornography, they remain free to walk into a multitude of retail establishments without fear of criminal sanction. Texas law 'serves to disrespect and subordinate' only those individuals whose sex lives lean heavily on so-called obscene devices.[72]

Third, it is a plausible conclusion that the 'obscene device' statute emerged from the hostility of Texas lawmakers to women and sexual minorities, or at least to members of those groups who fail to conform to traditional stereotypes.[73] As observed by legal scholar Kim Shayo Buchanan, 'the legal treatment of sex toys … is marked by legislative hostility and judicial ambivalence that betrays a fundamental societal discomfort with the nonprocreative sexual pleasure of women and sexual minorities.'[74] Indeed, the State here made little attempt to veil its efforts to reinforce gender and sexual norms; it asserted an interest in 'discouraging prurient interests in autonomous sex and the pursuit of gratification unrelated to procreation.'[75] By discouraging gratification unrelated to procreation, the State is communicating that it disapproves of those sexual activities that are unable to produce offspring, which would include all (cisgender) same-sex sexual activity. And although hostility towards 'autonomous sex' might seem evenhanded, the 'obscene device' statute is unlikely to have much impact on (normative) male masturbation. Regardless, the State's invocations of 'public morality' are ultimately just a more palatable way of expressing hostility towards those who violate traditional norms of sex and gender.

The *Reliable Consultants* majority was likely aware of these equality concerns, but nevertheless it never surfaced them. To the extent the majority acknowledged *any* burden of the law on specific individuals or populations, it was with respect to individuals who were using sexual devices in order to treat medical conditions or to repair a marriage under stress:

> For some couples in which one partner may be physically unable to engage in intercourse, or in which a contagious disease, such as HIV, precludes intercourse, these devices may be one of the only ways to engage in a safe, sexual relationship. Others use sexual devices to treat a variety of therapeutic needs, such as erectile dysfunction … Still other individuals use sexual devices for nontherapeutic personal reasons, such as a desire to refrain from premarital intercourse.[76]

Although the needs of these individuals are certainly important, the majority opinion focuses only on the most widely sympathetic, least-controversial use-cases for sexual devices. Within the universe of customers highlighted by the majority, sexual technologies are useful for avoiding disease, for treating sex-related ailments, or for keeping relationships intact. None of the cited individuals are seeking to *enhance* their

---

72. *Obergefell*, 576 U.S. at 675.
73. *United States v Windsor*, 570 U.S. 744, 770 (2013) (striking down the Defense of Marriage Act where there was 'strong evidence of a law having the purpose and effect of disapproval of' people in same-sex marriages); *Romer v Evans*, 517 U.S. 620, 632 (1996) ('[T]he amendment seems inexplicable by anything but animus toward the class it affects.').
74. Kim Shayo Buchanan, '*Lawrence v Geduldig*: Regulating women's sexuality,' *Emory Law Journal* 56 (2006), 1235, 1249.
75. *Reliable Consultants*, 517 F.3d at 745.
76. 517 F.3d at 742.

sex lives or to discover new forms of pleasure.[77] To the extent that sexual devices are used for 'nontherapeutic personal reasons' in the majority opinion, they are a helpful means of staying away from sexual intercourse until marriage. Although the majority opinion appropriately acknowledges that sexual devices may be especially important to people with certain physical disabilities, it nonetheless says little about the diverse uses of sexual devices by the broad range of purchasers.[78] As a result, it becomes difficult to identify the autonomy and equality concerns that I see at the core of this dispute. The majority focused solely on sexual devices used in connection with medical treatment and relationship therapy, and all other interests in accessing sexual devices disappeared into the zone of privacy.

I understand my colleagues' discomfort with discussing sexuality explicitly, especially given the absence of such discussions in any of the cases they relied upon to strike down the Texas statute.[79] But nothing in *Lawrence* or its progeny forecloses a transparent assessment of how individual autonomy is connected with sexual pleasure and is vulnerable to outmoded gender and sexual stereotypes. Especially in light of the Supreme Court's recent willingness to reconsider core pieces of its Due Process Clause jurisprudence, it is crucial for lower courts to spell out what is at stake for actual citizens affected by morality-infused legislation. If all that is at stake in the regulation of sexual devices is the ability to go to a store and purchase a vibrating phallus for use with a spouse or medical professional, then the broader social and political context disappears. The hostile deployment of traditional sexual morality goes unchecked, and the considerable impact on marginalized groups becomes both invisible and irrelevant.

Once we acknowledge the value of sexual technologies for large swaths of our society, the stakes of this dispute become clear. On one side of the dispute are businesses catering to the desire of individuals to pursue sexual pleasure for their own physical, emotional, and social well-being, often in defiance of traditional stereotypes. On the other side are lawmakers seeking to reinforce these stereotypes through criminal law. Pure disapproval of consensual, uncoerced sexual activity is an illegitimate basis for government action.

---

77. Lindemann, 'Pathology Full Circle,' 345; Buchanan, '*Lawrence v Geduldig*,' 1250.
78. *Reliable Consultants*, 517 F.3d at 742 ('For some couples in which one partner may be physically unable to engage in intercourse ... these devices may be one of the only ways to engage in a safe, sexual relationship.').
79. David S. Cohen, 'Silence of the Liberals: When Supreme Court Justices Fail to Speak Up for LGBT Rights,' *University of Richmond Law Review* 53 (2019), 1085–1147. Cohen observes that since the Supreme Court's decision in *Bowers v Hardwick*, 'no liberal Justice ... put forth a substantive argument for constitutional protection for gay rights.' *Id.* at 1089. He observes the dangers of this silence: 'By doing so, they lost an opportunity to use separate opinions to influence the trajectory of the law on gay and trans rights [and] solidify the societal and legal gains that may be threatened in the wake of Justice Kennedy's departure from the Court.' *Id.* at 1090.

10

NSW Registrar of Births, Deaths and Marriages v Norrie (Australia):

A Trickster's Jurisprudence

Odette Mazel, Claerwen O'Hara and Dianne Otto

Introduction

'I do have a specific sex, in terms of male or female that's "non-specific." That's what my specific sex is ... I'm 58 and I went to the High Court to establish that people had a right to be identified as neither male or female, and through that process, the High Court announced that I have a specific sex and that specific sex is non-specific ... I smashed the binary, what else makes sense after that? There's no gay and straight after binaries.'[1]

Norrie, who uses the pronouns 'they' and 'she,' has been a drag queen, sex worker, public servant, outreach worker, and stunt double, amongst other things. She underwent gender affirmation surgery in the late 1980s and lived as a woman, but then started questioning the rules around sex/gender.[2] In 2009, Norrie applied to have their sex/gender descriptor changed on their birth certificate to 'non-specific.' As required, their application was accompanied by statutory declarations from two medical practitioners who confirmed Norrie had undergone a sex affirmation procedure. Both declarations also expressed support for Norrie's claim that her sex was 'non-specific,' although this was not required by the legislation. After several appeals, Norrie's request was granted in 2014 by the final court of appeal, the High Court of Australia,[3] which found registering 'sex' under the relevant legislation was not confined to 'male' or 'female.'[4] Before explaining why this judgment needed further queering despite its finding

---

1. Norrie, interview by Odette Mazel, Waterloo, NSW, 22 August 2019.
2. Historically, the term sex has been associated with a binary construction (male or female) of biological characteristics, whilst gender [identity] has been understood as socially constructed and not necessarily aligned with biological characteristics. We start from the premise that both these terms are culturally constructed, multiplicitous, fluid and performative. We use the term sex/gender to indicate this understanding. See Judith Butler, *Gender Trouble: Feminism and the Subversion of Identity* (Routledge, 1990).
3. Australia is a colonial federation and New South Wales (NSW) is one of its States. Sydney, where Norrie lives, is the capital of NSW and is located on the lands of the Gadigal People of the Eora Nation which have never been ceded.
4. *NSW Registrar of Births, Deaths and Marriages v Norrie* [2014] HCA 11 (2 April 2014) (*Norrie* HCA).

in Norrie's favour, and discussing the legal methods we found helpful in doing so, we want to explain why we describe Norrie's engagement with law as that of a trickster.[5]

Tricksters are evident in diverse oral and literary sources, across different locations, cultures and temporalities. They are transgressive figures, sexually and gender ambiguous, androgenous or polymorphous,[6] shapeshifters: 'uncanny, perverse, flamboyant and unsettl[ing].'[7] They are queer. The trickster's appearance is an intervention—their role is to expose the contingency in any situation, to bring into question conventional practices and disrupt long held beliefs. They make fun of mainstream norms, trouble existing knowledge structures, flout authority and challenge power. While tricksters deconstruct accepted rules and behaviours, their revelations, once accepted, open the space for communal practices to be 're-constructed and defined anew.'[8]

Norrie's legal intervention is emblematic of the trickster. In exposing the limitations of the law, Norrie brought into plain sight the absurdity of the binary construction of male and female that had been read into Australian law since colonisation.[9] She challenged law makers to reject the legal dualism of male and female that is used to justify the policing, punishment and pathologization of non-compliant sex/gender identification and expression. Their truth-telling is a powerful personal act, but more significantly, a collective act, undertaken in the spirit of creating change for the broader queer community.

In this re-visiting of the judgment, we pay tribute to Norrie's shapeshifting bravery and her resolve to use the law to change the law. Theirs is a story of activism, disruption, flamboyance and transgression. A trickster's jurisprudence.

The Original Judgment of the High Court of Australia

'Surviving adversity is good. Anything that doesn't kill you, makes you prettier... I had no idea what I was getting into.'[10]

'Not all human beings can be classified by sex as either male or female.'[11] This was the very promising opening sentence of the High Court of Australia's unanimous judgment in Norrie's case. The judgment goes on to confirm that it is within the power of the Registrar, under the Births, Deaths and Marriages Registration Act 1995 (NSW), to record Norrie's sex as 'non-specific,' as she requested. This outcome was ground-breaking and there was clearly much to celebrate.[12] So why would we consider this judgment in need of 'queering'?

---

5. Thanks, Odette, for bringing this idea into this commentary.

6. Jacob W Glazier, 'Only a Trickster Can Save Us: Hypercommandeering Queer Identity Positions,' *International Journal of Humanities and Social Science Invention* 3/11 (2014), 28.

7. Glazier, 'Only a Trickster Can Save Us,' 28.

8. Kaisa Ilmonen, 'From Borders to Bridges: Trickster Aesthetics in the Novels of Michelle Cliff,' *American Studies in Scandinavia* 37 (2005), 89.

9. Sandy O'Sullivan, 'The Colonial Project of Gender (and Everything Else),' *Genealogy* 5/3 (2021), 67.

10. Norrie, interview by Odette Mazel.

11. *Norrie* HCA, [1].

12. Human Rights Law Centre, 'High Court Rejects Outdated Notions of Gender,' Human Rights Law Centre, 2 April 2014, accessed 10 November 2023, https://www.hrlc.org.au/news/media-release-high-court-rejects-outdated-notions-of-gender.

Despite its opening sentence, the Norrie judgment does not come close to recognizing sex/gender as a self-determined category as indicated by international human rights law at the time,[13] and recommended by the Australian Human Rights Commission.[14] Indeed, the High Court, in its exercise of statutory interpretation, failed to address Norrie's application as raising human rights issues at all. In our queering of the judgment, we utilized several principles of statutory interpretation that would have enabled the High Court to consider Australia's international human rights obligations and examine the context and purpose of the legislation more critically.

However, the biggest hurdle for queering the judgment was presented by the wording of the legislation, which makes 'sex affirmation surgery' a precondition to making an application for change of sex.[15] This wording (re)confirms the male/female duality as the norm and sex/gender identity as biologically based. Indeed, the High Court accepted the Registrar's submission that 'the Act recognizes only male or female as registrable classes of sex.'[16] The judgment then continues this obfuscation:

> But to accept [the Registrar's] submission does not mean that the Act requires that this classification can apply, or is to be applied, to everyone. And there is nothing in the Act which suggests that the Registrar is entitled, much less duty-bound, to register the classification of a person's sex inaccurately as male or female having regard to the information which the Act requires to be provided by the applicant.[17]

With these words, the High Court significantly qualifies its opening sentence by affirming the binary categorisation of legal gender as the dominant (normal) framework and recognizing merely 'that there exists some interstitial space between "female" and "male" into which some may fall.'[18] We wanted to show that, despite the precondition of sex affirmation surgery, the High Court could have rejected the harmful assumption that there must be an alignment between physical sex/gender characteristics and social sex/gender identity or expression before a change of sex could be recorded. For us, their judgment depended far too much on the medical practitioners' assessment that Norrie's sex could be physically classified as 'non-specific,' rather than on Norrie's self-identification.[19]

Finally, the legislation not only requires an applicant to subject themselves to sex affirmation procedure, but also that the applicant not be married.[20] While these requirements were not at issue in Norrie's case because she satisfied them both, we wanted to show the High Court had the opportunity to express its judicial opinion, known as *obiter dicta*, about these absurd injurious requirements.

---

13. *Yogyakarta Principles on the Application of International Human Rights Law in relation to Sexual Orientation and Gender Identity,* March 2007, Principle 3.

14. Australian Human Rights Commission, *Sex Files: the Legal Recognition of Sex in Documents and Government Records,* March 2009.

15. Births, Deaths and Marriages Registration Act 1995 (NSW), section 32DA(1)(c).

16. *Norrie* HCA, [32].

17. *Norrie* HCA, [32].

18. John Eldridge and Rebecca McEwen, 'A Call to Arms: *Norrie,*' 2014 39/3 *Alternative Law Journal* 189, 190.

19. *Norrie* HCA, [39].

20. Births, Deaths and Marriages Registration Act 1995 (NSW), section 32DA(1)(d).

Queering the Judgment

> 'I just thought this is what's right. Everyone will see this is right, won't they? This is right. [But] [i]t's not as straightforward as I thought it would be ... Change takes foolishness—people foolish enough to believe they can change the world.'[21]

In our queer reconsideration of the High Court's judgment, we try to centre Norrie's voice and tricksterism to resist the abstraction of the subject that occurs in most formal legal reasoning. In making this move we also want to acknowledge the (oral) tradition of storytelling, which is central to queer, feminist praxis and a foundation of Indigenous legal systems.[22] In addition, we found several common law legal methods to be helpful. As this was essentially a case of statutory interpretation, we employed those rules of interpretation that enabled us to broaden the usual scope of reasoning, including by expanding the range of relevant 'extrinsic materials,' which can be used to interpret the Act. In the trickster spirit, our expansive use of *obiter dicta* enabled us to trouble accepted 'truths'—a method which is often unfairly derided as 'judicial activism.' Whilst there were no prescribed parameters to this rewriting exercise, we decided to see how far we could queer the judgment by using the law and materials that existed in 2014, at the time of the original judgment.

The 'contextual' approach, which is the main method of statutory interpretation in Australia, provided us with two principles with troublemaking potential. One was the 'mischief rule,' which is the principle that the interpreter should read a statute in light of the 'mischief' or 'problem' that prompted the relevant statute.[23] To us, the mischief rule has resonances with the idea of the trickster. It provides an opportunity to disrupt the established order of life by inviting the interpreter to step out of the confines of accepted legal norms and question why they exist in the first place, creating space for those norms to be 're-constructed and defined anew.'[24] The mischief rule allowed us to go back in time and query how and why the practice of recording sex/gender in western civil registration systems came about. We did somewhat break our own rules in this instance by drawing on Lena Holzer's 2021 doctoral research on this history,[25] which we presented as an *amicus curiae* (friend of the court) submission. Her work enabled us to make visible the patriarchal and heteronormative underpinnings of the legal practice of recording sex/gender and denaturalize its necessity.[26]

---

21. Norrie, interview by Odette Mazel.
22. Irene Watson, 'First Nations Stories, Grandmother's Law: Too Many Stories to Tell,' in *Australian Feminist Judgments: Righting and Rewriting Law*, ed. Heather Douglas, Francesca Bartlett, Trish Luker and Rosemary Hunter (London: Hart Publishing, 2014), 46.
23. Samuel L Bray, 'The Mischief Rule,' *Georgetown Law Journal* 109 (2021), 967.
24. Ilmonen, 'From Borders to Bridges,' 89.
25. Lena Holzer, 'The Binary Gendering of Individuals in International Law: A Plurality of Assembled Norms and Productive Powers of the Legal Registration of Gender' (PhD Thesis, Graduate Institute of International and Development Studies, Geneva, 2022).
26. We would also like to acknowledge here the excellent work on decertifying legal sex occurring as part of 'The Future of Legal Gender' Project led by Davina Cooper at The Dickson Poon School of Law, King's College London, accessed 28 July 2023, https://futureoflegalgender.kcl.ac.uk/people/. See also Davina Cooper and Flora Renz, eds., 'Special Issue: Decertifying Legal Sex—Prefigurative Law Reform and the Future of Legal Gender' *Feminist Legal Studies* 31/1 (2023).

The second principle of statutory interpretation that made space for queer reconstruction was the requirement that the meaning of terms be considered in light of the object and purpose of the legislation. This purposive approach is different from the mischief rule in that it is focused on the aims of the statute itself, rather than the conditions that gave rise to a particular legislative enactment. This approach allowed us to centre Norrie's voice by taking up two submissions (stories) that they made to the Court regarding the purpose of the Act. The first was Norrie's contention that 'the primary purpose of a statute dealing with the registration of a person's birth, death and marriage, as well as, a person's sex, is to record the *truth* about those matters in so far as they concern that person.'[27] Norrie's emphasis on truth-telling invited us to read the term 'sex' in the Act in a way that prioritizes lived reality over the imposition of surgical alignment of physical and social sex/gender. For this, we also drew on another interpretive principle which requires reading the text of an Act as speaking continuously in the present (with contemporary meaning).

Norrie's second submission, related to the purpose of the Act, was that it should be construed as beneficial—as conferring a benefit or operating in a remedial way—because, in contemporary times, such a statute is linked with the protection and enforcement of human rights.[28] This submission drew on the principle that beneficial legislation should be given a broad construction, rather than a 'literal or technical' one.[29] This principle allowed us, as queer judges, to consider extrinsic materials relating to international and domestic human rights law and policy. In doing so, we were able to highlight the human rights materials that were in fact 'beneficial' because they recognized sex/gender categories other than 'male' and 'female,' as well as the right for people to self-determine their sex/gender. Together with Norrie's emphasis on truth-telling, these materials enabled us to conclude not only that the term 'sex' in the Act could accommodate a third, non-binary category, but that it was capable of recording *any* descriptor of sex/gender.

Reframing the issue as a question of human rights was significant because neither the NSW Court of Appeal nor the High Court referred to the main human rights law materials relating to sex/gender that existed at the time in their judgments. Yet, we were uncomfortable with uncritically seeking queer solutions in a human rights paradigm with imperial and liberal origins. We share Ratna Kapur's concern that, despite being held out as a mechanism for achieving freedom, the human rights framework can often operate to discipline, regulate and exclude the very subjects it purports to free.[30] At the same time, and working within the limits of settler-colonial heteronormative law, recourse to human rights law provided a way to read the statute in ways that would empower Norrie, render her legible to law, and ultimately give effect to their truth.

---

27. Norrie, 'Respondent's Submissions,' Submission in *NSW Registrar of Births, Deaths and Marriages v Norrie* [2014] HCA 11 (2 April 2014), 16 January 2014, [9].
28. Norrie, 'Respondent's Submissions,' [17], [46].
29. *IW v City of Perth* (1997) 191 CLR 1 at 12.
30. Ratna Kapur, *Gender, Alterity and Human Rights: Freedom in a Fishbowl* (Northampton: Edward Elgar Publishing, 2018).

In this regard, the two themes running through our rewritten judgment—mischief and critique on the one hand, and truth-telling and repair on the other—reflect a tension that often arises in queer engagements with the law.[31] While the anti-normative orientation of queer theory prompts queer scholars and activists to be suspicious of law and rights-based legal solutions, the lived reality often leads us back, necessitating ways to work within hostile systems in queer ways. This tension is even more acute in the case of queer judgment writing, which, by its very nature, centres law as (part of) the solution.

We have also endeavoured to make the settler-colonial context of Norrie's case visible. Anglo-Australian law was introduced just over 200 years ago based on a lie: that the land was *terra nullius* (land belonging to no-one) at the time of colonization/ invasion. This legal fiction was finally overturned by the High Court in 1992, when it recognized that Indigenous peoples and their laws (but not their sovereignty) had always existed, and that these laws and customs were fundamental to a traditional system of ownership, rights and obligations to land.[32] However, the court's (mis) treatment of sovereignty reinforced, rather than undermined, 'the supremacy of the Australian legal framework' over that of Indigenous peoples.[33] Arguing against the legitimacy of this claim in her contribution to the Australian Feminist Judgements Project, Irene Watson contests the jurisdiction of Australian law and highlights that the form of a legal judgment is antipathetic to the laws of Indigenous[34] oral traditions.[35] We believe that it is incumbent upon us here to open spaces of respect for Indigenous peoples, their laws and customs, and to trouble the boundaries of conventional legal reasoning in the ways that we can, and in the interests of justice more broadly.

There is a final point we would like to note. Following the NSW Court of Appeal's earlier judgment,[36] the Organisation Intersex International (OII) Australia (now Intersex Human Rights Australia) questioned the suggestion that 'intersex' may be a possible descriptor for Norrie, arguing that the term has a particular (biological) meaning and that departure from this meaning would have adverse effects for the intersex community.[37] We do not address this issue in our judgment, but want to note

---

31. Odette Mazel, 'Queer Jurisprudence: Reparative Practice in International Law,' *AJIL Unbound* 116 (2022), 10.

32. *Mabo v Queensland* (No2) (1992) 175 CLR 1.

33. Stuart Bradfield, 'Separatism or Status-Quo? Indigenous Affairs from the Birth of Land Rights to the Death of ATSIC,' *Australian Journal of Politics and History* 52/1(2006), 91.

34. We use the term 'Indigenous' to describe Aboriginal and Torres Strait Islander people of Australia, for ease of the reader, but acknowledge that the preferred nomenclature is Aboriginal and Torres Strait Islander people and that some people prefer First Peoples or First Nations.

35. Watson, 'First Nations Stories, Grandmother's Law,' 53. See, also, Nicole Watson, '*In the Matter of Djaparri (Re Tuckiar)* [2035] First Nations Court of Australia 1,' in *Australian Feminist Judgments: Righting and Rewriting Law*, ed. Heather Douglas, Francesca Bartlett, Trish Luker and Rosemary Hunter (London: Hart Publishing, 2014), 442 [2].

36. *Norrie v NSW Registrar of Births, Deaths and Marriages* [2013] NSWCA 145 (*Norrie CoA*).

37. 'Submissions on behalf of A Gender Agenda Inc., Seeking leave to appear as Amicus Curiae,' Submission in *NSW Registrar of Births, Deaths and Marriages v Norrie* [2014] HCA 11 (2 April 2014), 23 January 2014, [61]; Organisation Intersex International (OII) Australia, 'NSW Registrar of Births, Deaths and Marriages v Norrie: Implications for intersex people,' 10 February 2014, accessed 28 July 2023, https://ihra.org.au/

that these concerns were raised at the time, and that the organisation was pleased with the High Court's recognition of Norrie's gender classification as 'non-specific.'[38]

Conclusion

> 'Whether foolishly, arrogantly, or bravely, tricksters face the monstrous, transforming the chaotic to create new worlds and new cultures.'[39]

In 2009, following the release of the Australian Human Rights Commission's report,[40] Norrie's attention was drawn to Recommendation 5 which stated that: 'A person over the age of 18 years should be able to choose to have an unspecified sex noted on documents and records.' Norrie decided to test the NSW Government's commitment:

> The government had said they would approve a third gender, or a non-male/female option... So, I carried through with it... to hold them to their word. To see if this principle could work, [to see if] we could have identification and equality for non-binary people, to create a safe space for other people to choose that identity if they want.[41]

Following the High Court's judgment, Norrie reflected on how it had changed their life:

> I remember walking into the driver's license people... I had the letter from [the Registrar of] Births, Deaths and Marriages saying that my sex was non-specific... it was just a relief for me to be able to present as totally non-binary as I want and then have paperwork backing that up.[42]

Norrie is a boundary crosser, a mischief maker (Fig. 1). Her bravery—and foolishness—has made many lives more liveable. In queering the judgment, we have endeavoured to 'face the monstrous'[43] by honouring Norrie's engagement with law as a trickster.

wp-content/uploads/2014/01/OII-Aus-NSW-v-Norrie-High-Court.pdf.

38. Organisation Intersex International (OII) Australia, 'High Court Recognizes "Non-Specific" Gender Identity, Implications for Intersex People,' 2 April 2014, accessed 28 July 2023, https://ihra.org.au/25214/media-release-intersex-community-on-edge-high-court-contemplates-transgender-case/.

39. Jeanne Rosier Smith, *Writing Tricksters* (Berkeley: University of California Press, 1997), 2.

40. Australian Human Rights Commission, *Sex Files*.

41. Norrie, interview by Odette Mazel.

42. Norrie, interview by Odette Mazel.

43. Norrie, interview by Odette Mazel.

Fig. 1: Norrie on their bubble bike (photo provided with permission: Richard Hedger).

New South Wales (NSW) Registrar of Births, Deaths and Marriages v Norrie [2014] HCA 11 (2 April 2014)

Mazel, O'Hara and Otto JJ:

Introduction

[1] The applicant, whose legal name is Norrie and who is also known as Norrie May-Welby, applied to the New South Wales (NSW) Registrar of Births, Deaths and Marriages to change their legal sex from 'male' (as recorded at birth in Scotland in 1961) to 'non-specific.' Norrie uses the pronouns 'she/her' and 'they/them' and we will use both in this judgment.

[2] To make this application on 26 November 2009, Norrie went to the Office of the Registrar in Sydney, which is located on the unceded lands of the Gadigal People of the Eora Nation.

[3] Three months later, on 24 February 2010, the Registrar wrote to Norrie approving her application, although the Recognized Details (Change of Sex) Certificate recorded Norrie's sex as 'not specified,' which was not the change requested. It was nevertheless celebrated by Norrie.

[4] Three weeks later, the celebrations were brought to a halt when the Registrar wrote again, informing Norrie the Recognized Details (Change of Sex) Certificate had been reissued because the earlier one had been issued in error and was invalid. This time, Norrie's sex was recorded as 'not stated.'

[5] Norrie appealed against the decision of the Registrar to the NSW Administrative Decisions Tribunal (ADT), which affirmed the Registrar's power was confined to registering sex as either 'male' or 'female.' The ADT Appeal Panel followed suit. Norrie then appealed to the NSW Court of Appeal (CoA) which, on 31 May 2013, found in Norrie's favour.

[6] The NSW CoA determined the power of the Registrar is not limited to registering sex as either 'male' or 'female,' and that 'sex' in the Births, Deaths and Marriages Registration Act 1995 (NSW) does not have a binary meaning. The case before us is an appeal by the NSW Registrar of Births, Deaths and Marriages against that decision.

The Settler-Colonial Legislative Framework

[7] This Court was established pursuant to the Australian Constitution, which was drafted by the British colonizers and came into effect in 1901. It fails to recognize the dispossession of the Indigenous peoples who had occupied the land for thousands of years and makes no reference to their laws and customs. While this Court is thereby formally limited to consideration of settler-colonial laws, we recognize this is not the only law that runs in Australia.

[8] In NSW, the power of the Registrar to register a change of legal sex is set out in the Births, Deaths and Marriages Registration Act 1995 (NSW) (the Act). This Act has its origins in the English system of birth registration which was adopted in 1836 and then introduced in the former colony of NSW.[44]

[9] An application for registration of 'change of sex' is dealt with in Part 5A of the Act. A number of preconditions must be satisfied before a change of sex/gender will be approved. As Norrie was born in Scotland, their birth had not been previously registered in NSW, so the relevant section is 32DA:

> 32DA Application to register change of sex
> 1. A person who is 18 or above:
>   a. who is an Australian citizen or permanent resident of Australia, and
>   b. who lives, and has lived for at least one year, in New South Wales, and
>   c. who has undergone a sex affirmation procedure, and
>   d. who is not married,[45] and
>   e. whose birth is not registered under this Act or a corresponding law, may apply to the Registrar, in a form approved by the Registrar, for the registration of the person's sex in the Register.

[10] Norrie met all these conditions. Norrie argued the sex affirmation procedure they had undergone in 1989 had failed to resolve their sex ambiguity and they wanted their legal sex to reflect 'the truth,' which was that their sex was 'non-specific.'[46]

[11] The central issue in Norrie's case is the proper construction of section 32DC(1), which sets out the scope of the Registrar's power to enter a person's 'change of sex' in the Register:

---

44. An Act for registering Births, Deaths, and Marriages in England [17 August 1836] 6 & 7 Will. IV. c.86; submission on behalf of Lena Holzer seeking leave to appear as *amicus curiae*: Lena Holzer, 'The Binary Gendering of Individuals in International Law: A Plurality of assembled norms and productive powers of the legal registration of gender' (PhD Thesis, Graduate Institute of International and Development Studies, Geneva, 2022), 67.
45. Note for the future: The requirement not to be married was removed following the legalization of same-sex marriage by the Marriage Amendment (Definition and Religious Freedoms) Act (Cth) 2017.
46. Respondent's Submissions, 16 January 2014, [9].

32DC Decision to register change of sex
  1. The Registrar is to determine an application under section 32DA by registering the person's change of sex or refusing to register the person's change of sex.

[12] The question of law, raised by this appeal, is whether the Registrar's power extends to registering a person's sex/gender as something other than 'male' or 'female.'

Principles of Statutory Interpretation

[13] The modern approach to statutory interpretation is 'contextual.' While it must begin with consideration of the statutory text, that text must also be considered within its wider context.[47]

[14] Looking to the context of the statute involves considering its object and purpose. It also requires consideration of the 'mischief' or 'problem' in the world that 'the statute was intended to remedy.'[48]

[15] Accordingly, our analysis begins with the text of the statute, before turning to its purpose and the mischief to which relevant parts are addressed.

The Meaning of 'Sex'

[16] The terms 'sex' and 'change of sex' are not defined in the Act.

[17] The Registrar argued that, in the absence of a statutory definition of the terms, the words should be given 'their natural and ordinary meaning.' Thus, given the 'deeply engrained and very long-standing' binary construction of the term 'sex,' the Registrar contended its ordinary meaning is confined to either male or female.[49]

[18] We do not accept the meaning of 'sex' is, or ever has been, so clear-cut. First, as the NSW CoA's interchangeable use of the term 'sex' with 'gender' demonstrates, the notion of 'sex' is fluid and has long been entangled with other concepts.

[19] Indeed, the Meriam-Webster Dictionary states the terms 'sex' and 'gender' have a long and intertwined history, and that common usage (or ordinary meaning) of the two terms is by no means settled. While in technical and medical contexts, the term 'sex' has been understood to refer to biological forms, and gender has been understood to refer to psychological and sociocultural traits, outside those specific contexts, 'there is no clear delineation, and the status of the words remains complicated.'[50]

---

47. *Commissioner of Taxation v Consolidated Media Holdings Ltd* [2012] HCA 55, [39].
48. *Baini v The Queen* [2012] HCA 59; 87 ALJR 180, at [42].
49. Appellant's Submissions, 13 December 2013, [29].
50. Meriam-Webster Dictionary Online, accessed 28 July 2023, https://www.merriam-webster.com/dictionary/sex#usage-1.

[20] We also note that queer and feminist scholars have contested the distinction between sex (biology) and gender (social construction) insisting both categories are socio-culturally constructed and are for most, if not all, purposes indistinguishable.[51]

[21] Accordingly, in this judgment, the Court has chosen to reflect the unsettled nature of the terms, 'sex' and 'gender,' by using the expression 'sex/gender' when not referring to a particular textual usage.

[22] Turning to the Registrar's submission that the term 'sex' should be confined to the categories of 'male' and 'female' due to its 'long-standing' meaning, the Court notes this binary conception of sex/gender has been applied on the Australian continent through the processes of colonisation and does not necessarily reflect the experiences and much longer history of the first inhabitants of this land. In this context, the Court acknowledges the long-established cultural identities of (in English) 'brotherboy' and 'sistergirl' in some Aboriginal and Torres Strait Islander communities to describe those who do not identify as male or female.[52]

[23] Further, it is a well-established principle of statutory interpretation that 'the text of a statute is ordinarily to be read as speaking continuously in the present.'[53] In the NSW CoA judgment, Preston CJ explained it thus:

> Where a statute uses words in their ordinary sense, absent a contrary intention, the statute is to be construed as 'always speaking,' so that the words are to be interpreted in accordance with their current meaning. The language of the statute is regarded as ambulatory, embracing changes that occur in the subject matter.[54]

[24] As such, what is relevant here is not the 'long-standing' meaning of 'sex,' as contended by the Registrar, but rather its contemporary meaning, as applied throughout different cultural communities in Australia today.

[25] This Court has previously had occasion to consider the contemporary meaning of 'sex.' In *AB v Western Australia*, it acknowledged that 'the sex of a person is not, and a person's gender characteristics are not, in every case unequivocally male or female.'[55]

[26] Even more significantly from the perspective of statutory interpretation, there are indications in the Act itself that 'sex' need not be understood in a binary sense. Section 32A(b) provides:

---

51. Margaret Davies, 'Taking the Inside Out: Sex and Gender in the Legal Subject,' in *Sexing the Subject of Law*, ed. Ngaire Naffine and Rosemary J Owens (North Ryde: LBC Information Services, 1997), 25–46.
52. Andrew Farrell, 'Archiving the Aboriginal Rainbow: Building an Aboriginal LGBTIQ Portal,' *Australasian Journal of Information Systems* 21 (2017), 2–3.
53. *Commissioner of Police v Eaton* (2013) 252 CLR 1, [97] (Gageler J, dissenting on result).
54. *Norrie v NSW Registrar of Births, Deaths and Marriages* [2013] NSWCA 145, [288] (*Norrie* CoA).
55. *AB v Western Australia* (2011) 244 CLR 390, [23].

sex affirmation procedure means a surgical procedure involving the alteration of a person's reproductive organs carried out: ... (b) to correct or eliminate *ambiguities relating to the sex of the person*. (Emphasis added)

[27] Norrie submitted the recognition of ambiguity in s 32A(b) negates a binary definition of 'sex' for the purposes of the Act.[56] As the CoA observed, there is merit to this submission.[57]

The Purpose of the Legislation

[28] Section 33 of the Interpretation Act 1987 (NSW) provides that preference must be given to 'a construction that would promote the purpose or object underlying the Act' over 'a construction that would not promote that purpose or object.'

[29] In her judgment in this matter, Beazley ACJ noted the requirement that legislation must be construed in light of its context and purpose is reinforced by the canon of construction that beneficial legislation—legislation that confers a benefit or operates in a remedial way—is to be given a broad construction, rather than a 'literal or technical' one that is 'unreasonable or unnatural.'[58] A similar approach is taken in respect of legislation involving human rights.[59]

The parties' submissions

[30] In her submissions, Norrie stated '[t]he primary purpose of a statute dealing with the registration of a person's birth, death and marriage, as well as, a person's sex, is to record the truth about those matters in so far as they concern that person.'[60]

[31] The Registrar did not make submissions as to the general purpose of civil registration. With respect to purpose and mischief, the Registrar focused on Pt 5A of the Act. We will address those submissions below.

[32] Norrie further contended the Act should be construed as beneficial legislation because it is linked with the protection and enforcement of human rights.[61] The Registrar did not dispute this submission.

The Act

[33] The objects of the Act, set out in section 3, make it clear the Act is aimed at maintaining a system for registering births, adoptions, deaths, marriages, registered relationships, changes of name and changes of sex/gender, but provides little guidance

---

56. Respondent's Submissions, [18].
57. *Norrie* CoA, [244] (Sackville AJA).
58. *Norrie* CoA, [73] (Beazley ACJ).
59. *Waters v Public Transport Corporation* [1991] HCA 49; 173 CLR 349, 359 (Mason CJ and Gaudron J).
60. Respondent's Submissions, [9].
61. Respondent's Submissions, [17], [46].

as to the underlying purpose of such a system. The only exception to this is section 3(g) which refers to 'the collection and dissemination of statistical information,' establishing a link between data collection and civil registration.

Recourse to extrinsic materials

[34] Section 34(1)(b)(i) of the Interpretation Act 1987 (NSW) allows resort to extrinsic materials to determine the meaning of the provision 'if the provision is ambiguous or obscure.' Ambiguity here 'extends to circumstances in which the intention of the legislature is, for whatever reason, doubtful,'[62] as in this case.

[35] At common law, the principle is even broader. Reference to extrinsic material is permitted even without some ambiguity arising.[63] Further, any material considered relevant to the context of the legislation may be considered by a court undertaking statutory interpretation.[64]

[36] To ascertain the underlying purpose of the NSW civil registration scheme, the Court has reviewed academic literature on the subject, along with materials pertaining to international human rights law.

[37] As the NSW CoA set out in its judgment in this matter, the task of statutory interpretation permits recourse to writings of experts on the physical, medical, social and other sciences in order to ascertain the validity and scope of a law.[65]

[38] Further, there is a well-established interpretive presumption that 'the courts should not impute to the legislature an intention to interfere with fundamental rights.'[66] A similar presumption applies regarding consistency with international law obligations, including human rights treaty obligations.[67] These presumptions make it clear that, along with academic sources, materials pertaining to international human rights law can form part of the interpretive tool kit.

Extrinsic materials on the purpose of civil registration

[39] Based on the legal and academic materials before the Court, civil registration appears to have two underlying purposes.

---

62. *Repatriation Commission v Vietnam Veterans' Association of Australia (NSW Branch) Inc* [2000] NSWCA 65; (2000) 48 NSWLR 548 at [116] (per Spigelman CJ; Handley JA agreeing).
63. *A-G (Cth) v Oates* (1999) 198 CLR 162, [28].
64. *CIC Insurance Ltd v Bankstown Football Club Ltd* (1997) 187 CLR 384, 408.
65. *Norrie CoA*, [91]–[104] (Beazley ACJ).
66. *Coco v The Queen* (1994) 179 CLR 427 at 437.
67. *Minister of State for Immigration & Ethnic Affairs v Ah Hin Teoh* [1995] HCA 20; (1995) 183 CLR 273 [26] (Mason CJ and Deane J). Although this case concerned federal legislation, as Australia's international human rights obligations extend to all parts of the federation, we consider it applicable to NSW legislation concerned with human rights.

[40] First, civil registration plays a role in the State's data collection, as section 3(g) of the Act makes clear. Scholars have suggested the introduction of compulsory civil registration in Australia was the result of concerns relating to white settler population decline and a perceived need for the State to have better access to this demographic data.[68]

[41] Today, the data collected through civil registration assists governments to plan, allocate resources and deliver services. The United Nations Office of the High Commissioner on Human Rights (OHCHR) has observed that birth registration has:

> vital importance for the State, and a profound effect on governance at the national and international levels in improving services and ensuring accountability.[69]

[42] Second, civil registration has, at least since the mid-twentieth century, played an important role in the promotion and realisation of human rights. Birth registration is itself a fundamental human right. Article 24(2) of the International Covenant on Civil and Political Rights (ICCPR), to which Australia is a party, provides: '[e]very child shall be registered immediately after birth and shall have a name.' It is notable the ICCPR does not require registration of sex/gender.

[43] In addition, birth registration helps to ensure other human rights are upheld. In particular, it supports the right to recognition everywhere as a person before the law (Article 16 of the ICCPR). Through its connection to legal recognition, civil registration also provides access to other human, common law and citizenship rights in Australia, including a birth certificate.[70]

[44] This second, rights-based purpose of civil registration, supports Norrie's submission the Act should be construed as beneficial legislation, pointing towards a wide interpretation of the term 'sex,' if its registration is required.

[45] Further, Norrie's submission that civil registration should 'record the truth,' is supported by both the data-based and rights-based purposes of civil registration.

[46] First, given that the demographic data collected through civil registration is used to plan, allocate resources, and deliver services, the State has an interest in that data being as accurate as possible.

[47] Second, inaccurate or 'untrue' information in the register can interfere with the rights-based purpose of civil registration. An inconsistency between a person's registered

---

68.   Brian Reid, 'Masculinity of Birth Registrations in Australia, 1880–1915: Another Aspect of the Population Debate,' *Health and History* 2 (2000), 144, 152.
69.   United Nations Office of the High Commissioner for Human Rights, 'Birth registration and the right of everyone to recognition everywhere as a person before the law,' UN Doc. A/HRC/27/22 (17 June 2014) [38].
70.   Victorian Law Reform Commission, *Birth Registration and Birth Certificates* (Report August 2013), 13.

details and that person's social reality can hinder their access to the rights and services that civil registration aims to guarantee.

The Mischief and Registering / Changing 'Sex' under Pt 5A of the Act

The parties' submissions

[48] Part 5A was introduced into the Act by the Transgender (Anti-Discrimination and Other Acts Amendment) Act 1996 (1996 Act), Sch 2, cl 4. Part 5A deals with applications to alter the civil register to record a 'change of sex.'

[49] Both parties made submissions about the 'mischief' that the enactment of Pt 5A was intended to remedy.

[50] The Registrar contended the 'mischief' that Pt 5A aimed to rectify was any inconsistency between a person's sexual status and the larger body of laws of the State, which themselves operate on the assumption that sex/gender is binary. In the Registrar's view, any registration of a person's sex as 'non-specific' would undermine this process of legal alignment.[71]

[51] In contrast, Norrie submitted the 'mischief' that Pt 5A was designed to remedy was 'the difficulties confronted by persons unable to conform to traditional notions of sex identification, and to improve their lives by providing them with legal recognition of the person's perception of their gender.'[72]

The purpose of registering 'sex'

[52] At the heart of the Registrar's submission is the idea that '[r]egistration is not merely a matter of publicly recognizing a person's private identity—it confers a legal status upon a person.'[73] To address this submission, the Court must consider the purpose of registering sex/gender in the first place and, in particular, its relationship with legal status. On this issue, the *amicus* submission of Dr Lena Holzer has been particularly instructive.

[53] According to Dr Holzer, the purpose of registering sex/gender at birth, as required by England's new birth registration system in 1836, was to facilitate gendered differences in the enjoyment of rights and assist the military conscription of men.[74] In the context of the industrial revolution, particular emphasis was placed on excluding women from private property and inheritance rights.[75] Consequently, the registration of sex/gender supported the gendered division of labour, unequal pay, and a myriad

---

71. *Norrie* CoA, [122].
72. Respondent's Submissions, 16 January 2014, [45].
73. Appellant's Submissions [38].
74. Lena Holzer, 'The Binary Gendering of Individuals in International Law,' 59–64.
75. Lena Holzer, 'The Binary Gendering of Individuals in International Law,' 67–71.

of other laws and practices that instituted women's disadvantage, as compared to men. That is, it aimed to assist in the consolidation of *unequal* access to rights and duties on the grounds of sex/gender.

[54] In contemporary NSW, where the equal enjoyment of rights by everyone is a paramount legal and social value, the purpose of registering sex/gender must surely have changed. Indeed, the High Court's original view was that '[t]he chief, perhaps the only, case where the sex of the parties to the relationship is legally significant is marriage.'[76]

[55] In the present-day human rights-based approach to birth registration, the recording of sex/gender is widely viewed as unnecessary. In 2009, the Australian Human Rights Commission's report, which involved consultation with State governments including NSW, recommended that a person's sex/gender *not* be recorded on government documents 'unless there is a particular necessity to do so.'[77]

[56] The Commission identified only three cases of such necessity: where the recording of sex/gender is required for security reasons, to ensure a person can access appropriate benefits from Medicare or Centrelink and to gather data for the purpose of monitoring progress in achieving gender equality.[78]

[57] Acting on the recommendations of the Commission, the Australian Government introduced guidelines on the recognition of sex/gender for the purposes of government records in 2013.[79] These guidelines require all departments and agencies to remove sex/gender information from their records unless it is necessary for the performance of their specific functions.[80] The guidelines do, however, identify the collection of sex/gender-disaggregated data as 'crucial' for the purpose of 'the ongoing monitoring of equality.'[81]

[58] The limited number of purposes identified suggests registration of sex/gender no longer carries the legal importance the Registrar assigns to it.

[59] While the monitoring of sex/gender equality may well be an important reason for registering sex/gender, the discriminatory history of the practice necessitates caution about the way this data is used.[82] Further, to the extent that data collection can be used

---

76. *NSW Registrar of Births, Deaths and Marriages v Norrie* [2014] HCA 11 (2 April 2014), [42].
77. Australian Human Rights Commission, *Sex Files: the Legal Recognition of Sex in Documents and Government Records* (Concluding Report, March 2009), 34.
78. Australian Human Rights Commission, *Sex Files*, 34.
79. Australia Government, *Australian Government Guidelines on the Recognition of Sex and Gender*, (July 2013), with the implementation of practices to be fulfilled by 2016.
80. Australia Government, *Guidelines on Sex and Gender*, [26].
81. Australia Government, *Guidelines on Sex and Gender*, [27].
82. Travis SK Kong, Dan Mahoney and Ken Plummer, 'Queering the Interview,' in *Handbook of Interview Research*, ed. James A Holstein and Jaber E Gubrium (Thousand Oaks, California: Sage Publications, 2001), 236.

to support gender equality, this would again support Norrie's submission that civil registration should record the truth about a person's sex/gender, and that categories beyond 'male' and 'female' are therefore necessary. It is difficult to see how collecting data about a person that does not align with their lived reality could help to promote their equality in terms of sex/gender.

The purpose of recording 'change of sex'

[60] To determine the purpose of recording *change* of sex, the Court again turns to extrinsic materials and, in particular, the Second Reading Speech to the 1996 Act, which introduced Pt 5A.[83]

[61] In the Second Reading Speech, the Minister quotes a 1998 judgment by Justice Matthews in *Harris v McGuiness*, where she said not having the ability to change sex/gender would be to subject gender diverse people to a life of legal limbo and 'perpetual masquerade.'[84]

[62] The Minister's reliance on this passage lends weight to Norrie's submission that Pt 5A was introduced 'to recognize the difficulties confronted by persons unable to conform to traditional notions of sex identification.'[85]

[63] The idea that the purpose of recognizing a person's change of sex/gender in law is to avoid subjecting them to a life of pretence also accords with contemporary international human rights law. The Yogyakarta Principles, adopted in 2007, recognize the right to recognition as a person before the law, protected by Article 16 of the ICCPR, includes recognition of each person's *self-defined* gender identity because it is 'integral to their personality and is one of the most basic aspects of self-determination, dignity and freedom.'[86] This emphasis on self-definition goes to the heart of Norrie's claim that, in registering a change of sex/gender under the Act, an individual should be able to record *their* 'truth.'

Recording the Truth

[64] Norrie argued that '[t]he true position ... after the surgery, is that, *physically* she is not unequivocally male or female and, *psychologically* she does not specifically identify as male or female.' In this regard, they contended that the '[t]he record of alteration,

---

83. The Hon JW Shaw, Transgender (Anti-Discrimination and Other Acts Amendment) Bill, Second Reading, 30 May 1996, accessed 28 July 2023, https://www.parliament.nsw.gov.au/Hansard/Pages/HansardResult.aspx#/docid/HANSARD-1820781676-64715.
84. The Hon JW Shaw, Second Reading, citing *R v Harris and McGuiness* (1988) 17 NSWLR 158.
85. Respondent's Submission, [45].
86. *Yogyakarta Principles on the Application of International Human Rights Law in relation to Sexual Orientation and Gender Identity*, March 2007, Principle 3 (emphasis added).

or "change" of sex, following that surgery, on an official register should reflect that position.'[87]

[65] We understand Norrie's reliance on 'truth' in the sense that truth is subjective and a reflection of lived experience, rather than something defined or imposed by law or social convention. Truth can be disruptive of other claimed truths and can itself change over time.

[66] Given that the term 'sex' is capable of including non-binary sexes/genders in both its contemporary usage and within the Act, and given the beneficial rights-based purpose of both civil registration and Pt 5A specifically, the term 'sex' in s 32DC(1) can and should be construed in a way that can accommodate Norrie's true experience of sex/gender.

[67] It cannot be the case that Parliament expects Norrie, or others in a similar position, to choose a sex/gender identity that is not their own and live with the consequences of a legal status that does not accord with their truth.

[68] There are a wide range of terms used in the Australian community to describe people who are sex/gender diverse.[88] In light of this, the Australian Human Rights Commission recommends that 'a person over the age of 18 should be able to choose to have an unspecified sex noted on documents and records.'[89]

[69] The Australian Government Sex and Gender Guidelines recommended where sex/gender information is collected and recorded in a personal record, individuals should be given the option to select M (male), F (female) or X (Indeterminate/Intersex/Unspecified).[90] We would go further and suggest any descriptor of sex/gender should be recorded to give effect to that individual's truth.

[70] With respect to the Registrar's concerns about maintaining legislative consistency, and the problems that may be caused by an indeterminate number of categories of legal sex/gender, we agree with Beazley ACJ that any difficulties caused by the construction adopted 'is a matter for consideration by the legislature and/or law reform bodies.'[91]

[71] It is not necessary in this appeal to deal with the precise terminology which is appropriate for Norrie. Suffice it to say 'not specified' is inappropriate because it suggests a mere omission to complete a form, although this was the original term proposed by the Registrar. It is for the Registrar to record the truth of a person's sex/gender.

---

87. Respondent's Submissions, [22].
88. Australian Human Rights Commission, *Sex Files*, 8.
89. Australian Human Rights Commission, *Sex Files*, Recommendation 5.
90. Australian Government, *Guidelines on Sex and Gender*, [18].
91. *Norrie* CoA, [191].

[72] The question in this appeal was whether it was within the Registrar's power to register a person's sex/gender as something other than 'male' or 'female.' The question should be answered in the affirmative and Norrie's sex/gender should be recorded as 'non-specific,' as requested.

Self-Determination Beyond the Word 'Sex'

[73] Although the requirements that a person not be married and have undergone a 'sex affirmation procedure' are not at issue in this case, it is our view these preconditions to registration of 'change of sex' need urgent reconsideration by the NSW Parliament.

[74] The Yogyakarta Principles specify marriage should not be a relevant consideration in the registration of a legal change of sex/gender,[92] and they state categorically that '[n]o one shall be forced to undergo medical procedures, including sex reassignment surgery, sterilisation or hormonal therapy, as a requirement for legal recognition of their gender identity.'[93]

[75] These preconditions amount to human rights violations and unjustifiably limit the beneficial effects of our decision to those in NSW who meet these restrictive and harmful criteria.

---

92. *Yogyakarta Principles*, Principle 3.
93. *Yogyakarta Principles*, Principle 3.

11

R (On the Application of Hopkins) v Sodexo / HMP Bronzefield QB (Administrative Court) (United Kingdom):

Dehumanization, Infantilization & the Erasure of Disabled Lived Experiences in the Prison

Felicity Adams and Fabienne Emmerich

Introduction

Hopkins and Sodexo is a 2016 High Court decision in which queer people in prison in long-term relationships disrupt the fabric and essence of the prison system.[1] In the case, Michelle Hopkins challenged the decision to move her civil partner, Stephanie Hopkins, out of their shared cell into an adjacent cell after an initial three months in prison sharing a cell together. HMP Bronzefield, a privately run prison by Sodexo, based their decision on their 'Decency/Managing Relationships Policy' which banned women who were in a relationship from sharing a cell. Counsel for Michelle Hopkins made a number of claims that can be grouped together in three sets of issues: technical administrative law issues questioning the legality of the policy; preventing Michelle and her civil partner from sharing a cell as a violation of her rights under Article 3 and 8 European Convention of Human Rights (ECHR); a failure to recognize that Michelle suffered from a disability under the 2010 Equality Act (EqA 2010) and to make reasonable adjustments that included sharing a cell to ensure support and care.

Lord Justice (LJ) Silber rejected the application on all issues. He accepted that the 'Intimate Relationship Policy' (IRP) (as an element of the 'Decency/Managing Relationships Policy') was enforceable under the remit of 'Maintenance of order and discipline'—Rule 6 of the Prison Rules 1999—and that the lack of flexibility of the policy was lawful in order to prevent 'an important statutory policy' from being undermined (i.e. 'maintaining order and discipline in prison').[2] LJ Silber also held that Michelle Hopkins' rights had not been violated. He found that the withdrawal of her carer during lock up did not amount to ill treatment and, in any case, this did not meet

---

1. *R (on the application of Hopkins) v Sodexo / HMP Bronzefield QB* (Administrative Court) [2016] EWHC 606 (Admin).
2. *Hopkins v Sodexo* [2016]: 31–37, 40–45.

the threshold for Article 3 ECHR. Similarly, in relation to Article 8 ECHR, he found that as a prisoner she did not have the right to be cared for by her partner during lock up. Moreover, she was 'able to have substantial regular daily contact' with her partner, which meant that she had no recourse under Article 8 ECHR. He concluded that both women were first and foremost prisoners and this meant they could no longer choose 'in whose company they can sleep.'[3] He found no violation of Section 149 and Section 20 EqA 2010, which refer to the public sector equalities duties applicable to public institutions including prisons and the duty to make reasonable adjustments, respectively. He held that the private management of the prison did consider and have due regard to Michelle's disability before Stephanie was moved out, and they had taken all reasonable steps to avoid the disadvantage.

In this chapter, we co-produce a counter-judgment of *Hopkins v Sodexo*, technically in the form of a decision by the Court of Appeal on a fictional appeal against the original High Court decision, as well as this commentary, where we build on previously published work.[4] We invoke an abolitionist lens that foregrounds a disability justice outlook with a view to disrupting dominant approaches to judgment writing in rights-based cases. For the purposes of this piece, we centre our counter-judgment on Article 8 ECHR and Sections 20 and 149 EqA 2010. This is not to diminish the importance of the issues raised under Article 3 ECHR, but rather to provide us with enough space to engage more thoroughly with the interconnected issues raised by these aspects of the judgment.

In this commentary, we briefly set out our approach to queering judgment writing before we move on to examine how conceptions of sex, sexuality, gender, and disability in relationships are produced in the case. We consider how queer relationships centred on care and interdependence challenge and disrupt the cultures of ableism and heteronormativity produced by the prison system. We connect our discussion of the case to the erosion of relations of care in the broader prison context. We do this through a focus on three areas, namely: the presentation of the facts; dehumanization, invisibilizing and infantilizing language; and the erasure of lived experiences. We argue that invoking an abolitionist approach that foregrounds a disability justice lens opens up the potential of fracturing ableist and heteronormative conventions embedded in traditional judgment writing and resisting broader institutional restrictions that place limits on our collective capacities to be in relation with one another.

Our 'Queering': Our positions

The 'queer' in 'queer judgment' also connects with our personal social locations, as queer, white, able-bodied, neuro-diverse, non-incarcerated socio-legal scholars collaboratively writing a queer judgment. Our belonging to these systems accords us with multi-layered privileges and experiences of oppression. Our experiences of 'queerness'

---

3. *Hopkins v Sodexo* [2016]: 59–60.
4. Felicity Adams and Fabienne Emmerich, 'Mapping the Manifestations of Exclusion: Challenging the Incarceration of Queer People,' in *The Queer Outside in Law*, ed. Senthorun Raj and Peter Dunne (London: Palgrave, 2020), 107–140.

and what it means to be 'queer' and to engage in queer relationships are complex and non-linear, with our horizons continuously expanding. We have shared these positions to counter the hegemonic culture of silence in relation to positionality that is engrained in the traditional judicial decision making process. That is, judges omit information about their personal positions/experiences from the judgment, thus making the potential influences on their approaches less accessible to the reader. We seek to be upfront about our positions and collaborative approach to enable readers to question how these implicitly and explicitly influence our approaches.

By performing a queer judgment, we do not intend to absolve ourselves of those interlocking systems of power and violence that the carceral system is predicated on, and the imperialist, colonial foundations of law. We recognize that, in their current configuration, these systems delimit and actively endanger our collective capacities to survive and thrive, particularly for marginalized people in queer and or disabled communities. In many ways, these systems privilege assimilation above queer people's collective liberation, particularly those who are more marginalized in our communities.[5] By engaging with this project, we do not seek to label ourselves as 'good queer people,' to develop on Sara Ahmed's conceptualization of the 'good white people' who are said to adopt 'whiteness that is anxious about itself' as a strategy to achieve social justice.[6] Rather, we seek to authentically experiment with this approach and confront some of the core challenges that constitute this methodology. In essence, we approach the queer judgment as a counter-judgment.

Disability Justice

Disability Justice is an intersectional framework that works to build a more 'complex, whole and interconnected' understanding of disability that recognizes the distinct nature of all bodies, their needs and their strengths, and how bodies are influenced by intersecting systems of oppression.[7] The framework responds to the marginalization of diverse forms of disability, particularly Black and Brown people's experiences of disability in the Disability Rights movement.[8] We recognize the inherent tensions between utilizing a disability justice lens that seeks to transcend law and policy related work in order to 'affirm and support all people's inherent right to live and thrive' and proposing a counter-judgment of a legal case that centres on issues pertaining predominantly to a rights framework.[9] We see it as an important mechanism to both re-centre disabled

5. Sarah Lamble, 'Transforming Carceral Logics: 10 Reasons to Dismantle the Prison Industrial Complex Using a Queer/Trans Analysis' in *Captive Genders: Trans Embodiment and the Prison Industrial Complex*, ed. Nat Smith and Eric A Stanley (Oakland, US: AK Press, 2011), 235–266.

6. Sara Ahmed, 'Declarations of Whiteness: The Non-Performativity of Anti-Racism,' *Borderlands* 3(2) (2004).

7. Patty Berne, 'Review of Disability Justice—a Working Draft by Patty Berne,' Sins Invalid: an Unshamed Claim to Beauty in the Face of Invisibility (blog), accessed 1 January 2023, https://www.sinsinvalid.org/blog/disability-justice-a-working-draft-by-patty-berne.

8. Mia Mingus, 'Changing the Framework: Disability Justice,' *Leaving Evidence*, 12 February 2011, accessed 2 January 2023, https://leavingevidence.wordpress.com/2011/02/12/changing-the-framework-disability-justice/.

9. Talila 'TL' Lewis, 'Review of *Disability Justice Is an Essential Part of Abolishing Police and Prisons*,' *Level* (blog), 7 September 2020, accessed 1 January 2023, https://level.medium.com/

people in prison, whose bodies and identities are historically invisibilized, and to simultaneously illuminate the violence of law in contouring disabled people's experiences and producing ableist logics.[10] At the same time, we see developing layers to our collective knowledge, in relation to how the law operates in this context, through this lens as an important step in building towards more equitable and helpful modes of justice.

Ingredients

We felt deeply unsettled by the framing of the facts that form the basis of the original judgment and the use of dehumanizing language that resulted in the erasure of Michelle and Stephanie Hopkins' lived experiences as disabled queer incarcerated people, as well as the production of a narrative to undermine Michelle's disability claims. To support us in undertaking the counter-judgment, we have undertaken a queering of the original principles established by The Feminist Judgments Project in England and Wales.[11] These are ingredients that are intended to guide our exploration into *Hopkins and Sodexo*, in that they will produce an outcome that enriches our collective knowledge in relation to the intersection between judgment writing, disability, gender, and sexuality, while deviating from the original recipe and method. Although we do not specifically hinge the counter-judgment on these ingredients, they form the basis of our approach and the outcome.[12]

Presentation of the Facts

The presentation of the facts and evidence were spread across different parts of the original judgment: 'The Factual Background' and 'Evidence on the steps taken by Sodexo and medical notes' compiled by Counsel for Sodexo.[13] There was no indication of how the information was compiled and why certain pieces were included as important, nor was there any attempt to highlight gaps in the evidence. We spent quite some time making sense of the facts in the way they were presented in the original judgment to unpack them and then reassemble them into a narrative that, in our opinion, highlighted the gaps and opened up space to expose ableism.

The most obvious omission is the lack of follow-up information after Michelle's referral and two appointments with a consultant spinal surgeon, MRI scan, and referral to a pain clinic. This reflects a systemic approach to both delegitimize and undermine Michelle, but also to fix her in a permanent state of being that does not accurately represent her experience of her body. To compound this, LJ Silber seems to accept without question pieces of evidence presented in the medical notes that repeatedly question the nature of her condition. These are value-laden and judgmental comments

disability-justice-is-an-essential- part-of-abolishing-police-and-prisons-2b4a019b5730.
10. Mingus, 'Changing the Framework: Disability Justice.'
11. Rosemary Hunter, Clare McGlynn, and Ericka Rackley, eds, *Feminist Judgments: From Theory to Practice* (London: Bloomsbury Publishing, 2010).
12. We plan to publish our methodology at a later date.
13. *Hopkins v Sodexo*, 6–19, 56, 96, and 57.

from unspecified physicians and medical professionals to support the narrative that Michelle Hopkins is inauthentically presenting her disability.

This is not to position medicalization as the preferred default way of engaging with disability. We appreciate the multi-layered tensions with this approach through our personal experiences and through the work by disability justice activists. Rather, it is to suggest that those using this approach must capture a complex and authentic image of the person's experiences in order to make an informed decision.

Dehumanization, Invisibilizing, and Infantilizing Language

The language of the judgment reproduces processes of dehumanization. Michelle and Stephanie Hopkins' identities and lives were progressively eroded through the course of the judgment. The choice to replace their names with impersonal/general signifiers, 'the claimant [sic]' and 'the Interested Party' is an exercise of judicial power that invisibilizes people and their complex intersected identities. In contrast, all prison, medical and nursing professionals are named throughout with title and role. This approach, even if common in judicial writing, is particularly destructive in cases that centre on identity and disability, because the subject matter of the claim reaches to the core of personhood and citizenship. Michelle was challenging the decision to remove her partner from their shared living quarters to a cell on the same wing. In effect, this meant being separated daily during routine lock ups middays from 12.30pm to 2pm and evenings and nights from 6.45pm to 8am four days per week and from 5.15pm to 8am three days per week. We elected to refer to Michelle and Stephanie Hopkins by their first names, rather than adopting legalese, as a small way to inject their humanity and 'wholeness' into the judgment and reflect the overarching aims of the disability justice framework.

LJ Silber extends the dehumanizing approach towards judgment making through his inclusion of value laden, derogatory, and ableist comments. When considering submissions made under Section 20(3) EqA 2010, LJ Silber reflects on the evidence presented by Counsel for Sodexo and utilizes the word 'malingering.'[14] The use of the verb 'malinger,' meaning to pretend in order to avoid certain circumstances, reflects the hierarchization of disability that demarcates specific disabilities as 'authentic' whilst problematizing or viewing others with scepticism. LJ Silber simultaneously conveys disability as an undesirable state of being and locates this as an individual 'flaw' rather than as something that is produced by or dependent on the social context.[15]

Erasure of Lived Experiences

Most noticeable throughout the judgment is the absence of Michelle and Stephanie's voices. They are the subject matter of the comments, reports, and assessments, and are sometimes cited within those, but they are never heard in their own voice talking

---

14. *Hopkins v Sodexo*, 57.
15. Mingus, 'Changing the Framework: Disability Justice.'

about their experiences. The absence of their narratives reflects the historically ableist foundations of the law and how this institution excludes people with disabilities whose understanding of their life experiences are deemed to be insignificant, while simultaneously imposing life-altering consequences onto their bodies.[16] Even when LJ Silber remarks that Michelle declined to share what steps she preferred Sodexo to undertake in relation to Section 20 EqA 2010, he does so without exploring the motivations behind this decision, e.g. her sole wishes for Stephanie to remain her carer, potential distrust in State institutions, and resistance. Invoking a disability justice lens within the judgment would require LJ Silber to present a fuller and complex body of evidence that engages directly with Michelle and Stephanie's respective experiences and responses to their treatment in the prison. We appreciate, however, that Michelle and Stephanie may not desire to share this personal information with the court for a myriad of reasons, especially given their treatment in the prison. Should this be the case, this contributes an additional layer to the call by proponents of the disability justice framework for the abolition of harmful institutions that promote intersectional harms.

In the original judgment, LJ Silber does not reflect on the potential additional stress and anxiety produced by the removal of Stephanie from the cell, as people sharing in mutual care of one another. The facts illustrate that it took 102 days to reach a decision to separate Michelle and Stephanie into separate cells. While we cannot capture the full extent of the impact of both the delay and the decision, as there is no incorporation of reflections by Michelle or Stephanie, we can imagine the potential anxiety that may be produced through the potential loss of a loved one who provides sole care.

The decision to separate Michelle and Stephanie, the delay in admitting Michelle to Healthcare, and the lack of engagement with what this delay may mean for Michelle and Stephanie, are all indicators of the ableist logics that undergird *Hopkins v Sodexo* and the penal system, but also judicial decision making as an institution. This is because, together, these institutions devalue the interdependent modes of care shared between Michelle and Stephanie and they demarcate their approach to care as inferior.[17] Similarly, central to the function of the penal system is the separation of people from others with whom they are in relation, so that any mental health suffering resulting from that is normalized. The lack of reference to the potential suffering in this regard cements the normalization of these ableist practices.

Conclusion

We embarked on this process, albeit with a sense of trepidation, as an experiment to explore the potential for queering a judgment within a queer-abolitionist and disability justice framework. It has become painfully obvious that this is not a viable pathway. Nevertheless, this experience provided us with the opportunity to illuminate the violence of judgment-making and how this practice is specifically directed towards

---

16. Mia Mingus, 'Ableism,' *UnLeading*, accessed 15 January 2023, https://www.yorku.ca/edu/unleading/ableism/.
17. Mia Mingus, 'Ableism.'

disabled queer people in prison. This experiment has created the space to think of 'tactical' ways to disrupt judicial reasoning to expose systemic ableism that is also influenced by interlocking systems of oppression.[18] Fundamentally, we have been able to look beyond and outside the law, especially in terms of expanding our imaginations to build beyond the Prison Industrial Complex.

18. Natalie Oswin, 'On Normal Life: Dean Spade, Interviewed by Natalie Oswin,' Society and Space, 15 January 2014, accessed 11 November 2023, https://www.societyandspace.org/articles/on-normal-life.

R (ON THE APPLICATION OF HOPKINS) v SODEXO /

HMP BRONZEFIELD QB (COURT OF APPEAL)

Before Adams and Emmerich in the Court of Appeal.[19]

[1] Michelle Hopkins and her civil partner Stephanie Hopkins were incarcerated together at HMP Bronzefield on 6 November 2014, managed by Sodexo. They spent 102 days (3 months and 10 days) sharing the same cell together until 16 February 2015 when they were informed by the prison that Stephanie would be moved to another cell on the same wing. The decision to separate them was based on the 'Intimate Relationship Policy' (IRP), which is part of Sodexo's Decency/Managing Relationships Policy: 'It is not accepted that women within in [sic] an intimate relationship are to share a cell.' Michelle Hopkins challenged the decision before Lord Justice (LJ) Silber KBE of the Queen's Bench Division.[20]

The Issues in the Case of Michelle Hopkins

[2] The two issues that arise on this appeal: LJ Silber has erred in his decision that:
1. There has been no violation of the Claimant's rights under Article 8 of the ECHR even if those rights were engaged; and that
2. The Claimant is not a 'disabled person' within the meaning EqA 2010 and, even if she was, Sections 20 and 149 of that Act have not been contravened.

The Facts[21]

[3] The High Court decision illuminates the treatment of people with intersecting identities, needs and desires by State institutions and their multi-layered experiences, particularly in the prison context. The following overview of the facts, in this case, are taken largely from the original judgment written by LJ Silber, in addition to insights available in the public domain. Therefore, they do not capture or convey the full extent of Michelle Hopkins (Claimant) or Stephanie Hopkins' (Interested Party) experiences

---

19. We are writing this as a collaborative judgment. We have elected to utilize our names combined here and the pronoun 'we' to reflect this.

20. *R (on the application of Hopkins) v Sodexo / HMP Bronzefield QB* (Administrative Court) [2016] EWHC 606 (Admin).

21. *Hopkins* [2016], 1–19, 56,57 and 95.

of the prison as an institution or their feelings in relation to their treatment. However, drawing on the summary of the medical and prison reports, we attempt to provide a fuller illustration of the circumstances that LJ Silber eschews in his presentation of the original case facts.

[4] Michelle and Stephanie had been together since June 2010 and in a civil partnership since June 2013, when they were sentenced to prison on the same indictment for child cruelty on 6 November 2014.

[5] Michelle and her partner both had underlying health conditions when they entered prison. Both suffered from mental health problems that are not explained in more detail by LJ Silber. Michelle had experienced severe pain in her middle and lower back following a period of unexplained paralysis from the waist down in January 2012, which was diagnosed as a minor disc degeneration. Completely in line with the nature of a caring and loving relationship and within the paradigm of state-sanctioned relationships, civil partnership (or marriage), Michelle relied on Stephanie for her care needs, which included help to bathe and to dress. Equally, Michelle provided emotional support and care to Stephanie for her mental health needs.

[6] When they were placed in prison, Michelle and Stephanie declared that they were carers for each other. The prison then allowed them to share a cell together until they had assessed the care needs of both partners. To the knowledge of the Head of Residence at the prison, this was the first time two women had declared their caring responsibilities for each other. There is no mention that this also included women declaring civil partnerships. The process to reach the decision to separate Michelle and Stephanie took 102 days.

[7] The Occupational Therapy Report (7 January 2015) mentions that Michelle was struggling to use the toilet unassisted, but that she was able to transfer from her wheelchair onto the toilet. The report made three recommendations, two relating to reasonable adjustments (installation of a plastic fluted grab rail and the provision of a chair with arms) and a GP referral for a physiotherapy review of mobility and balance. The Prison decided that they would provide the chair, but not mount the handrails as a safeguarding response to prevent any self-harm.[22] Michelle was referred to a consultant spinal surgeon, who saw her twice and ordered an MRI scan as well as a referral to a pain clinic (physiotherapy). LJ Silber provides no information on the outcome of the specialist consultations or MRI scan, or any notes from the pain clinic. This leaves significant questions unanswered in relation to Michelle's condition or its effect upon her well-being and ability to carry out everyday activities unassisted.

[8] On 20 January 2015, Michelle disclosed to prison medical staff that a minor disc degeneration was diagnosed in 2012 and that she had bought the wheelchair

---

22. It is questionable whether ligature points at waist height pose a danger. It is not clear whether LJ Silber questioned this comment.

herself. The doctor recorded: 'It appears unusual to decide to use a wheelchair for this diagnosis.'[23]

[9] There were two multidisciplinary meetings held one week apart sometime prior to 16 February 2015, when the decision to remove Stephanie was communicated.[24] This was the catalyst for the complaint. At the first multidisciplinary meeting, a decision was made that the Primary Care Nursing Manager at Sodexo would consult Michelle's GP. It is unclear whether they had a reply before they held the second multidisciplinary meeting. At that second meeting, 'It was reported that the Claimant did not need a carer, i.e. someone to be specifically allotted to assist her.' They therefore made the decision to separate Michelle and Stephanie following the IRP and they decided to admit Michelle to Healthcare to be assessed further.

[10] Following the decision, Michelle contacted medical staff, according to the medical notes from 19 February 2015, to inform them that she needed 24-hour care for her condition, because she was unable to turn during the night. Again, the notes for 24 February 2015 state that Michelle saw the Primary Care Nurse to say she was not coping at night due to 'weakness of her left side and migraine headaches[,] therefore will require assistance at night.'[25] The Primary Care Nurse offered for Michelle to be admitted to the Healthcare Centre for assessment. Michelle refused the offer, because she was worried that she might be transferred to a different wing following her assessment and consequently she would lose her daily contact with Stephanie.

[11] We have found the determination and relaying of the facts very problematic. LJ Silber relies almost exclusively on evidence presented by Counsel for the prison/ Secretary of State. This evidence in many cases lacks the specificity of the physician or examining professional and in a number of cases reflects either irrelevant considerations or outright discreditation. For instance, the entry in the medical notes for 25 February 2015 state: 'Concerns were recorded by the doctor at HMP Bronzefield that the Claimant may be malingering.' And on 30 March 2015 the medical notes state: 'the Claimant was observed to stand unaided from her wheelchair, step onto scales, stand until a reading was obtained and then step back down again before sitting back in her wheelchair and wheeling herself out of the room.'

[12] We are deeply concerned that LJ Silber fails to question why evidence from medical notes where the physician is either unspecified or no reference is made to the examining professional is presented, whereas there is no mention of the professional opinion of a consultant spinal surgeon or the results of the MRI scan. Moreover, medical notes that refer to Michelle's suspicions that her partner may be unfaithful are included without any question as to their relevance. It produces a strong suspicion that there was a concerted effort to discredit Michelle's account of her disability.

---

23. *Hopkins*, 57, Medical Notes as summarized by Counsel for Sodexo.
24. LJ Silber's description of the facts lack specificity here.
25. The same entry then continues: 'This is contrary to the Social Care Report [2/56/502] (prepared on 3 July 2015), which records that there had been no such migraine episodes': *Hopkins* [2016], 57.

The Policy

[13] HMP Bronzefield prison is a women's prison privately run by Sodexo (First Defendant). Sodexo has a Decency/Managing Relationships Policy. The relevant provision is the IRP: 'It is not accepted that women within in [sic] an intimate relationship are to share a cell.'

It was argued that the 'IRP' was lawful to prevent 'an important statutory policy' from being undermined. LJ Silber agreed that the inflexibility of the policy was necessary to maintain order and discipline in prison.[26]

1st Issue—Article 8 of the ECHR—Violation of the Right to Private and Family Life

[14] LJ Silber first considered whether Article 8 rights were engaged and then whether Article 8 rights were violated. In both issues he held that they were not. We conclude that he erred on both these issues.

[15] According to Article 8(1) ECHR, 'Everyone has the right to respect for his private and family life, his home and his correspondence.' For people in prison, the European Court of Human Rights (ECtHR, Strasbourg Court) in *Nowicka v Poland* (2003) explains:

> 71. Moreover, normal restrictions and limitations consequent on prison life and discipline during lawful detention are not matters which would constitute in principle a violation of Article 8 either because they are considered not to constitute an interference with the detainee's private and family life or because any such interference would be justified (see the D.G. judgment cited above, § 105).[27]

Therefore, it is crucial that alleged violations of prisoners' right to privacy and family life, in this case the separation from a civil partner (a State-sanctioned relationship), are considered by the courts.

[16] It is accepted that, when determining a violation of Article 8(2) ECHR, the Court needs to consider whether the limitation in question (in this case the ban on sharing a cell with a queer partner) is in 'accordance with the law' and whether it is proportionate. In an earlier judgment, this Court in *Bright and Keeley* [2014] added a third question: whether incarcerated people are given the opportunity to make representations before the decision to separate is made.[28]

In accordance with the law

[17] The power to make rules in relation to the governance of prison life and the control of prisons lies with the Secretary of State as per Section 47(1) of the Prison Act 1952.

---

26. *Hopkins*, 40–5.
27. *Nowicka v Poland*, Application no. 30218/96 (EctHR, 3. March 2003).
28. *R (on the application of Bright) v Secretary of State for Justice, Bright v Governor of Whitemoor Prison CA* (Civil Division) [2014] EWCA Civ 1628; [2015] 1 WLR 723; [2014] 12 WLUK 564.

The Prison Rules 1999 derive their legality from this power. We agree with LJ Silber that the Decency/Managing Relationship policy which contains the 'IRP' comes within the remit of Rule 6(1) of the Prison Rules 1999:

> Order and Discipline shall be maintained with fairness, but with no more restriction than is required for safe custody and well ordered community life.

Whether the Ban on Sharing a Cell with a Queer Partner Is Proportionate

[18] The now accepted proportionality test in UK law was laid out by the Supreme Court in *Bank Mellat (Appellant) v HM Treasury Respondent (No.2)*:

> 20. (…) (i) whether its objective is sufficiently important to justify the limitation of a fundamental right; (ii) whether it is rationally connected to the objective; (iii) whether a less intrusive measure could have been used; and (iv) whether, having regard to these matters and to the severity of the consequences, a fair balance has been struck between the rights of the individual and the interests of the community.[29]

[19] First, we need to establish the objective of the 'IRP.' Sodexo/Secretary of State for Justice suggest that the policy was required to maintain 'order and discipline' in the prison. They submit that IRP is in compliance with Rule 6(1) of the Prison Rules 1999. Pursuing good order and discipline in prison has long been accepted by the courts as a legitimate aim that is 'sufficiently important' to justify restricting prisoners' rights.[30] Deferring to specialist knowledge, LJ Silber accepts Sodexo's justification.[31]

[20] Second, we are now urged to determine whether the intimate relationship policy that informed the decision to move Stephanie out of the shared cell was 'rationally connected' to achieving the stated aim, namely the prevention of disorder in the prison. We maintain that deference to specialist knowledge of Sodexo and the Ministry of Justice still requires evidence and data to be submitted, so the courts can assess whether the decision maker can demonstrate a link between the objective and the restriction. No such evidence was provided beyond statements that queer couples sharing a cell led to the perception that the prison was condoning sex; Sodexo was not able to determine whether people engaged in sex of a voluntary nature; to put processes in place would 'be resource-intensive and … would require very intrusive inquiries'; and that this would lead to disorder.[32] A rational connection is therefore not established.

---

29. *Bank Mellat v HM Treasury*, [2013] UKSC 38, UKSC 39, 3 WLR 179 (2013).

30. For an overview, see Dirk Van Zyl Smit, 'Prisoners' Rights,' in *Handbook on Prisons*, ed. Yvonne Jewkes (Cullompton: Willan, 2007), 566–84.

31. *Hopkins*, 77. LJ Silber then adds an irrelevant consideration, which has no bearing on the question of the pursuit of a legitimate aim, namely that Stephanie Hopkins was moved out of the cell once the GP had confirmed that Michelle Hopkins did not need a carer.

32. Evidence by the Head of Safer Custody Casework at the National Offender Management Service ('NOMS'), 33–5.

[21] Third, we need to determine whether a less intrusive measure could have been used. At present we have a disparity in the articulation of the ban on people in intimate relationships sharing a cell in the private and public prison estate. This Court in *Bright and Keeley* [2014] upheld the Secretary of State's view that it was unworkable to develop a policy providing guidance on long-term relationships. While the public prison sector has no policy, in this case Sodexo, a privately-run prison has developed a policy on Decency/Managing Relationships.

[22] It is well-founded in evidence-based research that sex takes place in prison. While it is not condoned by staff, it is ignored if it is 'discreet.'[33] The Howard League Commission on Sex in Prison produced a number of Recommendations that list a number of measures less intrusive than prohibiting sex altogether, which include clear, consistent policies framed within the reality of consensual and coercive sex in prison, coherent safeguarding framework for vulnerable groups, appropriate staff training, and access to sexual healthcare equivalent to that available on the outside.[34]

[23] Merely referring to resource implications without presenting detailed evidence, is not enough to justify the restriction of incarcerated peoples' Article 8 rights, in this case banning incarcerated queer people in relationships from sharing a living space.[35] To counter the exclusion of marginalized groups in prison through interlocking systems of harm inherent in a capitalist system that produces ableism, racism, classism, hetero/cis-normativity, and ageism, any detailed consideration of alternative measures should centre a disability justice lens as outlined in the grounds protected in the EqA 2010.

[24] Fourth, we need to determine whether 'a fair balance has been struck between the rights of the individual and the interests of the community' or alternatively whether the measure was disproportionate.

[25] The IRP is a blanket ban, which results in banning queer people in a relationship from sharing a cell. Blanket bans require particular scrutiny, because they prevent any consideration of individual experiences and the particular circumstances of individual cases, in this case those of queer people.[36] It is documented that many queer people feel unsafe to be open about their identity/sexuality, because they face a multiplicity of harms and violence on both a systemic and inter-personal level. This is particularly the case in men's prisons, where a toxic hypermasculinity is tolerated, including with acceptance of violence.[37] At institutional level the response is often to segregate queer

---

33. See Alisa Stevens, 'Sex in Prison: Experiences of Former Prisoners,' Howard League for Penal Reform, 2015, accessed 20 January 2022, https://howardleague.org/wp-content/uploads/2016/03/Sex-in-prison-web.pdf.

34. Stevens, 'Sex in Prison.'

35. *R (on the application of AB) v Secretary of State for Justice* [2009] EWHC 2220, [2009] All ER.

36. *R v Secretary of State for the Home Department, ex parte Daly* [2001] 3 All ER 433.

37. Joe Sim, *'Tougher than the Rest? Men in Prison,'* in *Men, Masculinities and Crime*, ed. Tim Newborn and Elizabeth A. Stanko (London: Routledge, 1994), 100–118.

people, who are produced as vulnerable, rather than dealing with or addressing systemic violence.[38]

[26] LJ Silber highlighted that blanket bans have been accepted by the Strasbourg authorities. He relied on two fairly dated decisions by the European Commission of Human Rights that accepted States' margin of appreciation to set blanket bans on conjugal visits in prison.[39] We maintain that LJ Silber erred in dismissing the applicability of the ruling in *Dickson v UK* by the Strasbourg Court.[40] The Strasbourg Court in *Dickson* drew on the challenge in *Hirst v UK* (2005) to the UK's blanket ban on prisoner disenfranchisement.[41] In *Dickson*, it acknowledged that the policy of refusing to facilitate the artificial insemination process for a person in prison was not a blanket ban as in *Hirst*, as any prisoner was able to apply. The Court held, however, that in its effect it amounted to a blanket ban, because 'the Policy did not permit the required proportionality assessment in an individual case.'[42]

[27] We find that an application and the opportunity to make representations to the Residential Manager to be placed on the same wing, as was the case for Michelle, does not mitigate the question of proportionality of the blanket ban.

[28] Sodexo, in particular the Residential Manager, made the decision to circumvent the 'IRP' on the grounds that both women had expressed that they fulfilled mutual caring roles. Michelle and Stephanie shared a cell for 102 days before the decision to move Stephanie out of the shared cell was communicated. These two points are particularly relevant. First, the prison was prepared to set aside the blanket ban and let both Michelle and Stephanie share a cell on account of their mutual caring responsibilities. Caring and nurturing is integral to long-term relationships. It is perfectly understandable that Michelle and Stephanie wanted to care for one another. This should not have to be medicalized and externally assessed in order to prevail. Second, the prison provided no evidence that both women sharing a cell for 102 days caused any problems relating to disorder in the wing or to the prison as a whole. More specifically, Sodexo stated that there had been no indication that Michelle and Stephanie had had sex while they were sharing the cell.

[29] It is a particularly cruel feature of imprisonment that it predominantly involves the separation from loved ones, also for queer prisoners. Yet, there may be instances, as in the case of Michelle and Stephanie, where people in a long-term relationship are sentenced and detained together. It seems particularly forced and artificial to inflict an intentional separation of the living arrangements of two incarcerated people who would otherwise be able to care and nurture for one another, in order to uphold a dangerous and exclusionary approach, namely that the prison is not perceived to condone sex.

---

38. *R (on the application of AB) v Secretary of State for Justice.*
39. *X and Y v Switzerland* (1978) 13 DR 241; *ELH and PBH v UK* [1998] EHLR 231.
40. *Dickson v The United Kingdom* (44362/04) [2007] 12 WLUK 23.
41. *Hirst v United Kingdom* (No.2) 74025/01 [2005] ECHR 681.
42. *Hopkins v Sodexo*, 84.

[30] Queer relationships in prison challenge the fabric of a punitive system centred on segregating along the gender binary and that perpetuates homophobia and transphobia. We cannot subsume them to the fiction of the normal prisoner, homogenizing and erasing identities and lived experiences. Homogenization produces the fiction of the normal prisoner that reinforces sexist, classist, racist, homophobic/transphobic and ableist stereotypes through a binary of inclusion/exclusion. We need to *see* people in prison, the complexities of their intersecting identities, and the multiplicity of their lived experiences and relationships.

2nd Issue—Section 20 and Section 149 EqA 2010

Is Michelle Hopkins a 'disabled person' within the meaning EqA 2010?

[31] Disability is a protected characteristic under Section 6 EqA 2010. Section 6(1) defines disability as when a person has a 'physical or mental impairment' and when this has a 'substantial and long-term adverse effect' on their performance of everyday activities. We reiterate our deep concern about the process for gathering evidence about Michelle's disability. The absence of Michelle's voice and experiences of her condition, pain and effect on her well-being together with no evidence of the professional opinion of the consultant spinal surgeon, no results from the MRI scan, or any notes from the chronic pain clinic, point to a misconception of disability and a lack of legitimacy and integrity in the process.

[32] While we recognize that there are different models of disability, such as the medical and social model, we draw on the crip model, where disability is a dynamic and changeable state of being that is dependent on context. Liat Ben Moshe et al. outline:

> Disability is fluid and contextual rather than biological. This does not mean that biology does not play out in our minds and bodies, but that the definition of disability is imposed upon certain kinds of minds and bodies... But more than that, disability, if understood as constructed through historical and cultural processes, should be seen not as binary but as a continuum. One is always dis/abled in relation to the context in which one is put.[43]

[33] We apply a disability justice lens in an attempt to both centre the specific expressed needs for interdependent modes of care for Michelle as a disabled person and to complicate the static and simplified conceptions of disability presented in the original judgment. This is important to avoid a singular, pre-ordained category of disability that delimits both the potential for multi-layered embodiments of disability and interdependence, and to facilitate courts in the interim in being more attuned to the constantly evolving nature of bodies and identities over time, across space, and in response to their material conditions.[44]

---

43. Liat Ben Moshe, Anthony J. Nocella, and A. J Withers, 'Queer-Cripping Anarchism: Inter-sections and Reflections on Anarchism, Queer-ness, and Dis-Ability,' in *Queering Anarchism*, ed. C. B. Daring, J. Rogue, Deric Shannon, and Abbey Volcano (Oakland, CA: AK Press, 2013), 210–211.
44. Mingus, 'Changing the Framework: Disability Justice.'

[34] We maintain that it is proper and fair to recognize Michelle's account of disability, that she suffered from a long-term physical impairment throughout her period of incarceration, and that Section 6(1) EqA 2010 is engaged.

Duty to make reasonable adjustments under Section 20(3) and (4) EqA 2010

[35] Recognizing Michelle's disability, we turn to the question whether the prison complied with the duty to make reasonable adjustments. Section 20(3) and (4) EqA 2010 set out the requirements, namely 'to take such steps as it is reasonable to have to take to avoid ... [putting a disabled person at a substantial] disadvantage.'

[36] The lack of detail and diversity in the evidence drawn by LJ Silber, including reflections by Michelle herself, those with whom she is in relation, and those recognized as medical experts, especially given the nature of Michelle's disability and pain, creates multi-layered challenges for the court and an incomplete illustration of the circum-stances. Firstly, it creates difficulty in delivering a fully-informed position in relation to Sections 20 (3) and (4) EqA 2010. Secondly, it facilitates the use of a medicalized model of disability that places pain within a hierarchy, and subtly casts doubt over Michelle's status as a disabled person and her experiences of pain.

[37] Simultaneously, this presentation of evidence undermines Michelle's need to access resources that support her daily functioning in the prison. It appears to demarcate Michelle as permanently in a position to function without support and constructs disability in linear terms. In the process, this fixes her body, disallows its potential flow from one state of being to another, and minimizes her need for care by her partner and other potentially supportive material resources.

[38] Similarly, Michelle's request to remain sharing a cell with her civil partner as a viable pathway is delegitimized. Her request is cast as non-engagement with officials in relation to potential steps forward and a refusal to consider any other option from sharing her cell with her civil partner. We maintain that there needs to be space for listening to potential justifications for Michelle's decision not to engage with the process beyond her initial request with the prison authorities.

[39] We do not accept the prison's framing of Michelle's needs that foreground her 'general' and 'ordinary' ability to utilize the toilet and attend to her needs unless she was experiencing 'a particularly bad day.' In this sense, the use of evidence here operates as a basis to render her requests exceptional, and to minimize the need for the prison to take 'steps' to provide her with modes of care that align more effectively with her requests and make her daily life 'easier' in a physical sense. Again, the prison provided limited information as to, e.g. the background to Michelle's suicide ideation, how this manifests, and how this developed. In this context it seems unreasonable to reject

the recommendation by the Occupational Therapist to install the grabrail in the cell. In this instance, 'risk' and safeguarding seem to have been used as mechanisms to circumvent statutory duties under Sections 20 (3) and (4) EqA 2010. We maintain that when reviewing its duties to make reasonable adjustments the prison should have centred the evidence illustrating the more challenging and varied periods for Michelle's health.

[41] We maintain that the prison failed to comply with Section 20(3) and (4) EqA 2010. It therefore did not comply with its duties to prevent discrimination against Michelle under Section 21 EqA 2010.

Has the Prison complied with the public sector duty Section 149 (1) EqA 2010?

[42] Through the IRP, the prison is preoccupied with preventing people from engaging in acts of sexual intimacy. It has eschewed the potential desires/needs of disabled people to receive support from a person with whom they are in a relationship, while equating their relationships with sex. This is despite the reality that queer and disabled people's distinct positions mean that they are ideally situated to support one another 'without primarily relying on the State … [that disabled people] have most often been forced to rely on for care, sometimes, well, often, with abuse and lack of control.'[45] Sharing a cell with her civil partner would have enabled interdependent mutual modes of care with Stephanie and would legitimate her chosen material support.[46] Their distinct positions and experiences place them at a distinct disadvantage in comparison with the mainstream prison population. In essence, the policy produces only minimal acknowledgement of disability and disabled people's needs rather than a 'due regard' as required under Section 149 EqA 2010.

[43] We maintain that there is a violation of Section 149 (1) EqA 2010. The prison's implementation of the IRP in and of itself fosters multiple harms against people on the grounds of disability and sexual orientation (Section 149(1)(a)), regresses equality of opportunity (Section 149(1)(b)), and hinders good relations between disabled people and the mainstream prison population (Section 149(1)(c)).

Sexuality and disability: the importance of combined discrimination (Section 14 EqA 2010)

[44] We maintain that submissions made in relation to Section 149 EqA 2010 should consider both sexual orientation *and* disability as combined discrimination, reflecting Section 14 EqA 2010. This is because ableism is intrinsically connected with intersecting categories of identity, including, in the present case, sexual orientation. While Section 14

---

45. Leah Lakshmi Piepzna-Samarasinha, *Care Work: Dreaming Disability Justice* (Vancouver: Arsenal Pulp Press, 2018), 33.
46. Leah Lakshmi Piepzna-Samarasinha, *Care Work*, 33.

EqA 2010 is not currently in force, this must be urgently remedied.[47] The prohibition of combined discrimination could better reflect the intersectional nature of Michelle's experiences as a disabled and queer person in the prison environment and rectify to some extent the compartmentalized and inauthentic hetero-narrative of her experiences.

Conclusion

[45] We uphold the appeal on both grounds. First, there has been a violation of Article 8(2) ECHR, for Sodexo did not provide evidence to demonstrate a rational connection between the IRP and the prevention of disorder, and there was no consideration of whether a less intrusive measure was possible. Moreover, the IRP as a blanket ban is directed at queer people and is exclusionary. It did not allow for Michelle's individual experiences and circumstances to be taken into consideration and a proportionality assessment to be made. Second, we maintain that LJ Silber's construction of Michelle's circumstances in relation to claims under Article 8 ECHR and the EqA 2010 reinforces the well-established violence of law in contouring people's narratives in an attempt to remain faithful to judicial conventions and to simultaneously discredit or to implicitly position people who deviate from the normative standard as inconsistent.[48]

[46] We reiterate that merely stating that resource implications are prohibitive in upholding the rights of prisoners under Article 8 ECHR, in particular queer prisoners, is insufficient. The Secretary of State and the National Offender Management Service (NOMS) must consider the complex realities of all people reaching out to one another in prison for nurture and care. We must ensure that queer and/or disabled prisoners are as safe as is feasible within an environment that is centred on deprivation and harm. However, we caution that any steps, e.g. guidance on long-term queer relationships in prison, must only be used in the interim. They must be formed within a disability justice framework that centres the transcending of adversarial legal systems that reduce people's lived realities as in the present case.[49] We appreciate that this is a fine balance to achieve, however, we also recognize the urgent need to engage with the realities of marginalized people in prison.

---

47. This is not to position the law as the desired or sole strategy that may support disabled and/or queer people in prison, but rather as a 'tactic' to experiment with how this may provide immediate relief or to support with alleviating specific harms with the foresight that investing in the law will not achieve our collective 'survival': Oswin, 'On Normal Life.'

48. Linda Steele, 'Disability, Abnormality and Criminal Law: Sterilization as Lawful and "Good" Violence,' Griffith Law Review 23 (3)(2014), 467–97.

49. Linda Steele, 'Disability, Abnormality and Criminal Law,' 467–97.

12

Prosecutor v Ahmad Al Faqi Al Mahdi (Reparations) (International Criminal Court):

Queering Cultural Heritage Law
& the Identities It Enshrines

Lucas Lixinski

Introduction

In 2016, the International Criminal Court (ICC) decided the first case in history about the destruction of cultural heritage as an international crime. *Prosecutor v Al Mahdi* was about the destruction by Islamic extremists of parts of the World Heritage Site of Timbuktu during the civil war in Mali.[1] The site is composed, among other things, of mausoleums containing the remains of Muslim Saints.[2] Previous jurisprudence in other international courts about the destruction of cultural heritage often made the destruction of heritage an element to a crime, rather than a crime itself. Therefore, *Al Mahdi* innovates by centring cultural heritage. Its 2017 order on reparations further innovates by giving fuller consideration to how an international court values heritage, for whom, and what it means to engage with heritage and identities in the aftermath of a major international crime.[3] This order on reparations is the judgment I chose to rewrite.

I seek to offer a queer perspective on this judgment as a pathway to queer international cultural heritage law (ICHL) and even heritage studies more broadly, so as to query the use of binaries in how we define heritage and its uses. Queer theory will

---

1. *Prosecutor v Al Mahdi* (Judgment and Sentence) (International Criminal Court Trial Chamber VIII, ICC-01/12-01/15), judgment of 27 September 2016 (hereafter cited in text as PAM).
2. I use the terminology of 'Muslim Saints' because that is the terminology used by the victims of the case when they are quoted by the ICC, and by the ICC itself.
3. *Prosecutor v Al Mahdi* (Reparations Order) (International Criminal Court Trial Chamber VIII, ICC-01/12-01/15), judgment of 17 August 2017 (hereafter cited in text as PAMR). Note that there was also an appeal to the reparations order, which partially informs my rewriting but which I will not describe in any detail in this commentary: *Prosecutor v Al Mahdi* (Judgment on the appeal of the victims against the 'Reparations Order') (International Criminal Court Appeals Chamber, ICC-01/12-01/15 A), judgment of 8 March 2018.

also be useful in strengthening the links between the legal mechanisms around heritage and the multiple, messy, and oftentimes contradictory identities that rely upon cultural heritage as their markers.

In terms of my method of rewriting, I adapt a 'checklist' Rosemary Hunter developed for feminist judgments.[4] Hunter's methodology of feminist judgments requires six things in the context of my adaptation for the queer context and the judgment I have re-written, in no particular order: (1) centring the queer person question; (2) ensuring participation in decision making; (3) challenging discriminatory biases; (4) paying attention to lived experience (which is a problem in a judicial context that tends to overlook sexuality in the composition of courts);[5] (5) actively seeking to overcome injustices based on discriminatory lines (while, I would add from a queer perspective, being wary of how equality can engender problematic 'tolerance' by flattening difference through a colonial prism);[6] and (6) being informed by queer scholarship. To these, and guided by point (6), I add the following steps informed by queer theory: (7) identifying and problematizing binaries underlying the status quo of the law's operation; (8) recasting the work of the law in terms of violence to introduce a certain wariness about the cavalier or saviour role of the law and lawyers and of the language of rights as a panacea.[7]

The most central tenet of the methodology, too, merits some revision. In asking a queer question, it is important that we should widen a queer question not just to think of queerness as an identity anchored in sexual orientation and/or gender identity, but more broadly to reimagine and centre otherness as a pathway to create relational opposition to an imagined 'normal' to unpack othering effects and embrace complexity and plurality, rather than create another binary. It is fairly obvious that asking a queer question and centring queer identities means asking 'whose experiences are excluded when the crime is applied in the real world,' and it can easily apply to crimes such as the destruction of heritage.[8] So, imagining a queer question in terms of queerness as otherness compels us to unpack the othering effects of international law and institutions across the board, which is relevant in thinking about the *Al Mahdi* case.

I argue that queering ICHL offers us a pathway to reimagine the way cultural identities are bound up in international legal categories. While queer theory does similar work to other forms of theory in heritage studies (as I show below), it can shed new light by asking the same questions differently, or by prioritizing questions in a different order. The enforcement of ICHL through the ICC forces a confrontation with

---

4.   Rosemary Hunter, 'An Account of Feminist Judging,' in *Feminist Judgments: From Theory to Practice*, ed. Rosemary Hunter, Clare McGlynn and Erika Rackley (Oxford: Hart Publishing, 2010), 30, 35.
5.   Leslie Moran, 'The Judicial Virtue of Sexuality,' in *Queer Theory: Law, Culture, Empire*, ed. Robert Leckey and Kim Brooks (Abingdon: Routledge, 2010), 86.
6.   Ratna Kapur, 'De-Radicalising the Rights Claims of Sexual Subalterns Through "Tolerance",' in *Queer Theory: Law, Culture, Empire*, ed. Robert Leckey and Kim Brooks (Abingdon: Routledge, 2010), 37, 46–47.
7.   Vanja Hamzić, 'International Law as Violence: Competing Absences of the Other,' in *Queering International Law: Possibilities, Alliances, Complicities, Risks*, ed. Dianne Otto (Abingdon: Routledge, 2018), 77.
8.   Rosemary Grey, Kcasey McLoughlin and Louise Chappell, 'Gender and Judging at the International Criminal Court: Lessons from "Feminist Judgment Projects",' *Leiden Journal of International Law* 34/1 (2021), 247, 259.

the 'human dimension' of heritage.[9] While the ICC has done terrific work that in some respects is itself already a queerer version of ICHL, it remained wedded to problematic binaries and categories that are worth further unpacking.

In order to introduce the rewritten judgment and pursue my thesis, the remainder of this commentary offers first my argument for why to queer and rewrite ICHL. I then provide some background to the original *Al Mahdi* judgments, alongside a justification for my choice of the reparations order. Next, I point to the main differences between the original and the rewritten reparations order.

Why Rewrite International Cultural Heritage Law?

ICHL for present purposes is the series of regimes for different types or domains of heritage. The most relevant domains for our present purposes are heritage in wartime,[10] world heritage,[11] and intangible cultural heritage,[12] since they come up more clearly in the *Al Mahdi* context.

ICHL protects identities inasmuch as they are cast as national identities, because ICHL is eminently a state-centric endeavour, despite proclamations of heritage being of value to all of humanity.[13] This problematic dichotomy between states and humanity renders us unable to see that there are other actors (particularly communities) for whom heritage matters most to create and galvanize identity, even mobilizing that identity for political purposes.[14] Queer theory, borrowing from postcolonial theory, destabilizes the concepts of global and local, and, with it, the centring of state narratives.[15] And, within the state, subaltern identities are only protected via heritage in sanitized forms that strip away any radical content or emancipatory claim, so they can be packaged to serve an authorized form of national identity.[16] Queer theory, as (a relatively small and underexplored) part of the package of critical projects that form critical heritage studies,[17] allows us to not only note this displacement of subaltern identity but also

---

9. Francesco Francioni, 'The Human Dimension of International Cultural Heritage Law: An Introduction,' *European Journal of International Law* 22/1 (2011), 9.

10. Convention for the Protection of Cultural Property in the Event of Armed Conflict with Regulations for the Execution of the Convention 1954 (adopted 14 May 1954, entered into force 7 August 1956) 249 UNTS 240 (1954 Hague Convention); Protocol to the Convention for the Protection of Cultural Property in the Event of Armed Conflict (adopted 14 May 1954, entered into force 7 August 1956) 249 UNTS 358 (Hague Protocol I); and Second Protocol to the Hague Convention of 1954 for the Protection of Cultural Property in the Event of Armed Conflict (adopted 26 March 1999, entered into force 9 March 2004) 2253 UNTS 172 (Hague Protocol II).

11. Convention concerning the Protection of the World Cultural and Natural Heritage 1972 (adopted 23 November 1972, entered into force 15 December 1975) 1037 UNTS 151 (WHC).

12. Convention for Safeguarding of the Intangible Cultural Heritage 2003 (adopted 17 October 2003, entered into force 20 April 2006) 2368 UNTS 3 (ICHC).

13. Lucas Lixinski, *International Heritage Law for Communities: Exclusion and Re-Imagination* (Oxford: Oxford University Press, 2019).

14. On a critique of this binary more broadly, see Lucas Lixinski, 'A Third Way of Thinking About Cultural Property,' *Brooklyn Journal of International Law* 44/2 (2019), 563.

15. Bruno Perreau, *Queer Theory: The French Response* (Stanford: Stanford University Press, 2016), 183.

16. Laurajane Smith, *Uses of Heritage* (Abingdon: Routledge, 2006), 76.

17. Colin Sterling, 'Critical Heritage and the Posthumanities: Problems and Prospects,' *International Journal*

to imagine what recentring it might look like, whether it is in relation to the state or the experts that often speak instead of communities in heritage contexts.[18]

Part of the effect of ICHL being split across domains is to reinforce a fiction of different categories. The most prominent division is the binary that separates heritage between tangible (that is, physically existing) and intangible (what one might call folklore). This binary effectively works to separate heritage from the people who practice and live in, with, or around it.[19] A critical perspective forces us to be suspicious of this binary and its clear division, and allows us to understand that heritage is not a thing, but a relationship, and, in this way, all heritage is in fact intangible.[20] What queer theory adds to this conversation is the idea of heritage as being created by affective relationships, which forces us to query not only the divide between tangible and intangible heritage, but also the consequences of doing away with this binary which shows that heritage matters to communities first and foremost, and that it is intangible practices that both are heritage and keep it alive and relevant.

Critical legal studies and critical heritage studies are key to unpacking the work that ICHL does. They also do much of the heavy lifting in the existing literature. What queer theory does that these larger critical traditions fail to do, at least as fully as queer theory, is to recentre debates around the idea of violence (rather than simply power), which forces us to query assumptions about whether the power contained in and wielded through heritage, identity, and the legal regimes around it is desirable in the first place, and whether that power can offer redress for the violence heritage holders experience. Further, queer theory helps identify and problematize binaries in ways that other approaches only do indirectly or less overtly. Also, queer theory calls stronger attention to subaltern narratives of heritage in its value, in a way that is warier of the language of rights. The language of rights is often seen in critical heritage contexts as a pathway to spelling out the fact that heritage embodies and channels power, and to shift that power in favour of communities and away from states. A wariness of rights borrowed from queer theory, however, also calls attention to the trade-offs in that embrace of rights, and the agency-stripping consequences of that language.

Background to the Original Judgment and the Case for Rewriting the Reparations Order

The *Al Mahdi* case involves charges of destruction of heritage in the context of a non-international armed conflict, in potential breach of Article 8(2)(e)(iv) of the Rome Statute.[21] The ICC undertook some interpretation of the crime and its elements because

of Heritage Studies 26/11 (2020), 1029, 1030.

18. Lixinski, *International Heritage Law for Communities*.

19. Lixinski, *International Heritage Law for Communities*, 3.

20. Smith, *Uses of Heritage*, 81.

21. The provision addresses the crime of '[i]ntentionally directing attacks against buildings dedicated to religion, education, art, science or charitable purposes, historic monuments, hospitals and places where the sick and wounded are collected, provided they are not military objectives.'

it was the first time it appeared on the docket (PAM, para. 13). The ICC discussed the context of the conflict, and Al Mahdi's participation in a morality brigade, as an expert on religion (PAM, paras. 31–32). Even though he initially advised against the destruction of the mausoleums (with an eye to keeping good relations between the insurgents and the local population), he ultimately directed the attack (PAM, paras. 36–37).

The ICC established the site as 'an integral part of the religious life of its inhabitants,' 'frequently visited by the residents.' (PAM, para. 34) They were also mostly part of a UNESCO World Heritage Site (PAM, para. 39), and as such had 'special importance to international cultural heritage' (PAM, para. 46). Nonetheless, Al Mahdi saw his role as more broadly contributing to eliminating superstition and 'backwards' practices, particularly those based on invented myths (PAM, para. 38(viii)). He also referred to the international prominence of the site as being created by '[t]hose UNESCO jackasses' (PAM, para. 46), in a rejection of international legal regimes and their imposition of rules onto local contexts. Ultimately, the Court sentenced Al Mahdi to nine years of imprisonment (PAM, paras. 105–109).

Less than one year later, in *Al Mahdi Reparations*, the ICC had a better opportunity to speak to the value of heritage, and the actual impact its destruction had on the lives of communities. Confronted with 139 reparations applicants, it had to engage with their voices, as well as with their calls for individual and collective reparations measures (PAMR, para. 9). The defence attempted to undermine these efforts by requiring demonstration of 'direct kinship between the people claiming the harm and the deceased whose mausoleums were attacked' (PAMR, para. 11), a call which the ICC rejected based on a broader (and queerer) understanding of kinship that was not dependent on specific descent or location, but rather on affective relationships.[22] The defence also called for predominantly collective reparations, and the use of modern and traditional justice mechanisms, among other forms of relief (PAMR, para. 12). The ICC determined that reparations amounted to 2.7 million euros, and gave instructions for implementation of the order (PAMR, paras. 134–148).

Key Differences

Based on my discussion of queering ICHL and the key features of the *Al Mahdi* judgments, I can now highlight some of the key differences between the original reparations order and my rewriting of it. I point to these differences to draw the reader's attention to contributions of queer theory to ICHL and how I attempted to articulate them within the formal constraints of a reparations order. This description serves as a guide to reading the rewritten judgment. I will speak to these differences using the steps in the methodology for queer judgment rewriting in Section 1.

First, in centring the queer person, or, for our purposes, 'the other,' the first key difference is that I placed victims' voices at the front and centre of the discussion

---

22. Dianne Otto, 'Resisting the Heteronormative Imaginary of the Nation-State: Rethinking Kinship and Border Protection,' in *Queering International Law: Possibilities, Alliances, Complicities, Risks*, ed. Dianne Otto (Abingdon: Routledge, 2018), 236.

of the impact of the crime. Drawing from quotes that are in the original reparations order, but placing them at the front of the Court's consideration, recentres lived experience and community voices over the views of experts on which the 'actual' ICC relied heavily. Drawing out these quotes speaks to ensuring participation in decision making (the second element of the methodology), but I added further elements by centring victims directly, and their representations, above the ICC's default choice of referring to legal representatives. In doing so, I nod to the filtering of voices through legal representatives and experts, which, while unavoidable in a judicial context, can still be tampered down with lived experience voices.

In terms of challenging discriminatory biases, the ICC's original reparations order is very mindful of doing so, highlighting time and again that reparations should not be pursued when they can have discriminatory effects, and that they should in fact be implemented to directly confront and overcome discrimination (PAMR, paras. 34, 105, 147). The ICC is mindful of the use of culture to oppress certain segments of society, particularly women (as the ICC spells out) and queer people (as I add in my rewritten judgment). There is thus no major change here, other than saying 'queer' out loud.

Foregrounding community voices is also a means to pay attention to lived experiences (fourth element). As I indicated above, the ICC does a relatively good job with that element in their original order, but community voices are often framed around the parameters set by expert opinion (PAMR 13–22—where, speaking to the importance of cultural heritage, the ICC Chamber only refers to expert opinion—and 106–108—on the moral harm experienced by communities). I largely do away with expert voices in the rewritten judgment, and defer much more to the lived experiences of the local community.

On the fifth element of the methodology—to actively seek to overcome injustices based on discrimination, –I already indicated above that the ICC does a relatively good job here. The key difference in the rewritten judgment is that I made sure to speak to the importance of maintaining difference. Even if the ICC did not seek to flatten difference directly, the treatment of individual victims as receiving equal compensation can be read as dismissing individual circumstances triggered by gender, class, sexuality, or other forms of diversity. The latter are very hard to account for in full in a large reparations order, in my view, but I at least acknowledged the Court's need to flatten some aspects of difference in the rewritten order, and attempted to frame it as a palatable and visible trade-off, rather than unspoken and naturalized consequence.

On the rewritten judgment being informed by queer scholarship (step six), I chose not to directly quote scholarly materials in the rewritten order, since the ICC also does not do it in the original order. But I hope the influence of queer scholarship is clear in the text, and throughout this commentary.

Step seven requires the identification of binaries. I do so in the rewritten judgment, particularly through the relationship between tangible and intangible cultural heritage, and the national and international heritage binary. The former is a relationship the ICC acknowledged in the original order (PAMR, para. 15), but does not problematize; the latter is a binary that the ICC leans into in determining (admittedly secondary) victimhood for the state and the international community (PAMR 51), a proposition

I reject altogether in the rewritten order. Acknowledging these binaries and their problematic work in the rewritten order allows me to focus more on the interests and voices of the community.

Lastly, the original order does not speak to the violence the law and legal institutions engender. While understandable (since it would mean the ICC undermining its own role and legitimacy in the case), I grapple with these questions in the rewritten order at least as means of acknowledging the limits of the law's operation, and nodding to the need to avoid legal violence in the implementation of reparations measures. I also attempt to avoid further violence in the implementation of reparations by suggesting communities, rather than ICC institutions, take the lead in implementation (and their will is supported, rather than directed or replaced, by ICC institutions).

INTERNATIONAL CRIMINAL COURT

TRIAL CHAMBER VIII

SITUATION IN THE REPUBLIC OF MALI

Prosecutor v Ahmad Al Faqi Al Mahdi (Reparations)

17 August 2017

Procedural History

[1] On 27 September 2016, after having pleaded guilty, the Chamber convicted Mr Al Mahdi of the war crime of attacking protected objects as a co-perpetrator under Articles 8(2)(e)(iv) and 25(3)(a) of the Rome Statute. Mr Al Mahdi directed attacks against ten protected buildings, nine of which formed part of a World Heritage Site.

[2] Based on his guilty plea, the Chamber determined a term of imprisonment for Mr Al Mahdi, and set a reparations phase calendar. This phase prompted a series of representations by: the Representatives of the Victims; victims themselves directly via their applications for reparations; the defence for Mr Al Mahdi; the Court's Prosecutor; and several amici curiae briefs, including one by the United Nations Educational, Scientific, and Cultural Organization (UNESCO).

[3] The Chamber further appointed four experts, two drawn from the local community in Timbuktu, to assist in the determination of reparations. The reports from these experts were made available to the parties, in redacted form. The Court understands the 'parties' to this reparations phase to be the victims (including their legal representatives), and the defence.

Overview

[4] The victims and their representatives comprise 139 reparations applicants. They maintain that the primary reparations measures that the Chamber should order are collective reparations in relation to the destroyed buildings. They also seek individual reparations for financial loss and mental harm experienced by certain members of the community.

[5] The Defence submits that primarily collective reparations are appropriate, as no bodily harm was suffered. The Defence argues that financial losses must be proven and limited to the period during which the destroyed monuments had not yet been rebuilt by UNESCO. The Defence also submits that psychological harm must be proven by way of showing a direct kinship between the people claiming the harm and the deceased whose mausoleums were attacked.[23]

The Importance of Cultural Heritage

[6] Since the Chamber had little opportunity to reflect on the value of heritage in the original judgment and sentence, and considering it is important to assess the value of this heritage for the purposes of deciding upon and quantifying reparations, the Chamber will now speak to the importance of cultural heritage in general as a matter of international law, and in the specific context of Timbuktu.

[7] The Chamber determined in its original judgment and sentence that the importance of Timbuktu was partly established by its status as a World Heritage Site. It noted that most of the destroyed buildings were part of the World Heritage Site.[24] It also noted that the targeting of Timbuktu stemmed partly because of its World Heritage status, which reflected the 'special importance' of Timbuktu, and informed Mr Al Mahdi's attitude towards these sites, when he referred to '[t]hose UNESCO jackasses.'[25] The presence of this site on the World Heritage List in particular spoke to the gravity of the crime, making it more significant.[26]

[8] The same original judgment and sentence also speak to the importance of Timbuktu as a heritage site for the local community, as a place of worship, social connection, economic activity, and exercise of cultural rights. These factors also spoke directly to elevating the gravity of the crime perpetrated by Mr Al Mahdi.[27]

[9] The Chamber now considers these elements anew, and in the context of reparations. Whereas the previous considerations were important to assess the gravity of the crime, the determination of reparations requires the Chamber to consider more closely the importance of Timbuktu as a heritage site, and of cultural heritage more broadly in relation to its impact on the victims of the crime.

[10] Even though the crime is that of destruction of cultural heritage, the heritage itself is not a victim of the crime. Rather, it is the communities that live in, with, or around the heritage that are the victims of this crime. To assume otherwise is to reify heritage

---

23. The language with the full list of relief sought is in *Al Mahdi Reparations Order* (ICC-01/12-01/15), at paras. 10–12.
24. *Prosecutor v Al Mahdi Judgment and Sentence* (ICC-01/12-01/15), para. 39.
25. *Prosecutor v Al Mahdi Judgment and Sentence* (ICC-01/12-01/15), para. 46.
26. *Prosecutor v Al Mahdi Judgment and Sentence* (ICC-01/12-01/15), para. 80.
27. *Prosecutor v Al Mahdi Judgment and Sentence* (ICC-01/12-01/15), paras. 79–80.

in ways that hide the relationships between people, peoples, and their identities. It is those relationships that are at the core of what heritage is, and why it matters.

[11] Heritage is often classified as being either tangible or intangible (the latter being the cultural practices that underpin social structures, such as storytelling, performances, ways of seeing the world, among others). In the case of Timbuktu, the focus of UNESCO World Heritage listing is on the tangible heritage, which is built monuments and mausoleums. However, what makes these buildings relevant is the ways in which the local community has related to them over centuries, and continues to relate to them. These relationships, which are fundamentally intangible cultural heritage, showcase the community's ongoing commitment to these buildings, the history and religion they embody, and keep the community connected both within and beyond the geographical territory of Timbuktu or Mali. They create a community around notions of kinship that are not based on specific assumptions about descent and geography, and are based instead on the affective relationships people have with their heritage. It is the case, in other words, that all heritage is in fact intangible, and the way we understand harm to heritage must focus on those relationships, with the physical structures only working as conduits for those practices, rather than being themselves the heritage.

[12] The loss and harm victims have experienced is to their inability to continue these relationships temporarily, but it is a relationship that can survive and be modified. The Chamber does not seek here to diminish the sense of cultural and religious loss experienced by the victims, but rather to contextualize it, so that reparations ordered do not assume that the heritage of Timbuktu is somehow lost forever because of its irreplaceability. The community has been harmed by these attacks on their heritage, which speaks to an attack on their collective identity, but they can also overcome this harm and become more resilient precisely because of and through their ongoing cultural relationships to Timbuktu. It is on facilitating community resilience that the Chamber focuses for the purposes of determining reparations.

[13] Therefore, the value of heritage as perceived through international recognition is secondary now. While useful to assessing the gravity of the crime, inasmuch as it was part of the motivation for destruction, it is the importance to the local community that is most centrally relevant for our purposes. International importance will be relevant further below, as it aids in assessing economic loss for the community that relied on Timbuktu for their livelihoods as providers for tourists and pilgrims that came to visit the site.

[14] That the local importance of Timbuktu is the most relevant factor, it bears stressing, does not mean that the importance of Timbuktu is determined by the nation-state. To the contrary. While international cultural heritage law has long been founded on a false dichotomy between national and international heritage, this dichotomy glosses over the central importance of communities as the actors who create, practice, and keep alive heritage. It is therefore to the local community, rather than the state of Mali,

that we must turn our primary focus in assessing and determining reparations. The role of the Court and its Trust Fund for Victims is to assist, but never displace or replace, the local community.

[15] The local community has been fragmented as a result of the conflict in Mali, of which the destruction of Timbuktu is a small part. Multiple members have left the region and restarted their lives elsewhere. They experience ongoing harm as a result of their lack of proximity to the site, but still feel bound to it, and see it as a part of their identity. The Chamber considers them to also be victims of the crimes of which Mr Al Mahdi is convicted.

[16] Although many of the buildings in the cultural heritage site of Timbuktu have been destroyed, their loss is not irreparable. The Chamber notes that a number of these mausoleums have already been reconstructed, via direct action of the local community and with some national and international funding support. The reconstruction of this heritage does not in any way diminish their worth or 'authenticity,' which is a concern for their value as tangible heritage under international law. In the Chamber's view, to the contrary, their reconstruction renews the community's relationship to their own heritage, and offers them an opportunity to come together and enhance their internal ties and resilience. That said, it is nonetheless a loss they have experienced, and that has caused significant anguish, and needs repairing. Despite the Chamber considering that the reconstruction of this heritage is a welcome step, it is possible that the original destruction and loss of 'authenticity' affects tourist appetite to visit the site, a consideration which we will reflect below in speaking to economic loss.

[17] The cultural identities at stake in this case are complex. They comprise cultural, economic, social, and religious connections to Timbuktu and its heritage. More than one of these connections co-exist for most of the victims in this case. The religious value of the site can be particularly problematic, in that it can engender a view of religion and religious practice that drives discriminatory assessments about minorities on the basis of gender, social status, religion, sexual orientation or gender identity, among others. The Chamber, while mindful not to replace the cultural practices and identities of the victims with its own value judgments, is also mindful that the relationships embodied in cultural heritage are at their best when difference is celebrated and used to create and reinforce, rather than exclude, kinship.

[18] Further, the Chamber acknowledges that communities have a right to participate in their cultural life, a right protected under international instruments. Further, the Chamber notes that communities have the right to control their own cultural heritage. That the cultural rights of the victims have been violated inevitably places them in the role of victims, but this violation also creates important opportunities for the community to exercise their agency in renewing their cultural heritage, their cultural identities, and their relationships of kinship.

[19] In conclusion, the value of heritage is central to our consideration of reparations. But this value can only be assessed adequately through the voices of communities. The community is multi-faceted, and their relationships cannot be assessed monolithically. There are, thus, multiple categories of victims, which the Chamber acknowledges in their plurality and complexity. For the purposes of this case and reparations order, however, the Court needs to make some generalizations about victims and their interests, which we hope will be accepted by communities in good faith, and as acknowledgment of the common bonds that tie the community to the heritage of Timbuktu.

Principles on Reparations

[20] As per Article 75(1) of the Rome Statute,

> [t]he Court shall establish principles relating to reparations to, or in respect of, victims, including restitution, compensation and rehabilitation. On this basis, in its decision the Court may, either upon request or on its own motion in exceptional circumstances, determine the scope and extent of any damage, loss and injury to, or in respect of, victims and will state the principles on which it is acting.

[21] The Court stresses, on the basis of its past jurisprudence, that reparations are aimed at redressing harm, which is a key measure of accountability. That is not to say that the purpose of reparations is punitive—rather, it is about the victims and the harm they experienced, and not the perpetrator. The purpose of reparations is to recover the dignity of the victims and allow them to develop, through their kinship ties, the necessary social and cultural tools to further their resilience. It is a tool of resilience, and, in some respects, reconciliation.

[22] Reparations are to be administered fairly, in a way that does not foster or perpetuate discriminatory practices. It is centred on the victims and their agency. It pays attention to the lived experiences of these communities and their diversity. It seeks to redress, rather than impose old or new violence upon victims. The participation of victims should be substantive and effective.

[23] Reparations need to be appropriate, adequate, and prompt. They should reflect local and customary practices unless these are discriminatory or exclusionary. They should respect the multiple ways in which kinship is created and harm is experienced, while also being achievable in their implementation. We note in particular the use of traditional cultural practices and heritage around the world to foster discriminatory practices, and reject reparations that renew or reinforce those aspects of cultural heritage.

[24] Reparations programmes need to be self-sustaining and support victim agency for not only repairing past harm and reverting to the status quo prior to the harm, but also making sure that the structural conditions that may have contributed to the harm are displaced, and replaced instead with community-centred action. Financial

compensation, in particular, should aim at redressing these structural causes, rather than over-individualizing victimhood in ways that dismisses structural causes of harm.

[25] The rights of Mr Al Mahdi need to be taken into account in ordering reparations, and balanced against victims' expectations.

[26] In sum, a reparations order must: (i) centre victims and their experience; (ii) directly address the convicted person as the one who is responsible for making reparations; (iii) set out the parameters of the liability that underpins reparations; (iv) specify and justify the types of reparations ordered, whether individual or collective, and the balance between these forms as appropriate; (v) it must identify the victims eligible for reparations based on the link between the harm suffered and the conduct of the convicted person.

Reparations in the Case

Victims

[27] The Chamber notes that reparations can be issued individually or collectively. Individual reparations can also be granted to legal entities that are direct victims of the crimes committed, such as cultural institutions, non-profit organizations, statutory bodies, corporations, and other partnerships.

[28] In this case, the local communities have been the principal victims of the crime of destruction of their heritage. The national community of Mali, or the international community as represented by UNESCO, have certainly been affected by the destruction of this site, but they have experienced no significant harm to their identities or livelihoods. And, to the extent heritage exists and is relevant because of connections to local communities, rather than national or international status, it is on those communities' concerns that we must focus.

[29] These communities can apply for reparations collectively, or members of the community can apply individually. Individual applications for reparations, however, should not detract from the more important work of collective reparations. Further, the individualization of reparations should not work to excuse the violence perpetrated collectively against these communities, nor should itself become a form of violence and erasure of community life. When individual reparations are owed, individual victims have a right to privacy and to have their claims heard confidentially by the Trust Fund for Victims, as per their expressed wishes before this Chamber.

[30] A key factor in considering eligibility for individual reparations from within the community is to consider each applying individual's kinship relationships within the community, as well as their stated relationship to the destroyed tangible heritage and the intangible heritage social and cultural practices that underpin it. This kinship

exists both locally and beyond, given the displacement of multiple members of the community from Timbuktu as a result of the conflict within which the destruction of cultural heritage took place. Individual victims who have moved away are less likely to benefit from collective reparations that centre only on the geographical boundaries of Timbuktu. Therefore, some of those collective reparation measures should aim at creating incentives for the return of those individuals to Timbuktu, if they so choose, or other ways to maintain those cultural and social ties to Timbuktu and its heritage alive from a distance.

Types and modalities of harm and reparations

[31] Reparations can be either individual or collective. They involve restitution, compensation, and rehabilitation.

[32] Restitution involves a return to the *status quo ante*, that is, recreating the conditions that existed before the crime occurred. In this context, restitution is neither possible nor desirable. It is impossible because the physical heritage has been destroyed, and its reconstruction, however important in the eyes of the community and already largely executed, will never fully restore the site to what it was beforehand. But said outcome would not in any event be desirable. Intangible cultural heritage, which is at the core of the crime perpetrated here, is meant to change over time. Cultural practices and relationships evolve, and the destruction of their physical markers will inevitably affect them. Further, and importantly, it would be undesirable to revert to the *status quo ante* without attention to the structural factors and conditions that contributed to the destruction of the heritage in the first place. Rather, it would be preferable if the community took advantage of this context to enhance their resilience and have a choice as to what elements of the culture represented by the destroyed mausoleums they wish to recover, and which ones need change.

[33] Compensation is the resources, typically financial, awarded to victims in recognition of their harm. It is an important consideration in this case, and it involves an assessment of the measurability of physical, emotional, and cultural harm.

[34] Rehabilitation seeks to restore the agency of victims. It may include economic development programmes or social, medical, or legal services. It can also include guarantees of non-repetition. It is centred on the lived experiences of victims. In this context, it is worth remarking, rehabilitation highlights the limits of the law in making adequate reparations for the harm to identities and kinship. It invites solutions that fall outside immediate legal scrutiny, and are driven by the community, to restore affective relationships that the law cannot adequately perceive.

Individual v Collective Harm

[35] As indicated above in this Order, the primary type of harm with which this Chamber is concerned is collective harm. That is because cultural heritage is created

and experienced collectively, it is a marker of identity that is held collectively. While individuals have experienced, according to their testimonies before this Chamber, different types of harm depending on the specific overlapping and interrelated relationships they each had with Timbuktu and the heritage therein, fundamentally those different relationships are underpinned by a sense of community and collective endeavour. Therefore, the Chamber will primarily focus on collective forms of reparation.

The Crime's Impact

[36] Communities and their members experienced the impact of the destruction of the tangible cultural heritage of Timbuktu on their intangible cultural relationships in different ways. It is important to centre their voices and experiences in our assessment of the impact of the crime to cede authority to the community to decide what justice means in this case, prior to determining appropriate reparations. The following extracts are drawn from the translations of application forms for victim status in this case:[28]

'I would like the ICC to give money or building materials for the upkeep of the mausoleums.'

'The Court must provide money to fix and care for (protect) the mausoleums. A wall should be built to protect the mausoleums.'

'I would like the Court to give money to help us build and maintain the holy sites. This will give us relief and help us make some progress.'

'In reparation for the harm, compensation to be used to support activities to foster resilience to the effects of the destruction, to overcome them and to re-establish stronger emotional and spiritual ties to this cultural property is desirable.'

'I was completely emotionally devastated by the destruction of the mausoleums.'

'I was a victim of the destruction of the mausoleum, upset and shaken in my body and to the depths of my being.'

'I have never suffered so deeply in my life [...] Mentally, I was devastated. I felt humiliated by the destruction. I am still suffering [...] I am still affected mentally.'

'I was so shocked and hurt on the day of the destruction that I could have died.'

'[M]y faith shattered and my belief unsettled.'

'I lost everything with the destruction—my childhood, my belief and my attachment.'

'My faith is shattered. My family fled [.] [...] I lost everything and all my faith.'

---

28. These quotes are drawn, verbatim, from *Al Mahdi Reparations Order*, paras. 61 (the first four quotes) and 85 (the remainder of the quotes). Footnotes omitted.

'The whole city suffered on the day the mausoleums were destroyed. I wept and many others wept, because we were in great pain. The saints are all important to us. They are ancestors of all of us. We used to seek blessings from them and make offerings to them at every milestone in our lives: births, deaths, sickness, travel, etc. That's why the destruction harmed us. We didn't think it was possible.'

'I cried a lot on the day of the destruction. My family, my friends and all the people of Timbuktu suffered. We will never forget. The Saints of Timbuktu are the descendants of Allah. When we used to ask for their blessings, they would be given. When the mausoleums were destroyed, we were shattered as well. The pain is still there today. The city has changed. Timbuktu is no longer what it was; even if the saints protect us still, it's not the same as before. We lost everything; today we have nothing.'

'The destruction of the sacred shrines of my ancestors caused me suffering [...] I suffered, as did the other members of my family. When there was a problem in our family, it was the only place in which we gathered and prayed for protection.'

[37] In other words, the destruction of tangible heritage and the disruption of intangible cultural heritage in this case gave rise to deep and consequential harm, which must be redressed.

Damage to Heritage

[38] The damage to the tangible heritage structures is the key act of the crime, and triggered the harm experienced by communities. Therefore, reparations must aim to reconstruct this heritage, in the terms set by the communities, and relying as much as possible on their expertise to imbue the site's external appearance, materials, and construction processes with cultural meaning relevant to the local community. Further, whenever possible, local workers, builders, and craftspeople should be used for this reconstruction. International expertise and assistance should be extremely limited to instances in which the community chooses to invite outside expertise and assistance, and should work subsidiarily to the interests, and under the direction, of the local community and its leaders.

[39] The reconstruction of these sites is a form of collective reparation. Using local workforces to do so is a form of individual reparation. Based on the calculations provided to the Chamber by the experts indicated above, the Chamber determines that 100,000 euros be used to pay for the work of reconstruction, whether the one already executed, or the one still to be done.

Consequential Economic Loss

[40] Economic losses are experienced on the basis of loss of income from local community members, particularly those whose livelihood depended upon tourism to the site. The Chamber understands that it is difficult, as the victims themselves told us, to fully individualize these members and reparations, given local kinship systems

that determine forms of distribution of monies earned from tourism in the area. This system of kinship requires us to treat these reparations as also primarily collective, even if there are significant individual components at play.

[41] The Chamber also recalls that the international status of Timbuktu as a World Heritage Site becomes relevant here, because this status helps attract tourists to the site. This status, and its requirement of authenticity that means the reconstructed mausoleums may be deemed as somehow 'less than' the ones destroyed, should be factored into the calculations of economic loss in the site.

[42] In terms of individual reparations, the Chamber estimates that the 139 identified individual victims be each awarded 2,000 euros for their economic loss, recommending that these individuals use these moneys in the way they deem appropriate. The payments should be made as lump sums. In the event of victims who have left Timbuktu as a result of the conflict or destruction of the mausoleums, a further 1,000 euros should be granted to each of these victims (in other words, 3,000 in total per victim), either to give them the means to allow them to relocate should they wish to do so, or to give them the resources to, at least temporarily, maintain their cultural connections to Timbuktu. The Chamber estimates that fifty-two of the identified individual victims fall in this category.

[43] In terms of collective reparations, the Chamber orders that 500,000 euros be made available to the community for the design and implementation of local development, educational, and job-creating programs. These programs can also extend outside the local geographical area, to account for those victims who have left Timbuktu.

[44] Local authorities should endeavour to adopt measures to avoid and control inflation that may arise as a consequence of the sudden influx of cash in the community.

Moral Harm

[45] An apology for the destruction of the tangible heritage, that also acknowledges the deeper impacts in terms of intangible cultural heritage and relationships, is owed to the community. This apology should come directly from Mr Al Mahdi, and should be made live during a large community gathering, with a recording made available to other members of the local community who may not have been able to attend. At this community gathering, the community is also invited to come together socially and in celebration, as a means to help re-establish and strengthen their kinship ties frayed by the crimes perpetrated by Mr Al Mahdi. This measure of collective reparation is important to redress some of the moral harm experienced.

[46] Further, the harm experienced by the community is deep, as indicated by their representations quoted above. There was community-wide moral harm, as well as harm to specific groups and kinship systems. These harms do not depend on individuals

proving direct descendancy from the people buried in the destroyed mausoleums, since they have been largely treated by the community as Saints whose existences transcend specific familial ties.

[47] Given the extensive harm experienced by the community, the Chamber orders 2,000,000 euros to be paid in moral harm damages, to be used by the community in terms similar to those outlined above in relation to collective economic loss, in addition to programs like psychological counselling individually or through collective group therapy, and other forms of cultural revitalization of the tangible and intangible cultural heritage of Timbuktu.

Implementation

[48] It is not for the Chamber to give detailed directions on implementation. However, it notes that the Trust Fund for Victims, working closely with and under the direction of the local community and its representatives, will be essential for the adequate implementation of this order. The Chamber further notes the key objectives of reparations, as outlined above, namely fostering the well-being and resilience of the community, with special attention to collective forms of reparation, should be at the forefront of all implementation activity.

Disposition

FOR THE FOREGOING REASONS, THE CHAMBER THEREFORE

ORDERS individual and collective reparations for the community of Timbuktu, in the terms specified above in the present order;

ACKNOWLEDGES that the harm to tangible cultural heritage in Timbuktu has impacted on intangible cultural heritage in Timbuktu;

ACKNOWLEDGES that the reparations are aimed primarily at the intangible cultural heritage associated with Timbuktu, to the extent it creates identity, kinship, and resilience for the communities in the area;

ASSESSES Mr Al Mahdi's financial liability to be in the amount of 2,930,000 euros;

ENCOURAGES the victims and their legal representatives to use the reparations resources so as to further their collective identity and resilience, while being mindful to at the same time redress and change, rather than simply repair, the root causes of violence on cultural or religious grounds in the region;

ORDERS the registry of the Court to oversee the implementation of this order;

SETS a deadline for the Trust Fund for Victims to offer a draft implementation plan within six months of this order;

DIRECTS the legal representatives and defence to file any observations on the draft implementation plan within 30 days of notification.

Dated 17 August 2017
At The Hague, The Netherlands

13

MB v Secretary of State for Work and Pensions (European Union):

A Transgender Studies Rewriting of the *MB* Judgment by the Court of Justice of the EU

Mariza Avgeri

The Case

In *MB*, the Court of Justice of the European Union (CJEU) considered whether Article 4(1) of Directive 79/7/EEC, taken together with Articles 3(1)(a) and 7(1)(a) of the same Directive, precluded national legislation from imposing discriminatory standards requiring a married transsexual person (the term that the Court uses) to fulfil specific criteria in order to qualify for a statutory retirement pension.[1] B was a transgender male-to-female individual. Since 1974, she had been married to a woman. Since 1991, she had lived as a woman, and in 1995 she underwent 'gender reassignment surgery,' according to the Court's terminology. She turned 60 in 2008, the legal retirement age for women in the UK at the time. She applied for a State pension upon retirement. The application was denied because MB had not followed the legal procedure for gender reassignment recognition. Therefore, under national law, she remained male.

MB decided not to apply for gender recognition under the applicable procedure. The UK did not allow same-sex marriage at the time, so one of the requirements for legal recognition was that she be 'unmarried.' That would require MB to obtain an annulment of her marriage, which she and her spouse opposed. In light of these facts, the UK Supreme Court posed a straightforward question: Is the requirement to be unmarried contrary to Directive 79/7/EEC's prohibition on discrimination on the basis of sex in matters of social security?

This case's facts and claim are similar to those in *Richards*.[2] However, *Richards* was concerned with the applicant's inability to have her gender reassignment legally

---

1. Case C-451/16, *MB v Secretary of State for Work and Pensions* [2016] ECLI:EU:C:2018:492.
2. Case C-423/04, *Sarah Margaret Richards v Secretary of State of Work and Pensions*, ECLI:EU:C:2006:256.

recognized. Since the Gender Recognition Act of 2004 went into effect, this is no longer the case. However, while the passage of the Act of 2004 has made recognition possible, it has also raised a number of new questions. Does Directive 79/7 apply to the conditions outlined in national law for gender reassignment recognition? At what point does a transgender individual receive protection under Directive 79/7? Does the prohibition against discrimination on the basis of sex between transgender and cisgender individuals only apply when gender reassignment has been legally recognized under national law?

The CJEU concluded that the UK legislation in question constituted direct sex discrimination and rejected the UK's argument that it is for the Member States to determine the conditions under which legal recognition is given to the change of gender of a person. The Court therefore concluded that national legislation which precludes a transsexual (using the Court's terminology), in the absence of recognition of their new gender, from fulfilling a requirement which must be met in order to be entitled to a right protected by EU law must be regarded as being, in principle, incompatible with the requirements of EU law. According to the Court, under national law, a person who has had gender affirmation surgery after marrying was treated less favourably than a person who had not had such surgery but was married, since the marriage annulment condition applied to the former but not to the latter for the purpose of statutory retirement pension entitlement.[3]

In light of the foregoing, it is reasonable to conclude that the CJEU has thus far only addressed cases involving transgender people who have undergone or want to undergo gender affirmation surgery. The Court was willing to protect this group by including gender reassignment discrimination within the prohibition on sex discrimination. This is something the Court first did in *P. v S.*.[4] It has done so since, mostly where discrimination was directly related to binary legal gender reassignment, but also in instances where discrimination resulted from an inability to meet specific prerequisites and thus enjoy certain Union-protected rights.

In the *MB* judgment, the Court seems to equate female trans status with the medical transition of MB in the absence of her legal gender recognition. What it fails to consider is that transness is not a matter of gender reassignment procedures but of self-determination, and any law that does not recognize gender on the basis of psychosocial self-identification deprives trans people from their rights, which has a material and social impact on them as with MB's pension.

On that basis, I rewrite the *MB* judgment based on Transgender Studies' theoretical assumptions outlined below, and I compare a married trans woman who has not obtained legal recognition for her acquired gender (as MB) with a married trans woman who has obtained legal recognition for her acquired gender. In this process, I do not deal at all with medical transition, which is a pathologizing discourse and is not a replacement for legal gender recognition, as the Court's decision seems to imply. In this light, I try to reveal the impact of the exclusion of trans identities by the (limited) protection afforded by the law due to its cis-homonormativity.

---

3.   *MB v Secretary of State for Work and Pensions*, para. 52.
4.   C-13/94, *P. v S. and Cornwall County Council*, 30 April 1996, ECLI:EU:C:1996:170.

Transgender Studies and the *MB* Case

Transgender studies arguably first came to the foreground as a distinct field with Sandy Stone's foundational book, firstly presented at a conference in 1988, 'Posttranssexual Manifesto,'[5] which was published in 1991.

Stone attempted to explore the concept of the 'transsexual' that was often experienced by people leading transsexual lives as a category limiting transgender people to mainstream narratives and forcing them to be silent about their own stories in order to access the legal and medical procedures that they needed. Stone attempted to break the silence surrounding the issue and reshape what she saw as 'textual violence inscribed in the transsexual body' into a challenging 'reconstructive force.'[6] In order to pursue this disruption and reconfiguration, Stone juxtaposed 'medically constituted transsexual embodiments against the backdrop of culturally intelligible gendered bodies.'[7] Her goal was to 'to take advantage of the dissonances created by such a juxtaposition to fragment and reconstitute the elements of gender in new and unexpected geometries.'[8] One can understand that Stone's attempt was both one of deconstruction and validation of marginalized gender variety. She embarked on an exploratory project that went beyond the then meaning of 'transsexual' and gave birth to new sets of questions and phenomena 'whose potential for productive disruption of structured sexualities and spectra of desire has yet to be explored.'[9]

Stryker uses the term transgender 'to refer to people who move away from the gender they were assigned at birth, people who cross over (trans-) the boundaries constructed by their culture to define and contain that gender.'[10] In this way, Transgender Studies encompasses both gender identity and gender expression, including all these locations that challenge established gender norms. It includes those who feel they belong to another gender than that which they were assigned at birth, and those who strive to find another not yet defined, acknowledged and already occupied gender location/space to express/be themselves. Transgender studies encompass the need to break away from conventional expectations that are prescribed to the gender positions that subjects are initially given and acknowledges the need to transcend this position or its prerequisites as something completely valid with no need of further explanation. That is transgender studies' main ontological assumption, which lies beyond the reality of gender categories as they are assigned and developed in mainstream western gender ideology.[11] We see

---

5. Sandy Stone, 'The Empire Strikes Back: A Posttranssexual Manifesto,' in *Body Guards: The Cultural Politics of Gender Ambiguity*, ed. Julia Epstein and Kristina Straub (New York: Routledge, 1991), 280–304.
6. Sandy Stone, 'The Empire Strikes Back,' 295.
7. Susan Stryker and Paisley Currah, 'Introduction,' *TSQ: Transgender Studies Quarterly* 1 (2014), 1, 3.
8. Stone, 'The Empire Strikes Back.'
9. Stone, 'The Empire Strikes Back.'
10. Susan Stryker, *Transgender History* (Berkeley: Seal Press, 2008), 1.
11. Dominant gender ideology excludes transgender and gender nonconforming subjectivities from the protection of European and EU Law by assuming sex/gender incongruence only as an exception and validating it only when fulfilling certain arbitrary and narrow legal or medical standards. See Jenny Andrine and Madsen Evang, 'Is "Gender Ideology" Western Colonialism?: Anti-gender Rhetoric and the Misappropriation of Postcolonial Language,' *TSQ* 9/3 (2022), 365–386; and Teresa Toldy and Júlia Garraio, 'Gender Ideology: A Discourse That Threatens Gender Equality,' in *Gender Equality. Encyclopedia of the*

that in this definition both gender expression and nonbinary identities are included, but on the other hand the foundational aspects of any trans identity are not doubted.

For Transgender Studies there is no such thing as the 'single organically unified natural object characterised by one and only one of two available sex statuses.'[12] The sex of the body is understood to be 'an interpretive fiction that narrates a complex amalgamation of gland secretions and reproductive organs, chromosomes and genes, morphological characteristics and physiognomic features.'[13] It is the core assumption of Transgender Studies that there are more than two viable configurations of bodily sexed being. The questions that Transgender Studies attempt to ask are: what are the purposes and the cost behind the collapse of the diversity of embodiment to two mutually exclusive categories of man and woman and through which means is this institutionalized. It is also a call to acknowledge that the given pronouns 'he' and 'she' enable personhood that we learn to claim in these institutional, material and societal terms and that there is agency and a process as well as a right in disavowing these pronouns as the cost of finding a location that accommodates the self. These are questions usually delegated to the fields of psychology and biology, but Transgender Studies help us to think about them through a different lens that challenges mainstream/normative gender ideology and classification.

On this basis, I try to offer a rewriting of MB based on Transgender Studies in order to open up a reparative potential of CJEU's jurisprudence on trans cases—*P. v S.*, *K.B.*, and *Richards*—that have not yet provided a viable solution for future instances involving non-binary or genderqueer persons. These judgments have not even appeared to leave an open door in that regard, because the Court examined the concept of sex and its boundaries in the (limited) manner in which it was presented, perhaps to avoid certain complexities, or perhaps to adhere to the key elements of each case to be decided. It has also failed to address the issue of transgender people who do not wish to undergo gender affirmation surgery or people who do not suffer from gender dysphoria,[14] thus avoiding extending the meaning of reassignment (affirmation) to social transition (name, mannerism, dress) or non-conforming gender expression beyond identitarian claims. Gender is also something that the Court and EU law have not dealt with explicitly, therefore leaving discrimination on grounds of gender identity and expression to fall under discrimination on grounds of sex. That potentially leaves more space for a binary, genitocentric and medical understanding of gender transition and does not extend protection to all genderqueer and nonbinary identities, as well as to gender nonconformity as a form of protected experience and expression that does not adhere to sex assigned at birth.

UN Sustainable Development Goals, ed. Walter Leal Filho, Anabela Marisa Azul, Luciana Brandli, Amanda Lange Salvia and Tony Wall (Cham: Springer Publishing, 2021).

12.   Susan Stryker, 'Transgender Feminism: Queering the Woman Question,' in *Third Wave Feminism: A Critical Exploration*, ed. Stacy Gillis, Gillian Howie and Rebecca Munford (London: Palgrave Macmillan, 2007), 59–70, 62.

13.   Stryker, 'Transgender Feminism.'

14.   Jack Drescher, Peggy Cohen-Kettenis and Sam Winter, 'Minding the Body: Situating Gender Diagnoses in the ICD-11,' *International Review of Psychiatry* 24/6 (2012), 568–577.

Gender nonconformity and genderqueer and nonbinary identity could well be protected under non-discrimination based on expectations that derive from sex assigned at birth, but we have not seen such a reading yet from the CJEU and the European Court of Human Rights (ECtHR). Franke argues that the law needs to accommodate the experiences of persons that lie beyond the hegemonic ideas of sex and gender.[15] Although she challenges the legal persistence on biological sex given that 'every sexual biological fact is meaningful only within a gendered frame of reference,'[16] Franke suggests that one should acknowledge the gender-conformity imperatives that derive from biological sex. which lead to discrimination against non-conforming individuals *because* of sex.[17] Understanding sex and gender as socially mediated constructs challenges the idea of sex as natural and fixed and gender as plainly cultural and constructed, and redefines sexual agency beyond biological and constructionist determinism. The insight provided by such a perspective becomes an even stronger imperative in the context of LGBTI related jurisprudence, since, as Shultz argues,[18] courts are not mere factfinders on issues of sex and gender; instead, they hold the ability to reinforce normatively accepted ideas that have led to the disenfranchisement and oppression of various experiences by presenting as 'foundational *fact* that which is really an *effect* of gender ideology.'[19]

As far as the legal superstructure's function and role in the regulation of gender go, one could recall queer theorist Butler's own words that 'identity categories tend to be instruments of regulatory regimes, whether as the normalizing categories of oppressive structures or as the rallying points for a liberatory contestation of that very oppression.'[20] Transgender studies, on the other hand, are not so suspicious of identities and labels, depending on how they are employed. Currah underlines, rightly so, that queer theorists have highlighted that identity-based political claims do not challenge categories of homosexuality and heterosexuality upon which subjection is based. Lisa Bower, for example, also claims that the 'politics of official recognition' are an attempt to 'fit the "queer other" within some space already acknowledged by the liberal nation-state.'[21] Currah's viewpoint mediates both identity iconoclasm versus identity fundamentalism and State-centred political intervention versus cultural interventions, which is what I also attempt with the rewriting of MB. As he explains, seeing the above concepts in opposing terms has 'sometimes had the unfortunate effect

15. Katherine M. Franke, 'The Central Mistake of Sex Discrimination Law: The Disaggregation of Sex from Gender,' *University of Pennsylvania Law Review* 144/1 (1995), 1, 8.
16. Franke, 'The Central Mistake of Sex Discrimination Law'; see, also, Judith Butler, *Gender Trouble: Feminism and the Subversion of Identity* (New York: Routledge, 1990).
17. Franke, 'The Central Mistake of Sex Discrimination Law,' 2.
18. Vicky Schultz, 'Women "Before" the Law: Judicial Stories About Women, Work, and Sex Segregation on the Job,' in *Feminists Theorize the Political*, ed. Judith Butler and Joan W. Scott (New York: Routledge, 1992), 297–338.
19. Franke, 'The Central Mistake of Sex Discrimination Law,' 2.
20. Judith Butler, 'Imitation and Gender Insubordination,' in *Inside/Out*, ed. Diana Fuss (New York: Routledge, 1991), 13–14.
21. Lisa Bower, 'Queer Problems/Straight Solutions: The Limits of a Politics of "Official Recognition",' in *Playing with Fire: Queer Politics, Queer Theories*, ed. Shane Phelan (New York: Routledge, 1997), 268–269.

of eliding the very material violence that people suffer from the discursive construction of the identity categories that many queer theorists are so eager to dismantle.'[22]

The reformist project of law, then, has to balance between deconstructing the productive capacity of law that shapes dominant exclusionary gender ideology, and providing institutional protection and validation to marginalized geometries of sex/gender/expression through affirmative inclusion, open to new reconfigurations of (a) gendered subjectivities that must and should become 'liveable.'

Currah stresses the need for political action addressed towards the State. He argues that identity-based political claims should not be abandoned before the system of sex/gender as regulated by the State is dismissed. Indeed, he argues that these aims—freeing queer and transgender identities from official classification that reproduces hierarchies and freeing them from State-sponsored violence and discrimination based on legal provisions—can be articulated together. Transgender studies coupled with queer theory (with the former being seen as the latter's 'evil twin'[23]) can 'defend the claim that transness requires that we understand, as we never have before, what it means to be attached to a norm—by desire, by habit, by survival'[24] while dismantling its primacy.

Hopefully the rewriting of the MB case that follows adds to reforming the law in the direction of making the protection afforded more encompassing, while destabilizing the hierarchy produced by the use of identities and labels, finding ways to make the latter one's tools for extending inclusion. The MB judgment is a good judgment in terms of protecting transexual people from discrimination because of sex, but the rationale of the judgment can be revisited from a Transgender Studies lens, whereby binarism and medicalization of transness is not the default.

---

22. Currah, 'Defending Genders,' 1365.
23. Stryker, 'Transgender Studies,' 212.
24. Andrea Long Chu and Emmett Harsin Drager, 'After Trans Studies,' *TSQ: Transgender Studies Quarterly* 6 (2019), 108.

JUDGMENT OF THE COURT
(Grand Chamber)

26 June 2018

In Case C451/16,
(...)

MB
v
Secretary of State for Work and Pensions,

THE COURT (Grand Chamber),
(...)
gives the following

Judgment

[1] This request for a preliminary ruling concerns the interpretation of Council Directive 79/7/EEC of 1978 on the progressive implementation of the principle of equal treatment for people in matters of social security.[25]

[2] The request has been made in proceedings between MB and the Secretary of State for Work and Pensions concerning the refusal to grant MB a State retirement pension as from the statutory pensionable age for persons of the gender that she acquired as a result of a change of gender.

Legal context

EU law

[3] The third indent of Article 3(1)(a) of Directive 79/7 provides that that directive is to apply to statutory schemes which provide protection against old age.

[4] Under Article 4(1) of that directive: 'The principle of equal treatment means that there shall be no discrimination whatsoever on ground of sex either directly, or indirectly by reference in particular to marital or family status, in particular as concerns: the scope of the schemes and the conditions of access thereto...'

---

25. OJ 1979 L 6, p. 24.

[5] Article 7(1)(a) of that directive provides: 'This Directive shall be without prejudice to the right of the Member States to exclude from its scope:(a) the determination of pensionable age for the purposes of granting old-age and retirement pensions and the possible consequences thereof for other benefits.'

[6] Article 2(1)(a) of Directive 2006/54/EC of the European Parliament and of the Council of 5 July 2006 on the implementation of the principle of equal opportunities and equal treatment of men and women in matters of employment and occupation,[26] provides: 'For the purposes of this Directive, the following definitions shall apply: (a) "direct discrimination": where one person is treated less favourably on grounds of sex than another is, has been or would be treated in a comparable situation.'

United Kingdom law

[7] In accordance with section 44 of the Social Security Contributions and Benefits Act 1992, read in conjunction with section 122 of that Act and with Schedule 4, paragraph 1, of the Pensions Act 1995, a woman born before 6 April 1950 becomes eligible for the State retirement pension (referred to in the legislation as a 'Category A retirement pension') at the age of 60, and a man born before 6 December 1953 becomes eligible at the age of 65.

[8] Section 1 of the Gender Recognition Act 2004 ('the GRA') provided, in its version applicable to the dispute in the main proceedings, that a person who was aged at least 18 should apply to a Gender Recognition Panel ('GRP') for a full gender recognition certificate recording a change of his or her gender on the basis of living as a person of the other gender.
     According to that provision, the new gender of the person requesting such a certificate was to be referred to as 'the acquired gender.'

[9] Section 2(1) of that Act provided that the GRP was required to grant a gender recognition certificate where the applicant:'(a) has or has had gender dysphoria, (b) has lived in the acquired gender throughout the period of two years ending with the date on which the application is made, (c) intends to continue to live in the acquired gender until death, and (d) complies with the requirements imposed by and under section 3 [of the GRA].'

[10] In order to obtain that certificate, according to section 3 of that Act, entitled 'Evidence,' the applicant was required to provide a report from two medical practitioners or from a medical practitioner and a psychologist.

[11] Subsection (2) of section 4 of the GRA, entitled 'Successful applications,' provided that an unmarried applicant was entitled to a full gender recognition certificate,

---

26. OJ 2006 L 204, p. 23.

whereas, pursuant to section 4(3), a married applicant was entitled only to an interim gender recognition certificate.

[12] Section 9(1) of that Act provided that, where a full gender recognition certificate was issued, the acquired gender thereafter became the person's gender for all purposes.

According to Schedule 5, paragraph 7, of the GRA 2004, which dealt specifically with the effect of a full gender recognition certificate on eligibility for State retirement pensions, once the certificate had been issued, any question of entitlement to a State retirement pension was to be decided as if the person's gender had always been the acquired gender.

[13] An interim gender recognition certificate allowed a married applicant to apply to have their marriage annulled by a court. According to section 5(1) of the GRA, the court granting the decree of nullity was then required to issue a full gender recognition certificate.

[14] Section 11(c) of the Matrimonial Causes Act 1973, in its version applicable during the period at issue in the main proceedings, provided that a valid marriage could legally exist only between a male and a female.

[15] The Marriage (Same Sex Couples) Act 2013, which came into force on 10 December 2014, allows persons of the same sex to marry. Schedule 5 of that Act amended section 4 of the GRA so as to provide that a GRP must issue a full gender recognition certificate to a married applicant if the applicant's spouse consents. However, The Marriage (Same Sex Couples) Act 2013 is not applicable to the dispute in the main proceedings.

The dispute in the main proceedings and the question referred for a preliminary ruling

[16] MB was born a male in 1948 and married in 1974. She began to live as a woman in 1991 and underwent gender affirmation surgery in 1995.

[17] MB does not, however, hold a full certificate of recognition of her change of gender, since, pursuant to the national legislation at issue in the main proceedings, in order for that certificate to be granted her marriage had to be annulled. She and her wife wish to remain married for religious reasons.

[18] In 2008 MB, having reached the age of 60 — that is to say, the age at which women born before 6 April 1950 may, under national law, receive a 'Category A' retirement pension from the State — applied for such a pension as from that age by virtue of the contributions paid into the State pension scheme while she was working.

[19] Her application was rejected by a decision of 2 September 2008 on the ground that, in the absence of a full gender recognition certificate, MB could not be treated as a woman for the purposes of determining her statutory pensionable age.

[20] The action brought by MB against that decision was dismissed by the First-tier Tribunal, the Upper Tribunal and the Court of Appeal.

[21] MB brought an appeal before the Supreme Court of the United Kingdom, claiming that the national legislation at issue in the main proceedings is discriminatory on grounds of sex, which is prohibited by Article 4(1) of Directive 79/7. When one refers to discrimination because of sex, we refer to discrimination based also on everything that derives from the sex assumed at birth, namely discrimination because of transgender status, gender identity and gender expression.

[22] According to the information provided in the order for reference, MB fulfils the social and psychological criteria that determine the acquired gender in a framework of self-determination. On the other hand, the national legislation on civil status at issue in the main proceedings for the purposes of a legal recognition of a change of gender requires the existence of gender dysphoria as well, and the annulment of marriage with a same gender partner. One sees here that the UK GRA 2004 concerns only individuals that are pathologized, although gender dysphoria does not necessarily correlate with gender incongruence. This though is important to take into consideration, since depathologization has been a long-standing demand of the transgender community. Moreover, transgender identity does not always manifest itself through specific external presentations that are stereotlong-standingibuted to one gender or the other, i.e. there can be masculine transgender women and feminine transgender men, trans women and men that 'pass' and others who do not. Finally, there are non-binary transgender individuals who do not conform to the psychological profile of experiencing themselves from an early age as identifying with the opposite gender. In this context, the GRA 2004 seems parochial and is not based on the dignity of the applicant, as it does not acknowledge the self determination of applicants and the psychosocial character of the transition to their true gender.

The referring court points out, however, that, at the time of the facts giving rise to the dispute in the main proceedings, the national legislation made such recognition, as well as the issuing of the certificate referred to in paragraph 17 above, conditional on the annulment of any marriage entered into before such a change took place. According to the referring court, such annulment was also required in order for a person who had changed gender, such as MB, to access the State retirement pension as from the statutory pensionable age of persons of the gender acquired by that person. This is discriminatory to married transgender persons before the Marriage Act 2013 took place, and the latter should have protected the former within it.

[23] Before the referring court, the Secretary of State for Work and Pensions submitted that, according to the Court's case-law resulting from the judgments of 7 January 2004, K. B.[27] and of 27 April 2006, Richards,[28] it is for the Member States to determine

---

27. C-117/01 [2004] EU:C:2004:7, para. 35.
28. C-423/04 [2006] EU:C:2006:256, para. 21.

the conditions under which a person's change of gender may be legally recognised. The Court's opinion is that nevertheless, when these conditions come within the scope of EU law, then EU law takes primacy and they may be considered discriminatory and not aligning with the interpretation of the right on non-discrimination (Article 21) and the right to dignity (Article 1) under the EU Charter of Fundamental Rights (CFR). Marriage annulment and gender dysphoria are medicalized and discriminatory prerequisites for gender recognition.[29] They prescribe the exclusion not only of homosexual transgender people but also erase non-binary and genderqueer identities and kinship. Marriage annulment and medical restrictions on legal gender recognition for non-cis and non-straight couples equals discrimination because of sex since it presupposes gender congruence/conformity as the legal default and favours cis straight couples and individuals over queer and transgender people.

Although, when it comes to marriage and family formation, Article 9 of the CFR differs from Article 12 of the ECHR, Article 9 is based on Article 12 of the ECHR. The language of Article 9 of the CFR has been updated and states that '[t]he right to marry and the right to establish a family shall be guaranteed in accordance with national laws governing the exercise of these rights.' This must be the legal framework that takes primacy when matters of the Member States enter the scope of EU law.[30] In this respect, affording marriage only to straight couples is direct discrimination according to sex in EU primary law, and cannot be accepted when it impacts on areas of competence of the EU. In comparison, Article 12 of the ECHR states that '[m]en and women of marriageable age have the right to marry.' This is especially significant in light of the fact that case law interpreting Articles 8 and 12 of the ECHR has created confusion, as evidenced by the number of cases brought to clarify, for example, who may legally marry, most notably transsexuals.[31] Thus, Article 9 of the CFR is comparable to the ECHR's Article 12, but its scope may be expanded if national legislation so provides. Moreover, given the prohibition of discrimination on the basis of sex that Article 21 CFR provides, it becomes clear that for all matters within the scope of EU law the differential treatment of people according to what is expected on the basis of their sex/gender, namely the configuration of sex characteristics/gender/gender identity and expression, is illegitimate. Indeed, the European Court of Human Rights (ECtHR) stated in 2002 in *Goodwin*: 'The Court would also note that Article 9 of the recently adopted Charter of Fundamental Rights of the European Union departs, no doubt intentionally, from the wording of Article 12 of the Convention by removing the reference to men and women.'[32] In 2018, the Court ruled that Member States must protect and recognize the rights of same-sex married couples, particularly in terms of free movement and citizenship, even if the State in question does not recognize same-sex unions legally.[33]

29. Alex Sharpe, 'A Critique of the Gender Recognition Act 2004,' *Bioethical Inquiry* 4 (2007), 33–42.

30. Steve Peers 'Taking rights away? Limitations and derogations,' in *The EU Charter of Fundamental Rights*, ed. Steve Peers and Angela Ward (Oxford: Hart Publishing, 2004), 141–157.

31. *Rees v UK*, App no 9532/81 (ECHR, 17 October 1986); *Cossey v UK*, App no 10843/84 (ECHR, 27 September); *Sheffield and Horsham v UK*, App no 23390/94 (ECHR, 30 July 1998); *Goodwin v UK*, App no 28957/95 (ECHR, 11 July 2002); *Karner v Austria*, App no 40016/98 (ECHR, 11 September 2001).

32. *Goodwin v UK*, App no 28957/95 (ECHR, 11 July 2002).

33. *Coman and Others v General Inspectorate for Immigration and Ministry of the Interior*, Case C-673/16

[24] In that context, the Secretary of State for Work and Pensions noted that the European Court of Human Rights has recognised that Member States may make recognition of a change of gender conditional on the annulment of that person's marriage.[34] It submitted that, although the ECHR requires States Parties to recognise the acquired gender of transsexual persons[35]it does not require them to allow marriages between same-sex couples. Indeed, the objective of maintaining the traditional concept of marriage as being a union between a man and a woman could, it was argued, justify making recognition of a change of gender subject to such a condition.

[25] In those circumstances, the Supreme Court of the United Kingdom decided to stay the proceedings and to refer the following question to the Court of Justice for a preliminary ruling:

'Does Council Directive 79/7/EEC preclude the imposition in national law of a requirement that, in addition to satisfying the physical, social and psychological criteria for recognizing a change of gender, a person who has changed gender must also be unmarried in order to qualify for a State retirement pension?'

Consideration of the question referred

[26] By its question, the referring court asks, in essence, whether Directive 79/7, in particular the first indent of Article 4(1), read in conjunction with the third indent of Article 3(1)(a) and Article 7(1)(a) thereof, must be interpreted as precluding national legislation that requires a person who has changed gender not only to fulfil physical, social and psychological criteria but also to satisfy the condition of not being married to a person of the gender that they have acquired as a result of that change, in order to be able to claim a State retirement pension as from the statutory pensionable age applicable to persons of that acquired gender.

[27] As a preliminary point, it must be noted that the case in the main proceedings and the question referred to the Court concern only the conditions for entitlement to the State retirement pension at issue in the main proceedings. Accordingly, the Court is not being asked to consider, generally, whether the legal recognition of a change of gender may be conditional on the annulment of a marriage entered into before that change of gender.

[28] The United Kingdom Government claims that marriage and the legal recognition of change of gender are matters which fall within the competence of the Member States with regard to civil status. In its view, in exercizing that competence, Member States not permitting marriage between persons of the same sex may, therefore, make

---

[2018] ECLI:EU:C:2018:385; see, also, Steve Peers, 'Taking rights away?'

34. *Hämäläinen v Finland*, App no 37359/09 (ECHR,16 July 2014).

35. As opposed here to 'transgender persons'—a language not used by the Court—a term that may include all aspects of transgender phenomena and not just binary trans binary medically transitioned manifestations.

the payment of a State retirement pension dependent on the annulment of an earlier marriage between such persons.

[29] In that regard, it must be noted that, although EU law does not detract from the competence of the Member States in matters of civil status and legal recognition of the change of a person's gender, Member States must, when exercizing that competence, comply with EU law and, in particular, with the provisions relating to the principle of non-discrimination.[36]

[30] Thus, it is clear, inter alia, from the Court's case-law that national legislation making eligibility for a pension benefit subject to a condition relating to civil status cannot be placed outside the scope of the principle of non-discrimination on grounds of sex set out in Article 157 of the Treaty on the Functioning of the EU (TFEU) in the area of workers' remuneration.[37]

[31] It follows that Article 4(1) of Directive 79/7, which implements the principle of non-discrimination on grounds of sex as regards social security, must be complied with by the Member States when they exercise their powers in the area of civil status.

[32] The first indent of Article 4(1), read in conjunction with the third indent of Article 3(1)(a) of that directive, prohibits all discrimination on grounds of sex as regards, inter alia, the conditions for access to statutory schemes ensuring protection against the risks of old age. Here the Court understands as sex the self-determined gendered experience by which the applicant presents themselves in society and must be acknowledged by the State if the person so wishes. Discrimination because of sex can have to do with discrimination based on what is expected and assumed based on the sex assigned at birth and the sex characteristics of the applicant. The two statements above in conjunction indicate that discrimination based on the hindrance of the applicant to identify psychosocially as the gender that they wish is illegitimate in EU law.

[33] It is not disputed by the parties to the main proceedings that the State retirement pension scheme at issue is such a statutory scheme.

[34] As is clear from Article 2(1)(a) of Directive 2006/54, there is direct discrimination based on sex if one person is treated less favourably on grounds of sex than another person is, has been or would be treated in a comparable situation. That concept must be understood in the same way in the context of Directive 79/7.

[35] In accordance with the Court's settled case-law, the scope of the latter directive, in view of its purpose and the nature of the rights which it seeks to safeguard, is also such

---

36. See, to that effect, inter alia, judgments of 27 April 2006, *Richards*, C-423/04, EU:C:2006:256, paras. 21 to 24; of 1 April 2008, *Maruko*, C-267/06, EU:C:2008:179, para. 59; and of 5 June 2018, *Coman and Others*, C-673/16, EU:C:2018:385, paras. 37 and 38 and the case law cited therein.

37. See, to that effect, judgment of 7 January 2004, *K.B.*, C-117/01, EU:C:2004:7, paras. 34 to 36.

as to apply to discrimination arising from gender affirming procedures and transition.[38] By that the Court means that differential treatment between a person that has legally changed gender and a transgender person that has not legally been able or willing to change gender is unlawful, especially when the prerequisites for changing gender are in breach of EU law and have an impact within its scope as with GRA 2004 in the matter of MB. For the Court, although, as it was noted in paragraph 29 of the present judgment, it is for the Member States to establish the conditions for legal recognition of a person's change of gender, the fact remains that, for the purposes of the application of Directive 79/7, it is unlawful treatment to expect transgender people to obtain legal recognition of their gender by annulling their marriage, or undergo a gender affirming operation due to gender dysphoria or acknowledging their experience only if they present as the opposite sex. This medicalizes trans experience and excludes transgender, gender nonconforming people and nonbinary people, who are also discriminated on the basis of the cultural signifiers of sex.

[36] In the present case, the national legislation at issue in the main proceedings makes access by persons who have changed gender to a State retirement pension as from the statutory pensionable age for persons of the acquired gender subject to, inter alia, the annulment of any marriage into which they may have entered before that change. By contrast, according to the information in the file before the Court, that marriage annulment condition does not apply to persons who have retained their birth gender and are married, who accordingly may receive a State retirement pension as from the statutory pensionable age for persons of that gender irrespective of their marital status. Instead of comparing cis heterosexual status with trans homosexual status, the Court finds that it is better to compare people with trans status that have legally changed gender with people with trans status that have not legally transitioned for the purposes of national law regardless of sexual orientation. This comparison renders visible the shortcomings both in legal gender recognition that is not inclusive and the sex discrimination in family formation.

[37] The Court considers that cis and trans people of any gender must be treated equally, whether they have acquired a legal gender certificate or just identify as trans gender. In this respect, the Court holds that it is discriminatory treatment to treat less favourably trans people who have officially acquired a new gender than trans and gender nonconforming people whose existence is erased by civil status or is acknowledged in parochial and discriminatory or degrading terms (they are not recognized as the gender they identify by law and the law treats them according to the gender assigned to them at birth). In this way, the Court compares 'legal gender' to 'gender identity,' in order to expand the scope of the concept of sex/gender in its effort to combat structural discrimination both towards binary transgender persons, and other (a)gendered experiences.

---

38. See, to that effect, judgment of 27 April 2006, *Richards*, C-423/04, EU:C:2006:256, paras. 23 and 24 and the case-law cited therein.

[38] Such less favourable treatment is based on sex and may constitute direct discrimination within the meaning of Article 4(1) of Directive 79/7.

[39] It is further necessary to establish whether the situation of a person who changed gender after marrying and the situation of a person who has retained their birth gender and is married are comparable. In this attempt, the Court equates all geometries of sex/gender and also affirms them, namely configurations of sex characteristics/gender identity/expression whether they are legally certified or not. The Court stands with an expansive view on gender

[40] The United Kingdom Government takes the view that those situations are not comparable on the ground that the marital statuses of the persons in question are different. A person who has changed gender after marrying finds themself married to a person of the gender that they have acquired, in contrast to a person who has retained their birth gender and is married to a person of the opposite sex. According to the United Kingdom Government, having regard to the purpose of the marriage annulment condition at issue in the main proceedings — which is to avoid the existence of marriages between persons of the same sex — such a difference means that the situations of those persons are not comparable.

[41] In that regard, it must be noted that the requirement relating to the comparability of situations does not require those situations to be identical, but only similar.[39]

[42] The comparability of situations must be assessed not in a global and abstract manner, but in a specific and concrete manner having regard to all the elements which characterise them, in the light, in particular, of the subject matter and purpose of the national legislation which makes the distinction at issue, as well as, where appropriate, in the light of the principles and objectives pertaining to the field to which that national legislation relates.[40]

[43] In the present case, it is clear from the information provided in the order for reference that the subject matter of the national legislation at issue in the main proceedings is the granting of a 'Category A' State retirement pension which can be claimed by persons who have reached the statutory pensionable age. The parties to the main proceedings clarified, during the hearing before the Court, that national law grants such a retirement pension to all persons who have reached that age and who have made adequate contributions to the United Kingdom's State pension scheme. Accordingly, it appears that the State statutory retirement pension scheme at issue in the main proceedings protects against the risks of old age by conferring on the person concerned

---

39. See, to that effect, judgments of 10 May 2011, *Römer*, C-147/08, EU:C:2011:286, para. 42, and of 19 July 2017, *Abercrombie & Fitch Italia*, C-143/16, EU:C:2017:566, para. 25 and the case law cited therein.
40. See, to that effect, judgments of 16 December 2008, *Arcelor Atlantique et Lorraine and Others*, C-127/07, EU:C:2008:728, paras. 25 and 26; of 16 July 2015, *CHEZ Razpredelenie Bulgaria*, C-83/14, EU:C:2015:480, paras. 89 and 90; and of 9 March 2017, *Milkova*, C-406/15, EU:C:2017:198, paras. 56 and 57 and the case-law cited therein.

the right to a retirement pension acquired in relation to the contributions paid by that person during his or her working life, irrespective of marital status.

[44] Thus, in the light of the subject matter of the retirement pension and the conditions under which it is granted, as set out in the previous paragraph, the situation of a person who changed gender after marrying and that of a person who has kept his or her birth gender and is married are comparable. This second comparison is between a trans and a cis married person.

[45] As the Advocate General observed in point 43 of his Opinion, the United Kingdom Government's argument, which emphasises the difference in the marital status of those persons, has the effect of making that difference the decisive element in determining the comparability of the situations at issue, whereas marital status, in itself, is not relevant for the purposes of the granting of the State retirement pension at issue in the main proceedings, as has been noted in paragraph 43 above.

[46] Moreover, the purpose of the marriage annulment condition invoked by that Government —namely, to avoid marriage between persons of the same sex — is unrelated to that retirement pension scheme and discriminatory. As a result, that purpose does not affect the comparability of the situation of a person who changed gender after marrying and that of a person who kept their birth gender and is married, in the light of the subject matter and the conditions under which that retirement pension is granted, as set out in paragraph 43 of this judgment.

[47] That interpretation does not follow the case-law of the European Court of Human Rights, to which the United Kingdom Government also refers in order to contest the comparability of the situation of those persons. As the Advocate General stated in point 44 of his Opinion, the European Court of Human Rights, in its judgment in *Hämäläinen v Finland*,[41] assessed whether or not the situation of a person who had undergone gender affirmation surgery after marrying was comparable to the situation of a married person who had not changed gender, in the light of the subject matter of the national legislation at issue, which concerned the legal recognition of a change of gender with regard to civil status. This Court does not view physical transition as necessary and just compares cis hetero and trans homosexual married persons for the purposes pension under UK law. This Court then sees a double discrimination, one against same sex family formation and one against trans status. The Court considers that cishomonormative discrimination based on sex whose impact enters the scope of EU law is unlawful, as EU law takes primacy within areas of competence of the EU.

[48] Therefore, it must be held that the national legislation at issue in the main proceedings accords less favourable treatment, directly based on sex, to a person who changed gender after marrying, than that accorded to a person who has kept their birth gender and is married, even though those persons are in comparable situations.

---

41. *Hämäläinen v Finland*, App no 37359/09 (ECHR, 16 July 2014), paras. 111 and 112.

[49] The United Kingdom Government submits, nevertheless, that the purpose of avoiding the existence of a marriage between persons of the same sex could justify the application only to persons who have changed gender of a requirement to annul any marriage previously entered into by such a person when national law did not, at the time of the facts giving rise to the main proceedings, allow marriage between persons of the same sex.

[50] However, according to the case-law of the Court, a derogation from the prohibition, set out in Article 4(1) of Directive 79/7, of all direct discrimination on grounds of sex is possible only in the situations exhaustively set out in the provisions of that directive.[42] As it is, the objective invoked by the United Kingdom Government does not correspond to any of the derogations allowed by that directive.

[51] With more specific regard to the derogation provided for in Article 7(1)(a) of Directive 79/7, the Court has already held that it does not allow Member States to treat differently persons who have changed gender after marrying and persons who have kept their birth gender and are married, with regard to the age of entitlement to a State retirement pension.[43]

[52] Consequently, the national legislation at issue in the main proceedings constitutes direct discrimination on grounds of sex and is, therefore, prohibited by Directive 79/7.

ON THOSE GROUNDS, THE COURT (GRAND CHAMBER) HEREBY RULES:

Council Directive 79/7/EEC of 19 December 1978 on the progressive implementation of the principle of equal treatment for men and women [and other genders] in matters of social security, in particular the first indent of Article 4(1), read in conjunction with the third indent of Article 3(1)(a) and Article 7(1)(a) thereof, must be interpreted as precluding national legislation which requires a person who has changed gender to fulfil particular physical, social and psychological criteria besides self-determination in order to change their legal gender. In addition, within the scope of EU law, persons of any gender have equal legal status and cannot be discriminated against because of trans or gender nonconforming status in order to be able to claim a State retirement pension as from the statutory pensionable age applicable to persons of their acquired gender.

[Signatures]

---

42. See, to that effect, judgments of 21 July 2005, *Vergani*, C-207/04, EU:C:2005:495, paras. 34 and 35, and of 3 September 2014, X, C-318/13, EU:C:2014:2133, paras. 34 and 35.
43. See, to that effect, judgment of 27 April 2006, *Richards*, C-423/04, EU:C:2006:256, paras. 37 and 38.

14

Elan-Cane (United Kingdom)

Carolynn Gray

Introduction

Ten years ago, very few people in the UK were talking about non-binary gender iden-tity, never mind challenging for legal recognition in the courts. However, non-binary identities are not new and have existed for as long as humanity. The question to be asked is why has it taken so long for legal recognition of non-binary gender identity to come to the fore? The *Elan-Cane* case which culminated in the UK Supreme Court in 2021,[1] combined with the decisions of both the UK and Scottish Governments to no longer pursue reform of the Gender Recognition Act 2004 to include a legal right to non-binary identity,[2] seems to have closed off the possibility of such legal recognition in the United Kingdom for the time being. The alternate dissenting judgment was written to show how, at the time of the Supreme Court judgment, it would have been possible for the Court to have taken a different approach and to have reached a different outcome without fundamentally changing any of the existing laws at the time.

Overview of the case

The dissenting judgment provides an overview of the facts of the case, the arguments presented, and the judgments of the Administrative Court,[3] the Court of Appeal,[4] and then the Supreme Court.[5] For the purpose of brevity they will not be repeated here in detail. *Elan-Cane* was a very straightforward case of limited legal importance, but paradoxically also an incredibly important case with all possibility of setting in motion a complete change of direction in relation to the rights of non-binary individuals.

---

1. [2021] UKSC 56; [2023] A.C. 559.
2. The UK government held a consultation on reform of the GRA 2004 from 3 July 2018 until 22 October 2018 and the Scottish government held a consultation on reform of the GRA 2004 from 9 November 2017 to 1 March 2018 and again from 17 December 2019 until 17 March 2020, following which decisions were made not to progress non-binary legal recognition.
3. [2018] EWHC 1530 (Admin).
4. [2020] EWCA Civ 363.
5. [2021] UKSC 56.

The case was about whether someone could have X as their gender marker on their passport; the simple answer is yes. Part 4 of the International Civil Aviation Organization's (ICAO) Document 9303, *Machine Readable Travel Documents*, to which the United Kingdom is bound, provides that the sex of the passport holder must be recorded on the passport 'by use of the single initial commonly used in the language of the State or organization where the document is issued.'[6] Where translation into English, Frensh or Spanish is required, the recorded sex must be followed by an oblique and one of the following capital letters: M (male), F (female), or X (unspecified). These three commonly used letters are to be recognised by all contracting States, but it is for individual States to determine how sex will be denoted on passports issued. So, X is a recognised sex marker on passports and the UK is bound to recognise passports from other countries using X as a sex marker, but the UK is not bound to issue passports which use X as a sex marker. There was nothing particularly complex about the *Elan-Cane* case from this perspective; should the UK choose to use X as a sex marker on passports, this would be permissible.

The complexity of *Elan-Cane* came when considering the politics of the case and the approach that the Justices deemed appropriate to take in relation to the role of courts and legislature. Changing UK passports to allow for X gender markers would not have necessarily changed the law for non-binary people; a passport is not a birth certificate and, in the UK, legal rights and recognition flow from birth certificates (or gender recognition certificates) but not from passports, driving licences or any other form of officially issued ID. The UK Supreme Court would therefore have been allowed to agree with Christie Elan-Cane that not only was Article 8 (right to private and family life) of the European Convention on Human Rights (ECHR) engaged, but that the refusal of the United Kingdom Passport Office (UKPO) to issue such passports was an infringement upon that right taken in conjunction with Article 14 (the right to not be discriminated against).

The original judgment was interesting because it evidenced how the Court shapes law through interpretative mechanisms and through selective application of legal rules. In the case, Majewski argues, 'the Supreme Court revised its previous approach to the margin of appreciation doctrine of the European Court of Human Rights.'[7] Majewski describes the Supreme Court's approach in the case as 'flat' rather than 'multi-level,'[8] and argues that it was entirely permissible for the Supreme Court to have adopted the multi-level approach which could have enabled a different outcome to have been reached. The decision of the Supreme Court in *Elan-Cane* was unanimous in denying the appeal. The Supreme Court adhered strongly to the idea that national law should not overtake developments within the European Court of Human Rights (ECtHR) when it comes to the interpretation of Convention rights and their applicability in contracting States.

The alternate judgment that accompanies this commentary takes a multi-level approach to understanding the Convention rights,[9] which means that while the ECtHR

---

6. International Civil Aviation Organization, *Machine Readable Travel Documents*, Doc 9303, 13.
7. Kaeper Majewski, 'Mirroring the Margin,' *Public Law* Oct (2022), 553.
8. Majewski, 'Mirroring the Margin,' 553.
9. Majewski, 'Mirroring the Margin,' 555.

may interpret a Convention right in a particular way, that does not mean that the domestic courts cannot interpret it differently in accordance with domestic law. In so doing, the alternate judgment applies that approach to reach the conclusion that not allowing Christie Elan-Cane to have an X on their passport amounts to a breach of their Articles 8 and 14 rights. A dissenting opinion was written because the UK Supreme Court, at this time of fluctuating politics, is taking a conservative approach to decision making and therefore a majority decision which found a breach of Elan-Cane's rights would never have been reached by this bench; a different bench may well have found differently.

Part of the problem for the Supreme Court was that there was no jurisprudence from the ECtHR—based in Strasbourg—directly on point, so the Supreme Court had to determine the amount of scope available in reaching the decision. Since the *Elan-Cane* judgment was handed down, in January 2023 the ECtHR decided, in the case of *Y v France* (no. 76888/17), that in failing to allow the applicant, an intersex person, to be registered as neutral or intersex on their birth certificate rather than male, France had not violated the applicant's Article 8 ECHR rights.

In *Elan-Cane*, the claimant, Christie Elan-Cane, argued that had there been Strasbourg jurisprudence on point, or even if it could be reasonably expected that the ECtHR, if determining such a case, would hold that the issue fell within the UK's margin of appreciation, it was 'open to the Supreme Court to "fill in" that margin and answer the question in the affirmative.'[10] Elan-Cane also argued that the approach taken by the UKPO breached their rights under Articles 8 and 14 ECHR. In dealing with this issue, the Supreme Court denied such competence. However, the situation is not as clear cut as it would seem from reading the original judgment and, although the case is ostensibly about the right of a non-binary person to use the X gender marker on their passport, a right which is in accordance with the Civil Aviation Authority (CAA) guidelines, it is also about the role of the UK's highest court in a time of political flux in which, it could be argued, we are witnessing a retreat of the UK from the global stage and a growing domestic backlash against LGBTQI+ rights in general. The Supreme Court's unanimous decision must be situated in this political context,[11] because, as the dissenting judgment below shows, it would have been possible to find in favour of the claimant without stretching the existing law and legal principles at all.

The issue for the Supreme Court in *Elan-Cane* was the extent to which the mirror principle, established in the case of *R (on the application of Ullah) v Special Adjudicator*,[12] applied. The mirror principle derives from the dicta of Lord Bingham in *Ullah* where he said, 'the duty of national courts is to keep pace with the Strasbourg jurisprudence as it evolves over time: no more, but certainly no less.'[13] The problem though is that there was no direct ECtHR jurisprudence to follow or from which

---

10. Majewski, 'Mirroring the Margin,' 553.
11. See Carolynn Gray, 'The evolution of LGBT Rights in the UK: is the Tide Starting to Turn?' in *Justice after Stonewall: LGBT Life between Challenge and Change*, ed. Paul Behrens and Sean Becker (London: Routledge, 2023).
12. *R (on the application of Ullah) v Special adjudicator* [2004] UKHL 26.
13. *R (on the application of Ullah) v Special adjudicator* at [20].

to depart, so the question became one of judicial creation and scope; if there was no ECtHR jurisprudence with which to keep pace, and Bingham was correct that it is not for the national courts to go beyond the Strasbourg court's interpretation of the rights embodied in the ECHR, then the judgment of the Supreme Court would have been correct. However, as the dissenting judgment shows, there is considerable debate about how national courts interpret Strasbourg jurisprudence and the application of the mirror principle.[14] The way in which the Court or individual Justices approach this interpretation reflects the extent to which there is desire to develop a particular area of national law, or indeed to not develop such an area of law. The dissenting opinion was written from an inclusive perspective: from a perspective which takes respect for non-binary identity as a basic human right, and from the perspective that law is not a fixed entity but rather ought to reflect contemporary society as far as possible. As such, it fits within the wider work being done to challenge the requirement to have sex as a legal classificatory concept, and within the calls for decertification of legal sex.[15]

Sex, Gender and Cisgenderism

The *Elan-Cane* judgment highlighted the systemic reliance on cisgenderism[16] and bigenderism[17] that is prevalent in the UK. The judgment also reflects the political move away from the furtherance of trans rights and, instead, towards a consolidation of the current position that UK citizens are sexed at birth for all legal purposes and the only possible change to that is where the person has a Gender Recognition Certificate (GRC) granted under the restrictive criteria set out in the Gender Recognition Act 2004. The Supreme Court's judgment in *Elan-Cane* did nothing to develop an understanding of non-binary identity in the UK and further entrenched the idea that being trans, in UK law, is a binary identity; one is either male or female (sex), identifies as such (gender), and is therefore legally defined as such with corresponding rights afforded.

The position being taken in UK law seems progressive in that trans people are provided with legal recognition, but this is dependent on adhering to a binary trans identity regardless of whether one has physically transitioned. Currently, in the UK, individuals can obtain a GRC without undertaking any physical transition: a purely legal transition.[18] However, the only option is to be legally recognised as the sex opposite to the one registered at birth. Sex, then, in UK law is both a legal and physical

---

14. Nuno Ferreira, 'The Supreme Court in a Final Push to go Beyond Strasbourg,' *Public Law* Jul (2015), 367–375.

15. For more on this, see: accessed on 19 January 2024, https://futureoflegalgender.kcl.ac.uk/, and the special issue of Feminist Legal Studies, ed. Davina Cooper et al, 31/1, 1–169.

16. Lucy Nicholas, 'Queer Ethics and Fostering Positive Mindsets Towards Non-Binary Gender, Genderqueer, and Gender Ambiguity,' *International Journal of Transgenderism* 20/2–3 (2019), 170.

17. Miqqi Alicia Gilbert, 'Defeating Bigenderism: Changing Gender Assumptions in the Twenty-first Century,' *Hypatia* 24/3 (2009), 93–112.

18. See also Carolynn Gray, 'A Critique of the Legal Recognition of Transsexuals in UK Law,' PhD Thesis, Glasgow University, 2015; Sharon Cowan, '"Gender is No Substitute for Sex": a Comparative Human Rights Analysis of the Legal Regulation of Sexual Identity,' *Feminist Legal Studies* 13 (2005), 74; Sharon Cowan, 'Looking Back (to)wards the Body: Medicalization and the GRA,' *Social and Legal Studies* 18/2 (2009), 247.

concept and individuals can, in theory within the law, be physically one sex and legally the other; but they cannot be legally neither sex, nor neutral, e.g. X.

The *Elan-Cane* case raised the question of gender, both as a legal concept and as a theoretical concept which needs to be explored. The calls to reform the GRA to include non-binary people reflect the importance of gender identity rather than physical/legal sex.[19] Arguably the gender recognition laws in the UK are about gender identity already, because the GRA 2004 provides that no body modification procedures need to be completed (or even planned or desired) for the applicant to be able to be granted a GRC, thus recognizing that a person's gender identity as the primary criterion within the existing legislation. *Elan-Cane* was the opportunity for the Supreme Court to consider how the law interacts with those who have a non-binary identity which sits outwith the scope of current UK legal recognition.

The emergence of non-binary identity and historical context

It is important at this point to spend some time exploring terminology. 'Non-binary' is a recent umbrella term which has roots in the queer movement of the 1990s and onwards and is akin, but not identical, to the term 'genderqueer,' which, Monro claims, 'emerged in the 1990s.'[20] However, the concept of gender fluidity is not new and certainly not an invention of the twentieth century. Herdt provides an excellent overview of this history of what would now be called non-binary or genderqueer identity,[21] as does Vincent.[22] Contemporaneously, though, non-binary or genderqueer identity can be defined as 'any type of trans identity that is not always male or female. It is [also] where people feel they are a mixture of male and female,'[23] and the current social recognition of such identities in recent years has enabled them to be described as emergent identities,[24] in that they have 'emerged against the binary gendered expectations that have dominated society in recent history.'[25] The non-binary identities have had to emerge in response to another system of thinking about sex and gender—cisgenderism—which is 'the assumption that assigned sex determines gender [and] [t]he assumption that there are only two genders.'[26]

As noted in the previous section, *Elan-Cane* highlights that cisgenderism is the default position in UK law and, therefore, trans people remain outwith this norm,

19. Gray, 'A Critique of the Legal Recognition of Transsexuals in UK Law'; Hannah Newman and Elizabeth Peel, '"An impossible dream"? Non-Binary People's Perceptions of Legal Gender Status and Reform in the UK,' *Psychology & Sexuality* 13/5 (2022), 1381–1395.
20. Surya Monro 'Non-Binary and Genderqueer: An Overview of the Field,' *International Journal of Transgenderism* 20/2–3 (2019), 126.
21. Gilbert Herdt, *Third Sex Third Gender: Beyond Sexual Dimorphism in Culture and History* (New York: Zone Books, 1996).
22. Ben Vincent, *Non-Binary Genders: Navigating Communities, Identities, and Healthcare* (Bristol: Policy Press, 2020).
23. Monro, 'Non-Binary and Genderqueer,' 126.
24. Rob Cover, *Emergent Identities: New Sexualities, Genders and Relationships in a Digital Era* (London: Routledge, 2019).
25. Newman and Peel, '"An Impossible Dream"?'
26. Newman and Peel, '"An Impossible Dream"?' 2.

rather than consider the possibility that gender itself is a construct, a spectrum along which everyone experiences their sense of self which is inherently fluid. The latter understanding of gender would frame non-binary gender as the norm and recognition of such as a fundamental human right. Just as binary trans identity has, somewhat, been de-pathologised in recent iterations of the medical diagnostic criteria, it is important to also note that non-binary identity is not a pathological identity, in that it is not a medical or psychiatric disorder. Richards *et al* note that 'there are a significant number of people who do not have an (observable) intersex/DSD condition, but who nonetheless identify outside of the gender binary.'[27] The medical literature is clear that non-binary individuals are not disordered, even if 'little is known about the identity development of non-binary individuals.'[28] However, 'newer research on nonbinary identity development focuses less on linear paths and more on the confluence of societal expectations and embracing cognitive flexibility for endless possibilities for gender identities,'[29] thus reiterating that non-binary identity is simply a way of experiencing gender along a spectrum of possibilities.

The problem for non-binary people, though, is that the natural experiencing and expression of one's gender that sits outwith the cisgendered, and indeed binary, expectation is not recognised by the system; this systemic invisibility is reinforced by the legal system. Non-binary individuals, such as Christie Elan-Cane, who have the courage to challenge the law, engage in something much larger than an individual quest for recognition: they challenge and contest the very naturalness of the binary gender/sex systems upon which contemporary society is based.[30] Such individuals are required to constantly decide, when interacting with systems such as the law, how to interact with a system which cannot see them. Many non-binary people interact with systems, including the legal system, by using their 'birth-assigned gender as a matter of necessity in day-to-day business and bureaucracy due to the fact that many systems [...] and social circles only recognize binary genders.'[31] This forces non-binary individuals to choose between visibility and authenticity in these interactions, which in itself is a form of both legal and psychic erasure.

As a result of this systemic invisibility and unintelligibility, 'non-binary people experience higher rates of discrimination due to the societal consequences of their rejection of the gender binary,'[32] but additionally many non-binary people 'experience macro and micro aggressions insinuating they are invisible, less legitimate, or need to justify their identity,'[33] even within the wider trans community.[34]

---

27. Christina Richards, Walter Bouman, Leighton Seal, Meg John Barker, Timo Nieder and Guy T'Sjoen, 'Non-binary or genderqueer genders,' *International Review of Psychiatry* 28/1 (2016), 95.

28. Emmie Matsuno and Stephanie Budge, 'Non/binary/Genderqueer Identities: a Critical Review of the Literature,' *Current Sexual Health Reports* 9 (2017), 118.

29. Matsuno and Budge, 'Non/binary/Genderqueer Identities,' 118.

30. Newman and Peel, '"An Impossible Dream"?'

31. Richards *et al*, 'Non-Binary or Genderqueer Genders,' 97.

32. Matsuno and Budge, 'Non/binary/Genderqueer Identities,' 119.

33. Matsuno and Budge, 'Non/binary/Genderqueer Identities,' 119.

34. Matsuno and Budge, 'Non/binary/Genderqueer Identities,' 119.

Elan-Cane in the context of current legal developments

The unintelligibility of non-binary people within the laws of the UK jurisdictions, although presented as absolute unintelligibility above, is somewhat mitigated in an employment context, and presumably in other areas where the legal issue is covered by the provisions of the Equality Act 2010, in particular its section 7, which prohibits discrimination on the grounds of 'gender reassignment' and has been interpreted to mean gender identity rather than whether or not one has physically transitioned. This slight divergence between different areas of law further highlights the political nature of the Supreme Court's *Elan-Cane* judgment. In 2016, I wrote that section 7 of the Equality Act 2010 was inadequate to protect non-binary people from discrimination, as it was unclear at the time whether this norm could be read as including non-binary people.[35] *Taylor v Jaguar Land Rover* has since clarified the legal position and held that non-binary people cannot be discriminated against in the context of employment.[36] Although of limited significance because it is a decision of the Employment Tribunal, this case has begun to clarify the position for non-binary people, albeit only in the context of discrimination in the field of employment.

Unfortunately, non-binary people have an additional hurdle to overcome in relation to the quest for legal recognition that was not faced by those seeking binary recognition of gender identity: the growing gender critical movement,[37] which has started to mobilise against the rights of not just trans individuals but which can be placed within the wider context of a societal push against the rights of the wider LGBTQI+ community.[38]

Conclusion

The *Elan-Cane* Supreme Court judgment was disappointing. The fictional dissenting judgment that I propose uses the same laws and same legal rules and knowledge that were available to the Supreme Court Justices at the time the case was decided and yet, as is shown, an alternate judgment could have been reached: a judgment in which the Supreme Court was willing to apply the reasoning of the ECtHR in the case of *Goodwin v United Kingdom* almost twenty years previous. Reaching this decision would not have fundamentally changed UK law; indeed, it would only have applied in the very limited context of UK passports. But it would have had a fundamental impact on the individual; it would have been one step towards Christie Elan-Cane and other non-binary individuals being intelligible within the UK administrative system and would have amounted to a reinforcement of their sense of self and of their ability to live authentically.

---

35. Carolynn Gray, 'The Genderqueer in UK Law: Why Current Laws are Insufficient,' in *Subjectivity, Citizenship and Belonging in Law: Identities and Intersections*, ed. Anne Griffiths, Sanna Mustasaari, and Anna Mäki-Petäjä-Leinonen (London: Routledge, 2016).

36. 1304471/2018.

37. For example, see *Forstater v CGD Europe* [2021] ICR 1; *Fair Play for Women Ltd v Registrar General for Scotland* [2022] CSOH 20; *For Women Scotland Ltd v Scottish Ministers* [2022] CSOH 90.

38. For more on this, see Carolynn Gray, 'The Evolution of LGBT Rights in the UK: Is the Tide Starting to Turn?' in *Justice after Stonewall: LGBT Life Between Challenge and Change*, ed. Paul Behrens and Sean Becker (London: Routledge, 2023).

R (ON THE APPLICATION OF ELAN-CANE)

v SECRETARY OF STATE FOR THE HOME DEPARTMENT

Dissenting Opinion

Lady Carolynn Gray

I have had the pleasure of reading the judgments of Lord Reed, Lord Lloyd-Jones, Lady Arden, Lord Sales, and Lady Rose. I accept their summary of the relevant facts, summarised below, although I differ from them in my conclusion.

The appeal is based on two fundamental questions:

i.   Is there an obligation on a contracting state under Article 8 of the European Convention for the Protection of Human Rights and Fundamental Freedoms (ECHR), either read alone or in conjunction with Article 14, to issue passports which do not specify the sex of the holder by means of using X gender marker rather than specifying the holder as male (M) or female (F)?

ii. If the above is answered in the negative, does the Human Rights Act 1998 impose such an obligation on the Home Secretary?

Contrary to my esteemed peers, I answer both questions in the affirmative.

Importance of Terminology

Lord Reed in his judgment provided a concise note on the use of terminology in his majority judgment and, while exceptionally useful, I take this opportunity to further comment on the importance of such terminology by this court in this case. The claimant self-identifies as non-gendered and, therefore, although legally registered as female, this judgment will refer to the claimant using the gender-neutral pronouns they and them. It is important that the court recognise and respect the identity of the claimant throughout, regardless of the decision being reached in relation to the obligations on the state to afford legal recognition of the claimant's gender identity.

Summary of the facts

The Claimant

For clarity, I seek to outline the relevant facts of this case once again in my judgment. The claimant, Christie Elan-Cane, was born with female sex characteristics and assigned female at birth although they identify as non-gendered. The claimant underwent medical procedures, some of which were funded privately and some funded by the NHS, to alter their body in ways which enabled them to live comfortably, having experienced dysphoria as a result of living as, and being perceived by others, as female. The claimant campaigns for legal recognition of non-gendered individuals. One of the key campaign areas for the claimant is around obtaining passports showing X gender marker; this is the focus of the present appeal.

The Policy

The instant appeal before this court is based on the policy of Her Majesty's Passport Office (HMPO) to only issue passports indicating a male (M) or female (F) sex. Should an applicant for a UK passport not declare a gender on their application, the gender stated on the supporting documents is used. It is therefore not possible under the HMPO policy to have a UK passport which does not state that one is male or female. It is possible for transgender people to have a passport issued which reflects their acquired gender, but it remains impossible to have a non-gendered passport. The issue of gender markers on UK passports was considered in a review by HMPO, concluded in 2014, the findings of which are set out in *Gender Marking in Passports—Internal Review of Existing Arrangements and Possible Future Options*, where it was reiterated that non-gendered passports would not be issued in the UK and that this was in line with wider UK legislative provisions which only recognise male and female as gender identities. The issue of non-binary legal recognition has been considered, and dismissed, by both the UK Government and devolved administrations, namely the Scottish Government, in recent reviews of gender recognition laws.

The Claimant's Argument

The claimant argued that the policy of HMPO to issue passports denoting male or female sex of the holder amounted to an interference with their right to respect for family life guaranteed by Article 8 of the ECHR; alternatively, that the policy was discriminatory to those who identified as non-gendered under Article 14 ECHR and that there was a positive obligation to recognise non-gendered identity for the purpose of UK passports.

Summary of judgments

Administrative Court

In 2018, in an application for judicial review of the HMPO policy, Justice Baker (Queen's Bench) dismissed the claim that HMPO's policy breached the applicant's right to private and family life under Article 8 ECHR, that it breached the applicant's rights under Article 14 ECHR, that it was irrational and that it had failed to take into account relevant considerations while taking into account irrelevant considerations ([2018] 1 W.L.R. 5119). Baker J held that although the right to private life under Article 8 ECHR was engaged and does indeed include a right to respect for one's gender identity, including a non-gendered identity, there was no positive obligation on the state to ensure that non-gendered identity was recognised. One of the factors enabling Baker J to reach this conclusion was the lack of European consensus regarding non-gendered identity in law and therefore the scope of the margin of appreciation to be afforded to the state. Additionally, Baker J relied on the argument that there were security-related justifications for not issuing passports using X gender markers and that there was a legitimate aim of 'maintaining an administratively coherent system of gender recognition across all government areas and legislation' [117]. As there were no plans to provide for recognition of non-gendered identity in other areas of law, it was legitimate for the Government to refuse to recognise non-gendered identity for the purpose of passports.

Court of Appeal

The decision of the Administrative Court was upheld by the Court of Appeal ([2020] QB 929). Although the Court of Appeal accepted that Article 8 ECHR included a right to non-gendered identity as a part of one's private life, there remained no positive obligation on the state to issue a passport to reflect this and HMPO's policy of not issuing non-gendered passports did not constitute an unlawful interference with the rights under Article 8. The Court of Appeal relied upon the lack of European consensus in relation to legal recognition of non-gendered identity in general and also upon the lack of consensus regarding the issuing of passports using X gender marker. However, the argument of the Secretary of State that there were security issues which prevented the issue of non-gendered passports was rejected by the Court of Appeal [73]. The issue of administrative coherence was upheld by the Court of Appeal, which held that the passport was not to be considered in isolation and the consequence of having non-gendered passports would inevitably lead to a wider legal challenge of binary gender within the law when it was clear that Government had rejected developing the law in this way. Therefore, the margin of appreciation afforded to the state was wide, the policy fell within this margin, and there was no breach of the claimant's Article 8 rights. The court acknowledged that there was a difference in treatment between binary gendered and non-gendered individuals under HMPO's policy, as binary gendered individuals could obtain a passport to recognise their gender identity whereas non-gendered individuals could not. However, it was held that the argument under Article 14 was essentially the same as that under Article 8 and this argument failed.

The relevant law

Article 8 has been broadly interpreted by the European Court of Human Rights (ECtHR) which has shown increased willingness to find in favour of citizens in areas relating to personal identity (*Brüggemann and Scheuten v Germany* (6959/75), *Goodwin v United Kingdom* (28957/95), *Hämäläinen v Finland* (37359/09)). Although, at this time, there is no case law relating to a right to respect for non-binary gender identity, arguably the ECtHR could be said to be heading in such a direction with the development of personal life under Article 8 embodying a right to the development of one's identity, including one's gender identity. The issue under consideration in this case is encompassed by the right to protection for identity and autonomy; this is an established area of protection under the Convention and, as such, the right to development of one's personality, including one's gender identity, is protected (*Brüggemann and Scheuten v Germany* (6959/75), *Goodwin v United Kingdom* (28957/95), *Hämäläinen v Finland* (37359/09)).

Perhaps the most important Strasbourg judgment relevant for this appeal was the judgment handed down in *Goodwin v United Kingdom* (28957/95); a judgment which is of crucial importance in this appeal as it held that the rights of the applicant under Article 8 ECHR had been illegally interfered with when UK law did not provide her with legal recognition of her gender. *Goodwin* indicated a shift in the balance between the rights of the individual, on the one hand, and the rights and interests of others and the state, on the other. *Goodwin* is a landmark decision and one to which we must give serious consideration in determining the outcome of this appeal, because *Goodwin* represented a different way of reasoning such cases. Applicable to this appeal is that, first, the ECtHR in *Goodwin* was willing to depart from previous case law in a fundamental manner: the court shifted the balance in such cases and gave much greater weight to the rights of individuals over the interests of the state. Second, the court also showed ability to depart from the concept of European consensus and, instead, considered international trends; more importantly, the court changed the way in which such applications were considered. Third, the court in *Goodwin* determined that the starting point was to consider the impact on the individual of the policy or law in question, rather than starting from the position of maintaining the state's interest in a coherent administrative system. This third shift in reasoning is crucial in this appeal.

Following the reasoning of the ECtHR in *Goodwin*, the starting question for this court, which has failed to be considered thus far in the current appeal, ought to be whether or not there is, or likely could be, 'concrete or substantial hardship or detriment to the public interest' which would 'flow from any change to the status of [the claimant]' (*Goodwin* (28957/95), [91]). Can it reasonably be said that there will be a concrete or substantial hardship or detriment to the public interest flowing from providing passports with X gender markers? I argue that such cannot be said to be the case. Therefore, rather than require the claimant to prove hardship or detriment, it is now 'incumbent upon the state to show an overwhelming interest in preserving the conflict [...] between law and social reality' for those in the position such as the claimant.[39] The right to personal autonomy, as protected under Article 8, necessitates such a change of focus, and I hold that the state has not shown that the continued policy of HMPO is necessary.

The concept of human dignity as a foundation of the ECHR has been stated throughout Article 8 case law, and *Goodwin* provided that personal autonomy was a fundamental aspect of human dignity, which necessitates a shift in focus from

---

39.   B. Rudolf, 'European Court of Human Rights: Legal Status of Postoperative Transsexuals,' *International Journal of Constitutional Law* 1/4 (2003), 721.

the needs of the state to the rights of the individual. Following *Goodwin*, the state's margin of appreciation in issues such as personal identity rights should be construed much more narrowly than it would otherwise be. Relevant to this instant appeal are two of the *Goodwin* considerations: (i) the lack of a European consensus, which meant that the ECtHR looked outward towards international approaches, and (ii) the relationship between individual rights and the state's administrative system. Prior to *Goodwin*, Strasbourg had repeatedly found against the right to recognition of gender identity, as there was deemed to be no positive obligation on contracting states to provide such recognition (*Rees* (A/106), [42]-[44]; *Cossey* (10843/84), [40]; *Sheffield and Horsham* (22985/93), [61]) and the state's margin of appreciation in relation to this was held to be wide (*Rees* (A/106), [37]; *Cossey* (10843/84), [40]; *Sheffield and Horsham* (22985/93), [58]) which enabled the court to determine that there had been no violation of Article 8 (*Rees* (A/106), [46]; *Cossey* (10843/84), [42]; *Sheffield and Horsham* (22985/93), [61]).

In contrast, in *Goodwin*, the ECtHR began by stating:

> [i]n determining whether or not a positive obligation exists, regard must also be had to the fair balance that has to be struck between the general interest of the community and the interests of the individual, the search for which balance is inherent in the whole of the Convention (*Goodwin* (28957/95), [72]).

The court continued that:

> since the Convention is first and foremost a system for the protection of human rights, the court must have regard to the changing conditions within the respondent state and within contracting states generally and respond [...] to any evolving convergence as to the standards to be achieved (*Goodwin* (28957/95), [74]).

Therefore, the ECtHR, and indeed national courts, can and should depart from previous decisions where to do so protects the rights in question and where there is evidence that changing social conditions would require to do so, because '[i]t is of crucial importance that the Convention is interpreted and applied in a manner which renders its rights practical and effective, not theoretical and illusory' (*Goodwin* (28957/95), [74]). By reiterating the purpose of the Convention as protecting human rights and reinforcing the idea that the Convention is a 'living instrument' which ought to be interpreted in a manner compatible with evolving social conditions and standards, the ECtHR in *Goodwin* has laid the foundations for this court to reconsider the rights of the claimant under Article 8 ECHR. The question for this court is not to what extent does the claimant's claim place a burden on the administrative systems of the state, but rather to what extent does the state's administrative system negatively impact on the applicant's development of identity and personal autonomy. The ECtHR acknowledged in *Goodwin* that 'serious interference with private life can arise where the state of domestic law conflicts with an important aspect of personal identity' (*Goodwin* (28957/95), [77]). Thus, the court was firmly placing the interests of the individual in developing their personal identity above the interests of the state in maintaining the *status quo*: a position of which this court ought to be mindful. In *Goodwin*, the court continued:

> [t]he stress and alienation arising from a discordance between the position in society assumed by a post-operative transsexual and the status imposed by law which refuses to recognise the change of gender cannot, in the court's view, be regarded as a minor inconvenience arising from a formality (*Goodwin* (28957/95), [77]).

In stating this, the interests of the individual were given primacy, as the court was swayed by the impact of interference with a fundamental aspect of oneself. In this regard, the ECtHR noted that, at the time of the *Goodwin* application, 'a conflict between social reality and law arises which places the transsexual in an anomalous position, in which he or she may experience feelings of vulnerability, humiliation and anxiety' (*Goodwin* (28957/95), [77]). Although the claimant is not transsexual (in that they do not seek to transition from female to male), the reasoning in *Goodwin* is just as applicable to the claimant's position. The social reality for the claimant is that they live as, and are perceived to be, gender neutral. The continued reminder on their passport that the state considers them to be female, places them in an anomalous position analogous to that of the applicant in *Goodwin*.

The Administrative Court and the Court of Appeal held that public interest outweighed the rights of the claimant, as did my esteemed colleagues in the majority decision. Public interest encompasses the need for a coherent administrative system and for ensuring security of the nation, although the latter was dismissed in the Court of Appeal and ought not to be a convincing argument in this appeal. The issue of a coherent administrative system was considered in *Goodwin*. In determining the importance of maintaining coherence against the rights of individuals, the ECtHR examined the previous decisions regarding the right to recognition of gender identity which had been decided in the 1980s and 1990s. In returning to these cases, the court was attempting to consider the public interest argument which had been put forward in those cases and observed that, in them, one fact which counted against those applicants was the 'the impact of any changes to the current birth register system' (*Goodwin* (28957/95), [80]). Moreover, in determining the scope of the margin of appreciation, the ECtHR considered the extent of consensus between states on issuing non-gendered passports. In this appeal, and in the judgments of the Administrative Court and the Court of Appeal, it was held that the overall lack of European consensus regarding issuing passports which use X gender markers meant that there is no requirement on HMPO to change their policy and issue such passports. However, we must be mindful of *Goodwin* once again, in which the ECtHR noted that although, as early as *Sheffield and Horsham v United Kingdom* (22985/93), there was growing recognition of the rights of those who transitioned, there was no clear consensus on how to provide recognition. The ECtHR, in *Goodwin*, noted that lack of a clear consensus in the contracting states was 'hardly surprising,' given the 'widely diverse legal systems and traditions' (*Goodwin* (28957/95), [85]) and the wide margin of appreciation afforded to contracting states in deciding 'on the measures necessary to secure Convention rights within their jurisdictions' (*Goodwin* (28957/95), [85]). Therefore, the ECtHR attached:

less importance to the lack of evidence of a common European approach to the resolution of the legal and practical problems posed, than to the clear and uncontested evidence of a continuing international trend in favour not only of increased social acceptance of transsexuals but of legal recognition of the new sexual identity of post-operative transsexuals (*Goodwin* (28957/95), [85]).

In largely dismissing the state of European consensus as a determinative factor, the ECtHR was again in effect strengthening the rights of the individual against the state in an area of private life which could be deemed intimate to the individual. In so doing, the ECtHR was giving primacy to the individual's identity over the state's maintenance of the *status quo*.

In *Goodwin*, the ECtHR strongly emphasised that, in some areas of one's private life, the individual's sense of identity will be protected notwithstanding a lack of European consensus on the matter in question; arguably this is the interpretation that this court should take, leading it to find in favour of the claimant.

This leaves the issue of the impact of finding in favour of the claimant on the state's administrative system, and once again *Goodwin* can provide direction. In that respect, the ECtHR noted that 'on the basis of the material before it at this time [it did not find] that any real prospect of prejudice [to others] has been identified as likely to arise if changes were made to the current system' (*Goodwin* (28957/95), [87]). The alleged problems identified in the Government's response in this appeal are merely hypothetical, and the challenges faced by the state by HMPO issuing such passports as requested by the claimant can easily be overcome and ought to not outweigh the rights of an individual to have one's identity recognised and respected.

Whereas colleagues in this court and in the lower courts based their judgments on the wide margin of appreciation to be afforded to the state in this appeal, *Goodwin* encourages restricting such a wide margin. As this appeal centres around the right to personal identity, the margin of appreciation ought to be very narrowly construed.

Human Rights Act 1998

Had the first question on which this appeal was based been decided in the negative, it would have been fundamental to the outcome of the appeal to consider the second question: whether the Human Rights Act 1998 imposes on the Secretary of State an obligation to provide passports which denote gender using X gender markers. As the first question was answered in the affirmative above, it is only tangentially important to now consider the second question. The Human Rights Act 1998 s.2(1)(a) provides that '[a] court or tribunal determining a question which has arisen in connection with a Convention right must take into account any judgment, decision, declaration or advisory opinion of the European Court of Human Rights.' Lord Bingham's dicta in *R (on the application of Ullah) v Special Adjudicator* ([2004] UKHL 26; [2004] 2 AC 232) is often deemed to be the leading authority on the meaning of s.2. According to Bingham's interpretation of s.2, all national courts—when considering an issue of a Convention right—are bound to 'keep pace with the Strasbourg jurisprudence as it evolves over time: no more but certainly no less' (*Ullah* [20]). This forces this court into a difficult position as, in the present case, there is no Strasbourg jurisprudence directly on point with which to keep pace. In such an instance, to what extent can a national court, indeed the Supreme Court in this instance, move beyond Strasbourg and develop national law? My esteemed colleagues considered this and adopted a restrictive interpretation of s.2 and of Lord Bingham's *Ullah* dicta—an approach which has been elsewhere referred to by academic commentators as a 'flat... analysis of Convention rights.'[40] However, this is not the only possible analysis of the *Ullah* dicta.

As noted, a question arises as to the role of the national courts where Strasbourg has been silent on a particular issue or where Strasbourg has determined an issue is within the states' margin of appreciation without providing further analysis. As discussed in the answer to the first point of appeal contained above, there is no direct Strasbourg jurisprudence to be followed but there is considerable guidance given in the *Goodwin* reasoning. The majority judgment held that it was not for the domestic courts to fill in the states' margin of appreciation. Contrarily, I would hold that it is *entirely* the responsibility of this court to do so and to determine the extent to which the Secretary of State should be obligated to alter HMPO policy. This analysis is based on the dicta of Lord Hoffmann in *Re G (A Child)(Adoption: Unmarried Couple)* ([2008] UKHL 38; [2009] 1 AC 173), in which he said *Ullah* should not apply 'in a case in which Strasbourg has deliberately declined to lay down an interpretation for all member states, as it does when it says that the question is within the margin of appreciation' (*Re G* [36]). It is not outwith the realm of possibility—indeed, it is likely—that should Strasbourg consider an application such as that brought by the claimant, it would be held that the issue falls within the state's margin of appreciation either in relation to the rights in question, or in relation to the mechanism by which a state must provide for the protection of those rights. Therefore, using the reasoning of Lord Hoffmann:

> [i]n such a case, it is for the court in the United Kingdom to interpret articles 8 and 14 and to apply the division between the decision-making powers of courts and Parliament in the way which appears appropriate for the United Kingdom. The margin of appreciation is there for division between the three branches of government according to our principles of the separation of powers. There is no principle by which it is automatically appropriated by the legislative branch (*Re G* [37]).

Using this reasoning, it is incumbent upon this court to decide what is appropriate for this state and we ought not defer automatically to Parliament. It is perfectly acceptable for this court to take into account the judgment of the ECtHR in *Goodwin*, and all other Article 8 jurisprudence, and hold that, as gender identity is a fundamental aspect of personal identity and autonomy, and is crucial to one's ability to live authentically in relation with others and with the state, the second point of appeal should also be answered in the affirmative.

---

40. Nuno Ferreira, 'The Supreme Court in a Final Push to go Beyond Strasbourg,' *Public Law* Jul (2015), 367–375.

Conclusions

This appeal was based on two arguments: (i) that Article 8 ECHR, either read alone or in conjunction with Article 14, imposes on the Secretary of State an obligation to provide the claimant with a passport on which their gender is denoted as X rather than as male (M) or female (F), and (ii) that if such an argument in (i) was deemed to fail, the Human Rights Act 1998 imposes an obligation on the Secretary of State to do the same. Although there is no jurisprudence in which the Strasbourg court has considered the rights of non-binary individuals to obtain 'genderless' passports, gender identity is protected under Article 8 ECHR. Growing international recognition of non-binary identity and international best practice in relation to legal recognition of gender identity is moving in favour of protecting the rights of non-binary individuals. Based on the approach taken by the European Court of Human Rights twenty years ago in *Goodwin v United Kingdom*, this growing international trend and emphasis on the rights of the individual versus the needs of the mechanisms of the state cannot be ignored. Additionally, the margin of appreciation does not need to be a restrictive mechanism as was applied in the majority judgment; there is scope within the interpretive tools of the ECtHR to allow contracting states to develop their own jurisprudence beyond the jurisprudence of the ECtHR. I am reminded once again of Lord Bingham in *Ullah* and the so-called mirror principle. This has been interpreted in a way which restricts the development of national law in ways which would be deemed to go beyond Strasbourg. Yet, in areas in which there is no Strasbourg jurisprudence, or a slowly developing jurisprudence, with which to keep pace, then national courts have every right to develop the law in ways which could be deemed to 'go beyond' Strasbourg.

For the reasons set out above, I would have allowed this appeal.

PART 3

FAMILY AND PARENTHOOD

15

Joslin et al. v New Zealand
(United Nations Human Rights Committee):

Queering the UN Human Rights Committee

Rafael Carrano Lelis and Paula Gerber[*]

Introduction

Form matters a great deal – above all in the juridical field.[1] For this very reason, challenging or subverting form is an important undertaking that can take many different configurations. Sally Engle Merry observes that the appropriation of the law and the use of legal terms and forms is an important mode of vernacularisation and of subversion of Western-produced legality.[2] Likewise, parody plays its role in the ambivalence between reaffirming the violence perpetrated by the legal form and subverting it by dislodging it from the 'original' context.[3]

The idea of rewriting judgments similarly falls within a realm that enables subversive reappropriation. This is even more so if we take as reference approaches such as queer theory that, at first glance, are completely refractory to the limits imposed by law and by legal form.

This chapter provides a reimagining of the *judgment*[4] in the View of the United

---

* The authors are deeply grateful for comments made to previous drafts of this chapter by the organisers of the Queer Judgments Project – Nuno Ferreira, Maria Federica Moscati, and Senthorun Raj – and by another contributor of the project, Daryl Yang. An initial draft of the chapter was presented by one of the authors at the Geneva Graduate Institute 'International Law PhD Roundtables,' the author is thankful for all of the participants' engagement with the paper, especially to Irene Manganini and Dena Kirpalani for their insightful comments.

1. Pierre Bourdieu, 'La force du droit : Eléments pour une sociologie du champ juridique,' *Actes de la recherche en sciences sociales* 64 (1986).
2. Sally Engle Merry, 'Legal Vernacularization and Ka Ho'okolokolonui Kanaka Maoli, The People's International Tribunal, Hawai'i 1993,' *PoLAR: Political and Legal Anthropology Review* 19/1 (1996).
3. Judith Butler, *Bodies That Matter: On the Discursive Limits of 'Sex'* (New York: Routledge, 1993).
4. 'View' is the technical name for decisions issued by the HRC. However, we chose to frame it as a judgment, because it both values the importance of the HRC's views and repurposes the labels of legal categories that may attribute hierarchical value to distinct documents in international law. For a detailed explanation of the HRC, see Nigel S. Rodley, 'The Role and Impact of Treaty Bodies,' in *The Oxford Handbook of International Human Rights Law*, ed. Dinah Shelton (Oxford: Oxford University Press, 2013), 621–648.

Nations Human Rights Committee (HRC) in *Joslin v New Zealand* (*Joslin*).[5] This communication was the first time a UN treaty body was required to directly address the right of same-sex couples to marry. To this day, *Joslin* remains the HRC's only authoritative interpretation of the International Covenant on Civil and Political Rights (ICCPR) as it relates to marriage and the sexual orientation of individuals seeking to marry.

The complaint in *Joslin* was brought by two lesbian couples from New Zealand who had been denied a marriage licence by the Registrar-General, on the basis that the *Marriage Act 1955* did not provide for the right of same-sex couples to marry. After exhausting domestic remedies, the authors submitted a complaint to the HRC, claiming that their human rights had been violated, in particular:

i.   Article 16 (recognition before the law);
ii.   Article 17 (interference with privacy and family) on its own and in conjunction with 2(1) (enjoyment of rights without discrimination);
iii. Article 23(1) (family) in conjunction with Article 2(1); and
iv.   Article 23(2) (marriage) in conjunction with Articles 2(1) and 26 (non-discrimination and equal protection).

The HRC, in a very brief decision, found no violation of the complainants' ICCPR rights. The View offers a deeply heteronormative judgment that cries out for a queer analysis and reimagining of how international human rights law (IHRL) might be used to protect rather than persecute persons who do not neatly fit into societal norms about gender and sexuality.

The Committee limited its analysis to Article 23 of the ICCPR, on the basis that the existence of a specific provision on the right to marry meant that any claims regarding this right should be considered taking into account only this Article. The HRC determined that Article 23 of the ICCPR recognises marriage as being the union *only* between a man and a woman wishing to marry each other. Therefore, the HRC concluded that a refusal to provide for marriage between same-sex couples did not violate the ICCPR. The rewritten view presented here reaches the opposite conclusion.

Since the View was delivered by the HRC, more than 20 years ago, the HRC's legal reasoning has been the subject of much scholarly analysis, and several different shortcomings have been noted. For example, Kristie Bluett considered the main reasonings that supported the HRC's view and presented legal arguments to counter these. She suggested that the time might be ripe for the Committee to revisit whether same-sex couples have a right to marry under the ICCPR and identified new challenges that could be raised, including the need for a contextual reading of Article 23 and for a harmonisation of the 'contradictory approaches' taken by the HRC in the *Joslin* and *Toonen cases*.[6] Paula Gerber, Kristine Tay, and Adiva Sifris combined an analysis of *Joslin* and the provisions of the ICCPR with an examination of other core human rights treaties. Through this, they concluded that the HRC's interpretation in *Joslin*

---

5. *Joslin et al. v New Zealand* [2002] United Nations Human Rights Committee (UN HRC), Communication No. 902/1999, U.N. Doc. CCPR/C/75/D/902/1999 [*Joslin v New Zealand*].

6. Kristie A. Bluett, 'Marriage Equality under the ICCPR: How the Human Rights Committee got it wrong and why it's time to get it right,' *American University International Law Review* 35/4 (2020).

no longer stands, considering both the rules of treaty interpretation and other developments observed in IHRL.[7] Similarly, Oscar Roos and Anita Mackay argued for an 'evolutionary interpretation' of Article 23(2) of the ICCPR to encompass same-sex couples' right to marry, and recall the counter-majoritarian function of human rights law in stating that consensus among State Parties to the Covenant should not be a prerequisite to the HRC expanding its interpretation of the provision.[8]

Conversely, in 2017, Malcolm Langford drew on one of the same methodological tools we employ in this chapter and offered a rewritten View of the HRC's decision in *Joslin*. However, he differently argues that 'the *Joslin* decision should be rewritten but only to provide a conditional right of same-sex couples to marry, as well as provide the basis for advancing a range of other LGBTI rights on a global basis.'[9] His rewritten piece reaches the same conclusion as the HRC in 2002 – that the 'mere refusal to provide for marriage between homosexual couples' does not amount to a violation of ICCPR provisions.[10] He concludes that 'even if a more progressive approach is legally justifiable, it is unlikely to be politically and practically advisable.'[11] As we set out in Section 3 below, there have been many positive developments since Langford's piece. However, they are not needed to draw a different conclusion. It is possible to rewrite the *Joslin* View, and reach a different conclusion, using only the legal arguments available at the time of the original judgment.[12] One important contrast in adopting a queer vantage point for this rewriting exercise is that we openly accept the assumption that our legal analysis is informed by both queer ethics and queer politics.

This commentary on the queer rewriting of the *Joslin* View consists of four sections. After this Introduction, Section 2 explores some of the methodological challenges in using queer theory in the legal field. In particular, we identify some of the experimental methods in this attempt at *queering* the jurisprudence of the HRC. We then elaborate on the queer approach adopted in the rewritten judgment. For example, although it mimics the structure that the HRC uses in its Views, and is written in the same time frame as the original judgment in *Joslin v New Zealand*, i.e. 2002, it adds elements to *trouble* its content. Developments since *Joslin*, although not considered in the rewriting process, are relevant to how we now consider that decision, and are discussed in Section 3.

---

7. Paula Gerber, Kristine Tay, and Adiva Sifris, 'Marriage: A Human Right for All?' *Sydney Law Review* 36/4 (2014), 643-667.

8. Oscar Roos and Anita Mackay, 'The Evolutionary Interpretation of Treaties and the Right to Marry: Why Article 23 (2) of the ICCPR Should Be Reinterpreted to Encompass Same-Sex Marriage,' *George Washington International Law Review* 49 (4) (2017), 890.

9. Malcolm Langford, 'Revisiting Joslin v New Zealand: Same-Sex Marriage in Polarised Times,' in *Integrated Human Rights in Practice: Rewriting Human Rights Decisions*, ed. E. Brems and E. Desmet (Cheltenham: Edward Elgar, 2017), 123.

10. *Joslin v New Zealand*, 11.

11. Malcolm Langford, 'Revisiting Joslin v New Zealand: Same-Sex Marriage in Polarised Times,' in Brems and Desmet, *Integrated Human Rights in Practice*, 138.

12. In the rewritten judgment, we always include as the main source for the argument material that was already available before the original date of the View. The only exception regards material that we only had access to through recent editions but that was nevertheless already available at the time (e.g. the *travaux préparatoires* of the UDHR). We also indicate when scholars have developed a similar argument to the one we make, even if after the original judgment, despite indicating as the main source the predated material. We do this as a matter of research ethics to give the authors due recognition for their ideas.

Finally, the last section concludes the commentary, emphasizing the value of queer engagement with the law and amplifying Dianne Otto's call to queer international law by 'changing meanings, unsettling taxonomies and inverting conventions,' so that we can 'imagine a more peaceful, equitable and inclusionary world.'[13]

Methodological Challenges in Queering Judgments

Why rewrite a judgment? What is the aim of doing something like this? Several answers are available to these questions, one of them being to frame the rewritten piece as a form of *queer counter-interpellation*.[14] In rewriting the view of the Human Rights Committee in *Joslin v New Zealand*, the intention is to circulate a queer counter-discourse, one that interpellates international legal bodies and exposes the heteronormative structure that underpins international law itself.

There is an evident challenge in mobilizing the law through queer terms. If we take anything from queer theory in that regard, it is that the legal field is an instrument of violence and regulation of queer bodies.[15] It is something to be deconstructed and broken down rather than engaged with, at the risk of legitimizing this constraining system. However, short of a queer revolution, we still need alternative ways to challenge legal power and discourse, to question it from the standpoint of 'queer curiosity.'[16]

The first, more legalistic, step in this exercise is perhaps the easiest one. We are mobilizing different legal arguments to support a more progressive outcome for the case. To do this, we explore different possibilities that allow for the interpretation of the ICCPR in a way that recognises that people of diverse sexual orientations, gender identities and expressions and sex characteristics (SOGIESC), have the right to marry people of any SOGIESC.

Nonetheless, by choosing to rewrite a judgment, we must accept that we are somewhat constrained by the legal form – the one set by the judging body, in this case, the UN HRC.[17] While one might consider the mere exercise of rewriting a judgment as something subversive in itself, a mere change in the delivered outcome is not enough to bring along queer subversiveness. For this reason, we propose an experimental approach to rewriting *Joslin*, which we call *counter-slurring*. As the case was brought to the HRC by two lesbian couples seeking recognition of their right to marry, we chose to disrupt the form by replacing references to the authors and to 'homosexual

---

13. Dianne Otto, 'Introduction: Embracing Queer Curiosity,' in *Queering International Law: Possibilities, Alliances, Complicities, Risks*, ed. Dianne Otto (London: Routledge, 2018), 2.

14. Rafael Carrano Lelis, 'Queer Unconventionality and Counter-Discourses of International Legality: Alternative Law-Making by LGBTI Transnational Activism' (paper presented at ESIL Interest Group on Social Sciences and International Law pre-conference workshop at the annual conference of the European Society of International Law, Aix-en-Provence, France, 30 August 2023); Jean-Jacques Lecercle, *De l'interpellation: sujet, langage, idéologie* (Paris: Éditions Amsterdam, 2019).

15. Ratna Kapur, 'The (Im)Possibility of Queering International Human Rights Law,' in *Queering International Law: Possibilities, Alliances, Complicities, Risks*, ed. Dianne Otto (London: Routledge, 2018), 131-147; Judith Butler, *Excitable Speech: A Politics of the Performative* (New York: Routledge, 1997).

16. Dianne Otto, 'Introduction: Embracing Queer Curiosity,' in Otto, *Queering International Law*, 1-11.

17. Rosemary Hunter, Clare McGlynn, Erika Rackley, eds., *Feminist Judgments: From Theory to Practice* (Oxford: Hart Publishing, 2010).

couples' with the words *dyke* and *faggot*. Even though these two slurs have been equally resignified by LGBTI+ communities, their injurious potential to individuals remains greater than the word *queer*, which one might say has been 'banalised' and lost its potential not only to injure but also to act in conferring this form of subversive agency.

We are aware of the uncomfortable effect that the use of the terms dyke and faggot may have on the reader; it is equally uncomfortable for those who are writing, proof-reading, and editing this work, but the use of this language is important and intentional. The purpose of doing this is twofold. First, it allows these terms to penetrate the legal form from a site other than that of injury;[18] from a position of rights claiming and recognition. Second, it follows Monique Wittig's call to avoid the discursive categories set by the 'straight mind.'[19]

In proposing the use of these words, a caveat is necessary. We cannot forget that these (the authors of the communication to the HRC) are real people, who were fighting the violation of their human rights. The use of the proposed terms ('dykes' and 'faggots') is not intended to establish these as the identities of the authors (or anyone else). Rather, they are used as discursive positions that resignify injury, so as to allow collective agency. In this sense, and again following Wittig, these categories should not be viewed as gendered or binary. Rather, they are introduced as a new linguistical framework that should not be reduced to the heteronormative interpretation of language. This means, therefore, that using these terms in no way excludes bisexual, gender non-binary, or any other individuals in the queer spectrum of gender and sexuality. The discomfort that reading these terms in the text may generate is deliberate. It seeks to engage the reader's perception of violence that can be produced by legal discourse, and to stimulate reflections on the heteronormative structures of international law. This replacement of words also has the goal of *troubling* the reader.

Having said that, we still understand that what separates emancipatory and subversive employments of slurs from their violent and derogatory use, are very blurry lines. We only proceed to do so because we (the authors of this chapter) have no problem identifying as a *dyke* and a *faggot*. This, we believe, is a crucial point in understanding the emancipatory potential of the reclaiming we propose. Following our theoretical framework, this could only be done by people, like us, who would potentially be hurt by these same terms.[20] In this sense, the use of these terms does not concern the original authors of the rewritten judgment – on behalf of whom we could never speak and who might very well reject such use. It does concern, however, both of us as writers and the larger collective of queer people who are affected by those slurs. That is why we have adopted this approach as a collective rather than a personal reclaiming exercise. The use of these terms in the rewritten judgment is partially what produces the emancipatory effect and drains the violent power of these words. Nevertheless, we take this opportunity to invite you to consider the effect that the repetition of these words might have on you, before reading the rewritten judgment. While it was a liberating exercise for us, it might not be for you.

---

18. Butler, *Excitable Speech*.
19. Monique Wittig, 'The Straight Mind,' *Feminist Issues* 1/1 (1980),103–11.
20. Butler, *Excitable Speech*.

Another pressing point is the extent to which the content of the rewritten judgment is restricted to what a given court or body would normally address. In this area, adopting a queer approach allows some room to go beyond the strict limits of the legal claims presented. In particular, it opens doors to question how the reading would (and should) also benefit other minoritised groups or identities. In this sense, it is an exercise of queer utopia, entailing not only imagining how a queer decision-maker might decide a case, but also how queer theory can stretch legal norms to establish new forms of universality.[21]

The last challenge is how to integrate queer theory into the rewritten judgment. As we are *re*writing, it is often the case that sentences or paragraphs of the original document will be entirely replicated, for example, to emulate the formality of the legal discourse. Therefore, the question arose as to how we could incorporate critical contributions offered by queer theorists while preserving the writing style. And indeed, whether we *should* even be seeking to preserve it? In the text to come, we frequently invite queer theorists to speak with and for the Committee, including some citations at length in different parts of the text, as if they were themselves ruling on the case. This, we hope, creates some *trouble* in the often-plain legal writing style.

In addition to the challenges explored above, in the rewritten judgment that follows, we also took advantage of the freedom this exercise provides to introduce a few changes in the way the HRC usually addresses individual communications. Notably, we have prioritised the merits rather than questions of admissibility. Even though admissibility is an important procedural stage in accessing treaty body mechanisms, it often works as an overly formal and bureaucratic barrier to realising justice for those who have experienced human rights violations. Moreover, the extended attention given to admissibility issues (sometimes three or more times the attention that is given to the merits) takes the focus away from the most relevant aspect of these proceedings, i.e. assessing and acknowledging the grave human rights violations allegedly perpetrated by States against individuals. Therefore, our reimagined View expands on many aspects that were under-addressed or entirely unaddressed by the HRC. Additionally, on the specific issue of admissibility in *Joslin*, the HRC positively assessed the matter and proceeded to the analysis of the merits.

Something else that is enabled by our queer rewriting is the expansion of the protective scope of the View. We can adopt a more fluid position in understanding the legal matters that are being analysed and, therefore, are not as limited, as the HRC would normally be, in responding to the claims made by both the authors and the State. This allows us, for example, to broaden the decision to embrace other non-normative persons, and to offer an interpretation of the provisions that is inclusive of queer people beyond the subject of marriage – such as addressing the prohibition of discrimination based on gender identity and sex characteristics.

---

21. Many developments have happened since and if adopted today the View might be an entirely different one. However, the reimagined judgment is still utopian for not constraining itself by all the Committee's legal or formal requirements; as well as for applying queer lenses to judge and pushing for a subversive understanding of heterosexual institutions.

Finally, our queer rewriting seeks to avoid the 'assimilative and normative gravitational pull of human rights.'[22] In bringing together these seemingly irreconcilable spheres – queer theory and IHRL – we use queer theory to undo many of the (hetero) normative assumptions underpinning the international human rights system. In this sense, our rewriting is a practice of queer imagination. It seeks to rethink a scenario in which both queer justice and human rights come together to overcome structures of violence and discrimination.

Subsequent developments

The HRC's View has not withstood the test of time. In the two decades since the *Joslin* decision, thirty-four countries have reformed their laws to provide that same-sex couples can marry on an equal footing with different-sex couples.[23] In the Advisory Opinion OC-24/17 of November 2017, the Inter-American Court of Human Rights recognised the right of same-sex couples to marry under international law. Following the request made by Costa Rica, the Court held that the American Convention on Human Rights 'does not protect a *single or a specific* model of a family.'[24] In interpreting Article 17(2) of the Convention, which like the ICCPR refers to 'men and women,' the Court stated that 'this wording does not necessarily mean either that this is the only form of family protected by the American Convention.'[25] The Court adopted an 'evolutive interpretation' to establish the obligation of States to ensure same-sex couples access to all 'legal institutions that exist in their domestic laws to guarantee the protection of all the rights of families,' which includes the right to marry.[26]

More recently, in March 2022, the CEDAW Committee issued its View on the communication *Rosanna Flamer-Caldera v Sri Lanka*.[27] The complaint concerned the criminalisation of same-sex sexual activity in Sri Lanka, which applies to both men and women.[28] The author – a lesbian activist from Sri Lanka – submitted that this was a violation of, among others, her right to non-discrimination based on gender and sexual orientation under Articles 2(a) and (d)–(g) of the Convention.[29] In its analysis of the merits, the CEDAW Committee not only identified a breach of several rights in the Convention, but also found that 'the rights enshrined in the Convention belong to all women, including lesbian, bisexual, transgender and intersex women, and that *article*

---

22. Kapur, 'The (Im)Possibility of Queering International Human Rights Law.'

23. ILGA World, 'ILGA World Database: Same-Sex Marriage and Civil Unions,' accessed 6 September 2023, https://database.ilga.org/same-sex-marriage-civil-unions.

24. *Advisory Opinion OC-24/17* (Inter-American Court of Human Rights, 24 November 2017), 71, emphasis added.

25. *Advisory Opinion OC-24/17*, 71.

26. *Advisory Opinion OC-24/17*, 82.

27. *Rosanna Flamer-Caldera v Sri Lanka* [2022] United Nations Committee on the Elimination of Discrimination against Women (UN CEDAW Committee), Communication No. 134/2018, U.N. Doc. CEDAW/C/81/D/134/2018 [*Rosanna Flamer-Caldera v Sri Lanka*].

28. ILGA World, 'ILGA World Database: Criminalisation of consensual same-sex sexual acts,' accessed 6 September 2023, https://database.ilga.org/criminalisation-consensual-same-sex-sexual-acts.

29. *Rosanna Flamer-Caldera v Sri Lanka*.

16 of the Convention applies also to non-heterosexual relations.[30] This reference is highly relevant to this chapter, since Article 16 addresses the right to marry. Thus, the CEDAW Committee issued a clear indication that the right of two women to marry is both recognised and protected under international law.

Conclusion

Although Juliet Joslin, Jennifer Rowan, Margaret Pearl, and Lindsay Zelf were unsuccessful in their complaint to the HRC, they can take some small comfort from the fact that some 20 years later, law and society have changed to such an extent that same-sex couples cannot only marry in New Zealand but in every continent around the globe. And they have played a part in the queering of international law.[31]

The history of frustrated encounters between queer and the (international) law, such as in *Joslin,* is also an integral part of this engagement and disengagement between the queer and the legal field. Denied claims expose many of the cis and heteronormative underpinnings of international human rights law. They also play an important role in bringing such topics to the public sphere, allowing marginalized themes and subjects to enter the public debate and discourse. Thus, these judgments serve as performative calls that initiate the process of recognition of non-normative bodies and identities under IHRL. Simultaneously, they are transforming this same law into something new – different from what they were initially engaging with – instead of merely assimilating to the norms dictated by it.

In conclusion, adopting Odette Mazel's reading of Eve Sedgwick's work in searching for reparative practices when queering international law, we offer this queer rewriting of the HRC's decision in *Joslin* as our attempt to use the law 'not as complicit or co-opting but as radical and defiant, empowering and transformative.'[32]

---

30. *Rosanna Flamer-Caldera v Sri Lanka,* 11, emphasis added.
31. In a happy footnote, Juliet Joslin and Jennifer Rowan did get married in Canada in 2008, and on 17 April 2013, were in the public gallery of New Zealand Parliament to witness the passage of the Marriage (Definition of Marriage) Amendment Act which allowed same-sex couples to marry in New Zealand and recognised their Canadian marriage. See https://www.rnz.co.nz/national/programmes/eyewitness/audio/201813826/jenny-and-jools.
32. Odette Mazel, 'The Texture of "Lives Lived with Law": Methods for Queering International Law,' *Australian Feminist Law Journal* 49/1(2023), 75.

VIEW OF THE HUMAN RIGHTS COMMITTEE UNDER ARTICLE
5, PARAGRAPH 4, OF THE OPTIONAL PROTOCOL TO THE
INTERNATIONAL COVENANT ON CIVIL AND POLITICAL RIGHTS

Seventy-fifth session

Concerning

Communication No. 902/1999

Submitted by:	Ms. Juliet Joslin et al. (represented by counsel Mr. Nigel C. Christie)
Alleged victim:	The authors
State party:	New Zealand
Date of communication:	30 November 1998 (initial submission)

The Human Rights Committee, established under Article 28 of the International Covenant on Civil and Political Rights

Meeting on 17 July 2002,

Having concluded its consideration of communication No. 902/1999, submitted to the Human Rights Committee by Ms. Juliet Joslin et al. under the Optional Protocol to the International Covenant on Civil and Political Rights,

Having taken into account all written information made available to it by the author of the communication and the State party,

Adopts the following:

Views under Article 5(4) of the Optional Protocol

[1] The authors of the communication are Juliet Joslin, Jennifer Rowan, Margaret Pearl and Lindsay Zelf who are all of New Zealand nationality. The *dykes*[33] claim to

---

33. For a detailed explanation regarding the use of the terms *dyke* and *faggot*, see Section 2 of the commentary preceding the rewritten judgment.

be victims of a violation by New Zealand of Article 16; Article 17, on its own and in conjunction with Article 2(1); Article 23(1), in conjunction with Article 2(1); Article 23(2), in conjunction with Article 2(1); and Article 26.

The facts as presented by the authors

[2.1] Both couples have been in lesbian relationships for several years, living together and sharing the responsibility for children and financial expenses. They maintain sexual relations. On different occasions between 1995–96, they applied for a marriage licence at the local Registry Office, under the *Marriage Act 1955*. The applications were rejected. The refusal was justified by the Registrar-General on the basis that the Registrar was acting lawfully in interpreting the *Marriage Act* as confined to marriage between a man and a woman, and did not, therefore, apply to couples comprised of *dykes* or *faggots*.

[2.2] All four *dykes* applied to the High Court, seeking a ruling that, as couples, they were lawfully entitled to obtain a marriage licence and to marry pursuant to the *Marriage Act 1955*. The Court rejected the application and the *dykes* appealed to the Full Bench of the Court of Appeal. The Court of Appeal denied the appeal. Having pursued their claim for a marriage license to the highest court in New Zealand, the Committee is satisfied that the *dykes* have exhausted domestic remedies, and the claim is admissible.

The complaint and arguments by the authors

[3.1] The authors claim that the decision to interpret the *Marriage Act* as excluding *dykes* and *faggots* from the institution of marriage violates Article 26 by discriminating against them directly on the basis of sex and indirectly on the basis of sexual orientation, which causes them to suffer 'a real adverse impact' in several ways.

[3.2] The *dykes* also claim a violation of Article 16. They assert that Article 16 is aimed at permitting persons to assert their essential dignity, through their recognition as proper subjects of law, both as individuals and as members of a couple, which recognition is being prevented by the State party's *heteronormative* reading of the *Marriage Act*.

[3.3] The authors further claim a violation of Article 17, both on its own and in conjunction with Article 2(1), in that the restriction of marriage to heterosexual couples violates the *dykes'* rights to family and privacy.

[3.4] The authors also claim a violation of Article 23(1), in conjunction with Article 2(1), submitting that this provision of the Covenant requires a non-discriminatory recognition of family. They assert that the only way in which their families differ from heterosexual families is that they are *dykes*.[34]

[3.5] Finally, the authors claim a violation of Article 23(2), in conjunction with Article 2(1). They contend that the right of men and women to marry must be interpreted in light of Article 2(1), which forbids distinctions of any kind. They assert that because the *Marriage Act* has been interpreted in a manner that distinguishes between couples on the prohibited ground of sex, which includes within its ambit sexual orientation, the *dykes'* rights in these respects have been violated.

[3.6] The *dykes* reject the State party's submissions on the merits. They argue that: (i) as *dykes* and *faggots* they are treated differently from heterosexuals with respect to marriage, (ii) this differential treatment is based on sex and sexual orientation, and (iii) *dyke* and *faggot* couples thereby suffer substantive detriment and stigmatisation based on the State party's discriminatory interpretation of the *Marriage Act*.

[3.7] The *dykes* go on to argue that the courts wrongly referred to a fixed 'traditional' understanding of marriage, contending that past discrimination cannot justify ongoing discrimination and that such a view ignores evolving social constructions. Since marriage is a social construct, the *dykes* argue that it can be socially deconstructed and/or reconstructed. They contend that society and the State party have programmed their selective memories to construct marriage as inherently and naturally heterosexual, thereby excluding access by 'deviant others' to marriage.

[3.8] Finally, as to State practice, the authors note that there is precedent for *dyke* and *faggot* marriages, with the Netherlands, in 2001, opening up civil marriage to *dyke* and *faggot* couples.

The State party's response to the complaint

[4.1] The State party rejects the authors' arguments that the Covenant requires States parties to enable *dykes* and *faggots* to marry. It asserts that marriage in the Covenant, and in other international instruments, such as, the Universal Declaration of Human Rights (UDHR), applies exclusively to heterosexual couples, that is, marriage is limited to being between a man and a woman.

[4.2] The State party's overarching argument is that the terms of Article 23(2), of the Covenant clearly envisage that State parties may define marriage in terms of couples of different sexes.[35] The State party places a great deal of emphasis on the fact that Article 23(2) is the only substantive Article in the Covenant which uses the gender-specific

---

34. The original claim stated that 'legal recognition' of their family was the feature missing to guarantee equal treatment between heterosexual families and theirs.

35. The use of a binary ('opposite') and biological determinism ('sex' instead of 'gender') exposes the State party's heteronormative bias.

terms of 'men and women;' all other provisions in the Covenant use gender-neutral terms.

[4.3] The State party further emphasises that this provision should be interpreted with reference to the Latin maxim *generalia specialibus non derogant*. That is, the meaning of Article 23(2) excludes a contrary interpretation being derived from other more general provisions of the Covenant. In this sense, the State party argues that the mention of 'men and women' in Article 23 introduces a more specific provision the interpretation of which cannot be altered by more general provisions within the Covenant, such as the obligations regarding non-discrimination and equality before the law in Article 26.

[4.4] The State party further contends that Article 16 confers individual rights and does not apply to the recognition of relationships.

[4.5] As to Article 17, both on its own and in conjunction with Article 2(1), the State party submits that the *dykes* have not endured any interference or attack on their family or privacy.

[4.6] As to Article 23(1), in conjunction with Article 2(1), the State party asserts that it does recognise the *dykes* as families, with or without their children.

[4.7] As to Article 26, the State party emphasises that the inability of *dykes* and *faggots* to marry flows directly from Article 23(2) of the Covenant and cannot, therefore, constitute discrimination in terms of Article 26. The State party further submits that marriage is *universally* understood as open only to individuals of opposite sexes.

[4.8] In any event, the inability of *dyke* or *faggot* couples to marry under New Zealand law is not a distinction or differentiation based on sex or sexual orientation. It is not the fact that they are *dykes,* but rather that they are a *dyke couple* that is determinative.[36] The *Marriage Act* grants all persons equal rights to marriage, regardless of sex or sexual orientation, and does not differentiate between persons on any such basis.

Committee's Views

[5.1] The Committee has considered the communication in light of all the information made available to it by the parties, as provided in Article 5(1) of the Optional Protocol.

[5.2] The authors' essential claim is that the Covenant obliges States parties to confer upon *dyke* and *faggot* couples the capacity to marry and that, by denying the authors this capacity, the State party is violating their rights under Articles 16, 17, 23 and 26 of the Covenant. The Committee notes that Article 23(2) of the Covenant expressly

---

36. In the HRC view, the State party submission was summarized as follows: 'it is the nature of the couple, rather than that of individual members, that is determinative.'

addresses the issue of the right to marry. Given the existence of a specific provision in the Covenant on the right to marriage, it is appropriate to first analyse the claims in light of this provision.

The State party invoked the maxim *generalia specialibus non derogant* to argue that other provisions of the Covenant could not be used to interpret the right to marriage, because of a specific exception established by the provision in Article 23(2). This would be the case if the provision included an explicit exclusion, for example, if it stated that '*dyke* and *faggot* couples do not have the right to marry under this Article.' However, no such explicit exclusion forms part of Article 23(2). The State party also asserted that marriage is 'inherently' heterosexual. If it seems so, it is only a consequence of the cultural imposition of compulsory heterosexuality, which seeks to establish causal links between biological sex, culturally established gender and their effect on sexual practices and desire.[37] In this sense, the Committee understands that asserting a unity between sex, gender and desire, wrongly assumes the heterosexuality of such desire through the differentiation of oppositional sexes and genders.[38] This is what underpins a binary system that excludes couples such as the authors. The Committee understands that the social expectation of a specific form of coherence between known features of sex, gender and sexuality creates pressure for relationships to be shaped in line with the heterosexual norm.[39] However, this social construct is not reflected in the wording of Article 23(2) of the Covenant.

The State party also asserted that the words 'men and women' in Article 23(2) should be interpreted as excluding the possibility of marriage for *dyke* and *faggot* couples, and that this is consistent with the *travaux préparatoires* of the Covenant. The Committee finds this argument lacks merit. Despite acknowledgements in social sciences of the culturally constructed concepts that shape social reality, some of these concepts, including the differentiation between 'man' and 'woman,' resist critical examination because they are supposedly an essential core of nature. The result would be to prevent an analysis of whether these concepts act to establish social obligations to maintain heterosexual relationships as the rule of normalcy.[40] Therefore, the State party's interpretation of Article 23 sustains a 'totalizing interpretation of history, social reality, culture, and language.'[41] The Committee rejects the State party's assertion that the *travaux préparatoires* support this contention.

Article 23 was drawn directly from Article 16 of the Universal Declaration of Human Rights (UDHR).[42] A careful analysis of the *travaux préparatoires* of the UDHR reveals that the inclusion of this language was intended to reinforce gender equality, not to exclude *dykes* and *faggots* from the right to marry.[43] The Committee recalls that:

---

37. Judith Butler, *Gender Trouble: Feminism and the Subversion of Identity* (New York: Routledge, 1999), 23.
38. Butler, *Gender Trouble*, 30.
39. Butler, *Gender Trouble*, 30.
40. Wittig, 'The Straight Mind,' 105.
41. Wittig, 'The Straight Mind,' 105.
42. Marc J. Bossuyt, *Guide to the 'Travaux Préparatoires' of the International Covenant on Civil and Political Rights* (Dordrecht and Boston: M. Nijhoff, 1987), 441.
43. William A. Schabas, *The Universal Declaration of Human Rights: The Travaux Préparatoires* (Cambridge: Cambridge University Press, 2013). After the View, this argument was developed by Gerber,

> The discourses which particularly oppress all lesbians, women, and homosexual men, are those discourses which take for granted that what found society, any society, is heterosexuality. These discourses speak about them and claim to say the truth in an apolitical field, as if anything of that which signifies could escape the political in this moment of history, and as if, in what concerns them, politically insignificant signs could exist. These discourses of heterosexuality oppress them in the sense that it prevents them from speaking on their own terms. Everything which puts them into question is at once disregarded as elementary.[44]

The State's party assumption of said founding heterosexuality leads it to an incorrect interpretation of Article 23(2), notwithstanding its correct understanding of the Article's drafting stages. The correct interpretation of Article 23 requires the suspension of any assumption of heteronormativity. The outcome of lifting this default heteronormative framing is that forms of kinship and bonding between persons are not restricted to gender binary and heterosexual couples. Likewise, when the words 'men' and 'women' are put together in a text, they cannot be presumed to automatically refer to a connection between the two that takes the form of a sexual or affective relationship.

The inclusion of the language of 'men and women' in Article 23(2) also serves the purpose of limiting the institution of marriage to adults rather than children. This interpretation is reinforced by the inclusion of the words 'marriageable age.' Furthermore, 'men and women' are inscribed in plural form which, interpreted in its ordinary meaning in reference to Article 31(1) of the VLTC, denotes the meaning of men as a group and women as a group. Thus, this provision does not mean that a man can only marry a woman and vice versa, but rather that women enjoy the right to marriage to the same extent as men, reinforcing the need to ensure *gender equality*. In this sense, the provision cannot be understood as prohibiting marriage between persons of diverse gender identities and expressions, most of whom were still unnamed as identities in the public sphere and therefore unknown by the drafters and could not have been foreseen at the time. Accordingly, State parties cannot impose any conditions that may impair the full enjoyment of the right to marry by intersex and non-binary persons. Article 23(2) does not in any way restrict or inhibit the right of persons to marry, based on gender identity, expression, or sex characteristics (GIESC).

This finding introduces a crucial distinction that opens the right to marry, as protected by the Covenant, to include non-binary persons, as well as polyamorous relationships. This is important in keeping open the frame of recognition, whereby recognizing the right of *dykes* and *faggots* to marry does not foreclose the future recognition of other possibilities of relationship, marriage or otherwise, under the provisions of the Covenant. Such an interpretation removes an imposition of certain relationship arrangements as a prerequisite to accessing legal protection.

Any recognition of marriage cannot serve to exclude other forms of relationship from accessing all rights enshrined in the Covenant. Furthermore, the diversity of forms

---

Tay, Sifris, 'Marriage,' 643–68; Kees Waaldijk, 'The Right to Marry as a Right to Equality: About Same-Sex Couples, the Phrase "Men and Women," and the Travaux Préparatoires of the Universal Declaration,' in *Furthering the Frontiers of International Law: Sovereignty, Human Rights, Sustainable Development*, ed. Niels Blokke, Daniëlla Dam-de Jong, and Vid Prislan (Leiden & Boston: Brill Nijhoff, 2021), 457–72.
44. Wittig, 'The Straight Mind,' 105.

of marriage in the different States that have ratified the Covenant, including polygamous marriages, speaks to the open interpretation that this provision should receive, proscribing any restrictive understanding of the right to marry.

The Committee recalls that Article 31(1) of the Vienna Convention on the Law of Treaties (VLTC) also requires that the context and purpose of a treaty must be taken into account in its interpretation. With regard to its context, there was no discussion of non-heterosexual marriage at the time that the Covenant was drafted. There were no organised groups of *dykes* and *faggots* advocating for the right to marry.[45] The very absence of contemplation of this is evidence that the Article was not intended to exclude it. Moreover, the purpose of the Covenant, as well as the UDHR, is to guarantee the protection of *everyone*'s human rights. A different interpretation would mean excluding *a priori* an entire group of people from the enjoyment of said rights.

Finally, the Committee notes that the State party has entered other treaties, before and after the adoption of the Covenant, that also address the right to marriage. Pursuant to Article 31(3)(c) of the VLTC, this can be taken into account for the purpose of interpreting the provisions. With that regard, the State party ratified the Convention on the Elimination of All Forms of Racial Discrimination in 1972 and the Convention on the Elimination of All Forms of Discrimination against Women in 1985. Articles 5(d)(iv) and 16(1)(a) of these treaties, respectively, provide for the right to marry *without* referring to 'men and women.'[46] The latter explicitly states, in Article 16(1), that the mention of 'men and women' shall have equality as its basis. These provisions further demonstrate that the wording of Article 23(2) of the Covenant cannot be interpreted as denying *dykes* and *faggots* the right to marry. Such an interpretation is only ever assumed because of the 'bias of compulsory heterosexuality' that renders other possibilities invisible and outside its purview.[47] The Committee rejects the idea that heterosexuality should be presumed as the sexual orientation of most people, either implicitly or explicitly.[48] The Committee recalls that 'heterosexuality has been both forcibly and subliminally imposed on women, yet everywhere women have resisted it, often at the cost of physical torture, imprisonment, psychosurgery, social ostracism, and extreme poverty.'[49] In this sense, adopting the State party's arguments would result in a continuation of the imposition of heterosexuality on *dykes* and *faggots*, prolonging this process of violence with the aid of legal discourse.

For the reasons outlined above, the Committee finds that Article 23(2) of the Covenant applies to *dyke* and *faggot* couples, and they are entitled to enjoy the right to marry to the same degree as heterosexual couples.

---

45. See historical accounts in different national contexts, e.g. James Green, *Beyond carnival: male homosexuality in twentieth-century Brazil* (Chicago: University of Chicago Press, 2000); Eric Marcus, *Making history: the struggle for gay and lesbian equal rights, 1945-1990* (New York: Perennial, 1992). After the initial View, see Waaldijk, 'The Right to Marry as a Right to Equality,' in Blokke, Dam-de Jong, and Prislan, *Furthering the Frontiers of International Law.*

46. The Articles indicate, respectively: 'The right to marriage and choice of spouse' and 'the same right to enter into marriage.'

47. Adrienne Rich, 'Compulsory Heterosexuality and Lesbian Existence,' *Signs* 5/4 (1980), 632.

48. Rich, 'Compulsory Heterosexuality,' 633.

49. Rich, 'Compulsory Heterosexuality,' 653.

[5.3] In addition to recognizing the right to marry in the context of *dyke* and *faggot* couples, the Committee also notes that the institution of marriage should not be used to regulate access to any rights, or limit social or legal recognition, under any circumstances. Therefore, State recognition of relationships cannot be invoked to justify differential treatment between its citizens. This would amount to discriminatory practice prohibited under Article 26 of the Covenant.

[5.4] Given the Committee's finding that Article 23(2) does not limit marriage to only heterosexual couples, the Committee turns to a consideration of the authors' claims of a violation of Article 23 in conjunction with Article 2(1).

This Committee noted in *Toonen v Australia* that the reference to 'sex' in Articles 2 and 26 is to be taken as including sexual orientation.[50] Therefore, reading Article 23, in conjunction with Article 2, the Committee concludes that the denial of marriage to *dykes* and *faggots* constitutes a violation of their right to access family protection (paragraph 1) and to marry (paragraph 2) without distinction of any kind under the Covenant, which includes sexual orientation.

[5.5] In addition to this Committee's View in *Toonen*, we note that sexual orientation also falls within the ambit of 'other status' for the purposes of Article 26. As a consequence, the same applies to Article 2(1). The different statuses enumerated in each of these Articles constitute an exemplary rather than exhaustive list of protected grounds from discrimination. The inclusion of 'other status' was intended to ensure the protection of *any* ground of discrimination, including those that could not be foreseen by the drafters at the time. This interpretation recognises the reality of *dykes* and *faggots*, and detaches the right to non-discrimination from any biological criterion, particularly when considering the cultural determination of this so-called biological aspect. In other words, 'what counts as sex is equally culturally determined and obtained.'[51] In addition, this interpretation of other statuses means that GIESC are also protected by the non-discrimination provisions of the Covenant, both by the term 'sex' and by the term 'other status.' The Committee finds that any denial of *dykes'* and *faggots'* right to marry *because* of their sexual orientation is a violation of the right to equal protection before the law.

[6] The Committee, acting under Article 5(4) of the Optional Protocol, is of the view that the facts before it reveal a violation of Article 23, in conjunction with Articles 2(1) and 26 of the Covenant.

[7] Under Article 2(3)(a), the *dykes*, having been denied their rights under the Covenant are entitled to a remedy. An effective remedy in these circumstances is for the State party to grant the authors a marriage licence, and for the State party's Registrar-General

---

50. *Toonen v Australia* [1994] United Nations Human Rights Committee (UN HRC), Communication No. 488/1992, U.N. Doc CCPR/C/50/D/488/1992.
51. Gayle Rubin, 'The Traffic in Women: Notes on the "Political Economy" of Sex,' in *Toward an Anthropology of Women*, ed. Rayna R. Reiter (New York and London: Monthly Review Press, 1975), 165.

to recognise that *dykes* and *faggots* have the right to marry, and that the *Marriage Act 1955* must be interpreted accordingly. Moreover, the State party should amend the *Marriage Act 1955* to explicitly recognise that all persons enjoy the right to marry, regardless of sexual orientation, gender identity and expression, and sex characteristics (SOGIESC).

[8] As the Committee has found there to be a violation of Article 23, in conjunction with Articles 2 and 26, the Committee is not required to consider whether there has also been a violation of Articles 16 and 17, both on its own and in conjunction with Article 2 of the Covenant. Nevertheless, the Committee notes, for future reference, that the right to recognition before the law enshrined in Article 16 applies to everyone regardless of SOGIESC, on the same basis reasoned above concerning the right to marry. Furthermore, the Committee recalls that the right to marry cannot be invoked to restrict any person's enjoyment of their rights under Article 16. In this sense, the Committee emphasises that there cannot be the imposition of any conditions (such as spousal consent) which may interfere with access to legal gender recognition by trans persons. Article 17 should likewise be interpreted under the framework set out above. Thus, the mention of 'family' in the provision must be read as not excluding any type of arrangement from its scope.

[9] The Committee requests that the State party, within 90 days of the date of the transmittal of its Views, provide the Committee with information regarding the measures it has taken to give effect to the Views.

[Adopted in English, which is the original version.]

16

EB v France: Lesbian Adoption in the European Court of Human Rights

Sanna Elfving, Katie Jukes, Miriam Schwarz and Surabhi Shukla[1]

The following pieces of work offer different approaches to queering of the *EB v France* judgment. We invite the reader to choose and read in the order and at the pace that suits them, and hope that our texts offer both a thorough understanding of the original judgment and joy as they offer themselves as companions in witnessing queer history.

URL: manypsychologistshavesaid/talk.eu

The following play rewrites the *EB v France* judgment by the European Court of Human Rights (ECtHR). To a large extent, the text has been taken from the original without indicating where it cites from it verbatim, and where it paraphrases or elaborates. Any resemblance of the characters with the protagonists in the original is intended.

Years active: 1998-2008

Archived: 22 January 2008

ACT 1

ACT I SCENE I SPRING 1998

14:38 26 February 1998   25 y
@theapplicant *added* @JuraSocialServicesDepartment

---

1. We have worked on this queered judgment as co-authors, contributing, critiquing, and building on each other's work. We would like to thank Claire O'Connell and Po-Han Lee, and their colleagues, contributors to this volume, who provided us feedback on an earlier draft. Thank you also to SJ Cooper-Knock who very kindly set some of the songs to music.

Since 1966, adopting a child as a single person has been possible in France. However, Phillippe Fretté was refused authorisation to adopt a child three years ago because of his *choix de vie...* I am hoping for a positive response.

@theapplicant *has left the chat*	*25 y*
@JuraSocialServicesDepartment *added* @Socio-EducationalAssistantAndNurse	*25 y*
@JuraSocialServicesDepartment *added* @Psychologist1	*25 y*
@JuraSocialServicesDepartment *added* @TechnicalOfficerChildren'sWelfareoffice	*25 y*
@JuraSocialServicesDepartment *added* @PsychologistChildren'sWelfareOffice	*25 y*
@JuraSocialServicesDepartment *added* @AdoptionBoard'sRepresentative	*25 y*
@JuraSocialServicesDepartment *added* @Board'sRepresentativeFamilyCouncil	*25 y*
@JuraSocialServicesDepartment *added* @HeadChildren'sWelfareService	*25 y*

ACT I SCENE II SPRING 1998

@JuraSocialServicesDepartment *wrote on 8 March 1998*   *25 y*

The first step is to assess whether @theapplicant is psychologically suitable to be a parent. This is of course no one's concern when people have biological children. The State trusts that when people have biological children, they are destined to be parents until the opposite is found to be true. Some EU member states therefore make psychological counselling a requirement for those who decide against a pregnancy. You see, we are generally quite suspicious of people who make conscious decisions about parenting. There must be something wrong with them.

ACT I SCENE III SUMMER 1998

@Socio-EducationalAssistantAndNurse *wrote*   *25 y*

@JuraSocialServicesDepartment, I have met @theapplicant for an interview to assess her psychological state. Ms EB is broad-minded, cultured, emotionally responsive, and seems to have a clear-sighted approach to child-rearing. Despite the fact that @theapplicant is applying to adopt as a single person, I enquired about the relationship she has with the woman with whom she lives. I note that the two women are in a long and stable relationship. I find this lifestyle most worrying and do not consider this to be a good environment for a child. There is a rich history of burning childless lesbians and refusing unmarried women the right to adopt. Seems like Ms EB is more comfortable telling the child that they have previously had a mother and father rather than living with a man.

@Psychologist1 *wrote*   *25 y*

> Indeed, @theapplicant has all the qualities to be able to raise a
> child as she is enthusiastic and warm-hearted and comes across as
> very protective of others and her ideas about child-rearing appear
> very positive. I think that some free association on our side will be
> helpful.

@Socio-EducationalAssistantAndNurse *wrote*   *25 y*

> Excellent idea. I was just about to suggest that because, after all,
> the adoption process raises the idea of a fault-finding mission to a
> new height.

Jacqueline Rose,
*Mothers: An Essay
on Love and Cruelty*
(London: Faber &
Faber, 2019), 209.

@Psychologist1 *wrote*   *25 y*

> Thank you, so nice of you to say so. Is she not seeking to avoid the
> violence of giving birth and genetic anxiety regarding a biological
> child? Is she not idealising the idea of having a child and under-es-
> timating the difficulties inherent in providing one with a home? Is
> she not fantasizing about being able to fully mend a child's past?

@Socio-EducationalAssistantAndNurse *wrote*   *25 y*

> Ah, very good points, while not at all related to the adoption proce-
> dure and what she said in the interview – yet so relevant.

@Psychologist1 *wrote*   *25 y*

> I also think that we agree on the fact that all the studies on parent-
> hood show that a child needs both their parents.

@Socio-EducationalAssistantAndNurse *wrote*   *25 y*

> Yes, absolutely, that is obvious. Let's not waste any time producing
> them here.

@Psychologist1 *wrote*   *25 y*

> Also, please note that I am saying 'both parents' and not 'two
> parents.' Sexual difference – that is, the binary which we think of
> as man and woman – is the foundational binary of our society.

Alterité Sexuelle
– a model of sexual
difference with a
referent man and a
referent woman that
conceives heterosexual
marriage and kinship
as the basis of French
society.

@Socio-EducationalAssistantAndNurse *wrote*

> Indeed. As Francoise Heritier has eloquently said, 'the fact that it is the woman who carries the children is at the basis of the fundamental opposition which allows us to think.' And I deduce from this: children parented by a single – not to mention queer – parent basically would not be able to think properly. These are indeed the unsurpassable limits of our thought, 'like the opposition between night and day.'

25 y

Françoise Héritier, 'Pacte civil de solidarité: "Aucune société n'admet la parenté homosexuelle"' Interview with Marianne Gomez, La Croix 9 Novembre 1998: Societé 16.

@Psychologist1 *wrote*

25 y

> I am so pleased that we agree on this. All these invigorating thoughts have made me forget about the time, and now, it is already night. Let's call it a day and hand in these notes.

ACT I SCENE III – AUTUMN 1998

@TechnicalOfficerChildren'sWelfareoffice @JuraSocialServicesDepartment

25 y

> I have also seen @theapplicant for an interview. And after the many useful things that @Socio-EducationalAssistantAndNurse and @psychologist1 have deduced, there is not much to add. @theapplicant has not given the question of a male role model sufficient thought. I also wonder about the role of Ms R., the partner of the applicant. However, it remains unclear what my qualification in adoption matters even is.

@PsychologistChildren'sWelfareOffice @JuraSocialServicesDepartment

25 y

> I have noted that @theapplicant has played a parental role with respect to her sisters and one of her parents. Is she trying to correct her feelings of worthlessness by becoming a mother? I daresay I have outdone myself with this insight.

> While I am on a roll, I note the unusual attitude of @theapplicant towards men, and ask, is the rejection of the male figure not a rejection of the child's own self-image? After all, this child would have a father but can the symbolic existence of the father be preserved within @theapplicant's capabilities?

@AdoptionBoard'sRepresentative @JuraSocialServicesDepartment *wrote*   *25 y*

> Thank you so much, dear colleagues, for your insightful contributions. I would like to add something from my own personal experience of living with a foster family. From that single subjective perspective, I can generalise that the mother and father figures fulfil complementary but different roles in parenting a child.

@PsychologistChildren'sWelfareOffice *wrote*   *25 y*

> Since under Article 343 of the Civil Code a single person *can* adopt a child, your observations in effect replace the law with illegal considerations. Surely, your experience is relevant.

@Board'sRepresentativeFamilyCouncil *wrote*   *25 y*

> I have something else to add. That is, @theapplicant's partner is not interested in parenting it seems. I shall suggest that @theapplicant could move house to raise the kid alone, which will in turn require sorting out material circumstances. That will obviously make things complicated.

@AdoptionBoard'sRepresentative *wrote*   *25 y*

> Thank you, it's good that you just made this up, now it can be used as an argument against @theapplicant.

@HeadofChildren'sWelfareService *wrote*   *25 y*

> By the way, I agree that the girlfriend does not seem to be interested. On top of that, she takes up all the space of any potential 'male referent' for the child.

@PresidentofTheCouncilforTheDépartement *wrote*   *25 y*

> The application for authorisation has been declined. Mostly because there will be two female parents but no male parent present for the kid, and that is just one woman too many and one man missing. On top of that, a woman who is living in the same house as the child and is the partner of the mother, shouldn't be allowed to take herself out of the parenting equation. This is a privilege we reserve for men in our culture.

@PresidentofTheCouncilforTheDépartement *closed this chatroom*

ACT II SCENE I WINTER/SPRING 1999

@theapplicant *has reopened the chatroom*   *24 y*
@theapplicant *added* @PresidentofTheCouncilforTheDépartement   *24 y*

> I request a reconsideration of the decision.

@theapplicant *has left the chat*   *24 y*
@PresidentofTheCouncilforTheDépartement *added* @Children'sWelfareService   *24 y*
@Children'sWelfareService *added* @clinicalpsychologist   *24 y*
@clinicalpsychologist *wrote*   *24 y*

> While @theapplicant has everything that one might look for in a
> mother, I think the authorisation should be denied as she has not
> figured out every single pedagogical approach to raising a child and
> I am also confused by the presence of the other mother.

@PresidentofTheCouncilforTheDépartement *wrote*   *24 y*

> One additional check should be enough. I am closing this chatroom.

@PresidentofTheCouncilforTheDépartement *has closed this chatroom*   *24 y*

ACT II SCENE II SPRING 1999

@theapplicant *reopened the chatroom*   *24 y*
@theapplicant *added* @BesançonAdministrativeCourt   *24 y*

> I request that the administrative decisions of 26 November 1998
> and 17 March 1999 be set aside.

@theapplicant *has left the chat*   *24 y*

ACT II SCENE III SPRING 2000

@BesançonAdministrativeCourt *added* @JuraSocialServicesDepartment   *23 y*

> The administrative decisions of 26 November 1998 and 17 March
> 1999 are set aside because the following reasons given by the *dépar-*
> *tement* are not sufficient for refusal:

> > A missing male referent and the uncertainty about which role
> > @theapplicant's partner will play in the child's life.

However, while this was an inadmissible reason, we think it wise to have spent two years discussing these important issues.

ACT II SCENE IV WINTER 2000

@JuraSocialServicesDepartment *added* @NancyAdministrativeCourtofAppeal   *23 y*

Appeal.

@NancyAdministrativeCourtofAppealjudge1   *23 y*

We do not agree with @BesançonAdministrativeCourt. The reasons of @theapplicant to request the decisions of 26 November 1998 and 17 March 1999 to be set aside are not valid. @theapplicant never asked for the personality test that she now complains was never sent to her. It is therefore lawful to document personality test results for her without talking to her.

@NancyAdministrativeCourtofAppealjudge2   *23 y*

We would like to add that, from our perspective, the decision to refuse the adoption authorisation was not based on @theapplicant's lifestyle, although this was referred to several times in the process. We were especially careful to use 'identification markers' and 'family safeguards.' There is nothing homophobic about this.

@NancyAdministrativeCourtofAppeal *closed the chatroom*   *23 y*

ACT II SCENE V SUMMER 2002

@theapplicant *reopened the chatroom*   *21 y*
@theapplicant *added* @Conseild'État   *21 y*
@theapplicant *wrote*   *21 y*

Appeal on points of law.

@theapplicant *left the chat*   *21 y*
@Conseil d'État

Even if a single person applies for authorisation of adoption, we still have to make sure that at least some men will be present in the vicinity of the potential child. In order to make this sound less like we are scared of women and more as if we had unequivocal scientific backing, we reason with the lack of a 'paternal referent.' The association with divorced or lesbian friends should be avoided in questions of childcare, which we will mask as concern about the partner's commitment. For both reasons, @theapplicant's appeal was not justified.

Rose, *Mothers*, 99

ACT III SCENE I

[The case has left the French courts and entered the European Court of Human Rights. The chatroom is exchanged for a theatre and the clacking of the keyboard is replaced by musical tones. Stage Left: In the Grand Chamber of the ECHR, a suited booted Law in white tie, a walking stick, and a hat takes EB through the different possibilities while giving her a tour of the court. The music is hopeful, but energetic and a little frantic— filled with the promise of rights realisation. The Law is not singing at this point, only talking animatedly, like a salesman.]

Law: Welcome, EB, is it?

Welcome EB, let me give you a tour.

This is the European Court of Human Rights.

Don't let the name fool you. We're all nice people here *[fake self-deprecating laugh]*. Now, if you'll follow me. Oops, careful over there, and can you fix up your hair? We are in the grand Chamber after all!

[The music picks up.]

*Song - Welcome to the Courtroom! *

[The Law is tap-dancing to this song. The music is now joyful and uncomplicated]

Well…

This is it!

This is where dreams come true,

This is where the flowers bloom,

This is where the skies are blue,

And day and night,

It's rights, rights, rights!

We can give you compensation,

To suit your situation.

We can give you remedies, and fast!

We can give orders to governments,

They cannot disobey,

Oh baby, we can make them last!

Don't worry, my dear,

now that you're here,

We'll turn your human wrongs to human rights.

…

[Law blushes with pride. Catches itself before it goes overboard. EB's face is unreadable. A little pause. The music lowers but continues in the background as the law speaks]

Law: Now, let's see.
You're from France, aren't you?
And you're here on an adoption matter?

[EB nods]

Law: Well, you're in luck!
There's a lot that we've been doing on adoption!
There's the Draft European Convention on the Adoption of Children,
The International Convention on the Rights of the Child,
The Hague Convention on the Protection of Children
And of course, the French Law…

[The beat changes and the music picks up again. The Law sings enticingly to a confused and dazed but slightly hopeful EB]

Law: Are you 28?

Think children are your fate?

Well, there's adoption!

There is adoption!

Do you love a child?

Got emotional ties?

Well, there's adoption!

Adoption!

There is adoption!

[Music stops]

[Sternly and point blank] We'll give you 5 years.

[The music continues in the background as the Law resumes its dancing once again in a jolly mood, oblivious to EB The Law is also going over EB's papers as it is doing so.

Law reads something. Stops. The music dies as it dawns on Law that EB is a lesbian.]

Law: Hang on. Wait. *[thinks]*. You didn't say you were gay. *[searches for words]* Oh well, that does not matter. I am sure we can find something for you... oh, there's France now, such good timing *[laughs sheepishly]*. France, this lady says that she has been discriminated against. Well, that's awkward but I am sure you can sort it out...hehehe. Oh well, is that the time?

[quite suddenly] Goodbye.

ACT III SCENE II TIME IS EXHAUSTED

[With the Law gone, now only EB and France remain on stage. They take a minute to take each other in. Slowly France comes to terms with what is being alleged. Its temperature rises. The lights on stage change to suggest an acrimonious mood. The piano begins to play angrily, choppily, in the background.]

France: Discrimination!

On sexual orientation!

[Haughtily, like the French]

How grand!

Obviously, you misunderstand.

[Then quite suddenly, as if France has taken a deep breath, the music stops, and France begins to sing as sweetly as it can.]

Song - Everybody Needs a Daddy

Everybody needs a daddy,

To do daddy things with them.

EB: what are daddy things?

France: *[stammers]*...you know, *groans*, *grunts*, *flexes muscles*

[starts again]

France: Everybody needs a daddy,

To do daddy things with them.

Every child needs a papa,

A papi, An Appa, A Baba, An Abba,

A *père,*

to care,

For them!

Paternal referent,

Now, that's a compliment.

Sexual difference,

We have confidence,

In this absolutely

Anthropologically.

Sociologically.

Epistemologically.

CENTRE OF OUR THOUGHT!

[music stops]

France: And the scientists also agree with us.

EB: Actually, the scientists don't agree.

France: SHHHHHH!!!!!

[the music starts up again]

France: Everybody needs a daddy,

Everybody needs a daddy,

Everybody needs a daddy,

[music swells]

My daaaddy told meeee sooo!

[The music dies down for a second but picks up again changing in beat and tone. This new music is contentious as EB fights back. EB's not singing right now, but one can see that she is gearing up to.]

EB: I thought it would be simple,
Or simpler in any case,
To adopt a child singly,
Than to do it with my partner or to adopt my partner's child,
Anyway, those options are not available since we are not married.
Never mind that we can't be!
Adopting singly is the only option available to me,
And I'm being refused because I'm applying singly.
This is a sick game.

Speaking of games…
Let's play a game.
The game is called 'Foul Play.'
I'll give you a scenario,
You say yay or nay.

I'll start you off.

[the music picks up for this rap song]

Song - Foul Play

EB: This ain't no itty-bitty treat,

It's nuanced and gritty.

It's got tons of rights,

I'll start a family life.

[EB to audience: is that foul play? Nah, not yet.]

I'm gonna be a mom,

And so I filled up a form.

Now I may not be straight,

Hey, I got Article 8!

[EB to audience: how about now? Someone from somewhere: still sounds good to me]

Cue up reality,

They hate my sexuality,

My scary lifestyle,

My girlfriend wife-style.

[someone from somewhere: oh, that's…. FOUL PLAY!]

Then they resolved,

That she won't be involved,

[someone asks]: Is that what she said?

EB: Nah, but they never cared.

[more people now]: FOUL PLAY!

[the music changes and gets more contemplative]

They say that the kid may become

Psychologically disturbed

And may face homophobic prejudice

Where do they get this?

And would they have said this

To a single straight woman?

Here's what it is though.

There's no evidence,

There's no proof,

But the government's scared,

That my kid will be a poof.

[pause]

poof.

[song ends abruptly]

ACT III SCENE III LAST WORDS

Song - Sorry, Not Sorry

[Judges are sitting around an oval table. This scene shows judges in conference as opposed to on the bench. 10 out of a 17-judge bench have decided that EB has been discriminated against on the basis of her sexual orientation. The song follows the majority judgment. The music begins and one judge calls the attention of the others to the matter at hand.]

Judge 1: Brother, brother, brother, brother, brother, brother, bro, br... sister? sister, sis?

[The judges turn one by one to face the singing judge as they are called out]

Judge 1: What will it be?

I feel confidently,

As I sip my tea,

[A little pause and then judges 1 and 2 in unison]

Quite contrary.

Judge 3: And arbitrary.

Judge 4: To insist on a father to be.

[Pause]

[Mini chorus - all four judges together]

> Heteronormativity,
>
> With State complicity.
>
> *[oh, that's dangerous]*
>
> Heteronormativity,
>
> With State complicity.
>
> *[thank god for us]*

[Judges look around the table. After a short pause...]

> Judge 5: There's no justification,
>
> For France as a nation.
>
> To insist on her homosexuality,
>
> Disproportionately.
>
> Judge 6: I agree.
>
> Judges 7, 8, 9: WE agree.
>
> Judge 10: Her relationship's stable,
>
> And so they are able,
>
> To cope with the upheaval
>
> Of a child.

[Judges all in unison]

> And while the kid's interests are paramount,
>
> That cannot surmount,
>
> The simple fact,

That this is not about that.

Because it's really about...

[Mini chorus]

Heteronormativity,

With State complicity.

[oh, that's dangerous]

Heteronormativity,

With State complicity.

[thank god for us]

Back-door Heteronormativity.

Hete

Ro

NORMATIVITY!

[Song Ends]

EB: That's great! Does this mean I get to adopt?

Judges: Now now, it only means that France refused authorisation on illegal grounds. We will ask France to look at your form again... Umm, but since you're old now, 46 [heehee], you're not too likely to succeed. [Awkward silence]. Here's 10,000 euros.

[The judges continue singing and dancing in self-congratulations while EB watches confused. They slowly process out of the stage while dancing. The music is joyful like upbeat choir music]

Heteronormativity

Lalala heteronormativi...

END.

Introduction: ECtHR and Same-Sex Adoption

Our re-written judgment challenges the way in which the legal systems of France and the European Court of Human Rights (ECtHR) treat parenthood, focussing on the experiences of lesbian and queer women as mothers. In considering the ways in which motherhood, parenthood, and the *ideal* family are implicated in this judgment, we draw on recent scholarship that disrupts the ways in which these norms are 'constantly defined and regulated by State power, legal and economic systems.'[2]

We have chosen this judgment as it provides an opportunity to queer the approach of the law to lesbian motherhood, lesbian adoption, and queer issues more widely. There have been developments in ECtHR jurisprudence and French law since the judgment was issued. Nevertheless, *EB v France* is unique in the insights it offers about the ECtHR's heteronormative approach to lesbian motherhood and adoption. Furthermore, the case continues to be relevant to the present time. In October 2023, the highest courts in India have found that while single queers could adopt, the law deprived them of this ability when they became coupled, limiting coupled adoption to married heterosexual couples exclusively. This state of law was found to be valid in the best interests of the child.[3] *EB v France* therefore provides a reflection point for observers of the Indian law. It shows us that the positions of law thrown up by the case continue to resonate with the legal imagination even today.

The claim in *EB v France* before the ECtHR concerned an unsuccessful adoption application by EB, a French nursery teacher. She alleged that the French adoption authorities' negative decision was influenced by prejudicial attitudes towards her as a lesbian woman. Although the authorities denied that their decision was based on her sexual orientation, the majority of the Court was satisfied that this was a decisive factor leading to the refusal to adopt. The ECtHR subsequently upheld EB's complaint that she had suffered discrimination on the grounds of her sexual orientation contrary to the provisions of the European Convention on Human Rights (ECHR).[4] Therefore, the Court concluded that France had violated EB's rights to be free from discrimination and to respect her private and family life (Article 14 taken in conjunction with Article 8).[5]

It is obvious from the written evidence submitted to the Court that the domestic authorities' decision was influenced by the *ideal* adoptive parents: a heterosexual couple. The evidence, which consisted largely of the adoption authorities' written assessments and reports about EB's adoption application, focused on the assumed need to have both maternal and paternal guardians, suggesting that having single parents or same-sex parents was harmful to the child's development.[6] In its assessment of the case, the ECtHR was quick to highlight that the Convention itself contained no express right

---

2. Judith Butler, 'Kinship Beyond the Bloodline,' in *Queer Kinship: Race, Sex, Belonging, Form*, ed. Tyler Bradway and Elizabeth Freeman (Durham: Duke University Press, 2022), 22-47.
3. *Supriyo @ Supriya Chakraborty & Anr v Union of India* 2023 INSC 920 (Supreme Court of India, 17 October 2023).
4. Convention for the Protection of Human Rights and Fundamental Freedoms (European Convention on Human Rights, as amended) (adopted 4 November 1950, entry into force 3 September 1953).
5. *EB v France*, para. 2 of the reasons section of the judgment.
6. *EB v France*, paras. 37-38.

to adopt for couples or individuals.[7] However, France had enacted national legislation allowing single persons to adopt, thereby going 'beyond its obligations under Article 8.'[8] Consequently, the French government could not take discriminatory measures within the meaning of Article 14 in the application of that right.[9]

The ECtHR has decided cases concerning the rights of the queer community since the 1950s.[10] While its judgments concerning queer parenting have prompted many observers to hail its progressive attitude, a closer look at the judgments reveals an inconsistent and somewhat incoherent approach.[11] Examples include restrictive second-parent adoption and assisted reproduction regimes which require same-sex couples to undertake additional legal steps to assert their parenting rights.[12] Some more recent judgments concerning the refusal to grant legal recognition to parent-child relationships legally established outside Europe between children born as a result of surrogacy demonstrate some of the legal barriers faced by intended parents, particularly if they are not related to the child. In one of the two recent cases concerning queer parenting, the ECtHR concluded that the Swiss authorities' failure to recognise the parent-child relationship between the child and the intended father, who was also the donor, and was married to a man, violated the child's rights under Article 8 ECHR.[13] In contrast, the authorities' failure to recognise the parent-child relationship between the child born in the United States through surrogacy and the intended mothers, a married lesbian couple, did not violate Article 8 when the national law required the couple to foster and subsequently submit an adoption application because the child was not biologically related to either woman.[14]

Although *EB v France* has sometimes been seen as a judgment that advances the rights of the queer community because the national authorities can no longer evaluate a request for adoption based on the prospective parent's sexual orientation, the judgment portrays lesbians very stereotypically, as illustrated by the five separate opinions annexed to the majority judgment. We explore those stereotypes in depth in our submission. While the ECtHR's judgments can be influential in shaping public

---

7. *EB v France*, para. 41: 'the provisions of Article 8 do not guarantee either the right to found a family or to adopt.'

8. *EB v France*, para. 49.

9. Lydia Bracken, 'Strasbourg's Response to Gay and Lesbian Parenting: Progress, then Plateau,' *International Journal of Child Rights* 24 (2016), 358, 361.

10. Loveday Hodson, 'Sexual Orientation and the European Convention on Human Rights: What of the "L" in LGBT?,' *Journal of Lesbian Studies* 23/3 (2019), 383.

11. Henriette Jakobien Liesker, 'Caught in a Balancing Act: The European Court of Human Rights and the Road to Recognition for Sexual Minorities,' *Oslo Law Review* 4/3 (2017), 172, 183; Paul Johnson, 'Heteronormativity and the European Court of Human Rights,' *Law and Critique* 23/1 (2012), 43; Brian Tobin, 'The European Court of Human Rights' Inconsistent and Incoherent Approach to Second-Parent Adoption,' *European Human Rights Law Review* 1 (2017), 59.

12. *Gas and Dubois* v *France* App no 25951/07 (ECtHR, 15 March 2012); *X and Others* v *Austria* App no 19010/07 (ECtHR, 19 February 2013), para. 153 (The Court found a violation of Article 14 and Article 8 in a case concerning an unmarried lesbian couple when it was impossible for the non-biological mother to adopt the other partner's son).

13. *DB and Others* v *Switzerland* App nos 58817/15 and 58252/15 (ECtHR, 22 November 2022) (The Court also noted that the State had no margin of appreciation in the area of birth registrations).

14. *Valdís Fjölnisdóttir and Others* v *Iceland* App no 71552/17 (ECtHR, 18 May 2021).

attitudes, it is worrying that stigmatizing attitudes are adopted by members of a leading international human rights court.

Another significant barrier for equal parenting rights is the considerable differences in national law, policy and practice of adoption and the legal recognition of equal marriage and parental status among Council of Europe (CoE) member States — largely because most national legislation continues to privilege the heteronormative two-parent family model.[15] In fact, the judgment in *EB v France* did not translate into any kind of collective recognition of adoption rights for gay men or lesbian women in all forty-six CoE member States.[16] By contrast, in some parts of Europe, LGBT+ rights are in retreat due to anti-abortion, anti-LGBT+ laws, constitutional bans on equal marriage, and the preservation of 'traditional' family values.[17] Many States continue to inadequately protect the interests of the parents who wish to raise their children 'outside the paradigm of the conjugal couple relationship.'[18]

Recent scholarship contends that in its judgments, the Court has been cautious in overstepping the State's discretion when legislating on 'sensitive' areas such as adoption.[19] Consequently, it has been criticised for allowing States a wide 'margin of appreciation' when dealing with issues ranging from adoption rights for single men and women, to access to reproductive technologies and surrogacy.[20] When the Court allows States a certain leeway to interpret Convention rights more restrictively, it frequently cites the lack of consensus amongst the CoE member States.[21] In this respect, the Court offers a significant and decisive role to positions supported by the majority of States as a reason to find no violation.[22] Although in *EB v France* the Court cited the lack of common European ground on adoption by same-sex couples, it noted that emerging

---

15. See Kerry O'Halloran, *The Politics of Adoption* (Cham: Springer, 2021); Nicola Surtees and Philip Bremner, 'Gay and Lesbian Collaborative Co-Parenting in New Zealand and the United Kingdom: "The Law Doesn't Protect the Third Parent",' *Social and Legal Studies* 29/4 (2020), 507.

16. Liesker, 'Caught in a Balancing Act,' 183.

17. Peter Dunne, 'Who Is a Parent and Who Is a Child in a Same-Sex Family? Legislative and Judicial Issues for LGBT Families Post-Separation, Part I: The European Perspective,' *Journal of the American Academy of Matrimonial Lawyers* 30/1 (2017), 27.

18. Surtees and Bremner, 'Gay and Lesbian,' 507.

19. Francesca Romana Ammaturo, 'The Council of Europe and the Creation of LGBT Identities Through Language and Discourse: A Critical Analysis of Case Law and Institutional Practices,' *The International Journal of Human Rights* 23/4 (2019), 575, 578.

20. See e.g. Ammaturo, 'The Council of Europe,' 577; Andrea Mulligan, 'Identity Rights and Sensitive Ethical Questions: The European Convention on Human Rights and the Regulation of Surrogacy Arrangements,' *Medical Law Review* 26/3 (2018), 449.

21. See *Fretté v France* App no 36515/97 (ECtHR, 26 May 2002), paras. 35-36 (the rejection of the adoption request by a single gay man was not a violation of Article 8 in conjunction with Article 14); *Evans v UK* App no 6339/05 (ECtHR, 10 April 2007) paras. 70-80, 90 (the ECtHR found no violation of Article 8), national law prohibited Ms Evans from using her frozen embryos after her ex-husband withdrew his consent); *Parrillo v Italy* App no 46470/11 (ECtHR, 27 August 2015), para. 176 (no violation of Article 8 where Italian law prohibited the use of embryos *post mortem* after Ms Parrillo's had died at the war in Iraq).

22. See e.g. Paul Johnson, *Homosexuality and the European Court of Human Rights* (London: Routledge, 2012); Kanstantsin Dzehtsiarou, *European Consensus and the Legitimacy of the European Court of Human Rights* (Cambridge: Cambridge University Press, 2015); Sabrina Ragone and Valentina Volpe, 'An Emerging Right to a "Gay" Family Life? The Case *Oliari v Italy* in a Comparative Perspective,' *German Law Journal* 17/3 (2019), 451.

European scientific consensus and general consensus demonstrated no differences in children brought up by lesbian, gay, or heterosexual couples.[23]

In conclusion, this judgment provides a window onto the complex stance taken by the Court in cases involving queer lives and rights and throws up more questions than it answers.

Methods and Reader

Our rewritten judgment uses drama and poetry as methods with which to queer the text. In her discussion of the relationship between the case of the *Zong* slave ship (discussed further below) and the black Atlantic literary tradition, Anita Rupprecht observes that re-assembling the official record using fiction and poetry is 'a project of nourishment rather than exorcism.'[24] Similarly, Eve Kosofsky Sedgwick has argued that queer approaches too often rely on paranoid reading; in the belief that language always already reveals its violent potential, and that this potential needs to be uncovered and explicated. While paranoid reading has proven to be very productive, she suggests 'reparative reading' as a possibility to expand the approaches of queer theory. She contrasts the two styles of reading in reference to camp style. A paranoid reading of the practice of camp, for example, might view it as 'parody, denaturalization, demystification, and mocking exposure of the elements and assumptions of dominant culture.'[25] But a reparative reading might see camp style as an 'additive, accretive' impulse that responds to the realistic fear that 'the culture surrounding it is inadequate or inimical to its nurture; it wants to assemble and confer plenitude to an object that then will have resources to offer to an inchoate self.'[26]

Our approach to queering the judgment is therefore (at least) two-fold. On the one hand, it dissects and deconstructs the original text to uncover the misogynist and homophobic lines of argument on which it relies. On the other, it transforms the judgment into a different form in which we hope it may offer something more, perhaps even laughter, surprise, or a new understanding, and different perspectives. We hope that the result of this rewriting includes a change in who is a default reader of this text,[27] in other words, who perceives to be addressed by it, or even to be included in its voice. Academic writing is of course exclusive in many ways, and so is literary writing. Yet, through the multitude of forms, poetic, dramatic, lyrical and academic, we hope to offer, at least, several options of experiencing the judgment's significance and its implications.

---

23. *EB v France*, paras. 46 and 92.

24. Anita Rupprecht, '"A Limited Sort of Property": History, Memory and the Slave Ship *Zong*,' *Slavery & Abolition* 29/2 (2008), 265.

25. Eve Kosofsky Sedgwick, 'Paranoid Reading and Reparative Reading, or, You're So Paranoid, You Probably Think This Introduction Is About You,' in *Novel Gazing: Queer Readings in Fiction* (New York, USA: Duke University Press, 1997), 27.

26. Sedgwick, 'Paranoid Reading,' 28.

27. Hanna Kubowitz, 'The Default Reader and a Model of Queer Reading and Writing Strategies Or: Obituary for the Implied Reader,' *Style* 46/2 (2012), 201.

In order to find this new perspective, to disrupt and reshape, to fill in the silence surrounding the judgment, poetic tools, such as rhyme, meter and rhythm, framed within recognised poetic forms such as odes, erasure poetry and blank verse, have been adopted. This road has been travelled before. A recent standout example is by the Canadian poet and lawyer Marlene NourbeSe Philip, who excavates the legal judgment in *Gregson* v *Gilbert*,[28] in her book *Zong!*[29] named after the slave ship whose owners murdered 130 enslaved African people by throwing them overboard and subsequently claiming on their insurance policy for loss of cargo. Discussing her project, Philip says, '[l]aw and poetry both share an inexorable concern with language – the "right" use of the "right" words, phrases, or even marks of punctuation; precision of expression is the goal shared by both.'[30] In the *Gregson* v *Gilbert* case, slaves aboard a ship were treated as 'property' for purposes of a contract of insurance. The owners of the ship could not be treated as murderers, even if they had ordered more than 130 slaves to be thrown overboard, because, for legal purposes, it was not possible to murder 'property.' This is a stark but powerful illustration of what Philip means when she says: '[i]n its potent ability to decree that what is and is not, as in a human ceasing to be and becoming an object, a thing, a chattel, the law approaches the realm of magic and religion.'[31] Philip uses only words from the judgment itself, erasing, reversing, re-ordering, in order to create a new text. The result is a work of poetry that the reader must struggle to make sense of and is as powerful visually as it is semantically. Rupprecht's analysis is helpful here:

> As a literary technique, rather than seeking to fill in the gaps in the record, this approach aims to disrupt false beginnings, progressions and closures associated with the very idea of the narrative process itself. As a comment on the difficulty of relating slavery as narrative, such writing unsettles precisely by disallowing any recuperative movement that might be secured by narrative closure.[32]

In discussing her work, Philip quotes the author James Walvin: 'The line of dissent from the *Zong* case to the successful campaign for the abolition of slavery was direct and unbroken, however protracted and uneven.'[33]

Similarly, here, the case of *EB* v *France* is a link in a chain of cases challenging discrimination against lesbians and can be held up to the light, revealing a spectrum of ideas, meanings and prejudices brought to bear on the queer community by the State as explored above. In this case, EB ceases to be human. Rather than becoming a chattel of a slave owner, she becomes a symbol of the other, the feared, the woman who does not need a man and demands to have a child. In desiring adoption, she represents a challenge to reproduction-centred family formation; she represents, in Edelman's words, the death of the family:

---

28. *Gregson* v *Gilbert* [1783] 3 Doug. KB 232.
29. M. NourbeSe Philip, *Zong!* (Middletown: Wesleyan University Press, 2012).
30. Philip, *Zong!*, 191.
31. Philip, *Zong!*, 196.
32. Rupprecht, 'A Limited Sort of Property,' 4.
33. Philip, *Zong!*, 189.

The child remains the perpetual horizon of every acknowledged politics, the fantasmic beneficiary of every political intervention… queerness names the side of those not 'fighting for the children,' the side outside the consensus by which all politics confirms the absolute value of reproductive futurism.[34]

Turning now from the use of drama and poetry to the content of the poems included here, queer theorists, including Michel Foucault, Judith Butler and Sara Ahmed, have emphasised the importance of the body as a site for theorizing law.[35] As Ahmed asserts, absent the body, law risks material harm not only to queer people, but to other minoritarians who may be commodified and objectified through both overt discrimination as well as more subtle forms of ignoring and misperceiving. Without the body, law fails to inform a functioning society and assure protection for people under its jurisdiction.[36]

In the context of *EB v France*, Katie Jukes' poems in our rewritten judgment consider the anatomy, the body, of the adoptive mother. The mother without child, with no reproductive demand or rights, she who has no blood ties, but all the responsibility, with her child. From this perspective, there is something queer about any adoptive maternal body — a body that poses yet is not a birth mother; a body that presupposes, yet is defined in opposition to, procreative activity; a body that is marked as defective by others yet is chosen as capable. The position of the adoptive maternal body on the borderlands of maternity — a body that has been given an entry visa, but not full citizenship in motherhood — provides the opportunity for a queer poetic critical perspective on this judgment.[37]

Family and the French Polemic

In 1998, when the applicant had originally filed her adoption application, France was a bundle of interesting contradictions as far as LGBT+ rights were concerned. While sexual orientation discrimination had been outlawed since 1985, thus asserting the moral equality of lesbians and gays, the recognition of their intimacies was limited to a civil partnership (PACS) granted in 1999 — which gave some, but not all the rights available to a married heterosexual couple.[38] Adoption, for instance, remained a heavily guarded territory and was not available to PACS couples, either heterosexual or queer. Contrarily, adoption remained available to singles regardless of their sexual orientation and gender identity, at least on paper. Therefore, when EB applied for the adoption, she was in a way, simultaneously eligible and ineligible for it. She was eligible in her capacity as a single adoptive parent, which she desired to be, but she was also

---

34. Lee Edelman, *No Future: Queer Theory and the Death Drive* (Durham: Duke University Press, 2004).
35. See e.g. Michel Foucault, *The History of Sexuality: An Introduction* (New York: Pantheon Books, 1978); Judith Butler, *Gender Trouble: Feminism and the Subversion of Identity* (New York: Routledge, 1990); Sarah Ahmed, 'Deconstruction and Law's Other: Towards a Feminist Theory of Embodied Legal Rights,' *Social and Legal Studies* 4/1 (1995), 55.
36. Ahmed, 'Deconstruction.'
37. Shelley M. Park, *Mothering Queerly, Queering Motherhood: Resisting Monomaternalism in Adoptive, Lesbian, Blended, and Polygamous Families* (New York: State University of New York Press, 2013).
38. PACS stands for Pacte Civil de Solidarité.

ineligible because she was in a same-sex coupling with R and could not have applied as a couple.

The simultaneous assertion and denial of the moral worth of LGBT+ people/couples through these legal gymnastics was the expression of deeply held beliefs in French thought. Bruno Perreau argues that in the last four decades or so, with the loss of imperialist justifications for its political projects, France increasingly sought refuge in anthropology to justify its politics, and this can be seen in its justification on issues ranging from immigration and housing to hijab and the rights of LGBT+ people. This focus on anthropology was manifested through a 'meticulous focus on the body.'[39] In Perreau's words, the 'citizen's gendered body is considered to be the very site from which the social body draws its identity.'[40]

In the specific case of family law, its foundational texts in France, that is, the 1804 Napoleonic Code and the 1939 Family Code, have always set up the family as the best way to organise political consensus and solidarity. Therefore, in the French polemic, the family is never just a private entity: it is intimately connected to the public. It is the foundation of the social order. In other words, there is no social contract without the heterosexual family.[41]

Further, France's particular brand of secularism meant that politicians could not really resort to their religious views regarding adoption and family. Further, the stated equality of LGBT+ people/couples with heterosexuals meant that their unequal adoption status could not be justified on those grounds either. These political commitments meant that a new justificatory source had to be found, and Claude Lévi-Strauss and Jacques Lacan became the unlikely and perhaps unwilling heroes of the anti-LGBT movement. French Parliamentarians cited Levi-Strauss' *The Elementary Structures of Kinship* to argue that sexual difference and generational difference were the two pillars of society.[42] Sexual difference is the idea that the two sexes — male and the female — have unique roles to play in parenting, and the child takes their place in society by confronting the other sex and forming an identity and their subjectivity in negotiation with the two sexes.[43] This was in no way homophobic, the Parliamentarians asserted. Children raised in the absence of this dialectic would be 'symbolically modified.'[44]

It is in this context that the repeated reference by the French administration to the 'paternal referent,'[45] and a desire to preserve the symbolic existence of the father[46] to ensure a 'child's stable and well-adjusted development'[47] reveals a new layer of,

---

39. Bruno Perreau, *The Politics of Adoption: Gender and Making of French Citizenship* (Boston: MIT, 2014), xii.
40. Id.
41. Camille Robcis, *The Law of Kinship: Anthropology, Psychoanalysis, and the Family in France* (Ithaca, NY: Cornell University Press, 2013), 4.
42. Robcis, *The Law of Kinship*, 2-3.
43. Débats parlementaires, Assemblée nationale, 7 November 1998 ; and Débats parlementaires, Assemblée nationale, 30 March 1999.
44. Jean-Pierre Winter, 'Gare aux enfants symboliquement modifiés,' *Le Monde des Débats*, March 2000.
45. *EB v France*, paras. 11, 15, 36.
46. *EB v France*, para. 13.
47. *EB v France*, para. 10.

and provides an insight into, French society. These scientific sounding, hard facts of life sounded universalist, truer than objections driven by emotions or deeply held beliefs, and had the cool, detached air of erudition celebrated in French public life. For this reason, they have been hard to shake off and were repeated in the 'marriage for all' debates in France in 2013: '*1 papa, 1 maman, on ne ment pas aux enfants,*'[48] '*non à la filiation-fiction.*'[49] Adoption finally became available to married same-sex couples in 2013. However, same-sex adoption typically takes a long time, both because of the continuing hold of these psychic beliefs on people, and because many countries which partner with France for adoption do not permit children to be matched with LGBT+ people/couples. It is estimated that only 200 same-sex parenting families have succeeded in adopting since 2013.[50]

---

48. One papa, one mama, we won't lie to children.
49. No to fictional filiation.
50. Marine Delrue, 'Ten Years of Same-Sex Marriage in France, in Graphs,' *Le Monde*, 24 April 2023, accessed 26 April 2024, https://www.lemonde.fr/en/france/article/2023/04/23/ten-years-of-same-sex-marriage-in-france-in-graphs_6023942_7.html

Thirteen Ways of Looking at a Judgment

I

among volumes of legal judgments

none are transcendent

objective or universal

II

language of the victims

is awkward, rank and damp

haunted by ghosts of miscarriage

III

one judgment swirls in the wind

disembodied and disappearing

IV

trees are growing

judges dress

V

black shoes glisten

white wigs

blue gowns

matching white lace collars

VI

the lesbian wears

a pink tutu

fake snakeskin stilettos

yellow eyeshadow

to match

VII

homosexual

bull dagger

boi

femme

invert

VIII

a child

will have no family image

a child

will be unstable and maladjusted

IX

outside the Grand Chamber

the mood in the streets

is changing

shadows fall

a blackbird squawks

X

days become queer

damages to the dyke

a small part of the show

XI

the lesbian is

too old to adopt a child is

bankrupt, is

legal history

XII

the judgment sits in a tree

XIII

a blackbird abandons its nest

Ode to The Judges of the Grand Chamber

O Christos   hold me in your paper arms

O Nicolas   sync our lips

O Jean-Paul this salty tongue leaks

O Boštjan   your words secrete imaginary milk

O Danuté   wipe me clean

O Peer   a puppet speaks

O Françoise your inky eyes

O Loukis   my narrow hips

O Ireneu   bless our anatomies

O Riza   your queer anxieties

O Sverre   behold this smoke

O Mindia   myths that twist and bulge

O Antonella your thick curls

O Elisabeth don't forget

O Elisabet we are sick

O Egbert   evangelist brother

O Dragoljub our bodies our lot

Erasure

expose   risks

unclear   unspoken

ambiguity   risk

rejected.   extreme,   rejection   rejection

A Field of Mothers

Once upon a time, there was a mother,

her great limbs sheltered the children

in summer like a canopy of leaves, &

a patchwork blanket sewn by her mother

and her mother before, squares of worn

cotton & corduroy, blues & browns, held

the weight of her baking. Another mother

wandered restless through knee-high grass,

gathering frogs and toads, to sketch their skin

in a notebook packed with dried beech, maple

& oak, a host of wildflowers, stork's bill,

meadow vetchling, forget-me-knots, pressed

between thick paper leaves, preserved worlds.

A third mother climbed trees, scraping her knees,

calling to the children from high branches,

a lighthouse, *careful, don't fall, you can see*

the island from here. Her light bounced

from rock to wave, keeping the darkness safe.

Together they grew a knot of roots, tethered

leaves, tendrils of their days, gentle winds

dispersing their inheritance, like seeds.

Staking A Claim

was it irresistible   the pull of a win

forms to live in   official din

was it the fizz   a child's cry   wick

of your rage   a broken wing,

or was it a road you glimpsed, a track,

a fingertip found on a map,

or was it the stain of your menstrual blood

or a fly you heard buzz   in your brain?

17

McD v L and M (Ireland):
The Case for Procreative Liberty for LGBT+ Families

Claire O'Connell (Judgment) and James Rooney (Commentary)

Introduction

Our contribution to this collection is a critical re-examination and re-imagination of the Irish decision in *McD v L*, where the Supreme Court held a sperm donor had greater rights over a child conceived with his sperm than a child's non-genetic, intended mother.[1] I provide a background to the judgment, situating it within Irish constitutional jurisprudence on family rights. I also give a summary of the Supreme Court's decision and O'Connell J's reimagined dissent, before providing additional commentary on the decision.

Case History

The first McD v L Case

Briefly stated, *McD v L* concerns a long-running guardianship dispute between a lesbian couple ('L' and 'M') and a gay man ('McD'), the sperm donor in the conception of their first child ('HL').[2] Whilst McD was a friend of L and M's prior to HL's conception, they were not especially close, and he signed a (legally unenforceable) contract to not take on any parenting role and instead to be a 'favourite uncle' to HL.[3] However, McD sought an increasingly parental role with greater access and decision-making over HL in breach of the prior agreement,[4] ultimately culminating in him going to court to seek legal recognition as a guardian of HL.

After the birth, L, the gestational mother, became unwell and wished to travel with M and HL to Australia, where her family were based. In March 2007, two days before their scheduled departure, McD was granted an injunction from the High Court

---

1. *McD v L* [2010] 2 IR 199.
2. For an overview of the decision, see also Andrea Mulligan, 'Constitutional Parenthood in the Age of Assisted Reproduction,' *Irish Jurist* 51/1 (2014), 90.
3. [2010] 2 IR 199, [14].
4. [2010] 2 IR 199, [37].

prohibiting the removal of HL from the jurisdiction.[5] This injunction was granted as McD had an arguable case that he, as sperm donor, *could* acquire guardianship rights over HL.[6] As moving HL to Australia without McD's permission would negate his ability to acquire guardianship, the High Court prevented HL's removal from Ireland, and appointed a child psychiatrist, Dr Gerard Byrne, to monitor interactions between HL and McD, and to assess whether the best interests of the child lay in McD being made a guardian.

L and M appealed this injunction to the Supreme Court, which concluded McD had an arguable case that, as sperm donor and thereby 'biological father' of HL, he had a right to have his guardianship claim processed.[7] Having prohibited the removal of HL to Australia, the matter was remitted back to the High Court, to determine whether McD should be appointed as a guardian.

The Second McD v L Case in the High Court

In determining the legal standing of L and M on the one hand, and McD on the other, the High Court engaged with the rights of parents under the Constitution of Ireland.[8] Article 41.1 of the Constitution states: '[t]he State recognises the Family as the natural and primary unit group of society' and 'guarantees to protect the Family in its constitution and authority.'[9] Later in Article 41, '[t]he State pledges itself to guard with special care the institution of Marriage, on which the Family is founded, and to protect it against attack.'[10] Interpreting these provisions alongside one another, the Supreme Court found that the family which is protected under the Constitution is exclusively the *marital* family which, prior to 2015, meant exclusively heterosexual families.[11]

The Supreme Court has also found additional, unenumerated constitutional rights of unmarried 'natural mothers to the custody and care of her child,'[12] as well as much less expansive rights of natural fathers to seek access to or guardianship of their child.[13]

---

5. *McD v L* [2007] IESC 28.
6. S.6A of the Guardianship of Infants Act, 1964, as amended, provides, '*where the father and mother of an infant have not married each other, the Court may on the application of the father, by order appoint him to be the guardian of the infant.*'
7. [2007] IESC 28 at [32].
8. Hereinafter 'The Constitution.'
9. Article 41.1.1° of the Constitution of Ireland, 1937 (capitalisations in original text).
10. Article 41.1.3° of the Constitution of Ireland, 1937 (capitalisations in original text).
11. In *The State (Nicolaou) v An Bord Uchtála* [1966] IR 1R 567, the Supreme Court held at 643 that 'the family referred to in [Article 41] is the family which is founded on the institution of marriage.' Indeed, 'to award equal constitutional protection to the family founded on marriage and the "family" founded on an extra-marital union would in effect be a disregard of the pledge which the State gives in Article 41.3.1 to guard with special care the institution of marriage.' This judgment was cited affirmatively in *McD v L* [2010] 2 IR 199, [142]-[143].
12. [1966] IR 567, 644. See also *G v An Bord Uchtála* [1980] IR 32, and Máiréad Enright, 'Involuntary Patriotism: Judgment, Women and National Identity on the Island of Ireland,' in *Northern/Irish Feminist Judgments: Judges' Troubles and the Gendered Politics of Identity*, eds. Máiréad Enright, Julie McCandless and Aoife O'Donoghue (Dublin: Bloomsbury, 2017), 27.
13. [1966] IR 567, 644.

The variation in rights protection between unmarried fathers and mothers is unambiguously grounded upon an understanding by the Courts that women are preternaturally maternal and thereby the natural custodian of children, whereas, per the Supreme Court:

> it is rare for a natural father to take any interest in his offspring [particularly] when it is considered that an illegitimate child may be begotten by an act of rape, by a callous seduction or by an act of casual commerce by a man with a woman.[14]

This dictum on the rights of unmarried fathers over their children has never been overturned, and was applied affirmatively by the Supreme Court as recently as 2021.[15] It is in the context of this understanding of families as composed of either heterosexual married couples, or unmarried relationships between men and women, that the Court came to decide *McD v L*. Hedigan J in the High Court concluded the unit of L and M and their son could not constitute a 'family' under the Constitution, as they were unmarried and could not be married. As the genetic and gestational – and thereby, in the Court's language, the 'natural' – mother, Hedigan J found L was the only lawful parent of HL.[16] Hedigan J also held McD as the sperm donor was the natural father, and thereby entitled to seek guardianship.[17] However, Hedigan J held this right to seek guardianship had to be balanced against the importance of maintaining the integrity of the 'de facto family' of HL with his mothers.[18] This concept of a *de facto family* had not previously been considered in Irish law, and in substantiating this concept, Hedigan J relied upon Article 8 jurisprudence of the European Court on Human Rights,[19] particularly *Keegan v Ireland*,[20] and *X, Y, and Z v United Kingdom*.[21]

Hedigan J placed weight upon the report of Dr Byrne, who inveighed against guardianship or access rights for McD, and found McD 'should not have any role that gives him rights that could interfere with the child's family life with the respondents.'[22] With reference to these conclusions, Hedigan J found against McD, holding that granting him guardianship would compromise the integrity of the 'de facto family' unit.[23] As O'Shea noted, 'in recognising the lesbian couple as a family, Hedigan J did not see the need to also find a place for the father's relationship with the child.'[24] McD appealed against this judgment to the Supreme Court.

---

14. [1966] IR 567, 641.

15. *In Re JJ* [2021] IESC 1.

16. [2010] 2 IR 199, [94].

17. [2010] 2 IR 199, [100].

18. [2010] 2 IR 199, [106]-[122].

19. Hereinafter, 'the ECtHR' or 'Strasbourg.'

20. *Keegan v Ireland* (1994) 18 EHRR 342.

21. *X, Y and Z v United Kingdom* (1997) 24 EHRR 143.

22. [2010] 2 IR 199, [128].

23. [2010] 2 IR 199, [143].

24. Nykol O'Shea, 'Can Ireland's Constitution Remain Premised on the "Inalienable" Protection of the Marital Family Unit Without Continuing to Fail its International Obligations on the Rights of the Child,' *Irish Journal of Family Law* 15/4 (2012), 87.

The Second McD v L Case in the Supreme Court

The Supreme Court, in the decision to which O'Connell J has given her dissent below, held that 'there is no institution in Ireland of a de facto family' deserving of legal recognition.[25] The Supreme Court held Hedigan J erred in relying on Strasbourg's jurisprudence, given the ECHR is incorporated on a sub-constitutional level in Ireland. Furthermore, the Supreme Court found that 'the trial judge erred in not giving sufficient weight to the status of the applicant as the father of the child' and gave undue weight to the report of Dr Byrne.[26] In determining whether it was in HL's best interests to have McD instated as a guardian, the Supreme Court placed greater reliance on 'the natural and, in a sense, perfectly human excitement on the part of the applicant at the birth of what he regarded as and *what was in fact his own child*.'[27] According to Fennelly J:

> The blood link, as a matter of almost universal experience, exerts a powerful influence on people. The applicant, in the present case, stands as proof that participation in the limited role of sperm donor under the terms of a restrictive agreement does not prevent the development of unforeseen but powerful paternal instincts.[28]

Alongside this elevation of the parental claim of McD, the Supreme Court denied any legal recognition to the relationship between HL and M, his non-genetic mother:

> The respondents do not form a de facto family in Irish law. The first respondent, as the mother of the child, has a natural right guaranteed by the Constitution to his custody and to look after his general care, his nurture, his physical and moral wellbeing and his education, in every respect. The child has corresponding rights as a human person to those benefits. *The second respondent has no legally or constitutionally recognisable family relationship with the child.*[29]

Through this, the Supreme Court adjudicated upon the matter as if HL was not being raised by two women at all, but by one woman whose parentage of her child had to be considered alongside the potential guardianship role of the child's father.[30] Having reversed Hedigan J's decision, the Supreme Court once again remitted the matter back to the High Court. On remittal, Hedigan J ordered that McD was entitled to access to, but not guardianship, of HL.[31] Further:

> the respondents will encourage HL to develop friendly relations with the applicant on the basis of 'a favourite uncle' type of relationship. At their discretion, when they consider it age appropriate, the respondents will reveal to HL that the applicant is his biological father.[32]

---

25. [2010] 2 IR 199, [146].
26. [2010] 2 IR 199, [126].
27. [2010] 2 IR 199, [195] (emphasis added).
28. [2010] 2 IR 199, [304].
29. [2010] 2 IR 199, [338] (emphasis added).
30. As Tobin noted, 'the Supreme Court's decision makes it clear that if a female same-sex couple uses sperm from a known donor to conceive a child at home, then the known donor will be treated in law as being akin to any other natural unmarried father, with the rights that accompany that status.' Brian Tobin, 'Regulating Non-Clinical Donor-Assisted Human Reproduction in Ireland,' *Irish Jurist* (2018), 179.
31. *McD v L* [2010] IEHC 120.
32. [2010] IEHC 120, [10].

In return, McD was ordered:

> to play the role of 'favourite uncle' until the true nature of his relationship is revealed to HL. He will not reveal to HL his biological paternity and agrees to defer to the respondents in their choice of timing to make that revelation.

McD was further ordered to seek no paternal role in HL's upbringing and to acknowledge and 'respect the *familial integrity* of the respondents and HL.'[33]

The Judgment Reimagined

O'Connell J strongly dissents from the decision of her colleagues on four main points. First, O'Connell J affirms the reliance placed by Hedigan J on Dr Byrne's report, especially given the absence of statutory guidance contradicting such reliance. Second, O'Connell J considers Hedigan J to have correctly weighted the *'blood link'* between McD and HL, given the absence of any relationship between McD and the child, and the breakdown of relationship between McD and the child's mothers. To O'Connell J, the manifest 'loving, supportive, and consistent nurturing that the Respondents offer the child' merits greater recognition than the blood link between the child and McD. In this, O'Connell J inverts the biologically-determinist reasoning of the Supreme Court that a 'natural father' must, by virtue of their blood link, be entitled to make a claim over H, unlike HL's mother M, who has no biological link to her son.

Third, O'Connell J critiques the majority's assessment that relying on European Court of Human Rights (ECtHR) jurisprudence was inappropriate, finding instead that Hedigan J gave appropriate weight to Strasbourg case law. Finally, and perhaps most significantly, O'Connell J departed from her colleagues in her interpretation of the family rights protections contained within the Constitution. Citing Supreme Court precedent placing value on sexual privacy, O'Connell J finds a right to procreative liberty is unenumerated and latent within the Constitution. On the basis of this right, O'Connell J affirms the decision of Hedigan J, and refuses guardianship or access rights to McD.

Commentary

Queer people throughout history have raised families, in almost all instances without legal protection or recognition – and indeed, in defiance of legal prescriptions on who can or cannot parent. Whilst L and M are perhaps the most high profile lesbian couple to have had their roles as parents questioned by the courts in Ireland, they are far from the first.[34] In this case, the Supreme Court imposed on a pair of lesbian parents

---

33. [2010] IEHC 120, [11] (emphasis added).
34. Per McDonagh, 'in Ireland and England there had been a number of cases [in the 1980s] where divorced women have wanted to retain custody of their own children. Usually, in these countries women are awarded custody of their children, because women usually have responsibility for children. But if a woman is a lesbian, the usual procedure is suddenly reversed. Then it is considered better for the children if the father is given custody.' Patrick McDonagh, *Gay and Lesbian Activism in the Republic of Ireland* (Dublin: Bloomsbury 2021), 52.

who had – with informed consent by the father, expressly and in writing – excluded the 'natural father' from any parenting role, a biologically-determinist understanding of who can be a parent. Illustrative of this, only L is ever termed HL's 'mother' in the Supreme Court judgment, with M termed 'the Second Respondent.' This approach is based upon a heteronormative understanding of the family as based on mothers and fathers which necessarily excluded L and M.

In the years since *McD v L*, several significant changes have been made in regards the recognition of queer relationships in Ireland. The most high-profile change was the amendment to the Constitution to permit same-sex marriage, after an almost 2:1 popular vote in favour in 2015.[35] This change has entitled same-sex married parents to the same family rights over their children as heterosexual married parents.[36] Alongside this, the Children and Family Relationships Act 2015 provided, for the first time, a legal process whereby some non-gestational mothers can be registered as parents on their child's birth certificate. For children born before 4 May 2020, this process of recognition was only available if their sperm donor was anonymous. As Tobin noted, 'the requirement that the gamete donor must be unknown to the parties respects the decision in *McD v L* where the Supreme Court held that a known donor has rights akin to a natural parent.'[37] Thus, whilst certainly a positive development, this Act only permits recognition of non-gestational mothers in circumstances so narrow that M would still be unable to make use of this process to be recognized as HL's mother.

Even with the considerable social progress for LGBT+ parents in Ireland since *McD v L*, the legal and constitutional understanding of 'parenthood' in Ireland remains grounded in an assumption that the 'ideal' or 'normal' family is heterosexual.[38] Only if the sperm donor is anonymous, and thereby the possibility of a relationship between the child and the donor is foreclosed, could both of HL's mothers be recognised as such under the law. As well as the expressive harm this erasure causes, this is more importantly a bad outcome for children, as it leaves parents such as M in a 'legal half world,' in which they are not authorised to make important decisions on behalf of their own children.[39] In contrast to this, in the judgment provided here, O'Connell J offers us an alternative jurisprudence, one in which 'loving, supportive and consistent nurturing' is considered parenthood worthy of greater legal recognition than the act of donating sperm.

---

35. Article 41.4 of the Constitution of Ireland, 1937 now states: 'Marriage may be contracted in accordance with law by two persons without distinction as to their sex.'

36. And, as noted above, as a married couple, to greater protection than unmarried parents, including unmarried heterosexual parents. Per Hogan, in *McD*, 'the Supreme Court's broad rejection of the concept of a de facto family in Irish law is one which applies to both heterosexual and gay people.' See, also, Claire Hogan, '*JMcD v PL and BM* Sperm Donor Fathers and De Facto Families,' *Irish Journal of Family Law* 13/4 (2010), 83.

37. Brian Tobin, 'Assisted Reproductive Techniques and Irish Law: No Child Left Behind?,' *Irish Jurist* 64 (2020), 138, 142.

38. Lydia Bracken, 'Challenging Normative Constructions of Parentage in Ireland,' *Journal of Social Welfare and Family Law* 39(3) (2017), 316. See also Jenni Millbank, 'Reproductive Outsiders – the perils and disruptive potential of reproductive coalitions,' in *Queer Theory, Law Culture and Empire*, eds. Robert Lecky and Kim Brooks (London: Routledge, 2010).

39. Per O'Donnell J in *MR v An tArd Chláraitheoir* [2014] IESC 60, [211].

J McD v PL and BM [2010] 2 IR 199

RECORD NO. 26M/2007

THE SUPREME COURT

IN THE MATTER OF THE GUARDIANSHIP OF INFANTS ACT 1964,
IN THE MATTER OF THE FAMILY LAW ACT 1995, IN THE MATTER
OF THE CHILD ABDUCTION AND ENFORCEMENT OF CUSTODY
ORDER ACT 1991 AND IN THE MATTER OF HL, AN INFANT

BETWEEN

J MCD

APPELLANT

AND
PL AND BM

RESPONDENTS

AND
THE ATTORNEY GENERAL

NOTICE PARTY

Dissenting Judgment of Mx Justice O'Connell delivered on the 10th of December 2009.

Facts and Issues

The facts arising within this case begin with an agreement between the Appellant and the Respondents, in circumstances where the Appellant agreed to act as a sperm donor for the Respondents who are in a committed and loving same-sex female relationship. This relationship was solemnized by a civil union in the United Kingdom in 2006. Their child was born on 2 May 2006.

The role to be played by the Appellant was agreed between the parties and intended to be that of a 'favourite uncle,' with his part in the child's conception to be disclosed to the child at the discretion of the Respondents. Similarly, access between the Appellant and the child was to be at the discretion of the Respondents.

The agreement between the parties was made in the absence of any legislative framework in relation to donor insemination and resulting parentage. As a result, the Appellant, by virtue of his gamete donation, is the child's legal father under Irish law. Notably, there is no dispute between the parties that the Appellant is in fact the child's genetic father.

The application before this Court is an appeal in respect of the High Court's decision to refuse the Appellant's claims for guardianship and access to the child under section 6A and section 11(2)(a) of the Guardianship of Infants Act 1964 [hereinafter 'the 1964 Act'] respectively. A summary of the key issues to be determined by this Court is as follows:

1. The enforceability of a private agreement to opt out of or regulate parentage,
2. The weight to be attached by the Court to a section 47 Report,
3. The correlation of rights as they apply between the mother, sperm donor, and child in Irish law,
4. The status of the "*de facto*" family in Irish law, and
5. The application of the European Convention on Human Rights Act 2003.

Reservations with the Majority Judgment

It is tempting to simply relay each sentiment expressed by the learned trial judge in the High Court with my endorsement, given the considered nature of the decision rendered. However, my colleagues have expressed sentiments in relation to the High Court findings that I find do not reflect the positions held by Hedigan J and, in doing so, cause them to allow the appeal. For that reason, I will briefly and expressly demonstrate where I believe the majority have erred in finding fault with the judgment in the High Court. Having had the benefit of the judgments of my colleagues, I note that there exist three primary and repeating issues taken with the judgment of the learned High Court judge.

The Section 47 Report

The first is the weight he attaches to the section 47 report authored by the court appointed psychiatrist, Dr Gerard Byrne. Specifically, Denham J has found disfavour with the finding of the trial judge that 'save for grave reasons again, which I think the court should set out clearly, the s. 47 report ought to be accepted in its recommendations.' She believes that such a finding is erroneous and would alter the role of the Court. Similarly, Murray CJ has described Hedigan J as having afforded 'undue weight' to the section 47 report.

Respectfully, I must disagree. As the learned trial judge noted, there is no statutory guidance or otherwise in relation to the weight attaching to the section 47 report. The role of the assessor often involves a psychological or psychiatric component or an assessment of the attachment of the child to either parent. Such matters are uniquely within the expertise of the assessor and not the Court. The parties are also entitled to engage a second opinion and cross-examine the assessor on their recommendations and other points of contention. The Court obtains the benefit of this challenge and analysis. This report and its recommendations are often the key independent source of evidence in a contested application for guardianship, custody, or access.

I can find nothing in the judgment of Hedigan J that removes the power of the Court to act as final arbiter, having considered the section 47 report, together with the evidence and all other relevant factors. The findings of the learned trial judge pose no obstacle to the Court in diverting from the recommendations of the report where it deems it necessary, and, as a matter of fair procedures, acknowledges the duty imposed on the Court to give reasons for such diversions.

Insufficient Weight Being Attached to the Blood Link

The second issue of concern among my learned colleagues is the learned trial judge affording insufficient weight to the status of the Appellant as the father of the child. This position is taken by Denham J and endorsed by both Murray CJ and Geoghegan J. In the first instance, I cannot agree with my learned colleagues that disproportionate weight was placed on any particular factor but, more to the point, I do not believe it is the task of this Court to critique the weight attached to the various relevant factors by the learned trial judge, save any conflict with wider constitutional principles and protections. In this regard, I note with approval the authorities cited by Hedigan J in establishing the constitutional parameters to consider, namely that of the unmarried mother and the unmarried father in Irish law, the latter of which I will discuss further below.

The applications brought before the High Court are subject to one key principle, contained within section 3 of the 1964 Act:

> Where in any proceedings before any court the custody, guardianship or upbringing of a child
> … is in question, the court, in deciding that question, shall regard the welfare of the child as
> the first and paramount consideration.

The impact of this principle in the case at hand is that the learned trial judge had considerable discretion to determine where the welfare of the child lies, and what weight to attribute to any particular substantive factor found within the substantial evidence presented. While all relevant factors must be considered to some degree, the weight attached to such factors is for the trial judge to determine having regard to the circumstances of the case as a whole, and primarily as they relate to the child's welfare. To focus too readily on the blood link present in this case would be to disproportionately focus on the adult Appellant, when the first and paramount consideration is the welfare of the child. In this regard, I would also reiterate the finding of Finlay CJ in *JK v VW* [1989] 2 IR 437 at p. 447 that:

> The blood link between the infant and the father and the possibility for the infant to have the
> benefit of the guardianship by and the society of its father is one of many factors which may
> be viewed by the court as relevant to its welfare.

This was reiterated by Hamilton CJ in *WOR v EH* [1996] 2 IR 248 at 269:

> The blood link between the natural father and the children will be one of the many factors
> for the judge to consider, and the weight it will be given will depend on the circumstances as
> a whole.

A summary of the key factors considered by the learned trial judge are usefully set out in paragraph 273 of the judgment of Fennelly J. Therefore, I do not deem it necessary to reiterate them here. I do wish, however, to expand upon the role of the Appellant and the impact of the blood link.

Firstly, I note that the Appellant's status as an unmarried father is not a constitution-ally protected legal status. His rights are statutory only, and the determination by this Court of his statutory rights to guardianship and access are subject to the welfare of the child. It is also correct to say that the blood link, or the genetic link, upon which a father's legal parentage is established, has been a historically malleable concept, based on the exact circumstances of the case. This has been borne out by the prescription by the Irish courts of a spectrum of significance in relation to the blood link by itself in *JK v VW* [1989] 2 IR 437, where this Court held at p 447 that:

> The range of variation would, I am satisfied, extend from the situation of the father of a child conceived as the result of a casual intercourse, where the rights might well be so minimal as practically to be non-existent, to the situation of a child born as the result of a stable and established relationship and nurtured at the commencement of his life by his father and mother in a situation bearing nearly all of the characteristics of a constitutionally protected family, when the rights would be very extensive indeed.

The Court in *JK* concluded that the extent and character of the rights of the genetic father accrue from the relationship with the child. It held that the blood link is of small weight and would not be a determining factor if considered in the absence of other factors beneficial to the children and in the presence of factors negative to the children's welfare.

In the first instance, I find that the 'sperm donor' is a status that now falls within the spectrum of fathers' rights and agree in full with paragraphs 202-204 of the judg-ment of Geoghegan J in this regard. Sperm donors are characterised by the voluntary contribution of their gamete to the planned conception by others and their agreement prior to conception to abdicate any parental role in relation to the child.

In turning to consider the specific facts of this case, I note that the child has been found to have formed no attachment or bond with the Appellant. The Appellant had no prior relationship with the child's mother and the nature of the acquaintance between the parties was contractual. Each action taken by the Respondents was with a view to set boundaries, to limit the expectation of any parental role, and to instil the knowledge in the Appellant to accept the restricted role into which he volunteered to step. I find that these circumstances set the blood link arising in this case at the lowest possible end of the spectrum, worthy of little to no weight, save for in the context of the child's identity.

Therefore, I cannot find any fault with the trial judge's assessment of, and conclu-sions on, the lack of the Appellant's constitutional status, nor do I find any difficulty in his extensive assessment, or the weight he attaches to the individual circumstances of the case, including the blood link, in reaching his determination.

The European Convention on Human Rights and De Facto Families

The third factor proposed by my learned colleagues in setting aside the decision of the High Court and allowing the appeal was the perception that Hedigan J unlawfully and without authority:

a. Directly applied and/or gave Direct Effect to Article 8 of the European Convention on Human Rights (the ECHR) in Irish law.
b. Conferred the status of "family" on the Respondents in Irish law.
c. Misapplied the European Convention on Human Rights Act 2003.

With all respect to my learned colleagues, I cannot agree with their assessment of the High Court judgment as it relates to these issues. The Chief Justice provides a commendable summary of the applicability of the ECHR in this jurisdiction together with the provisions of the 2003 Act. Regrettably, however, he, together with Denham and Fennelly JJ continue to de-contextualise the references of the learned High Court judge, and his application of Article 8.

For the sake of clarity, I shall set out, in summary form, the findings of the High Court in this regard:

1. The Second Respondents and their child constitute a *de facto* family, distinguishable from a constitutional family.
2. Irish constitutional law does not recognise either same sex or opposite sex *de facto* families. Nonetheless, *de facto* families consist of a status that has been recognised by the Supreme Court as having certain rights and duties, albeit not a constitutional status.
3. Domestic courts have the primary obligation to interpret and apply the ECHR but the European Court of Human Rights (ECtHR) is primarily a supervisory body and is subsidiary to the national systems safeguarding human rights.
4. The Constitution prevails in Ireland over the ECHR and, therefore, any rights that the Court finds to arise under the ECHR can only be applied by the Court absent a constitutional conflict.
5. If a case was taken to the ECtHR, the Court, having had regard to the committed relationship and close personal ties between the Respondents, would recognise them as a *de facto* family under Article 8 of the ECHR.
6. The Respondents and the child enjoying a *de facto* family is a factor which must be considered in determining where the welfare of the child lies.

I cannot find a singular fault with such conclusions, and I would add that the learned High Court judge at no point bestowed a legal status upon the Respondents and the child as a unit, beyond the fact that such a unit must be considered within the Court's subjective and discretionary determination of the child's welfare. Hedigan J did not equate family life under Article 8 to the 'protection of the natural primary and fundamental unit group of society' under Article 41. He did not find any breach of the parties' rights under the ECHR, nor did he make a declaration of incompatibility. He simply, as a former member of the ECtHR for a period of nine years, explored the parameters of judicial discretion with rights-based thinking.

Finally, Murray CJ and Fennelly J refer to the fact that Hedigan J did not identify the specific provision or rule of law that he was interpreting when applying the ECHR. My opinion is that this was so plain on the face of the High Court judgment so as to negate any need for explicit citation. It is evident from the judgment of the High Court that the sole consideration of Hedigan J lay within section 3 of the 1964 Act in determining how the welfare of the child could be best served. In this regard, Hedigan J clearly and effectively acted within the confines of the discretion afforded to him under section 3 of the 1964 Act and the boundaries imposed on him by the 2003 Act.

Dissenting Judgment

While my learned colleagues take issue with the trial judge's perceived direct application of the ECHR, particularly in light of the lack of necessity of same in arriving at his conclusions, I believe the only potential for error amidst the trial judge's considered and humane judgment was that he did not base his assertions slightly closer to home. Article 40.3.1 of the Constitution protects a number of unenumerated personal rights that are recognised and declared, as opposed to conferred, by the Superior Courts of Ireland. Amongst these rights is the right to marital privacy as espoused by Walsh J in the judgment in *McGee v Attorney General* [1974] IR 284. In this case, Walsh J held that:

> the sexual life of a husband and wife is of necessity and by its nature an area of particular privacy. If the husband and wife decide to limit their family or to avoid having children by use of contraceptives, it is a matter peculiarly within the joint decision of the husband and wife and one into which the State cannot intrude unless its intrusion can be justified by the exigencies of the common good ... it is outside the authority of the State to endeavour to intrude into the privacy of the husband and wife relationship for the sake of imposing a code of private morality upon that husband and wife which they do not desire.

This case took place in 1974 and revolved around the use of contraception within the marital family, to control the expansion of one's family. Today, it is common case that contraception is legally obtainable by unmarried individuals either for casual encounters or those in committed relationships. It is a tool for independence, autonomy, and agency. It is used to delimit the reproduction of persons who wish to express and enjoy their sexual freedom without necessarily procreating. In this manner, the right to obtain and use contraception safe from state intervention is certainly encompassed within an individual's right to privacy in sexual matters under Article 40.3.1, found by the majority of this Court in *McGee* to constitute a personal right. It is my view that this tool of expression, and of the dignity in the realisation of reproductive choices, has a counterpart within the right to privacy and that is the right of procreative liberty. In this regard I would echo the judgment of Griffin J within the same case in observing that 'what more personal right could there be in a citizen than the right to determine in marriage his attitude and resolve his mode of life concerning the procreation of children.'

While Griffin J refers to such determination arising in the context of marriage, I would also refer to the judgment of Costello J in *Murray v Ireland* [1991] ILRM 465, wherein the right to beget a child, procreate, and resolve matters relating to the procreation of children was held to be a personal right under Article 40.3.1, as opposed to a right encompassed within Article 41, applying only to married couples.

The Respondents in this case are a same-sex female couple who have taken the courageous step to love one another. This, I am certain, they are entitled to do without the judgment, imposition, or interference of the institutions which govern this State. Their relationship naturally creates a private universe onto themselves within the ether of modern day living. It is safe, it is secure, and it is theirs.

The Respondents decided to grow their universe to include a child. However, their child could not have been formed without a third party, and without risk, given the lack of protections offered to their family by the legislature. This was a biological necessity which they did not choose. Without a best practice model guiding couples towards a pathway to parentage, any person engaging in assisted human reproduction in this country is in a legislative lacuna with neither incentives nor deterrents in balancing the rights of those involved. The couple in this case knew this. The Respondents knew that by introducing a known donor into their lives, and into the conception of their child, they ran the risk of upsetting their own personal and peaceful familial eco-system. The Respondents could have obtained a sperm sample online through several unregulated websites or international sperm banks. Instead, they chose to ensure that their child would have their right to identity vindicated, that the child would know their genetic origins and have access to a biological progenitor should they wish.

At this juncture, it is important to take note of the novel and formidable aspects of assisted human reproduction, namely the fact that roles, rights, and responsibilities can be considered and opted into by the parties involved, preceding, as opposed to arising from, a set of inescapable circumstances. I find that this aspect of assisted human reproduction is transformative in terms of the opposing rights that generally arise within a child's conception, such as those of the marital family, unmarried mother, or father. The Appellant in this case is a single man who was approached by the Respondents with the intention of becoming a sperm donor. The Respondents provided him with a written contract setting out the roles and obligations of each party to the agreement. There is a consensus among the learned trial judge and my learned colleagues that such an agreement would only be enforceable insofar as it vindicated the rights of the child. I would add that any agreement that imposes finality in terms of the welfare, rights, and interests of a child and impedes recourse to independent adjudication process is similarly unenforceable. The final arbiter of the child's welfare is the Court.

The agreement between the parties was drafted by the Respondents and reviewed by the Appellant prior to conception. It is within the autonomy and agency of any individual in the place of the Appellant to walk away from this agreement, to revoke his consent prior to any insemination or embryo formation, and to relieve himself of any and all unwanted burdens. This is evidenced by the Appellant availing of such relief, in changing his mind, before eventually deciding to proceed. The Appellant also availed of the opportunity to amend the agreement and impose his own conditions.

The Respondents provided the Appellant with reading materials. His evidence is that he did not read these extensively. I can only conclude that any such lack of preparation arises from the Appellant's failing as opposed to any inadequacies in the careful safeguards imposed by the Respondents. The Respondents sought that the Appellant engage in medical screening, and he obliged, sharing his results with them once obtained.

I find the learned trial judge's description of these events, the conflicts in the parties' evidence, and his concluding opinions as to the credibility of same, to be comprehensive, reasonable, and rational. Having reviewed the transcripts, it is clear that the Appellant offered his free, full, and informed consent to becoming a 'favourite uncle' to the child; a person who is known to the child and involved in their life to the extent facilitated by the Respondents, but not fulfilling a paternal role.

I note from my learned colleagues' judgments that some emphasis is placed upon the Appellant's natural and understandable desire, upon seeing the child, to become more involved in their life. I find that such an inference negates the clear ability of the Appellant to consider the risk, if not the likelihood, of such an emotional response, prior to the conception of the child. While I agree that there exists an innate connection between persons and children with whom they share a genetic link, I cannot accept that such a bond was unforeseen or unavoidable. Nor do I find that such a foreseeable bond justifies the level of interference with the family life of conscientious parents, such as the Respondents.

I further believe that this approach does not pay sufficient attentiveness to the natural desire of the Respondents and their entitlement to resolve matters relating to the procreation of their child within the auspices of their right to procreative liberty, which I have deemed to be a personal right under Article 40.3.1. I find that this right enables an individual, either by themselves, or together with their partner, to shape and determine the nature of their child's conception insofar as such does not breach the constitutional or fundamental rights of another. I further note that this right is the right of the individual, and not only the individual who can contribute a genetic or gestational link to the child, but all individuals who responsibly exercise their right to create their family through assisted human reproduction. In addition, I find that within this right exists a corresponding duty on the State to respect and recognise the resulting parentage arising from such efforts.

While the exact scope of this right is a living and breathable concept, in this case, I see it as a vital right of those who engage in assisted human reproduction - a process engaged prior to the conception of the child. While I do not wish to enter a realm of such level of prescription as to be considered to be creating law, it seems incumbent upon me, in setting out this right, to adequately prescribe loose parameters. Such parameters may be expanded or restricted within the gift of the legislature who will be uniquely placed to propose and implement specific criteria in this regard. Insofar as the rights of others can be stated within the context of this case, I find that a high standard should be imposed before an interference with the right to procreative liberty can be justified, particularly in circumstances like the present ones: the person asserting the right has vindicated both the child's identity in ensuring that the child can identify their gamete donor, and the right of a person not to parent a child in ensuring that the agreement of an individual to act as a donor, or indeed a surrogate, is borne from voluntary and informed consent.

The impact of such a constitutional right in this case is that it cannot be disregarded in its entirety and, moreover, significant weight must be attached to it in the determination by the Court under section 3 of the 1964 Act, given the voluntary and proactive efforts made by the Respondents in safeguarding the process of conception. In determining the weight to be attached to this right, within a consideration of the welfare of the child, I make the following observations:

1. The Respondents could not have reasonably done more to properly and attentively facilitate their child's conception. I would reiterate the belief of the learned High Court judge that their approach was both 'thoroughly practical and intelligent.'
2. The final contract included a provision that the Appellant would be consulted in respect of the child's testamentary guardianship arrangements in the event of the death of both of the Respondents. The Appellant did not seek to act as the testamentary guardian of the child at any point prior to the birth of the child.
3. The relationship between the parties was one that was mired by distrust, betrayal, and discomfort. The Appellant lacked a considerable level of tact, sensitivity and insight in his interference with the couple in the early life of their child. In this regard, I note the tactless comments of his dinner accompaniment, the eager attempts of the Appellant to impose himself on the Respondents' family life shortly after the birth, the self-invitations, and the increasing use of legalistic language.
4. The relationship of the Respondents became strained and disrupted as a result of the increasing level of involvement sought by the Appellant.

Taken together, these observations demonstrate the most severe interference with the right of the Respondents to have their procreative liberty respected. This severity is borne from the high standard of preparations and safeguards on behalf of the Respondents and the corresponding thwarting of the agreement by the Appellant in a manner that impacted the right of the child to the peaceful enjoyment of their familial environment.

Furthermore, I am conscious of the chilling effect this judgment may have if a sperm donor who intended and consented to act as a 'favourite uncle' only, was treated in Irish law for the same intents and purposes as a father who was at all times intent on parenting his child. This would naturally result in the use of anonymous sperm donors, thus denying the child a pathway to access their genetic origins. From this perspective alone, I would refuse the Appellant's reliefs for guardianship and access.

The result of my learned colleagues' judgment in allowing the appeal is that the agency and autonomy of individuals in entering into agreements prior to the conception of the child cannot be upheld. It ensures that no same-sex female couple can carefully and responsibly facilitate or plan the conception of their child to the exclusion of third parties, without interfering with their child's right to identity or risk third party interferences such as those claimed by the Appellant. I cannot, and do not, agree.

Finally, there is no question within these proceedings that the Second Respondent would accrue any rights by virtue of the refusal of the Appellant's reliefs. That is a matter for the legislature, not the judiciary. This can only be borne out through a standalone legislative framework that has yet to be established in Ireland, to the detriment of its people and specifically its children. It is also, as a result of this judgment, a legislative absence that falls foul of the constitutionally protected right to procreative freedom.

Reliefs

At present, the imposition of the Appellant in the lives of the Respondents in my opinion would naturally create a tension that is not worthy of a child's formative years. While the legislature has not yet seen fit to create such a framework, it is within my discretion pursuant to section 3 of the 1964 Act to take account of the loving, supportive, and consistent nurturing that the Respondents offer the child and to determine that the child's welfare, while in my hands, is best protected through the vindication of the child's right to identity and the right to the peaceful enjoyment of their familial environment, with due regard for the Respondents' constitutional right to procreative liberty.

I would therefore have made no order as to access or guardianship but would, however, have put the matter back in before the Court within a period of two years in order for an updated section 47 report to be furnished to the Court. I would have ordered that the assessor facilitate a discussion between the Respondents and the child in relation to the identity and the presently limited role of the Appellant. At that point, I would have sought the assessor to incorporate the child's views into their assessment as to whether the child wishes to have knowledge of the Appellant, resulting in limited access orders being considered if, and as, necessary.

18

Constitutional Court, Judgment no. 138, 14 April 2010 (Italy):

Finally, Even the Judges See that Same-Sex Couples Exist!

Yàdad De Guerre and Marica Moscati[1]

> To a precious friend

Introduction

'Cose da pazzi il matrimonio gay alla Corte Costituzionale.'[2] This is what an usher whispered while walking through the room of the hearing that was held on 23 March 2010 at Palazzo della Consulta in Rome – the house of the Constitutional Court of Italy – which dealt with whether Italian law infringed upon the rights of same-sex couples.[3]

This commentary starts with that quote for three reasons. First, it captures the striking peculiarity of that moment, that even visually showed the contradictions of the Italian context.[4] The formality of the proceeding, the sumptuosity of the room, the presence of the Army of Carabinieri,[5] the astonished laughs of some from the audience still lingering in the past, while the topic to be discussed during the hearing, the hopes of the couples in the room, the hugs amongst the lawyers, were all proudly and fiercely trying to push Italy into a future of acknowledgment, respect and visibility not only for couples, but for all LGBTIQ+ people in Italy. Indeed, as we will explain in more detail below, until 2008 (when same-sex marriage cases were dealt with by the Constitutional Court) talking about same-sex marriage was not on the main agenda of academics, lawyers or judges.

---

1. In this paper we prefer to use the names all our friends call us: Yàdad (Davide) and Marica (Maria Federica).
2. Authors' translation: 'This is crazy stuff – gay marriage at the Constitutional Court.'
3. Hereinafter 'the couples,' as the case dealt only with same-sex couples.
4. Maria Federica Moscati, *Pasolini's Italian Premonitions: Same-Sex Unions and the Law in Comparative Perspective* (London: Wildy, Simmonds & Hill, 2014).
5. The Army of Carabinieri is one of the Italian police forces (accessed 18 December 2023, www.carabinieri.it). Carabinieri are often employed during court hearings.

Second, the quote above gives a human dimension to what, at the time, was mainly portrayed as a surreal legal moment. Both the hearing and the human experiences leading to it were very intense, and in our rewritten judgment we make that clear. The third reason for starting the commentary with this quote relates to our own positioning vis-à-vis this judgment. Marica attended the hearing, and the quote that starts this commentary was taken from the ethnographic notes she wrote during the hearing. We were both involved to different extents in what happened before, during and after the hearing in question. Until 2020, we were both members of Rete Lenford – Avvocatura per i Diritti LGBTI, which, as will be discussed below, spearheaded the litigation strategy that led to the hearing.

Although quite some time has passed since then, discussing judgment no. 138/2010 has cemented our friendship and we have realised that what follows is a more mature reading of the original judgment than those readings we both have done in the past.

Thus, we present our commentary in the form of a conversation we had in Rome on 17 August 2023. As this was just one of the countless conversations about this judgment that we had over the last ten years, this conversational commentary tries to condense our reflections during the years and builds on Marica's ethnographic notes and participant observations collected between 2008 and 2020. Witnessing those events had effects on our lives that we are still processing emotionally, professionally, and in our relations with some members of the LGBTIQ+ movement in Italy. We hope that rendering the reader an observer of our conversation, will offer a more realistic picture of the genesis of strategic litigation, and of the journeys that LGBTIQ+ people and their allies struggling for equality go through. The first part of our conversation describes the day of the hearing and discusses the judgment of the Italian Constitutional Court.

Then we offer the reader an account of the events that led to the hearing and conclude with some reflections on our re-written judgment.

To ease *you*[6] – the reader – into the scene, we would like *you* to look at the pictures in the chapter. We took them on 17 August 2022; we were in Rome at 6:00pm at one of the tables of Necci, a cocktail bar located in an area called Pigneto, when we started talking. Then, we moved to a restaurant close by, and later on kept talking while walking towards an area called San Giovanni until 2:00am, when we hugged each other and took separate ways home.

Fig. 1[7]

---

6. In the online version of the chapter, we use rainbow flag colours to emphasise words and celebrate queerness. For several reasons, the printed version of the chapter is in black and white. Thus, dear reader, feel free to be inspired by your own inner colours and give to all words in italics the colours you like.

7. We are the authors of this picture.

Judgment No. 138/2010 and its influence

Marica: Yàdad, yesterday I passed by Palazzo della Consulta... it's unbelievable how, after so many years, the memories of that day are so vivid... I still feel the adrenaline!

Yàdad: I know... it's a rhetorical question, as I imagine what the answer is, but is *that day 23 March 2010*?

Marica: Yep! I kept the dress I was wearing that day somewhere at home! Apart from the fashion reference, attending the hearing was not only emotional, but also a moment of learning... I used that opportunity to do some court ethnography, and I could collect data for my research on law in action, and cause lawyers... I approached the collection of data following Gramsci's suggestion to avoid separating the intellectual from feelings.[8]

Yàdad: What did you look at and what did you find?

Marica: Drawing on the literature about court ethnography, I looked at the environment and the interactions between judges, lawyers, and audience... I took notes from the moment we – lawyers of Rete Lenford – met in Piazza del Quirinale at the entrance of Palazzo della Consulta. We passed the security check and then we walked to the hearing room. The Palazzo is magnificent and beautifully decorated with paintings and sculptures. The room of the hearing wasn't very big, but it was sumptuous – I admired the golden decorations, the huge chandeliers, the precious rugs... let's say that if you are looking for evidence of how architecture is used to visualise the power that the law and courts have, then Palazzo della Consulta is the place to go.[9] It reminded me of what Mirjan Damaška labels as the policy-implementing process of hierarchical officialdom.[10] The performativity of power was also encapsulated in the entrance of the judges through a back door; one by one, they sat while the audience stood. However, the rush of the audience to get into the seats, the exchange of looks between the couples, *the lawyers of Rete Lenford hugging each other*, the words and body language of some of the lawyers representing the couples, were all clearly *resisting the power* of the Court and *transgressing* the (re)production of heteronormative law in Italy. Putting it like Goffman, everyone that day, including myself, was a performer and a character.[11]

Yàdad: Marica, you know that I am always up for a discussion on that day and the subsequent judgment of the Constitutional Court... and by the way, we should start writing for the Queer Judgments Project... I know we both have written about

---

8. Antonio Gramsci, *Quaderni dal Carcere* (V.Gerratana ed ,Turin: Einaudi, 2014).

9. Judith Resnik, Dennis E. Curtis and Allison Anna, Tait, 'Constructing Courts: Architecture, the Ideology of Judging, and the Public Sphere, in Law,' in *Law, Culture and Visual Studies*, eds. Anne Wagner and Richard K. Sherwin (New York, London: Springer, 2014), 515.

10. Mirjan Damaška, *The Faces of Justice and State Authority* (Yale: Yale University Press, 1991).

11. Erving Goffman, *The Presentation of Self in everyday Life* (London: Penguin Books, 1959).

the judgment of the Constitutional Court already,[12] but some time has passed since then, and we need to reflect more on the effects of that decision; only then we can re-write the judgment.

Marica: What about making a move and continuing our chat while we find something to eat? We are coming closer to talk about the no. 138/2010 judgment, and I need energy to listen to you, ha ha ha!

Yàdad: You are soooooo funny!... I have spent years reading and studying the judgment... anyway...

We walk through Pigneto and reach the restaurant Fuori, where we grab a table outside and keep talking.

Marica: Go on! I will take notes while you talk, so we can use them for the Queer Judgments Project.

Yàdad: The judgment of the Constitutional Court is...

Marica: Wait! For the Queer Judgments Project, we should give a bit of context first and then comment on the judgment... well, the facts of the case are included in the re-written judgment, but maybe we should just say that: the Italian Constitutional Court was called upon to determine whether some of the articles of the Italian Civil Code that concern marriage were unconstitutional and the Court ruled that they weren't.

Yàdad: Can I say what I think, now, my lovely lawyer?

Marica: No need for sarcasm, my queer independent researcher... for Italy, the judgment was ground-breaking, but we cannot assume all readers are acquainted with the judgment, so we should provide all the information. So, we should say that the Court recognised that same-sex couples deserved legal protection as all social groups do. However, the Court specified that such recognition should be different from marriage between a man and a woman.

Yàdad: Although some Italian legal scholars and part of the LGBTIQ+ movement in Italy welcomed the decision and to some extent considered it as a positive outcome, our reading of it suggests that the judgment delivered by the Constitutional Court is a homophobic decision! It reproduces structural violence against LGBTIQ+ people in Italy, homophobia, and exclusion.

---

12. Moscati, *Pasolini's Premonitions*, 190-192; Yàdad De Guerre, 'Le frocie società naturali,' *Jacobin Italia,* 16 April 2021.

Marica: I would also say that it's a fascist judgment, and that the legislative developments that followed are similarly fascist. The fascist imprint is evident in paragraph 9 of the judgment, where the Court decouples same-sex unions from procreation and, therefore, essentialises biology and reproduces binarism.[13] The Court shapes the bodies of same-sex couples as infertile… it sterilized their bodies… and, what's more insulting, it disrespectfully seems to insinuate that same-sex parents are not good parents. In this sense, it is fascist, in my view.

Yàdad: Totally agree. This judgment was fascist and authoritarian for me too, in the same sense that you're saying: it defines same-sex couples through a heteronormative institutional interpretation of the Italian family based on the marriage between a man and a woman with the aim to generate children for the country – an interpretation that de-historicizes same-sex love, relationships, and families… an interpretation that keeps overlooking queer people and their voice within Italian history.[14]

Marica: And why do you think the judgment is homophobic?

Yàdad: It's homophobic because it consciously avoids recognizing the love that same-sex partners feel for each other and…

Marica: Sorry for interrupting you, but during the hearing I thought that the body language that some of the judges had, was also homophobic – some of them didn't even look at the lawyers representing the couples. Go ahead.

Yàdad: Marica, it's not easy to finish a sentence when speaking with you! The Court included same-sex couples within the social groups protected under Article 2 of the Constitution. Although the Court said that the notion of social group 'must also include homosexual unions, understood as the stable cohabitation of two individuals of the same sex,'[15] the Court didn't consider what same-sex couples were asking for, namely that they are two people who love each other and consciously *decide to create a family* based on that love. The decision does not see same-sex couples as a basis to start a family, although families are protected under Article 29 of the Italian Constitution and are a specific kind of 'social group' as well.

---

13. See para. 9 of the judgment: 'Moreover, it is not by chance that, after addressing marriage, the Constitution considered it necessary to deal with the protection of children (Article 30), guaranteeing equal treatment also to those born outside marriage, provided that this is compatible with the members of the legitimate [marriage-based] family. The necessary and fair protection guaranteed to biological children does not undermine the constitutional significance attributed to the legitimate family and the (potential) [pro] creative purpose of marriage which distinguishes it from homosexual unions.' This is the official translation of the judgment, accessed 18 December 2023, https://www.cortecostituzionale.it/documenti/download/doc/recent_judgments/S2010138_en.pdf. We have added some words to the translation by using square brackets.
14. For an overview on family law during fascism in Italy, see Paolo Ungari, *Storia del diritto di famiglia in Italia, 1796-1975* (Bologna: Il Mulino, 2002).
15. Para. 8.

Marica: But don't you think – as our wonderful Sen suggests – that accepting same-sex marriage only because they mirror opposite-sex couples in terms of love is heteronormative?[16]

Yàdad: I agree with Sen, but I also believe that it depends on what the couples asked for... if they wanted their love to be recognised, then, *queerly*, the judge should do that.

Marica: It's all about the family in Italy... isn't it?

Yàdad: Hmmm... yes... After reading the judgment so many times, I have realised that the core question the Court had to deal with was: could these couples be included within the concept of 'natural society' as per Article 29 of the Constitution?[17] This article provides that '[t]he Republic shall recognise the rights of the family as a natural society founded on marriage.'[18] The Court logically had to determine whether these couples could be considered a 'natural society.' Only after ascertaining that a same-sex couple was a 'natural society,' could the Court then apply the principle of equality and determine whether and how marriage should be extended to same-sex couples. 'Natural' means that a social phenomenon pre-exists State law and, therefore, State law cannot affect it. The Court said that 'the intention [of the Constituent Assembly] was to stress that the family contemplated under the provision had original rights which pre-existed the State, and which the latter was obliged to recognise.'[19] To be considered as 'natural society,' a phenomenon should emerge from society because it pre-exists the written law, and then it may be regulated by the law through marriage. The Court looked at the travaux préparatoires of the Italian Constitution, the Civil Code, legal amendments to family law legislation... And of course, it couldn't find a trace of same-sex couples.

Marica: Well, I believe the trace was there already!

Yàdad: Exactly! The Court – and I believe it did so consciously – decided to overlook not only the same-sex couples standing before them, but also the court cases they filed, the conference and the publication organised before the hearing by academics who discussed same-sex marriage (you too published that paper on the variety of marriages to show that the Court didn't have to invent anything and was not being asked to transgress its role, as same-sex marriage had always been there).[20] In my view, if the Court had considered all this as evidence that same-sex couples were already part

---

16. Senthorun Raj, *Feeling Queer Jurisprudence: Injury, Intimacy, Identity* (Abingdon: Routledge, 2020).

17. Throughout the commentary, we use quotation marks for 'natural society' as direct quote to Article 29 of the Constitution.

18. Official translation of the Italian Constitution, accessed 18 December 2023, https://www.senato.it/sites/default/files/media-documents/Costituzione_INGLESE_2023.pdf.

19. Decision 138/2010, para. 9.

20. Maria Federica Moscati, 'Tre Motivi Empirici e Legali per Dire Si al Matrimonio tra Persone dello Stesso Sesso,' in *La Societa' Naturale e i Suoi nemici. Sul Paradigma Eterosessuale del Matrimonio*, ed. Roberto Bin et al., (Torino: Giappichelli Editore, 2010), 281.

of the Italian society, then the conclusion of the judgment would have been different: a *queer natural society* was speaking, and acting right before them, but the Court wasn't willing to listen to them.

Marica: Maybe the judges of the Constitutional Court knew that the Italian legislator would not have the intellectual sophisticatedness to understand the original text of the Constitution and would instead pay attention only to the immediate practical implications of Article 29.

Yàdad: Speaking of which, we should talk about the effects of this judgment on the law… although I believe that the long-term effects of this decision have not yet materialised.

Marica: Why do you want me to get angry tonight? You know already what I think… We should distinguish the consequences of the judgment from the consequences of the conventional interpretation of the judgment. This interpretation has focused on three points of the judgment. First, the paragraph of the judgment in which the Court says that the Italian Parliament has the authority and responsibility to determine the way same-sex unions should be given legal recognition.[21] Second, when the Court says that a legal recognition of same-sex unions could not be based on a 'simple equalisation of same-sex unions to marriage.'[22] Finally, and this makes me so angry, this interpretation has taken for granted the separation between procreation and parenting, on the one hand, and same-sex couples, on the other. Consequently, the legal effects of this judgment have been horrifically condensed in Law no. 76/2016 on civil unions. It is a piece of segregating legislation that has legalized discrimination against same-sex couples and made them unworthy of marriage and parenting. Regardless of what the proponent of the law and several people within the LGBTIQ+ movement in Italy assert, I will keep loudly arguing that the law on civil unions is the product of a political compromise that infringes upon the rights of the children of same-sex couples. But we have already said, reiterated, and shouted this so many times… we have even ended friendships within the movement because of our criticism towards this law and its supporters.

Yàdad: Ok, ok, I can relate to that… glass of water?

Marica: No, thank you…

Giving a Voice to the Invisible: Affermazione Civile

Yàdad: I think the judges had all the elements they needed to understand that same-sex couples were already part of society… after all, the hearing was prompted by lower court cases filed by same-sex couples. The revolution was that same-sex couples entered court rooms, they challenged Italian law and its legal culture.

---

21. Decision 138/2010, para. 8.
22. Decision 138/2010, para. 9.

Marica: Yàdad, but that was something that Affermazione Civile (AC) did. AC aimed at extending marriage to same-sex couples in Italy. It started as an individual initiative by a same-sex couple, and then developed into a more structured form of strategic litigation led by Rete Lenford, an association of lawyers, and supported by Certi Diritti, a charity working on civil rights. The strategic litigation was accompanied by an awareness campaign.[23]

Yàdad: Exactly! For the first time, strategic litigation was set in motion to support same-sex marriage in Italy... set in motion by those couples, their lawyers, their allies, including Stefano Rodotà. That meant that same-sex couples were speaking and were listened to, were supported, and recognized... they existed and were acknowledged by society... so, going back to what I said about Article 29 and the interpretation of 'natural society,' what else did the Court need to understand that same-sex couples were already there before the law existed? I know you have already written about AC, your involvement with it, the support from international cause lawyers and activists, the chats with Paula Ettelbrick... But time has passed since then and maybe you should reflect on whether and how AC transformed Italian legal culture and yourself, first as a PhD student, then as a cause lawyer, and finally as a friend... I understand that you were so passionate about the campaign that you even changed the focus of your PhD.

Marica: Yes, I did. I will explain. Give me five minutes to call home and I will come back to this.

Marica leaves the table and calls her partner... she comes back five minutes later.

Yàdad: Also, I think that including your ethnographic notes in the commentary for the Queer Judgments Project would show that a judgment is just the last part of a story.

Marica: Ahaha! Ok, then... I agree, it's time to vent, and talking about all this while we are here in Rome, where everything started, and sitting at a table from which we can see a picture of Pasolini, has an important symbolic meaning. For me, personally, AC was essentially a story of *friendship, joyful activism, and intense transformations*! Yes, I changed the focus of my research, I prioritised activism over career, I moved back to Italy, I joined Rete Lenford and became a cause lawyer.[24] But what occurred to me is marginal. More broadly and importantly, AC and what happened during the months before the hearing and the judgment is a story of *pride, solidarity and visibility*. For the first time, same-sex couples were made visible, with a voice, and claimed their rights.... This, I think, was clamorous, also within the LGBTIQ+ community, as historically LGBTIQ+ people in Italy ironically and sadly paid the price of invisibility for not being criminalized.[25]

---

23. For full details see: Moscati, *Pasolini's Premonitions*, 190-192.
24. Austin Sarat and Stuart A. Scheingold (eds), *Cause Lawyers and Social Movements* (Stanford: Stanford University Press, 2006). For details on Rete Lenford see, accessed 22 April 2024, https://www.retelenford.it/.
25. Moscati, *Pasolini's Premonitions*, 14.

Yàdad: Yes, I agree, and we should include this in our re-written judgment.

Marica: AC was *a vision of one lawyer who understood how to turn a bottom-up initiative – a same-sex couple asking for legal advice on how to register their marriage – into a collective effort…* an effort that to different extents influenced Italian legal culture, the LGBTIQ+ movement, political parties, and academia. *It was about affirmation, validation, and access to justice.* This brought to the hearing at the Constitutional Court an intersection of friendship, alliances, legal challenges, emotions, political struggles, and vision. *It made queer bodies visible…* but not anymore stereotypically depicted… now the bodies of *two same-sex partners were visible and together as a couple, raising their voice in court for the first time and wanting to create a family.* AC broke the hegemony on the bodies that for ages the Italian culture, politics, and laws have used to hide the existence of same-sex couples.

Yàdad: Yes! That's what the judges didn't want to see. And that's why I think it was possible to think about same-sex couples as a 'natural society.' There was a path that led to the process of coming out and speaking up – and that's queer history, which exists in Italian culture too, whether the Court wanted to recognize it or not.

Marica: Of course. And I believe that AC had a transformative effect on how some lawyers in Italy perceived themselves… not only lawyers in general, but also LGBTIQ+ lawyers in particular. I did interviews with lawyers who told me that being involved in AC helped them to come out as LGBTIQ+. At that time, I don't think we were aware of what the consequences of AC would be in the long term…. we just threw ourselves into it with all our passion. We were ready to do everything from photocopying to studying, from preparing the cases to organizing conferences…. Ah, there was also the fact that we wanted to create awareness… our conferences were about topics, like same-sex marriage, that – paraphrasing Pasolini – would *scandalize the sceptical… those, in particular lawyers and legal scholars, who refused to see that the queers were there!*

Yàdad: Yes. And one could never understand all these things simply by reading the judgment. There were couples asking to get married, but also lawyers who were not just lawyers, who were making a political and personal point in the legal sphere and beyond. There were academics, judges, and activists involved in the process… A lot of people tried to reflect on same-sex marriage because of AC, at the same time re-positioning themselves as straight or queer, as political, or non-political, as left-wing or right-wing, as resistant or institutional…

Marica: There was an idea of broad change – and not only for LGBTIQ+ people – based on the opportunity to claim social justice. By asking the Constitutional Court to rule on same-sex marriage, we also asked it to (re)define the meaning of family in Italy. And that requires reflecting on the Italian society as a whole, given the country we're talking about. And the Constitution itself.

Yàdad: Somehow, we should put all this in our judgment. So, how are we going to write it?

Our judgment

Marica: As a preliminary observation, I want to say that my work on our rewriting of the judgment is premised upon conflicting beliefs and emotions that I hold. The influence that queer theory and the work of Pasolini or Foucault or Mieli have had on me, push me to consider courts as an expression of oppressive power.[26] My personal experience – even embodiment – of reviving some memories has been painful – emotionally, mentally, and physically. The time before, during and after the judgment was intense, and reviving some of those memories, while missing some of the companions in that endeavour, has not been easy to deal with. For these reasons, to deny the power of law and protect myself through avoidance,[27] I should submit a blank page to this project. However, my experience as activist lawyer and as a teacher has taught me that every occasion should be used to raise awareness. So, I am working on our re-writing of this judgment with the hope that it will prove useful to judges who will adjudicate similar cases in the future.

Yàdad: Exactly. In our judgment, by drawing upon the Italian Constitution, we should consider *the families created by same-sex couples as the main actor. We do not deny their capacity to procreate* and, *we do not overlook their love and the families they create because of that love.* Further, we do not link marriage and procreation, as if marriage existed for the sole purpose of procreation. But *we do link same-sex couples, marriage, procreation, and parenting. Thus, we assert that same-sex couples can marry, and can have and raise children! Arguing otherwise would be offensive for the children of same-sex couples.* To be honest, I think that the Italian Constitution lends itself to a queer interpretation, as it was written with the aim of trying to stem future fascist manipulations, and so it leaves room for inclusion beyond the normative.

Marica: Ours will be a *restitution*: *the existence of same-sex couples* is the principle that will inspire our judgment. Using this approach, we will interpret Article 29 of the Italian Constitution and, building upon the work of AC, we will have the evidence that same-sex couples are part of society in Italy regardless of the legislator acknowledging their existence or not. But how exactly do you suggest we re-write the judgment?

Yàdad: First, we need to explain to the reader that, unlike other courts in other legal systems, dissenting opinions are not included in the final judgments of the Italian Constitutional Court. Decisions are taken in the council chamber and it's not possible

---

26. On the 'queer/law' see: Alex Sharpe, 'Queering Judgment: The Case of Gender Identity Fraud,' *The Journal of Criminal Law* 81 (2017), 422.
27. Stanley Rachman, Adam S. Radomsky and Roz Shafran, 'Safety Behaviour: A Reconsideration,' *Behaviour Research and Therapy* 46/2 (2008), 163-173.

to know how judges voted. We also need to say that one of the judges oversees the writing up of the final text, which will then be published.

Marica: Yes, good point. And I would suggest you be that judge.

Yàdad: Maybe we could use parts of the original text and queer syntax, terminology and punctuation. The Court uses grammar, language, and punctuation politically. For example, it puts important words like same-sex couples/family/love in brackets. To me, that suggests that the Court uses grammar and punctuation to neglect/hide that same-sex couples exist. Another example of this is that the Court uses the word 'problem' to qualify homosexuality. Thus, if punctuation is performative,[28] we will express our respect for same-sex couples and their families by using punctuation in a certain way too... we will not put the words same-sex couples in brackets. Ah, we should not use the word homosexuals – I know that some members of the queer community in Italy might still use it, but in my view, judges should not.

Fig. 2[29]

Marica: I like that, and since it's already 2:00am, I would suggest meeting up tomorrow and deciding about our individual tasks and deadlines.

Yàdad: Ok, ciao!

Marica: Ciao... love you *assai*[30]... *sono felice di fare sta cosa con te*.[31]

---

28. Jennifer DeVere Body, *Punctuation: Art, Politics, and Play* (Durham: Duke University Press, 2008).
29. Yàdad took this picture.
30. 'A lot,' an expression that is mainly used in the South of Italy where Marica and Yàdad come from.
31. 'I am happy to be doing this with you.'

JUDGMENT No. 138[32]

YEAR 2010

REPUBLIC OF ITALY

IN THE NAME OF THE ITALIAN PEOPLE

THE CONSTITUTIONAL COURT

gives the following

Judgment

in proceedings concerning the constitutionality of Articles 93, 96, 98, 107, 108, 143, 143a and 156a of the Civil Code, initiated by the Tribunal of Venice and by the Trento Court of Appeal

having heard the Judge Rapporteur Yàdad De Guerre;

The Facts of the Case

[1] The Tribunal of Venice meeting collectively, with the referral order indicated in the epigraph, raised, with reference to Articles 2, 3, 29 and 117, first paragraph, of the Constitution, the question of constitutional legitimacy of Articles 93, 96, 98, 107, 108, 143, 143-a, 156-bis of the civil code, 'in the part in which, systematically interpreted, they do not allow people to marry people of the same sex.'

The referring judge states that the tribunal has been requested to rule in proceedings initiated by Messrs G. M. and S. G., both male, concerning an objection pursuant to Article 98 of the Civil Code against the decision of 3 July 2008, whereby the registrar at the Municipality of Venice refused to publish notice of their intention to marry, as requested by them.

---

32. For the Facts of the Case, we have used some text from the official translation of the judgment and then queerly re-written or queerly modified it as suggested in our Commentary; we have followed the style of the Italian Constitutional Court where possible. See footnote 6 above for the use of colours in the text.

The official, in fact, considered the publication as unlawful, because it was in contrast with the current constitutional and ordinary legislation that suggests that the institution of marriage in the Italian legal system is unequivocally focused on the gender diversity of the spouses.

The Tribunal of Venice recalls the arguments made by the appellants, who noted that Italian law does not provide a definition of marriage, nor an express prohibition of marriage between persons of the same sex.

It also observes the applicants asked to order the registrar of the Municipality of Venice to proceed with the publication of the notice of the appellants' intention to marry; subordinately, to raise the question of constitutional legitimacy of Articles 107, 108, 143, 143-a and 156-bis of the Civil Code, with reference to the Articles 2, 3, 10, second paragraph, 13 and 29 of the Constitution.

The Tribunal of Venice points out that, one cannot ignore the rapid transformation of society and customs that has taken place in recent decades, during which we have witnessed the overcoming of the monopoly held by the traditional family model and the simultaneous spontaneous rise of different, forms of cohabitation, which ask for protection.

According to the Tribunal of Venice, the first principle is that laid down by Article 2 of the Constitution, which recognizes the inviolable rights of human beings not only within the individual sphere but also, and perhaps above all, within the social sphere.

The Tribunal of Venice also states that the right to marry constitutes a fundamental right of individuals, recognized at a supranational level as well as at a national level. The Tribunal continues by suggesting that the freedom to marry or not to marry, and to choose a spouse autonomously, concerns the sphere of autonomy and individuality, so that it results in a choice with which the State cannot interfere, if there are no prevailing incompatible interests, which in this case are not identifiable.

The Tribunal of Venice argued that it cannot share opinions contrary to the recognition of the freedom of marriage between persons of the same sex based on ethical reasons, linked to tradition or to nature, both due to the radical transformations that have taken place in family customs and to the fact that this would involve dangerous arguments, which have been used in the past to defend serious forms of discrimination.

The Tribunal of Venice, in relation to Article 29, first paragraph of the Constitution, observes that the meaning of that provision is not that of recognizing the foundation of the family as a kind of 'natural right,' but that of affirming the pre-existence and autonomy of the family with respect to the State. This interpretation imposes limits to the power of the state legislator, as it emerges from the records of the debate conducted within the Constituent Assembly, recalling the abuses previously committed against a certain type of family.

Furthermore, the Tribunal of Venice asserted that legislative developments from 1948 until today – including divorce – demonstrate that the protection of tradition does not fall within the purposes of Article 29 of the Constitution and that family and marriage are institutions open to transformations. *Therefore, justifying the alleged prohibition of same-sex marriage by resorting to arguments related to same-sex couples' supposed lack of procreative capacity and the protection of procreation is groundless.*

Having excluded that a difference in treatment between same-sex couples and opposite-sex couples can be based on Article 29 of the Constitution, the Tribunal of Venice states that Article 29 should not constitute an obstacle to the legal recognition of marriage between persons of the same sex. In fact, this provision should rather be reinterpreted considering current social developments.

Moreover, the referring court points to Article 117(1) of the Constitution, which requires the legislature to respect the limitations resulting from European Union law and international law obligations, such as Articles 8, 12 and 14 of the European Convention on Human Rights (ECHR).

Finally, the referring court points out that the legal systems of many countries with a legal tradition similar to the Italian one, are moving towards a *concept of family relations that can include same-sex couples.*

On the basis of these considerations, the Tribunal of Venice reaches the conclusion that the question of constitutionality raised is not manifestly groundless, and also finds that it is relevant because the application of the contested provisions cannot be avoided in the logical and legal reasons to be considered in order to reach a decision in this case.

[2] Messrs G. M. and S. G. entered an appearance in the proceedings before the Constitutional Court, with written statement filed on 20 July 2009.

After setting out the facts on which the case is based and reporting the contents of the referral order, the private parties highlight the relevance of the question proposed and observe that the referring court has recognised an incontrovertible fact, namely that the law does not currently impose any express prohibition preventing two persons of the same sex from contracting marriage. The requirement that marriage should be between people of the opposite sex is claimed to be the result of an interpretative tradition arising within a social context that was entirely different from the current one and which has been handed down from one generation to the next, including through the residual influence of canon law on the institution of marriage under civil law.

However, the private parties claim that this historical dimension cannot prevent the question from being revisited, similar to what other foreign constitutional courts have done. Nor can it be inferred that opposite sex is a mandatory characteristic of marriage, because Article 29 does not constitutionalise the characteristics of the institution of marriage provided for under ordinary legislation or emerging from its settled interpretation. The Civil Code is claimed to constitute the object and not the parameter for the proceedings and, in any case, cannot end up as a key with which to read constitutional law.

Therefore, the private parties argue that it is necessary to identify the meaning of the words marriage and family used in Article 29 in light of the principle of self-determination which pervades the entire Constitution. That provision privileges families founded on marriage. In the opinion of the private parties, this means that if in our society two people of the same sex can also establish a de facto family, *their exclusion from the bond of marriage will not only result in irrational discrimination, but also lead to thousands of citizens being denied the protection from the State.*

Having recalled the notion of family as a natural society, contained in the referral order, the private parties observe that Article 29, which protects from undue interference of the State, is the right to self-determination of the individual. For LGBTIQ+ people, this right would currently be violated by depriving them of the possibility to marry people of the same sex.

However, according to the private parties, this situation should not prevent a rereading of the law, in consideration of the changed social and legal conditions, given the relevance, in this respect, of European Convention of Human Rights, and the principles of equality (and therefore non-discrimination) and the protection of fundamental rights. Nor would it be possible for marriage to be understood as a necessary place of procreation since civil marriage is no longer institutionally oriented towards this purpose.

The private parties emphasize the need for the fundamental right to marry to be guaranteed for everyone without any distinction. In the presence of a fundamental right, it is up to the Constitutional Court to remove the obstacles that prevent anyone from enjoying it, especially if we consider that we are not talking about a regulatory prohibition but a mere interpretative practice.

The private parties then refer to the interpretation that Article 29 of the Constitution excludes the legal recognition of same-sex couples, noting that the said article cannot be interpreted in such a way as to violate the principle of equality and that in our society the principle of equality promotes pluralism and social inclusion.

[3] The President of the Council of Ministers, represented by the State Attorney's Office, intervened in these constitutionality proceedings by writ filed on 21 July 2009, asking that the question be ruled inadmissible or otherwise manifestly groundless.

The State attorney argues that under both private law and constitutional law, marriage refers without doubt to the union between persons of the opposite sex.

The State attorney claims that there is no violation of the principle of equality laid down by Article 3 of the Constitution, because the latter requires equal treatment for identical situations and different treatment in *de facto* different situations.

The State attorney further claims that as regards Article 29 of the Constitution, family law stresses the pre-legal nature of the family, identifying one single unequivocal and stable model, whilst legislation dedicated to other types of social groups acknowledges Article 29 as having a content that changes in line with the evolution of social customs.

Finally, the State attorney claims that there is no contrast with Article 117(1) of the Constitution, regarding the limitations resulting from EU law and international law obligations.

The State representative points out that EU law has not enacted legislation on marriage but has rather limited itself in various resolutions to laying down criteria and principles, leaving to the individual Member States the question as to whether national legislation needs to be adapted.

As regards international law obligations, and in particular compliance with the ECHR, the State attorney asserts that the aforementioned provisions of the Italian

Civil Code do not appear to contrast in particular with Article 12 ECHR. This norm not only reasserts that the institution of marriage concerns persons of the opposite sex but also reserves the determination of the conditions governing the exercise of the right to national law.

The State attorney further argues that, in any case, a proactive intervention by the Constitutional Court could not be achieved through a lexical operation involving merely the replacement of the words 'husband' and 'wife' with the word 'spouses.' Such a move would involve the inclusion of a new family figure into the normative framework of the Civil Code notwithstanding a constitutional rule which refers precisely to 'family,' whereas this task is necessarily reserved to Parliament.

[4] By the other referral order mentioned in the headnote, the Trento Court of Appeal raised a question concerning the constitutionality of several norms too. According to the Trento Court of Appeal it is necessary to ask whether preventing marriage between partners of the same sex is lawful, or marriage must be guaranteed to all.

Conclusions on points of law

[1] Since the two proceedings concern the same question, they are to be joined for decision in a single judgment.

[2] For reasons of logical priority, it is necessary to start our considerations from Article 29 of the Constitution and the reasons for the specific language used in it. It provides in paragraph one that '[t]he Republic recognises the rights of the family as a natural society founded on marriage,' whilst the second paragraph adds that 'Marriage shall be based on the moral and legal equality of the spouses within the limits laid down by law to ensure family unity.'

This provision, which has given rise to a lively debate within the academic literature that is still ongoing, defines 'family' as a 'natural society' recognised by the State through the institution of marriage. The intention was to stress that the notion of 'family' contemplated in this provision had original rights which pre-existed the State, and which the latter was obliged to recognise. *This expression, thus, puts limits on the intervention of the State in the relationships between individuals who freely decide to create a family, as it was the case during the fascist regime.*

In view of the above, the concepts of family and marriage cannot be considered to have been crystallised with reference to the time when the Constitution was written and entered into force. *Both family and marriage are endowed with the flexibility that is inherent within constitutional principles* and are therefore to be interpreted taking account of the evolution of society and customs.

In this regard, it is evident that at this moment in time, *families are formed, structured, performed and perceived in diverse and dynamic ways*. It is also evident that *in the future even more types of families will be created*. Thus, discussing whether different families exist would be anachronistic today. The focus of this hearing is on whether and how the choice to create a family in all forms should be protected.

Some who create families do not necessarily wish to marry, but others might wish to. While waiting to have the opportunity to marry, some same-sex couples continue to create their families. Should they be left without legal protection? *This Court, looking at the anti-fascist identity of our Constitution, can only answer: no, those couples should not be left without legal protection.*

More importantly, the hearing today is about children too. This Court, the Italian legislator, the whole Italian society are bound to respect children's rights and to implement the best interests of every child regardless of the way they have been conceived, the relationship of their parents, the sexuality of their parents, and the identity of those looking after them. *In Italy, children raised in families not based on opposite-sex marriage are lively members of the Italian society*, and they should be protected. At the moment, however, the law neglects them and their families. The rights of these children emerge as being shaped by the limitative interpretation of Article 29, the law governing recourse to assisted reproductive techniques (ARTs), and a heteronormative politics of reproduction rights and parenting roles. Overlooking the rights of these children is contrary to our Constitution.

Therefore, *the concepts of family and marriage must also include same-sex partners*, who should be recognised the fundamental right to live their relationships freely and *to obtain full legal protection* thereof along with all associated rights and duties, *including parenting rights, rights to adoption, and rights to reproduction*. In fact, given the meaning of the expression 'natural society,' which imposes on the State the duty to recognise the family with its original rights, it is not possible for a Republican institution to deny such rights to same-sex relationships that, although socially ostracized to some extent, *have been for a long while in the fabric of the Italian society*. The presence of same-sex couples here today, at this hearing, shows that the sex difference of the spouses, interpreted so far as an essential characteristic of marriage, is no longer respectful and appropriate.

Regardless of the different positions on the subject, it is sufficient to take into consideration *that same-sex relationships as a 'natural society' are effectively acknowledged by all who accept or condemn it*. Such acknowledgment entails that the State recognises the original rights that this 'natural society' deserves through the institution of marriage. The State cannot refuse this recognition on the grounds of morality, approval by majority or the longevity of one concept. The marriage of the many opposite-sex couples cannot be considered a barrier to the marriage of same-sex couples or other relationships. It is the genesis of the Constitution and its content that today tell us that the main task of the Italian Republic after the fascist regime is precisely to remove the obstacles 'which, by limiting the freedom and equality of citizens, prevent the full development of the natural person' (Article 3). It is not to the State to decide what a 'natural society' is, but rather to see those families and protect them.

[3] Furthermore, when asked to recognise the rights claimed by same-sex couples who want to marry, the State must consider these couples as 'natural society' and not only as a particular kind of social grouping, as protected under Article 2 of the Constitution. This norm provides that the Republic recognises and guarantees the inviolable rights

of human beings, both as individuals and as social groupings in which they express their personality, and requires compliance with the mandatory duties of political, economic and social solidarity.

[4] Accordingly, social groupings must be deemed to include all forms of simple or complex communities that can *nurture* the free development of the person through relationships, within a context that promotes and *celebrates diversity*.

However, this Court finds that the aspiration to legal recognition of same-sex relationships can be achieved only by rendering them equivalent to opposite-sex relationships, which means having the *possibility to choose* marriage. In fact, at this very historical time in Italy, it is through marriage that an individual may be fully protected as a family if they so wish.

It must be said, though, that the family contemplated under Article 29 may be seen as a specific social grouping whose rights derive merely as a consequence of constituting a group; on the contrary, the citizen has individual rights in a social grouping that depend on timescales, procedures and limits specified by law. Therefore, to avoid future restrictions to various adult relationships and family structures, including those *with more than two partners*, the legislator should find mechanisms that provide appropriate protection in a timely fashion for those families too.

On this basis, it may be inferred that *every kind of family in a pluralistic society has its original rights that the Republic must recognise*. It therefore follows that it is for Parliament to determine – exercising its full discretion – the forms of guarantee and recognition for unmarried couples, be they same or opposite sex. However, *such discretion cannot be exercised to limit the rights of couples who are not opposite-sex*. The Italian Constitution, the variety of families that characterise Italian society, the couples in this hearing, the several other couples that are not here today but expressed their voice through Affermazione Civile, and this Court, compel the Parliament to be guided by the principle of equality enshrined in Article 3 of the Constitution while legislating. Such a trajectory is even more crucial when considering the arguments of the lawyers representing the couples today. Their reading of the Civil Code and the Constitution reveals how linking marriage to procreation is so inadequate and contrary to Article 3.

Therefore, any laws aiming at regulating relationships between partners of the same-sex or other forms of adult relationships, cannot grant to these relationships less rights than those provided for opposite-sex couples that marry, or even limit protection only to relationships with two partners.

On These Grounds

THE CONSTITUTIONAL COURT

hereby:

a. *rules* that, with reference to Articles 2 and 117(1) of the Constitution, the question concerning the constitutionality of Articles 93, 96, 98, 107, 108, 143, 143a and 156-bis of the Civil Code raised by the Tribunal of Venice and the Trento Court of Appeal by the referral orders mentioned in the headnote is *admissible*;
b. *rules* that, with reference to Articles 3 and 29 of the Constitution, the question concerning the constitutionality of the aforementioned Articles of the Civil Code raised by the Tribunal of Venice and the Trento Court of Appeal by the same referral orders *is grounded*.

Decided in Rome at the seat of the Constitutional Court, *Palazzo della Consulta*, on 14 April 2010.

19

UKM v Attorney-General (Singapore):

Same-Sex Parenting and the Legal Closet in Singapore

Daryl WJ Yang

Introduction

In 1999, Baden Offord penned an article which described the 'homosexual burden' that queer Singaporeans bear because of the Singapore state's construction of non-normative sexualities as a social difference to 'consolidate an imagined border that somehow delineates Singapore from Western society.'[1] Twenty years later, however, a reader may mistakenly think that the 'homosexual burden' has since disappeared when they peruse the Singapore High Court's decision in *UKM v Attorney-General*.[2] After all, nowhere in the judgment did Chief Justice of Singapore Sundaresh Menon acknowledge or address the challenges that the appellant and his life partner have had to endure in their pursuit of parenthood, and which ultimately led them to appear before the court.

The appellant in *UKM v Attorney-General* is a gay Singaporean man who had been in a long-term relationship with his same-sex partner of the same age and nationality for around 13 years at the time of the litigation. After exploring several ways to become parents in Singapore, the couple eventually had a son (the 'Child') who was born in November 2013 via gestational surrogacy in the United States of America ('USA'). The son grew up under the couple's care in Singapore and the family was largely able to live their lives as freely as possible in a country that – at the time of the judgment – still criminalized male same-sex sexual conduct under Section 377A of the Penal Code 1871.

However, the appellant was forced to seek the court's assistance after he failed to obtain Singaporean citizenship for the Child (who has American citizenship by virtue of his being born in the USA). As a child considered to be 'illegitimate' under Singapore law (since the appellant was not married to the surrogate mother), the Child could not

---

1. Baden Offord, 'The Burden of (Homo)sexual Identity in Singapore,' *Social Semiotics* 9/ 3 (1999), 309.
2. [2018] SGHCF 18.

acquire Singaporean citizenship by descent as a matter of right under Article 122 of the Constitution of the Republic of Singapore ('Constitution'), which states that a person born outside Singapore shall be a Singaporean citizen by descent if, at the time of his birth, either his father or mother is a Singaporean citizen. This is because paragraph 15 (1) of the Third Schedule to the Constitution ('Paragraph 15(1)') states that references to an 'illegitimate' person's father or parent shall be construed as references to their mother. As a result, since the surrogate mother is an American citizen, the Child was not entitled to Singaporean citizenship by descent.

As an alternative, the appellant decided to legally adopt the Child to increase the child's chances of becoming a Singaporean under Article 124 of the Constitution, which allows a minor under the age of 21 years (as defined in the constitutional provision) who is the child of a Singaporean citizen to be registered as a Singaporean citizen. An adoption order was therefore necessary to establish that the Child is the appellant's child under Article 124. This is because, under paragraph 15(2) of the Third Schedule to the Constitution, references to an adopted child's parent are to be construed as references to the adopter. The question before the court was therefore a simple one: should an adoption order be granted to the appellant under the Adoption of Children Act 1939 ('ACA') to adopt his own biological son born overseas through gestational surrogacy?

Though the High Court granted the adoption order and reversed the lower court's dismissal of the application, I argue that the judgment is a legally closeted one that fails to explicitly engage with the discrimination that the appellant and his family had to confront as a family that falls outside Singapore's heteronormative imagination. Bringing into dialogue Offord's concept of the 'homosexual burden' with Eve Kosofsky-Sedgwick's metaphor of the closet,[3] the concurring Opinion I have written forces the 'homosexual burden' to 'come out' by making explicit the ways in which it ultimately led the appellant to seek the High Court's assistance so that the Child could remain in Singapore as a citizen, like his parents are. In this regard, I am guided by what Sedgwick described as the 'satisfaction in dwelling on the degree to which the power of our enemies over us is implicated, not in their command of knowledge, but precisely in their ignorance.'[4]

To come out or not to come out, that is the question

The judgment in *UKM v Attorney-General* opens with a declaratory statement: 'The appellant is a gay man.'[5] At face value, one might mistakenly assume that this is a queer judgment that attends to the injustices faced by the appellant and his family because of his and his partner's sexual orientation. Instead, I suggest that, quite contrary to this opening statement, the decision is more appropriately characterised as a *legally closeted judgment*. This refers to a judicial decision that fails or refuses to engage

3. Eve Kosofsky Sedgwick, *Epistemology of the Closet* (Berkeley: University of California Press, 1990).
4. Sedgwick, *Epistemology of the Closet*, 7.
5. *UKM v Attorney-General*, [1].

with the appellant's sexual orientation and the discriminatory treatment that he has experienced because he did not conform to the heteronormative conception of family in Singapore, both legally and socially.

As a preliminary point, the fact that this judgment was closeted may be attributed to the appellant's decision *not* to file a constitutional challenge against the heteronormative laws and policies that led him and his family to come before the court in the first place. My concurring Opinion raises two potential aspects that could have been challenged in this case: first, the government's policy against supporting adoption by same-sex couples and, second, the gendered definition of parent under Paragraph 15(1) which meant that the Child was not entitled to citizenship by descent as a matter of right. Many queer people remain closeted because coming out is unsafe for them, and this has served as a strategy of self-preservation. In the same way, the appellant successfully sought refuge in the legal closet that he and his lawyers had constructed by operating within the confines of the existing legal framework rather than openly challenge it. In doing so, they succeeded in obtaining what he needed: the adoption order that established a legal relationship between him and his son.

It is not surprising why the appellant – and his lawyers – would make such a strategic choice. In the first place, constitutional challenges are rare in Singapore and successful ones are even rarer.[6] In the specific context of gender and sexuality, constitutional challenges have not been particularly successful, and positive reforms have mostly been achieved through 'a pragmatic strategy of [political] engagement.'[7] In this regard, the legal strategy that the appellant adopted is reminiscent of Lynette Chua's observation that gay rights activists in Singapore employ 'pragmatic resistance' in their advocacy, where the goal is to 'stay alive and advance with skirmishes rather than court demise by declaring open warfare on grander principles.'[8] Indeed, it is difficult to overstate the narrowness of the decision in this case.[9] In this regard, the appellant's legal strategy may be characterised as a closeted one in that his sexual orientation was deliberately under-emphasised. Indeed, as the District Judge noted in her judgment, '[t]he case before me was no different from most other adoption cases from the standpoint of the intentions of the applicant.'[10] On one hand, this is of course uncontroversial from a queer perspective: a gay parent should be and is in fact no different from a heterosexual parent. On the other hand, as my concurring Opinion makes clear, the case cannot be any *more* different from other adoption cases: if the appellant was not a gay man, he would not have had to travel across the world to realize his desire to be a parent with his partner by assisted reproductive technology (ART) and surrogacy.

6. Jack Lee, 'Foreign Precedents in Constitutional Adjudication by the Supreme Court of Singapore, 1963-2013,' *Washington International Law Journal* 24 (2015), 249.

7. Daryl WJ Yang and Jaclyn L Neo, 'Gender Equality in Singapore: Whither the Constitution?' in *Gender, Sexuality and Constitutionalism in Asia*, ed. Wen-Chen Chang, et al. (Bloomsbury Publishing, 2023).

8. Lynette J Chua, *Mobilizing Gay Singapore: Rights and Resistance in an Authoritarian State* (Singapore: NUS Press, 2014), 17.

9. See also Remy Choo, 'Gay Adoption and Judicial Decision Making, Singapore Style | LinkedIn' (*LinkedIn*, 20 December 2018), accessed 31 December 2022, https://www.linkedin.com/pulse/gay-adoption-judicial-decision-making-singapore-style-choo-zheng-xi/.

10. *Re UKM* [2018] SGFC 20, [5].

The foregoing discussion brings to mind Sedgwick's characterization of the closet as 'the defining structure for gay oppression.'[11] In the context of USA jurisprudence, she highlighted how the court has 'codifie[d] an excruciating system of double binds, systematically oppressing gay people, identities and acts by undermining through contradictory constraints on discourse the grounds of their very being.'[12] Put simply, a queer person's non-conforming sexual identity can harm them either way, whether they are in or out of the closet: damned if you do (come out), damned if you don't. A similar phenomenon can be observed in the Singaporean context. Under Singapore law, the appellant could have become a parent if he was in the closet: as a matter of law, it is possible for a single man to adopt under the ACA (though he would only be permitted to adopt a male child unless special circumstances exist, an issue that raises even more questions from constitutional, queer and feminist perspectives). However, as a matter of policy, he would only have been able to do so if he was not in a same-sex relationship, because the Ministry of Social and Family Development ('MSF') is unwilling to recommend adoption of children by non-heterosexual couples. Insofar as being in a same-sex relationship requires one to come out (at least to themselves and their partner, if not to others), then coming out and parenting are directly in tension (at least insofar as parenting through adoption goes). This describes part of the 'homosexual burden' that Offord referred to when it comes to a cisgender gay man's aspiration towards parenthood:[13] if you wish to one day become a parent, then you must stay in the closet.[14]

Knocking down the closet door: The incoherence of compulsory heterosexuality

Harvey Milk famously proclaimed that coming out is a critical feature of queer justice; otherwise, if they remain in the closet and stay invisible, queer people 'remain in limbo – a myth, a person with no parents, no brothers, no sisters, no friends who are straight…'[15] While existing scholarship on queer visibility has focused on the politics of recognition which allows activists to lay claim to rights and demand equal justice,[16] it may also expose the 'incoherences and contradictions of homosexual identity … and … the incoherences and contradictions of compulsory heterosexuality.'[17]

While the appellant in *UKM v Attorney-General* opted to stay in the closet in terms of his legal strategy, he was nevertheless forced to come out when he sought the court's

---

11. Sedgwick, *Epistemology of the Closet*, 71.
12. Sedgwick, *Epistemology of the Closet*, 70.
13. Offord, 'The Burden of (Homo)sexual Identity.'
14. For a more general discussion of same-sex parenting in Singapore, see Shawna Tang, 'Same-Sex Partnering and Same-Sex Parented Families in Singapore' in *Family and Population Changes in Singapore*, ed. Wei-Jun Jean Yeung and Shu Hu (London: Routledge, 2018).
15. Harvey Milk, *An Archive of Hope: Harvey Milk's Speeches and Writings* (Berkeley: University of California Press, 2013), 153. See also Suzanna Danuta Walters, *All the Rage: The Story of Gay Visibility in America* (Chicago: University of Chicago Press, 2003).
16. Emil Edenborg, 'Visibility in Global Queer Politics' in *The Oxford Handbook of Global LGBT and Sexual Diversity Politics,* ed. Michael J. Bosia, Sandra M. McEvoy, and Momin Rahman (Oxford: Oxford University Press, 2019).
17. Sedgwick, *Epistemology of the Closet*, 81.

assistance to grant an adoption order so that the Child could acquire Singaporean citizenship. In doing so, the 'incoherences and contradictions' of both queerness and compulsory heterosexuality were brought to the fore.[18]

The first such contradiction is how the legal proceedings exposed the so-called traditional family as a mere ideological preference given the court's affirmation – and the government's concession – that there is no real or material difference in terms of the welfare of a child brought up by a heterosexual or same-sex couple. There was no dispute over whether the Child will be cared for by his parents or whether being brought up by a gay person would adversely affect the welfare of a child. Yet, as if without a hint of irony, one of the grounds for the government's opposition to the adoption application was its concern for the Child's welfare 'arising from the fact that he is being brought up in what would be regarded in [Singapore] society as an unconventional household with same-sex parents.'[19] Same-sex parenting is considered to be 'unconventional' in Singapore precisely because the Singapore government made it so – by refusing (until recently) to decriminalize same-sex sexual conduct and privileging the heterosexual nuclear family over other types of family arrangements. This raises the question: what is the underlying justification for the government's disavowal of same-sex parenting in Singapore?

This case is therefore fascinating when one considers Lee Edelman's polemical construction of queerness as the opposite of 'fighting for the children.'[20] By forcing the government to publicly acknowledge that queer parents are no less capable of raising their children, the appellant has – perhaps unwittingly – inverted the logic of reproductive futurism. Whereas 'the children' are usually invoked to justify queer oppression, it is precisely because the welfare of the child is the paramount consideration of the court that the appellant was able to obtain the adoption order.

The second incoherence emerges in respect of how *UKM v Attorney-General* challenges the common law concept of legitimacy as well as the law's gendered norms. Both the High Court and the government's counsel were at pains to insist that a child's legitimacy status is practically irrelevant in Singapore. Yet, it obviously remains a legally valid concept with real implications: as my concurring Opinion highlights, if not for the concept of legitimacy and the gendered definition of parent in Paragraph 15(1) which recognises only the mother, but not the father, of an 'illegitimate child' as their parent, the Child would have been able to obtain citizenship by descent via Article 122 of the Constitution.[21] It is also notable that the idea of legitimacy, as a legal concept received from the common law, was alien to Chinese, Indian and even Malay/Muslim culture in Singapore, as the Singapore courts have expressly acknowledged.[22]

---

18. Ruthann Robson, 'Compulsory Matrimony' in *Feminist and Queer Legal Theory: Intimate Encounters, Uncomfortable Conversations*, ed. Martha Fineman, Jack E Jackson and Adam P Romero (London: Taylor & Francis, 2009).

19. *UKM v Attorney-General*, [81].

20. Lee Edelman, *No Future: Queer Theory and the Death Drive* (Durham: Duke University Press 2004), 3.

21. Article 122 states that a person born outside Singapore shall be a citizen of Singapore by descent if, at the time of their birth, either their father or mother is a citizen of Singapore, by birth, registration or descent.

22. Wai Kum Leong, 'The Next Fifty Years of the Women's Charter,' *Singapore Journal of Legal Studies* (2011), 157-160.

Nevertheless, this did not stop its applicability under Singapore law despite its foreign origins. Contrast this with the rejection of queerness in Singapore on the basis that it is a Western construct and import;[23] the inconsistency is difficult to ignore.

In considering the continued relevance of legitimacy as a legal concept in Singapore family law, the High Court referred to a parliamentary debate where the government rejected the abolition of the concept of legitimacy on the basis that Singapore society 'continues to desire parenthood within marriages.'[24] However, as Leong Wai Kum forcefully argued, the effects of illegitimacy on a child do not 'sit well with the concern for [their] wellbeing.'[25] Yet again, compulsory heterosexuality is exposed for not truly being about 'the children.'

Finally, and most pertinently, the High Court's readiness in finding that there is a public policy against the formation of families with same-sex parents (which the court refers to as same-sex family units), is striking when one compares it with the court's much more cautious approach in finding that there was no settled policy against surrogacy. Notably, the High Court did not shy away from inferring a policy against the formation of same-sex family units from two legislative provisions that are related only because they deal with issues relating to sexual orientation as well: the criminalization of male same-sex sexual conduct under Section 377A of the Penal Code and a prohibition against same-sex marriage in Section 12 of the Women's Charter. Though the Court insisted that the appellant's sexual orientation was 'made relevant by the law as we understand it,'[26] it is more likely that the logic operated in the opposite direction. Put another way, the Court's conflation of – and simplistic understanding of – the concepts of marriage, family, gender, and sexuality led it to the conclusion that a prohibition against same-sex sexual conduct and same-sex marriage means that there also exists a prohibition against same-sex family units.

The heteronormative state strikes back: Legislative reforms to the law on adoption

Notwithstanding its exposure of the contradictions in Singapore's heteronormative hegemony and the burden borne by the appellant and other non-heterosexual persons, queer visibility is ultimately a 'double-edged sword,' in that it may also invite backlash from state and non-state actors to maintain the subjugation of queer subjects in society.[27]

Despite the spotlight placed on compulsory heterosexuality and the state's narrow definition of family by the appellant by bringing this case before the High Court, what ensued was not a reimagination or reconfiguration of Singapore's family law. Instead, shortly after the judgment was issued, the state doubled down, announcing

---

23. Offord, 'The Burden of (Homo)sexual Identity;' Simon Oberndof, 'Both Contagion and Cure: Queer Politics in the Global City-State,' in *Queer Singapore: Illiberal Citizenship and Mediated Cultures*, ed. Audrey Yue and Jun Zubillaga-Pow (Hong Kong: Hong Kong University Press, 2012).
24. *UKM v Attorney-General*, [188].
25. Leong, 'The Next Fifty Years,' 162.
26. *UKM v Attorney-General*, [209].
27. Edenborg, 'Visibility in Global Queer Politics,' 353.

its intention to amend the Adoption of Children Act. In a speech in response to numerous parliamentary questions, the Minister for Social and Family Development noted that 'while the welfare of the child should always be a very important consideration in adoption proceedings, we are looking at whether the Adoption of Children Act needs to be amended so that a better balance can be struck when important public policy considerations are involved.'[28]

The amendments were subsequently passed in April 2022, and require the Guardian-in-Adoption and the court to consider the applicants' 'suitability to adopt' under Section 7 of the new Adoption of Children Act 2022 as defined by the factors prescribed by regulations and any applicable ruling, decision, or judicial pronouncement by any court. In the Minister's speech introducing the Bill, it was explained that the public policy against the formation of same-sex family units is to be taken into account in adoption proceedings under this Section 7.[29] In addition, the new legislation expressly stipulates that a joint adoption order may only be made by two individuals married to each other because Singapore's public policy encourages parenthood within marriage.

In an analysis of the law's function in enforcing heteronormativity in European cases on non-binary gender, Grietje Baars writes:

> Through living queer lives we wrench the frames of law, yet law adapts to us – or we to it – and seduces us (the more privileged among us) into accepting our legal framing, our box – where, we if we sit still inside of it, we don't feel our chains.[30]

Baars' observations resonate with the events that followed the Singapore High Court's granting of the adoption order to the appellant which highlight the difficulty of 'accepting... our box.' Because the appellant pursued a closeted legal strategy, the law was able to adapt and refashion itself into a more powerful set of rules to enforce compulsory heterosexual matrimony and close any loophole that offered at least some breathing room to us queers living under its shackles.

At the same time, as discussed above, it is also entirely possible that a non-closeted legal strategy that involved constitutional arguments could have led to the same (or an even worse) outcome. This was the case with the decriminalization of male same-sex sexual conduct. Although the Singapore government repealed Section 377A of the Penal Code in 2022 because of the purported risk of it being struck down by a future court for violating the constitutional right to equality, the repeal was coupled with a new constitutional amendment immunizing any law or policy that is informed by the heterosexual definition of marriage from being struck down for violating any person's

---

28.   Singapore Parliamentary Debates, Official Report (14 January 2019) vol 94 'Government's Position on Court Ruling to Award Adoption to Man in Same-sex Relationship' (Minister for Social & Family Development, Mr Desmond Lee), accessed 21 January 2024, https://sprs.parl.gov.sg/search/#/sprs3topic?reportid=oral-answer-1859.
29.   Singapore Parliamentary Debates, Official Report (14 January 2019) vol 95 'Second Reading of the Adoption of Children Bill' (Minister for Social & Family Development, Mr Masagos Zulkifli B M M), accessed 21 January 2024, https://sprs.parl.gov.sg/search/#/sprs3topic?reportid=oral-answer-1859.
30.   Grietje Baars, 'Queer Cases Unmake Gendered Law, Or, Fucking Law's Gendering Function,' *Australian Feminist Law Journal* 45/1 (2019), 61.

constitutional rights under Part 4 of the Constitution.[31] Specifically, the new Article 156 of the Constitution (titled 'Institution of marriage') states that nothing in Part 4 of the Constitution invalidates a law or exercise of executive authority by reason that the law or executive action is based on a definition of marriage as a union between a man and a woman.

Taken together, the possibility of achieving same-sex marriage and parenthood through the courts appears fully shut in Singapore. This is yet another facet of the 'homosexual burden' in Singapore: one's access to justice through the courts is limited by virtue of one's sexual orientation. While the High Court in *UKM v Attorney-General* chose to hide in the closet by turning a blind eye to queer injustice in its decision, the subsequent legislative response has written into law a legal closet that potentially forestalls any future ventilation of queer inequality or oppression before the courts. It remains to be seen whether and how gay rights activists and future plaintiffs can navigate their way around this legal closet to pursue queer justice and equality, which operates as the new 'homosexual burden' that we must bear in a post-decriminalization Singapore.

---

31. Yang and Neo, 'Whither the Constitution?'

UKM v Attorney-General [2018] SGHCF 18

Daryl WJ Yang

Concurring Opinion

Introduction

[1] The question presented in this appeal is whether an adoption order should be granted to a gay man seeking to adopt his own biological son born overseas through gestational surrogacy, whom I shall refer to as the Child. While I agree with the majority's conclusion in the majority decision by the Honourable Chief Justice Sundaresh Menon (*Majority Opinion* or *MO*) that the adoption order sought should be granted, I disagree with the majority's view that (i) there is a public policy against the formation of same-sex family units (*the Policy*) and (ii) insofar as the majority is correct that the Policy does exist, that making the adoption order breaches the Policy.

[2] Before turning to the facts of this case, I make three preliminary comments on what this case is and is not about.

[3] First, like the majority, I am mindful that this is a highly controversial case in the court of public opinion, which 'challenges the mores of a largely conservative society' (MO at [1]). However, while I agree with the majority that this court must therefore only 'apply the law… to determine the particular dispute in the case at hand' and not 'determine social policy,' I am concerned that the majority may have inadvertently done so, by finding in favour of the existence of the Policy.

[4] Second, while it is up to the appellant and his counsel how he wishes to run his case, I note that he has elected not to challenge the constitutionality of the Policy (MO at [203]) and it is not for this court to consider questions that are not raised before it. This is remarkable against the backdrop of the ongoing constitutional challenges against section 377A of the Penal Code 1871 (*Section 377A*), which criminalizes 'gross indecency' between men. Notably, the majority accepted the reliance by the Director of Social Welfare of the Ministry of Social & Family Development ('the Guardian') on the existence of Section 377A in support of a finding that there is public policy against the formation of same-sex family units (MO at [206]). I elaborate on this point below.

[5] Third, this case calls into question the role that law plays – and should play – in (in)validating the intimate relationships between individuals within society. As will become evident in the next section, there is no question that the appellant will continue to love and care for his biological Child together with his partner regardless of the outcome of this appeal. Notably, although the couple jointly decided to have the child and are raising the Child together, only the appellant has sought the adoption order to establish a legal relationship between the Child and himself.

[6] In my view, this case is not about the appellant's desire for the law's recognition of his family. Rather, it stems from a solely practical concern: to increase his Child's chances of obtaining Singaporean citizenship. As the facts will show, this is an issue that almost no other Singaporean parent – except male same-sex couples – have to concern themselves with because their children would be guaranteed Singaporean citizenship as a matter of right under the Constitution of the Republic of Singapore (Constitution).

The factual backdrop

[7] The appellant is a 46-year-old gay Singaporean man who has been in a long-term relationship with another man of the same age and nationality for around 13 years. The couple have cohabited since about 2003 and live together with their Child who was born on 19 November 2013 via gestational surrogacy in the United States of America (USA). The appellant was listed as the Child's father on the Child's birth certificate issued by the state of Pennsylvania while the surrogate mother was listed as the Child's mother. While the fact that the Child was born via gestational surrogacy featured significantly in the parties' arguments, I agree with the majority that it has no bearing on the outcome of this appeal.

[8] Why did the couple go halfway across the world to conceive the child via gestational surrogacy? I note that the appellant and his partner had initially sought to adopt a child in Singapore but were informed that they would not be allowed to do so because of their non-heterosexual orientation. Serendipitously, it is for this very same reason that the appellant has come before this court: to adopt a child, albeit his own biological Child.

[9] After the couple returned to Singapore, an application for Singaporean citizenship was made on behalf of the Child. However, in August 2014, the Child's citizenship application was rejected. Instead, the Child was granted permission to remain in Singapore on a yearly basis under a long-term visit pass (LTVP).

[10] The failure of the appellant to obtain Singaporean citizenship by descent under Article 122 of the Constitution for his Child led him to apply for the adoption order sought in this appeal. This is because paragraph 15(2) of the Third Schedule to the Constitution (Paragraph 15(2)) states that if a child is adopted, then references to the child's father or parent are to be construed as references to the adopter.

[11] The appellant thus wishes to apply for Singaporean citizenship for his Child under Article 124(1) of the Constitution, which allows the Government to register a child under the age of 21 years as a Singaporean citizen if two requirements are satisfied: first, they are *a child of a Singaporean citizen* and second, the child is residing in Singapore. The adoption order will allow the Child to satisfy the former requirement though this does not guarantee that the Child will succeed in his citizenship application: Article 124(1) ultimately confers the discretion whether to grant the application on the Government.

[12] The adoption order was not granted by the Family Court in *Re UKM* [2018] SGFC 20 (FC Decision) on the basis that granting it would 'smear the thin line between the rights and interests of adults and those of children' (at [44]) given that the applicant was attempting to 'obtain a desired result – that is, formalizing the parent-child relationship, by walking through the back door of the system when the front door was firmly shut' (at [33]). This is because, in the learned District Judge's view, assisted reproductive technologies (ART) were only permitted to be offered to heterosexual married couples in Singapore and surrogacy services are not permitted by virtue of clause 5.48 of the Licensing Terms and Conditions on Assisted Reproduction Services (26 April 2011) (ART Licensing Terms) promulgated under s 6(5) of the Private Hospitals and Medical Clinics Act 1980. Furthermore, the District Judge did not consider that the welfare of the Child demanded the granting of the adoption order because the Child will 'continue to have shelter, food on his table, a good education and a sound support system in the shape of an extended family' (at [33]).

[13] The appellant now appeals against the FC Decision on the basis that the adoption order would be for the Child's welfare and the public policy considerations raised by the Guardian do not outweigh the Child's welfare.

The obstacles to same-sex parenting in Singapore

[14] The facts of this case should make clear that the present appeal arises from a rather peculiar set of facts and law. First, as a mixed matter of fact and law, this case would likely have not arisen if the appellant and/or his partner had been able to conceive or adopt a child in Singapore. More specifically, this case could only have been brought by a gay man or same-sex couple because of the serious practical difficulties that they face or would face conceiving or adopting a child in Singapore. Second, as a matter of law, this appeal would not have arisen if not for paragraph 15(1), which states that:

Illegitimate children and adopted children

15.— (1) For the purposes of Part 10 [Citizenship], references to a person's father or to his parent or to one of his parents shall, in relation to a person who is illegitimate, be construed as references to his mother.

While they are not strictly in issue in this appeal, these points deserve some elaboration to provide the appropriate socio-legal context.

[15] In my view, it was unfortunate that the appellant elected not to challenge the prevailing policies against the use of ART by a same-sex couple, and/or Paragraph 15(1). Had the appellant and his partner been heterosexual or if either of them had been biologically capable of becoming pregnant, they would have been able to conceive their child within Singapore (whether through birth or adoption) and would not have faced the present challenge of obtaining Singaporean citizenship for his biological Child. That this is something only a person of a particular gender and sexual orientation would face surely engages the appellant's constitutional right to equality under Article 12 of the Constitution.

[16] Yet, as the constitutionality of the relevant laws and policies was not argued before this Court, I will not comment further on this issue. Instead, I will simply briefly describe the factual context that has given rise to this appeal.

Appellant's inability to conceive or adopt a child in Singapore

[17] This case arose from the appellant's inability to conceive or adopt a child in Singapore. Had the appellant been able to do so, the present challenge in obtaining Singaporean citizenship for his Child would not have arisen.

[18] First, in terms of conceiving a child that has a biological link with him, the appellant would have to conceive a child through the use of assisted reproductive technology and surrogacy services. However, as noted at [12] above, surrogacy services cannot be provided in Singapore – regardless of the sexual orientation of the couple. Consequently, the appellant had to seek out surrogacy services overseas. This culminated in the present appeal because his Child could not obtain Singaporean citizenship by birth under Article 121 of the Constitution, which provides that every person born in Singapore shall be a citizen of Singapore by birth if at least one of their parents is a citizen of Singapore.

[19] At the same time, the appellant was not the first or only parent who had conceived their child through surrogacy services. Instead, as the Guardian conceded, it has supported 10 adoption applications by married heterosexual couples where their child was conceived through surrogacy. The only difference here is that the appellant is not heterosexual and is not married, which is a consequence of his sexual orientation considering that same-sex marriage is not legally recognised in Singapore by virtue of section 12 of the Women's Charter 1961, which states that marriages solemnized in Singapore or elsewhere between persons who are not respectively male and female at the date of marriage are void.

[20] Second, the appellant is unlikely to have been able to adopt a child in Singapore considering that he is in a long-term relationship with another man. Strictly speaking, and as a matter of law, the appellant can adopt a male child in Singapore as a single man.

Section 4(3) of the Adoption of Children Act 1939 only stipulates that an adoption order cannot be made where the sole appellant is a male and the infant in respect of whom the application is made is a female except in special circumstances. As this is not an issue before this court, I would only note that this gendered distinction potentially raises a question as to whether it may be inconsistent with the guarantee of equality under Article 12 of the Constitution.

[21] Nevertheless, as noted in the decision of the lower court, the applicant and his partner had approached the Ministry of Social and Family Development (MSF) and were advised that the Ministry was unlikely to recommend adoption of children by parties who were in a same-sex relationship (FC Decision at [5]). This is because of the Ministry's view that allowing adoption by same-sex couples would be against Singaporean public policy regarding the composition of a family unit and parenthood within the confines of a heterosexual marriage.

Paragraph 15(1) of the Third Schedule to the Constitution

[22] Ordinarily, a child of a Singaporean citizen who is born overseas is entitled to acquire Singaporean citizenship by descent pursuant to Article 122 of the Constitution. Specifically, Article 122(1)(b) provides that:

> a person born outside Singapore after 16 September 1963 shall be a citizen of Singapore by descent if, at the time of his birth … either his father or mother is a citizen of Singapore, by birth, registration or descent.

[23] However, in this case, the Child is regarded by the law as an 'illegitimate' child, having been born out of wedlock. This is because the appellant was not married to the mother of the Child at the time of the birth.

[24] According to Paragraph 15(1), references to an illegitimate person's father or parent are to be construed as references to that person's mother. The Child therefore cannot acquire Singaporean citizenship by descent pursuant to Article 122 because his mother, i.e. the gestational surrogate, was a citizen of the USA, not Singapore.

[25] In this regard, it is curious that the majority suggested at [77] of the MO that 'the distinction between legitimate and illegitimate children has indeed been eroded, and it is significant today *only* for the purposes of succession law.' Clearly, as the present case demonstrates, the concept of legitimacy remains relevant in the context of citizenship law as well. Also, with respect, Professor Leong Wai Kum - whom the majority cites in support of the proposition that legitimacy is only relevant to succession law - did not make such an assertion. Rather, the scholar asserted that the disadvantageous effects of being an illegitimate child are of 'residual nature' and one such residual area is succession. It is quite clear that the Professor Leong was not suggesting that succession law was the only area where illegitimacy continues to have an impact.

[26] The Guardian also submitted that 'the distinction between legitimate and illegitimate children is today virtually inconsequential' (MO at [27(b)]). This is not true. The Child in this case would have obtained Singaporean citizenship by virtue of Article 122 if not for Paragraph 15(1). It is incorrect to say that the distinction between legitimate and illegitimate children is 'inconsequential' when clearly this Child was deprived of the opportunity to acquire Singaporean citizenship because of his illegitimate status.

[27] The appellant could have, but did not, invite this Court to consider whether Paragraph 15(1) violates his or the Child's right to equality under Article 12 of the Constitution. There are two potential violations here. First, Paragraph 15(1) discriminates on the basis of gender by defining the parent of an illegitimate child as their mother only. Second, Paragraph 15(1) discriminates against an illegitimate child by halving their chance of acquiring citizenship. This is because a 'legitimate' child may obtain Singaporean citizenship so long as *either* parent is a Singaporean. In contrast, an 'illegitimate' child may obtain Singaporean citizenship *only if* their mother is Singaporean.

My reasoning on the granting of the adoption order

[28] Like the majority, I agree that the adoption order should be granted. However, I find that there is no public policy against the formation of same-sex families in Singapore that the court should consider when considering the appellant's adoption application. Even if there were such a Policy, I do not think that the majority was correct in its finding that the Policy militates against granting the adoption order.

Whether making the adoption order is for the welfare of the child

[29] As a starting point, I agree with the majority that the court must consider the welfare of the Child. This is by virtue of Section 3 of the Guardianship of Infants Act 1934 (2020 Rev Ed), which states that:

> Where in any proceedings before any court the custody or upbringing of an infant or the administration of any property belonging to or held in trust for an infant or the application of the income thereof is in question, the court, in deciding that question, shall regard the welfare of the infant as the first and paramount consideration...

[30] I also agree with the majority that making the adoption order would be for the welfare of the Child because it increases his prospects of securing Singaporean citizenship and long-term residence here where his family is located (MO at [67] and [84]).

[31] I also agree with the majority that the fact that the Child is being raised by a same-sex couple has no bearing on the Child's welfare (MO at [83]).

[32] While I agree with the majority that the legitimation of the legal relationship between the appellant and the Child would confer social, psychological, and emotional benefits on the Child, I do not share the majority's qualification that such benefits would be

less weighty than the social, emotional and psychological benefits conferred by the Child's potential acquisition of Singaporean citizenship. While the latter appears to be more tangible as a matter of geographical certainty, it is not appropriate or feasible to measure that against the intangible value of having one's relationship with their child legally recognized through adoption. The fact that legitimacy remains a valid legal concept in Singapore gives pause to any claim that whether or not a child is 'legitimate' has no or limited impact on the lived realities of those whose relationship with their loved ones is defined as being 'illegitimate.' It is time that this court or the legislature expressly retire the concept of legitimacy from our legal framework if it is no longer relevant to our modern society.

[33] I am somewhat confused by the Guardian's arguments on the welfare of the Child. The Guardian's initial objection to the appellant's application for an adoption order was that it would be 'contrary to public policy to allow for an adoption in this case where the applicant is in effect seeking the court's endorsement of his intent to form a family unit with his male partner' (FC Decision at [14]). On appeal, the Guardian now argues that granting the adoption order would not be for the welfare of the Child. This is quite remarkable given that it was the MSF itself (which the Guardian is part of) that advised the appellant to adopt his Child to establish a legal nexus between them, so that the Child can obtain Singaporean citizenship and remain in Singapore (MO at [12]).

Whether there exists a public policy against the formation of same-sex families

[34] Turning to the nub of this appeal, the majority found that there exists a public policy against the formation of same-sex families which militates against the making of the adoption order. According to the majority, this public policy means that the Government is 'opposed to the advancement of any right claimed by a homosexual for the purpose of forming a same-sex family unit' (MO at [202]). This is defined as a family where there are two same-sex co-parenting individuals as well as a family where there is a single non-heterosexual parent and a child.

[35] I agree with the majority that public policy must be 'clearly expressed in order to be persuasive' (MO at [144]) and the source of a public policy must be 'relevant to establishing that policy' (MO at [146]).

[36] The majority relies on the following evidence in support of this finding.

[37] The first is Prime Minister Lee Hsien Loong's parliamentary speech in 2007 on the Government's decision not to repeal Section 377A, wherein he stated that 'we have also been right to adapt, to accommodate homosexuals in our society, but not to allow or encourage activists to champion gay rights as they do in the West' (MO at [204]). According to the majority, this speech indicates that the Government's position is 'to maintain the status quo such that the traditional family unit remains the societal norm' (MO at [205]).

[38] The second is Section 377A itself, which 'continues to signal public sentiment against sexual conduct between males, even in private' (MO at [206]).

[39] The third is Section 12(1) of the Women's Charter 1961 (Rev Ed 2020) ('Section 12(1)'), which stipulates that a marriage between persons who, at the date of the marriage, are not respectively male and female is void. The majority understands this to 'communicate that society does not accept same-sex family units' (MO at [206]).

[40] The majority's logic in relation to Section 377A and the Prime Minister's speech is unpersuasive. In my view, this criminal provision has little to do with the formation of same-sex family units except that both are generally related to same-sex relationships. However, as the Court of Appeal has previously observed, 'Section 377A prohibits, at its core, sexual acts between males' (*Lim Meng Suang v Attorney-General* [2015] 1 SLR 26 at [51]). A law criminalizing male same-sex sexual conduct has no direct, or indirect, relationship with the *formation* of same-sex family units. The former is a matter of criminal law and sexual conduct, while the latter is a matter of family law and familial relations.

[41] It appears that the majority has read the formation of same-sex family units into the term 'gay rights' as employed by the Prime Minister in his speech quoted above. Alternatively, it may be that the majority is of the view that Section 377A represents a general social disavowal of same-sex relationships which should also extend to a disavowal of same-sex family units. I am unable to agree with the majority that either the Prime Minister's speech or the continued criminalization of 'gross indecency' between men under Section 377A is evidence of a public policy against the formation of same-sex family units. Any tangential relationship between the criminalization of male same-sex sexual conduct and the formation of same-sex family units is insufficiently clear or relevant to justify the existence of a public policy against the latter.

[42] As for Section 12(1), the majority has conflated the institution of marriage with the institution of family itself. While they are closely related concepts, marriage and family are not interchangeable. Specifically, Section 12(1) prohibits same-sex *marriage* but does not say anything about same-sex *family units*.

[43] Like the majority, I accept that the Government has a public policy in favour of parenthood within marriage (MO at [191]). However, the majority noted that this is not the same as a public policy against other forms of parenthood (MO at [192]). Just because it is desirable in the Government's view that a family comprise of 'a married heterosexual couple having and raising children within that household' (MO at [187]) does not mean that the Government is opposed to family units that do not conform to that particular family arrangement. A same-sex family may not necessarily comprise a married same-sex couple nor is it necessary that a same-sex couple has to be married to *form* a same-sex family unit.

[44] Accordingly, a prohibition against same-sex marriage is not the same as a public policy against same-sex family units. A same-sex family unit can exist without contravening the prohibition against same-sex marriage, as is the case with the appellant and his family. The appellant is not married to his partner. Further, while it is entirely possible that the majority is correct that Singapore society does not accept same-sex family units, the existence of Section 12(1) itself is insufficient authority for this claim. At most, Section 12(1) demonstrates that Singapore society does not accept same-sex marriage.

[45] It could be argued that there is a public policy against the formation of same-sex family units if, for example, the Government enacted a law to remove a child from the custody of their same-sex parents. An express prohibition on non-heterosexual persons adopting a child on the basis of their sexual orientation under the Adoption of Children Act 1939 would also be evidence of the existence of such a public policy. Short of such evidence, it is difficult to see how a law prohibiting same-sex marriage leads to the conclusion that there exists a public policy against same-sex family units.

[46] In conclusion, just as the majority did not consider that there was sufficient evidence in support of a public policy against planned and deliberate parenthood by unmarried persons through the use of ART of surrogacy (MO at [195]), there is insufficient evidence to support a finding that there is a public policy against the formation of same-sex family units. Section 377A and Section 12(1) are neither clear nor relevant authorities for such a proposition. Just because they are both also related to same-sex relationships and non-heterosexual persons does not mean that they also represent or support the specific public policy in question in relation to the formation of same-sex family units.

[47] I therefore cannot concur with the majority's assertion that the appellant and his partner's sexual orientation was only 'made relevant by the law' (MO at [209]). While it is true that Section 377A and Section 12(1) are laws relating to sexual orientation, specifically non-heterosexual orientations, they do not say anything about the formation of same-sex family units *per se*. The majority assumed that those laws were relevant to the question of whether there exists a public policy against the formation of same-sex family units simply because they also relate to non-heterosexual orientations. However, Section 377A and Section 12(1) cannot be relied upon to support any and all alleged public policies that are disadvantageous or unfavourable to non-heterosexual persons, relationships or communities.

Conclusion

[48] As there is no public policy against the formation of same-sex family units, there is no need to proceed to the second step of the analytical framework to balance the Child's welfare against any public policy considerations. Accordingly, I would make the adoption order, it being for the welfare of the Child and there is nothing to militate against the making of such the order.

[49] As a final note, the majority emphasised that it 'express[ed] no subjective personal judgment on the appellant's attempt to form a same-sex family unit' (MO at [208]). I agree that the appellant's sexual orientation and his desire to raise his own Child with his same-sex partner are irrelevant to *whether the adoption order should be made.* However, as I have explained in this Opinion, the appellant's sexual orientation is very relevant as to *why the adoption order was even sought* through these proceedings in the first place.

PART 4

HEALTH AND REPRODUCTION

20

R *(on the application of A and B)* v *Secretary of State for Health* (United Kingdom):

What is the Cost of Reproductive Rights?

Lynsey Mitchell

Introduction

R (on the application of A and B) v Secretary of State for Health (hereinafter *A and B*) was heard at the UK Supreme Court amid growing media attention paid to the prohibition on abortion in Northern Ireland (NI) and against the backdrop of the Campaign to Repeal the Eighth Amendment in Ireland.[1]

The Abortion Act 1967 was not extended to NI, which meant that abortion provision has always existed in something of a legal vacuum there. Rather than the framework adopted in England, Scotland and Wales that allows doctors to provide abortions if certain criteria are met, abortions could only be legally carried out in NI when there was a threat to the woman's physical or mental health or life.[2] This meant that there was some provision of legal abortion in NI but the vast majority of people needing an abortion were forced to travel to Great Britain to seek abortion care.[3] The lack of guidance on when an abortion was legal meant that there was a series of cases seeking judicial clarity on the matter.[4]

---

1. For an overview of the Repeal the Eighth Campaign and its wider significance, see Ruth Fletcher, '#RepealedThe8th: Translating Travesty, Global Conversation, and the Irish Abortion Referendum,' *Feminist Legal Studies* 26 (2018), 233; Máiréad Enright et al., 'Abortion Law Reform in Ireland: A Model for Change,' *Feminists@Law* 5(1) (June 29, 2015).

2. Abortion is criminalised in England and Wales by s.58 and s.59 of the Offences Against the Persons Act 1861, which also applied to Northern Ireland until 2020. The blanket prohibition on abortion was challenged in 1939 by an English doctor who instigated his own prosecution after performing an abortion on a thirteen-year-old rape victim. The Court interpreted s.58 and s.59 as allowing for some abortions and determined that these included where there was a threat to the woman's physical or mental health or life. See *R v Bourne* [1939] 1 KB 687.

3. Between 2020 and 2021, 63 abortions were carried out; in 2019-2020 there were 22; in 2018-19 there were 8; and in 2017-18 there were 12: Department of Health, 'Northern Ireland Termination of Pregnancy Statistics' (Hospital Information Branch), accessed 11 August 2023, https://www.health-ni.gov.uk/articles/termination-pregnancy.

4. *Northern Health and Social Services Board v F and G* [1993] NILR 268; *Northern Health and Social Services Board v A and others* [1994] NIJB 1; *Western Health and Social Services Board v CMB* (Unreported),

Background

The case was brought by A and B, a daughter and a mother respectively. A was a fifteen-year-old girl who was pregnant and wished to have an abortion and B supported this. However, the fact that A and B resided in NI meant that A could not access an abortion there and her best alternative option was to travel to England. As well as the inconvenience and stress of travel, B had to raise money to pay for the termination as people from NI could not access National Health Service (NHS) funded abortions in England. Had A resided in England, the abortion would have been provided for free.

A and B was the first Northern Irish abortion case to reach the Supreme Court, and activists were hopeful that the court would determine that discrimination against Northern Irish people[5] when it came to accessing funded abortions in England was unlawful and a violation of human rights. This case was not about the lack of abortion provision in NI; it was solely focussed on the discriminatory treatment afforded to those who travelled to England to have an abortion. Around the same time, the Northern Irish Human Rights Commission instituted judicial review proceedings, asking the Northern Irish High Court to rule that the lack of provision of abortion in cases of rape, incest, fatal foetal abnormality and serious malformation of the foetus was a contravention of human rights.[6] Horner LJ declared the law incompatible with article 8 of the European Convention on Human Rights (ECHR) and issued a declaration of incompatibility under section 4 of the Human Rights Act 1998 (HRA), which was overturned on appeal.[7]

There was also growing recognition internationally that lack of access to abortion could constitute a violation of human rights,[8] and UN treaty bodies called on States to reform abortion laws and remove criminal sanctions.[9] The UK has been repeatedly

---

High Court (Family Division), 29 September 1995; *Down Lisburn Health and Social Services Board v CH and LAH* (Unreported), High Court (Family Division), 18 October 1995.

5. This commentary and judgment use the term 'pregnant people' recognizing that trans men and non-binary people also experience pregnancy and may require access to abortion care. Recognizing that trans and non-binary people need abortion care is important and adopting more inclusive language around pregnancy and abortion may help to improve access. Adopting inclusive language that challenges the assumption that only women can experience pregnancy and abortion also helps to dismantle the patriarchal narratives and norms applied to abortion and pregnancy. However, abortion law generally uses the term 'woman' to refer to those seeking abortion. The original judgment refers to 'women' (both the applicants specifically, and others seeking abortion more generally). Where possible, this commentary and rewritten judgment use the term 'pregnant people' but for clarity it uses the term 'woman' when referring to the original judgment or to legislation.

6. *In the Matter of an Application for Judicial Review by the Northern Ireland Human Rights Commission in the Matter of the Law on Termination of Pregnancy in Northern Ireland* [2015] NIQB 96.

7. *Attorney General for Northern Ireland v Northern Ireland Human Rights Commission* [2017] NICA 42 and *In the matter of an application by the Northern Ireland Human Rights Commission for Judicial Review (Northern Ireland)* [2018] UKSC 27.

8. Human Rights Committee (HRC), *Amanda Mellet v Ireland* (9 June 2016, CCPR/C/116/D/2324/2013); HRC, *KL v Peru* (22 November 2005, CCPR/C/85/D/1153/2003); CEDAW, *LC v Peru* (4 November 2011, CEDAW/C/50/D/22/2009); HRC, *LMR v Argentina* (28 April 2011, CCPR/C/101/D/1608/2007).

9. The Committee on Economic, Social and Cultural Rights (CESCR) has called on states parties to the International Convention on Economic, Social and Cultural Rights to 'liberalize restrictive abortion laws; to guarantee women and girls access to safe abortion services and quality post-abortion care': CESCR,

criticised by UN treaty bodies for failing to redress the situation.[10] Northern Irish activists and lawyers referred the UK Government to the UN Committee on the Elimination of Discrimination Against Women (CEDAW) over the lack of abortion provision in NI.[11]

The Secretary of State for Health acknowledged that A and B had been treated differently when accessing abortion care in England.[12] His argument, which was accepted by the majority of the judges, was that treating people differently based on residence was justified and that it did not amount to discrimination under the ECHR. He argued that it was acceptable to force people from NI to endure serious financial and mental hardship because their needs were secondary to the devolved health settlement and because of the need to demonstrate respect for the wishes of the Northern Irish Assembly.[13] However, neither the Secretary of State nor the majority of the judges explained why allowing people from NI to access the same funded abortions available to everyone else in the UK would threaten the devolution or democratic settlement in NI.

I find the framing of this case by the Government as a devolution issue rather than a reproductive rights issue particularly troubling given the conceptualisation of reproductive rights within the international legal regime's right to health. Framing abortion as an elective treatment which depends on the devolved political settlement elevates abortion to a position of great consequence in politics, while simultaneously de-prioritising it as a gendered health issue worthy of time or debate.[14] This sends the message that reproductive rights can be bartered away,[15] and positions

---

General Comment No. 22: The Right to Sexual and Reproductive Health, (2016) UN Doc. E/C.12/GC/22 (2016), para. 10.

10. In 2016, CESCR recommended that the UK should 'amend the legislation on termination of pregnancy in Northern Ireland to make it compatible with other fundamental rights, such as women's rights to health, life and dignity': CESCR, *Concluding Observations on the Sixth Periodic Report of the United Kingdom of Great Britain and Northern Ireland*, UN Doc. E/C.12/GBR/CO/6 (2016), para. 62. The Committee on the Rights of the Child (CRC) has also advocated that abortion be decriminalised and called on the UK to 'review its legislation': CRC, *Concluding Observations on the Fifth Periodic Report of the United Kingdom of Great Britain and Northern Ireland*, UN Doc. CRC/C/GBR/CO/5 (2016), para. 65(c). CEDAW has repeatedly challenged the NI regime in its UK reports: for example, CEDAW, *Concluding Observations on the Seventh Periodic Report of the United Kingdom of Great Britain and Northern Ireland*, UN Doc. CEDAW/C/GBR/CO/7, para. 51, and *Concluding Observations on the Sixth Periodic Report of the United Kingdom of Great Britain and Northern Ireland*, UN Doc.C/UK/CO/6, para. 289.

11. FPANI, Northern Ireland Women's European Platform and Alliance for Choice, *Submission of Evidence to the CEDAW Committee Optional Protocol: Inquiry Procedure*, Transitional Justice Institute Research paper (No 15-01), 60-61. For commentary on the utility of leveraging international human rights law, see Catherine O'Rourke, 'Bridging the Enforcement Gap - Evaluating the Inquiry Procedure of the CEDAW Optional Protocol,' *American University Journal of Gender Social Policy & the Law* 27 (2018), 1.

12. *R (on the application of A and B) v Secretary of State for Health*, [20].

13. The UK devolves certain areas of law (known as competencies) to the devolved nations—Scotland, Wales and Northern Ireland—which each have their own parliament or law making assembly. In Northern Ireland, health is a devolved competency under the Northern Ireland Act 1998. The devolution settlement sets out that the UK Parliament should not legislate in areas that are devolved.

14. The appellants cited a variety of international human rights law documents and decisions on abortion access, but their weight was considered 'slight' by the Court: *R (on the application of A and B) v Secretary of State for Health*, [35].

15. Nicholas Hellen and Caroline Wheeler, 'Abortion Reform "Blocked to Protect DUP Deal,"'

abortion not as a right but as a privilege that is only granted when the political or social conditions allow.[16]

Queering Abortion Law?

The Court did not consider forced pregnancy to be a gross violation of bodily autonomy and human rights. I suggest this is because pregnancy and motherhood are still positioned as a gendered norm and ideal, rendering abortion a last resort, necessary in only the most extreme circumstances, rather than routine reproductive healthcare. Those who need abortions are constructed as tragic victims needing the legal and medical establishment's pity and paternalistic permission to access abortion.[17] Human rights law has been of limited utility, securing access to abortion only where those who need abortions can demonstrate suitable justifications such as a threat to life.[18] Since A did not fall within this category, the majority of the judges appeared content to view her quest to obtain an abortion as nothing more than the pursuit of elective treatment that would logically incur costs. That these costs were the main barrier to her accessing an abortion is not understood as a problem, or certainly not one serious enough to merit legal redress.

There was no claim or consideration that the failure to provide funded abortions on the NHS to people from NI was a violation not only of article 14 (the right to enjoy the convention rights without discrimination) in conjunction with article 8 ECHR (the right to private and family life), but also of article 3 ECHR (The prohibition on torture and inhuman or degrading treatment). The failure to engage with the reality of A's circumstances appears to be another instance of pregnant people's suffering meriting sympathy, but not being considered serious enough to be a violation of human rights.[19] Implicit within this is the idea that simply being forced to remain pregnant cannot be construed as a violation of human rights and that enduring hardship or suffering to procure an abortion is acceptable. A and B told the Court how the failure to fund abortions caused them severe trauma and suffering, yet this was not enough to engage article 3. However, a queer lens allows us to start from the position that actual trauma and suffering caused by the State's lack of protection for bodily autonomy is a violation of article 3, on the basis that the physical and mental hardships this causes reach the threshold for inhuman or degrading treatment.[20]

The Times, 27 January 2019, accessed 11 August 2023, https://www.thetimes.co.uk/article/abortion-reform-blocked-to-protect-dup-deal-kpbw8vltt.

16. Lynsey Mitchell, 'Reading Narratives of Privilege and Paternalism: The Limited Utility of Human Rights Law on the Journey to Reform Northern Irish Abortion Law,' *NILQ* 7/1 (2021), 89.

17. Rosamund Scott, 'Risks, Reasons, and Rights: The European Convention on Human Rights and English Abortion Law,' *Medical Law Review* 24 (2015), 1, 2.

18. Brid Ní Ghráinne and Aisling McMahon, 'Abortion in Northern Ireland and the European Convention on Human Rights: Reflections from the UK Supreme Court,' *International and Comparative Law Quarterly* 68/2 (2019), 490.

19. For a discussion of the failure of abortion trauma to engage article 3, see Ní Ghráinne and McMahon, 'Abortion in Northern Ireland and the European Convention on Human Rights.'

20. Alyson Zureick, '(En)Gendering Suffering: Denial of Abortion as a Form of Cruel, Inhuman, or Degrading Treatment,' *Fordham International Law Journal* 38 (2015), 99.

Ludlow has highlighted this hierarchy within discourse about abortion, whereby narratives of 'traumatized' abortion stories resplendent with suffering eclipse those stories that reinforce the ordinary and routine nature of abortion.[21] The implicit demand that 'abortion be the exception, and not a normal part of women's lives' reinforces the association between abortion and trauma, shame, violence, and abuse:

> Because they are presented so frequently, these circumstances [rape and abuse, medically dangerous pregnancies] have become reinscribed as the 'appropriate reasons' to have an abortion, and they render all other reasons for aborting questionable at best, and frivolous at worst.[22]

This case positions pregnancy and childbirth as *normal* and abortion as *exceptional* and *elective*, rather than routine healthcare that is fundamental to respecting bodily autonomy and so, the law's ability to offer redress to those needing to end a pregnancy is limited. This is because of the powerful heteronormative framing in which pregnancy is positioned as normal and desirable. This results in State regulation in the way of abortion restrictions being understood as justified.

Reproductive Justice

While abortion regulation may seem a firmly established feminist domain of legal critique, this case offers an important opportunity to demonstrate how a queer perspective allows for an alternative decision that would situate bodily autonomy, choice, physical and mental health at its centre, but also engage with wider social factors that are central to the reproductive justice movement. Reproductive justice is a term coined by Black and ethnic minority women that seeks to go beyond the narrow binaries of pro-choice and anti-choice which had become the focus of the reproductive rights campaign.[23]

In attempting to conceptualise what queer reproductive justice would look like, many acknowledge a clash of ideologies.[24] Thomas and Morrison concede that a queer reproductive politic may appear 'paradoxical,' as feminist and reproductive rights movements have long sought refuge in political and legal protectionism while queer theory has produced 'some of the most incisive critiques of identity politics and appeals to State protection.'[25] However, they demonstrate that insightful and powerful

---

21. Jeannie Ludlow, 'The Things We Cannot Say: Witnessing the Traumatization of Abortion in the United States,' *Women's Studies Quarterly* 36/1-2 (2008), 28, 41.

22. Ludlow, 'The Things We Cannot Say.'

23. See Justin Murray et al., 'Introduction' in *In Search of Common Ground on Abortion: From Culture War to Reproductive Justice*, ed. Robin West, Justin Murray and Meredith Esser (Farnham: Taylor and Francis, 2014), 4; Loretta J. Ross and Rickie Solinger, *Reproductive Justice: An Introduction* (Oakley: University of California Press, 2017); Laura Nixon, 'The Right to (Trans) Parent: A Reproductive Justice Approach to Reproductive Rights, Fertility, and Family-Building Issues Facing Transgender People,' *William & Mary Journal of Law, Race, Gender and Social Justice* 20/1 (2013), 73, 79-80.

24. Mimi Marinucci, *Feminism is Queer* (London: Zed Books, 2016).

25. Carly Thomsen and Grace Tacherra Morrison, 'Abortion as Gender Transgression: Reproductive Justice, Queer Theory, and Anti–Crisis Pregnancy Center Activism,' *Signs: Journal of Women in Culture and Society* 45/3 (2020), 705.

activism and alternative conceptualizations can emerge when feminist and queer theory approaches are united to champion reproductive justice:[26]

> We argue for reading abortion as gender transgression and suggest that approaching something as wildly ordinary as abortion—nearly one-quarter of US women obtain an abortion in their lifetime, after all—as transgressive encourages broadening queer conceptualizations of normativity and transgression, allowing us to recognize deeper connections between queer and reproductive issues and, further, to complicate this very distinction.[27]

The case of *A and B* demonstrates society's and the judiciary's inherent patriarchal construction of those who need abortions as deserving sympathy, while mandating that they justify their need to have an abortion. Anyone who does not fit this narrow stereotype of having a tragic circumstance necessitating an abortion is therefore viewed as deviant. In rewriting this judgment, I wanted to subvert the law's continued adherence to stereotypical gendered attitudes and assumptions about pregnant people that deny agency and bodily autonomy when it comes to sex and reproductive decision making. The majority judgment in *A and B* refused to grapple with the wider reality for people like A, i.e., they cannot afford the cost of an abortion in England, so the real barrier is socio-economic. I wanted to centre this perspective and offer an alternative interpretation of abortion rights that was rooted in reproductive justice.

By adopting a queer perspective, I acknowledge that we can conceptualize access to abortion as constituting more than just a negative duty. Such a conceptualization as a negative duty does not engage with the reality of people's lives and is overly deferential to a heteronormative system in which abortion is positioned as deviant and destructive. As Cohen argues, queer politics will be most powerful when it engages with those who have not benefited from heteronormativity (e.g. Black single mothers) rather than being limited to LGBTQ-identified people.[28] For reproductive justice scholars and activists, a wider conceptualization of pro-choice advocacy borne of a queer lens is necessary because the right to legal abortion will 'not resolve the barriers to having children that many women of color and low-income women face.'[29]

Therefore, to truly have reproductive choice, critiques of barriers to abortion must include social and economic barriers, otherwise decisions around whether to become a parent cannot be made freely by everyone. It cannot be the case that reproductive freedom is only available to those with economic means. Not only do barriers to abortion perpetuate discrimination, but they reinforce the dominance of certain lifestyles.

---

26. Thomsen and Morrison note that in 2013 there was almost no mention of the term queer reproductive justice, but that in the past decade, this has changed. In 2014, Unite for Reproductive and Gender Equity (URGE, formerly Choice-USA) added a 'Queering Reproductive Justice' page to its website. In 2015, the University of Michigan organized an event called 'Queering Reproductive Justice: Opportunities and Challenges.' In 2017, SisterSong held a 'Queering Reproductive Justice 101' workshop, and the National LGBTQ Task Force created 'Queering Reproductive Justice: A Toolkit.' See also Barbara Sutton & Elizabeth Borland, 'Queering Abortion Rights: Notes from Argentina,' *Culture, Health & Sexuality* 20/12 (2018), 1378.
27. Thomsen and Morrison, 'Abortion as Gender Transgression,' 703.
28. Cathy J. Cohen, 'Punks, Bulldaggers, and Welfare Queens: The Radical Potential of Queer Politics,' *GLQ* 3/4 (1997), 437.
29. Zakiya Luna and Kristin Luker, 'Reproductive Justice,' *Annual Review of Law and Science* 9 (2013), 327, 328.

This is especially true around pregnancy and child rearing, where heteronormativity seeks to capture those with reproductive capacity:

> [W]e cannot challenge dominant ideas about gender without taking reproductive norms seriously ... Because requirements for being considered a 'good' woman are sutured to what it means to be a 'good' mother, any work to upend gender norms requires critical engagement with ideas about reproduction—even for those of us who plan to avoid parenthood or do not have heterosexual sex.[30]

In this judgment, I aim to similarly acknowledge the emancipatory potential of queer reproductive justice as a means to move beyond heteronormative narratives that position abortion as a tragedy or procedure of last resort or an elective procedure only for those with money. Instead, a queer lens offers the potential to disrupt the positioning of pregnancy as *normal* and *natural* with abortion juxtaposed as *exceptional* and *deviant*. It acknowledges that a society that values true reproductive freedom should determine that lack of access to funded abortion constitutes a human rights violation because a lack of funded abortion is, for many, a barrier to abortion.

In this judgment, I also draw a parallel with other teenagers like A who seek healthcare but are forced to gain parental help to validate those decisions. Despite well settled case law on teenagers being able to consent to healthcare decisions privately,[31] there are still situations, mainly around contraception, abortion, and gender affirming healthcare[32] where teenagers are not considered to have agency, and this is reflected in State regulation of such care. True reproductive justice can empower teenagers and young adults to seek the care they need without overly burdensome State regulation making this impossible.

---

30. Thomsen and Morrison, 'Abortion as Gender Transgression,' 719.
31. See, e.g. *Gillick v West Norfolk & Wisbeck Area Health Authority* [1986] AC 112, *Re R (A Minor) (Wardship: Consent to Treatment)* [1991] 3 WLR 592, and *Re E (A Minor) (Wardship: Medical Treatment)* [1993] 1 FLR 386.
32. *R (Bell) v Tavistock and Portman NHS Foundation Trust* [2021] EWCA Civ 1363.

THE SUPREME COURT OF THE UNITED KINGDOM

Easter Term
[2023] UKSC 7
On appeal from: [2015] EWCA Civ 771

R (on the application of A and B) v Secretary of State for Health

before
Lady Mitchell

JUDGMENT GIVEN ON
10 August 2023

Heard on 15 and 16 March 2023

Introduction

[1] This case concerns the provision of NHS-funded abortions to pregnant people from Northern Ireland (NI). The question for the court is whether it is lawful for the Secretary of State for Health (the respondent) to exclude A (a woman from NI who travelled to England to receive abortion care) from the provision of NHS-funded abortions.

The Abortion Act 1967

[2] The Abortion Act 1967 (the 1967 Act) regulates the provision of abortion care in England, Wales and Scotland. It created a set of exceptions to the general criminalisation of abortion. S.1 lists four grounds on which an abortion can lawfully be provided. These are:

    a.   that the pregnancy has not exceeded its twenty-fourth week and that the continuance of the pregnancy would involve risk, greater than if the pregnancy were terminated, of injury to the physical or mental health of the pregnant woman or any existing children of her family; or

b. that the termination is necessary to prevent grave permanent injury to the physical or mental health of the pregnant woman; or

c. that the continuance of the pregnancy would involve risk to the life of the pregnant woman, greater than if the pregnancy were terminated; or

d. that there is a substantial risk that if the child were born it would suffer from such physical or mental abnormalities as to be seriously handicapped.

[3] The Act did not decriminalise abortion. It provides permittable exceptions to criminalisation. S.5 states that any abortion that is performed outwith the grounds stated in s.1 remains a criminal act (*Greater Glasgow Health Board v Doogan and another (Scotland)* [2014] UKSC 68).

[4] While the 1967 Act was considered a radical piece of legislation allowing doctors to provide abortions free from criminal sanction, it was not extended to NI as set out in s.7(3). Abortion remained criminalised there under the Offences Against the Persons Act 1861 and the Criminal Justice (Northern Ireland) Act 1945. Abortion in NI is allowed only when continuing the pregnancy would threaten the life of the woman, or her physical or mental health (*Family Planning Association of Northern Ireland v Minister of health and Social Services and Public Safety* [2004] NICA 37). The grounds on which a person can seek an abortion in NI are therefore much narrower than the grounds in the rest of the UK.

[5] Consequently, most people who need an abortion in NI are forced to travel to Great Britain or elsewhere to obtain an abortion. This incurs significant costs.

Facts

[6] The appellants (A and B) are both Northern Irish women. A was fifteen years old when she found out she was pregnant. B is A's mother. A wished to have an abortion. B helped to organise this and accompanied A to Manchester, where the procedure was carried out. The procedure and travel costs amounted to £900. Neither A nor B could readily afford this. B was able to raise £500 by borrowing money from friends. The other £400 was contributed by the charity Abortion Support Network, who intervened in this case. The stress of having to raise money urgently was a particular strain on A and B and caused particular difficulties.

Due in part to the virtual prohibition on abortion in NI, many medical practitioners are reluctant to even provide information on abortion due to fear of prosecution, a situation that the UN Committee on the Elimination of Discrimination Against Women called 'chilling' (CEDAW Committee, Inquiry Concerning the United Kingdom of Great Britain and Northern Ireland under article 8 of the Optional Protocol to the Convention on the Elimination of All Forms of Discrimination against Women, Report of the Committee, 6th March 2018, UN Doc. CEDAW/C/OP.8/GBR/1.)

[7] Despite the European Court of Human Rights (ECtHR) making it clear that even in states where abortion is prohibited, the provision of information on abortion services comes within the ambit of article 10 of the European Convention on Human Rights (ECHR) (*Open Door and Dublin Well Woman v Ireland*, Application no. 14234/88, 1992), the fear of prosecution meant that A had little advice and no opportunity to discuss abortion with medical professionals. This lack of information contributes to the stigma and fear of discussing abortion, which creates further obstacles for those trying to plan travel and secure funds to do so. It may also significantly delay the organisation of travel and abortion care.

[8] Statistics show that approximately 1,000 pregnant people travel from NI to England for abortion care each year.[1] However, the true figure is much higher because many do not disclose they are from NI, and some travel to Scotland or Wales or further afield to undergo abortions. Changes to the law in the Republic of Ireland to allow for lawful abortion care means that some are now likely to travel there for abortion care.[2]

[9] If a pregnant person is not able to raise the funds to travel for an abortion, they are either forced to continue with a pregnancy they do not want and ultimately raise a child in circumstances that they would not have chosen, or they choose to undertake illegal self-administered abortions. 'Back-street' or self-administered abortions are the leading cause of death during pregnancy: 10,000 women and pregnant people die annually worldwide from unsafe abortions and the UN cites lack of access to safe abortion as a risk to health and life.[3] While modern medical abortion is safe and poses less risk than pregnancy, criminal crackdowns and seizures of abortion medication means people may be forced to resort to unsafe non-medical self-administered abortions. Those who undertake self-administered abortions in NI are liable to criminal prosecution and several people have been prosecuted.[4] However, the availability and reliability

---

1.   1,014 women travelled from Northern Ireland in 2019. In 2020 and 2021 the numbers were lower (371 and 161) but this is attributed to the travel restrictions in place due to the COVID-19 pandemic: 'Abortion Statistics for England and Wales,' accessed 11 August 2023, https://www.gov.uk/government/statistics/abortion-statistics-for-england-and-wales-2020/abortion-statistics-england-and-wales-2020.
2.   In 2021, five people from Northern Ireland officially had abortions in the Republic of Ireland. The numbers are thought to be higher. See 'Department of Health Ireland Annual Report,' accessed 11 August 2023, https://www.gov.ie/pdf/?file=https://assets.gov.ie/229909/2e7c74df-8c05-4263-be47-5ffe1b435250.pdf#page=null.
3.   World Health Organisation (WHO), 'Abortion factsheet,' accessed 11 August 2023, https://www.who.int/news-room/fact-sheets/detail/abortion.
4.   In 2016, a student who miscarried after taking pills purchased online was found guilty and sentenced to three months of imprisonment (suspended): Henry McDonald, 'Northern Irish Woman Given Suspended Sentence Over Self Induced Abortion,' The Guardian, 4 April 2016, accessed 11 August 2023, https://www.theguardian.com/uk-news/2016/apr/04/northern-irish-woman-suspended-sentence-self-induced-abortion. The facts are narrated in *In the matter of an application by the Northern Ireland Human Rights Commission for Judicial Review (Northern Ireland)* [2018] UKSC 27 [89]. In 2017, a mother was charged with procuring pills for her 15-year-old daughter. The judge ordered the jury to acquit her following amendments to the law on 22 October 2019. The case is unreported but the decision to prosecute was the subject of a judicial review: *In the Matter of an application for judicial review by JR76 and in the matter of a continuing decision by the Director of Public Prosecutions to prosecute the first applicant* [2019] NIQB 103.

of abortion pills means that many in NI attempt to obtain these from abroad, so the true number of abortions carried out in NI is unclear.

Abortion in Great Britain

[10] The vast majority of abortions carried out in Great Britain are medical abortions.[5] Those seeking treatment are prescribed mifepristone and misoprostol. These drugs are considered safe and effective by the World Health Organisation (WHO).[6] At the time A sought an abortion, pregnant people in England were required to attend in person to obtain treatment. Subsequent amendments have allowed pregnant people's homes to be classed as a suitable place of treatment, thus allowing abortions to effectively take place at home following a consultation and prescription of medication.

Grounds of Challenge

[11] The appellants argue that the respondent's failure to provide an NHS-funded abortion for A (a UK citizen ordinarily resident in NI) was unlawful in public law and a breach of A's human rights.

The NHS in England

[12] Section 1(1) of the National Health Service Act 2006 (the 2006 Act) places a duty on the respondent to promote a comprehensive health service in England, designed to secure improvement in '(a) the physical and mental health of the people of England, and (b) in the prevention, diagnosis and treatment of physical and mental illness.' The Act states that the respondent must provide services in accordance with the Act and exercise their functions so as to secure that such services are provided.

[13] The respondent's argument is that, since the 2006 Act refers to the 'people of England,' they were obligated to only provide abortion services for those ordinarily resident in England, which would exclude any duty to people from NI, since they are not ordinarily resident in England. The respondent also claims that, since the system of devolved healthcare places a similar duty on the Northern Irish Health Secretary to provide healthcare for the people of NI, it would be incorrect for the respondent to include people from NI within the confines of the services provided to the 'people of England.' Regulation 3(2) of the National Health Service (Functions of Strategic Health Authorities and Primary Care Trusts and Admissions Arrangements) (England) Regulations (SI 2002/2375) delegates the operation of the respondent's functions

---

5. In 2021, 87% of abortions in England and Wales were medical abortions: 'Abortion Statistics England and Wales,' accessed 11 August 2023, https://www.gov.uk/government/statistics/abortion-statistics-for-england-and-wales-2021/abortion-statistics-england-and-wales-2021. In Scotland, 98.8% of abortions were medical: 'Abortion Statistics Scotland, accessed 11 August 2023, https://publichealthscotland.scot/media/19737/2023-05-30-terminations-2022-report.pdf.
6. World Health Organisation (WHO), 'Clinical practice handbook for safe abortion' (WHO: Geneva, 2014).

to primary care trusts. Regulation 3(7) sets out the categories of persons for whom the trust should exercise these functions:

a. Persons registered, other than temporarily, with a GP in the area of the trust;
b. Persons 'usually resident in the area';
c. Persons resident outside the UK who were present in its area (albeit that other regulations required a trust to charge such persons for services);
d. Persons suffering serious mental illness who were resident in other parts of the UK and who were present in its area; and
e. All persons present in its area but only for the provision to them of emergency and analogous services, treatment for certain infectious diseases and 'any other services which the [respondent] may direct.'

[14] The appellants argue that it was within the powers of the respondent under regulation 3(7)(e) and s.7(1) of the 2006 Act to dictate to trusts that the provision of abortion services should include those who were UK citizens resident in another part of the UK. Had the respondent done this, A would have been entitled to an NHS-funded abortion in England. The appellants argue that the failure of the respondent to exercise this power was irrational and a violation of their human rights.

Public Law

[15] The respondent acknowledges that it was within his power to choose to include people from NI in his direction to trusts when commissioning services. However, he argues that his decision not to exercise this power is justified, as he did so to respect the devolved system of healthcare throughout the UK and the democratic mandate in NI that chose not to provide abortions and continues to criminalise them. It was argued that allowing people from NI to access NHS services in England would contribute to wider 'health tourism' that would undermine the devolved system of healthcare.

[16] The issue to be decided here is whether the respondent should have directed trusts to allow people from NI who needed abortions access to the funded regime in England. Since Northern Irish people can already receive NHS-funded care if they happen to need it when in England, it is strange and absurd to suggest that allowing access to NHS-funded abortions would create a precedent for health tourism. Despite the respondent's duty being to the people of England, those from the rest of the UK and abroad can receive treatment via the NHS in England. Someone ordinarily resident in NI who develops acute appendicitis while visiting England would receive an appendectomy free on the NHS. That same person has to pay if they require an abortion. The respondent justifies this discrepancy by claiming he is respecting the system of devolved healthcare in the UK. The case in question relates to abortion care, which is unique as it is healthcare that cannot be accessed in NI. People from NI are not travelling to England for better abortion treatment, they are forced to travel to obtain abortion care because they cannot have this treatment legally at home. It is not

the funding that is enticing them to England, but the fact that there is no option to have the treatment in NI.

[17] In respect of the argument that the respondent's decision to deny funding stems from a desire to respect the will of the Northern Irish Assembly (which continues to criminalise abortion), I am unconvinced. Permitting Northern Irish people to travel to Great Britain to access abortion is understood to respect the will of the Northern Irish Assembly, therefore I am unconvinced that extending funded care to those same people somehow tips the balance into disrespect.

[18] I therefore find that the respondent was remiss in not exercising his powers to direct trusts to fund abortions for those from NI. I do not find his reasoning compelling and do not agree that excluding people from NI from any possibility of funded abortion care in the UK is a legitimate aim.

Human Rights

[19] The appellants argue that the failure of the respondent to exercise his power to make provision for people from NI to have funded abortions violates article 14 (right to enjoy Convention rights without discrimination on any ground) of the ECHR in conjunction with article 8 (the right to respect for family and private life).

Article 8 ECHR

[20] It is established that decisions over abortion engage article 8 (*A, B & C v Ireland*, Application no. 25579/05, 2011). While the ECtHR makes clear that article 8 does not confer a right to abortion, state decisions to prohibit or limit abortion come within the parameters of article 8. This was accepted by the respondent.

Article 14 ECHR

[21] Article 14 provides that persons will not be discriminated against in the application of the Convention. The applicants' argument is that they are being discriminated against because they are from NI, and had they been from another region of the UK, then they would have been able to access an NHS-funded abortion in England. The respondent does not dispute this but claims that it amounts to different treatment and not discrimination within the ambit of article 14, because his decision struck a fair balance and was not manifestly without reasonable foundation.

Residency

[22] While residency is not specified as a ground in article 14, it does fall under 'other status' (*Carson v United Kingdom* 51 EHRR 13 [70]). The respondent relied heavily on *Magee v UK* ((2000) 31 EHRR 35). Here the applicant was a man ordinarily

resident in England, who was arrested while visiting NI. He complained that he was treated differently based on residency, because had he been in England, he would have received better treatment after his arrest. However, the situation here is not analogous. It is not a case of a person from England arguing that they are being discriminated against because they have less access to abortion in NI than they would in England. It is a case of a person from NI arguing that they are in England, and the only reason for denying them access to funded NHS care is their residency in NI and the fact that the care they need is abortion care. The appellants are being treated differently because they normally reside in NI.

Is the Difference in Treatment Justified?

[23] Someone present in England would be treated free of charge by the NHS in England if they were from NI and required immediate medical care in any other situation. This appears uncontroversial. However, in excepting abortion care from this understanding, those who travel to England for an abortion are being singled out solely on the basis that they are seeking abortion care, and they are from NI. If Northern Irish people who are not pregnant are entitled to free NHS treatment in England should they require it, and this is considered uncontroversial, then it is difficult to understand why providing free abortion care to pregnant people from NI is controversial. Abortion care, which is healthcare, is being singled out as different from routine healthcare.

Did the Difference in Treatment Pursue a Legitimate Aim?

[24] The respondent does not clarify why he believes he should defer to the fact that abortion is criminalised in NI when making decisions about funding abortion care in England. Were the respondent's explicit aim to prevent pregnant people from NI from seeking abortions in England,[7] this could at least be said to be respecting the democratic will of the Northern Irish Assembly, as this position would be logically coherent, although unlawful. However, the fact that over 1,000 people travel to England annually for abortion care demonstrates that the respondent's decision not to provide funded abortions for people from NI does not prevent abortions, it simply makes them harder, more costly, and more traumatic to obtain. Preventing abortion cannot be his aim. The logic behind his decision seems less about being respectful of democratic will and devolution and more about being punitive to those seeking abortions. It is not clear how this respects the devolution settlement. The UK Government maintains overall responsibility for meeting the UK's human rights obligations and reproductive healthcare is one such obligation.

[25] Attempting to reproduce the criminality of abortion and the restricted access to all but the most extreme cases would mean denying the majority of Northern Irish

---

7. Preventing people from accessing abortion is a violation of the ECHR. In *P & S v Poland*, application no 57375/08 (ECHR, 30 October 2012), the ECtHR held that Poland had violated the applicant's article 8 rights.

pregnant people seeking abortion any effective access to abortion in Great Britain, ultimately forcing them to carry pregnancies to term against their will, forcing them to resort to unsafe or illegal abortions, or forcing to travel abroad to access abortion services. While people are not explicitly prohibited from travelling outside NI to have an abortion, the very real effect of the respondent's decision is that at best it frustrates and encumbers those seeking to travel for abortion care, and at worst prevents it entirely. I am not convinced that the cost of abortions being prohibitive to many can be considered anything other than a direct consequence of the respondent's decision. Nor is this an unintended consequence. By claiming to respect the democratic and devolution settlement in NI, the respondent can only intend to frustrate access to abortion for people from NI. I do not find his justifications for treating those from NI differently compelling, nor do I find that they constituted a legitimate aim or struck a fair balance.

Young people and body autonomy

[26] At the time she found out she was pregnant, A was 15. Courts have previously been asked to determine the limits of young persons' ability to consent to medical treatment (*Gillick v West Norfolk & Wisbeck Area Health Authority* [1986] AC 112 House of Lords; *R (Bell) v Tavistock and Portman NHS Foundation Trust* [2021] EWCA Civ 1363). However, in this case, both mother and daughter agreed about the best treatment for A. The lack of abortion provision in NI meant that the only way to achieve this was by travelling to Great Britain. The initial barrier to A receiving abortion care was the lack of provision, and criminal sanctions for abortion, in NI. A further barrier was the respondent's decision to exclude pregnant people from NI from funded abortion services that he commissioned.

[27] Article 12 of the United Nations Convention on the Rights of the Child (UNCRC) provides that 'States Parties shall assure to the child who is capable of forming his or her own views the right to express those views freely in all matters affecting the child, the views of the child being given due weight in accordance with the age and maturity of the child.' In domestic law, as Gillick and subsequent cases have set out, in almost all other medical situations, young people's views are respected, and parents should not be informed against their children's wishes. This case involved an abortion about which both mother and daughter agreed. It would be almost impossible for a young person who did not have parental support, or did not wish to inform their parents, to navigate such a system. These consequences would have been known by the respondent and considered acceptable.

Intersectional barriers due to age and socio-economic background

[28] The respondent's position is that pregnant people were not prevented from leaving NI to obtain abortion care. Here the respondent frames his obligations to NI people needing abortion care only in a negative context. While at no point did the State detain

or actively seek to prevent A from travelling to Great Britain to obtain an abortion, the reality is that the respondent's decision to exclude her and others like her from funded abortion care services creates a real barrier to access. In many cases, this will prevent people from accessing an abortion. This is surely much more so when the persons involved are under 18 and unlikely to be able to access the necessary funds. They will be unprepared for navigating the complexities of booking an abortion and travel to Great Britain, especially if they are trying to do this without informing a parent or guardian and without any professional guidance or support.

[29] The appellants' case was that A had been discriminated against on the basis of residency. However, it was open to them to argue that A was also discriminated against on grounds of age, sex, and the fact that she was pregnant. Had A wished to obtain an abortion and not inform her mother, she would have found the barriers almost unsurmountable. The practical effect of the respondent's decision is that young people like A face an almost virtual prohibition on leaving NI to obtain an abortion. This amounts to discrimination against people from NI, particularly young pregnant people. This creates trauma and embeds stereotypes around pregnancy and abortion.

Conclusion

[30] The question for the court was whether the respondent's decision to exclude people from NI from accessing NHS abortion care was a dereliction of his duty under public law and whether this decision violated A's human rights. The fact that A was ultimately supported by her mother to have an abortion, does not detract from the harsh realities that the respondent's decision created for people like A.

[31] He argued that his decision to exclude pregnant people from NI from funded abortions was motivated by desire to afford respect to the devolved healthcare system and democratic decision making in NI. He did not explain why he should be motivated by this in respect of provision of abortion care in England. Regardless, I am not convinced by his argument that his decision was justified.

[32] It is my view that the respondent deferred too much to the fact that abortion is criminalised in NI. The fact is that abortion is still effectively criminalised throughout the UK. The Abortion Act 1967 did not repeal the underlying criminal law, but instead merely created legal exceptions that escape criminalisation. The difference in NI is not that abortion is criminalised; the difference is that the regime for commissioning legal abortion care services under the 1967 Act was never extended to NI. While it is true that NI has therefore retained the pre-1967 position and allows for abortion only in situations where the pregnant person's life or physical or mental health is at risk (*R v Bourne* [1939] 1 KB 687), it is the case that some abortions are legally carried out there. A did not meet the criteria for a legal abortion in NI, but the respondent appears to have sought to replicate many of the barriers to abortion care for Northern Irish people in England. It is not clear why.

[33] In excluding Northern Irish pregnant people from funded abortion care, the respondent has effectively sought to allow abortion for those from NI in only the narrowest circumstances. Rather than criminalisation, the barriers these people face in England are costs and ability to travel. While not explicitly preventing them from obtaining an abortion in England, for many, his decision has that practical effect. In my mind, this is exactly what the respondent means when he says that he is respecting the system of devolved health care and respecting the democratic mandate in NI. He is doing so by deliberately making it difficult for people from NI to obtain abortion care. However, his duty is not to Northern Irish law makers, but to facilitate healthcare for the people of England (which can include people from NI).

[34] The respondent agreed that because of his decision, people from NI were treated differently, but claimed this did not meet the threshold for violating article 14 as his decision to treat NI people differently pursued a legitimate aim and was proportionate. It is not clear what the respondent's aim was, and his claim that he was respecting the devolved system of healthcare and the democratic mandate of the Northern Irish Assembly is unconvincing and illogical. I therefore find that his decision to treat people from NI differently amounts to discrimination under article 14. A was a child who was pregnant and from NI. For all of these reasons she was discriminated against.

[35] I find that the respondent's decision not to exercise his duties and not to fund A's abortion, amounted to a violation of the appellants' article 14 rights in conjunction with article 8. She was excluded from necessary healthcare and treated less favourably because she was from NI. While it was not open to me to consider whether this treatment amounts to a violation of article 3, it is clear to me that the effect of the respondent's decision was real suffering, trauma, and hardship.

For these reasons I would allow the appeal.

21

McConnell and YY v The Registrar General for England and Wales (United Kingdom):

Reflections and Hopes for the Future

*Liam Davis**

Introduction

Families have always existed in various shapes and sizes. Whether or not they are able to be adequately accommodated by UK law – given its insistence on the traditional, nuclear, two-parent, cisgender, heterosexual paradigm – is another question.[1] It may be unsurprising therefore that many queer families which are not, in their view, adequately recognised by law have begun seeking formal (legal) equality. One such example is the case of Alfred (Freddy) McConnell, a trans man who gave birth and wanted to be registered as his child's 'father' or 'parent' on the birth certificate. It was ultimately decided that he should be registered as 'mother,' which has been defined legally as the person who gives birth.[2] I will consider this decision below in a fictional appeal to the UK Supreme Court.

Seeking formal legal equality may not, however, be the prerogative of all queer people and families. Rather than seeking legitimation from the law/state, some queer people may actively rebel against state-approved bureaucracy as a form of activism against any *right* way to exist.[3] Following this line of thinking, one may question the usefulness of engaging in a project which aims, albeit queerly, to rewrite/invent

* I would like to thank everyone involved in the Queer Judgments Project for making this collection happen. I would also like to thank the editors, and Liam Evans and Lynsey Mitchell, for their comments on earlier drafts.

1. Martha Fineman, *The Neutered Mother, The Sexual Family and Other Twentieth Century Tragedies* (New York: Routledge, 1995); Liam Davis, 'Deconstructing Tradition: Trans Reproduction and the Need to Reform Birth Registration in England and Wales,' *International Journal of Transgender Health* 22 (2021), 179; Alan Brown, *What Is the Family of Law?: The Influence of the Nuclear Family* (Oxford: Hart Publishing, 2019).

2. *R (on the application of McConnell) v The Registrar General for England and Wales* [2020] EWCA Civ 559 (hereafter *McConnell*).

3. J Michael Ryan, 'Born Again?: (Non-)Motivations to Alter Sex/Gender Identity Markers on Birth Certificates,' *Journal of Gender Studies* 29 (2020), 269; Sue Westwood, '"My Friends Are My Family": An Argument about the Limitations of Contemporary Law's Recognition of Relationships in Later Life,' *Journal of Social Welfare and Family Law* 35 (2013), 347; Sophie Lewis, *Abolish the Family: A Manifesto for Care and Liberation* (London: Verso, 2022).

legal judgments if – for those adopting a specific kind of queer critique – seeking formal equality is a fruitless pursuit. However, as Sharpe aptly points out, if 'queer (or feminism) renunciate judgment, then the space of judgment will continue to be monopolised by the judiciary, and therefore is likely to be animated by hegemonic discourses.'[4]

In the judgment below, I did not feel able to provide Freddy with his desired outcome of being registered as a 'father' or 'parent' simply because of the rigidity of the current law, infused with cis-heteronormativity. Herein lies the tension, though: attempting to apply law to families which are generally not within the purview of lawmakers at the time seldom generates positive results. Despite this, I did feel able to issue a declaration of incompatibility under the Human Rights Act 1998 (HRA) so that Parliament could review the issues at hand. This is still, however, potential legitimation by way of state approval, and it is arguable whether we should internalise the norms propagated by the state or strive for something more (and this could be the abolition of requiring state legitimacy to live our lives).[5] While liberal law reform projects will only ever capture a subset of those who want recognition, this is not to say that such projects do not have a place within resistance against the state and are not helpful strategies through which to mobilise. They should not, however, be a central demand within such resistance, nor should changing the law (even if favourably) be construed as the end goal.[6]

In writing this reflection, I want to highlight two things: first, how the coherence and certainty requirement introduced by the courts in the *McConnell* judgments operate to favour the traditional nuclear family; and second, to introduce a more sceptical view on law's function(s), inspired by queer and trans activism and scholarship.

A queer perspective

The italicised *a* in this section's title is deliberate, highlighting the many different conceptualisations of 'queer' – even if they might share some common themes. It is generally accepted that queer theory aims to 'challenge, interrogate, destabilise and subvert'[7] values consistent with cis-heteronormativity which are used to marginalize those who fail to conform with hegemonic ideas of any right way to exist (the *right* way being cisgender and heterosexual, among many other things). Accordingly, a large proportion of queer critique is anti-law/state, insofar as what the law says about queer people is unlikely to change their material circumstances.

This section analyses two different aspects of the *McConnell* judgments, also from two different queer perspectives. The first considers the law's need for coherence and certainty of the birth registration system and how, in practice, this requirement

---

4. Alex Sharpe, 'Queering Judgment: The Case of Gender Identity Fraud,' *The Journal of Criminal Law* 81 (2017), 425.
5. Edward Higgs, 'UK Birth Registration and Its Present Discontents,' *Reproductive Biomedicine and Society Online* 5 (2018), 36
6. Dean Spade, 'Law as Tactics,' *Columbia Journal of Gender and Law* 21 (2011), 442; Dean Spade, *Normal Life: Administrative Violence, Critical Trans Politics, and the Limits of Law* (Durham: Duke University Press, 2015).
7. Hannah McCann and Whitney Monaghan, *Queer Theory Now: From Foundations to Futures* (London: Red Globe Press, 2019), 1.

is cis-heteronormative. It suggests a type of queer critique which might enable the law to expand its understanding of family and parenthood. The second considers a life outside of law, or at least being more sceptical of law's regulatory function.

The desire for coherency and certainty

The desire for coherence and certainty of the birth registration system was one of two factors justifying why the courts considered it proportionate that Freddy be required to register as his child's mother – the other was the rights and protection of wider society. I have written about the requirement for coherence and certainty more extensively elsewhere.[8] For the courts in this case, coherence and certainty could only be fulfilled by ensuring that anyone who gives birth – regardless of their legal sex/gender status – is registered as 'mother,' as this supposedly ensures the child knows who gave birth to them and allows them to be aware of their biogenetic origins. As Fenton-Glynn points out though, the right to know who gave birth (if such a right exists) does not necessitate the use of the term 'mother' and could just as easily be achieved through 'altering the legal nomenclature to reflect the individual's biological role without the connotations of gender.'[9] It remains to be seen how onerous it would be to substitute 'mother' in legislation for a gender-neutral term such as 'gestational parent' (if indeed knowing who gave birth is decided something worth making explicit – which it may be, for various reasons). Also, time will tell how far this gender-neutral term would contribute to the gender-neutralizing of motherhood in general, not just legally.

It is clear from *McConnell* that if people who give birth are registered as anything other than 'mother,' the child will seemingly not know who gave birth to them; or, if registered differently, the child will be given inaccurate information. This is problematic for two reasons. First, allowing trans men who give birth to register as 'father' does not mean the child is unable to locate their biogenetic heritage, it simply means their parent is registered in the social and factual role they will fulfil. Second, to frame the situation otherwise suggests that trans parents are inherently deceitful and will seek to hide the circumstances surrounding their child's birth (this presumed dishonesty has been documented in other areas, such as marriage, sexual intimacy and gender identity 'fraud').[10]

The operation of this requirement of coherence and certainty is therefore cisnormative and heteronormative, given law's insistence on gendered terminology and requiring trans people to register inconsistently with their gender identity. This is explicitly seen in the Court of Appeal's judgment in *McConnell*, in which the judges stated they were unaware of how the majority of society would feel if they were referred to as 'parent 1'

---

8. Davis, 'Deconstructing Tradition,' 186-188; Liam Davis, 'The Evolution of Birth Registration in England and Wales and its Place in Contemporary Law and Society,' *Modern Law Review* 87 (2024), 317.

9. Claire Fenton-Glynn, 'Deconstructing Parenthood: What Makes a Mother?,' *Cambridge Law Journal* 79 (2020), 37.

10. Flora Renz, 'Consenting to Gender? Trans Spouses after Same-Sex Marriage' in *From Civil Partnership to Same-Sex Marriage 2004-2014: Interdisciplinary Reflections*, ed. Nicola Barker and Daniel Monk (Oxford: Routledge, 2015), 83-97; Alex Sharpe, *Sexual Intimacy and Gender Identity 'Fraud': Reframing the Legal and Ethical Debate* (Oxford: Routledge, 2018).

and 'parent 2' as opposed to mother and father.[11] In other words, the judges had at the forefront of their reasoning the traditional (cis, heterosexual) family and therefore could not entertain a decision in favour of a relatively small proportion of society. Viewed this way, and as suggested in the rewritten/invented judgment below, the current law disproportionately impacts trans parents by not allowing them to register in their social and factual role. Cis parents are unlikely to feel discomfort, or the same discomfort, at being labelled a gendered term that is consistent with their gender identity (that is, women being registered as mothers and men as fathers). Some cis parents may prefer to be registered as 'parent,' but this is different to being forcibly registered in a gendered term unaligned to one's own identification. In the case of trans men, the current legal framework seemingly views them as 'part-man'[12] and not 'male enough' to ascend to fatherhood.[13]

Given law's inability to adequately cater for trans parents, and some queer families generally, it is helpful to discuss the usefulness of seeking recognition from the law/state, or whether doing so perpetuates the notion that what the law/state says is sacrosanct.

The limits of law: approaching law as tactics and the benefits of being on the outside

From birth (if not before, through medical ultrasounds), we are assigned a binary sex/gender: female/male. This is subsequently registered on the birth certificate and can only be changed, in the UK, upon legally updating one's sex/gender under the Gender Recognition Act 2004 (GRA). It is not just sex/gender that is important on the birth certificate, however. For parents, this is also the document which will list them as parents to their children and, in the vast majority of circumstances, it will do so using gendered language: mother/father.[14] This is one example of an extension of the state (the registry office) 'administering sexage and gendering.'[15]

Dean Spade's analysis of law as tactics has been instrumental in illustrating how law is deployed tactfully and how we need to understand law this way in return. Understanding law tactfully – by which Spade means being aware of the broader context in which law operates, intersecting with other systems of power and how they work in tandem – allows us to understand more fully the system(s) in which we are operating and resisting. For Spade, there is a danger of 'merely tinkering with the legal window dressing' as doing so perpetuates the fiction that 'if we change what the law

---

11. *McConnell*, [81].

12. Craig Lind, 'Perception of Sex in the Legal Determination of Fatherhood: X, Y and Z v UK,' *Child and Family Law Quarterly* 9 (1997), 408

13. Alice Margaria, 'Trans Men Giving Birth and Reflections on Fatherhood: What to Expect?,' *International Journal of Law, Policy and the Family* 34 (2020), 234.

14. If the conception is brought about through assisted reproduction, the non-birth giver can be registered as 'parent': Human Fertilisation and Embryology Act 2008, ss 42, 43. Likewise, 'parent' is the default language used on parental orders (used in surrogacy) since 2010: Law Commission of England and Wales and Scottish Law Commission, *Building Families through Surrogacy: A New Law*, Law Com No 411, Scottish Law Com No 262 (2023), para. 13.18; The Parental Orders (Prescribed Particulars and Forms of Entry) Regulations 2010 Sched 1. 'Parent' is also used on adoption certificates.

15. Grietje Baars, 'Queer Cases Unmake Gendered Law, Or, Fucking Law's Gendering Function,' *Australian Feminist Law Journal* 45 (2019), 60.

says about a vulnerable population, we will necessarily change the key conditions of vulnerability.'[16] In other words, we should strive not to 'internali[se] the norms of the bureaucratic state'[17] by attaching significant meaning to what is printed on a piece of paper, but instead to think about a life outside of law, or one which acknowledges how law is deployed to meet certain ends – like prioritising certain gender identities, expressions and family types. Within this line of thinking, it is not the end goal to reform the law to allow trans parents to register as they wish on the birth certificate; rather, it is about creating conditions in which trans parents – and *all* queer people and families – can flourish without necessarily having recourse to the law. After all, it is the state, and law generally, which is largely responsible for the multitude of queerphobic attacks endured in society and for creating the dire material conditions in which queer people find themselves.

It is of little surprise, then, that some queer people do not want to engage with the (state) law and this maybe highlights a distinction between those who are more likely to desire formal legal equality and those who are not. Applying this to birth registration specifically, some queer people may be sceptical of this state bureaucracy not least because of its regulation of sex/gender and parenthood, but also because of its bordering and racialisation functions. Birth registration's bordering and racialised functions are made more salient through the fact that it is controlled by the Home Office: the same department responsible for, in its own words, 'security and economic prosperity' (by which it means the violent enforcement of borders).[18]

To approach birth registration from the perspective of law as tactics means, among other things, to question the fundamental need for birth registration. For which purpose(s) do we register births? It could be for many reasons: to monitor population size; to enable people to locate their (biogenetic) heritage; or, it could have multiple intersecting purposes, such as using the information recorded as a form of biopower through which the state quite literally decides who is alive, while also using this information to propagate its gender normativity and racialised bordering functions.[19] Even after asking questions like this, it is still not enough to simply change the law and policy surrounding birth registration. What needs to change is the material circumstances which enable birth registration to operate this way, and to perhaps strive for a world where registration is unnecessary (or at least where it does not have such insidious effects).

Conclusion

This reflection perhaps raises more questions than it answers and highlights two opposing, but potentially complementary, queer critiques. On one hand, it explored the value of expanding law's regulatory function to accommodate the various queer families

---

16. Spade, 'Law as Tactics,' 57.
17. Higgs, 'Birth Registration,' 36.
18. 'Home Office,' accessed 20 July 2023, https://www.gov.uk/government/organisations/home-office.
19. Michel Foucault, *The History of Sexuality, Volume I: An Introduction* (New York: Pantheon Books, 1978).

and lives that cannot currently be adequately recognised. This approach highlighted the 'stability, predictability and categories'[20] required by law in order to survive: anything outside the traditional ideal is either given recognition on the basis of assimilation or is simply not recognised. This approach is not without its benefits, as it can be used as a steppingstone through which to organise for more collective change that helps everyone – not just those seeking formal legal equality. This is where living outside law, or approaching law tactfully, comes into play and it becomes necessary to question the end goal(s) of effective resistance. Is it simply to change what the law says about us, so that we can benefit from equality laws? Or, to change the material circumstances in which queer people and families find themselves so that, outside law, they are still able to live a liveable life?[21]

The tension between expanding laws to accommodate minority groups and wanting to live outside law or approach law tactfully is something to which I often find myself returning. The two positions need not be mutually exclusive. Taking part in this project has enabled me to confront this tension head on, yet again, and has led to some helpful thoughts behind using law reform as the primary medium through which to enact meaningful and long-lasting change. Ending with the words of Grietje Baars, 'can we say that it is possible to queer the legal structures that seek to contain our genders and sexualities, or is now the time to say "fuck law"'?[22] I think: fuck law. That being said, it is hard to effectively say 'fuck law' while still operating within the confines of a legal system as we know it, especially with rewriting/inventing a legal judgment.

---

20. Adam Romero, 'Methodological Descriptions: Feminist and Queer Legal Theories' in *Feminist and Queer Legal Theory: Intimate Encounters, Uncomfortable Conversations*, ed. Martha Fineman, Jack Jackson and Adam Romero (Oxford: Routledge 2009), 191.
21. Judith Butler, *Undoing Gender* (London: Psychology Press, 2004).
22. Baars, 'Queer Cases,' 60.

THE SUPREME COURT OF THE UNITED KINGDOM

Trinity Term
[2023] UKSC 7
On appeal from: [2020] EWCA Civ 559

JUDGMENT

McConnell and YY (by his litigation friend) (Appellants) v The Registrar General for England and Wales (Respondent)

before
Lord Davis, President

JUDGMENT GIVEN ON
21 July 2023

Heard on 18 and 19 April 2023

Lord Davis:

Introduction

1. The central question at the heart of this appeal is: who, or what, is a 'mother'? Indeed, the first instance decision ([2019] EWHC 2384 (Fam)) marked the first time the UK courts had to confront this question head on at common law.

2. Applying this question to the current case, this Court is tasked with deciding whether Alfred McConnell, a transgender man in receipt of a Gender Recognition Certificate (GRC) – granted under the Gender Recognition Act (GRA) 2004 – is entitled to be registered as his child's 'father,' or otherwise as a 'gestational parent' or 'parent' on the child's birth certificate, as opposed to 'mother.'

3. That this case engages the appellant's rights under the European Convention on Human Rights (ECHR) – specifically Article 8 (the right to respect for his family and private life) – is undisputed (see Court of Appeal decision: [2020] EWCA Civ 559, at [55]). The fact the Appellant has, thus far, been told he would have to register his child's birth as a 'mother' – a term which is not consistent with his own gender identity and contradicts the social and factual reality of the parent-child relationship – serves as proof of the interference with his Article 8 rights.

4.   While courts are supposed to apply the law as it reads on the statute, it is critical in cases like this to consider the wider context and the potential ramifications of not redressing what may be considered by some as a flaw in the law. Many of us cannot begin to imagine the deep distress it must cause not to have one's identity recognised in all aspects of life and without prejudice. As a result, I am surprised that the Court of Appeal did not decide to engage in the more normative, difficult, underlying questions – such as what constitutes a 'mother' – with the same rigour the President of the Family Division, Sir Andrew McFarlane, did at first instance in the High Court. None of this should be construed as the courts bending to the political will of others, nor that the court is unusually considering the political climate in its reasoning – although I am not convinced this is always a bad thing. While politics should not necessarily inform a judge's reasoning, it is important to be attentive to the effects a judgment may have on the group(s) to which it pertains, particularly if that judgment may be viewed as negative by the group(s) affected. Context is important; families have always come in different shapes and sizes. Law does not exist in a vacuum and it is important it recognises and affords protection to all families.

5.   For reasons that will be explained, I have concluded that a declaration of incompatibility pursuant to section 4 of the Human Rights Act (HRA) 1998 must be granted in relation to sections 9 and 12 of the GRA 2004 to the extent that these sections preclude trans parents from registering their child's birth in accordance with the social role they will have in that child's life. I also grant a declaration of incompatibility in relation to the relevant provisions of the Births and Deaths Registration Act (BDRA) 1953 and Schedule 7(2) of The Registration of Births and Deaths Regulations 1987 for the same reasons.

6.   Before explaining those reasons, I would like to bring awareness to some semantics. This judgment uses the term 'gender' in preference to 'sex' unless this would be technically incorrect. For example, on a UK birth certificate, 'sex' is registered at birth, not 'gender.' This should not be construed as drawing a distinction between sex and gender. Indeed, section 9(1) of the GRA 2004 says that, when a GRC is issued, a person's 'acquired' gender becomes their 'acquired' sex, too. There is, however, a general exception to this found in section 9(2), which states that subsection (1) 'does not affect things done, or events occurring, before the certificate is issued.'

The facts

7.   Mr McConnell was registered as female at birth. Aged 22, he began transitioning to the male gender. He began testosterone treatment in 2013 and underwent a double mastectomy in 2014. Both his passport and NHS records were amended to reflect his male gender. Doing so does not require a GRC.

8. In September 2016, under medical guidance, Mr McConnell suspended treatment in the hope of becoming pregnant. He commenced fertility treatment at a licensed clinic registered for such purposes under the Human Fertilisation and Embryology Act (HFEA) 1990, as amended by the HFEA 2008. He was registered as 'M' for male on clinical records.

9. Shortly after suspending testosterone treatment, Mr McConnell applied for a GRC under section 1 of the GRA 2004 to confirm his status as male and to receive an amended birth certificate. As part of this, Mr McConnell submitted a declaration that he 'intend[ed] to continue to live in the acquired gender until death.' The GRA panel granted the application, and a GRC confirming Mr McConnell's male status was issued on 11 April 2017. Under section 9(1) of the GRA 2004, the gender of the person named on the certificate 'becomes for all purposes the acquired gender.' However, this is subject to various exceptions, one of which is parenthood. This will be explored in more detail below.

Issues on appeal

10. Having set out the factual background, I now turn to the issues concerned in this appeal:
    i. The meaning of 'mother' at common law.
    ii. The correct interpretation of the GRA, particularly sections 9 and 12.
    iii. Whether sections 9 and 12 violate the Appellant's Article 8 rights.
    iv. If the answer to (iii) is yes, whether this Court can interpret the legislation in a manner compatible with the Appellant's Convention rights, as required by section 3 HRA. If this is not possible, this Court can consider whether it should issue a declaration of incompatibility pursuant to section 4 HRA.

The meaning of 'mother'

11. For reasons to be explained, I have determined that, based on the current operation of the law, the term 'mother' is to be used to refer to those who give birth for the purposes of birth registration. This is irrespective of that person's gender identity, or the sex they were assigned at birth.

12. Before the current proceedings, there was a dearth of authority on the definition of 'mother' at common law. As the President in the High Court stated, this is perhaps unsurprising given that until recently and to the majority of (mostly cisgender, heterosexual) society, it was assumed that a 'mother' is the person who gives birth (at [131]). Indeed, the physiology associated with the ability to gestate has typically been coded 'female.' That is why, over 30 years ago, Lord Simon felt comfortable observing that '[m]otherhood, although a legal relationship, is based on a fact, being proved demonstrably by parturition' (*The Ampthill Peerage* [1977] AC 547 at 577). The President rightly stated that such

an observation was *obiter* and should be approached with caution, but was correct in saying it was a statement of what, at the time, was considered to be obvious to the vast majority (at [131]). This has been codified in statute too, with 'mother' being defined for the purposes of assisted reproduction as the 'woman who is carrying or has carried a child as a result of the placing in her of an embryo or of eggs and sperm, and no other woman' (section 33(1) HFEA 2008).

13. The High Court and the Court of Appeal took slightly different approaches as to the gendered nature of 'mother.' The President undertook an extensive, normative analysis of the meaning of 'mother' and disentangled 'mother' from being exclusively associated with women. For him, 'mother' was not gender-specific but simply related to the 'biological process of conception, pregnancy and birth' (at [280]). It was in this regard, after legally disassociating the meaning of 'mother' and 'father' from their day-to-day, societally gendered underpinnings that the President felt able to speak of 'male mothers' and 'female fathers' (at [141-142]).

14. The Court of Appeal, on the other hand, did not engage with the normative analysis of 'mother.' Instead, it adopted a much narrower focus. It avoided commenting on the feasibility of 'male mothers' and 'female fathers,' other than to say that it is not possible to say that 'Parliament has "de-coupled" the concept of "mother" from gender' (at [54]). Despite agreeing with the Court of Appeal for reasons I will discuss next, the Court could have explained in more detail why it thought it was not possible to say Parliament had de-coupled 'mother' from 'gender.'

15. The President in the High Court should be commended for attempting to disentangle 'mother' from its gendered underpinnings, at least in a legal sense. And it is this qualifier – in a *legal* sense – which is important. I confess that I am not sure how useful it is to make a legal distinction that will not – for almost all intents and purposes – make a difference to a trans person's daily life within society. This is because, to the average person walking down the street, Mr McConnell is likely to be perceived as male. When telling people who are unaware of his transition that he is a parent, they are likely to assume he is a father. This may change if, and when, Mr McConnell discloses the fact he gave birth. In this circumstance, people are perhaps likely to misgender Mr McConnell and refer to him as a 'mother' because this term is socially synonymous with giving birth and being a woman. To me, being able to say he is (legally) a 'male mother' makes no difference to the perception that Mr McConnell is likely to be viewed as a woman due to having given birth.

16. That being said, I accept that registering trans men who give birth as 'mother' is a natural consequence of how the law is to be applied currently. Section 12 of the GRA operates as an exception to the general rule in section 9(1) that a trans person's 'acquired' gender becomes their acquired gender 'for all purposes' (I will discuss the correct interpretation of sections 9 and 12 in the next section). Delving into,

REFLECTIONS AND HOPES FOR THE FUTURE 411

and attempting to disassociate, gendered terminology within a legal judgment (while with laudable intentions) muddies the already muddy water. Put simply, no legal acrobatics is likely to change the fact that many in society will probably perceive Mr McConnell as a 'mother' upon finding out he gave birth.

17. Due to the history of the common law, then, I agree that people who give birth should be registered on the birth certificate as a 'mother.' While this decision engages the Appellant's human rights under Article 8, whether it is justified and proportionate remains to be determined below.

18. Despite being a natural consequence of how the law operates, I do not agree with the legal creation of 'male mothers' and 'female fathers' insofar as these terms preclude trans parents from registering in their social and factual role. Such terminology is likely to cause confusion and, on the basis of how these terms are likely to be understood by the majority of society, constitute an oxymoron. Also, like the Court of Appeal, I do not think Parliament has given sufficient thought to the decoupling of 'mother' from gender and therefore this is not a tenable interpretation of the law at present.

Interpretation of sections 9 and 12 of the GRA

19. I will deal with the interpretation issue quickly. Key to determine here is whether section 12 GRA is only retrospective (as the Appellant argues), or whether it is both prospective and retrospective (as the Respondent argues). While I agree, mostly, with the Court of Appeal's analysis that section 12 is both prospective and retrospective, there are a few additional points I would like to mention.

20. Sections 9 and 12 state:

9 General

1. Where a full gender recognition certificate is issued to a person, the person's gender becomes for all purposes the acquired gender (so that, if the acquired gender is the male gender, the person's sex becomes that of a man and, if it is the female gender, the person's sex becomes that of a woman).

2. Subsection (1) does not affect things done, or events occurring, before the certificate is issued; but it does operate for the interpretation of enactments passed, and instruments and other documents made, before the certificate is issued (as well as those passed or made afterwards).

3. (…)

12 Parenthood

1. The fact that a person's gender has become the acquired gender under this Act does not affect the status of the person as the father or mother of a child.

21. Something that was not engaged with – but was acknowledged – by both lower courts is the effect of Schedule 7(2) of The Births and Deaths Regulations 1987. This Schedule says that 'the particulars to be recorded in respect of the parents of a child shall be those appropriate *as at the date of its birth*' (emphasis added). Counsel for the Appellant argued that, provided a child's birth occurs after the issuance of a GRC, section 9 GRA should operate to recognise a trans parent in their 'acquired' gender, meaning section 12 should not restrict or modify the effect of a GRC (High Court judgment, at [65]). However, in relation to the present case, this falls to be determined on how 'mother' status is to be ascribed. As stated above, 'mother' status is to be afforded to all those who give birth, regardless of gender identity. Therefore, while there is merit in Counsel's argument, and while it does potentially highlight an incongruence between law and lived reality, the registering of Mr McConnell as 'mother' is 'appropriate' at the date of birth within the wording of Schedule 7(2).

22. This aside, I agree with the Court of Appeal's reasoning regarding the interpretation of sections 9 and 12 (at [29-33]). I also agree that, on the face of it, section 12 is not limited to events only occurring before a GRC is issued, and where that was Parliament's intention, it made express provision to this effect (as in, for example, section 16).

23. Thus concluding that section 12 is to be applied both prospectively and retrospectively, I now turn to whether the interference caused as a result of those sections is compatible with the Appellant's human rights under the ECHR.

The human rights dimension

24. Where I diverge most from the lower courts' reasoning is in applying the ECHR.

25. The HRA 1998 gave further effect to the ECHR in UK law. Under section 3, the courts must interpret any legislation in a way that is compatible with Convention rights. Crucially, the courts must do this '[s]o far as it is possible.' If the court is satisfied legislation is incompatible with Convention rights, it is able to issue a declaration of incompatibility under section 4.

Article 8

26. The Respondents, correctly in my view, concede that there is an interference with the Appellant's Article 8 ECHR rights.

27. The interference with the Appellant's Article 8 rights stems from the exceptions granted in the GRA, particularly section 12 regarding parenthood. I have reached my decision above regarding the correct interpretation of section 12 (that it be applied both retrospectively and prospectively) when read in conjunction with section 9. If a trans person obtains a GRC, they are to be treated as the 'acquired'

gender, save for when an exception applies, in which case they are to be treated as their birth sex. This goes to the heart of the Appellant's appeal. If 'mother' is to be understood as a (female) gendered term, as I have suggested above it is, then the current operation of the birth registration system is an example of the state requiring (some might say forcing) a trans person to declare that their sex is not the sex they were assigned at birth.

28. The interference with Mr McConnell's Article 8 rights is thus two-fold: (i) it interferes with his right to private life, as the outcome of the registration would not be congruent with his own sense of identity; and (ii) it interferes with his right to a family life as the long-form of YY's birth certificate would list Mr McConnell as a 'mother' when, in day-to-day life, he is YY's 'father.' It is only the long-form version of the birth certificate that includes details about parentage. The short-form version does not include this information: see section 33(2) BDRA 1953.

29. Accepting that there is an interference under Article 8(1), I turn to the provisions under Article 8(2) to assess whether the interference is capable of being justified. It must be assessed:
    i.   Whether the interference is 'in accordance with the law.'
    ii. Whether there is a legitimate aim for the interference.
    iii. Whether the interference is proportionate.

30. On the first question, it has not been suggested that the interference is not in accordance with the law. It clearly is. The matter is governed by legislation and thus concerns 'law' for the purposes of the Convention.

31. The second question is whether there is a legitimate aim for the interference. This is where I depart from the reasoning adopted by both the High Court and Court of Appeal.

32. The Court of Appeal suggested that the interference's aim is legitimate because it consists of the 'protection of the rights of others' and the 'maintenance of a clear and coherent registration of births' (at [58]). Also, that the question of whether the interference is legitimate is to be addressed generally, and not in relation to the particular facts before it. Hence, the question is not whether it would be in YY's best interests to have the person who gave birth to him registered as 'mother,' but whether the rights of children generally include the right to know who gave birth to them and that person's status.

33. I confess I find it hard to follow the Court of Appeal's reasoning, particularly on the latter point regarding a child's right to know who gave birth to them. It has been suggested by multiple academic commentators that the right of a child to know who gave birth to them does not necessitate the use of the word 'mother' (for example, Claire Fenton-Glynn, 'Deconstructing Parenthood: What Makes a Mother?' (2020) 79 *Cambridge Law Journal* 34).

34. Given trans men are generally able to produce their own eggs and gestate, the Respondent's concern in ensuring such children are able to locate who gave birth to them has perhaps been overstated. Should a trans man, for whatever reason, not be able to use his own eggs, he will have to pursue fertility treatment. However, he would still be giving birth to the child which is seemingly of most concern to the Respondents and any resulting child. If fertility treatment is conducted in the UK, there is ample chance for the child to locate their biological heritage through records kept by the Human Fertilisation and Embryology Authority. Much like the law has decoupled the provision of genetic material from parental status, perhaps one's identification as 'mother' or 'father' ought to be based on gender identity (Sheelagh McGuinness and Amel Alghrani, 'Gender and Parenthood: The Case for Realignment' (2008) 16 *Medical Law Review* 261, 280).

35. There is little research available regarding trans parents disclosing their trans status to their children. Where this is done, however, it is generally met with a positive attitude by children, and the younger the child is when disclosure occurs, the better children react (Trish Hafford-Letchfield and others, 'What Do We Know about Transgender Parenting? Findings from a Systematic Review' (2019) 27 *Health and Social Care in the Community* 1111).

36. It does not seem as though any research has been conducted specifically on the scenario presented in this case, that is, where a trans man gives birth as a father, raises their child as a father, and the impact on the child of realising a 'mother' did not give birth to them. Despite this, there is a general trend in assisted reproduction toward openness and transparency (Maria Tallandini and others, 'Parental Disclosure of Assisted Reproductive Technology (ART) Conception to Their Children: A Systematic and Meta-Analytic Review' (2016) 31 *Human Reproduction* 1275). There is nothing to suggest that trans parents would be any different in this regard, especially as other research indicates that children in trans families report positive relationships and good psychological adjustment (Susan Imrie and others, 'Children with Trans Parents: Parent–Child Relationship Quality and Psychological Well-Being' (2021) 21 *Parenting* 185).

37. Following this line of reasoning, then, reveals how registering the person who gave birth as the 'mother' is unnecessary and perhaps even harmful in the context of trans men who give birth.

38. Regarding the maintenance of a clear and coherent birth registration scheme, again, it is not clear why this necessitates using the term 'mother' to describe the person who gave birth. It is true, however, that this term is used in many other inter-linked pieces of legislation which may be affected if 'mother' no longer refers to the person who gave birth.

39. Counsel for the Respondents informed the Court of Appeal that 'mother' is used 45 times in the Children Act 1989 alone (at [64]). Crucially, under section 2(2)(a),

it is the 'mother' who automatically acquires parental responsibility of a child following birth. This is an operation of law and registration on the birth certificate is not required to confer parental responsibility on the mother. The same cannot be said of the father or second parent. While fathers and second parents who are married or civilly partnered to the mother have a right to automatically acquire parental responsibility, this is not on the same basis as the mother. There are additional steps involved. It may be that, after being told how the law operates, trans men who give birth would acquiesce – or even accept – being registered as a 'mother' if it means they benefit from the automatic acquisition of parental responsibility upon giving birth. There are clearly benefits to ensuring at least one person is responsible for a child upon birth. Still, while it would require wholesale reform to many inter-linked pieces of law (which would not be the prerogative of the court as that would amount to judicial law-making), it remains to be convincingly argued why the term 'mother' could not be substituted for a suitable alternative – such as 'gestational parent.'

40. To summarise, while there is a legitimate aim with regards to protecting others in ensuring they know who gave birth to them, this aim seems unsubstantiated (even irrelevant) when it comes to trans parents.

41. Despite finding that the interference is not in pursuit of a legitimate aim insofar as it applies to trans men who give birth, if I found it were in pursuit of a legitimate aim, I would have found that the interference was not proportionate. To me, the balancing exercise has been weighted too far in favour of the rights of others when compared with the right of the Appellant to register in his social and factual role as a father.

42. While the lower courts have correctly stated there is no consensus throughout European countries on how to register trans men who give birth (and how to register trans parents' parental status generally), neither court referenced two Swedish decisions which affirmed a trans parent's transition and allowed them to be registered with the gendered term socially applicable to them (Göteborg Administrative Court, Case no. 6186-14, 5 October 2015; Stockholm Administrative Court, Case no. 3201-14, 9 July 2015). These decisions concerned trans men who had given birth and wanted to be registered as 'father.' One of the trans men had transitioned prior to giving birth (Göteborg case) and the other transitioned after giving birth (Stockholm case). Due to the lack of European consensus on how to register trans parents, it is important to consider the legal framework in countries which legally validate a trans person's parental status. This is because, as discussed above, law does not exist in a vacuum and should, as far as possible, aim to protect all family types. Sweden is particularly important here, being one of few European countries which validates trans parents' desired parental terms, and because there is documented case law of trans men giving birth both before and after legally changing their gender.

43. Neither of the Swedish decisions are available in English and so I am grateful in particular to the work of Anniken Sørlie for their analysis in their book chapter 'Governing (trans)parenthood: The tenacious hold of biological connection and heterosexuality' in *Queering International Law: Possibilities, Alliances, Complicities, Risks*, ed. Diana Otto (Routledge, 2017), 171-190.

44. Sweden operates differently to the UK in terms of birth registration, but this is not material for my analysis. In both Swedish decisions, the trans men concerned were able to have their parental designation registered as 'father' and, crucially, the Swedish courts held that both Article 8 and Article 14 (equality in the enjoyment of other Convention rights) had been breached in relation to both the parent and child(ren). According to Sørlie, this is because registering trans parents in their social role was consistent with the aims of the Swedish population register: namely, to record correct and relevant information about people. Moreover, the Swedish courts considered that registering trans men as 'mothers' implied they were registered as a woman, meaning a trans man's gender identity was not fully legally recognised (Sørlie, 188).

45. In considering trans people and the ECHR, regard must also be given to the case of *Goodwin* and trans parents being made to live in an 'intermediate zone as not quite one gender or the other' (*Goodwin v UK*, no. 28957/95, judgment of 11 July 2002, at [90]). The kind of trans parent the Strasbourg Court had in mind was the 'fully achieved and post-operative' trans parent. However, Parliament took a different route when enacting the GRA 2004, going further than the Strasbourg Court by not requiring any surgical intervention.

46. In my view, the current law disproportionately impacts trans people and forces them to disclose their trans status. It is inappropriate, no matter the likelihood, that a document requires a trans person to register in a term that does not align with their identity and which could cause harm to both parents and children. In line with the Swedish decisions, this does not fully respect a trans person's rights under Article 8 and also outs, no matter how infrequently, a parent as trans. It follows that the interference with the Appellant's rights under Article 8 would not have been proportionate and would therefore be breached.

47. It is not possible, in my decision, to interpret the domestic legislation in a way that is compatible with Mr McConnell's Article 8 rights, as foreseen by section 3 HRA. This is principally because it would require the rewriting of multiple statutes which is a job for Parliament.

48. As the legislation cannot be interpreted compatibly with the Convention rights, the Court is asked whether it can issue a declaration of incompatibility under section 4 HRA. This is a discretionary power. Issuing a declaration does not force government or Parliament to do anything (*R (Nicklinson) v Ministry of Justice (CNK Alliance Ltd intervening)* [2015] AC 657, at [343]).

49. However, given the severity of the interference with the Appellant's Convention rights, I am convinced that, being given the power to issue a declaration of incompatibility, the Court should do so in the present case for the reasons stated above.

Article 14

50. Article 14 was not strictly raised in the present appeal, but if it were, the claim under this Article would have succeeded. This is because the interference with Mr McConnell's Article 8 right is likely to disproportionately impact trans parents and is thus contrary to Article 14.

51. As mentioned above, the disconnect between having to register in a term unaligned to one's identification is likely to cause discomfort. But this discomfort is unlikely to be the same for cis parents as it is for trans parents. While some cis parents may prefer to be registered as 'parent,' this is different to having to register in a gendered term which is not consistent with one's identity. I am surprised that neither the High Court nor the Court of Appeal expressly considered the impact a birth certificate that is not congruent with a child's lived experience would have on their sense of self and development. In my view, the lower courts placed too little importance on the opinion of Claire Brooks, YY's litigation friend, that 'it is important for YY's identity and self-esteem that his birth certificate reflects the reality of his life' and that '[a]nything else gives the impression of something secretive or shameful' (High Court judgment, at [59]). I am, of course, unable to say with certainty how much this incongruence would impact YY's well-being, as well as children in similar scenarios, but I do not think it is unreasonable to assume it would cause at least some problems.

52. Despite the law on birth registration requiring every person who gives birth to register as 'mother,' this has a disproportionate impact on trans men as it requires them to be registered in a way that is not congruent with their identity.

Conclusion

53. The legislative scheme of the GRA, in requiring Mr McConnell to be registered as a mother, violates his Article 8 right. Successfully rectifying this issue for the Appellant – namely, by registering him as a 'father' or 'parent' – would amount to judicial law-making and is therefore outside the scope of the Court. To that extent, I would allow the appeal and make a declaration that sections 9 and 12 GRA, and the relevant provisions of the BDRA 1953 and Schedule 7(2) of the associated Regulations, are incompatible with Article 8 ECHR.

22

Re Imogen (Australia)

Joanne Stagg

Introduction

Re Imogen (No. 6) was a single judge Australian Family Court decision dated 10 September 2020.[1] At issue was whether a 16-year-old transgender girl, Imogen, could undertake stage 2 hormone therapy.[2] She was already taking puberty blockers. Her separated parents disagreed on her medical care. Imogen's mother opposed her transition, while her father supported her desire to transition. The mother insisted Imogen was a boy with a psychological illness. Imogen's treating doctors confirmed she was a transgender girl and the appropriate medical care for her included medical transition. Both her father and doctors agreed she was competent to consent to medical treatment.

Though the judge ruled in Imogen's favour, allowing her to undergo hormone therapy, the judgment in *Re Imogen* reflected the dominant cisnormative discourse that medical transition care is abnormal, and potentially will be regretted [157-160]. Imogen's awareness of her gender was the subject of medicalised debate amongst experts, as is often the case for transgender people [171-182] and a possible result of social contagion [144-149 and 176]. Watts J allowed expert evidence from an anti-trans activist psychiatrist, rather than appropriately examining the witness' expertise and bias [throughout the judgment]. Finally, the judge carved out an exception to normal rules for adolescent medical decision-making competence, to create a separate rule for transgender health care which would allow a parent to override an otherwise competent person's consent to medical care [28-63]. These may appear at first glance to be individual issues, but all stem from a single cause: the construction of transgender people's experiences of adolescence and gender as aberrant and potentially inauthentic.

---

1. *Re Imogen (No 6)*, No. 761 (FamCA 10 September 2020) [2020] FamCA 761 (Hereafter cited as '*Re Imogen*'). 'Imogen' and most other names in the case are pseudonyms to protect the privacy of Imogen.
2. Adolescents' gender-affirming medical care is referred to as a three-stage process in Australian case law, as readers will see in cases referred to in this contribution, including *Re Alex: Hormonal Treatment for Gender Identity Dysphoria* [2004] FamCA 297, 93-175 (hereafter cited as '*Re Alex*'), *Re Jamie* [2013] FamCAFC 110 (hereafter cited as *Re Jamie*), *Re Imogen (No 6)* and *Re Kelvin* [2017] FamCAFC 258, (hereafter cited as '*Re Kelvin*'). The stages are: stage 1, puberty blockers from early adolescence; stage 2, so-called 'cross hormones' or the hormones appropriate to the person's gender rather than assigned sex at birth; and stage 3, various forms of gender-affirmation surgery.

After discussing briefly what it would mean to be a queer judge, this commentary will examine the law relating to gender-affirming care for transgender adolescents in Australia. It will then give a brief overview of the issues relating to the construction of transition care as suspicious, the expert evidence in *Re Imogen*, and adolescents' medical consent in Australia.

The judgment below is a fictional decision on an appeal against *Re Imogen*. It will demonstrate how treating queer people as authorities on their own lives, with ability to consent to medical care, would have led to different findings of law in *Re Imogen*. It will also examine how normal rules of evidence should be applied to deny hate groups space to treat transphobic denial of science as medical expertise.

The queer judge

My idealised queer judge embraces key aspects of queer theory and uses them to inform their approach to judging.[3] Queer judges themselves do not necessarily need to be queer. However, they should embrace Eve Sedgwick's conception of queerness as 'the open mesh of possibilities, gaps, overlaps, dissonances and resonances, lapses and excesses of meaning when the constituent elements of anyone's gender or anyone's sexuality aren't made (or *can't be*) made to signify monolithically.'[4] The queer judge would not assume that cis-heteronormativity signifies a monolithic 'norm' from which noncisgendered people or nonheterosexuals depart, nor a norm to which queer individuals should aspire. Instead, the queer judge would embrace the 'possibilities, gaps, overlaps, dissonances and resonances' of queerness as equally valid, equally intelligible, and equally honoured as cis-heteronormative experiences, lives, and stories. They may make the queer ordinary and the ordinary queer.

Using Butler's concept of 'performance,' the queer judge performs judging in ways that embody both judging and queerness. For Butler, performance 'is always a reiteration of a norm or a set of norms, and to the extent that it acquires an act-like status in the present, it conceals or dissimulates the convention of which it is a repetition.'[5] The queer judge relies for their authority on the institution and performance of the judicial role. The way in which they embody and perform that judicial role simultaneously gives authority to their judgments, creates, and reinforces the role of 'judge,' and may expand the act of 'judging' such that it may include queer perspectives.

The queer judge will, of course, interrogate and reject cis-heteronormativity in their approach to individual cases.[6] However, the queer judge will go further. The queer judge will bring the greater spirit of queerness and queer theory into their performance of judging. Thus, they may bring genuine queer curiosity, not only about queer lives,

---

3. Tamsin Phillipa Paige and Joanne Stagg, 'Queer Approaches to International Adjudication,' in *The Max Planck Encyclopedia of International Procedural Law* (Oxford: Oxford University Press, 2022), accessed 14 July 2023, www.opil.ouplaw.com/home/mpil.

4. Eve Kosofsky Sedgwick, *Tendencies* (Durham: Duke University Press, 2008), 8.

5. Judith Butler, *Bodies That Matter: On the Discursive Limits of 'Sex'* (Abingdon; New York: Routledge, 2011), xxi.

6. Alex Sharpe, 'Queering Judgment: The Case of Gender Identity Fraud,' *The Journal of Criminal Law* 81/5 (2017), 417–35.

but about normative presumptions and legal orthodoxies which underlie legal reasoning in case law. They will question their own presuppositions and be open to novel arguments and re-thinking the law.

In queering judging, the queer judge, like queers more generally, is constrained by the need to themselves remain acceptable to cis-heteronormative institutions with which they may wish to engage. For the queer judge, this creates a need for a form of judicial respectability, which translates into remaining within the constraints of their legal and judicial traditions. To use the judicial role, they cannot destabilise the judiciary nor their own authority within the judiciary. They may paradoxically reinforce cis-heteronormative patriarchy while being able to use the unique opportunity of judicial performance (itself a performance made possible by centuries of cis-heteronormative patriarchal power and institutions) to examine and even, perhaps, destabilise some facets of cis-heteronormativity. Thus, their queerness, like the tamed queerness of respectability discourse, cannot become either too exuberant or too challenging to cis-heteronormative society. The judgment below uses this framework for queer judging.

Gender-affirmation for young people in Australia

Until relatively recently, Australian courts required trans children's gender-affirming medical care to be subject to court supervision. This approach started with *Re Alex*, in 2004. *Re Alex* applied an older case, *Marion's case,* to gender-affirming care of adolescents.[7] In *Marion's case*, the High Court of Australia found that court approval would be required for nontherapeutic permanent surgical sterilisation of intellectually disabled children who would never be competent to consent to sterilisation.[8] The principle in *Marion's case* has been extended in Australia to any other nontherapeutic medical intervention with permanent effects for any child without the capacity to consent to the treatment.[9]

Marion's case also confirmed that *Gillick v West Norfolk and Wisbech Area Health Authority* would apply in Australia.[10] Under *Gillick*, a sufficiently competent adolescent could consent to medical care without parental intervention when they achieve 'a sufficient understanding and intelligence to enable him or her to understand fully what is proposed.'[11]

In *Re Alex*, the Family Court of Australia ordered that transition care could not be given to non-*Gillick* competent adolescents without court approval. They decided that both stage 1 care (reversible puberty blockers) and stage 2 care (cross-hormones appropriate to the affirmed gender) should be treated as a single medical process.

Re Alex was later reviewed in *Re Jamie*.[12] In that case, the court found that stage 1

---

7. *Secretary, Department of Health and Community Services v JWB and SMB* (1992) 175 CLR 218 (Usually referred to and hereafter cited as '*Marion's case*').
8. The High Court of Australia is the highest appellate court in Australia.
9. *Re Alex*.
10. *Marion's case*, 239 (Mason CJ, Dawson, Toohey and Gaudron JJ).
11. *Marion's case*, 237 (Mason CJ, Dawson, Toohey and Gaudron JJ), quoting *Gillick* at 189.
12. *Re Jamie* [108, 179, 193].

and stage 2 transition treatments were two separate medical interventions. They found that stage 1 treatment did not fall under the principle in *Marion's case*, because it was fully reversible. On the other hand, they decided that court approval would still be required for stage 2 treatment because it was, in the opinion of the court, irreversible, non-therapeutic, and would have significant permanent physical effects.[13] The judges considered that it was likely that a court would need to rule on the capacity of the trans adolescent before a doctor could undertake treatment of a *Gillick* competent trans adolescent.[14]

The requirement for a court to confirm *Gillick* competence before any transgender adolescent could consent to transition care was overturned by the Full Court of the Family Court of Australia in *Re Kelvin*, which established that if both parents and treating doctors agreed an adolescent was *Gillick* competent, then the trans adolescent could consent to their own transition care without a court ruling as to their competence. *Re Kelvin* also established that all stages of transition care were therapeutic treatment for gender dysphoria. Therefore, parents could consent to transition care for their transgender children without seeking court approval. However, the case did not make findings about the appropriate process when parents disagreed about a transgender adolescent's medical care.

Re Imogen

In *Re Imogen*, Imogen was a trans girl who was nearly 17. Imogen's father sought to have Imogen declared *Gillick* competent and/or to allow her to undergo stage 2 gender-affirmation care. Her mother did not accept that Imogen was a transgender girl. Prior to the trial in the case, Imogen had taken stage 1 medications (puberty blockers) and now sought to undertake stage 2 hormone treatment (feminizing hormones). By the time the matter came to court, Imogen had undertaken therapy to explore her gender and had also begun (illegally) securing cross hormones online without prescriptions.

In *Re Imogen*, Watts J ruled that, where a parent challenged either the teenager's competence or proposed gender-affirmation care, *Gillick* competent teenagers required a court ruling declaring their competence to allow them to seek gender-affirming health care.

Cisnormativity in Re Imogen

The idea that trans young people are at risk because they may regret gender-affirming care is mentioned throughout the case law and is a frequent trope amongst anti-trans groups. This anti-trans trope was debunked in evidence in *Re Imogen*. Several studies were submitted in evidence and listed in the judgment. One, by de Vries et al, showed that in a cohort of 70 adolescents treated between 2000 and 2008, no participant changed their mind about being trans and none desisted in their wish to medically transition.[15]

---

13. *Re Jamie*, [111, 181-186, 195-196].
14. *Re Jamie*, [111, 181-186, 195-196].
15. Annelou LC De Vries et al., 'Puberty Suppression in Adolescents with Gender Identity Disorder: A Prospective Follow-up Study,' *The Journal of Sexual Medicine* 8/8 (2011), 2276–83.

A follow up study on 55 of the same cohort showed none of those who underwent gender-affirmation surgery regretted their choices. Gender-affirmation care significantly improved participants' mental health, wellbeing and satisfaction with their bodies.[16] In addition, a large literature review presented to the court stated:

> data from numerous studies demonstrates a regret rate [for medical transition] ranging from [0].3 percent to 3.8 percent. Regrets are most likely to result from a lack of social support after transition or poor surgical outcomes using older techniques.[17]

The same review found that trans people who could not access gender-affirmation care suffered 'health challenges such as depression, anxiety, suicidality, and minority stress,' while transition substantially ameliorated gender dysphoria, anxiety, depression, suicidality, and substance abuse.[18] That beneficial effect was particularly strong where the trans person had social and familial support.[19]

The evidence about regret presented in *Re Imogen* is similar to other research that places regret rates at approximately 1%.[20] Regret rates are substantially lower than regret rates for many other types of surgery (e.g. regret for breast reconstructions after mastectomy may be as high as 40-47.2%).[21] In addition, research shows the effect of transition is overwhelmingly positive, with substantial reductions of serious adverse mental health conditions and lifesaving reductions in levels of suicidality.[22]

Anti-trans moral panic and anti-trans discourses often deploy claims of children being persuaded into erroneous diagnosis of pathologized transgender identities, leading to regretted medical interventions.[23] Such discourses often deploy the political emblem of an imaginary Child at risk of being coerced or peer pressured into a transition they will regret afterwards.[24] The imagined suffering of the idealised Child is then prioritised

---

16. Annelou LC De Vries et al., 'Young Adult Psychological Outcome after Puberty Suppression and Gender Reassignment,' *Pediatrics* 134/4 (2014), 696–704.

17. 'What Does the Scholarly Research Say about the Effect of Gender Transition on Transgender Well-Being?,' What We Know, accessed 11 December 2022, https://whatweknow.inequality.cornell.edu/topics/lgbt-equality/what-does-the-scholarly-research-say-about-the-well-being-of-transgender-people/, (Hereafter 'What Does the Scholarly Research Say').

18. 'What Does the Scholarly Research Say.'

19. 'What Does the Scholarly Research Say.' I note that the medicalization of the trans experience using the diagnosis of gender dysphoria as a necessary indicator is highly problematic, but that also some (not all) transgender people describe feeling dysphoric, e.g. as described in 'Dysphoria,' TransHub, accessed 23 October 2023, https://www.transhub.org.au/dysphoria.

20. Valeria P. Bustos et al., 'Regret after Gender-Affirmation Surgery: A Systematic Review and Meta-Analysis of Prevalence,' *Plastic and Reconstructive Surgery – Global Open* 9/3 (March 2021).

21. Joanne Sheehan et al., 'Regret Associated with the Decision for Breast Reconstruction: The Association of Negative Body Image, Distress and Surgery Characteristics with Decision Regret,' *Psychology & Health* 23/2 (2008), 207–19; Toni Zhong et al., 'Decision Regret Following Breast Reconstruction: The Role of Self-Efficacy and Satisfaction with Information in the Preoperative Period,' *Plastic and Reconstructive Surgery* 132/5 (November 2013), 724e–34.

22. 'What Does the Scholarly Research Say'; Jack L. Turban et al., 'Pubertal Suppression for Transgender Youth and Risk of Suicidal Ideation,' *Pediatrics* 145/2 (February 2020).

23. Van Slothouber, '(De)Trans Visibility: Moral Panic in Mainstream Media Reports on De/Retransition,' *European Journal of English Studies* 24/1 (2020), 89–99.

24. Lee Edelman, *No Future Queer Theory and the Death Drive* (Durham: Duke University Press, 2004); Slothouber, '(De)Trans Visibility,' 94.

over the actual suffering of real transgender children denied transition. This can only occur in the context of the weaponization of cisnormative discourses of the naturalness and normativity of cisgender experiences of gender, and of the deployment of moral panic discourses of transgender people as sinister persuaders of young people into a non-normative lifestyle. A concomitant concern with preserving fertility is often also deployed as part of the moral panic discourses about the harm of transition.[25] Both the political futurism of the imagined Child and the concern for procreation are deployments of heteronormative presumptions that a primary requirement for a fulfilled life is procreation. As soon as we decouple the welfare of young people from cis-heteronormative presumptions and consider transgender experiences as a natural variation of human experience – and reproduction as optional (as many queers do) – denying a trans adolescent highly effective medical care that substantially reduces real suffering becomes an act of abuse, rather than protection.

Gillick competence and cisnormativity in Re Imogen

The principles in *Gillick* as adopted in *Marion's case* mean an Australian adolescent who is capable of understanding and consenting to medical care could not have that consent overridden by a parent, though it may be overridden by a court only after exercise of serious caution where the child is at severe risk of death or serious harm.[26] There appears to be no case where a *Gillick* competent adolescent's consent has been overturned where they would benefit from the medical care they were seeking.

Despite the general Australian approach to *Gillick* competence, Watts J in *Re Imogen* restricts the decision-making of *Gillick* competent transgender adolescents where a parent does not want them to have gender-affirming care. This reflects cisnormative discourses about transgender people being mistaken about their own gender or being persuaded they are transgender through social contagion.[27] Reflecting concerns that medical professionals are failing to gatekeep transition care, courts would then become the opposing parent's desired gatekeeper, checking for true signs of transgender status.[28] *Re Imogen* creates a sub-class of *Gillick* competent adolescents who are subject to parental interference in and refusal of care because they are a gender minority. Such an approach – that a non-consenting parent can override a *Gillick* competent trans adolescent's consent to care – seems to directly contradict the High Court's acceptance of *Gillick* in Australia and the formulation of consent principles in the *Gillick* case itself.

Evidence of Dr D'Angelo

Expert witnesses are generally required to be unbiased and have sufficient relevant expert knowledge.[29] However, in *Re Imogen*, the mother's expert, Dr Robert D'Angelo,

---

25. Slothouber, '(De)Trans Visibility,' 94.
26. Pip Trowse, 'Refusal of Medical Treatment-a Child's Prerogative?,' *Law and Justice Journal* 10/2 (2010), 191–212.
27. Slothouber, '(De)Trans Visibility,' 95–96.
28. Slothouber, '(De)Trans Visibility,' 96.
29. Experts must have relevant demonstrated expertise: *R v Parenzee* [2007] SASC 143. The expert's duty is

was not an unbiased expert witness. D'Angelo is active in anti-trans and so-called 'gender critical' groups,[30] including the Society for Ethical Gender Medicine,[31] which the Southern Poverty Law Centre describes as one of several 'associations of anti-trans medical professionals' and as a far-right group 'flooding' US legislatures with anti-trans legislation.[32]

Dr D'Angelo is opposed to standard gender-affirmation care for trans young people.[33] He advocates that psychiatric care to persuade trans adolescents that they are not transgender would be more appropriate than gender-affirming care. This approach is dangerous. A summary of Australian standard care recommendations for trans young people states that 'psychological practices attempting to change a person's gender identity to be more aligned with their sex assigned at birth … lack efficacy, are considered unethical, and may cause lasting damage to an individual's social and emotional health and wellbeing.'[34]

The court's decision to give an anti-trans activist equal standing with doctors who promote gold-standard medical care appears to be influenced by cisnormative conceptions of gender-affirming care as controversial or aberrant.

The judgment

I present the alternative queer judgment below as an intermediate level appeal by the unsuccessful mother from the first instance decision in *Re Imogen* to the Full Court of the Family Court and Federal Circuit Court of Australia. In it, I explore the issues with the creation of new legal standards restricting *Gillick* competent decision-making for transgender adolescents, the positioning of transition care as controversial, and the problematic decision to allow the evidence of an anti-trans activist as appropriate expert evidence on the care of a trans child. In doing so, this queer judgment will attempt to make what is now queer to courts (health care for trans teens) ordinary and the ordinary (suspicion about transition and acceptance of anti-trans tropes) queer.

---

to give an 'objective and unbiased opinion' as required by r7.18 *Federal Circuit and Family Court of Australia (Family Law) Rules 2021* (Cth), mirroring the previous *Family Court Rules 1975* (Cth) in this respect.

30. 'Gender critical' is a term, like 'race realist,' used to codify bigotry: Lucy Nicholas and Sal Clark, 'Leave Those Kids Alone: On the Uses and Abuses and Feminist Queer Potential of Non-Binary and Genderqueer,' *INSEP–Journal of the International Network for Sexual Ethics and Politics* 8 (2020), 7–8; Katelyn Burns, 'The Rise of Anti-Trans "Radical" Feminists, Explained,' Vox, 5 September 2019, accessed 21 December 2022, https://www.vox.com/identities/2019/9/5/20840101/terfs-radical-feminists-gender-critical.

31. Alison Clayton, Roberto D'Angelo, and Patrick Clarke, 'Parental Consent and the Treatment of Transgender Youth: The Impact of Re Imogen,' *Medical Journal of Australia* 217/3 (2022), 167.

32. 'Far-Right Groups Flood State Legislatures With Anti-Trans Bills Targeting Children,' Southern Poverty Law Center, accessed 11 December 2022, https://www.splcenter.org/hatewatch/2021/04/26/far-right-groups-flood-state-legislatures-anti-trans-bills-targeting-children.

33. I will not cite each paper individually to avoid increasing Dr D'Angelo's citation index and promote his anti-trans activism. His papers are listed at https://www.researchgate.net/profile/Roberto-Dangelo-8, accessed 16 December 2023. That page lists thirteen anti-gender-affirmative care papers by Dr D'Angelo since 2018.

34. Michelle M Telfer et al., 'Australian Standards of Care and Treatment Guidelines for Transgender and Gender Diverse Children and Adolescents,' *Medical Journal of Australia* 209/3 (2018), 132–36.

Re Imogen
Judgment on appeal

FULL COURT OF THE FAMILY COURT AND FEDERAL CIRCUIT

COURT OF AUSTRALIA

APPELLANT:	The mother
RESPONDENT:	The father
FIRST INTERVENOR:	Australian Human Rights Commission
SECOND INTERVENOR:	Attorney-General of the Commonwealth
INDEPENDENT CHILDREN'S LAWYER:	[this lawyer is not named to maintain anonymity]

Joint judgment of the Full Court of the Federal Circuit and Family Court of Australia

Grounds for appeal

[1] The mother has brought an appeal against the decision of Watts J in the court below that Imogen is *Gillick* competent, and that Imogen be administered oestrogen as recommended by her treating medical practitioners.

[2] The father opposes the appeal. In addition, the father's counsel has argued that each of the following findings of Watts J were incorrect in law. Those findings were:
   a. If a parent or a medical practitioner of an adolescent disputes:
       i.   The *Gillick* competence of an adolescent; or
       ii. A diagnosis of gender dysphoria; or
       iii. Proposed treatment for gender dysphoria,
       an application to this court is mandatory;
   b.
       ...
   c. Notwithstanding a finding of *Gillick* competence, if there is a dispute about diagnosis or treatment, the court should:

      i.   Determine the diagnosis;

      ii. Determine whether treatment is appropriate, having regard to the adolescent's best interests as the paramount consideration; and

      iii. Make an order authorizing or not authorizing treatment pursuant to s 67ZC of the Act on best interest considerations;

  d. If a parent or legal guardian does not consent to an adolescent's treatment for gender dysphoria, a medical practitioner, who is willing to do so, should not administer treatment to an adolescent who wishes it, without court authorisation.

[3] This court finds for the reasons below that Watts J erred in findings a, c, and d. For the reasons below, we find the appropriate approach is:

  a. If an adolescent is *Gillick* competent for relevant medical care, including gender-affirmation care, they may consent to the medical care without parental intervention.

  b. If a parent brings an application to this court challenging the proposed medical care of an adolescent or *Gillick* competence of the adolescent, the following principles apply:

      i.   The court must first determine if the adolescent is *Gillick* competent. The court should make a declaration pursuant to s 34(1) of the Family Law Act 1975 (Cth) as to whether the adolescent is *Gillick* competent.

      ii. If the adolescent is *Gillick* competent, the adolescent may make all relevant medical decisions for which they are competent. This court and their parents will have no further role in supervising the *Gillick* competent adolescent's medical care, including gender-affirmation care.

      iii. *Only* if the adolescent is not *Gillick* competent, this court should make a finding as to the appropriate medical care for the adolescent and the appropriate orders to ensure the adolescent's best interests in that circumstance. That may include making orders authorizing appropriate medical care and/or giving parental responsibility for medical decisions to one parent or carer, rather than another.

  c. If an adolescent is *Gillick* competent in the opinion of their relevant medical practitioner, exercising appropriate medical discretion and applying the normal standards for determining *Gillick* competence used for all medical decision making, there is no requirement that a medical practitioner either seek parental consent nor court authorisation to administer gender-affirming health care to a *Gillick* competent adolescent. The lack of consent or refusal of care by a parent or legal guardian does not prevent a *Gillick* competent adolescent from consenting to medical care. The consent of the *Gillick* competent adolescent shall act as a full defence to any allegations of assault or battery.

  d. For clarity, parents do not have the right to override a *Gillick* competent adolescent's request for medical care. This is especially clear where the care is therapeutic and in the best interests of the adolescent, as is gender-affirming medical care for transgender adolescents.

Facts

[4] This is an appeal against a judgment of Watts J in the Family Court of Australia, delivered on 10 September 2020. This is not a rehearing of the matter. This court is bound by the trial judge's findings of fact unless no reasonable judge could have made such a finding. Watts J summarised the facts in this matter as follows:

> This case is about Imogen, aged 16 years and 8 months, and her future medical treatment. Imogen has been diagnosed with Gender Dysphoria and assessed as *Gillick* competent by her treating doctors. Imogen currently takes stage 1 puberty suppression medication and has expressed a consistent, persistent, and insistent view that she wishes to move to stage 2 gender-affirming hormone treatment. Imogen's mother disputes Imogen's diagnosis and that Imogen is *Gillick* competent. She says that Imogen is unable to fully and sufficiently understand the nature of the treatment proposed, lacks an understanding of and ability to assess the risks associated with stage 2 treatment and has a misplaced confidence in the positive effects of transitioning. Imogen's mother does not consent to gender-affirming hormone therapy.

Jurisdiction

[5] Jurisdiction is not in issue in this matter.

[6] Additionally, as the appellant court stated in *Re Kelvin*, there is a 'well settled principle that a later Full Court will consider itself free to depart from an earlier decision if that decision can be said to be "plainly wrong."'[35] This court may review and correct incorrect legal principles in previous cases of the Full Court of the Family Court, and of this court, when considering the appeal in this matter.

The status of gender-affirming care for trans youth

[7] Gender-affirming medical care for transgender children and adolescents is the subject of international and Australian standards of care, known respectively as the WPATH Standards and the AusPATH Standards.[36] Gender-affirming care for transgender adolescents is broken into three stages for trans children and adolescents. Before undergoing medical interventions, a trans child may socially transition, but have no medical interventions. This is the usual course of practice for a child before puberty. At the onset of puberty, transgender adolescents will be offered stage 1 care, the administration of puberty blockers, which delay puberty and are fully reversible. Stage 2 care involves the administration of so-called *cross hormones*, that is, feminizing hormones

---

35. *Re Kelvin*, [167], which cites: *Nguyen v Nguyen* (1990) 169 CLR 245, 268-270 (Dawson, Toohey and McHugh JJ); *Gett v Tabet* (2009) 254 ALR 504, [261]-[301]; and *F Firm & Ruane and Ors* (2014) FLC 93-611, [163].
36. E. Coleman et al., 'Standards of Care for the Health of Transgender and Gender Diverse People, Version 8,' *International Journal of Transgender Health* 23 (19 August 2022): S1–259; Coleman et al., 'Australian Standards of Care and Treatment Guidelines for Trans and Gender Diverse Children and Adolescents – AusPATH,' accessed 12 December 2022; Telfer et al., 'Australian Standards of Care and Treatment Guidelines for Transgender and Gender Diverse Children and Adolescents.'

for trans girls and masculinizing hormones for trans boys, as well as medications which may block the production or effects of natal hormones. Stage 3 care may involve various gender-affirming surgeries. Not all trans people choose to have hormonal or surgical interventions.

[8] Past case law, and the case in this appeal, have treated stage 2 gender-affirming medical care as being unusual or unsafe. In *Re Alex*, Nicholson CJ stated that:

> there are significant risks attendant to embarking on a process that will alter a child or young person who presents as physically of one sex in the direction of the opposite sex, even where the court is not asked to authorise surgery.[37]

The majority in *Re Kelvin* mirrored this concern when they said that 'the consequences of a wrong decision are particularly grave.'[38]

[9] In *Re Sam and Terry*, Murphy J stated that:

> The proposed stage 2 treatments for each of Terry and Sam carry significant risks and will also have irreversible effects on each of them in differing ways. For each, the proposed hormonal treatment carries an increased risk of breast cancer and may adversely affect fertility. The treatment will also have irreversible physical effects, such as, in Terry's case, the growth of facial hair and deepening of voice and, in Sam's case, the redistribution of muscle mass and body fat. Those side effects are significant in themselves, but they are also significant because they are side effects designed to effect hormonal changes and overt manifestations consistent with a gender different to each child's birth gender.[39]

[10] The judge in that case also implied that there was a risk that the trans person may change their mind, saying 'sometimes a longer view might also conflict with the immediate desires of children, even those whose views are mature.'[40]

[11] However, in the evidence before the court below, particularly scholarly articles appended to the affidavit of Dr C and the evidence of Dr C, showed that regret for transition is rare (none in studies by de Vries et al. and between only 0.3% and 3.2% in a literature review by Cornell University).[41] Regret appears to arise more commonly with older surgical techniques or where individuals faced lack of social support or discrimination, and did not appear to be about the effects of medical transition in the majority of the small percentage of cases in which there was some regret.[42] In addition, the evidence showed that gender-affirming medical care had substantial benefits

---

37. *Re Alex*, [196].
38. *Re Kelvin*, [116].
39. *Re Sam and Terry*, [100].
40. *Re Sam and Terry*, [103].
41. De Vries et al., 'Puberty Suppression in Adolescents with Gender Identity Disorder: A Prospective Follow-up Study'; De Vries et al., 'Young Adult Psychological Outcome after Puberty Suppression and Gender Reassignment'; 'What Does the Scholarly Research Say.'
42. 'What Does the Scholarly Research Say.'

in reducing suicidality, anxiety, depression, and gender dysphoria.[43] Based on similar evidence, gender-affirming care was found to be therapeutic by the Full Court of the Family Court in *Re Kelvin*.[44]

[12] Courts have also referred to healthcare for transgender people as being rapidly changing. For example, in *Re Kelvin*, the court pointed out:

> The change from the fourth edition to the fifth edition [of the Diagnostic and Statistical Manual of Mental Disorders] in May 2013 was significant. In the former edition the 'condition' was described as a Gender Identity Disorder, but in the latter edition it is described as Gender Dysphoria. Thus, it is no longer described as a 'disorder,' and further, and significantly, there was

> i. … a change from the recognition of gender identity disorder to a recognition of gender dysphoria and, of course, the latter focusses very much on the dysphoria as the disorder to be treated rather than the issue of identity, and identity itself is no longer regarded as any kind of pathology.

[13] The majority in *Re Kelvin* further noted the development of the WPATH and AusPATH standards.[45] They also mentioned awareness of the risks of failing to treat gender dysphoria, including social and psychological distress and suicidality.[46]

[14] Since at least *Re Alex* in the early 2000s, medical evidence has consistently asserted that failing to undertake appropriate transition care is harmful to transgender adolescents. The ongoing research identified in *Re Jamie, Re Kelvin* and research placed before the trial judge in this case clearly identifies that not only is it distressing and deleterious for trans adolescents to be prevented from transitioning, but delays in transitioning also carry a very real risk of causing suicidality for young trans people. For transgender people, it is clearly established that it is harmful and may even be deadly to prevent them from transitioning. This, of course, is why the majority in *Re Kelvin* found that Stage 2 care was therapeutic.[47]

[15] The staging and medications used in Stage 1 and Stage 2 care have been remarkably stable and consistent since at least the decision in *Re Alex* in 2004. The name and details of the relevant diagnosis may have changed over time, but the evidence put before the court showed that this so-called 'Dutch protocol' has been the 'gold-standard' approach to medical care for trans adolescents since the turn of the century.[48]

---

43. De Vries et al., 'Puberty Suppression in Adolescents with Gender Identity Disorder: A Prospective Follow-up Study'; De Vries et al., 'Young Adult Psychological Outcome after Puberty Suppression and Gender Reassignment'; 'What Does the Scholarly Research Say about the Effect of Gender Transition on Transgender Well-Being?'
44. *Re Kelvin*, [162-164].
45. *Re Kelvin*, [159-160].
46. *Re Kelvin*, [17 -23].
47. *Re Kelvin*, [162-164].
48. De Vries et al., 'Puberty Suppression in Adolescents with Gender Identity Disorder: A Prospective Follow-up Study'; De Vries et al., 'Young Adult Psychological Outcome after Puberty Suppression and Gender Reassignment'; Telfer et al., 'Australian Standards of Care and Treatment Guidelines for Transgender and Gender Diverse Children and Adolescents'; 'What Does the Scholarly Research Say.'

[16] Much of the trial judge's discussion about the uncertainty of appropriate care for transgender young people arose from the evidence of the mother's expert witness Dr D'Angelo.[49] He recommended that Imogen be placed in his psychiatric care, to undergo care focused on dissuading her from her transgender identity and focusing on pathologizing her perception of her gender as arising out of social contagion or trauma.

[17] Dr D'Angelo's approach was to seek 'a remission of gender and body dysphoria,' though he claimed the aim was 'not to get an adolescent to identify with their natal gender.'[50] He recommended that Imogen be denied stage 2 treatment and be removed from stage 1 treatment for at least 12 months. He attributes Imogen's perception of her gender as female to possible social contagion or as a reaction to stress from trauma suffered in her family.[51] He stated that an appropriate goal of his treatment would be for Imogen to no longer desire medical transition. It is clear that the doctor seeks to engage in treatment which would 'attempt to change or suppress a person's … gender identity,' which is a form of conversion therapy.[52] While such an approach is not illegal in Imogen's home state of New South Wales, the court notes both the adjoining state of Queensland and the Australian Capital Territory had already passed provisions criminalizing conversion therapy when the decision below was handed down on 10 September 2020.[53]

[18] The trial judge rejected Dr D'Angelo's evidence, in part because he relied upon a methodologically flawed study subject to strong criticisms and lengthy editorial correction,[54] and 'had not properly analysed' another study which he misstated in evidence.[55] The trial judge was rightly concerned about Dr D'Angelo repeating tropes about various pharmaceutical and social vested interests and 'agendas' in promotion of medical transition care and substantially overstating the likelihood of regret for transition care by orders of magnitude.[56] Watts J found that 'Dr D'Angelo presents as an advocate for an alternative approach to the treatment of adolescents present-ing with Gender Dysphoria.'[57] The evidence presented in the court below included standards that stated that such 'alternative approaches' 'lack efficacy, are considered unethical, and may cause lasting damage to an individual's social and emotional health and wellbeing.'[58]

---

49. *Re Imogen*, [137-164].
50. *Re Imogen*, [221].
51. *Re Imogen*, [120,175].
52. *Public Health Act 2005* (Qld), s213F.
53. *Public Health Act 2005* (Qld), Ch 5B; *Sexuality and Gender Identity Conversion Practices Act 2020* (ACT).
54. Lisa Littman, 'Parent Reports of Adolescents and Young Adults Perceived to Show Signs of a Rapid Onset of Gender Dysphoria' *PLoS One* 13/8 (2018) e0202330; Littman, 'Correction Parent Reports of Adolescents and Young Adults Perceived to Show Signs of a Rapid Onset of Gender Dysphoria,' *PLoS One* 14/3 (2019) e0214157; Arjee Javellana Restar, 'Methodological critique of Littman's (2018) parental-respondents accounts of "rapid-onset gender dysphoria."' *Archives of Sexual Behavior* 49/1 (2020), 61-66.
55. *Re Imogen*, [155].
56. *Re Imogen*, [159, 219, 230].
57. *Re Imogen*, [230].
58. Telfer et al., 'Australian Standards of Care and Treatment Guidelines for Transgender and Gender

[19] Accepting Dr D'Angelo as an expert in this case was inappropriate. Counsel for the father in this appeal referred to the case of *R v Parenzee*.[59] In that case, an alleged expert denied scientific consensus about HIV based on a fanatic belief, leading to a finding that they could not appropriately assist the court to understand relevant scientific opinions. This court would apply a similar approach to Dr D'Angelo in this case.[60] Since Dr D'Angelo apparently had a fixed ideological view that adolescents were generally unable to understand the potential effects of gender transition and, so, could never be *Gillick* competent to consent to the procedure, and also apparently had a fixed view that gender-affirming care and the general consensus on that care *must* be wrong (contrary to general scientific consensus), he was unable to assist the court in determining if Imogen was in fact *Gillick* competent or should transition.[61]

[20] Alleged experts whose rejection of scientific consensus appears to arise out of bias against particular social groups should be considered with especial scepticism. This court should not accept unsupported claims of individuals or groups which are hostile to the existence of transgender people or seek to routinely deny standard medical care for transgender people when deciding what approach the law should take to gender-affirming medical care for transgender adolescents. When establishing the expertise of the alleged 'expert,' the court must take care to examine whether the expert is qualified, able to assist the court, and unbiased, in the same way that the court should examine all experts' qualifications and alleged expertise. The evidence of someone who seeks to deny standard medical care to an entire minority group should not be treated as relevant to assist the court to understand medical care for an adolescent in that group.

Gillick *Competence*

[21] Watts J found that even where a child is *Gillick* competent, a court should still independently consider the appropriateness of gender-affirming care where one or both of the child's parents object to the child having gender-affirming care. The judge also found that a medical professional could not give a *Gillick* competent child gender-affirming medical care where a parent disagreed with that care, even if the *Gillick* competent child consented to the care. This is a misunderstanding of *Gillick* competence in Australia.

[22] Though the court in *Re Kelvin* clearly decided that parents could consent to Stage 2 care for an incompetent child where the child, parent, and relevant medical professionals agreed, that court stated:

> We note though that in answering that question we are not ... [saying] anything about the
> need for court authorisation where there is a genuine dispute or controversy as to whether

Diverse Children and Adolescents.'
59. *R v Parenzee*, [2007] SASC 143.
60. *Re Imogen*, [156-157].
61. *Re Imogen*, [189].

the treatment should be administered; e.g., if the parents, or the medical professionals are unable to agree. There is no doubt that the court has the jurisdiction and the power to address issues such as those.[62]

[23] It is into this gap that Watts J in *Re Imogen* was required to step, since the parents in the current case did not agree about Imogen's diagnosis of gender dysphoria nor her care. His Honour mentioned the principles from *Re Kelvin* but found that the decision of Bryant CJ in *Re Jamie* should guide his approach to whether an order for *Gillick* competence and then an order for treatment were required.

[24] Thackray, Strickland and Murphy JJ in *Re Kelvin* discussed Bryant's CJ's reasoning in *Re Jamie* on *Gillick* competence. They said:

> [181] … What her Honour is saying is that because court authorisation is required where there is the significant risk of making the wrong decision and the consequences of a wrong decision are particularly grave, it was also appropriate that the Court determine *Gillick* competence. In other words, the nature of the treatment requires that to be the case (also see Finn J at [185] – [186]).

> [182] Now, of course, if as appears to be the case, the nature of the treatment no longer justifies court authorisation, and the concerns do not apply, then there is also no longer a basis for the court to determine *Gillick* competence.

[25] Ainsley-Wallace and Ryan JJ gave a separate judgment in *Re Kelvin*, in which they agreed with the final orders but gave additional reasoning. They stated they 'agree with the conclusion reached, that a child who is capable of giving informed consent (*Gillick* competent) can authorise stage 2 treatment for Gender Dysphoria and it is not necessary for a court… so to find.'[63] They were correct to find that the decision in *Marion's case* does not 'erect a freestanding obligation to obtain a court finding that [a] child is *Gillick* competent before his or her consent can be given effect.'[64] However, for the reasons below, this court cannot fully accept their statement that, under *Marion's case*, 'the court has no role to play *unless there is a dispute about consent or treatment*' (emphasis added). Rather, courts have no role to play in deciding treatment once there is a finding that an adolescent is *Gillick* competent.

[26] Ainsley-Wallace and Ryan JJ themselves give the basis for this reasoning. They state, '[a]t common law, a parent is no longer capable of consenting on the child's behalf when the child achieves a sufficient understanding and intelligence to enable him or her to fully understand what is proposed (*Gillick* competent).'[65]

[27] This leaves us then to consider situations in which the child is thought to be *Gillick* competent by their treating medical professionals, but not by one or more of their parents. Can that child consent to transition medical care?

---

62. *Re Kelvin*, [167].
63. *Re Kelvin*, [187].
64. *Re Kelvin*, [189].
65. *Re Kelvin*, [199].

[28] To decide this, we must go back to *Marion's case*, and thence to *Gillick*'s case. The High Court in *Marion's case* stated that the approach in *Gillick v West Norfolk and Wisbech Area Health Authority* 'should be followed in this country as part of the common law' and '*Gillick* is taken to reflect the common law in Australia.'[66]

[29] The court in *Marion's case* first considered why consent to medical procedures is necessary. That is because surgery or other medical interference with one's body is a battery (or assault under some criminal law statutes) unless there is consent to the procedure.[67] A person with capacity to fully understand the procedure may consent to it. The majority in *Marion's case* stated that '[a] minor is, according to this principle [of *Gillick* competence] capable of giving informed consent when he or she "achieves a sufficient understanding and intelligence to enable him or her to understand fully what is proposed."'[68]

[30] It was also clear that it is only when 'the particular child is ... incapable of giving valid informed consent to medical treatment [that] the second question arises; namely whether there are kinds of intervention which are, as a general rule, excluded from the scope of parental power to consent to.'[69] It is clear from this approach that the court considered that requirements for parental or court consent to procedures only arose if the adolescent was not *Gillick* competent.

[31] In *Gillick* itself, Lord Fraser specifically considered whether a parent had 'the right to veto' medical care where the child in question was competent to consent.[70] He found that the parent does not and that a doctor may provide medical advice and treatment to a competent child without either informing the child's parent(s) or seeking their consent.[71]

[32] Similarly, Lord Scarman found that 'the parental right to determine whether or not their minor child ... will have medical treatment terminates if and when the child achieves a sufficient understanding and intelligence to enable him or her to understand fully what is proposed.'[72] Lord Bridge of Hardwick agreed with the reason of Lords Fraser and Scarman, creating a majority.[73]

[33] The novelty of treatment did not affect a competent adolescent's capacity to consent, since in *Gillick* several judges commented that the fact that the contraceptive

---

66. *Marion's case*, 238-239 (Mason CJ, Dawson, Toohey, and Gaudron JJ).
67. *Marion's case*, 232-235 (Mason CJ, Dawson, Toohey, and Gaudron JJ).
68. *Marion's case*, 237 (Mason CJ, Dawson, Toohey, and Gaudron JJ).
69. *Marion's case*, 239 (Mason CJ, Dawson, Toohey, and Gaudron JJ).
70. *Gillick*, 408-410 (Fraser LJ).
71. *Gillick*, 409 (Fraser LJ).
72. *Gillick*, 424, (Scarman LJ).
73. *Gillick*, 428 (Bridge of Hardwick LJ).

pill was a relatively new treatment was not grounds to find that parents or the court could veto the decisions of a competent child.[74]

[34] Since *Gillick* has been stated specifically by the High Court in *Marion's case* to be part of the common law in Australia, clearly a *Gillick* competent adolescent, that is, one who has 'sufficient understanding and intelligence to understand' medical treatment, has full capacity to consent to medical care, without veto by a parent. Courts below the High Court cannot override that principle.

[35] Ainsley-Wallace and Ryan JJ state in *Re Kelvin* that *Marion's case* 'does not … support court intervention in relation to therapeutic procedures to which a legally competent person can consent.'[75] This court agrees with their Honours on this point.

[36] The explicit adoption of *Gillick* in *Marion's case* and the care with which the High Court restricts their discussion of parental consent to non-*Gillick* competent children in *Marion's case* make it clear that the test of therapeutic benefit in *Marion's case* should not be applied to *Gillick* competent adolescents. Once a child is *Gillick* competent, there is no requirement to consider whether medical care is therapeutic or has permanent effects. Under *Marion's case*, that test is only relevant if the adolescent is not competent.

[37] This does not mean that any medical professional can be forced to carry out procedures against their better clinical judgment. However, once the child is *Gillick* competent to the extent required to understand the treatment, there is no longer any role for a court or a parent to intervene in the competent adolescent's decisions, beyond the scope for a court to override a competent adult's decisions.

[38] Transgender young people are no more or less likely to be *Gillick* competent than their peers. Watts J effectively granted parents of trans and gender diverse adolescents a power to interfere with their *Gillick* competent children's care. This separate rule for transgender adolescents cannot be maintained in light of the clear refusal to find that parents had the power to veto their competent children's medical consent in *Gillick* itself.

[39] Though this court can use the *parens patriae* jurisdiction to override the medical consent of a *Gillick* competent child,[76] it has long been established that this power should only be used in the most serious and life-threatening of situations and with the great caution.[77]

---

74. *Gillick*, 414, 419 (Scarman LJ).
75. *Re Kelvin*, [200].
76. This jurisdiction applies where the court is required to take steps to protect a child or other person of reduced capacity from harm: *Re Kara* [2020] NSWSC 1083.
77. Such cases have largely involved young people refusing medical care where there was a risk of death from lack of blood transfusions or refusal of care for anorexia nervosa. Case examples include *Department*

[40] This court should not lend itself to parental veto, which was clearly rejected in *Gillick,* simply because a competent adolescent is a member of a gender minority. Invocation of the *parens patriae* or ordinary jurisdiction of this court to enable such a veto is inappropriate considering the incorporation of *Gillick* into Australian law by the High Court in *Marion's case.*

---

of *Community Services v Y* [1999] NSWSC 644 and *Minister for Health v AS* [2004] WASC 286. Great caution: *Re Kara* [2020] NSWSC 1083, [63, 72].

23

Appeal-Review-(1)-Zi No. 162 (2021) (Taiwan):
Queering the Taiwan High Court Criminal Judgment

Po-Han Lee, Tsung-Han Yu, Titan Deng and Tzu-Wei Lin

Introduction

We decided to rewrite the 2022 judgment in Appeal-Review-(1)-Zi No. 162 (2021) (hereinafter the *AR-162 ruling*) by the Taiwan High Court from a queer critical perspective, to help us address the complexity and relationality of sexuality and the collaboration between biomedical and juridical powers. The case concerned the criminality of the defendant, Mr A's non-disclosure of his HIV-positive status before engaging in oral sex with Mr B under the influence of drugs.[1] This High Court's judgment was conclusive in terms of the factual findings regarding whether the sexual behaviour of Mr A to Mr B falls within the scope of 'unsafe sexual behaviour' criminalized by the HIV Infection Control and Patient Rights Protection Act (HIV Act).[2]

In summary, the defendant, Mr A, was HIV-positive and had not been constantly undetectable in terms of his viral load when he was accused of having unprotected oral sex in a chemsex encounter with Mr B, who claimed to be a *victim* of HIV transmission.[3] In Taiwan, intentionally infecting others with HIV still constitutes a crime. Although Mr B eventually tested negative, the potential consequences of causing significant harm to him led to the prosecution of Mr A, and the case experienced four levels of court hearings and five decisions, respectively, in 2019, 2020, 2021, and two in 2022.[4] In fact, following the AR-162 2022 ruling by the Taiwan High Court

---

1. Taiwan High Court Criminal Judgment Appeal-Review-(1)-Zi No. 162 (2021), 12 January 2022. Notably, Titan Deng was the legal representative of Mr A since the second instance of the criminal proceeding.

2. Supreme Court Criminal Judgment Tai-Appeal-Zi No. 55 (2021), 17 June 2021; HIV Infection Control and Patient Rights Protection Act, available at Laws & Regulations Database of the Republic of China (Taiwan), accessed 5 August 2023, https://law.moj.gov.tw/ENG/LawClass/LawAll.aspx?pcode=L0050004.

3. Chemsex refers to sexual activities combined with recreational drug use as an increasingly widespread sexual practice among gay and bisexual men who have sex with men. See Poyao Huang et al., 'An Object-oriented Analysis of Social Apps, Syringes and ARTs Within Gay Taiwanese Men's Chemsex Practices,' *Culture, Health & Sexuality* 26/4 (2023).

4. For the history of the case, see the Appendix below. We want to emphasise that both Mr A (the defendant) and the prosecutors appealed to the Taiwan High Court for different reasons. While Mr A pleaded total innocence, the prosecution argued against punishment reduction granted under Article 59 of the Criminal

that we have chosen to re-write, the prosecution appealed (again) to the Supreme Court, which dismissed and settled the case.[5] In Taiwan, the Supreme Court can only review and decide on the interpretation and application of the law.

A notable development of the process was that, on 2 July 2021, the Ministry of Health and Welfare revised the *Criteria of Unsafe Sexual Behaviour* and officially recognized the 'undetectable equals untransmittable' (U=U) discourse—i.e. someone with an undetectable viral load cannot sexually transmit HIV to others. Thus, the Ministry redefined the scope of 'unsafe sexual behaviour' from sexual contact with a 'potential' to a 'significant' risk of infection.[6] Moreover, the new criteria include a medical assessment of the 'risk' before prosecution is pursued. Before this policy revision, judicial decisions had equalled 'direct contact ... without isolation' to a medical assessment.[7] However, we expect this policy change to significantly reduce the findings of criminal motive and thus the chance for a prosecutor to file a case, especially in situations with no victim, namely no legal right or interest of any particular individual being harmed.

The first four judgments, in this case, employed different approaches to using U=U in legal reasoning and have thus reflected the contentiousness and inconsistency of legal and moral responsibility of HIV-positive persons regarding their exercise of sexual freedoms. Among them, the AR-162 judgment crystallizes a paradigm shift regarding the criminalization of people engaging in certain sexual practices. Eventually, the case was not about U=U since Mr A's viral load had not been consistent with the standard of so-called *undetectable*. Instead, the court considered the evidence regarding the low to ignorable risk of oral sex and declared Mr A as not guilty.

The persons and the behaviour in question had remained the same, yet their legal status changed. Is it because of HIV science? Yes and no. The biomedical discourse has changed based on new evidence since the early 2010s; this can be seen from the references relied on by the courts.[8] The new discourse did not directly affect the law's attitudes to the sexual lives of HIV-positive persons in Taiwan until the Ministry adopted this discourse and reflected it in an administrative order. This development reflects the temporal gaps between bioscience, health policymakers, and legal reasoning, in which one's criminal status is unforeseeable despite one's serostatus remaining

---

Code. For the convenience of the rewriting exercise, and since we conclude that Mr is not guilty, we did not consider the argument about punishment..

5. Supreme Court Criminal Judgment Tai-Appeal-Zi No. 2419 (2022), 14 July 2022.

6. Executive Yuan's General Description of the Draft Amendment to Article 2 of the Criteria of Unsafe Sexual Behaviour, Executive Yuan Gazette Vol. 27, Issue 60, No. 20210406 (2021), accessed 20 October 2022, https://gazette.nat.gov.tw/EG_FileManager/eguploadpub/eg027060/ch08/type3/gov70/num35/images/Eg01.pdf.

7. Titan Deng, 'Can the Undetectable be Unpunished? On U=U and the Crime of Attempting to Infecting HIV,' [測不到病毒可以無罪嗎？談U=U與蓄意傳染HIV罪] *Prevention of HIV/AIDS Quarterly*, 110 (2020).

8. UNAIDS, *Guidance Note on Ending Overly Broad HIV Criminalisation: Critical Scientific, Medical and Legal Considerations* (Geneva: Joint United Nations Programme on HIV/AIDS, 2013); Françoise Barré-Sinoussi et al., 'Expert Consensus Statement on the Science of HIV in the Context of Criminal Law,' *Journal of the International AIDS Society* 21/7 (2018).

the same.[9] Such indeterminacy of criminality has made us question the constitutionality of the relevant norms. For instance, in our rewritten judgment, we once considered suspending the proceedings and submitting a petition for constitutional review. However, following a conversation between ourselves, we decided to declare Mr A's innocence as the AR-162 ruling did, prioritizing the defendant's right to a speedy trial in criminal proceedings. Even so, as a reasonable lower-court judge would do, we mentioned our doubts regarding the constitutionality of the criminal punishment against HIV transmission.

Queering such a case is to recognize the agency of people who have sex with each other and to problematize HIV exceptionalism in Taiwan's criminal justice system. HIV exceptionalism denotes the global trend for treating HIV/AIDS in law and policy differently from other diseases.[10] We adopt a socio-relational approach to sex between persons living with HIV (PLHIV) and others, contrasting with the dominant medico-legal perspective that defines responsibility based on the risks of specific acts.[11] When focusing on the blameworthiness of PLHIV, the law reflects the state's desire to punish and depict the faults of those living with HIV/AIDS who are sexually active.[12] The law fails to capture the power dynamics of sexual encounters, suppresses the HIV-positive party's right to sexual autonomy, neglects the other parties' sexual agency, and potentially harms queer solidarity. The judgments at various levels on this case have painted contested images of *irresponsible gay men* regarding intimacy, risk management, and trustworthiness.

In our commentary, we first discuss the tension between the messiness of sex and the pursuit of specificity by law and science. In this context, we consider the implications of chemsex for the law on sex and that on drugs, both of which have failed to address the right to sexual autonomy, including the desire for intimacy involved with the materiality of narcotics. The idea and normative content of the right to sexual autonomy will be discussed in the rewritten judgment; hence, we herein focus on the intersection of sex and drugs. We thus argue for a shared responsibility for protecting sexual partners' right to sexual autonomy as the starting point for rethinking/queering a sexual encounter, with or without drugs. Lastly, from the perspective of shared responsibility, we demonstrate how punitive laws against HIV-positive persons harm the solidarity between sexual minority men, including not only gay and bisexual men, but queer and other men who have sex with men.

---

9.   Serostatus refers to the presence or absence of a serological marker in the blood. The presence of detectable levels of a specific marker within the serum is considered seropositivity, while the absence of such levels is considered seronegativity.

10.   The exceptionalist stance has, on the one hand, produced and reinforced HIV stigma, and yet, on the other hand, obtained extraordinary attention and resources from policymakers and the scientific community. See Shin-Rou Lin, 'HIV Screening and Informed Consent: An Analysis of the Changing Paradigm of HIV Exceptionalism and HIV Screening Laws in Taiwan,' [愛滋篩檢與告知後同意－愛滋例外主義轉向趨勢與臺灣法制之檢討] *Chengchi Law Review* 150 (2017).

11.   Po-Han Lee, 'Irreducible Interactional Dilemmas: Understanding "Infectious Sexualities" Sociologically,' [無法化約的互動困局：從社會學理解感染「性」] *Prevention of HIV/AIDS Quarterly* 113 (2020).

12.   Po-Chia Tseng, 'Subordinated Agency: Negotiating the Biomedicalisation of Masculinity Among Gay Men Living with HIV,' *Sociology of Health & Illness* 43/6 (2021); Alvaro Martinez-Lacabe, 'The Non-positive Antiretroviral Gay Body: The Biomedicalisation of Gay Sex in England,' *Culture, Health & Sexuality* 21/10 (2019).

Messy sex and unsexy law

In Mr A's case, his legal representative in the first trial focused on U=U. The prosecutor successfully challenged the U=U defence when the expert witness, Mr A's attending doctor, expressed the nature of uncertainty of science regarding how and whether the medication works. As Carl Stychin once identified, the law of modern times tends to seek specificity and regulate ambiguity even in the face of risk and uncertainty in contemporary societies.[13] The law's demand/desire can hardly be satisfied, especially when it is entangled with biomedical sciences, in which health and clinical uncertainties are folded in a complex combination of factors and are not necessarily unpackable.[14] Thus, legal and ethical challenges exist in the overreliance of judicial reasoning on science, which locates law in an opaque space where inconsistencies are almost unavoidable. This situation is further complicated by the need to legally characterize the sexual encounter of an HIV-positive person, whose serostatus and sexual behaviours must be first determined.

Criminal law requires an action/inaction to meet specified factual elements (described as *Tatbestand* in German legal terminology) to declare a crime has been committed. This ensures the foreseeability of committing an offence by the persons involved; otherwise, the person's action/inaction should not be punishable. However, circumstances (e.g. in public health and medical law) that constitute unspecified/blank elements (described as *Blankettatbestand* in German legal terminology) are allowed if the facticity of part of the offence is subject to the development of scientific understanding. The HIV Act is an example of this.[15] On this matter, the law—or judicial decisions relying on such law—tends to assume the comprehensiveness and certainty of science but fails to see the uncapturable and uncontrollable—thus excluded—messiness of interpersonal dynamics of sexual encounters by science.

Although science may acknowledge such limits, the law does not. In the context of the growing dominance of the U=U paradigm, one's viral load matters more than what happens in the sexual encounter. Yet, beyond such context, it matters whether one performs oral, anal, or vaginal sex; whether they have an erection or ejaculate or not; whether protected measures are taken; their sexual roles in each *scene* matter, signifying the ability of scientific discourse to dissect a sexual encounter. People engaging in a sexual encounter have also embodied the risk paradigm, informed by non-erection and non-ejaculation, usually taken as sexual dysfunction for a man, and which become risk aversion practices. A pathology in sexual medicine constitutes the protective factor for sexual health and, therefore, non-criminality.

Whether one has reached the state of viral suppression according to a blood test

---

13. Carl F. Stychin, *Law's Desire: Sexuality and the Limits of Justice* (London: Routledge, 1995).
14. Brian King, 'HIV as Uncertain Life,' *Geoforum* 123 (2021); Sonali P. Kulkarni et al., 'Clinical uncertainties, health service challenges, and ethical complexities of HIV "test-and-treat": A systematic review,' *American Journal of Public Health* 103/6 (2013).
15. Yu-Wei Hsieh, 'Legal Problems of Attempting to HIV Infection: The Dangerousness of Unsafe Sexual Behaviour,' [愛滋病毒蓄意傳染條款的法律問題：危險性行為的行為危險性] *Prevention of HIV/AIDS Quarterly* 97 (2016).

or not, conversations about their *infected* subjectivity are very complex and challenging, not only because of sexual and HIV stigmas but also due to the ethical burden embedded in *disclosure* decisions.[16] Considering the sexual encounter between Mr A and Mr B involved drug use, the *sex scenes*, in which the risk assessment may have been overshadowed by 'the moment of pleasure,'[17] must be messy, according to their narratives. Equating *intentional* non-disclosure with the *attempt* to infect others with HIV and considering it a crime, which demands the state's intervention, seems to paint a sexual relationship in which one is a stereotypical perpetrator and the other the victim, based on the serodiscordance between them. The set-up does not necessarily represent the power dynamics and interactions between all who engage in sex. Sex tends to unleash unbearable contradictions that all parties must bear,[18] such as moments of self-pleasure mixed with the responsibility for others and excitement/frustration, as well as (Mr B's) moments of intimacy and victimization and (Mr A's) moments of reluctance.

Whereas sex is messy, the law is not; it is even less sexy (less sex-positive) due to the uncertainty of science when the latter analyses a sexual encounter by segmenting it into separate acts, disregarding the contextual complexity. Informed by new evidence of HIV science, it is increasingly necessary for the law to balance its desire to capture and control sexualities, on the one hand, and the justification for restricting personal, sexual, and informational freedoms of PLHIV or persons identified as belonging to *high-risk populations*, on the other hand.[19] As mentioned earlier – and constituting one of the already discussed blank factual elements – Article 2 of the *Criteria of Unsafe Sexual Behaviour* defines 'unsafe sexual behaviour' and has been revised by the Ministry in 2021. It requires both a 'direct contact with the mucous membranes of organs or body fluids without isolation' and a medical assessment of 'a significant risk of causing HIV infection.' This revision reflects the health authority's updated understanding of HIV infection from a probable to significant risk—in addition to the new procedural requirement regarding medical assessment.[20]

HIV exceptionalism and queer solidarity

HIV criminalization is a result of HIV exceptionalism, which is evidenced by the fact that legislator removed the crime of transmitting venereal diseases (Article 285 of the Criminal Code) in 2019. The constitutionality of Article 21 of the HIV Act in and by itself is contested due to the lack of evidence that prohibitive and punitive policies are beneficial for achieving public health goals, while seriously limiting the sexual

---

16. Grant H. Roth et al., '"It's a Very Grey, Very Messy Area": A Qualitative Examination of Factors Influencing Undetectable Gay Men's HIV Status Disclosure to Sexual Partners,' *Culture, Health & Sexuality* 25/5 (2023).

17. Annette Houlihan, '(Ill-Legal) Lust is a Battlefield: HIV Risk, Socio-Sexuality and Criminality' (Doctor of Philosophy Griffith University, 2007), ii.

18. Lauren Berlant and Lee Edelman, *Sex, or the Unbearable* (Durham: Duke University Press, 2013).

19. See, for example, regarding HIV screening in Taiwan, Shin-Rou Lin, 'Not Truly Mandatory? Not Fully Voluntary? An Empirical Study of Taiwan's Implementation of HIV Screening Laws,' [非真正強制？不完全自主？臺灣愛滋篩檢法制之實證檢討與改革] *National Taiwan University Law Journal* 47/4 (2018).

20. Deng, 'Can the Undetectable be Unpunished? On U=U and the Crime of Attempting to Infecting HIV.'

autonomy and life of PLHIV.[21] HIV/AIDS prevention and treatment policy—or the lack of it—at both institutional and societal levels since the 1980s, is a history of the politics of survival entangled with the pursuit of a sense of belonging.[22] A counterpublic has been constituted in resisting the state's ignorance of queer people's health needs and overregulation of queer bodies.[23] Article 21 of the HIV Act signifies the state's invasion of queer private lives and matters.

The criminalization of HIV infection has harmed queer solidarity.[24] Not only has Mr A suffered a new depressive episode because of the criminal investigation that took place and, as a consequence, stopped taking TRIUMEQ regularly,[25] but Mr B has also forgiven Mr A and asserted that he should be less punished. Decriminalization does not mean non-responsibility for one's intentional transmission of HIV infection. Still, such instances should remain civil disputes in which the rights consciousness regarding a *damaged* body and feelings (should one feel and embody so) can be developed, and compensation can be claimed. Beyond tort law, a sexual-contractual obligation to respect and protect each other's sexual agency and health based on good faith may also be breached. Or, alternative dispute resolution mechanisms can be designed to facilitate reconciliation and provide redress for interested parties beyond the recourse to litigation or remedies for non-justiciable issues.[26] Decriminalizing HIV infections also aims to address negative sentiments of the general public and within queer communities due to an exceptionalist attitude towards HIV among sexually transmitted diseases,[27] and to rebuild queer solidarity through the exit of the state from the realm of sexuality.[28]

21. UNAIDS, *Guidance Note on Ending Overly Broad HIV Criminalisation: Critical Scientific, Medical and Legal Considerations* (Geneva: Joint United Nations Programme on HIV/AIDS, 2013); Barré-Sinoussi et al., 'Expert Consensus Statement on the Science of HIV in the Context of Criminal Law.'

22. João Biehl, *Will to Live: AIDS Therapies and the Politics of Survival* (Princeton: Princeton University Press, 2007).

23. Counterpublic signifies the collectivity of publics that conscientiously resists the dominant ideology and strategically subverts that ideology's construction in public discourse. See Ta-Wei Chi, 'Translation/Public: AIDS, "Tongzhi," and "Ku'er,"' [翻譯的公共：愛滋，同志，酷兒] *Bulletin of Taiwanese Literature* 26 (2015); Lauren Berlant and Michael Warner, 'Sex in Public,' *Critical Inquiry* 24/2 (1998).

24. For a similar discussion in other contexts where queer solidarity is also threatened by the law's repression of sexual autonomy in the name of (sexual) health, see Lucy Wanjiku Mung'ala and Anne de Jong, 'Health and Freedom: The Tense Interdependency of HIV/AIDS Interventions and LGBTIQ Activism in Kenya,' *Kohl: A Journal for Body and Gender Research* 6/1 (2020); Sarah Schulman, *Stagestruck Theater, AIDS, and the Marketing of Gay America* (Durham: Duke University Press, 1998); Justyna Struzik, 'Thick Times: Transformation, Activism and HIV in Poland,' *European Review of History* 28/4 (2021).

25. TRIUMEQ Film-Coated Tablets are a cocktail of dolutegravir, abacavir, and lamivudine, a prescription medicine used to treat HIV-1 infection in adults and children weighing over 40kg.

26. See David Barr, Joseph J. Amon, and Michaela Clayton, 'Articulating A Rights-Based Approach to HIV Treatment and Prevention Interventions,' *Current HIV Research* 9/6 (2011).

27. Heather Love, *Underdogs: Social Deviance and Queer Theory* (Chicago: University of Chicago Press, 2021). Some may argue that HIV exceptionalism has also led to more attention and specified allocation of resources and funding for HIV prevention and treatment from the government than is the case for other diseases. Yet, we do not agree that HIV exceptionalism aims to protect HIV-positive persons' rights beyond the law's public health goals – especially when considering the 'normalization' of public financing of HIV/AIDS care through payments from the specified budget of the Taiwan Centers for Disease Control to the National Health Insurance. See Hans Tao-Ming Huang, 'Medical Governance, Name-Based HIV Surveillance and the New Moral Authoritarianism.' [列管制度下的醫療治理：「人類免疫缺乏病毒傳染防治及感染者權益保障條例」與新道德權威] *Taiwan: A Radical Quarterly in Social Studies* 94 (2014).

28. Ellis Hanson, 'The Future's Eve: Reparative Reading after Sedgwick,' *South Atlantic Quarterly* 110/1

Therefore, we have rewritten the AR-162 ruling informed by a queer-relational approach to sexuality, which rejects stereotypes of pathways of HIV transmission and considers that the power relationship between sexual partners is unfixed and dynamic. Although the ruling was a landmark decision as the first judgment recognizing the legitimacy of the U=U defence and the exception of oral sex from the scope of unsafe sex, it did not go far enough to challenge the constitutionality of the law itself because it could not appreciate the messiness of sex and the uncertainty of science from a doctrinal perspective. This judgment marks the success of using an administrative order to introduce into the law new biomedical evidence about HIV infection, although this fails to see the sociality and agency of the persons involved in the voluntary sexual encounter. Thus, the judgment offers no alternative when criminal law is no longer a viable option for situations between safe and unsafe sex. Our rewritten judgment provides a reparative reading for the unfinished work left by the AR-162 ruling.

(2011); Odette Mazel, 'Queer Jurisprudence: Reparative Practice in International Law,' *AJIL Unbound* 116 (2022).

TAIWAN HIGH COURT CRIMINAL JUDGMENT

Appeal-Review-(1)-Zi No. 162 (2021)

Appellant: Taipei District Prosecutor's Office
Appellant and Defendant: Mr A

I. Decision

The original judgment—Taiwan Taipei District Court Criminal Judgment Prosecution-Zi No. 493 (2018) based on Indictment of Taiwan Taipei District Prosecutor's Office Investigation-Zi No. 7474 (2018), which ruled that Mr A committed the crime of attempting to infect others by having unsafe sex and concealing the fact that he had been infected with HIV and shall be sentenced to 1 year and 5 months in prison—is revoked.

Mr A is not guilty.

II. Facts

The defendant, Mr A, was infected with HIV on 27 June 2003, and has received antiretroviral treatment since 11 July 2003. The genotype testing report on 17 May 2016 showed that Mr A developed no drug resistance. On 21 October 2017, Mr A switched to taking the TRIUMEQ Film-Coated Tablets. In November 2017, he tested with a viral load of 48cp/ml. Viral load is the amount of HIV in the blood of someone who has HIV; adherence to taking HIV medicine can make the viral load low to the point that a test cannot detect it (below 200cp/ml, known as *undetectable viral load*). On 11 April 2017, Mr A was screened for a viral load of 15,400 cp/ml while receiving 28-day TRIUMEQ medicine on the same day. With the viral load having increased from 48 to 15,400 cp/ml, he tested no drug resistance after a test conducted by his attending doctor. In Taiwan, persons living with HIV (PLHIV) receive repeat prescriptions for patients with chronic conditions, which include a 28-day portion of drugs three times about every 3 months. Since the National Health Insurance Administration pays the medical expenses for blood tests four times a year, HIV-positive patients need to visit a doctor for blood tests and repeat prescriptions every 3 months. On 9 May 2017, when Mr A received 28-day TRIUMEQ medicine with his repeat prescription, no blood test was recorded.

From 22 to 24 May 2017, Mr A offered Mr B methamphetamine *for high fun*. During the same period, Mr A and the alleged victim, Mr B, performed oral sex to each other several times at Mr A's residence, although neither of them *came* (ejaculated). When Mr B surrendered himself to the police under the influence of drugs and was referred to the Taipei District Prosecutor's Office due to the violation of the Narcotics Hazard Prevention Act, the prosecutor learned that in addition to taking drugs, there were also matters potentially related to the breach of Article 21 of the HIV Infection Control and Patient Rights Protection Act (人類免疫缺乏病毒傳染防治及感染者權益保障條例, hereinafter 'HIV Act'). On 9 June 2017, Mr A received the other 28-day portion of TRIUMEQ medicine. However, Mr A reported that because of the relevant investigative procedures, he had developed depressive episodes, which prevented him from taking the medication regularly. That was why he was tested with a viral load of 12,100cp/ml on 14 July. Mr B underwent an HIV test on 26 October 2017, and the result was negative.

III. Reasoning

i. *The Prosecution contends that:*

Mr A knew he had AIDS due to infection with HIV and, thus, he was 'the infected' as defined by Article 3 of the HIV Act. He was also aware that condom-less oral or anal sex constitutes 'unsafe sexual behaviour,' according to the Criteria of Unsafe Sexual Behaviour defined by the Ministry of Health and Welfare. Such sexual behaviour would infect Mr B. Supposing Mr B were also 'the infected,' such unsafe sexual behaviour might also lead to so-called *HIV superinfection*, a condition in which a person with an established HIV infection acquires a second strain of HIV, often of a different subtype. Consequently, Mr A engaged in 'unsafe sexual behaviour,' although Mr A was aware that he was infected with HIV and that his blood test results in April 2017 showed a high viral load. That Mr A did not reveal his HIV status before having sex with Mr B is uncontested, and whether Mr A had an erection or ejaculated or not, and whether they stopped condom-less oral sex before having an erection, as argued by Mr A, is irrelevant.

ii. *This Court holds that:*

Relevant laws

[1] According to Article 21, Paragraph 1, of the HIV Act:

> Individuals who are fully aware that they are infected and have, by concealing the fact, unsafe sex with others…, and thus infect others, shall be sentenced to 5–12 years of imprisonment.

Paragraph 3:

> An attempt to commit the offence shall be punished.

Paragraph 4:

> The central competent authority shall formulate the definition of unsafe sex following the relevant regulations outlined by the World Health Organization.

[2] According to Article 2 of the Criteria of Unsafe Sexual Behaviour (version of 10 January 2008, effective when Mr A and B had sex):

> The scope of unsafe sexual behaviour refers to sexual behaviour that involves direct contact with the mucous membranes of organs or body fluids without isolation, medically assessed *as probably causing HIV infection* (emphasis added).

[3] According to the same Article (version of 2 July 2021):

> The scope of unsafe sexual behaviour refers to sexual behaviour that involves direct contact with the mucous membranes of organs or body fluids without isolation, and that has been medically assessed *as having a significant risk of causing HIV infection* (emphasis added).

[4] According to Article 10, Paragraph 5, of the Criminal Code:

> The term sexual intercourse means the following sexual acts that are not based on rightful purposes: (1) Insertion of a sexual organ into the reproductive organ, anus, or mouth of another person or an act of making them connected; (2) Insertion of a body part or an object other than a sexual organ into the reproductive organ or anus of another person or an act of making them connected.

MR A's CONDUCT DOES NOT SATISFY THE REQUIRED ELEMENTS OF THE CRIME

This point concerns the prosecutor's contention about anal sex yet there has been no evidence on this point other than Mr B's original statement. The lack of further proof results in the ambiguity of relevant facts and, based on the principle of *in dubio pro reo* ('when in doubt, rule for the accused'), this Court dismisses the contention that anal sex took place. U=U means that the virus cannot be continuously detected for 6 months. Mr A's viral load was detectable in April and July; thus, this Court cannot conclude that his situation meets the requisites for U=U. However, Mr A's attending doctor testified to the possibility of viral suppression to an undetectable level should Mr A have taken his medicine stably for more than 1 month before his sexual encounter with Mr B. Based on the principles of presumption of innocence and *nulla poena sine lege* ('no penalty without law'), the lack of further evidence has created reasonable doubt regarding the possibility of Mr A's HIV transmission through anal sex.

Regarding the act of oral sex performed by Mr A and Mr B to each other, the critical issue here is whether the circumstances surrounding *unprotected* oral sex constitute 'unsafe sex' under Article 21, Paragraph 1, of the HIV Act. The scope of 'unsafe sexual behaviour' provided in this provision is determined by the health authority mandated by Paragraph 4 of the same Article, constituting a so-called blank norm of criminal law to be completed by administrative acts and decisions. More precisely, the interpretation of the element of unsafe sexual behaviour depends on the definition given in Article 2 of the Criteria of Unsafe Sexual Behaviour, revised on 2 July 2021, considering the new evidence concerning HIV infection. The Ministry explicitly acknowledges that the report *Ending Overly Broad Criminalisation of HIV Non-Disclosure, Exposure and Transmission: Critical Scientific, Medical and Legal Considerations*, published by the Joint United Nations Programme on HIV/AIDS (UNAIDS) in 2013, is authoritative in determining the Ministry's revision. The Ministry also considered the *Expert Consensus Statement on the Science of HIV in the Context of Criminal Law* adopted at the 2018 International AIDS Conference among the best available scientific and medical evidence.[29]

The replies from the Ministry, Taiwan AIDS Society, and National Taiwan University Hospital to this court's earlier inquiry confirmed the credibility of both documents. Based on Documents 1 and 2, the studies of sexual transmission pathways and the possibility of infection with HIV have all considered sexual acts separately. For example, oral sex has been evaluated along with the presence/absence of ejaculation and erection. In the context of anal and vaginal sex, in addition to ejaculation or not, the sex role of the HIV-positive party (insertive or receptive) also matters. The UNAIDS report, in particular, considers the estimated per-act risk of HIV infection from oral sex (orogenital contact) from 0 to 0.04%,[30] recommending that:

> In no case should prosecution for HIV non-disclosure, exposure, or transmission proceed when one of the following circumstances exists: the person took reasonable measures to reduce the risk of HIV transmissions, such as practising safer sex through using a condom or engaging in non-penetrative sex or oral sex; the person believed that they could not transmit HIV given their effective treatment or low viral load.[31]

The Expert Consensus Statement also mentions that 'the possibility of HIV transmission from oral sex performed on an HIV-positive person varies from none to negligible, depending on the context.'[32] Article 21 of the HIV Act contains a constitutive element of 'infecting others;' it also punishes 'attempted offenders,' i.e. sexual behaviour is still punishable for its attempt, although it does not transmit the virus. The UNAIDS has recommended that the use of criminal law in the HIV context can be legitimate only 'where there is an actual and significant harm intentionally caused to another person;'[33] it is clearly unreasonable for the law to include a crime of *attempting* to infect others with HIV and equate it with the intention to cause harm.

---

29. Executive Yuan, General Description of the Draft Amendment to Article 2.
30. UNAIDS, *Ending Overly Broad Criminalisation of HIV Non-Disclosure, Exposure and Transmission: Critical Scientific, Medical and Legal Considerations* (Geneva: Joint United Nations Programme on HIV/AIDS, 2013), 17.
31. UNAIDS, *Ending Overly Broad Criminalisation of HIV Non-Disclosure, Exposure and Transmission: Critical Scientific, Medical and Legal Considerations*, 26. See, also, as cited in the UNAIDS report, Rebecca F. Baggaley, Richard G. White, and Marie-Claude Boily, 'Systematic Review of Orogenital HIV-1 Transmission Probabilities,' *International Journal of Epidemiology* 37, no. 6 (2008). This review mentioned that the upper range (0.04%) was related to unprotected receptive oral intercourse with ejaculation between men with an HIV-positive or unknown serostatus partner.
32. Françoise Barré-Sinoussi et al., 'Expert Consensus Statement on the Science of HIV in the Context of Criminal Law,' *Journal of the International AIDS Society* 21, no. 7 (2018), 5.
33. UNAIDS, *Ending Overly Broad Criminalisation of HIV Non-Disclosure, Exposure and Transmission: Critical Scientific, Medical and Legal Considerations*, 12.

AN UN-HOLISTIC NOTION OF 'SEXUAL BEHAVIOUR' AND THE LAW'S AMBIGUITY

This court has considered the status of 'unsafe sex behaviour' in law, namely the relationship between the concept of 'sex behaviour' referred to in the HIV Act and the notion of 'sexual intercourse' used in Article 10, Paragraph 5, of the Criminal Code. According to the Criminal Code, 'sexual intercourse' is defined explicitly to include vaginal intercourse, anal sex, oral sex, fingering, and so on. Yet, 'sexual behaviour' under the HIV Act refers to direct contact with the mucous membranes of organs or body fluids. In comparison, vaginal, anal, and oral intercourse should be included in the definition of sexual behaviour, whereas kissing, *scissoring*, and *rimming* are not considered sexual intercourse. The insertion of an object such as a dildo with sexual intent into the anus or vagina constitutes sexual intercourse, although this is not regarded as sexual behaviour, simply because it does not involve direct contact with mucous membranes or bodily fluids.

Therefore, the conceptual scopes of sexual intercourse and sexual behaviour are different; they partly overlap and are partly mutually exclusive. Accepting this conclusion, we need to see sexual behaviour between involved parties from a holistic perspective. The statements of prosecutors, the defendant's defence, expert appraisals and replies, as well as this court's past decisions, have all divided a sexual encounter into oral, anal, or vaginal sex, against which the risk is assessed respectively. Such a reductionist methodology is blind to the blurredness, messiness, and continuity of sexual action/inactions within an encounter and fails to appreciate sexual behaviour between the parties. Besides, the law has led us to only focus on oral sex between Mr A and Mr B, and whether oral sex entails the risk of infecting the sexual partner with HIV. The oversimplifying tendency of law has failed to consider the sexual intent and sex roles of both parties, the presence and absence of erection or ejaculation during oral sex, and the effect of methamphetamine on their bodies (e.g. sexual function and performance) and minds (e.g. confusion, delusion, and somatosensory amplification). The lack of clarity on this matter has rendered the sexual behaviour of Mr A and Mr B beyond the current scope of the law.

Accordingly, this court considers that the law should also evaluate the risk of the sexual behaviours at issue from a holistic perspective. Differentiating between oral, anal, and vaginal sex and assessing unsafety regardless of its interrelationship with dangerousness (in legal terms) and risk (in biomedical terms) cannot capture a sexual encounter in which multiple sexual acts—active or passive—are involved. This normative development reflects the paradigm shift concerning the U=U discourse, which, nevertheless, may hardly resolve the problem of the opaqueness and complexity of sexuality and intimacy, especially in the chemsex context. Out of this concern, the court has reasonable doubt concerning the adequacy and temporal relevance of Article 21 of the HIV Act in the U=U era, where PrEP (pre-exposure prophylaxis) becomes increasingly available.

POTENTIAL UNCONSTITUTIONALITY OF THE CURRENT ARTICLE 21 OF THE HIV ACT

Since the repeal of Article 285 of the Criminal Code on 29 May 2019, the sexual activities of persons with non-HIV venereal diseases are no longer considered a crime. Comparatively, the constitutionality of Article 21, Paragraphs 1 and 3, of the HIV Act is not without question, notably since the Constitutional Court reiterates the constitutional protection of the rights to sexual autonomy and privacy, whose legal restrictions need to be subjected to strict scrutiny,[34] including being the least restrictive possible and directly related to the compelling/overriding governmental aim. Article 21, Paragraphs 1 and 3, of the HIV Act aims to punish infected individuals who do not self-disclose their status before engaging in unsafe sexual behaviour with others. HIV-positive persons are legally obliged to disclose their HIV seropositive status or not engage in *unsafe* sexual behaviour. This rule has restricted a person's freedom to decide whether and with whom to have sex. The right to sexual autonomy is an integral part of an individual's right to self-determination and is a fundamental right guaranteed by Article 22 of the Constitution.

This court considers that the right to sexual autonomy is not limited to self-determination regarding whether and with whom to have sex, but also refers to self-determination on all matters related to sexuality, including gender identity and expression, sexual orientation, sexual preferences and how, where, and when, how intense, and how often to have sex, as well as the health risks of sexual behaviour under one's control. Apart from masturbation, most forms of sexual practice require the participation of others.[35] Thus, there is a necessity to legally characterize and define the exercise of sexual autonomy of all parties whose rights can potentially be in conflict within an imbalanced power relationship. Nevertheless, any interference and limitation on sexual autonomy for such a purpose must be subject to strict scrutiny due to the indivisibility of sexual autonomy and one's personality.

In this light, the blank norm of criminal law is hardly consistent with the principle of clarity and certainty of law in a strict sense.[36] The lack of clarity lies not only in the unpredictability of the scope of safe/unsafe sex along with the development of HIV science, but also in the categorization of sexual acts that omits the complexity of lived and embodied experiences. Moreover, such a restriction upon HIV-positive persons entails a much higher duty of care, legally and morally, than that imposed on the general population, especially the actors who equally participate in sex. The higher burden imposed on HIV-positive persons is not grounded on any evidence that criminal punishment is effective in suppressing HIV transmission.

The legislator is allowed to use the indefinite concept of 'unsafe sexual behaviour' when formulating Article 21, Paragraph 1, of the HIV Act, and when authorizing the executive branch to issue an administrative order to complement the blank law.[37]

---

34. See Judicial Yuan Constitutional Interpretation No. 791 (2020).
35. This by no means suggests that masturbation is beyond the scope of sexual autonomy; on the contrary, social and cultural taboos and discrimination against sexual masturbation should not be underestimated.
36. See Judicial Yuan Constitutional Interpretation No. 690 (2011).
37. See Judicial Yuan Constitutional Interpretation No. 680 (2010).

However, the concept of unsafe sexual behaviour is questionable. Ordinary and HIV-positive persons do not necessarily have the ability, competence, or confidence to evaluate the significance of such risk based on the best available scientific and medical evidence. The safety/unsafety of sexual behaviour is neither understandable based on legal interpretation nor precise enough through biomedical discourse, with which the law tends to fail to catch up. Consequently, the burden of foreseeability is clearly excessive for the HIV-positive party in sex. The existence of scientific uncertainty and the uncertainty of risk have disproportionately restricted PLHIV (particularly those whose viral loads are not stably undetectable) from having a sexual life and exercising sexual autonomy, not to mention the responsibility to prevent transmission only lying on their shoulders.

By restricting their sexual autonomy, the law also differentiates and punishes irresponsible HIV-positive persons from responsible ones. Regarding the scrutiny of the principle of proportionality, the legal interests to be protected by Article 21, Paragraphs 1 and 3 of the HIV Act include the legal interests of the body (personal sexual health) and society (public health). Comparing Article 21, Paragraph 1, of the HIV Act and the already-repealed Article 285 of the Criminal Code, we can find a difference in defining the criminal subjects. The HIV Act punishes the 'individuals who are fully aware that they are infected (of HIV),' while the Criminal Code criminalized the 'individuals who are fully aware that they have venereal diseases.' The former criminal subjects who are punishable are those living with the virus, whether or not the infected body develops into having the disease – namely, acquired immunodeficiency syndrome (AIDS). The latter became punishable when their bodies were diagnosed with non-HIV venereal diseases.

The law distinguishes those who are infected with non-HIV venereal diseases and can be exempted from regulation after recovery and non-reinfection from those infected with HIV and who will never be excused from monitoring and governing. The subjectivity of persons with non-HIV venereal diseases is subject to change, and thus may fall within or outside the scope of the law. In contrast, the subjectivity of PLHIV is assumed to be stable and always readily under control. Such an assumption might be acceptable because AIDS was incurable and HIV infection was non-suppressible when the law was enacted. However, until today, the status of *the infected* in the context of the HIV Act remains fixed, even if one's viral load is (once) undetectable, one's body fluids are not infectious, or one can be deemed as almost recovered. Their sexual behaviour, excluded from sexual autonomy, will always be regulated, and its safety/unsafety is never conclusive.

Regarding achieving the public health purpose of deterring unsafe sexual behaviours, the law is doubtful concerning its degree of restrictiveness of personal autonomy and the proportionality of the means employed. The UNAIDS report reveals that the broad application of punishment is not helpful, and is sometimes even harmful, for HIV prevention and control. Yet, the legislator has not assessed the use of administrative measures or civil liability as an alternative to criminalization. In criminal proceedings, uncovering intimate conversations between the parties, the steps of a sexual encounter, the defendant's medical records, and so forth, has allowed, almost unconditionally, the state to invade a person's very private sphere. The disadvantage of combining such serious interference with one's privacy and the degree to which Article 21, Paragraphs 1 and 3, of the HIV Act limit sexual autonomy is unreasonably disproportionate to the interests it declares to protect.[38]

The right to sexual autonomy is inseparable from the development and expression of personality, and is closely related to human dignity, belonging to an individual's most intimate and private sphere. We must be highly alert whenever state powers intend to enter this private remit. This does not mean a total ban on any intervention, yet great caution is required. Most sexual activities engage more than one party; however, that does not make them a matter of public interest, and the state is still prevented from interfering in this field except for a legitimate interest and necessity.[39] In the present case, Mr A and Mr B consented to oral sex, regardless of performance. Their agreement to have oral sex protects their primary sexual autonomies, and the physical and emotional reactions to sexual desire embody the secondary sexual autonomy, which is unlikely to be a matter worthy of a criminal court. Among the sexual acts between these two persons (and sometimes three), neither Mr A nor Mr B disclosed or asked about each other's HIV status. Under the influence of *high fun* in the chemsex context, neither might have been able to think carefully about sexual health risks.

For this court, if Mr A and Mr B engaged in sex voluntarily, their sexual behaviour shall remain a civil affair. Since Article 21 of the HIV Act has allowed for criminal charges without complaint, protecting Mr B's right to sexual autonomy is not the sole purpose of the law. Nevertheless, from the public health perspective, the evidence does not support criminal law as necessary and effective for HIV prevention. Instead, 'relying on disclosure to protect oneself … can and does lead to a false sense of security.'[40] Laying responsibility on one of the parties in sexual behaviour is not consistent with the notion of the right to sexual autonomy, which entails all parties bearing responsibility for each other.

Conclusion

In the present case, the defendant, Mr A, has been prosecuted for violating Article 21 of the HIV Act, by *attempting* to transmit HIV to Mr B, who was not infected after the sexual encounter in question and testing for HIV. The court finds that the sex encounter between Mr A and Mr B does not constitute unsafe sex behaviour; therefore, Mr A is not guilty. Meanwhile, the court also believes that on reasonable grounds, the validity of provisions as applied may be in contravention of the Constitution.

---

38. See Judicial Yuan Constitutional Interpretation No. 603 (2005).

39. The prohibition of domestic, sexual, and intimate partner violence, for example, requires the state to address victimization resulting from power imbalances within an interpersonal relationship.

40. UNAIDS, *Ending Overly Broad Criminalisation of HIV Non-Disclosure, Exposure and Transmission: Critical Scientific, Medical and Legal Considerations*, 44.

APPENDIX. THE HISTORY OF THE CASE

Trial	Judgment Number	Date	Judgment
First instance	Taiwan Taipei District Court Criminal Judgment Prosecution-Zi No. 493 (2018)	13 December 2019	Mr A (convinced by the judge to plead) guilty (for *pity* and punishment reduction, under Article 59 of the Criminal Code).
Second instance	Taiwan High Court Criminal Judgment Appeal-Prosecution-Zi No. 212 (2020)	9 June 2020	Mr A (withdrawing his plea as guilty and found) not guilty.
Third instance	Supreme Court Criminal Judgment Tai-Appeal-Zi No. 55 (2021)	17 June 2021	The second-instance judgment revoked, and the case returned for re-judging.
First review instance	Taiwan High Court Criminal Judgment Appeal-Review-(1)-Zi No. 162 (2021)	12 January 2022	Mr A not guilty.
Final instance	Supreme Court Criminal Judgment Tai-Appeal-Zi No. 2419 (2022)	14 July 2022	The appeal dismissed, and the whole case settled.

24

Nathaniel Le May v The General Manager, Ontario Health Insurance Plan (Canada):

Establishing the Legal Right to

Transition-Related Surgery for a Non-Binary Ontarian

Frank Nasca[1]

Introduction

In January 2023, I was scrolling through a Facebook group for transmasculine Canadians when I saw a post by Nathaniel Le May. Nathaniel's post described his experience of attempting to get funding from the Ontario Health Insurance Plan ['OHIP'] for phalloplasty surgery—a surgery that OHIP typically funds.[2] However, Nathaniel's surgical needs were somewhat non-normative. Although Nathaniel needed phalloplasty (the construction of a phallus) to relieve his gender dysphoria, he did not want or need hysterectomy and vaginectomy (the removal of his uterus and vagina).

Because Nathaniel did not want or need vaginectomy and hysterectomy, OHIP denied him funding for his surgery, even though he met all other funding approval criteria. The implications of this are profound: OHIP's stance was that trans people must undergo sterilization procedures to access medically necessary publicly funded care. In addition, OHIP's position was that Nathaniel's surgery was not a valid form of 'sex-reassignment surgery'—a position that clearly discriminates against non-binary trans people and other trans people that seek surgical outcomes other than a 'normal' penis or vagina.

By the time I saw Nathaniel's post, I had conducted extensive research into the intersection between law and transgender healthcare in Ontario in preparation for my initially proposed submission to this volume. Nathaniel's funding denial struck me as contrary to the current state of the law in Ontario, so I commented on Nathaniel's post. This began a fruitful legal collaboration and personal friendship between Nathaniel

---

1. I would like to thank Professor Bruce Ryder for his research support and Oliver Flis for his editing assistance.
2. OHIP is Ontario's single-payer public healthcare plan.

and me, which culminated in me representing Nathaniel at the Health Services Appeal and Review Board ['Board'] raising a challenge to OHIP's funding denial.

By the time I saw Nathaniel's post, he had been self-advocating to OHIP for over six months. Over the course of those months, Nathaniel repeatedly raised concerns that the Respondent (the General Manager of OHIP) was violating his human rights and discriminating against him. Despite persistently raising these concerns, the Respondent continued to hold firm in its position. Thus, at the Board, in addition to alleging that the Respondent misinterpreted the text of its enabling statutory and regulatory scheme, Nathaniel and I also alleged infringements to Nathaniel's right to be free from discrimination under the Ontario Human Rights Code ['Human Rights Code'][3] and his right to the equal protection and benefit of the law and to security of the person under s. 15(1) and s. 7 of the Canadian Charter of Rights and Freedoms ['Charter'].[4]

Nathaniel and I worked tirelessly over the course of the next six months to prepare legal submissions and a robust evidentiary record. Buoyed by the support of a phenomenal expert medical witness and by a community of legal mentors, we built a compelling and extensive case. We were set for a three-day hearing in June 2023, and were prepared to litigate all the legal issues raised. However, on the eve of hearing, the Respondent unilaterally decided to reverse course and fund Nathaniel's surgery. This decision was not a part of a negotiated settlement, and Nathaniel was clear that he was unwilling to settle the case without a commitment to systemic policy change at OHIP to guarantee that future patients would not meet the same barriers.

While the funding approval was a personal win for Nathaniel, it also enabled the Respondent to successfully request that the Board dismiss the case for mootness and lack of jurisdiction. This means that Nathaniel's Human Rights Code and Charter claims were not adjudicated, and that there is no public decision interpreting the Respondent's statutory and regulatory scheme. In short, OHIP was able to strategically avoid public scrutiny and full adjudication of the important legal issues raised.

The following fictional judgment is the judgment that Nathaniel should have received from the Board. It is the judgment that would have acknowledged the violations of his fundamental rights and that would have secured systemic change for future transgender Ontarians seeking surgical care. Prior to presenting the judgment, the rest of this commentary sets the context for the state of transgender healthcare in Ontario and the legal frameworks applicable to Nathaniel's case.

Context

In 2022, Canada became the first country in the world to release comprehensive national census data on its transgender and non-binary population.[5] At 0.33% of the population, one thing from the Statistics Canada report is resoundingly clear:

---

3. RSO 1990, c H 19.
4. Part I of the *Constitution Act, 1982*, being Schedule B to the *Canada Act 1982* (UK), 1982, c 11.
5. 'Canada is the First Country to Provide Census Data on Transgender and Non-Binary People,' Statistics Canada, 27 April 2022, accessed 26 September 2023, https://www150.statcan.gc.ca/n1/daily-quotidien/220427/dq220427b-eng.htm.

we make up an extreme minority. As such, our community often lacks the political power necessary to compel legislative or executive action to address our legal needs.

This reality is borne out on the ground, particularly in relation to access to transition-related healthcare. Although the Canada Health Act states that the 'primary objective of Canadian health care policy is to protect, promote, and restore the physical and mental well-being of residents of Canada and to facilitate reasonable access to health services without financial or other barriers,'[6] Nathaniel's story is one of many that shows that Canada (or at least Ontario) falls short of this objective. In fact, a 2020 report by TransPulse Canada found that 42% of transgender Ontarians had an unmet healthcare need that year. Further, only 25% had accessed all needed gender-affirming care, while 46% were attempting to access gender-affirming care but had not yet received care.[7] A 2018 report on legal problems facing transgender Ontarians found that 25% of participants faced a justiciable problem related to accessing medical treatment, relative to just 2.6% of the general population.[8]

As a parliamentary democracy, lawmaking power in Canada rests with a legislative branch that is elected not by minorities, but majorities. Regulation-making and resource allocation decisions are then carried out by an executive whose policy goals are set by the legislature. How, then, can the legal needs of the 0.33% be realized? One possible strategy is through Human Rights Code and Charter litigation like that brought by Nathaniel.

Relevant legal frameworks

Nathaniel asked the Board to decide four legal issues:
  a. What is the correct textual, contextual, and purposive interpretation of the statutory and regulatory regime that governs the Respondent?
  b. Were the Respondent's actions discriminatory under the Human Rights Code?
  c. Did the Respondent's actions deny Nathaniel his right to the equal protection and benefit of the law under s. 15(1) of the Charter? and
  d. Did the Respondent's actions infringe Nathaniel's right to security of the person under s.7 of the Charter?

To help situate readers in the Canadian legal context, I will provide a brief overview of the legal frameworks that underlie each of these four questions.

Statutory and Regulatory Framework Governing the Respondent

The Respondent General Manager of OHIP is appointed by the Lieutenant Governor pursuant to the Health Insurance Act ('HIA').[9] The General Manager's legal authority

---

6. RSC 1985, c C-6, s 3.
7. 'Report: Health and Healthcare Access for Transgender and Non-Binary People in Canada,' Trans PULSE Canada, 10 March 2020, accessed 17 November 2022, https://transpulsecanada.ca/results/report-1/, 10.
8. Julie James et al., 'Summary Report One: Legal Problems Facing Trans People in Ontario,' HIV & AIDS Legal Clinic Ontario, 6 September 2018, accessed 17 November 2022, https://www.rainbowhealthontario.ca/wp-content/uploads/2018/09/TransFJ-Report2018Sept-EN.pdf, 10.
9. RSO 1990, c H 6, s 4.

is set out in the HIA and circumscribed by the HIA. In other words, the General Manager does not have jurisdiction to decide to fund surgical procedures that are not prescribed as insured services under the HIA or the regulations thereunder. However, it also does not have the authority to arbitrarily deny funding for procedures that are set out in the statute and regulations.

At issue in Nathaniel's case was whether the Respondent misinterpreted provisions of the OHIP Schedule of Benefits. The Schedule of Benefits is part of a regulation under the HIA, and it sets out the scope, conditions, and limitations for public funding for healthcare. Nathaniel and I took the position that the Respondent's interpretation was legally incorrect, and thus it was acting outside of the scope of its statutory authority when it decided to deny Nathaniel funding for his surgery. Further, we submitted that the Respondent's interpretation was discriminatory and in contravention of the Charter.

The Ontario Human Rights Code

The Human Rights Code is a provincial statute. It provides Ontarians with the right to be free from discrimination based on a list of prohibited grounds (including gender identity and gender expression) in areas such as housing, employment, and the receipt of goods and services. The Code applies to both public and private agencies, and the statute specifically stipulates that it binds the Crown and every agency of the Crown, including the Respondent.[10]

Although it is a statutory instrument, the Code is often described as being 'quasi-constitutional' in character. This is because it has primacy over other legislative instruments—all other statutes and regulations in Ontario must conform with the Code, unless the statute or regulation specifically indicates that it applies despite the Code.[11] In the ordinary course, disputes related to the Code are adjudicated by an independent tribunal, the Human Rights Tribunal of Ontario. However, given the unique and quasi-constitutional character of the Code, other courts and tribunals sometimes exercise concurrent jurisdiction over Code-related issues. The Health Services Appeal and Review Board has acknowledged its jurisdiction to apply the Code, following guidance set out by the Supreme Court of Canada in *Tranchemontagne v Ontario (Director, Disability Support Program)*.[12]

The Canadian Charter of Rights and Freedoms

The Charter is a constitutional instrument that guarantees Canadians certain rights and freedoms, 'subject only to reasonable limits prescribed by law as can be demonstrably justified in a free and democratic society.'[13] The Charter was introduced in 1982 as a part of the patriation of the Canadian constitution. Unlike the Code, the Charter

---

10. *Human Rights Code*, s 47(1).
11. *Human Rights Code*, s 47(2).
12. *E.N.T. v Ontario (Health Insurance Plan)* 2018 CanLII 82192 (ON HSARB), [35], citing *Tranchemontagne v Ontario (Director, Disability Support Program)* [2006] 1 SCR 513.
13. *Charter*, s 1.

does not apply to private entities, and only laws and state actions are subject to Charter scrutiny.[14] In this case, Nathaniel did not allege that any statute or regulation contravened the Charter, and he was not seeking to declare any law unconstitutional. Rather, he claimed that the actions of the Respondent, a state actor, infringed his rights under ss. 7 and 15(1) of the Charter.

Section 7 of the Charter reads: 'Everyone has the right to life, liberty and security of the person and the right not to be deprived thereof except in accordance with the principles of fundamental justice.' On a plain reading of s. 7, it may not appear to be the most natural home for advancing transgender healthcare rights, particularly because s. 15(1) provides an equality guarantee. Further, in the early days of s. 7 jurisprudence, litigation took place primarily in the criminal law context. However, over the last three decades the s. 7 landscape has shifted significantly.[15] In my view, s. 7 is one of the most dynamic lines of jurisprudence in Canadian constitutional law, and Nathaniel's case presented strong and justiciable s. 7 arguments.

Section 7 jurisprudence has had a wide impact on the lives of marginalized people. Section 7 has recently been invoked to strike down repressive sex work laws,[16] create access to safe injection sites for intravenous drug users,[17] allow tent encampments to remain in place to shelter homeless people in British Columbia,[18] and create access to physician assisted dying[19]—a type of health care which, to a degree, parallels trans care, in that it is viewed by some segments of society as morally wrong. Even in the early days of s. 7 jurisprudence, the section was invoked to strike down laws criminalizing abortion,[20] and to ensure that Canadians could not be imprisoned for strict liability offences.[21] None of these cases had trans litigants or trans justice at their core, and therefore they may not appear to fit the descriptive mould of 'pro-LGBT cases' that animate much trans legal progress.[22] Nevertheless, each of them plays a role in advancing the interests of marginalized people most harmed by government

---

14. *Charter*, s 32.

15. To understand the shifts in s 7 jurisprudence, I recommend reading two pairs of cases: *Reference re ss 193 and 195.1(1)(C) of the Criminal Code (Man) (Prostitution Reference)* [1990] 1 SCR 1123 alongside *Canada (Attorney General) v Bedford (Bedford)* [2013] 3 SCR 1101; and *Rodriguez v British Columbia (Attorney General)* [1993] 3 SCR 519 alongside *Carter v Canada (Attorney General)* [2015] 1 SCR 331. The *Prostitution Reference* and *Rodriguez* cases are from the early 1990s. *Bedford* and *Carter* revisit substantively similar legal issues in the mid-2010s, but the legal framework for analysing s 7 claims—in particular the broader notion of the principles of fundamental justice—shifted so significantly that the Court was able to break from *stare decisis* and reach divergent conclusions from those reached in the 1990s.

16. *Bedford*. Note, the victory for sex workers rights in *Bedford* was short-lived, animating the limitations of using the judiciary to address systemic policy issues. Shortly after *Bedford*, Parliament passed new laws that addressed the Court's s 7 concerns, but are otherwise arguably more repressive because they make the *purchase* of sexual services illegal, thereby criminalizing sex in exchange for money for the first time in Canada.

17. *Canada (Attorney General) v PHS Community Services Society (PHS Community Services)* [2011] 3 SCR 134.

18. *Victoria (City) v Adams* 2009 BCCA 563.

19. *Carter*.

20. *R v Morgentaler* [1988] 1 SCR 30.

21. *Re BC Motor Vehicle Act* [1985] 2 SCR 486.

22. Senthorun Sunil Raj, *Feeling Queer Jurisprudence: Injury, Intimacy, Identity* (New York: Routledge, 2020), 8.

(in)action.[23] In light of the complex social, legal, and economic vulnerabilities faced by many trans people, s. 7 provides promise for far-reaching constitutional protections.

Viewed in this light, s. 7 is a natural fit for advancing access to trans healthcare. In the healthcare context, s. 7 has been a particularly successful legal tool. Courts have held that the rights to life and security of the person are engaged by state-created threats to claimants' lives due to restricting medical care,[24] state-imposed hardship in attaining care,[25] state-imposed threats to bodily integrity,[26] and denial of autonomy in medical decision-making.[27]

Furthermore, Section 15(1) of the Charter reads:

> Every individual is equal before and under the law and has the right to the equal protection and equal benefit of the law without discrimination and, in particular, without discrimination based on race, national or ethnic origin, colour, religion, sex, age or mental or physical disability.

From the early days of s. 15(1) jurisprudence, it has been interpreted as a broad substantive equality provision. It does more than require sameness or forbid formal distinctions; it also 'requires attention to the "full context of the claimant group's situation," to the "actual impact of the law on that situation," and to the "persistent systemic disadvantages [that] have operated to limit the opportunities available" to that group's members.'[28]

Litigation under s.15(1) has driven progress for lesbian, gay, bisexual, and queer people, but progress for the transgender community has been much slower. With respect to sexual orientation, *Egan v Canada* set the foundation for future litigation under s.15(1) when, in 1995, the Supreme Court of Canada held that sexual orientation is an 'analogous ground' under s.15(1).[29] This means that laws and government actions cannot discriminate against people on the basis of their sexual orientation,[30] and sexual orientation is treated as if it appears in the text of the provision. Three years later, in *Vriend v Alberta*, the Supreme Court found that Alberta's exclusion of sexual orientation from its provincial human rights statute violated s.15(1).[31] In 1999, *M. v H.* established that the exclusion of same-sex couples from a benefits regime under the Family Law Act was also an unjustified violation of s.15(1).[32] And, in 2003, Ontario became the first province in Canada to legalize same-sex marriage when the Court of Appeal for Ontario declared the common law definition of marriage in violation of s.15(1), and subsequently made same-sex marriage immediately available across the province in *Halpern v Canada (AG)*.[33]

---

23. Jennifer Koshan, 'Section 7: Superhero, Mere Mortal or Villain?' The Canadian Bar Association, 8 August 2016, accessed 17 November 2022, https://www.cba-alberta.org/Publications-Resources/Resources/Law-Matters/Law-Matters-Summer-2016-Issue/Section-7-Superhero,-Mere-Mortal-or-Villain.
24. *Chaoulli v Quebec (Attorney General)* [2005] 1 SCR 791.
25. *R v Morgentaler; PHS Community Services.*
26. *R v Morgentaler; Bedford.*
27. *Carter; R v Morgentaler.*
28. *Fraser v Canada (Attorney General)* [2020] 3 SCR 113, [40]-[42].
29. [1995] 2 SCR 513.
30. Subject to reasonable limits, as all Charter rights are subject to limits prescribed by law.
31. [1998] 1 SCR 493.
32. [1999] 2 SCR 3.
33. [2003] OJ No 2268.

Yet, despite this progress for lesbian, gay, and bisexual people (and despite the significant unmet legal needs of the transgender community), transgender people have often been left out of the s.15(1) discourse. In early 2023, the Supreme Court of Canada commented on the s.15(1) rights of transgender people for the first time in *Hansman v Neufeld*.[34] However, this case was not a direct Charter challenge—the issues in the case arose from a defamation claim involving a school board trustee who made transphobic remarks about the British Columbia Sexual Orientation and Gender Identity school curriculum. Since there was no direct Charter challenge, the Supreme Court did not make any substantive ruling on transgender rights under s.15(1). However, the Court commented that 'the transgender community is undeniably a marginalized group in Canadian society. The history of transgender individuals in our country has been marked by discrimination and disadvantage.'[35] The Court also indicated a judicial appetite for recognizing gender identity and gender expression as analogous grounds under s.15(1).[36]

With the growing judicial recognition of transgender legal issues and judicial acknowledgement of the need for equality protections for transgender people, I remain hopeful that cases like Nathaniel's will continue to shift the legal landscape for transgender Canadians. Although Nathaniel was denied the opportunity to have his rights adjudicated by an impartial and independent tribunal, this volume offers occasion to envision what could have been, had Nathaniel and I been allowed to litigate the case we prepared.

---

34. *Hansman v Neufeuld* 2023 SCC 14.
35. *Hansman* [84].
36. *Hansman* [88].

NATHANIEL LE MAY v THE GENERAL MANAGER,
ONTARIO HEALTH INSURANCE PLAN

Decision and Reasons of the Board

Overview

[1] The Appellant, Nathaniel Le May, is a transgender Ontarian seeking phalloplasty, a form of surgery enumerated as an insured service in the *Schedule of Benefits: Physician Services,* a schedule under Regulation 552 of the *Health Insurance Act* ('*Schedule of Benefits.*')[37]

[2] Mr. Le May has met all the prior authorization criteria outlined in Appendix D of the *Schedule of Benefits*, and the Respondent General Manager of the Ontario Health Insurance Plan ('Respondent') is willing to approve Mr. Le May's surgical funding if he also undergoes the removal of his reproductive organs, including his vagina and uterus.

[3] However, Mr. Le May does not medically require—or personally desire—the removal of these organs. Because Mr. Le May is not seeking a vaginectomy and hysterectomy concurrent to his phalloplasty, the Respondent has denied Mr. Le May funding for phalloplasty.

[4] Mr. Le May appeals this denial. He further submits that the Respondent's decision to deny funding is discriminatory under the Ontario's *Human Rights Code* and denies him the equal benefit and protection of the law guaranteed by s.15(1) of the *Canadian Charter of Rights and Freedoms* and his right to security of the person guaranteed by s.7 of the *Charter.*

[5] For the reasons that follow, the appeal is allowed. The Board finds that the Respondent is obligated to pay for Mr. Le May's surgery and makes a declaration that the Respondent violated Mr. Le May's rights under the *Human Rights Code* and the *Charter.*

---

37. Schedule of Benefits under RRO 1990, Reg 552 of the Health Insurance Act, RSO 1990, c. H 6, accessed 21 January 2024, https://www.health.gov.on.ca/en/pro/programs/ohip/sob/physserv/sob_master.pdf, AD8.

Facts

[6] Mr. Le May identifies as transmasculine nonbinary.

[7] In Fall of 2021, he determined that he required genital surgery to relieve his diagnosed gender dysphoria, and he began seeking a surgical referral from his endocrinologist.

[8] On December 1, 2021, Mr. Le May's endocrinologist and social worker jointly completed a Request for Prior Authorization for Sex-Reassignment Surgery and submitted it to OHIP. Mr. Le May's healthcare team assessed him and determined he met all the relevant prior authorization criteria for phalloplasty. Mr. Le May was clear at the time of his assessment that he did not require vaginectomy, hysterectomy, or urethral lengthening. His healthcare team noted this in their referring paperwork. His endocrinologist supported this treatment plan, writing:

> Nathaniel feels that to complete his transition/journey he wishes to pursue gender-affirming surgery via phalloplasty. Normally this procedure requires a vaginectomy, but Nathaniel feels very strongly that this is not appropriate in his case as his current organs do not cause him dysphoria per say [sic] and does not feel the need to remove structures which are not causing any harm/distress, he just wishes to have the structures which he is currently missing. I support Nathaniel's approach and desires and believe that everything should be done for him to live authentically as he feels is most appropriate for him.[38]

[9] On August 29, 2022, the Respondent issued a letter denying funding for Mr. Le May's surgery, stating:

> This request has been denied.
>
> Phalloplasty (including vaginectomy, urethroplasty, glansplasty) is an insured OHIP service when the criteria for payment is met, as set out in Appendix D of the Schedule of Benefits for Physician Services (the Schedule) under Regulation 552 of the *Health Insurance Act* (HIA). Phalloplasty (without vaginectomy) is not listed as an insured service in Appendix D of the Schedule.[39]

[10] After reviewing the text of Appendix D, Nathaniel sought clarification regarding which portion of Appendix D the Respondent was relying on to ground its denial. Nathaniel's position is that the surgery he seeks is listed separately from vaginectomy in Appendix D, and thus is an insured procedure (regardless of whether it is performed in a prescribed grouping with vaginectomy).

[11] Nathaniel's interpretation is supported by the expert evidence of Dr. O, who was qualified as an expert before the Board in the subject of transgender surgical care. Dr. O

---

38.   Referral letter from Mr. Le May's endocrinologist, on file with author and publicly accessible via a request for case documents made to the Health Services Appeal and Review Board.

39.   OHIP Denial Letter, on file with author and publicly accessible via a request for case documents made to the Health Services Appeal and Review Board.

assisted the Board by providing definitions of the medical terms contained in Appendix D. As Dr. O notes in his report:

> There are five separate surgical interventions discussed in this appeal: phalloplasty, glansplasty, vaginectomy, urethroplasty, and hysterectomy.
>
> a. Phalloplasty refers to the creation of a neophallus, or penis, using a tissue flap from another part of the patient's body.
>
> b. Glansplasty refers to the construction of the glans penis, or penis crown, from the cylindrical tissue flap, resulting in a penis (which appears circumcised).
>
> c. Vaginectomy refers to the surgical removal of the vaginal epithelium, resulting in the closure of the vaginal canal.
>
> d. Urethroplasty, in this context, refers to the creation of a neourethra that is routed through the neophallus, enabling the patient to void urine via the phallus. In other contexts, urethroplasty is a general urologic term that may refer to other procedures involving the repair or reconstruction of the urethra.
>
> e. Hysterectomy refers to the removal of the uterus. It is a pre-requisite for vaginectomy, so although it is not raised directly in this appeal, it is implied that if Mr. Le May must receive a vaginectomy, he must also receive a hysterectomy. This is because vaginectomy prevents the ability to perform cervical cancer screening and thus generally obligates hysterectomy as well.
>
> [...]
>
> Although the treatment plan for some transmasculine patients indicates that phalloplasty should be performed concurrently with vaginectomy and urethroplasty to address the patients' medical needs, there is no medical requirement to receive a vaginectomy or urethroplasty concurrently with phalloplasty in all cases.[40]

[12] Between receiving the denial letter in August 2022 and this hearing in June 2023, Nathaniel repeatedly requested that the Respondent provide additional clarity regarding which portion of Appendix D it was relying on to ground its refusal. The Respondent did not point Mr. Le May to any particular text or provision of Appendix D.

[13] In its Grounds of Response filed with this Board, the Respondent took the position that the words 'sex-reassignment surgery,' which appear in Appendix D, precluded coverage for Nathaniel's surgery, writing:

> The Respondent submits that the Applicant's request for funding of only the one specific external genital surgery identified in the Applicant's funding application is not a valid request for funding approval of *sex-reassignment surgery* insofar as the term – 'sex-reassignment surgery' –

---

40. Report of Dr. O, on file with author and publicly accessible via a request for case documents made to the Health Services Appeal and Review Board.

is 'prescribed' in the Schedule of Benefits and is, and has been, habitually interpreted, established, and understood in Appendix D since 2016 (emphasis added by Respondent).[41]

[14] The Respondent further relied on the text of its internal Request for Prior Authorization for Sex-Reassignment Surgery form ('Approval Form'), which contains a checkbox under the heading '*Proposed procedure(s) for which prior approval is requested*' which reads 'Phalloplasty (includes vaginectomy, urethroplasty, glansplasty).' The Respondent submits that the words 'includes vaginectomy, urethroplasty, glans-plasty' should be interpreted to mean that phalloplasty *must* include these additional procedures.

[15] Mr. Le May also presented the Board with numerous email communications between himself and the Respondent in which he raised concerns that his human rights were being violated, that he was experiencing discrimination, and that the Respondent's actions constituted coerced sterilization. In these email records, there is no indication that the Respondent took steps to investigate or address Mr. Le May's allegations. Mr. Le May raised human rights concerns as early as August 31, 2022, more than six months before this appeal was filed.

Issues

[16] Mr. Le May's appeal raises the following legal issues:
  i.   What is the correct textual, contextual, and purposive interpretation of Appendix D of the *Schedule of Benefits*? (i.e., is phalloplasty a funded procedure when pre-approval criteria are met, regardless of whether a patient also undergoes vaginectomy?)
  ii. Is the Respondent's interpretation of Appendix D discriminatory under the *Human Rights Code*?
  iii. Does the Respondent's interpretation of Appendix D deny Mr. Le May his right to the equal protection and benefit of the law under s.15(1) of the *Charter*?
  iv. Does the Respondent's interpretation of Appendix D infringe Mr. Le May's right to security of the person under s.7 of the *Charter*?

Analysis

Phalloplasty is a funded procedure under the Schedule of Benefits

[17] The Respondent erred in its interpretation of Appendix D of the Schedule of Benefits. The Board finds that the only reasonable textual, contextual, and purposive interpretation of Appendix D is that each enumerated genital surgery is independently funded when the criteria for approval are met.

[18] The relevant portion of Appendix D reads:

---

41. Grounds of Response, on file with author and publicly accessible via a request for case documents made to the Health Services Appeal and Review Board.

Sex-reassignment surgical procedures listed in this section are insured services when prior authorization has been obtained from the MOH [Ministry of Health].

[...]

Prior authorization for sex-reassignment surgery will only be provided [...] for the specific services listed:

External Genital Surgery (clitoral release, *glansplasty*, metoidioplasty, penile implant, *phalloplasty*, scrotoplasty, testicular implants, urethroplasty, vaginectomy, penectomy, vaginoplasty).[42]

[19] Since each surgical procedure is enumerated separately, the only reasonably available textual interpretation is that phalloplasty is a funded procedure when a patient meets the prior authorization requirements.

[20] Mr. Le May meets all the requirements listed in Appendix D, evidenced by the fact that the Respondent is willing to fund his procedure if he receives a concurrent vaginectomy.[43] Mr. Le May's supporting letters from his endocrinologist and social worker also confirm that he meets all prior authorization requirements.

[21] Moreover, the only published decision of this Board discussing the Respondent's funding of phalloplasty confirms that phalloplasty is an insured service. The decision does not state that coverage is contingent on receiving a vaginectomy.[44]

APPENDIX D MUST BE INTERPRETED IN LIGHT OF ITS STATUTORY AND REGULATORY CONTEXT AND PURPOSE

[22] A contextual and purposive approach to statutory interpretation also leads to the necessary conclusion that phalloplasty is a funded procedure. Appendix D exists as a Schedule of Regulation 552 under the *Health Insurance Act*. Relevant provisions of the *HIA* demonstrate that the purpose of Appendix D is to enumerate a list of insured services that support Ontarians to access gender-confirming care. For example, ss.11.2(1.1)-(1.2) of the *HIA* read:

Efforts to change sexual orientation or gender identity

11(1.1) Despite subsection (1) and subject to the regulations, if any, any services that seek to change the sexual orientation or gender identity of a person are not insured services. 2015, c. 18, s.1.

---

42. *Schedule of Benefits*, AD8 ['Appendix D'] (emphasis added).
43. OHIP Approval Letter, on file with author and publicly accessible via a request for case documents made to the Health Services Appeal and Review Board.
44. *M.L. v. Ontario (Health Insurance Plan)*, 2017 CanLII 44819 (ON HSARB).

Exception

11(1.2) The services mentioned in subsection (1.1) do not include,

> (a) services that provide acceptance, support or understanding of a person or the facilitation of a person's coping, social support or identity exploration or development; and

> (b) sex-reassignment surgery *or any services related to sex-reassignment surgery.* 2015, c. 18, s.1 (emphasis added).[45]

[23] These provisions establish that, while Ontario will not fund 'conversion therapies' aimed at changing a person's sexual orientation or gender identity, it has an express intent to fund services that help to better align one's physical and emotional self with one's sense of their gender identity.

[24] Critically, the provision provides that OHIP will fund any services related to sex-re-assignment surgery. This leads to the conclusion that the legislative intent was not to fund only certain prescribed groupings of surgeries (e.g., phalloplasty with vaginectomy, urethroplasty, and glansplasty), but to fund *any* necessary gender-affirming surgeries, subject only to the limitations and conditions enumerated in the *Schedule of Benefits*.

[25] This interpretation also accords with the medical reality of these procedures. Each of the procedures enumerated in Appendix D is a separate surgical intervention, which are sometimes (but not always) performed concurrently in groupings that can respond to an individual's experience of gender dysphoria.

[26] Nothing in the text of the *Schedule of Benefits, Regulation 552,* or the *HIA* supports the Respondent's interpretation that phalloplasty *must* include vaginectomy. This interpretation is contrary to the purpose of Ontario's gender-affirming surgery program and incongruous with the text, context, and purpose of the language contained in Appendix D and the surrounding statutory and regulatory provisions.

> *The Respondent's interpretation violates Mr. Le May's rights under the Human Rights Code*

[27] The Respondent's submissions to the Board rely in part on emphasizing the words 'sex-reassignment' to suggest that the surgeries sought by Mr. Le May are outside of the coverage provided in Appendix D. The Respondent submits:

> [T]he Applicant's request for funding of only the one specific external genital surgery identified in the Applicant's funding application is not a valid request for funding approval of *sex-reassignment surgery.* (emphasis added by Respondent)[46]

---

45. *Health Insurance Act*, s 11.2(1.1)-(1.2).
46. Grounds of Response, [24].

[28] The Respondent's interpretation of the words 'sex-reassignment' demonstrate that it does not view Mr. Le May's experience of his gender identity and his surgical goals to treat his diagnosed gender dysphoria as a valid form of sex-reassignment. Mr. Le May submits that this interpretation is discriminatory under the *Code*.

[29] The Respondent, as an agent of the Crown, is bound by the *Code*.[47] Moreover, the *Code* has primacy over other acts and regulations in Ontario, including in instances where the act or regulation 'purports to require or authorize conduct that is a contravention of Part I [of the *Code*].'[48]

[30] A *prima facie* breach of the *Code* is made out when three elements are in place. A claimant must demonstrate: 1) that they have a characteristic protected from discrimination (e.g., a ground of discrimination is present), 2) they have experienced an adverse impact within a social area protected by the *Code*, and 3) the protected characteristic was a factor in the adverse impact.[49] Once a claimant establishes a *prima facie* case, the burden switches to the respondent to justify why its actions were not discriminatory.

[31] In Mr. Le May's case, gender identity and gender expression are both characteristics protected from discrimination.[50] Therefore, he readily meets the first element of a *prima facie* case.

[32] He has experienced an adverse impact with respect to the receipt of services because he has been denied funding for a medically necessary surgery. Receipt of services is a social area protected by the *Code*.[51]

[33] Lastly, Mr. Le May's particular and individualized experiences of gender identity and gender dysphoria are the pivotal factor in the adverse treatment—the Respondent is clear that it is willing to fund surgical outcomes that it views as valid 'sex-reassignment,' including phalloplasty with vaginectomy. In fact, the Respondent approved Mr. Le May to undergo phalloplasty on the condition that he also receive vaginectomy, urethroplasty, and glansplasty.[52] But the Respondent is unwilling to fund the procedures that Mr. Le May requires to address his diagnosed gender dysphoria, procedures which are intimately connected to his gender identity and his expression of that identity.

[34] There is a clear nexus between Mr. Le May's gender identity and gender expression, and his denial of service by the Respondent. Therefore, the Respondent's actions constitute *prima facie* discrimination under the *Code*. The Respondent has advanced

---

47. *Human Rights Code*, s 47(1).
48. *Human Rights Code*, s 47(2).
49. See e.g. *Moore v British Columbia (Education)* [2012] 3 SCR 360; *R.B. v Keewatin-Patricia District School Board* [2013] HRTO 1436 [204].
50. *Human Rights Code*, s 1.
51. *Human Rights Code*, s 1.
52. OHIP Approval Letter dated September 13, 2022, Tab 1.

no plausible justification that rebuts the finding that it has acted in a discriminatory manner.

The Respondent's interpretation violates Mr. Le May's ss.15(1) and 7 Charter rights

[35] Mr. Le May submits that the Respondent's interpretation of Appendix D, and its subsequent actions in denying funding, violate his rights under s.15(1) and s.7 of the *Charter*.

[36] As a Crown agency, the Respondent's interpretation and application of Appendix D is a state action that is subject to *Charter* scrutiny.

[37] Although the jurisprudence is clear that 'the *Charter* does not confer a freestanding constitutional right to health care,' it is equally clear that 'where the government puts in place a scheme to provide health care, that scheme must comply with the *Charter*.'[53]

[38] In this case, the government has chosen to put in place a scheme to provide a particular form of healthcare—that is, transgender surgical care—and it is bound to deliver this scheme in a *Charter*-compliant manner.

Mr. Le May's s.15(1) rights have been infringed

[39] To make out a violation of s.15(1), Mr. Le May must demonstrate that: the impugned law or state action: [1] on its face or in its impact, creates a distinction based on enumerated or analogous grounds; and [2] imposes a burden or denies a benefit in a manner that has the effect of reinforcing, perpetuating, or exacerbating disadvantage.[54]

[40] Although gender identity and gender expression are not enumerated grounds in s. 15(1), the Supreme Court of Canada recently acknowledged that these traits carry the markers of analogous grounds. In *Hansman v Neufeld*, the Court wrote:

> [J]udicial recognition of the plight of transgender individuals in Canada is growing. And in 2021, the Superior Court of Quebec held that '[g]ender identity is analogous to the grounds listed at s. 15(1) of the Canadian Charter' because '[g]ender identity is an immutable personal characteristic.'[55]

[41] The Board agrees gender identity and expression should be considered analogous grounds under s. 15(1).

[42] The Respondent's interpretation is that Appendix D only insures binary 'sex-reassignment' outcomes. This creates a distinction on the basis of gender identity and expression.

---

53. *Chaoulli*, [104], see also *Eldridge v British Columbia (Attorney General)* [1997] 3 SCR 624.
54. *Fraser*, [27]; *R. v. Sharma* [2022] SCC 39, [28].
55. *Hansman*, [88] (citations omitted).

It precludes non-binary transgender individuals from accessing the same surgical care that is available to transgender people who are seeking conventionally binary surgical outcomes.

[43] This distinction clearly denies a benefit (i.e., surgical funding), and this denial has the effect of reinforcing, perpetuating, or exacerbating disadvantage.

[44] The denial of a benefit is evidenced by the fact that Respondent will not fund Mr. Le May's surgery, despite the fact that Mr. Le May meets all relevant prior approval criteria.

[45] The distinction created by the Respondent—the willingness to fund binary 'sex-reassignment procedures' while refusing to fund non-normative surgical outcomes—reinforces and perpetuates disadvantage for non-binary transgender individuals. Most shockingly, this distinction would require Mr. Le May and others in his circumstances to undergo state-mandated sterilization procedures in order to access the very surgical care that OHIP both purports to fund, and is willing to fund, for people who seek binary surgical outcomes.

[46] On this basis, the Board finds that Mr. Le May's s.15(1) rights have been violated.

MR. LE MAY'S S.7 RIGHTS HAVE BEEN INFRINGED

[47] The Respondent's interpretation of Appendix D leads to the conclusion that the benefits extended by Appendix D are only available if Mr. Le May submits himself to procedures that amount to sterilization. Mr. Le May argues that this is an arbitrary and grossly disproportionate intrusion on his right to security of the person under s. 7 of the *Charter.*

[48] Before addressing the substance of Mr. Le May's s. 7 claim, the Board first wishes to address the Respondent's argument that *Flora v Ontario Health Insurance Plan* ('*Flora*') precludes the Board from ordering the Respondent to fund Mr. Le May's surgery.[56]

[49] In the Grounds of Response, the Respondent relies on *Flora* for several general propositions regarding the obligations of the state to provide healthcare. Because the court in *Flora* dismissed a s. 7 challenge to components of the OHIP regime, it is necessary to discuss why Mr. Le May's case is distinguishable.

[50] The Respondent has misapplied the principles derived from *Flora* in at least two respects.

---

56. 2008 ONCA 538.

[51] First, the appellant in *Flora* sought a positive right to receive a type of care that OHIP did not otherwise fund. Mr. Flora was seeking re-imbursement for a surgery he attained abroad, which OHIP did not fund in the normal course.[57]

[52] In contrast, Mr. Le May seeks relief from an arbitrary requirement to remove his reproductive organs in order to access procedures that are enumerated in the *Schedule of Benefits*. Mr. Le May is not asking OHIP to fund any particular type of care other than that which it has already committed to fund in Appendix D. Thus, the requirement to receive vaginectomy in order to access funding for phalloplasty constitutes a deprivation of his right to security of the person under s. 7.

[53] In this regard, the Respondent's reliance on the statements in *Flora* that '[f]unding provided under the Act "does not extend to all medical treatments or procedures,": [and] "[n]either the Act nor the Regulation promise that insured Ontarians will receive public funding for all medically beneficial treatments"'[58] is misplaced, because these statements are not relevant on the facts of Mr. Le May's case. There is no dispute that Ontario retains discretion to determine what types of care it funds, but Mr. Le May is seeking a type of care which Ontario has—in fact and in law—already committed to funding.

[54] Additionally, in *Flora* the appellant had already been assessed in Ontario and deemed ineligible for the type of care he was seeking based on the relevant medical standards in Ontario.[59] In contrast, Mr. Le May's referring physicians have assessed him and determined that he meets all the eligibility criteria contained in Appendix D.

[55] The impugned provision in *Flora* only allowed out-of-province care to be funded if a patient was eligible for the care, but the procedure was not available in Ontario. This reflects a policy choice of the government regarding what types of care they chose to fund. Appendix D also reflects a policy choice—one to fund the enumerated genital surgeries.

[56] There is no tenable basis to exclude Mr. Le May from this funding, particularly because *Flora* establishes that it 'remains the task of health care professionals to determine the nature of the medical services to be provided to a particular patient.'[60]

[57] In this case, Mr. Le May's health care professionals have diagnosed him with gender dysphoria. They unequivocally support his need to receive phalloplasty, and unequivocally support his need *not* to undergo vaginectomy.

---

57. *Flora*, [1]-[5].
58. Grounds of Response, [29].
59. *Flora*, [11], [22], [58], [65].
60. *Flora*, [86].

[58] Rather than following the recommendations of Mr. Le May's healthcare team, the Respondent has substituted its own views regarding which types of care Mr. Le May should receive, contrary to the Court of Appeal for Ontario's guidance in *Flora*.

MR. LE MAY'S RIGHT TO SECURITY OF THE PERSON IS INFRINGED IN A MANNER THAT VIOLATES TWO PRINCIPLES OF FUNDAMENTAL JUSTICE

[59] To demonstrate that his s. 7 rights have been violated, Mr. Le May must first show that the Respondent's actions deprive him of his life, liberty, or security of the person. If Mr. Le May establishes that his s. 7 interests are engaged, he must then demonstrate that the deprivation runs afoul of the principles of fundamental justice.[61]

[60] The jurisprudence is clear that 'where a law creates a risk to health by preventing access to health care, a deprivation of the right to security of the person is made out.'[62]

[61] Mr. Le May is prevented from accessing healthcare that his physicians have deemed medically necessary, and for which he meets all the relevant pre-approval criteria. Thus, the Respondent's interpretation of Appendix D deprives him of his right to security of the person by preventing his access to healthcare.

[62] The infringement of Mr. Le May's right to security of the person offends two principles of fundamental justice: arbitrariness and gross disproportionality.

[63] The Respondent has drawn an entirely arbitrary line around which transgender people are worthy of accessing publicly funded care. According to the Supreme Court of Canada in *Canada (Attorney General) v Bedford*, a law or state action is arbitrary if there is no 'direct connection between the purpose of the law and the impugned effect on the individual, in the sense that the effect on the individual bears some relation to the law's purpose.'[63]

[64] Since the starting place of the analysis is the purpose of the law, purpose must be defined with precision for the arbitrariness analysis.[64]

[65] The purpose of Appendix D can be understood with reference to its statutory and regulatory context, set out above: the Appendix provides a list of surgical interventions that help transgender Ontarians better align their bodies with their identities, when they meet the criteria for pre-approval set out in the Appendix.

[66] This Board's decision in *M.L. v Ontario (Health Insurance Plan)* also discusses the purpose of the Regulations, noting that 'the change to the Regulation made

---

61. See e.g. *Carter*, [55]
62. *PHS Community Services*, [93].
63. *Bedford*, [111].
64. *Carter*, [78].

in March 2016 [...] was intended to broaden access to referrals for OHIP-funded SRS [sex-reassignment surgery] procedures.'[65]

[67] Thus, the regulation's purpose is to increase access to all OHIP-funded SRS procedures, which include phalloplasty.

[68] In light of this purpose, there is no medical basis to exclude Mr. Le May from this funding. There is no valid (e.g., non-discriminatory) policy reason for excluding Mr. Le May from this funding, particularly because Mr. Le May is, in fact, seeking a set of surgical interventions that will create a smaller resourcing demand on the public healthcare system. Mr. Le May is seeking only two surgical interventions—phalloplasty and glansplasty. If Mr. Le May were to proceed with the surgical interventions required by the Respondent, he would also need to undergo hysterectomy, vaginectomy, and urethroplasty. These additional three surgeries would create a higher resource burden on the public healthcare system.

[69] In addition to being arbitrary, the impacts of the Respondent's interpretation of Appendix D offend the principle against gross disproportionality, because the 'seriousness of the deprivation is totally out of sync with the objective of the measure.'[66] In fact, the Respondent advances no plausible objective tied to its interpretation of Appendix D that might come close to justifying the *carte blanche* exclusion of Mr. Le May (and other similarly situated transgender people) from accessing publicly-funded care unless they undergo sterilization procedures.

[70] Therefore, the Respondent's actions violate Mr. Le May's s. 7 rights.

Neither violation of Mr. Le May's Charter rights is justified pursuant to s. 1 of the Charter

[71] Once *Charter* rights are implicated in an administrative decision—as they are in the present case—reasonable limits on those rights are assessed using the administrative law framework set out in *Doré v Barreau du Québec*[67] and affirmed in *Loyola High School v Quebec (Attorney General)*[68] and *Law Society of British Columbia v Trinity Western University*.[69] The Supreme Court of Canada instructs:

> [T]he question becomes 'whether, in assessing the impact of the relevant *Charter* protection and given the nature of the decision and the statutory and factual contexts, the decision reflects a proportionate balancing of the *Charter* protections at play' (*Doré*, at para. 57; *Loyola*, at para. 39). The extent of the impact on the *Charter* protection must be proportionate in light of the statutory objectives.[70]

---

65. *M.L.*, [34].
66. *Bedford*, [120].
67. [2012] 1 SCR 395.
68. [2015] 1 SCR 613.
69. [2018] 2 SCR 293 ['*Trinity Western*'].
70. *Trinity Western*, [58].

[72] The Board finds that the *Charter* infringements experienced by Mr. Le May are significant—he has been denied both the equal protection and benefit of the law under s. 15(1) and has been denied his right to security of the person under s. 7.

[73] The Respondent's statutory objectives require it to administer the Ontario Health Insurance Plan in accordance with the framework set out in the *HIA* and its regulations.[71] However, the Board has already concluded that the Respondent has acted outside of its statutory objectives by denying Mr. Le May funding for a surgery that is, correctly interpreted, an insured service.

[74] Given that the Respondent is not legally empowered to exercise its discretion in a manner that places it outside its statutory jurisdiction, there is certainly no basis for it to act in a manner that is both beyond its statutory mandate and in violation of the *Charter*.

[75] Thus, the Respondent's actions are not proportionate to the infringements of Mr. Le May's *Charter* rights and are not justified.

Order

[76] The appeal is allowed.

[77] The Respondent is directed to fund Mr. Le May's phalloplasty and glansplasty surgeries.

[78] Furthermore, this Board makes the following declarations:
  a. A declaration that the Respondent violated Mr. Le May's right to be free from discrimination in the receipt of services pursuant to s. 1 of the *Human Rights Code;*
  b. A declaration that the Respondent's interpretation and application of Appendix D infringed Mr. Le May's right to the equal protection and benefit of the law under s. 15(1) of the *Charter* and is not justified pursuant to s.1 of the *Charter;*
  c. A declaration that the Respondent's interpretation and application of Appendix D infringed Mr. Le May's right to security of the person under s. 7 of the *Charter* and is not justified pursuant to s.1 of the *Charter.*

---

71. *Health Insurance Act*, s 4.

PART 5

ASYLUM AND MIGRATION

25

HJ (Iran) & HT (Cameroon) (United Kingdom):

Queer Reflections on a Landmark Case on the Rights of LGBT+ Refugees

Alex Powell

HJ (Iran) & HT (Cameroon) in Context

HJ (Iran) & HT (Cameroon) has generally been regarded as a major step forward in the protection of refugees of who are sexually diverse[1] in the UK.[2] For example, Rainbow Migration heralded the decision as a 'key factor in the improvement of first decisions.'[3] Much early critique of the decision centred on its failure to draw distinctions between incidental and core aspects of sexuality.[4] Later critique has also focused on the failure of the decision to offer concrete guidance for decision makers who are tasked with determining whether a particular claimant is a sexually diverse person,[5] and for retaining the role of discretion reasoning by asking decision makers to make judgments regarding future behaviour.[6] Despite these criticisms, the judgment has generally been regarded as a positive step towards greater protection for sexually diverse refugees.

---

1. While it would be more common to use terminology such as LGBT+ or SOGIE (Sexual Orientation and Gender Identity and Expression), I deploy this terminology in order to avoid the overly identitarian frameworks associated with sexuality. I have expanded on my reasons for this more fully elsewhere. See: Alex Powell, '"Sexuality" Through the Kaleidoscope: Sexual orientation, Identity and Behaviour in Asylum Claims in the United Kingdom,' *Laws* 10 (2021), 90.
2. *HJ (Iran) & HT (Cameroon) v Secretary of State for the Home Department* [2010] UKSC 31.
3. UK Lesbian and Gay Immigration Group (UKLGIG), Missing the Mark: Decision Making on Lesbian, Gay (Bisexual, Trans and Intersex) Asylum Claims (UKLGIG, 2013), accessed on 7 September 2023, https://www.rainbowmigration.org.uk/publications/missing-the-mark/.
4. See, for example, James C. Hathaway and Jason Pobjoy, 'Queer Cases Make Bad Law,' *New York University Journal of International Law and Politics* 44(2) (Winter 2012), 315–390.
5. Satvinder Juss, 'Sexual Orientation and the Sexualisation of Refugee Law,' *International Journal on Minority and Group Rights* 22 (2015), 128–53.
6. Jana Wessels, 'The Art of Drawing Lines: Future Behaviour and Refugee Status,' in *Research Handbook on International Refugee Law*, ed. Satvinder Juss (Edward Elgar, 2019); Jana Wessels, '*HJ (Iran) and HT (Cameroon)* – Reflections on a New Test for Sexuality-Based Asylum Claims in Britain,' 24 *International Journal of Refugee Law* 24 (2012), 815.

As I have made clear elsewhere, this is not a position I disagree with.[7] The decision in *HJ (Iran) & HT (Cameroon)* addressed a substantial deficiency with regard to how the Refugee Convention definition of a refugee was being applied to cases concerning sexuality or sexual diversity in the UK. However, as Adler has argued, even progressive movements, moments, and legal processes carry trade-offs.[8] It is in this register, linking to a history of queer critical analysis, that I seek to offer a queer re-writing of the judgment. This re-writing seeks to retain the progressive consequences of the decision, reaching substantially the same outcome as that reached by the Supreme Court. However, my judgment seeks to pay greater critical attention to the forms of knowledge regarding the nature, constitution, and ontological basis of sexual diversity that are promoted—both implicitly and explicitly—within the judgment. In particular, I seek to limit or restrain the movement from discretion to disbelief within the adjudication of refugee status that has generally been associated with both this decision and similar decisions in other jurisdictions.[9]

As such, my judgment seeks to avoid the homonormative,[10] homonationalist,[11] and overly fixed ways of conceptualizing sexual diversity displayed in the original judgment.[12] Otherwise put, I seek to offer a counter-judgment that is more attentive to the forms of essentialism, strategic or otherwise, at play when the law attempts to grasp at concepts such as sexuality.[13] The phrase strategic essentialism was coined by Spivak. She utilised this term to refer to the way social groups mobilize based on a shared characteristic and, in so doing, erase or ignore differences between members of those groups.[14] Through being attentive to these patterns, I seek to offer an 'ethical reimagining' that is more aligned with the experiences,[15] desires, and self-conceptions of sexually diverse refugees.

In offering this judgment, I share many of the concerns regarding the compatibility of queer theory with the practice of judgment writing, as expressed by Sharpe[16]

---

7. Powell, '"Sexuality" Through the Kaleidoscope'; Alex Powell, *Queering Refugee Law: A Study of Sexual Diversity in Asylum Policy and Practice in the United Kingdom* (PhD Thesis, City University of London, 2021).

8. Libby Adler, 'Life at the Corner of Poverty and Sexual Abjection: Lewdness, Indecency, and LGBTQ Youth,' in *Research Handbook on Gender, Sexuality and the Law,* ed. Chris Ashford and Alexander Maine (London: Edward Elgar, 2020).

9. Jenni Millbank, 'From Discretion to Disbelief: Recent Trends in Refugee Determinations on the Basis of Sexual Orientation in Australia and the United Kingdom,' *International Journal of Human Rights* 13:2–3 (2009), 391–414.

10. Lisa Duggan, 'The New Homonormativity: The Sexual Politics of Neoliberalism,' in *Materializing Democracy: Towards a Revitalized Cultural Politic,* ed. Russ Castronovo and Dana Nelson (New York: Duke University Press, 2002).

11. Jasbir Puar, 'Mapping US Homonormativities,' *Gender, Place and Culture* 13:1 (2006), 67–88; Jasbir Puar, *Terrorist Assemblages: Homonationalism in Queer Times* (New York: Duke University Press, 2012).

12. See, for discussion, Alex Powell, '"Sexuality" Through the Kaleidoscope.'

13. Gayatri Spivak, 'Criticism, Feminism and the Institution,' *Thesis Eleven*, 10-11(1) (1985), 175.

14. Spivak, 'Criticism, Feminism and the Institution,' 175–187.

15. Alex Sharpe, 'Queering Judgment: The Case of Gender Identity Fraud,' *The Journal of Criminal Law* 81 (2017), 417.

16. Sharpe, 'Queering Judgment,' 420–425.

and the Feminist Judgments Project.[17] These concerns were also discussed in further depth in the introduction to this volume. However, one area of distinction between this particular judgment and those projects is that my aim is not 'to demonstrate that, at the time a case was decided, it could, and should, have been decided differently.'[18] On the contrary, I agree with the final decision reached in *HJ (Iran) & HT (Cameroon)*. However, I want to challenge the particular epistemology of sexual diversity promoted within the case. That is to say that I wish to 'challenge the majority's story [on sexuality] and weaken its hold on our collective imagination.'[19] This is consistent with what Sharpe, herself drawing on the work of Valdes,[20] identifies as the core principles of queer legal theory, namely 'challenging dominant and binary understandings of the categories of sex, gender and sexuality, deconstructing ideas of normalcy and deviance, [and] defending desire.'[21] As such, while the judgment reached in *HJ (Iran) & HT (Cameroon)* is agreeable to me, the forms of truth cemented regarding the form and shape of sexual diversity demand a queer critical challenge.

The Counter and the Anti-Normative

In offering this counter judgment, I wish to make a direct interjection into the debate regarding the ability of queer theory to make and sustain normative claims. As Zanghellini has argued, queer theory is often seen as somewhat aloof and removed.[22] Indeed, at times, queer theory is framed as being anti-normative, a brand of critical theory that, while able to problematize existing schemas and systems of thought, fails to offer any suggestions regarding how things could be different.[23]

Zanghellini has posited that, instead of being viewed as anti-normative, queer theory can be understood as counter-normative.[24] Counter-normativity involves the deployment of queer theory's insights, attention to the socially disavowed, and awareness of power-relations, to put forward reform proposals that serve fundamentally humanistic aims.[25] In this sense, Zanghellini is proposing an approach through which queer theory can instead serve as a platform to critically evaluate, reassess, and reformulate our commitments to allow difference to be more genuinely valued within our societies.

Deployed in the manner proposed by Zanghellini, queer theory can offer practical solutions to social problems. It is in this sense that the judgment here is offered,

---

17. Rosemary Hunter, Clare McGlynn and Erika Rackley, eds., *Feminist Judgments: From Theory to Practice* (London: Hart Publishing, 2010).

18. Sharpe, 'Queering Judgment,' 417.

19. Erika Rackley, 'An Account of Feminist Judging,' in *Feminist Judgments: From Theory to Practice*, ed. Rosemary Hunter, Claire McGlynn and Erika Rackley (London: Hart Publishing, 2010), 33.

20. Francisco Valdes, 'Afterward and Prologue: Queer Legal Theory,' *Cardozo Law Review* 83 (1995), 344.

21. Sharpe, 'Queering Judgment,' 421.

22. Aleardo Zanghellini, 'Antihumanism in Queer Theory,' *Sexualities* 34 (2020), 530, 540.

23. See, for example, Martha Nussbaum, 'The Professor of Parody: The Hip Defeatism of Judith Butler,' The New Republic, 22 February 1999, accessed 20 December 2022, https://newrepublic.com/article/150687/professor-parody.

24. Aleardo Zanghellini, 'Queer, Antinormativity, Counter-Normativity and Abjection,' *Griffith Law Review* 18 (2009), 1.

25. Zanghellini, 'Queer, Antinormativity, Counter-Normativity and Abjection,' 4.

with a view to addressing the overreliance on identity politics within the asylum claims of people of diverse sexualities and promoting a more constructivist and relativist conception of sexual diversity.

As such, a part of the purpose of this counter-judgment lies in attempting to prove the clear, articulable, and fundamentally pragmatic implications that can flow from queer theory. This, alongside other judgments in this volume, speaks to the value of queer theory as a critical tool with which both lawyers and judges should be encouraged to engage.

The Original Judgment

HJ (Iran) and HT (Cameroon) is a set of combined appeals heard in the Supreme Court by a panel consisting of Lord Hope, Lord Rodger, Lord Walker, Lord Collins, and Sir John Dyson. The appeal concerned the issue of whether the 'reasonable tolerability' test, on the question of whether a claimant could be required to 'be discreet' regarding their sexual diversity in order to avoid persecution in their country of origin, was compatible with the Refugee Convention. Under the test as set down by the Court of Appeal in *J*, the question a decision maker should ask is whether discretion within the country of origin was a condition which the claimant could reasonably be expected to tolerate.[26] However, the Supreme Court in *HJ (Iran) and HT (Cameroon)* held that requiring discretion was incompatible with the Refugee Convention.

In the immediate case, both appellants were gay men who claimed a fear of persecution on the basis of sexual orientation, behaviour, or identity. HJ was, at the time of the Supreme Court decision, a 40-year-old Iranian man who had claimed asylum on his arrival in the UK in December 2001. HT was a 36-year-old Cameroonian man who had claimed asylum in January 2007, after being arrested at Gatwick airport for using a false passport. In the original judgment, both are described as 'practicing homosexuals,' which is presumably a sanitised way of saying both actively pursued sexual, social, and romantic relationships with other men [4].

In 2009, the case reached the Court of Appeal, with the claimants appealing against the test used to determine whether they had a well-founded fear under Article 1(A)2 of the Refugee Convention 1951. Their appeals were dismissed.[27] All parties to the hearing agreed that 'homosexuals' could constitute a particular social group for the purposes of the Convention. However, the issue in the case was whether a claimant should be expected to tolerate needing to be discreet in order to avoid persecution [6]. The Secretary of State argued that the question was always whether or not discretion upon return to the country of origin was something the claimant could reasonably be expected to tolerate. However, the appellants contended that such a proposition was not compatible with the UK's obligations under the Refugee Convention.

---

26. *J v Secretary of State for the Home Department* [2007] Imm AR 73.
27. [2009] EWCA Civ 172.

Queering *HJ and HT*

One of the fundamental issues when offering a queer judgment is an attempt to show that the decision—or logics employed therein—could have been different within the existing framework of the law. As such, my focus here is on putting forward a judgment consistent with the law as it was in 2010 which shows how the judges could have reached their decision without resorting to the essentialised forms of identity politics deployed within the judgment. As such, note should be taken that subsequent matters such as the Nationality and Borders Act 2022 or the Illegal Migration Act 2023 are not considered in this decision. Given the above focus, I reach conclusions that are highly similar to those reached in the original judgment. Namely, I agree that the test employed prior to the case reaching the Supreme Court was incompatible with the Refugee Convention. However, I depart from the original judgment in regard to the conceptions of sexual and gender diversity that inform my reasoning. In particular, I employ more relativist conceptions of sexual diversity—conceptions that are less moored to identity politics. As a result of this, my judgment also demonstrates a departure from the test which the Supreme Court established for decision makers reaching determinations regarding membership of a particular social group. I instead advance a test which devotes critical attention to the inter-relations between the construction of the particular social group and the way in which claimants demonstrate membership of that group.

A few key areas of difference are to be stressed. Firstly, the substantive decision rests entirely on law and scholarship prior to the 2010 decision. However, I utilise the terminology of 'sexual diversity' as outlined in my 2021 paper.[28] This terminology 'capture[s] anyone who engages in sexual activity with, is attracted to, or who identifies with, a culture founded around a non-normative sexual practice or partner.'[29] The point here is that something in regard to the sexual lives of the persons in question marks them out as different to the surrounding society, or as otherwise non-normative. In setting out this, I note that Dustin and Ferreira have been critical of this deployment of 'diverse' in the sense that it can be seen to reify the perceived distinction between heterosexuality and non-heterosexuality.[30] However, my use of the phrase is not intended to explicitly exclude those who are heterosexual, but rather to move us away from a focus on identities and instead to focus on the characteristics which lead people to be the targets of persecution. As such, I argue this conceptual shift moves us towards a more relativist and less fixed conception of sexual difference. In stating this, I note that alternative terminologies such as 'sexual orientation and gender identity and expression' (SOGIE) have also become increasingly utilised within refugee and migration literature.[31] More broadly, terms such as queer can be used to signify

---

28. Powell, '"Sexuality" Through the Kaleidoscope.'
29. Powell, *Queering Refugee Law*.
30. Moira Dustin and Nuno Ferreira, 'Canada's Guideline 9: Improving SOGIE claims assessment?' *Forced Migration Review* 56 (2017), 80.
31. See, for example, Nick J Mulé, 'Safe Haven Questioned: Proof of Identity Over Persecution of SOGIE Asylum Seekers and Refugee Claimants in Canada,' *Journal of Immigrant and Refugee Studies* 18 (2020),

the same characteristics without carrying implications of identity. However, I argue that a focus on sexual diversities provides the conceptual space to consider claimants' own frameworks for understanding their sexual lives without the conceptual baggage carried by ideas such as identity and orientation and without the theoretical baggage carried by queer theory. Secondly, the test I present requires decision makers to formulate a wider particular social group along the lines of sexually diverse people; this is to avoid the simplistic resort to identity as the framework through which sexual diversity is understood.

207; Nuno Ferreira, 'Utterly Unbelievable: The Discourse of Fake SOGI Asylum Claims as a form of Epistemic Injustice,' *International Journal of Refugee Law* 34 (2022), 303.

JUDGMENT

HJ (Iran) (FC) (Appellant) *v* Secretary of State for the Home
Department (Respondent) and one other action

HT (Cameroon) (FC) (Appellant) *v* Secretary of State for the
Home Department (Respondent) and one other action.

Alex Powell SCJ

Judgment Given on
7th July 2010
Heard on 10, 11 and 12 May 2010

[1] These appeals raise the question of which test should be applied when considering whether a sexually diverse person, or person who will be perceived as sexually diverse, who is claiming asylum under the Convention Relating to the Status of Refugees 1951, and its 1967 protocol, has a well-founded fear of persecution on the basis of that sexual diversity.

[2] Neither sexual orientation, nor sexual identity, was considered a ground for asylum by the High Contracting Parties at the time when the Convention was being drafted. However, precedent from *Islam v Secretary of State for the Home Department; R v Immigration Appeal Tribunal, Ex p Shah [1999] 2 AC 629* onwards has firmly established that people with diversities of gender and sexuality can be recognised as members of particular social groups for the purposes of the Convention and its protocol.

[3] Moreover, social divides have emerged with some recognizing sexual diversity as a part of the fabric of human existence deserving of social and legal protections and others either denying the existence of people who are sexually diverse or engaging in persecutory responses to their existence. Two such examples are relevant in the immediate case. Firstly, there is HJ, who is 40 years old and Iranian. He claimed asylum on his arrival in the United Kingdom in December 2001. In Iran, Article 233 of the Islamic Penal Code sets out that in a consensual relation the active (penetrating partner) shall receive 100 lashes while the passive partner shall be sentenced to death. HT, who is 36 years old, is from Cameroon. In Cameroon, Article 347 of the Penal Code provides for up to 5 years imprisonment for sexual relations with people of the same sex. Social discrimination is also rife in the country. HT arrived in the UK in January 2007.

[4] The remainder of the relevant facts, as well as the procedural history of the cases, can be found in the judgment of my learned friend, Lord Hope.

[5] In this Court, the Secretary of State submitted that the test of whether the appellants should be granted refugee status was correctly set out by the Court of Appeal in *J v Secretary of State for the Home Department* [2007] Imm AR 73. Namely, that the relevant test was whether or not discretion on return to the country of origin would be reasonably tolerable to the claimant. HJ, however, argued that the test as stated in *J v Secretary of State for the Home Department* was misconceived. He submitted that the test was not compatible with the definition of a refugee in Article 1A(2) of the Convention. This was argued on the basis that, in requiring the claimant to suppress their protected ground so as to avoid the potential persecution they may face if it were to become known, the very status to which the Convention protection attaches was denied. HT also contested the test utilised in the *J* case. He submitted that any applicant who was able to show a well-founded fear of persecution was entitled to refugee status and, thus, that a claimant should not be expected to demonstrate that concealment of their protected characteristic was something they could not be reasonably expected to tolerate.

[6] As per Article 1A(2) of the Convention, a refugee is a person who,

> Owing to well-founded fear of being persecuted for reasons of race, religion, nationality, membership of a particular social group or political opinion is outside the country of his nationality and is unable or, owing to such fear, unwilling to avail himself of the protection of that country.

[7] The meaning of Article 1A(2) is largely settled ground. There is no doubt that people who are sexually diverse, such as gay men, can constitute particular social groups. This was established in *Islam v Secretary of State for the Home Department; R v Immigration Appeal Tribunal, Ex p Shah* [1999] 2 AC 629, 643-644. Further, regulation 6(1)(e) of the Refugee or Person in Need of International Protection (Qualification) Regulations 2006 (SI 2006/2525) clearly identifies that sexual orientation can form the basis of a particular social group.

[8] As established by the Supreme Court of Canada in *Ward* [1993] 2 SCR 689, 709, the fundamental requirement for a particular social group to be said to exist is that the members of that group have a characteristic that either cannot be changed, or where changing it would be an affront to the human dignity of the members of the group. This point is further confirmed by the United Nations High Commissioner for Refugees (UNHCR) Guidance note on Refugee Claims Relating to Sexual Orientation (2008). As such, it is easy to see that sexual diversity can constitute a basis for the existence of a particular social group. This is so whether that sexual diversity registers as a form of identity, orientation, or behaviour.

[9] In this regard, note should be taken that the purpose of the Convention, its underlying rationale, is to provide a means for people to live their lives free from the prospect

of suffering serious harm as a result of their race, religion, nationality, membership of a particular social group, or political opinion. It seeks to do this by requiring signatories to provide surrogate protection where the country of origin, or previous habitual residence, from which someone comes is unable or unwilling to do so. As it was put by La Forest J in *Ward*:

> At the outset, it is useful to explore the rationale underlying the international refugee protection regime, for this permeates the interpretation of the various terms requiring examination. International refugee law was formulated to serve as a back-up to the protection one expects from the state of which an individual is national. It was meant to come into play only in situations when that protection is unavailable.

As such, we should start from the premise that signing the Refugee Convention binds states to offer surrogate protection to individuals from states who permit, facilitate, or engage in harm arising to such an intensity that it constitutes persecution. In this regard, at least at a general level, protection is an entitlement regardless of what action a given claimant might themselves be able to take to prevent such harm accruing.

[10] Furthermore, note should be taken that, as identified above, the very foundation of sexual diversity as a matter protected by the Convention is based on the fact that sexual diversity is widely socially recognised as something that distinguishes people from surrounding society. As identified in the (UNHCR) Guidance note on Refugee Claims Relating to Sexual Orientation (2008), this social recognition is adequate to show the existence of a particular social group. Having confirmed this, the only question is whether the claimant would have a well-founded fear on return. To make protection contingent on the behaviour of the claimant would undermine the very human dignity which the Convention sets out to protect.

Well-founded fear: The causal link

[11] In the immediate appeals, the fact that sexual diversity can provide a relevant particular social group for the purposes of the Refugee Convention is not at issue. However, the issue of refugee status does not end with the existence of a relevant particular social group. The Convention requires the claimant to have a "well-founded fear" of persecution for a Convention reason. This was well put by Simon Brown LJ in *Ahmed (Iftikhar) v Secretary of State for the Home Department* [2000] INLR 1, 7–8: 'In all asylum claims there is ultimately a single question to be asked: is there a serious risk that on return the applicant will be persecuted for a Convention reason?'

[12] I would endorse this as the appropriate question. The question makes clear that the pertinent issue is whether or not the claimant faces a well-founded fear of persecution, not whether such a fear will actually arise. Put another way, the fact that a claimant could avoid certain actions and, in so doing, avoid having a well-founded fear of persecution is not a relevant factor in deciding whether or not they are a refugee. This follows the reasoning in the Australian case *S395/2002 v Minister for Immigration and Multicultural Affairs* (2003) 216 CLR 473, where McHugh and Kirkby JJ

said that persecution does not cease to be persecution just because it would be possible for it to be avoided by some action on the part of the defendant.

[13] Before this Court, Mr Bourne has argued that discretion regarding the claimant's sexual diversity could be treated by analogy to the use of internal relocation. This is to say that, as with a claimant who is asked to internally relocate to avoid the threat of persecution, the appropriate question to ask with regard to whether or not a claimant might be asked to be 'discreet' or otherwise to conceal their sexual diversity is whether or not it would be reasonably tolerable for them to do so. This submission raises the core matter before this Court, namely whether the test outlined in paragraph 16 of *J* should be upheld.

[14] With regard to the analogy with internal relocation, I would endorse the views of Lord Hope, namely that the analogy can be dismissed because, in order for it to hold up, the Court would need to presume that the claimant would be both willing and able conceal their sexual diversity from those around them on return. As such, there should be no prospect of internal relocation and concomitant concealment in cases concerning sexual diversity because there is no way in which the claimant could make a new life for themselves without negating the very group membership protected by the Convention.

The Test in the *J* Case

[15] At paragraph 16 of *J*, Maurice K LJ provided a new test for the application of discretion. This test called on the decision maker to 'ask itself whether "discretion" is something that the appellant can reasonably be expected to tolerate, not only in the context of random sexual activity but in relation to "matters following from, and relevant to, sexual identity".'

[16] This sets up a situation where the question before the decision-maker, with regard to discretion, is effectively whether or not the application of discretion itself constitutes persecution in the terms set out in the Convention. Otherwise put, discretion which is tolerable to the claimant will mean that they do not have a well-founded fear of persecution. However, discretion which is not reasonably tolerable will itself constitute persecution.

[17] The test as it was articulated in *J* expanded on the Australian authority *S395/2002 v Minister of State for Immigration and Multicultural Affairs* (2003) 216 CLR 473. At paragraph 40 of that judgment, McHugh and Kirby JJ said that:

> The purpose of the Convention is to protect the individuals of every country from persecution on the grounds identified in the Convention whenever their governments wish to inflict, or are powerless to prevent, that persecution. Persecution covers many forms of harm ranging from physical harm to many intangibles, from death and torture to state sponsored or condoned discrimination in social life or employment. Whatever form the harm takes, it will constitute

persecution only if, *by reason of its intensity or duration, the person persecuted cannot reasonably be expected to tolerate it*. But persecution does not cease to be persecution for the purpose of the Convention because those persecuted can eliminate the harm by taking avoiding action within the country of nationality. The Convention would give no protection from persecution for reasons of religion or political opinion if it was condition of protection that the person affected must take steps—reasonably or otherwise—to avoid offending the wishes of the persecutors. Nor would it give protection to membership of many a "particular social group" if it were a condition of protection that its members hide their membership or modify some attribute or characteristic of the group to avoid persecution. (emphasis added)

The sentence regarding intensity, duration and reasonable toleration has, by the Court of Appeal in *J*, been interpreted as the core principle arising from the *S395/2002* decision. In giving his own judgment, Maurice J, identified that this standard had been adopted in *Z v Secretary of State for the Home Department* [2005] Imm AR 75, *Amare v Secretary of State for the Home Department* [2006] Imm Ar 217, and *RG (Colombia) v Secretary of State for the Home Department* [2006] EWCA Civ 57.

[18] However, as the above quote makes clear, paragraph 40 presents a relatively dense statement that contains complications which have led the Court of Appeal in *J* to err in their interpretation. Specifically, the judgment seems to miss the point that persecution does not cease to be persecution because there were actions that the claimant might take to avoid the risk of persecution. This is made even clearer in paragraph 50 of *S395/2002*, where McHugh and Kirby JJ stated that:

In so far as decisions in the Tribunal and Federal Court contain statements that asylum seekers are required, or can be expected, to take reasonable steps to avoid persecutory harm, they are wrong in principle and should not be followed.

[19] As such, the Court of Appeal's reliance on some sections of *S395/2002* does not sit at all comfortably with the overall thrust of the decision. Rather, the principle which the Court of Appeal should have taken was that a decision-maker cannot require a claimant to behave in any particular way. To require a claimant to behave in a given way in order to avoid having a well-founded fear of persecution is an unprincipled denial of the very protection which the Refugee Convention is intended to provide. As this was the test applied by the Court of Appeal, the decision of the Court of Appeal to dismiss these appeals was an error of law and must be set aside.

The test to be applied

[20] Having established that the test applied in the Court of Appeal was not correct, I now turn to considerations of what test is to be applied when a decision-maker is faced with having to determine whether or not a claimant is eligible for protection on a ground relating to their sexual diversity. In identifying this test, there are a range of relevant authorities from comparative jurisdictions. These are well explored by Lord Hope

at paragraphs [30 to 34][32] of his judgment[33] and I do not think anything needs be added to his interpretation at this time.

[21] In setting out this test, I depart from my fellow Judges Lord Rodger and Lord Hope, who set out their own tests at paragraphs [82] and [35][34] respectively. I do, however, concur with Lord Walker who points out at paragraph [98][35] that a decision-maker seeking to adjudicate an asylum claim relating to sexually diverse people is tasked with rendering an individual and fact-specific inquiry.

[22] While the jurisprudence regarding the possibility of people who are sexually diverse constituting a particular social group for the purposes of the Convention is settled, as addressed above at paragraphs 7 and 8, it is important to briefly revisit this. This is because the formulation of the particular social group inherently impacts both who can be a member of that group and how membership of that group might be determined. For example, the initial decision in this case recognised 'practicing homosexuals' as a particular social group. To determine if a given claimant is a member of a group such as 'practicing homosexuals' involves a far more conduct-driven group construction—and therefore analysis from decision makers—than a more identity-centred group such as gay men or lesbians. For this reason, it is necessary to carefully consider the exact group that is being claimed. In this regard, I take note of the extensive academic literature detailing the cultural specificity of sexually diverse identities. For example, Ratna Kapur, in her Book 'Erotic Justice: Law and the New Politics of Postcolonialism (Glass House Press 2005), pinpoints the problems that arise in attempts to universalize the approach to LGBTIQA+ rights adopted in the US or UK. As such, decision-makers should be mindful that while the Convention certainly does offer protection to sexually diverse people, this protection is not contingent on them presenting in a particular manner that corresponds to the ways in which sexual diversities and conceptualised in the UK.

[23] Given the above, I would construct the particular social group for both of the claimants in the immediate case as being 'sexually diverse people.' This is to say that the group is defined by social and sexual behaviour that marks them out as being different from surrounding society. In their Guidelines on International Protection No 3, the UNHCR identifies that a social group can be found to exist on the basis of one of two tests, namely, the 'protected characteristics' test or the 'social perception test.' Put another way, a particular social group can be found to exist either because they have a characteristic that is either innate or fundamental to human dignity or because there is a social perception that such a group exists.

---

32. Original Judgment.
33. For the purposes of clarity, references to the original judgment have been placed into square brackets.
34. Both Original Judgment.
35. Original Judgment.

[24] Generally speaking, sexuality claims are construed as falling under the first of these tests for a particular social group. This is to say that an identity such as gay is envisaged as being an innate or unchangeable characteristic, or as fundamental to human dignity. If one focuses on the 'innate or unchangeable characteristic' element, the result is that the particular social group is formed around elements of an identity that is assumed to be fixed. Here, I take note of scholarship establishing the difficult evidential burden that results for claimants from this fixed construction of a particular social group. However, it is noted that a particular social group does not require an innate protected characteristic at all. As the UNHCR clearly identifies, a particular social group can be founded either on such a characteristic *or* on the basis of a social perception that such a group exists. As such, given the extensive scholarship which calls into question the 'innateness' or 'unchangeability' of sexual diversity, a decision-maker can, and should, instead focus on the question of whether such a group is socially perceived as existing.

[25] This idea of social perception does not require widespread visibility or a framework of identity. Indeed, the social perception of a group could be show by the insertion of insidious or restrictive norms around a particular form of conduct. These norms are themselves a form of evidence that there is a social perception that breaching them marks one out as different. The key here is that social perception relates to particular activities, identities, or orientations that may, if they were to become know, mark one as somehow other when compared to the society around them.

[26] When the particular social group is founded on social perception, there is scope, for example, for such a group to be formed around a culturally specific behaviour. Further, there is scope for the group to be formed around a form of sexual difference that is not the same as the ones we may see every day. Rather, a group constructed around the sexual diversity of its members can be viewed as a group whose members, or perceived members, are viewed as different by the society around them. This view of them as different does not relate to what they do, who they spend time with, or the places they go. Instead, it may be a wholly passive association drawn from the perception of non-compliance with the sexual and social scripts of the society around them.

[27] In accordance with the above, decision-makers should be aware that there is no requirement for the claimant to understand their sexual diversity as an identity. They may not even understand their sexual diversity as being something that is significant. This would not stop them from being a potential target for persecution. As Lord Roger articulates at paragraph [79][36] of his own judgment in this matter, the Nazi period shows all too clearly that one's own views of the importance of a given characteristic is of little relevance if a persecutor has decided that they are defined by that characteristic. As such, even where the particular social group is articulated in the same terms as we have in the UK, decision-makers should harbour no expectations that they will be met with identities like those in the UK.

---

36. Original Judgment.

[28] As the above suggests, decision-makers should be careful when formulating particular social groups associated to sexual difference, so that they do not rely on the everyday examples of sexual difference they see in the UK. Instead, they should adopt particular social group formulations which do not overly constrain them when they turn to the issue of determining membership of the group.

[29] Once the appropriate particular social group has been selected, the next stage of the test for decision makers is to confirm that the claimant is a member of that group. Taking notice of the extensive academic literature detailing the complexities and difficulties of demonstrating membership of a particular social group relating to sexual diversity, I wish to impress upon decision-makers that they should be open minded with regard to the kinds of evidence received. This evidence can take a number of forms. While it would never be appropriate for a decision-maker to require or accept sexually explicit evidence, they should also not expect claimants to provide developed emotional accounts nor identifications with discrete identities or social groups. This much has been made clear by the European Court of Justice in their decision in the case of *A, B and C* in joined cases C148/13 to C150/13, where they identified that Council Directive 2005/85/EC prohibits enquiries premised on both sexually explicit evidence and stereotypes.

[30] In applying this identification stage of the test, decision-makers should also be mindful that human sexuality is rarely fixed in nature. This has, once again, been extensively demonstrated across academic scholarship. As such, it would be an unprincipled denial of protection for a decision-maker to seek to rely on the sexual history of a claimant to deny their claim. For example, the fact that a claimant may have been in a heterosexual marriage should not be regarded as determinative. Indeed, decision-makers should maintain an awareness that heterosexual marriage may be a natural course of action for any person seeking to avoid persecution linked to their sexual diversity. Given that refugee countries of origin may be more socially conservative than the UK, it is particularly incumbent upon decision-makers to avoid overly simplistic reasoning such as any suggestion that previous relationships show that a currently claimed status is not credible. Indeed, decision-makers should also be aware that, given sexual diversity is not fixed over a lifetime, it may simply be the case that a claimant's sexual and social identities, orientations and behaviours have not remained fixed across their life. As such, decision-makers should approach the issue of identifying group membership in a nuanced way. The exact vicissitudes of how this is to be done are doubtlessly a proper matter for Home Office policy. However, given the present dangers of elements of claimants' narratives being misinterpreted by decision-makers, significant scrutiny should be applied to group categorisation and how the claimant's membership thereof is evidenced.

[31] When addressing the issue of whether or not a given claimant is a member of the particular social group, decision-makers should also give appropriate weighting to self-identification as, for example, a lesbian or gay man. In the absence of reasons

to doubt the credibility of the claimant, self-identification should be taken as strong evidence that the person fits within the category with which they have identified themselves. In this regard, and as addressed further below, decision-makers should be mindful that where a claimant has self-identified with a particular group, there is a greater likelihood that—even if the decision-maker is not fully satisfied as to the validity of their self-identification—the claimant will be imputed to be a sexually diverse person by those within their country of origin.

[32] Finally, decision-makers should also be aware that it is not just group membership, but also imputed group membership that can satisfy the Convention ground. As such, if a claimant is able to show that they are at risk of persecution because they are suspected of being sexually diverse, including (but not exclusively) by showing a past history of such suspicions, then this would be sufficient to dispense with the identification stage of the test.

[33] Turning to the risk of persecution, it is important here to note that decision-makers are required to look to the situation within the country of origin with regard to the specific particular social group they have identified the claimant as being part of. As such, decision-makers should avoid any expectation that sexual diversity will either have manifested, or been suppressed, in ways similar to the UK. The pertinent issue is whether the claimant would be at risk of persecution due to their sexual diversity upon return. In answering this question, the decision-maker need not consider whether the claimant could keep aspects of their sexual diversity secret to avoid persecution. The protection of the Convention is from a fear of persecution for a Convention ground and that protection would be fatally undermined if it were subject to substitution for the claimant's capacity to hide their difference from surrounding society. In some cases, such as the situations in Iran and Cameroon, this may be easy to detect through the existence of enforced laws against certain behaviours. However, decision-makers should be aware that it is not necessary for criminal norms affecting sexually diverse people to exist and that an absence of information regarding the forms of sexual diversity within a refugee country of origin may well itself suggest the existence of persecution. This is because silence may be a strong indicator of intolerance towards sexual diversity. This is obvious from the history of the UK, where 'lesbianism' was never criminalised. Yet, this cannot be seen as a tolerant approach, but rather as part of a particular framing of women's sexuality that itself led to numerous forms of ill-treatment that we would now rightly regard as persecutory. Simply put, a sentence to non-existence can itself be said to be indicative of persecution.

[34] This second stage of the inquiry is necessarily future oriented. The question is whether the environment within the claimant's country of origin is one that could be regarded as persecutory at the point at which they are returned. If the answer is yes, then the core elements of refugee status have been found. In determining this, it is right that decision-makers should have reference to the Home Office Country Policy and Information Notes. However, as addressed above, when reviewing evidence of this kind,

note should be taken that an absence of mention of sexual diversity may well suggest a persecutory environment.

[35] Given that Home Office Country Policy and Information Notes frequently do not provide information on the treatment of sexual and gender diverse people, it is important to add that the determination of how sexually diverse people are treated should be undertaken on the basis of suitable evidence. This includes taking strong note of the fact that the experiences of tourists or visitors with a different cultural background and greater degrees of socio-economic capital and protection relative to the broader population in refugee countries of origin cannot be taken as representative. It is entirely possible that a country would be a safe place for those from the UK to visit and yet permit persecution to those who call that country home. As such, no weight should be placed on tourism sites or other forms of evidence that do not focus on the situation for permanent residents. Where suitable evidence does not exist, decision-makers should have reference to country experts. Decision-makers should also ensure that, where there are no reasons to doubt the personal credibility of the claimant, appropriate consideration is given to the principle of the benefit of the doubt.

[36] In looking at the future, it is important that decision-makers recognise that behaviour is often highly situational. Irrespective of the decision-makers' views on the claimant's future conduct, they should be clear that it is incompatible with the Refugee Convention to require the claimant to conceal their sexual, social, romantic, or identity-based positionality with regard to sexual diversity in any way. The enquiry must be squarely and exclusively focused on the situation facing sexually diverse people within the claimant's country of origin. When making this enquiry, decision-makers should also be mindful that claimants who are socialised in different contexts may not behave in an entirely predictable manner. As such, determinations regarding how the claimant might behave should be based on solid evidential foundations. Just as it would be contrary to the Refugee Convention to require the claimant to behave in a discreet manner, it would also be contrary to the Refugee Convention to deny international protection simply because the claimant would act discreetly because their behaviour is socially unacceptable in their country of origin.

[37] I have partly set out this test at such length as a response to issues in other jurisdictions, where moves away from discretion have concomitantly led to increased doubt being cast on whether a claimant is a sexually diverse person. Specifically, in other jurisdictions such as Australia, scholarship has noted that there has been a shift from discretion to disbelief, whereby claims are denied on the basis that the claimant is not a sexually diverse person (see Jenni Millbank, 'From Discretion to Disbelief: Recent Trends in Refugee Determinations on the Basis of Sexual Orientation in Australia and the United Kingdom,' *International Journal of Human Rights* 13:2–3 (2009), 391–414). In particular, I have sought to stress the importance that decision-makers do not mistake the social and cultural associations that often attach to LGBTIQA+ identities in the UK as an innate property that will be expressed by all people

who are sexually diverse. Otherwise put, the issue with the decision of the Court of Appeal in the immediate case is that, amongst other things, it conceives of sexual diversity in physical terms relating to participation in a sexual act and little more, and thus ignores the range of demands which being 'discreet' places upon an asylum claimant. However, this should not mean that decision-makers must adjudicate cases against a wider conception of identity such as that seen in the UK. While such identity is the most common way for sexual diversity to present in the UK—at least in a public facing manner—this is a result of a particular history. Decision-makers should not expect all claimants, who will have very different experiences, to understand or express their own experiences in similar terms.

[38] The embrace of a wider form of identity-based reasoning may, if done uncritically, lead to more cases being refused on the basis that the claimant has not been able to provide sufficient evidence that they are, or would be perceived as, sexually diverse in accordance with the particular social group outlined. It is for this reason that I have sought to be so clear and direct in warning decision-makers of the level of caution which should be exercised when formulating their own particular social groups.

The matters at hand

[39] At their core, both of these cases concern discretion reasoning. Specifically, they concern a conception of the law which saw claimants being denied because, for reasons entirely related to their fear of persecution, they would act in way that meant that potential persecutors would most likely not be aware of their sexual diversity. For the reasons addressed above, this conception of the law is to be rejected. Instead, the tests set out in this judgment should be applied.

[40] For the reasons given, I set aside the decisions of the Court of Appeal in both matters. These judgments were an error of law and the test set out by the Court of Appeal should not be used moving forward. Instead, the test which I have set out at paragraphs 20-35 should be used. Accordingly, this matter is remitted to the Tribunal for a reconsideration under the test set out here.

26

X, Y *and* Z (European Union):

Who is Protected as Queer Refugee by the Court of Justice of the European Union?

Carmelo Danisi (Commentary) and Nuno Ferreira (Re-written decision)

Introduction

The decision of the Court of Justice of the European Union (CJEU) in the joined cases of *X, Y and Z v Minister voor Immigratie en Asiel*,[1] in 2013, marked a turning point in EU asylum law concerning sexual minorities.[2] It clarified the (minimum) standard of protection which sexual minorities are entitled to under the Common European Asylum System (CEAS),[3] especially in relation to the key terms of the definition of refugee, and has become the point of reference for subsequent CJEU decisions concerning other substantive and procedural aspects of asylum claims based on sexual orientation.[4] It originated from three separate Dutch proceedings involving men fleeing, respectively, Sierra Leone (X), Uganda (Y) and Senegal (Z), and concerned their asylum claims submitted on the grounds of a fear of persecution for membership of a sexual minority. Before reaching its decision on these cases, the Council of State of the Netherlands (Raad van State) deemed it appropriate to submit a preliminary reference request to the CJEU to clarify how the Qualification Directive (QD) should

---

1. Joined Cases C-199/12, C-200/12 and C-201/12, 7 November 2013, ECLI:EU:C:2013:720. The number of commentaries dedicated to this judgment confirm its significance: e.g. Maarten Den Heijer, 'Persecution for Reason of Sexual Orientation: X, Y and Z,' *Common Market Law Review* (2014), 1217–1234. The commentary has been written thanks also to the support of the GenDJus project, which is funded by the NextGenerationEU through the Call PRIN 2022 PNRR DD No. 1409 of 14 September 2022, project proposal code P2022FNH9B – CUP J53D23017230001.
2. The expression 'sexual minorities' is used here in an encompassing way, as to include anyone who does not identify as heterosexual.
3. Nuno Ferreira, 'Reforming the Common European Asylum System: Enough Rainbow for Queer Asylum Seekers?' *GenIUS* 2 (2018), 25–42.
4. Joined Cases C-148/13 to C-150/13, *A, B and C v Staatssecretaris van Veiligheid en Justitie*, 2 December 2014, ECLI:EU:C:2014:2406; Case C-473/16, *F. v Bevándorlási és Állampolgársági Hivatal*, 25 January 2018, ECLI:EU:C:2018:36; Case C-18/20, *XY v Bundesamt für Fremdenwesen und Asyl*, 9 September 2021, ECLI:EU:C:2021:710.

be applied when sexual orientation is the reason for seeking international protection in an EU Member State.[5]

In laying the groundwork for a queer rewriting of the judgment, this commentary identifies the good, the bad and the ugly aspects of the CJEU's decision when analysed through the prism of international refugee and human rights law protecting the rights of queer people.[6] Indeed, EU asylum law is deeply informed by a combination of these legal frameworks: while the Geneva Convention on the Status of Refugees[7] is the cornerstone on which the CEAS is based, human rights standards as established by the EU Charter of Fundamental Rights (EU Charter)[8] and the European Convention on Human Rights (ECHR)[9] should be always applied when EU law is at stake.[10]

The X, Y and Z judgment provides a clear example of the Court's competence to interpret EU law to make sure that it is applied consistently across the entire Union. The CJEU is not entitled to recognize or reject refugee status or other forms of international protection in relation to non-EU nationals; it can, however, be called upon by courts of EU Member States to decide how the legislative acts forming the CEAS should be interpreted and applied across the EU. In the exercise of this competence, the CJEU's rulings are based on the questions formulated by national judges and, despite the option being available, the CJEU does not usually expand on its answers to offer broader (queer) considerations than those strictly required to clarify the correct interpretation of the specific EU law issues raised by the referring court. As we will see in the following sections, this is an important facet of the X, Y and Z case. The X, Y and Z judgment concerned the interpretation of the first Qualification Directive (QD), adopted in 2004, which was later replaced by the 2011 version, which also sought to embed in EU legislation the principles that had emerged in the CJEU case law on asylum in the meantime.[11]

Given these premises, the following sections discuss the three key points emerging from the X, Y and Z case: discretion reasoning as a basis for rejecting refugee status (section 'The Good'); identification of a Particular Social Group (PSG) as one of the grounds on the basis of which refugee status can be granted (section 'The Bad'); and the role

---

5. Council Directive 2004/83/EC of 29 April 2004 on Minimum Standards for the Qualification and Status of Third Country Nationals or Stateless Persons as Refugees or as Persons who otherwise Need International Protection and the Content of the Protection Granted, OJ L 304, 30.9.2004, p. 12–23. It was replaced by Directive 2011/95/EU of the European Parliament and of the Council of 13 December 2011, OJ L 337, 20.12.2011, p. 9–26. All references to QD in this contribution refer to the 2004 Directive.

6. 'Queer' is here understood as relating to anyone whose sexual orientation, gender identity or expression, or sex characteristics are non-normative in the broader social context.

7. UN General Assembly, Convention Relating to the Status of Refugees, 31 July 1951, UNTS vol. 189, p. 137, as complemented by the Protocol adopted on 31 January 1967, UNTS vol. 606, p. 267.

8. European Union, *Charter of Fundamental Rights of the European Union*, OJ C 326, 26.10.2012, p. 391–407.

9. Council of Europe, *European Convention for the Protection of Human Rights and Fundamental Rights*, 4 November 1950.

10. In accordance with Article 51 of the EU Charter and Article 6(3) of the Treaty on European Union (TEU). This obligation was also preliminarily acknowledged by the CJEU in X, Y and Z, paras. 39–40.

11. It also added gender identity as a relevant factor for the purposes of determining a Particular Social Group (PSG): see the recast version of Article 10(1)(d). For an overview of the QD and the CEAS, see Daniel Thym, *European Migration Law* (Oxford: OUP, 2023).

of criminalisation in the context of the notion of persecution (section 'The Ugly'). Drawing on this analysis, the re-written judgment that follows advances queerly framed solutions to these points.

Testing *X, Y and Z* as a Queer Judgment

When the Dutch Council of State requested a preliminary ruling on the correct interpretation of the QD, it formulated three main questions in a precise order: first, whether people 'with a homosexual orientation' form a PSG (para. 37); second, if such people can be expected to conceal their orientation to avoid persecution in their country of origin; and, third, whether the 'criminalisation of homosexual activities' (sic) amounts to an act of persecution. For the reasons that are discussed below, the CJEU decided to provide its answers in a different order. After confirming that sexual minorities did form a PSG in the countries of origin of the applicants in the domestic proceedings, the CJEU anticipated its answer on the issue of criminalisation before rejecting any sort of discretion reasoning under EU law. Given the significance of the rationale followed by the CJEU in its last answer, which is fully in line with the human rights-based approach to refugee law adopted in this commentary, we start our analysis of the judgment in *X, Y and Z* by looking at this very last point. After setting out the 'good' of the CJEU decision, we move on to an examination of the 'bad' aspect of the judgment, which deals with the notion of PSG, and finally we look at what appears to be the 'ugly' part of the *X, Y and Z* case: the rejection of criminalisation *per se* as persecution.

The Good: Castigating the Inhumanity of Discretion Reasoning

In what emerged as the most significant achievement of the *X, Y and Z* case for sexual minorities fleeing persecution, the CJEU highlighted that sexual orientation is a characteristic 'so fundamental to a person's identity that the persons concerned cannot be required to renounce it,' even in the form of concealment to escape persecution in their country of origin (paras. 62–63). It would be therefore unreasonable to expect sexual minorities to exercise any sort of restraint in expressing themselves.[12] Second, in answering the question on the possible distinction between 'core' and marginal areas of one's sexual orientation, the CJEU rejected the existence of 'non-core' aspects of sexual minorities' lives that may be deserving of less or no protection under EU asylum law. In doing so, the Court referred to the QD itself, where, when stating that a PSG can be formed by people having the same sexual orientation as the shared characteristic (Article 10(1)(d)), no limits are set out on how such people should live their identity or how they should behave both in private and public spaces. This understanding echoed the previous *Y and Z* case,[13] which concerned asylum claims submitted by religious minorities. According to the CJEU's findings in *Y and Z*, no distinction can be made

---

12. Janna Wessels, *The Concealment Controversy: Sexual Orientation, Discretion Reasoning and the Scope of Refugee Protection* (Cambridge: CUP, 2021).

13. Joined Cases C-71/11 and C-99/11, *Bundesrepublik Deutschland v Y and Z*, 5 September 2012, ECLI:EU:C:2012:518.

between expressing one's faith in public or in private for the purpose of granting refugee status, with the clear consequence of rejecting any expectation of concealment or restraint in the expression of one's religion or belief as a valid reason for denying international protection.

This interpretation of the QD on the concealment issue is in line with the UNHCR's reading of international refugee law enshrined in its 2012 SOGI Guidelines No. 9, despite the fact that these received no mention by the CJEU in *X, Y and Z*. In dealing with the persistence of the discretion reasoning in the evaluation of sexual minorities' asylum claims, these Guidelines state that the only question to be evaluated by decision makers is how a member of a sexual minority group would be treated if returned to their country of origin and if this amounts to persecution.[14] Moreover, the Guidelines highlight that being discreet does not guarantee avoiding persecution, as circumstances may change over time. Not only can a person's sexual orientation be discovered irrespective of their conduct, but also, and perhaps most importantly, it only needs to be imputed to them, for example for not complying with social traditional gender roles and expectations. Although the CJEU did not go that far in its conclusion, it certainly did not entertain possible reasons why a person claiming asylum should be discreet in their home country, as the re-written judgment specifies in stronger terms.

In any case, the broad understanding of sexual orientation and the findings on discretion are also compliant with consolidated human rights standards, at least from two different standpoints. First, they ensure that each person's dignity, inherently embedded in one's identity without distinction of any kind, is equally worth of protection as provided for by Article 1 of the EU Charter. Second, owing to the lack of a distinction between core and non-core areas of sexual orientation identity and behaviour, the Court avoided any inappropriate distinction within human rights when these are applied to sexual minorities. The 'good' of the *X, Y and Z* judgment indeed had the potential to prevent the emergence of a hierarchy of harms in the mistaken belief that sexual orientation is only attached to specific human rights and not to their whole spectrum. Yet, as we note below, such a risk was not entirely avoided owing to the contradictory interpretation of the QD that emerged in other parts of the judgment.

The Bad: A Cumulative Approach to Tests for Defining a PSG

Being based on the definition of refugee included in the Geneva Convention, Article 2(c) of the QD lists five grounds on the basis of which the fear of persecution of people seeking asylum should be well-founded: race, religion, nationality, political opinion or membership of a PSG. It is well-known that, although other grounds like religion or political opinion can be relevant for sexual minorities' asylum claims, membership of a PSG remains 'the' basis for most of these requests. Yet, unlike the Geneva Convention, where a definition of PSG is absent, the QD offers some indications

---

14. UNHCR, *Guidelines on International Protection No. 9: Claims to Refugee Status Based on Sexual Orientation and /or Gender Identity within the Context of Article 1A(2) of the 1951 Convention and/or its 1967 Protocol Relating to the Status of Refugees*, UNHCR (2012), para. 32 (hereinafter 'UNHCR SOGI Guidelines No. 9').

to identify a PSG for the purposes of granting refugee status. According to Article 10(1)(d), a group can be qualified as a PSG when 'in particular' two conditions are satisfied: the group shares a protected characteristic, be it innate, unchangeable or fundamental to one's identity (commonly known as the fundamental characteristic test), 'and' is perceived as having a distinct identity by the home country's society (commonly known as the social recognition test). Already at the time of the adoption of the QD, the UNHCR recommended that Member States adopt an alternative, rather than a cumulative, approach to these two different tests for finding a PSG.[15] In its authoritative guidance, the UNHCR has always supported such an alternative approach to these tests,[16] and the EU legislator could have followed this interpretation more clearly. Yet, the same QD's provision also specifies that, 'depending on the circumstances in the country of origin,' a PSG might include a group sharing a common sexual orientation (see Article 10(1)(d), second subparagraph).

In the *X, Y and Z* case, despite such a clear reference to sexual orientation, the CJEU replied to the question on whether 'foreign nationals with a homosexual orientation' form a PSG by adopting an overall literal and restrictive approach to the interpretation of the QD. Instead of simply using the QD's reference to PSGs based on sexual orientation, thus avoiding any rigid stance on the debate on the cumulative v alternative approach to the PSG tests, the CJEU decided to verify itself whether 'homosexuals' could qualify as a PSG. In doing so, the Court opted for applying the tests cumulatively, given that these are linked in the QD through the conjunction 'and' (paras. 45–48). This is so even though the tests are introduced with the expression 'in particular' (see above), which allowed for a more flexible interpretation of this provision, including each test sufficing for a finding of a PSG. Despite the final positive conclusion reached in this case by the CJEU, its approach required two separate tests: first, it was necessary to qualify sexual orientation as a protected fundamental characteristic ('fundamental characteristic test'), *and*, secondly, to verify the existence of a separate group formed by 'homosexuals' in the countries of origin of X, Y and Z ('social recognition test'). While the first test was unproblematic to be met and the CJEU's finding had positive implications for the interpretation of other parts of the QD when sexual minorities are involved (see section 'The Good'), the assessment of a distinct social visibility was connected to 'the existence of criminal laws [that] specifically target homosexuals' (para. 49) because of the way the questions had been framed by the national court. It follows that, beyond setting a mandatory cumulative approach to tests (including when sexual orientation is the basis for claiming asylum), the CJEU left the door open to restrictive interpretations of the social visibility test with respect to countries where no criminal laws target sexual minorities.[17]

---

15. UNHCR, *Annotated Comments on the EC Council Directive 2004/83/EC of 29 April 2004* (UNHCR, 2005), 23.

16. UNHCR, *Guidelines on International Protection No. 2: 'Membership of a Particular Social Group' within the Context of Article 1A(2) of the 1951 Convention and/or its 1967 Protocol Relating to the Status of Refugees* (UNHCR, 2002), para. 2.

17. International Commission of Jurists, *Refugee Status Claims based on Sexual Orientation and Gender Identity: A Practitioner's Guide* (ICJ, 2016), 201.

To address this criticism, the re-written judgment below adopts the more flexible interpretation of Article 10(1)(d) that was suggested above, thus showing that the alternative approach to PSG tests recommended in the UNHCR 2012 Guidelines No. 9 is actually supported by the same QD. In doing so, it avoids the reiteration of linear and fixed understandings of personal identities. Indeed, requiring individuals to also demonstrate a distinct identity from the rest of society leads to the risk of exclusion from protection of those members of sexual minorities who do not fall into clearly established categories.[18] Such a lack of understanding of queer realities is even more visible in the way the CJEU assessed the question on criminalisation, to which we finally turn.

The Ugly: Denying Criminalisation per se as a Form of Persecution

Despite the positive elements in the *X, Y and Z* judgment discussed above, the definition of persecution when sexual minorities claim international protection remains problematic under EU asylum law. The question asked by the Dutch Council of State specifically referred to the 'criminalisation of homosexual activities and the threat of imprisonment' (para. 34) and whether these could constitute an act of persecution. It took as its point of reference Article 9(1)(a) of the QD, read in conjunction with Article 9(2)(c). According to the CJEU, the mere criminalisation of homosexual acts does not amount to persecution, unless the criminal sanctions in question are applied in practice. In fact, it is only when criminalisation leads to a punishment that, if such punishment is disproportionate or discriminatory, it may amount to persecution (para. 61). In providing such an answer, the CJEU adopted a very conservative approach, one that reiterates the disputable definition of persecution included in the QD. In fact, the CJEU did not enquire into the appropriateness of the QD definition of persecution in terms of the Geneva Convention. The CJEU took for granted that persecution 'within the meaning of Article 1(A) of the Geneva Convention *must* be sufficiently serious by their nature or repetition as to constitute a severe violation of basic human rights, *in particular* the rights from which derogation cannot be made under Article 15(2) of the [ECHR]' (Article 9(1)(a) of the QD, emphasis added). However, the Geneva Convention does not specify what persecution is and, most importantly, does not establish a mandatory connection between the definition of refugee and human rights violations, whether absolute or otherwise. It supports, instead, a case-specific evaluation of the well-founded fear in the context in which the persecution occurred or would take place in case of return. As the UNHCR put it, persecution needs to be a 'flexible' and 'adaptable' concept, one that is 'sufficiently open to accommodate its changing forms' and 'cannot and should not be defined solely on the basis of serious or severe human rights violations.'[19] By contrast, irrespective of the recognition that the QD must be interpreted in a manner consistent with the Geneva Convention (para. 40) and the Directive's own wording ('in particular,' above), the CJEU read the QD in such

---

18.   Carmelo Danisi, Moira Dustin, Nuno Ferreira and Nina Held, *Queering Asylum in Europe: Legal and Social Experiences of Seeking International Protection on grounds of Sexual Orientation and Gender Identity* (Cham: Springer, 2021), ch. 3 and 267–269.

19.   UNHCR, *Annotated Comments on the EC Council Directive 2004/83/EC of 29 April 2004*, 20.

a way that restricts persecution only to those acts that amount to severe violations of non-derogable rights. In other words, where sexual minorities are involved, the CJEU transformed what in the QD was meant as an example of persecution into the *only* acts amounting to persecution. Yet, the consequence of this reasoning is worse than the reasoning itself. In a clear contradiction to the previous recognition of sexual orientation as a fundamental characteristic that, as such, finds expression in every facet of a person's life (see section 'The Good') and is protected by the indivisible spectrum of human rights, the CJEU affirmed that sexual orientation is 'specifically' connected with the right to private and family life (Arts. 8 ECHR and 7 EU Charter) (para. 54). Given that criminalisation in itself entails a violation of such a derogable right, in the Court's view it cannot be so severe as to constitute persecution.

We can find some support for the CJEU's interpretation in the UNHCR's position that persecution needs to concern the individual claiming asylum and, where taken in abstract terms, a general measure cannot have effect until it is applied to a specific person.[20] However, such an understanding contradicts the recognition that international and EU refugee law protects sexual minorities, who in such countries cannot express themselves freely due to the risk of being criminally sanctioned. In this sense, requiring a person to have been or risk being severely punished in order to satisfy the requirement of persecution seems to re-introduce discretion reasoning in other, more subtle, ways. Moreover, the CJEU's approach fails to consider the effects of the discriminatory nature of such laws on the everyday life of sexual minorities, owing to the 'oppressive atmosphere of intolerance' they generate and the impunity they grant to State and non-State persecutors.[21] When looking at these effects, the 2012 SOGI Guidelines do not distinguish between derogable and non-derogable rights, a distinction which, in any case, under international human rights law, is attached to public emergencies threatening the life of the nation (see Article 15 ECHR) and is not meant to relate to the definition of 'persecution.' Instead, the UNHCR insists on the need for a contextual assessment of every individual situation.[22]

In fact, only such an assessment verifies the detrimental cumulative—exogenous and endogenous—effect of criminal law on sexual minorities' everyday lives irrespective of the nature of the rights that have been or could be violated in case of return.[23] Criminalisation can make sexual minorities' life so insecure that, in light of each individual context, it may generate a well-founded fear that leads to forced departures from the country of origin as the only way out. In *X, Y and Z*, not only did the CJEU

20. Alice Edwards, '*X, Y and Z*: The "A, B, C" of Claims Based on SOGI?' presentation at the Experts Roundtable on asylum claims based on sexual orientation and gender identity or expression (Brussels, 27 June 2014), 2.

21. UNHCR, *UNHCR SOGI Guidelines No. 9*, paras. 26–27. See also the vivid accounts of people fleeing their home countries in Danisi et al., *Queering Asylum in Europe*, esp. ch. 5.

22. UNHCR, *UNHCR SOGI Guidelines No. 9*, para. 28. See, also, UNHCR, *Handbook on Procedures and Criteria for Determining Refugee Status under the 1951 Convention and the 1967 Protocol relating to the Status of Refugees* (UNHCR, 1992, reissued in 2019), paras. 51–53.

23. For a wider discussion, see Carmelo Danisi, 'Crossing Borders between International Refugee Law and International Human Rights Law in the European Context,' *Netherlands Quarterly of Human Rights* 37 (2019), 359–368.

fail to undertake such a contextual analysis, but also, in contrast to its approach to discretion (see section 'The Good'), the CJEU even ignored the reasoning already emerged in the previous *Y and Z* case where it considered that the exercise of freedom of religion—a derogable right—could amount to persecution in light of the consequences experienced by the concerned person, such as the genuine risk of being prosecuted.[24] Moreover, the Court failed to consider the possibility of qualifying criminalisation and its consequences under the QD's alternative definition of persecution: 'an accumulation of various measures, *including* violations of human rights which is sufficiently severe as to affect an individual in a similar manner as [provided in Article 9(1)(a)].'[25] Crucially, such a reasoning could also rely on one of the examples of persecution listed in—the equally ignored—Article 9(2)(b): 'legal, administrative, police, and/or judicial measures which are in themselves discriminatory or which are implemented in a discriminatory manner.' These norms require a proactive role on the part of asylum decision makers,[26] and an understanding of criminalisation at least as *prima facie* persecution, thus either reversing the burden of proof or moving the assessment onto the other elements of the refugee notion. [27]

The re-written judgment takes into account these developments by advancing an interpretation of the QD that, at the very least, always leads to a presumption of persecution when the applicant's country of origin criminalises same-sex sexual acts. The burden is then on decision makers to prove that there is not, in fact, a risk of persecution, despite the existence of such criminal law. In order to discharge such a burden of proof, in line with the UNHCR Guidelines No. 9 and procedural obligations set out in the same QD, decision makers are asked to carry out a contextual analysis of the situation of sexual minorities in their country of origin, one that considers the overall effects of the criminalisation on the applicant's own life, including (but not exclusively) whether it is applied and what sanctions it entails.

The way forward for a queer CJEU in asylum law

This commentary has shown the CJEU's mixed approach in interpreting EU asylum law when refugee status is requested on sexual orientation grounds. Although the limitations imposed by its role and competences cannot be underestimated, the CJEU could have navigated better the straits left open by the EU legislator to offer a truly queer interpretation of the QD, one that takes into account the specific conditions, needs and rights of sexual minorities along the lines suggested here. The re-written version of the original judgment in the *X, Y and Z* case that follows in the next pages shows exactly what the CJEU should have done differently to achieve a more appropriate

---

24. For a full comparison, see ICJ, *X, Y and Z*, paras. 54–58.
25. Article 9(1)(b) QD, emphasis added.
26. Danisi et al., *Queering Asylum in Europe*, ch. 6.
27. See Italian Supreme Court of Cassation, decision no. 15981, 20 September 2012, where the Court found that the criminalisation of same-sex sexual acts amounts to persecution because it entails a deprivation of the fundamental right to live freely one's sexual and emotional life.

interpretation—for both sexual minorities and asylum law as an international coherent system—of the legal framework that was available in November 2013.

Some preliminary clarifications about the re-written judgment are necessary. The re-written version adheres closely to the original wording and structure where those were generally unproblematic.[28] Instead, where the original judgment is problematic on account of its terminology or legal analysis, the wording has been changed and the structure has been adapted. Generally, the term 'homosexuals' was replaced with 'sexual minorities,' 'homosexuality' with 'sexual orientation,' and 'homosexual acts' with 'same-sex sexual acts,' to avoid the Western, medicalised and pathologizing history of the former term. Gender-neutral terminology was also favoured throughout, even though the judgment deals in particular with male applicants. We hope that our suggestions can inform not only the next wave of CJEU judgments on asylum claims based on sexual orientation and, possibly, gender identity, but also future EU asylum legislation.

---

28. Owing to the limited space available, several non-essential passages have been omitted, which is signalled by '(…).' Moreover, the numbering of the paragraphs in the re-written judgment does *not* correspond to the numbering of the original judgment.

JUDGMENT OF THE COURT (FOURTH CHAMBER)

7 November 2013

(...)

In Joined Cases C-199/12 to C-201/12,

REQUESTS for a preliminary ruling under Article 267 TFEU from the Raad van State (Netherlands), made by decision of 18 April 2012, received at the Court on 27 April 2012, in the proceedings

Minister voor Immigratie en Asiel

v

X (C-199/12),
Y (C-200/12),

and

Z

v

Minister voor Immigratie en Asiel (C-201/12),

intervening parties:

Hoog Commissariaat van de Verenigde Naties voor de Vluchtelingen (C-199/12 to C-201/12),

THE COURT (Fourth Chamber),
(...)
gives the following

Judgment

[1] These requests for a preliminary ruling concern the interpretation of Article 9(1) (a) of Council Directive 2004/83/EC (...) (OJ 2004 L 304, p. 12) ('the Directive'), read in conjunction with Article 9(2)(c) and Article 10(1)(d) thereof.

[2] The requests have been made in proceedings, first, between the Minister voor Immigratie en Asiel (Minister for Immigration and Asylum, 'the Minister') and X

and Y, nationals of Sierra Leone and Uganda respectively, in Cases C-199/12 and C-200/12, and second, in Case C-201/12, between Z, a Senegalese national and the Minister, concerning the rejection by the latter of their applications for residence permits for a fixed period (asylum) in the Netherlands.

Legal context

International law

THE CONVENTION RELATING TO THE STATUS OF REFUGEES ('THE GENEVA CONVENTION')

[3] (...)

[4] The first subparagraph of Article 1(A)(2) of the Geneva Convention provides that the term 'refugee' is to apply to any person who 'owing to well-founded fear of being persecuted for reasons of race, religion, nationality, membership of a particular social group or political opinion, is outside the country of [their] nationality and is unable or, owing to such fear, is unwilling to avail [themselves] of the protection of that country.'

[5] It is now consensual that international protection applications on grounds of sexual orientation or gender identity fall within the scope of international refugee law, and that international human rights law and the principle of non-refoulement apply to such applications, as enshrined in Principle 23 of the (non-legally binding but legally authoritative) Yogyakarta Principles.

[6] The UNHCR 2012 Guidelines on International Protection No. 9: Claims to Refugee Status based on Sexual Orientation and/or Gender Identity ('the UNHCR 2012 Guidelines No. 9') set out the key aspects that need to be considered when deciding on these applications.

THE EUROPEAN CONVENTION FOR THE PROTECTION OF HUMAN RIGHTS AND FUNDAMENTAL FREEDOMS ('THE ECHR')

[7] The ECHR, signed at Rome on 4 November 1950, protects several rights, including the 'Right to life' in Article 2, the 'Prohibition of torture' in Article 3, the 'Right to respect for private and family life' in Article 8, and the 'Prohibition of discrimination' in Article 14. (...)

European Union law

THE CHARTER OF FUNDAMENTAL RIGHTS OF THE EUROPEAN UNION ('THE CHARTER')

[8] Article 18 of the Charter protects the right to asylum 'with due respect for the rules of the Geneva Convention of 28 July 1951 and the Protocol of 31 January 1967 relating to the status of refugees,' as well as the EU Treaties.

[9] The Charter also protects the 'Right to life' in Article 2, the 'Prohibition of torture and inhuman or degrading treatment or punishment' in Article 4, 'Respect for private and family life' in Article 7, and 'Non-discrimination' (Article 21).

THE DIRECTIVE

[10] (...)

Netherlands law

[11] (...)

The disputes in the main proceedings and the questions referred for a preliminary ruling

[12] (...)

[13] In those circumstances, the Raad van State decided to stay the proceedings and to refer the following questions to the Court for a preliminary ruling which have been formulated in almost identical terms in each of the three cases:

'(1) Do foreign nationals with a homosexual orientation form a particular social group as referred to in Article 10(1)(d) [of the Directive]?

(2) If the first question is to be answered in the affirmative: which homosexual activities fall within the scope of the Directive and, in the case of acts of persecution in respect of those activities and if the other requirements are met, can that lead to the granting of refugee status? That question encompasses the following subquestions:

(a) Can foreign nationals with a homosexual orientation be expected to conceal their orientation from everyone in their [respective] country of origin in order to avoid persecution?

(b) If the previous question is to be answered in the negative, can foreign nationals with a homosexual orientation be expected to exercise restraint, and if so, to what extent, when giving expression to that orientation in their country of origin, in order to avoid persecution? Moreover, can greater restraint be expected of homosexuals than of heterosexuals?

(c) If, in that regard, a distinction can be made between forms of expression which relate to the core area of the orientation and forms of expression which do not, what should be understood to constitute the core area of the orientation and in what way can it be determined?

(3) Do the criminalisation of homosexual activities and the threat of imprisonment in relation thereto (…) constitute an act of persecution within the meaning of Article 9(1)(a), read in conjunction with Article 9(2)(c) of the Directive? If not, under what circumstances would that be the case?'

(…)

Consideration of the questions referred

Preliminary observations

[14] (…) The Directive must be interpreted in the light of the Geneva Convention's general scheme and purpose, and in a manner consistent with the Geneva Convention and the other relevant treaties referred to in Article 78(1) TFEU. As is apparent from recital 10 in the preamble thereto, the Directive must also be interpreted in a manner consistent with the rights recognised by the Charter (Case C-364/11 *Abed El Karem El Kott and Others* [2012] ECR, paragraph 48 and the case-law cited). In the case of asylum applications related to sexual orientation, the Directive should also be interpreted in a manner consistent with the UNHCR 2012 Guidelines No. 9.

The first question

[15] (…) To be recognised as a refugee, a third-country national must, on account of circumstances existing in their country of origin and the conduct of actors of persecution, have a well-founded fear that they personally will be subject to persecution for at least one of the five reasons listed in the Directive and the Geneva Convention, one such reason being 'membership of a particular social group' ('PSG').

[16] Article 10(1) of the Directive gives a definition of a PSG, membership of which may give rise to a genuine fear of persecution.

[17] According to that definition, a group is regarded as a PSG where, *in particular,* two conditions are met. First, members of that group share an innate characteristic, or a common background that cannot be changed, or share a characteristic or belief that is so fundamental to identity or conscience that a person should not be forced to renounce it. Second, that group has a distinct identity in the relevant country because it is perceived as being different by the surrounding society.

[18] As far as concerns the 'fundamental characteristic test,' it is common ground that a person's sexual orientation is a characteristic so fundamental to the identity of so many people that they should not be forced to renounce it. That interpretation is supported by the second subparagraph of Article 10(1)(d) of the Directive, from which it appears that, according to the conditions prevailing in the country of origin, a specific social group may be a group whose members have sexual orientation as the shared characteristic.

[19] The 'social recognition test' requires that, in the country of origin concerned, the group whose members share the same sexual orientation has a distinct identity because it is perceived by the surrounding society as being different.

[20] The UNHCR 2012 Guidelines No. 9 state, in paragraph 45, that the fundamental characteristic and the social recognition tests are *alternative*. In the case of the Directive, although the tests are connected with the word 'and,' they are introduced with the words 'in particular.' So, a PSG can be found in circumstances where these tests are not both fulfilled (for example, only one is fulfilled or none is fulfilled but there is still evidence of the existence of a particular social group).

[21] In that connection, the existence of criminal laws that specifically target members of sexual minorities, reinforces a finding that those persons form a separate group which is perceived by the surrounding society as being different. The lack of such criminal laws should not, however, be interpreted as sexual minorities not constituting a PSG.

[22] Therefore, the answer to the first question referred in each of the cases in the main proceedings is that Article 10(1)(d) of the Directive must be interpreted as meaning that the existence of criminal laws that specifically target sexual minorities (and knowing such minorities always share a fundamental characteristic), reinforces the finding that those persons must be regarded as forming a particular social group, even if such criminal laws are not at all a requirement for such finding.

The third question

[23] (...) In order to answer this question, it must be recalled that Article 9 of the Directive defines the elements which support the finding that acts constitute persecution within the meaning of Article 1(A) of the Geneva Convention. In that regard, Article 9(1)(a) of the Directive, to which the national court refers, states that the relevant acts must be 'sufficiently serious' by their nature or repetition as to constitute a 'severe violation of basic human rights,' *in particular*—but not exclusively—the unconditional rights from which there can be no derogation, in accordance with Article 15(2) of the ECHR.

[24] Moreover, Article 9(1)(b) of the Directive states that an accumulation of various measures, including violations of human rights, which is 'sufficiently severe' as to affect an individual in a manner similar to that referred to in Article 9(1)(a) of the Directive, must also be regarded as amounting to persecution.

[25] It is clear from those provisions that, for a violation of fundamental rights to constitute persecution within the meaning of Article 1(A) of the Geneva Convention, it must be sufficiently serious. Therefore, not all violations of fundamental rights suffered by an applicant with an application related to sexual orientation will necessarily reach that level of seriousness.

[26] Nonetheless, it is well established in international human rights law that 'sodomy laws' that criminalise same-sex sexual acts are a violation of human rights law, as stated since the 1980s in seminal cases by the UN Human Rights Committee (HRC) in *Toonen v Australia* (CCPR/C/50/D/488/1992, 4 April 1994) and the European Court of Human Rights in *Dudgeon v UK* (Application no. 7525/76, 22 October 1981), *Norris v Ireland* (Application no. 10581/83, 26 October 1988) and *Modinos v Cyprus* (Application no. 15070/89, 22 April 1993).

[27] Furthermore, the UNHCR 2012 Guidelines No. 9 state that while penalties such as death penalty, prison terms, or severe corporal punishment make their persecutory character particularly evident, even criminal laws prohibiting same-sex relations that are irregularly, rarely or never enforced can lead to an 'intolerable predicament for an LGB [lesbian, gay or bisexual] person rising to the level of persecution' (paragraphs 26–28). Indeed, despite the lack of actual prosecutions, criminal legislation may be used to facilitate blackmail, discrimination and harassment, including on the part of the police.

[28] Moreover, EU national highest jurisdictions such as the Italian Supreme Court have found that the criminalisation of same-sex sexual acts *in itself* constitutes persecution, whether or not it is effectively applied, on account of the human rights violation it entails (Corte di Cassazione, ordinanza n. 15981/12).

[29] Placing these criminal law norms within their broader societal context of discrimination and intolerance, and taking seriously the human rights violations in question, requires us to also consider that—at the very least—criminalisation of same-sex sexual acts should lead to a *presumption of persecution*, which places on asylum authorities the burden to prove that, despite such criminal laws, the overall social and legal conditions in the country of origin do not amount to persecution. In this sense, in line with the definition provided in Article 9(1)(b), persecution can be meant also as an accumulation of various measures, including violations of human rights, which is sufficiently severe as to affect an individual in a similar manner as resulting from acts provided in Article 9(1)(a).

[30] In those circumstances, the mere existence of legislation criminalizing same-sex sexual acts, including when it is accompanied by a term of imprisonment like those at issue in the main proceedings, should be always presumed to be an act affecting the applicant in a manner so significant that it reaches the level of seriousness necessary for a finding that it constitutes persecution within the meaning of Article 9(1) of the Directive.

[31] Furthermore, when this legislation provides for criminal sanctions like imprisonment, death penalty and so on, such sanctions constitute punishment which is disproportionate or discriminatory within the meaning of Article 9(2)(c) of the Directive, in line with the UNHCR 2012 Guidelines No. 9 (paragraph 26).

[32] Where an applicant for asylum relies on the existence in their country of origin of legislation criminalizing same-sex sexual acts, the burden is on the national authorities to examine all the relevant facts concerning that country of origin and prove that, despite the existence of criminal laws against same-sex sexual acts, the legal and social conditions in the country of origin do not amount to a risk of persecution for the applicant.

[33] Having regard to all of those considerations, the answer to the third question is that, in each of the cases in the main proceedings, Article 9(1) of the Directive, read together with Article 9(2)(c) thereof, must be interpreted as meaning that the criminalisation of same-sex sexual acts alone is, at least, an indication of persecution strong enough as to reverse the burden of proof and place on authorities the burden to prove that such criminal law norms, combined with the social conditions in the country of origin, do not create a risk of persecution for the applicant. Moreover, a term of imprisonment which sanctions same-sex sexual acts must be regarded as being a punishment which is disproportionate and discriminatory and thus constitutes an act of persecution under all circumstances.

The second question

PRELIMINARY OBSERVATIONS

[34] (…) The second question refers to a situation in which the applicant has not shown that they have already been persecuted or have already been subject to direct threats of persecution on account of their membership of a PSG whose members share the same sexual orientation.

THE SECOND QUESTION, PARTS (A) AND (B)

[35] (…) In connection with the second question, parts (a) and (b), it must be stated that nothing in the wording of Article 10(1)(d) suggests that the European Union legislature intended to exclude certain types of acts or expression linked to sexual orientation from the scope of that provision.

[36] Thus, Article 10(1)(d) of the Directive does not lay down limits on the conduct that the members of a PSG may adopt with respect to their identity or to behaviour which may or may not fall within the definition of sexual orientation for the purposes of that provision.

[37] In that connection, it is important to state that requiring members of a social group sharing the same sexual orientation to conceal that orientation is incompatible with the recognition of a characteristic so fundamental to a person's identity that the persons concerned cannot be required to renounce it.

[38] Therefore, applicants for asylum cannot be expected to conceal their sexuality in their country of origin in order to avoid persecution.

[39] In the system provided for by the Directive, when assessing whether an applicant has a well-founded fear of being persecuted, the competent authorities are required to ascertain whether or not the circumstances established constitute such a threat that the person concerned may reasonably fear, in the light of their individual situation, that they will in fact be subject to acts of persecution (see, to that effect, *Y and Z*, paragraph 76).

[40] That assessment of the extent of the risk, which must, in all cases, be carried out with vigilance and care (Joined Cases C-175/08, C-176/08, C-178/08 and C-179/08 *Salahadin Abdulla and Others* [2010] ECR I-1493, paragraph 90), will be based solely on a specific evaluation of the facts and circumstances, in accordance with the rules laid down in particular by Article 4 of the Directive (*Y and Z*, paragraph 77).

[41] It follows that the person concerned must be granted refugee status, in accordance with Article 13 of the Directive, where it is established that on return to their country of origin their sexuality would expose them to a genuine risk of persecution within the meaning of Article 9(1) thereof. The fact that they could avoid the risk by exercising greater restraint than a heterosexual in expressing their sexual orientation is not to be taken into account in that respect.

[42] Similarly, how asylum applicants expressed their sexuality in their countries of origin or how they would express it if they were returned, should not be used by asylum authorities to find that there is no risk of persecution. Even if an applicant may have successfully concealed their sexuality before departing and intend to conceal it if returned, the risk of persecution may remain on account of factors beyond the control of the applicant, such as relatives, neighbours, work colleagues and other people finding out about the applicant's sexuality, which can set in motion a range of social and legal harmful consequences.

[43] In the light of those considerations, the answer to parts (a) and (b) of the second question, referred in each of the three cases in the main proceedings, is that Article 10(1)(d) of the Directive, read together with Article 2(c) thereof, must be interpreted as meaning that, when assessing an application for refugee status, the competent authorities cannot reasonably expect, in order to avoid the risk of persecution, the applicant for asylum to conceal their sexuality in their country of origin or to exercise reserve in the expression of their sexual orientation. Any experience or intention of concealment and reserve do not, in fact, preclude in any way the risk of persecution.

THE SECOND QUESTION, PART (C)

[44] Having regard to the reply given to the first question, parts (a) and (b), there is therefore no need to reply to part (c) of the second question.

[45] Nevertheless, it must be recalled that, for the purpose of determining, specifically, which acts may be regarded as constituting persecution within the meaning of Article 9(1) of the Directive, it is unnecessary to distinguish acts that interfere with the core areas of the expression of sexual orientation, even assuming it were possible to identify them, from acts which do not affect those purported core areas (see, by analogy, *Y and Z*, paragraph 62).

(...)

On those grounds, the Court (Fourth Chamber) hereby rules:

[1] Article 10(1)(d) of Council Directive 2004/83/EC and the content of the protection granted must be interpreted as meaning that the existence of criminal laws, such as those at issue in each of the cases in the main proceedings, which specifically target sexual minorities (and knowing such minorities always share a fundamental characteristic), reinforces the finding that those persons must be regarded as forming a PSG, even if such criminal laws are not at all a requirement for such finding.

[2] Article 9(1) of the Directive, read together with Article 9(2)(c) thereof, must be interpreted as meaning that the criminalisation of same-sex sexual acts alone is, at least, an indication of persecution strong enough as to reverse the burden of proof and place on authorities the burden to prove that such criminal law norms, combined with the social conditions in the country of origin, do not create a risk of persecution for the applicant. Moreover, a term of imprisonment which sanctions same-sex sexual acts must be regarded as being a punishment which is disproportionate and discriminatory and thus constitutes an act of persecution under all circumstances.

[3] Article 10(1)(d) of the Directive, read together with Article 2(c) thereof, must be interpreted as meaning that, when assessing an application for refugee status, the competent authorities cannot reasonably expect, in order to avoid the risk of persecution, the applicant for asylum to conceal their sexuality in their country of origin or to exercise reserve in the expression of their sexual orientation. Any experience or intention of concealment and reserve do not, in fact, preclude in any way the risk of persecution.

[Signatures]

27

Coman and Others v Inspectoratul General Pentru Imigrări and Ministerul Afacerilor Interne (European Union):

Recognizing Married Same-Sex Couples
for the Purposes of EU Free Movement Law

Alina Tryfonidou

Background to the *Coman* Case

Having been originally established as a regional supranational organisation that was primarily concerned with economic objectives, the European Union (EU)[1] did not initially include the protection of human rights among its aims and objectives.[2] Needless to say, back in the 1950s, at a time when consensual sexual activities between men were, still, considered a criminal offence under the sodomy laws of some of the founding States of the EU and the Council of Europe,[3] the need to protect the rights of sexual minorities was very far from the EU Treaty drafters' minds. Yet, following a few slow steps in the 1980s and 1990s which consisted of the adoption of purely soft law measures aiming to protect the rights of sexual minorities,[4] in 1999 the EU acquired its first legal basis for legislative measures which would have as their aim prohibiting discrimination on a number of grounds, including discrimination based on sexual orientation.[5] This led to the adoption of Directive 2000/78, which prohibits discrimination based on, among other things, sexual orientation, albeit only in the context of employment.[6] Discrimination on the grounds of sexual orientation is, also,

---

1. In this commentary, for ease of reference, the term 'EU' will be used throughout, even when referring to the period before the establishment of the EU in 1993.
2. For an excellent analysis of the history of the EU, see Luuk Van Middelaar, *The Passage to Europe: How a Continent became a Union* (New Haven, CT: Yale University Press, 2014).
3. Namely Germany, Ireland, the United Kingdom and Norway.
4. For more on these, see Mark Bell and Lisa Waddington, 'The 1996 Intergovernmental Conference and the Prospects of a Non-Discrimination Treaty Article,' (1996) 25 ILJ 320.
5. At the time, this was Article 13 EC (European Community Treaty). This is, currently, Article 19 TFEU (Treaty on the Functioning of the EU).
6. Directive 2000/78 establishing a general framework for equal treatment in employment and occupation [2000] OJ L303/16. For an analysis of the prohibition of sexual orientation discrimination under this instrument, see Alina Tryfonidou, 'The Impact of the Framework Equality Directive on the Protection of

prohibited by Article 21(1) of the Charter of Fundamental Rights of the EU ('the Charter'), in all situations which fall within the Charter's scope of application as defined in Article 51 of the Charter.

Despite the fact that the EU over the last two decades has protected and respected the negative right of lesbian, gay, and bisexual (LGB) persons to be free from discrimination, EU law comes (mostly) empty-handed in relation to positive family rights, such as the right to marry and/or enter into a registered partnership and the right to become a parent.[7] This is not necessarily due to a lack of desire to protect such rights but simply because of the limited competence that the EU has in the family law field.[8] Consequently, from the EU's point of view, it is entirely up to each EU Member State to decide whether it will allow two persons of the same sex to marry in its territory and/or enter into a registered partnership, and whether two persons of the same sex can become the joint legal parents of a child.

It thus comes as no surprise that the first case which reached the European Court of Justice (ECJ) and which involved the refusal of a Member State (Romania) to recognize a same-sex marriage contracted in another Member State (Belgium) by a Union citizen—the *Coman* case[9]—was not presented as a case which focused on the rights of sexual minorities. Rather, it was approached as a case which sought to ensure that the right to free movement of *all* Union citizens should be respected.

The case is, in fact, a brilliant example of strategic litigation, as one of the applicants—the one who gave the case its name (Coman)—is a well-known LGBTQI+ rights activist. Coman holds Romanian nationality and is, thus, a Union citizen. Whilst in New York in 2002, Coman met Hamilton (an US citizen) and the two of them started a relationship which led to their marriage in 2010 in Brussels, whilst Coman was resident there. Shortly after they contracted their marriage, the couple approached the Romanian authorities to enquire whether Hamilton would be allowed to reside in Romania for more than three months, as the spouse of Coman. The argument of the couple was that Coman was a Union citizen who had exercised free movement rights within the EU (by moving from Romania to Belgium and—allegedly in the future—back to Romania) and, as such, was entitled under EU law to the right to be joined in his Member State of nationality by his spouse, who should be granted a right of residence in its territory for more than three months. The Romanian authorities, nonetheless, replied that due to the fact that Coman's spouse was a man and that Romania does not allow two persons of the same sex to marry, nor does it recognize same-sex marriages contracted abroad, Hamilton would not be granted a right of residence in Romania for more than three months. When the case reached the Romanian Constitutional Court,

---

LGB Persons and Same-Sex Couples from Discrimination under EU law,' in Uladzislau Belavusau and Kristin Henrard (eds), *EU Anti-Discrimination Law Beyond Gender* (Hart, 2019), 229.

7. Alina Tryfonidou, 'Positive State Obligations under European Law: A Tool for Achieving Substantive Equality for Sexual Minorities in Europe,' (2020) 13 *Erasmus Law Review* 98.

8. Which has been confirmed on a number of occasions in the case law of the European Court of Justice (ECJ): see, for instance, Case C-147/08 *Römer v Freie und Hansestadt Hamburg*, ECLI:EU:C:2011:286, para. 38.

9. Case C-673/16 *Coman and Others v Inspectoratul General pentru Imigrari and Ministerul Afacerilor Interne*, ECLI:EU:C:2018:385.

the latter made a reference for a preliminary ruling to the ECJ asking it, essentially, whether Romania was required by EU law to grant a right to family reunification to Coman with his same-sex spouse.

The Re-Written Judgment and the Gaps It Has Aimed to Cover

The judgment attracted wide scholarly attention and shall thus not be analysed here in detail.[10] Suffice it to say that the Court approached this case as an EU free movement case and confined itself to answering—in as narrow way as possible—the specific questions asked by the referring court, in this way leaving many questions unresolved.[11] The right to free movement is one of the fundamental freedoms that the Union has granted to Member State nationals since the beginning of its existence. Thus, Member State nationals should be free to move to, and reside on, the territory of a Member State other than that of their nationality, and to return to the Member State of their nationality from another Member State, unless limiting the exercise of this right can be justified on non-economic grounds. Although the right was initially granted only to Member State nationals whose movement between Member States had an economic purpose, in the 1990s this right was extended to *all* Member State nationals via their newly acquired status as Union citizens.[12]

Family reunification rights are a necessary complement to free movement rights: if Union citizens cannot be joined or accompanied in the Member State of destination by their family members, they may be deterred from moving.[13] After all, as the Court has noted in a number of its rulings—including in *Coman*—the right to lead a 'normal family life' in the Member State to which a Union citizen moves is one of the rights that stem from the right to free movement laid down in the Treaty. The Court has nowhere explained what it means by 'normal' family life. And although I have kept the reference to this right in the re-written judgment, *at least for the purposes of the re-written judgment* this should be taken to refer to family life 'devoid of any external interferences or obstacles to its enjoyment,' rather than as reflecting any moral ideas or choices with regard to what *can* constitute a *valid* familial relationship or a valid way of leading family life.

In *Coman*, the Court focused on examining whether the contested refusal of the Romanian authorities to recognize the same-sex marriage of the applicants for the purpose of the grant of EU family reunification rights amounted to an *unjustified*

---

10. See, for instance, Alina Tryfonidou, 'The EU top court rules that married same-sex couples can move freely between EU Member States as "spouses",' (2019) 27 FLS 211; Dimitry Kochenov and Uladzislau Belavusau, 'After the Celebration: Marriage Equality in EU Law Post-*Coman* in Eight Questions and Some Further Thoughts,' (2020) 27 MJ 549.

11. For a detailed analysis of these questions, see Alina Tryfonidou, 'The ECJ Recognises the Rights of Same-Sex Spouses to Move Freely between EU Member States: The *Coman* ruling,' (2019) 44 ELRev 663.

12. For a detailed analysis of the provisions governing the free movement of persons under EU law, see Catherine Barnard, *The Substantive Law of the EU: The Four Freedoms* (Oxford: OUP, 2022), chapters 6–9 and 12.

13. For an analytical examination of the family reunification rights that Union citizens enjoy under EU law, see Chiara Berneri, *Family Reunification in the EU: The Movement and Residence Rights of Third Country National Family Members of EU Citizens* (Oxford: Hart, 2019).

obstacle to the exercise of Coman's free movement rights. It concluded that it did. The Court was of the view that where a Union citizen has made use of EU free movement rights by moving and taking up genuine residence in a Member State other than that of their nationality and, whilst there, has created or strengthened a family life with a third-country national of the same sex with whom they contracted a marriage in that Member State, Article 21 TFEU (which grants the right to free movement and residence in another Member State to all Union citizens) precludes the authorities of that citizen's State of nationality from refusing to grant the same-sex spouse of the Union citizen a right of residence in its territory on the ground that the law of that Member State does not recognize same-sex marriage. It should be noted here that the case focused on examining whether there was a violation of Coman's free movement rights: fundamental human rights were only considered by the Court at the justification stage of the ruling, where it confined itself to recalling that—as established by the European Court of Human Rights (ECtHR)—the relationship of a same-sex couple may fall within the notion of 'private life' and 'family life' in the same way as the relationship of an opposite-sex couple.[14]

Accordingly, one of the criticisms levelled at the *Coman* judgment is that the Court avoided using human rights as the basis for a separate line of argumentation for finding a breach of EU law, preferring, instead, to follow the much less controversial free movement path. As a response to this criticism, the judgment has been re-written in a way which demonstrates that in addition to constituting a violation of the free movement provisions, the contested refusal can, also, constitute a violation of human rights which need to be protected under EU law. The re-written judgment, therefore, includes one paragraph (paragraph 36) that expressly notes the obligation of Member States to read the term 'spouse,' for the purposes of Directive 2004/38,[15] in a way which complies with the Charter, and another paragraph (paragraph 52) that explains why the contested refusal amounts to a breach of Article 7 of the Charter, which protects the right to respect for private and family life. The re-written judgment also refers to the judgment of the ECtHR in *Orlandi*,[16] where the Strasbourg court ruled that the European Convention on Human Rights (ECHR) requires States to recognize same-sex marriages concluded abroad, albeit not necessarily as *marriages*. *Orlandi*, therefore, imposes on ECHR signatory States both a wider and a narrower obligation than the one imposed on EU Member States by the judgment in *Coman*: wider in the sense that the cross-border recognition is required for *all* legal purposes in the State where it is sought; and narrower in that the obligation imposed requires ECHR signatory States to merely recognize *in some legal form* marriages contracted abroad, and not necessarily as marriages.

The re-written judgment, therefore, stretches the obligation imposed by EU law further, in order, exactly, to make it broader in all respects than the obligation imposed

---

14. *Coman*, para. 50.
15. Directive 2004/38 on the right of citizens of the Union and their family members to move and reside freely within the territory of the Member States [2004] OJ L158/77.
16. *Orlandi and others v Italy* App nos 26432/12, 26742/12, 44057/12 and 60088/12 (ECtHR, 14 December 2017).

by *Orlandi*. After all, as emphasized in the re-written judgment, Article 52(3) of the Charter provides that insofar as the Charter contains rights which correspond to rights guaranteed by the Convention, the meaning and scope of those rights shall be the same as those laid down by the Convention, *without this preventing Union law providing more extensive protection*. Thus, the re-written judgment includes *obiter statements*[17] which widen the obligation imposed by EU law by holding that same-sex marriages contracted abroad by an EU citizen who has exercised free movement rights, must be recognized by a Member State *for all legal purposes*, basing this again on a free movement rationale. Drawing on the Court's surnames case law,[18] the re-written judgment argues that a discrepancy in the recognition of a Union citizen's marital status in different Member States and the resultant difficulties—or, even, impossibility—in benefitting, in some Member States, from the legal effects of their marriage can, in itself, amount to an obstacle to the exercise of free movement rights.

Thus, in order to respect the limits placed on EU competences, the re-written judgment adopts a functional approach in order to expand the obligations imposed on EU Member States with regard to the cross-border recognition of (same-sex) marriages. Nonetheless, this approach is informed by queer theory in that it seeks to avoid embracing and perpetuating heteronormative ideas of marriage—that marriage is an institution for heterosexuals and that any other statuses that resemble marriage (in the traditional—heteronormative—sense) should have (only) *some* of the benefits attached to marriage extended to them (such as—as per *Coman*—the granting of family reunification rights).

The same 'queer rationale' lies behind the other important change made in the re-written judgment, which concerns the territorial scope of application of the obligation imposed by the original judgment. As noted elsewhere,[19] although the Advocate General in *Coman* emphasized in his Opinion that the term 'spouse' is 'independent of the place where it was contracted,'[20] the Court in its judgment made repeated references to marriages that were 'concluded in a Member State in accordance with the law of that State' or similar statements to that effect.[21] This seems to be limiting the territorial scope of the obligation to recognize marriages *contracted within the EU*, which would mean that if Mr Hamilton and Mr Coman happened to have contracted their marriage in the US or any other third country, Romania might not be obliged to recognize it. Such a limitation would, nonetheless, contradict the earlier pronouncement of the Court in *Metock* (a case which concerned *opposite-sex* marriages),[22] where it noted that 'neither

---

17. They are obiter in that the questions referred were, specifically, about the right of residence of the spouse of the Union citizen and not about whether the same-sex marriage of the applicants would be recognized in Romania for legal purposes other than the granting of that right.

18. Case C-148/02 *Garcia Avello v Belgian State* ECLI:EU:C:2003:539; and Case C-353/06 *Grunkin and Paul v Standesamt Niebüll* ECLI:EU:C:2008:559.

19. Alina Tryfonidou, 'The ECJ Recognises the Rights of Same-Sex Spouses to Move Freely between EU Member States,' 676.

20. Opinion of AG Wathelet in *Coman*, ECLI:EU:C:2018:2, para. 49.

21. *Coman*, paras. 33, 35, 36, 39, 40, 42, 45, 51, 52, and 56.

22. Case C-127/08 *Metock and others v Minister for Justice, Equality and Law Reform*, ECLI:EU:C:2008:449.

Article 3(1) nor any other provision of Directive 2004/38 contains requirements as to the place where the marriage of the Union citizen and the national of a non-member country is solemnized.'[23] Accordingly, and assuming that the Court—as would be logical—wishes to stand by its original pronouncement in *Metock*, when re-writing the judgment, all statements which limited the obligation to recognize marriages to those concluded within the EU have been removed or amended in order to extend the obligation of recognition to *all* marriages. After all, such an expansion or (depending on the Court's intention in *Coman*) clarification is required in order to avoid providing an interpretation of Directive 2004/38 which is discriminatory against same-sex couples, contrary to Recital 31 of that Directive and Article 21 of the Charter.

The re-written judgment, therefore, is an idealized (albeit realistic)[24] version of the original judgment, written from a queer perspective. In particular, it avoids reproducing heteronormative ideas of marriage by requiring that marriage—irrespective of the sexes of the parties to it—is considered as *one* institution. Thus, same-sex spouses should not just be given *some* of the rights and privileges which have, traditionally, been reserved for the 'gold standard' of marriage, namely, opposite-sex marriage. Rather, the approach should be that once a couple (whether opposite-sex or same-sex) is married, it is considered marriage for all legal purposes. It should, nonetheless, be acknowledged that both the Court's original judgment in *Coman* and the re-written judgment have the unintended consequence of creating a distinction among same-sex couples: on the one hand, there is the privileged class of same-sex couples who can travel and work abroad and can, thus, obtain access to marriage in States which allow this and—*relying on EU law*—require the Member State to which they move to recognize their same-sex marriage contracted abroad and, on the other hand, there is the less 'privileged' class of same-sex couples who do not have the socio-economic-cultural means to do so and are thus 'stuck' in their Member State of origin without legal protection. This resultant distinction is, nonetheless, an unintended consequence of the limited scope of application of EU law—and the limited competence of the EU in the family law field—and is bound to be eliminated in the (hopefully not too distant) future if *all* EU Member States will open marriage to same-sex couples.

The fact that at the time that it delivered its judgment the Court did have the tools to deliver a bolder judgment along the lines of the re-written judgment, should not lead us to an overly critical approach towards the Court's ruling. After all, the ruling *was* positive and the Court did rule—effectively—in favour of the applicants, securing the rights of sexual minorities *in the specific factual context of the case*. The fact that Romania, six years after the ruling, has still not complied with the judgment, demonstrates that the Court may have been right to choose making the smallest possible—albeit positive—steps required in order to protect the family rights of sexual minorities under EU law.

Finally, a few technical points should be made. Overall, the re-written version of the original judgment in the *Coman* case adheres closely to the original wording

---

23. *Metock*, para. 98.
24. Realistic, in that it takes into account the limits on the EU's competence.

and structure where those were unproblematic, though, as explained above, some new paragraphs have been added and this has resulted in the numbering of the paragraphs in this re-written judgment not corresponding to the numbering in the original judgment. Where problematic on account of its non-gender-neutral terminology, wording has been changed. Moreover, the phrase 'homosexual couple' was replaced with 'same-sex couple,' and 'heterosexual couple' with 'opposite-sex couple,' to avoid the Western, medicalized and pathologizing history of the term 'homosexual.' On account of the limited word count available, several non-essential passages have been omitted, including references to case law; the omitted passages are signalled by '(...).'

JUDGMENT OF THE COURT (Grand Chamber)

5 June 2018

(…)

In Case C673/16,

REQUEST for a preliminary ruling under Article 267 TFEU from the Curtea Constituțională (Constitutional Court, Romania), made by decision of 29 November 2016, received at the Court on 30 December 2016, in the proceedings

Relu Adrian Coman,
Robert Clabourn Hamilton,
Asociația Accept
v
Inspectoratul General pentru Imigrări,
Ministerul Afacerilor Interne,

intervener:
Consiliul Național pentru Combaterea Discriminării,

THE COURT (Grand Chamber),
(…)
gives the following

Judgment

[1] This request for a preliminary ruling concerns the interpretation of Article 2(2)(a), Article 3(1) and (2)(a) and (b) and Article 7(2) of Directive 2004/38/EC (…).

[2] The request has been made in proceedings between Mr Relu Adrian Coman, Mr. Robert Clabourn Hamilton and the Asociația Accept (together, 'Coman and Others'), on the one hand, and the Inspectoratul General pentru Imigrări (General Inspectorate for Immigration, Romania, 'the Inspectorate') and the Ministerul Afacerilor Interne (Ministry of the Interior, Romania) on the other, in connection with a request concerning the conditions under which Mr Hamilton may be granted the right to reside in Romania for more than three months.

Legal context

European Union law

[3] Recital 31 of Directive 2004/38 states as follows:

'This Directive respects the fundamental rights and freedoms and observes the principles recognized in particular by the Charter of Fundamental Rights of the European Union. In accordance with the prohibition of discrimination contained in the Charter, Member States should implement this Directive without discrimination between the beneficiaries of this Directive on grounds such as sex, race, colour, ethnic or social origin, genetic characteristics, language, religion or beliefs, political or other opinion, membership of an ethnic minority, property, birth, disability, age or sexual orientation.'

[4] Article 2 of that directive, entitled 'Definitions,' provides, in paragraph 2(a) and (b):

'For the purpose of this Directive:

(…)

(2) "family member" means:

a.   the spouse;

b.   the partner with whom the Union citizen has contracted a registered partnership, on the basis of the legislation of a Member State, if the legislation of the host Member State treats registered partnerships as equivalent to marriage, and in accordance with the conditions laid down in the relevant legislation of the host Member State;

…'

[5] Article 3 of Directive 2004/38, entitled 'Beneficiaries,' provides as follows:

'1. This Directive shall apply to all Union citizens who move to or reside in a Member State other than that of which they are a national, and to their family members as defined in point 2 of Article 2 who accompany or join them.

(…)

[6] Article 7 of that directive, entitled 'Right of residence for more than three months,' is worded as follows:

'(1) All Union citizens shall have the right of residence on the territory of another Member State for a period of longer than three months if they:

(…)

(d) are family members accompanying or joining a Union citizen who satisfies the conditions referred to in points (a), (b) or (c).

The right of residence provided for in paragraph 1 shall extend to family members who are not nationals of a Member State, accompanying or joining the Union citizen in the host Member State, provided that such Union citizen satisfies the conditions referred to in paragraph 1(a), (b) or (c).

(…).'

[7] Article 7 of the Charter of Fundamental Rights ('the Charter') provides that 'Everyone has the right to respect for his or her private and family life, home and communications.' Article 52(3) of the Charter notes that 'In so far as this Charter contains rights which correspond to rights guaranteed by the Convention for the Protection of Human Rights and Fundamental Freedoms, the meaning and scope of those rights shall be the same as those laid down by the said Convention. This provision shall not prevent Union law providing more extensive protection.'

European Convention on Human Rights

[8] Article 8(1) of the European Convention on Human Rights (ECHR) provides that everyone has the right to respect for his private and family life, his home and his correspondence.

Romanian Law

[9] Articles 259(1) and (2) of the Codul Civil (Civil Code) state as follows:

'1. Marriage is the union freely consented to of a man and a woman, entered into in accordance with the conditions laid down by law.

Men and women shall have the right to marry with a view to founding a family.'

[10] Article 227(1), (2) and (4) of the Civil Code is worded as follows:

'1. Marriage between persons of the same sex shall be prohibited.

2. Marriages between persons of the same sex entered into or contracted abroad by Romanian citizens or by foreigners shall not be recognized in Romania. ...

The legal provisions relating to freedom of movement on Romanian territory by citizens of the Member States of the European Union and the European Economic Area shall be applicable.'

The dispute in the main proceedings and the questions referred for a preliminary ruling

[11] Mr Coman, who holds Romanian and American citizenship, and Mr Hamilton, an American citizen, met in New York (United States) in June 2002 and lived there together from May 2005 to May 2009. Mr Coman then took up residence in Brussels (Belgium) in order to work at the European Parliament as a parliamentary assistant, while Mr Hamilton continued to live in New York. They were married in Brussels on 5 November 2010.

[12] In March 2012, Mr Coman ceased to work at the Parliament but continued to live in Brussels, where he received unemployment benefit until January 2013.

[13] In December 2012, Mr Coman and Mr Hamilton contacted the Inspectorate to request information on the procedure and conditions under which Mr Hamilton, a non-EU national, in his capacity as member of Mr Coman's family, could obtain the right to reside lawfully in Romania for more than three months.

[14] On 11 January 2013, in reply to that request, the Inspectorate informed Mr Coman and Mr Hamilton that the latter only had a right of residence for three months because, under the Civil Code, marriage between people of the same sex is not recognized, and that an extension of Mr Hamilton's right of temporary residence in Romania could not be granted on grounds of family reunion.

[15] On 28 October 2013, Coman and Others brought an action against the decision of the Inspectorate before the Judecătoria Sectorului 5 București (Court of First Instance, District 5, Bucharest, Romania) seeking a declaration of discrimination on the ground of sexual orientation as regards the exercise of the right of freedom of movement in the European Union, and requesting that the Inspectorate be ordered to end the discrimination and to pay compensation for the non-material damage suffered.

[16] In that dispute, they argued that Article 277(2) and (4) of the Civil Code is unconstitutional. (…)

[17] By order of 18 December 2015, the Judecătoria Sectorului 5 București (Court of First Instance, District 5, Bucharest) referred the matter to the Curtea Constituțională (Constitutional Court, Romania) for a ruling on that plea of unconstitutionality.

[18] The Curtea Constituțională (Constitutional Court) states that the present case relates to recognition of a marriage lawfully entered into abroad between a Union citizen and his spouse of the same sex, a third-country national, in the light of the right to family life and the right to freedom of movement, viewed from the perspective of the prohibition of discrimination on grounds of sexual orientation. In that context, that court had doubts as to the interpretation to be given to several terms employed in the relevant provisions of Directive 2004/38, read in the light of the Charter and of the recent case law of this Court and of the European Court of Human Rights.

[19] In those circumstances, the Curtea Constituțională (Constitutional Court) decided to stay the proceedings and to refer the following questions to the Court for a preliminary ruling:

'(1) Does the term "spouse" in Article 2(2)(a) of Directive 2004/38, read in the light of Articles 7, 9, 21 and 45 of the Charter, include the same-sex spouse, from a State which is not a Member State of the European Union, of a citizen of the European Union to whom that citizen is lawfully married in accordance with the law of a Member State other than the host Member State?

(2) If the answer [to the first question] is in the affirmative, do Articles 3(1) and 7([2]) of Directive 2004/38, read in the light of Articles 7, 9, 21 and 45 of the Charter, require the host

Member State to grant the right of residence in its territory for a period of longer than three months to the same-sex spouse of a citizen of the European Union?

(...)

Consideration of the questions referred

Preliminary observations

[20] It is the Court's established case law that the purpose of Directive 2004/38 is to facilitate the exercise of the primary and individual right to move and reside freely within the territory of the Member States, which is conferred directly on citizens of the Union by Article 21(1) TFEU, and that one of the objectives of that directive is to strengthen that right (...).

[21] Article 3(1) of Directive 2004/38 provides that the directive is to apply to all Union citizens who move to or reside in a Member State other than that of which they are a national, and to their family members, as defined in point 2 of Article 2 of the directive, who accompany or join them.

[22] In that regard, as the Court has held on a number of occasions, it follows from a literal, contextual and teleological interpretation of Directive 2004/38 that the directive governs only the conditions determining whether Union citizens can enter and reside in Member States other than that of which they are a national and does not confer a derived right of residence on third-country nationals who are family members of a Union citizen in the Member State of which that citizen is a national (...).

[23] (...) It follows that Directive 2004/38, which the national court has asked the Court of Justice to interpret, cannot confer a derived right of residence on Mr Hamilton.

(...).

[24] In that regard, the Court has previously acknowledged, in certain cases, that third-country nationals, family members of a Union citizen, who were not eligible, on the basis of Directive 2004/38, for a derived right of residence in the Member State of which that citizen is a national, could, nevertheless, be accorded such a right on the basis of Article 21(1) TFEU (...).

[25] In particular, the Court has held that, where, during the genuine residence of a Union citizen in a Member State other than that of which they are a national, pursuant to and in conformity with the conditions set out in Directive 2004/38, family life is created or strengthened in that Member State, the effectiveness of the rights conferred on the Union citizen by Article 21(1) TFEU requires that that citizen's family life in that Member State may continue when they return to the Member State of which they are a national, through the grant of a derived right of residence to the third-country

national family member concerned. If no such derived right of residence were granted, that Union citizen could be discouraged from leaving the Member State of which they are a national in order to exercise their right of residence under Article 21(1) TFEU in another Member State because they are uncertain whether they will be able to continue in their Member State of origin a family life which has been created or strengthened in the host Member State (...).

[26] As regards the conditions under which such a derived right of residence may be granted, the Court has stated that they must not be stricter than those laid down by Directive 2004/38 for the grant of a derived right of residence to a third-country national who is a family member of a Union citizen having exercised their right of freedom of movement by settling in a Member State other than that of which they are a national. That directive must be applied, by analogy, to the situation referred to in paragraph 25 above (...).

(...).

The first question

[27] By its first question, the referring court seeks to ascertain, in essence, whether (...) Article 21(1) TFEU must be interpreted as precluding the competent authorities of the Member State of which the Union citizen is a national from refusing to grant that third-country national a right of residence in the territory of that Member State on the ground that the law of that Member State does not recognize marriage between persons of the same sex.

[28] It should be recalled that, as a Romanian national, Mr Coman enjoys the status of a Union citizen under Article 20(1) TFEU.

[29] In that regard, the Court has held on numerous occasions that citizenship of the Union is intended to be the fundamental status of nationals of the Member States (...).

[30] As is apparent from the Court's case law, a national of a Member State who, as in the main proceedings, has exercised, in their capacity as a Union citizen, their freedom to move and reside within a Member State other than their Member State of origin, may rely on the rights pertaining to Union citizenship, in particular the rights provided for in Article 21(1) TFEU, including, where appropriate, against their Member State of origin (...).

[31] The rights which nationals of Member States enjoy under that provision include the right to lead a normal family life—in the sense of a family life devoid of any external inteferences or obstacles to its enjoyment—together with their family members, both in the host Member State and in the Member State of which they are nationals when they return to that Member State (...).

[32] As to whether the 'family members' referred to in the paragraph above include the third-country national of the same sex as the Union citizen, it should be recalled at the outset that Directive 2004/38 (…) specifically mentions the 'spouse' as 'family member' in Article 2(2)(a) of the directive.

[33] The term 'spouse' used in that provision refers to a person joined to another person by the bonds of marriage (…).

[34] As to whether that term includes a third-country national of the same sex as the Union citizen whose marriage to that citizen was concluded in a Member State in accordance with the law of that State, it should be pointed out, first of all, that the term 'spouse' within the meaning of Directive 2004/38 is gender-neutral and may therefore cover the same-sex spouse of the Union citizen concerned.

[35] Next, it should be noted that, whereas, for the purpose of determining whether a partner with whom a Union citizen has contracted a registered partnership on the basis of the legislation of a Member State enjoys the status of 'family member,' Article 2(2)(b) of Directive 2004/38 refers to the conditions laid down in the relevant legislation of the Member State to which that citizen intends to move or in which they intend to reside, Article 2(2)(a) of that directive, applicable by analogy in the present case, does not contain any such reference with regard to the concept of 'spouse' within the meaning of the directive.

[36] Finally, it should be pointed out that Recital 31 of Directive 2004/38 requires Member States to implement the Directive without discrimination on grounds such as sexual orientation. Such discrimination clearly ensues when Member States interpret the term 'spouse' as including only the opposite-sex spouse of a Union citizen. The same Recital also notes that the Directive 'respects the fundamental rights and freedoms and observes the principles recognized in particular by the Charter of Fundamental Rights.' As will be stressed subsequently, the refusal by Member States to recognize the marriages concluded in another State between a Union citizen who has exercised free movement rights and a third-country national can, itself, also amount to a violation of the right to respect for family life laid down in the Charter.

[37] It follows that a Member State cannot rely on its national law as justification for refusing to recognize in its territory, for the purpose of granting a derived right of residence to a third-country national, a marriage concluded by that national with a Union citizen of the same sex in another country.

[38] Admittedly, a person's status, which is relevant to the rules on marriage, is a matter that falls within the competence of the Member States and EU law does not detract from that competence (…). The Member States are thus free to decide whether or not to allow marriage for persons of the same sex within their territory (…).

[39] Nevertheless, it is well-established case law that, in exercising that competence, Member States must comply with EU law, in particular the Treaty provisions on the freedom conferred on all Union citizens to move and reside in the territory of the Member States (…).

[40] To allow Member States the freedom to grant or refuse entry into and residence in their territory by a third-country national married to a Union citizen, according to whether or not national law allows marriage by persons of the same sex, would have the effect that the freedom of movement of Union citizens who have already made use of that freedom would vary from one Member State to another, depending on whether such provisions of national law exist (…). Such a situation would be at odds with the Court's case law, cited by the Advocate General in point 73 of his Opinion, to the effect that, in the light of its context and objectives, the provisions of Directive 2004/38, applicable by analogy to the present case, may not be interpreted restrictively and must not be deprived of their effectiveness (…).

[41] It follows that the refusal by the authorities of a Member State to recognize, for the purpose of granting a derived right of residence to a third-country national, the marriage of that national to a Union citizen of the same sex which was contracted in another country, may interfere with the exercise of the right conferred on that citizen by Article 21(1) TFEU to move and reside freely in the territory of the Member States. Indeed, the effect of such a refusal is that such a Union citizen may be denied the possibility of returning to the Member State of which they are a national together with their spouse.

[42] Such an interference with the exercise of the right conferred on that citizen to move and reside freely in the territory of the Member States may also arise if the authorities of a Member State refuse to recognize the Union citizen's marriage to a third-country national of the same sex after the Union citizen and their same-sex spouse have been admitted into the territory of that State and for purposes other than granting a derived right of residence to the third-country national spouse. Such purposes can include taxation, inheritance, maintenance, and the taking out of health or life insurance. After all, as noted in paragraph 31 of this judgment, the rights which Union citizens enjoy under Article 21(1) TFEU include the right to lead a normal family life, together with their family members, both in the host Member State and in the Member State of which they are nationals when they return to that Member State. It is, nonetheless, clear that leading a normal family life requires not merely the possibility that the spouses live together in the same EU Member State (…) but, also, that the spouses are recognized as 'spouses' for all legal purposes, once they are within the territory of that Member State.

[43] Moreover, the Court has held in previous case law involving the cross-border recognition of the surnames of Union citizens that a discrepancy in surnames is liable to cause serious inconvenience for those concerned at both professional and private levels resulting from, inter alia, difficulties in benefitting, in the Member State of which they

are nationals, from the legal effects of diplomas or documents drawn up in the surname recognized in another Member State of which they are also nationals (...). Such serious inconvenience is even more likely to be caused from a discrepancy in the recognition of a Union citizen's marital status in different Member States and from the resultant difficulties—or, even, impossibility—in benefitting, in some Member States, from the legal effects of their marriage. Such serious inconvenience can, in itself, constitute an obstacle to the exercise of free movement rights.

[44] That said, it is established case law that a restriction on the right to freedom of movement for persons, which, as in the main proceedings, is independent of the nationality of the persons concerned, may be justified if it is based on objective public interest considerations and if it is proportionate to a legitimate objective pursued by national law (...). It is also apparent from the Court's case law that a measure is proportionate if, while appropriate for securing the attainment of the objective pursued, it does not go beyond what is necessary in order to attain that objective (...).

[45] As regards public interest considerations, a number of Governments that have submitted observations to the Court have referred in that regard to the fundamental nature of the institution of marriage and the intention of a number of Member States to maintain a conception of that institution as a union between a man and a woman, which is protected in some Member States by laws having constitutional status. The Latvian Government stated at the hearing that, even on the assumption that a refusal, in circumstances such as those of the main proceedings, (...) constitutes a restriction of Article 21 TFEU, such a restriction is justified on grounds of public policy and national identity, as referred to in Article 4(2) TEU.

(...)

[46] (...) [T]he Court has repeatedly held that the concept of public policy as justification for a derogation from a fundamental freedom must be interpreted strictly, with the result that its scope cannot be determined unilaterally by each Member State without any control by the EU institutions. It follows that public policy may be relied on only if there is a genuine and sufficiently serious threat to a fundamental interest of society (...).

[47] The Court finds, in that regard, that the obligation for a Member State to recognize a marriage between persons of the same sex concluded in accordance with the law of another State, does not undermine the institution of marriage in that Member State, which is defined by national law and, as indicated in paragraph 38 above, falls within the competence of the Member States. Such recognition does not require that Member State to provide, in its national law, for the institution of marriage between persons of the same sex. It is confined to the obligation to recognize such marriages, concluded in another State in accordance with the law of that State, for the sole purpose of enabling such persons to exercise the rights they enjoy under EU law.

[48] Accordingly, an obligation to recognize such marriages concluded in another State for the purpose of enabling Union citizens to exercise the rights they enjoy under EU law does not undermine the national identity or pose a threat to the public policy of the Member State concerned.

[49] It should be added that a national measure that is liable to obstruct the exercise of freedom of movement for persons may be justified only where such a measure is consistent with the fundamental rights guaranteed by the Charter, it being the task of the Court to ensure that those rights are respected (…).

[50] As regards the term 'spouse' in Article 2(2)(a) of Directive 2004/38, the right to respect for private and family life guaranteed by Article 7 of the Charter is a fundamental right.

[51] In that regard, as is apparent from the Explanations relating to the Charter of Fundamental Rights (…), in accordance with Article 52(3) of the Charter, the rights guaranteed by Article 7 thereof have the same meaning and the same scope as those guaranteed by Article 8 of the ECHR, (…) without this preventing Union law from providing more extensive protection.

[52] It is apparent from the case law of the European Court of Human Rights that the relationship of a same-sex couple may fall within the notions of 'private life' and 'family life' in the same way as the relationship of an opposite-sex couple in the same situation (…). Moreover, in its judgment in the *Orlandi* case in 2017 (…), the same Court held that Article 8 of the ECHR requires signatory States to the Convention to recognize marriages contracted abroad as a form of union. Given that the rights guaranteed by Article 7 of the Charter have the same meaning and the same scope as those guaranteed by Article 8 of the Convention, *without this preventing Union law from providing more extensive protection*, this means that EU Member States are required by Article 7 of the Charter to recognize same-sex marriages contracted abroad *at least* as a form of union, and this is for all legal purposes and not just for enabling Union citizens to exercise free movement rights deriving from EU law. Therefore, the refusal to recognize—in a situation which falls within the scope of application of the Charter—*at least* as a union a same-sex marriage contracted abroad can amount to a violation of Article 7 of the Charter.

[53] In the light of all the foregoing considerations, the answer to the first question is that, (…) Article 21(1) TFEU must be interpreted as precluding the competent authorities of the Member State of which a Union citizen is a national from refusing to grant that citizen's third-country national spouse a right of residence in the territory of that Member State on the ground that the law of that Member State does not recognize marriage between persons of the same sex.

(…)

On those grounds, the Court (Grand Chamber) hereby rules:

[1] In a situation in which a Union citizen has made use of their freedom of movement by moving to and taking up genuine residence, in accordance with the conditions laid down in Article 7(1) of Directive 2004/38/EC (…) in a Member State other than that of which they are a national, and, whilst there, has created or strengthened a family life with a third-country national of the same sex to whom they are joined by a marriage lawfully concluded in another State, Article 21(1) TFEU must be interpreted as precluding the competent authorities of the Member State of which the Union citizen is a national from refusing to grant that third-country national a right of residence in the territory of that Member State on the ground that the law of that Member State does not recognize marriage between persons of the same sex.

(…)

www.ingramcontent.com/pod-product-compliance
Lightning Source LLC
Chambersburg PA
CBHW051748200326
41597CB00025B/4482